Lecture Notes in Information Systems and Organisation

Volume 85

AF837866

Lecture Notes in Information Systems and Organization (LNISO) is a series of scientific books that explore the current state of information systems studies, in particular in the context of organizations, as well as behavioral and design aspects of information systems. The series offers an integrated publication platform for high-quality conferences, symposia and workshops proceedings. Books accepted for publication are selected based on a double-blind peer-review evaluation made by invited reviewers. The series is indexed in Scopus.

Christoph M. Flath · Gunther Gust ·
Frédéric Thiesse · Axel Winkelmann
Editors

Shaping the Digital Future Through Innovation and Practice

Proceedings of the 19th International Conference on Wirtschaftsinformatik, Würzburg, Germany, 2024—Vol. 4

Springer

Editors
Christoph M. Flath
Julius-Maximilian University of Würzburg
Würzburg, Germany

Gunther Gust
Julius-Maximilian University of Würzburg
Würzburg, Germany

Frédéric Thiesse
Julius-Maximilian University of Würzburg
Würzburg, Germany

Axel Winkelmann
Julius-Maximilian University of Würzburg
Würzburg, Germany

ISSN 2195-4968 ISSN 2195-4976 (electronic)
Lecture Notes in Information Systems and Organisation
ISBN 978-3-032-08488-0 ISBN 978-3-032-08489-7 (eBook)
https://doi.org/10.1007/978-3-032-08489-7

This Springer imprint is published by the registered company Springer Nature Switzerland AG
The registered company address is: Gewerbestrasse 11, 6330 Cham, Switzerland

Contents

Smart Cities & Digital Government

Cultural Digital Twin Cities—Accessing Cultural City Data from Unstructured Sources 3
Luca T. Bauer, Robin J. Fritzsche, Gerhard Klassen, Dulce M. Villegas Nunez, and Björn Niehaves

Data-Driven Micromobility Governance—A Stage Model 13
Felix N. Bäßmann, Daniela G. Waßmann, and Michael H. Breitner

Getting to Know Your Customer: Onboarding in an Urban Mobility Ecosystem 29
Daniel Richter and Jürgen Anke

Guiding Principles for Government as a Platform 45
Peter Kuhn, Luca Gastaldi, Dian Balta, and Florian Matthes

Supporting the Store-Based Retail with Big Data in German Towns—A Longitudinal Mixed-Method-Study 61
Cindy Kreuels, Aida Stelter, Bastian Kordyaka, and Björn Niehaves

Unlocking Value: Towards a Comprehensive Taxonomy for Commercializing Open Data in the Business Context 77
Eric Börner

Urban Gamification: Designing Municipal Websites for Enhanced Citizen Trust 93
Bastian Kordyaka, Sebastian Weber, Luca Bauer, Robin Fritzsche, Gerhard Klassen, Raphael Palombo, Dulce Villegas, Marc Wyszynski, and Bjoern Niehaves

Practice Track: Innovative Prototypes & Impact of IS

A Drift Detection Prototype for Quality Control in Manufacturing 105
Dharmil Rajesh Mehta, Safa Omri, Richard Zowalla, and Jens Neuhuettler

A Method for Performing Ontology-Based Computational Literature Reviews Exemplified for Design Science Research 119
Sebastian Huettemann, Roland M. Mueller, and Barbara Dinter

Addressing the Challenge to Measure Information Security Behavior: Toward a Holistic Metric with Scavenger Hunts 135
Martin Brehmer and Raphaela Stöckl

Cybersecurity Awareness Training for Industrial Software Developers via a Serious Game for Code Review 143
Andrei-Cristian Iosif, Ulrike Lechner, Maria Pinto-Albuquerque, and Tiago Espinha Gasiba

Digital Twins for Haptic Design Thinking: An Innovative Prototype 161
Alexander Voelz, Christian Muck, and Wilfird Utz

Enabling Smart Service Innovation in SMEs: The bi.smart Launchpad 171
Daniel Heinz, Carina Benz, Hitomi Bremmer, Yevgeni Paliyenko, and Christian Schiller

Two Sides of the Same Coin: An E-Commerce Ecosystem Agent-Based Simulation 187
Gero Strobel, Tobias Wulfert, and Leonardo Banh

Student Track

Evaluation of Hypothetical Document and Query Embeddings for Information Retrieval Enhancements in the Context of Diverse User Queries 203
Marten Jostmann and Hendrik Winkelmann

Exploring Themes in Digital Detox Research: Insights from a Literature Review 213
Marietta Forster, Fabian J. Stangl, and René Riedl

Fostering Inclusivity—Towards Principles for Inclusive Information Systems Design 239
Naveen Vimalan, Markus P. Zimmer, and Paul Drews

Hate Speech and Sentiment of YouTube Video Comments From Public and Private Sources Covering the Israel-Palestine Conflict 257
Simon Hofmann, Christoph Sommermann, Mathias Kraus, Patrick Zschech, and Julian Rosenberger

Investigation of Success Factors for Co-Creation Platforms for SMEs 273
Hanna Fritzke, Ann-Kristin Cordes, and Mitja Kulczynski

Knowledge Management Through Knowledge Repositories: Deriving Design Principles From Practice 287
Christian Gussew and Philipp zur Heiden

Perception and Management of Work Interruptions among Digital Business Professionals: An Updated Study 303
Volker Seiler, Fabian J. Stangl, and René Riedl

The Role of Data Management in Scaling AI Startups: A Practical Framework 321
Tilman Friedrich, Lukas Sanwald, and Isabelle Keutner

Understanding Similarities and Differences of Digital Health Platforms: Towards a Taxonomy 337
Finn Schubert, Jan Maschewski, and Paul Drews

AI Act Workshop

Assuring EU AI Act Compliance and Adversarial Robustness of LLMs 355
Tomas Bueno Momcilovic, Beat Buesser, Giulio Zizzo, Mark Purcell, and Dian Balta

The Impact of the AI-Act on the Implementation of Conversational Agents in Healthcare Processes 365
Björn-Lennart Eger, Daniel Rose, and Barbara Dinter

Contributors

Jürgen Anke HTWD University of Applied Sciences, Digital Service Systems Group, Dresden, Germany

Dian Balta Technical University Munich, Munich, Germany;
Fortiss, Munich, Germany

Leonardo Banh University of Duisburg-Essen, Essen, Germany

Luca T. Bauer Fachbereich 3—Mathematik und Informatik, University of Bremen, Bremen, Germany

Felix N. Bäßmann Information Systems Institute, Leibniz University Hannover, Hannover, Germany

Carina Benz Karlsruhe Institute of Technology, Karlsruhe, Germany

Eric Börner Chair of Business Information Systems, Esp. Information Systems in Industry and Trade, TU Dresden, Dresden, Germany

Martin Brehmer Faculty of Business and Economics, University of Augsburg, Augsburg, Germany

Michael H. Breitner Information Systems Institute, Leibniz University Hannover, Hannover, Germany

Hitomi Bremmer IBM Research Europe, Zurich, Switzerland

Tomas Bueno Momcilovic fortiss GmbH Research Institute, Munich, Germany

Beat Buesser EDI GmbH, Karlsruhe, Germany

Ann-Kristin Cordes Department of Computer Science, Kiel University, 24098 Kiel, Germany

Barbara Dinter Chair of Business Information Systems—Business Process and Information Management, Chemnitz University of Technology, Chemnitz, Germany

Paul Drews Institute of Information Systems, Leuphana University, Lüneburg, Germany

Björn-Lennart Eger Chair of Business Information Systems—Business Process and Information Management, Chemnitz University of Technology, Chemnitz, Germany

Marietta Forster Digital Business Institute, School of Business and Management, University of Applied Sciences Upper Austria, Steyr, Austria

Tilman Friedrich Freie Universität Berlin, Berlin, Germany

Robin J. Fritzsche Fachbereich—Mathematik und Informatik, University of Bremen, Bremen, Germany

Hanna Fritzke Department of Computer Science, Kiel University, 24098 Kiel, Germany

Tiago Espinha Gasiba Siemens AG, Munich, Germany

Luca Gastaldi Politecnico Di Milano, Milan, Italy

Christian Gussew Department of Management Information Systems, Paderborn University, Paderborn, Germany

Daniel Heinz Karlsruhe Institute of Technology, Karlsruhe, Germany

Simon Hofmann Friedrich-Alexander Universität Erlangen-Nürnberg, Nürnberg, Germany

Sebastian Huettemann Berlin School of Economics and Law, Berlin, Germany

Andrei-Cristian Iosif Siemens AG, Munich, Germany;
Universität der Bundeswehr München, Munich, Germany

Marten Jostmann viadee Unternehmensberatung AG, Münster, Germany

Isabelle Keutner Berlin School of Economics and Law, Berlin, Germany

Gerhard Klassen Freie Universität Berlin, Berlin, Germany

Bastian Kordyaka Faculty 3, Digital Public, University of Bremen, Bremen, Germany

Mathias Kraus Universität Regensburg, Regensburg, Germany

Cindy Kreuels University of Siegen, Siegen, Germany

Peter Kuhn Technical University Munich, Munich, Germany;
Fortiss, Munich, Germany

Mitja Kulczynski Department of Computer Science, Kiel University, 24098 Kiel, Germany

Ulrike Lechner Universität der Bundeswehr München, Munich, Germany

Jan Maschewski Institute of Information Systems, Leuphana University, Lüneburg, Germany

Florian Matthes Technical University Munich, Munich, Germany

Christian Muck OMiLAB NPO, Berlin, Germany

Roland M. Mueller Berlin School of Economics and Law, Berlin, Germany

Bjoern Niehaves Fachbereich 3—Mathematik und Informatik, University of Bremen, Bremen, Germany

Yevgeni Paliyenko University of Stuttgart, Stuttgart, Germany

Raphael Palombo Faculty 3, Digital Public, University of Bremen, Bremen, Germany

Maria Pinto-Albuquerque Instituto Universitário de Lisboa (ISCTE-IUL), ISTAR, Lisbon, Portugal

Mark Purcell IBM Research Europe, Dublin, Ireland

Daniel Richter HTWD University of Applied Sciences, Digital Service Systems Group, Dresden, Germany

René Riedl Digital Business Institute, School of Business and Management, University of Applied Sciences Upper Austria, Steyr, Austria;
Institute of Business Informatics—Information Engineering, Johannes Kepler University Linz, Linz, Austria

Daniel Rose Chair of Business Information Systems—Business Process and Information Management, Chemnitz University of Technology, Chemnitz, Germany

Julian Rosenberger Universität Regensburg, Regensburg, Germany

Lukas Sanwald Freie Universität Berlin, Berlin, Germany

Christian Schiller Fraunhofer IAO, Stuttgart, Germany

Finn Schubert Institute of Information Systems, Leuphana University, Lüneburg, Germany

Volker Seiler School of Management, Carinthia University of Applied Sciences, Villach, Austria

Christoph Sommermann Friedrich-Alexander Universität Erlangen-Nürnberg, Nürnberg, Germany

Fabian J. Stangl Digital Business Institute, School of Business and Management, University of Applied Sciences Upper Austria, Steyr, Austria

Aida Stelter University of Siegen, Siegen, Germany

Raphaela Stöckl Faculty of Business and Economics, University of Augsburg, Augsburg, Germany

Gero Strobel University of Duisburg-Essen, Essen, Germany

Dulce M. Villegas Nunez Fachbereich 3 - Mathematik und Informatik, University of Bremen, Bremen, Germany

Wilfird Utz OMiLAB NPO, Berlin, Germany

Naveen Vimalan Leuphana University Lüneburg, Lüneburg, Germany

Alexander Voelz Faculty of Computer Science, University of Vienna, Vienna, Austria

Daniela G. Waßmann Leibniz University Hannover, Hannover, Germany

Sebastian Weber Faculty 3, Digital Public, University of Bremen, Bremen, Germany

Hendrik Winkelmann viadee Unternehmensberatung AG, Münster, Germany

Tobias Wulfert University of Duisburg-Essen, Essen, Germany

Marc Wyszynski Faculty 3, Digital Public, University of Bremen, Bremen, Germany

Markus P. Zimmer Leuphana University Lüneburg, Lüneburg, Germany

Patrick Zschech TU Dresden, Dresden, Germany

Giulio Zizzo IBM Research Europe, Dublin, Ireland

Philipp zur Heiden Department of Management Information Systems, Paderborn University, Paderborn, Germany

Smart Cities & Digital Government

Cultural Digital Twin Cities—Accessing Cultural City Data from Unstructured Sources

Luca T. Bauer, Robin J. Fritzsche, Gerhard Klassen, Dulce M. Villegas Nunez, and Björn Niehaves

Abstract This working paper explores the concept of cultural digital twin cities, proposing a novel approach to incorporating cultural and social data into the digital modeling of urban environments. Recognizing the limitations of current digital twins, which largely focus on physical and infrastructural elements, this work in progress paper emphasizes the significance of uncurated data sources, such as open street map imagery, social media conversations, and its metadata. This approach not only enhances the understanding of urban life beyond tangible aspects, but also includes currently inaccessible aspects of the city in urban development. The paper sets a foundation for future research, development of frameworks, and software dedicated to the realization of 'other' digital twin cities, aiming to bridge the divide curated and uncurated urban dimensions.

1 Introduction

In digital times, the smart city is at the core of citizen centric policy. It is modeled on a structural digital copy, often lacking a cities socio-cultural fabric. Policymakers' vision and reality are seldomly congruent. Wanting to create data-based policy for their citizens, policymakers need to get as close of a model of their living space as

L. T. Bauer (✉) · R. J. Fritzsche · G. Klassen · D. M. Villegas Nunez · B. Niehaves
Fachbereich 3 - Mathematik und Informatik, University of Bremen, Bremen, Germany
e-mail: bauerl@uni-bremen.de

R. J. Fritzsche
e-mail: robfri@uni-bremen.de

G. Klassen
e-mail: gklassen@uni-bremen.de

D. M. Villegas Nunez
e-mail: villegas@uni-bremen.de

B. Niehaves
e-mail: niehaves@uni-bremen.de

C. M. Flath et al. (eds.), *Shaping the Digital Future Through Innovation and Practice*,
Lecture Notes in Information Systems and Organisation 85,
https://doi.org/10.1007/978-3-032-08489-7_1

possible. This purpose is currently often achieved by creating digital twins of the city [19]. However, these often only reflect the tangible surface area, leaving behind all social and cultural dimensions [1].

In our research we assess how to use uncurated data to generate a holistic picture of the culture of a city through the visualization in a digital twin. In this working paper, we give a theoretical background and propose exemplary use cases to build upon, where digital twins have a utilization for the social fabric of a city [3]. From recent research, we deduced that a combination of the structural and unstructured dimensions could be a vital step to a better understanding of the social fabric and culture of a city [1]. Cultural digital twin cities could be a tool that may revolutionize conceiving a city. For this we assessed three examples on how to approach the development.

Based on this, our working paper is guided by the following research question (RQ): *How does current research use uncurated data to assess cultural dimensions of digital twin cities?*

2 Theoretical Backdrop & Methodology

We employed a comprehensive literature review to explore current trends in research on the intersection between digital twin cities (DTC) and the cities' culture mapped on digital models. As this is a work in progress, the depicted methodology is purely literature review. Following, we introduce practical publications for scoping the topic and show synergies between currently seldomly linked concepts.

For this purpose, we did a systematic search of databases such as JSTOR, SCOPUS, and Google Scholar using a predefined set of keywords relevant to our study's focus. For this purpose we mapped a assessed a total of 922 publications Scopus and 1162 JSTOR publications using the search string *("digital twin" AND "culture") OR ("digital twin" AND "cultural") OR ("smart city" AND "culture") OR ("smart cities" AND "culture").* Exclusion criteria were set to omit non-peer-reviewed articles, editorial comments, and studies not directly addressing the core themes of our investigation. The presented working paper solely depicts the theoretical background upon which current tool development and research processes are based.

2.1 *The Smart City and Its Digital Twins*

Smart cities are generally seen as a change of paradigm regarding urban development. Even though they lie at the intersection between three strongly discussed issues of public policy, urban development and digital transformation, their concepts are often one-size-fits-all, lacking empirical and strategic depth [20, 21]. This is especially visible when looking at non-economic or intangible infrastructure.

Smart cities mostly revolve around citizen-centric urban development and participatory projects [7, 9]. Planning and operating a smart city as such is not only a bureaucratic and political project, but one of public–private partnership including every party concerned [24]. They are meant to enable policymakers and citizens alike [4, 27, 28]. The same applies to scholarly work. If the public sector aims to provide best possible, most need-based services to the city's residents, it needs to consider research from all disciplines, be it political sciences, information systems, engineering, sociology, architecture, anthropology, urban planning or many more. As Kitchin noted, there are many concerns to be addressed, like "[...] *the politics of big urban data, technocratic governance and city development, corporatization of city governance and technological lock-ins, buggy, brittle and hackable cities, and the panoptic city*" [19]. Here we see a need to not only apply their respective frames of reference to a given object, but rather to follow their lanes of research and identify uses of smart cities to address their challenges.

In the frame of smart cities, an often-used concept for policy creation is the digital twin. In the early 2000s [14], the concept of 'digital twins' emerged as a transformative paradigm in various domains, ranging from manufacturing and healthcare to urban planning and beyond. Digital twins represent a virtual counterpart or replica of a physical entity, system or process. In the rapidly evolving landscape of smart cities, the integration of cutting-edge technologies has given rise to the DTC, providing a virtual counterpart to physical entities and systems. A DTC describes the implementation of digital twin technologies on an urban scale [10]. The foundational idea involves creating a comprehensive, digital replica of a city's infrastructure, allowing for advanced analysis and data-driven decision-making.

Scientifically, the utilization of digital twin cities has been explored in various domains, including forecasting, simulation, and crisis management. Noteworthy examples include their role in handling health data during the COVID-19 pandemic [12] and optimizing energy resources [13]. Deng et al. predict that the development of digital twin cities will establish a new management paradigm, enabling the tracing of past events and the exploration of future directions—a trend expected to shape future research in this domain [10].

Still, in establishing a new paradigm of smart cities, what is often left behind is the social fabric and culture of the city as it cannot easily be depicted in the logic of a technological, mostly economic digital twin [1]. Here we see an untapped potential that could be realized by identifying data sources that can map out the social fabric of a city. This social fabric is sometimes not immediately visible in official data as it often comes from counter positions to prevalent political positions [6]. To make this social fabric visible is an ambitious task as culture is an often-intangible concept. The successful creation of a cultural digital twin of a city could have many benefits. On the one hand a new tool to inform policies. On the other hand, a better way to understand the life and culture in a city.

2.2 Culture in the City

Striving to access a city's cultural makeup through a digital twin, there is a need for a pragmatic understanding of culture. We need a definition of culture that can be used to identify which data can represent the culture of a city. The term culture has undergone many changes in the course of history and is often described as an overly broad and ambiguous concept [33]. Striving to define the term we see an opportunity to include a broad spectrum of versions of culture. Lenard identifies four approaches to define culture. These approaches are culture "*-as-encompassing-group; -as-social-formation; -as-dialogue and -as-identity*" [23]. Culture-as-encompassing-group can be understood as an encompassing value system that provides guidelines which provide the context for choice and meaning for members of a group. This account is criticized for drawing boundaries of a culture as determined and unchanging [25]. Culture-as-social-formation is an approach that tries to react to the critique of the culture-as-encompassing-group account but at the same time tries to retain most of its content. It understands culture as the shared experience of group members being subject of the same social formations and institutions. This approach acknowledges that culture has the tendency to change and develop over time. Culture-as-dialogue defines culture by the interaction of the members of a group and their engagement with each other. This account has the actions of the group members and their capacity to shape their culture in its focus. Culture-as-identity describes an account that sees an overlap between the concept of identity and the concept of culture. The things we identify with describe our culture. This account is preferred by some scholars as it incorporates a wide variety of cultural forms [11].

We chose the conception of culture specific to the context of cities and decided to work mainly with the culture-as-identity account, as we think that it is most inclusive to bottom-up initiatives. When understanding culture as identity or identification, we can infer that something is culturally relevant if people identify with it, exemplary social events such as festivities, traditions, or monuments people frequently visit, as well as create themselves through, i.e. street art.

To understand which data is feasible for this purpose, we need to understand that the data of a city can be fit into two dimensions: structured and unstructured dimensions. The structured dimension depicts what is usually associated with tangible and curated infrastructure, mobility, and economic data. The unstructured city on the other hand, is less palpable [22]. It, rather than being a documented, is the organic socio-political fabric [16]. Oftentimes the data that can be identified as unstructured is data that is not curated or provided by city or corporate officials. It can for example be social media data or crowd-sourced data. It is "*[...] the shapeless areas of the city where economic and socio-political structures are particularly unstable*" [16]. As such it can been seen as the organic fabric between structural components. To approach the identification with events or physical entities in cities, we identify currently unstructured data as a very important source.

The culture visible in this manner often shows data that goes against the focus of outward visible digitalization initiatives [17]. Our aim is to use unstructured, uncurated data to generate a holistic picture of the social parts of a city. Especially the social spaces of a city are often created, as their progenitors act on them out of a feeling of being left behind. As such, beside bottom-up initiatives, the whole city must be made accessible for policymakers for more inclusive urban development.

2.3 *The Cultural Digital Twin City*

For accessing current potential research on cultural digital twin cities, we conducted SCOPUS searches on the last ten years with the keywords "digital twin city" (69), "digital city twin" (2), "culture" AND "digital twin" (109), as well as "cultural" AND "digital twin" (219). Even though over 400 publications were identified as potentially useful, most of them revolved around cultural heritage preservation, which is used for historical and architectural documentation purposes, but is not of use for assessing the unstructured parts of a city in a digital twin [2, 3, 5, 26, 29]. Other publications revolved around social dimensions of cities in the sense of slums and settlements that are not scheduled in official city records [18]. Our research agenda understands the holistic city as the data about a city that is not curated and not provided by city officials or corporations. This can partly include settlements, but it is rather the social fabric dimension of the city that we are interested in. None of the publications developed a digital twin with this type of data of a city. We concur this as a gap in current research and see a need for a comprehensive framework. In developing a framework, we want to focus on technologies and use cases that could be beneficial in creating a CDTC.

3 Use-Cases for Cultural Digital Twin Cities

In this chapter we identify the use and current use cases of Cultural Digital Twin Cities (CDTC). CDTC can be seen as an asset for cities on many levels besides policymaking. They enable better social and cultural policy, they can be used to attract tourists and to shine a light on culture, art and traditions that are neglected in classical city guides [29]. This could open a new and innovative pathway to understanding city art and culture. The technology can be identified as a vital step towards more representation and therefore more participation. Furthermore, digital twins can be used to enhance future city planning to preserve this cultural heritage against external influence [8, 26]. In this we see direct impact in urban planning processes to integrate and visualize.

As visible, there is a current gap in CDTC-modelling regarding the unstructured city. Even though a coherent frame is lacking, we identified examples of data sources as most relevant empirical cases. We chose them, as they are both the most tangible with actual use for policymakers and they also show innovative capabilities for accessing cultural dimensions in a CDTC. Other examples often were either vague or did not provide practical solutions, but rather ideas. The most promising examples of data that could be useful in developing a CDTC are the following: (1) openly accessible street view data [15], (2) social media conversations data [31], (3) social media geo-tags metadata [32]. We have chosen these studies based on their innovativeness in applying technology on data.

Hao and Wang's paper introduces an approach to creating a Digital Twin (DT) for urban environments using computer vision and openly accessible street map imagery. Their framework aims at inventorying facilities across various types and locations by employing a DeepLab V3 semantic segmentation model, which is pre-trained on the CityScapes dataset. By detecting curb facilities from GSV images and using Inverse Perspective Mapping (IPM) to estimate their spatial locations, the researchers can aggregate and filter these estimations to build a comprehensive digital inventory [15]. They use uncurated data, but it is not for the purpose of building a CDTC. We could use their methods to identify changes over time in street structure and widen their approach to e.g. street art.

Scheibmeir and Malaiya's paper introduces an approach of analyzing social media conversations with natural language processing to build a digital twin. Their study employs social media data to construct a digital replica and simulate the spread of an invasive species across the United States. By merging socio-material assemblage theory with digital twin technology, they developed machine learning algorithms and an initial digital twin model to forecast the movements of these pests [30]. This approach of using social media discussions in combination with natural language processing and machine learning could be a promising way to map out culture in form of things people identify with in discussions under social media posts in a digital twin of a city, especially combined with picture-place recognition. To use this for our CDTC we need to develop indicators of identification in discussions linked to locality.

Sicari et al. use geotagging metadata of social media posts to construct a platform for enhancing 3D virtual indoor navigation [32]. In the case of cultural digital twin cities this could be an analysis of frequency or absolute number of geotagging metadata assessed by places in the city. From this information we infer identification with specific places or sights. But to be able to make this inference we need to compare if the pictures containing the geotagging have similar parts of a place e.g. monuments, graffiti, natural scenes in it. For this we could incorporate neural. network-based picture classification and pairwise comparison.

These three studies represent examples of which technologies could be used to assess the cultural dimension of a city. By synthesizing their approaches, it can possible develop a robust and multifaceted CDTC. This integrated model may not only document and preserve the cultural heritage of cities but also provide valuable insights for policymakers, urban planners, and cultural institutions. Nevertheless, a functional link is currently missing. All solutions presented provide value but are not possible to link in a user-friendly manner. For deeper impact an interoperable framework will be necessary on which visualization tools can depend.

4 Discussion and Outlook

As modern cities become increasingly more digital a holistic picture of the life and culture in a city is needed. This study highlights the growing digitalization of modern cities and the consequent need for a more comprehensive representation of urban life that encompasses all dimensions. Despite the advancement of digital twin technologies in capturing the physical and infrastructural aspects of cities, there remains a significant gap in their ability to represent the cultural fabric of urban environments.

Answering the RQ: *How does current research use uncurated data to assess cultural dimensions of digital twin cities?*, we introduced the concept of cultural digital twin cities as a solution to bridge this divide by integrating unstructured dimensions of city life through various uncurated data sources. This approach not only offers a more comprehensive view of urban environments, but also empowers citizens to engage with their city in ways not dictated by policy mandates.

Furthermore, our research lays the groundwork for future investigations into the application and impact of cultural digital twin cities. Regarding further research we plan to incorporate the identified methods and technologies on different uncurated data sources. This will be the next step in building a comprehensive Cultural Digital Twin City. Further research and application will be based upon the currently still in development DIN-SPEC 91607 for urban digital twins. Nevertheless, data on not only feasible, but most relevant use-cases for urban planners is inaccessible. Throughout our literature review, we were unable to find a empirical studies based on needs as articulated by citizens or urban planners. Creating a coherent framework for CDTCs technological capabilities will need more empirical data and the why's, not only the what's of integrating uncurated and cultural data.

In summary, our research presents a forward-looking perspective on the digital representation of cities, advocating for a more inclusive and culturally rich approach. By bridging the gap between the often seen as antagonistic dimensions of urban life, cultural digital twin cities promise to enhance the comprehensiveness, accuracy, and utility of digital urban models, paving the way for more responsive and inclusive urban environments. Nevertheless, singular approaches like the ones mentioned before, fall short in comparison to the overarching goals. Not interoperable solutions allow for first assessments but are unable to be linked properly.

References

1. Allam, Z., & Newman, P. (2018). Redefining the smart city: Culture, metabolism and governance. *Smart Cities, 1*(1), 4–25.
2. Banfi, F., et al. (2023). *Representing intangible cultural heritage of humanity: From the deep abyss of the past to digital twin and XR of the Neanderthal man and Lamalunga Cave (Altamura, Apulia).* The International Archives of the Photogrammetry, Remote Sensing and Spatial

Information Sciences, XLVIII-M-2-2023, pp. 171–181. https://doi.org/10.5194/isprs-archives-XLVIII-M-2-2023-171-2023
3. Brumana, R., et al. (2023). *Immersive Appian way health infrastructure: Human centric digital twin (the PAA archeological park of the Appian way 12km state-own section, UNESCO candidature).* The International Archives of the Photogrammetry, Remote Sensing and Spatial Information Sciences, XLVIII-M-2-2023, pp. 311–318. https://doi.org/10.5194/isprs-archives-XLVIII-M-2-2023-311-2023
4. Bunders, D. J., & Varró, K. (2019). Problematizing data-driven urban practices: Insights from five Dutch 'smart cities.' *Cities, 93*, 145–152.
5. Buonocore, S., Guidazzoli, A., Liguori, M. C., Zuzolo, P., & Monelli, M. (2023). Digital twin, from industry to cultural heritage. *Memorie della Società Astronomica Italiana Journal of the Italian Astronomical Society, 94*, 73.
6. Burns, R., & Andrucki, M. (2021). Smart cities: Who cares? *Environment and Planning A: Economy and Space, 53*(1), 12–30.
7. Capra, C. F. (2016). The Smart City and its citizens: Governance and citizen participation in Amsterdam Smart City. *International Journal of E-Planning Research (IJEPR), 5*(1), 20–38.
8. Caprari, G., Castelli, G., Montuori, M., Camardelli, M., & Malvezzi, R. (2022). Digital twin for urban planning in the green deal era: A state of the art and future perspectives. *Sustainability, 14*(10), 6263.
9. Cardullo, P., & Kitchin, R. (2019). Being a 'citizen' in the smart city: Up and down the scaffold of smart citizen participation in Dublin, Ireland. *GeoJournal, 84*(1), 1–13.
10. Deng, T., Zhang, K., & Shen, Z.-J.M. (2021). A systematic review of a digital twin city: A new pattern of urban governance toward smart cities. *Journal of Management Science and Engineering, 6*(2), 125–134.
11. Eisenberg, A. (2009). *Reasons of identity: A normative guide to the political and legal assessment of identity claims.* Oxford University Press. https://doi.org/10.1093/acprof:oso/9780199291304.001.0001
12. Ford, D. N., & Wolf, C. M. (2020). Smart cities with digital twin systems for disaster management. *Journal of Management in Engineering, 36*(4). https://doi.org/10.1061/(ASCE)ME.1943-5479.0000779
13. Francisco, A., Mohammadi, N., & Taylor, J. E. (2020). Smart city digital twin–enabled energy management: Toward real-time urban building energy benchmarking. *Journal of Management in Engineering, 36*(2), 04019045.
14. Grieves, M., & Vickers, J. (2017). Digital twin: Mitigating unpredictable, undesirable emergent behavior in complex systems. In *Transdisciplinary perspectives on complex systems: New findings and approaches* (pp. 85–113). Springer.
15. Hao, H., & Wang, Y. (2022). Smart curb digital twin: Inventorying curb environments using computer vision and street imagery. *IEEE Journal of Radio Frequency Identification, 7*, 168–172.
16. Hernandez, F., & Kellett, P. (2010). *Rethinking the informal city: Critical perspectives from latin America.* Berghahn Books. (Introduction: Reimagining the Informal in Latin America).
17. Jirón, P., Imilán, W. A., Lange, C., & Mansilla, P. (2021). Placebo urban interventions: Observing smart city narratives in Santiago de Chile. *Urban Studies, 58*(3), 601–620.
18. Khawte, S. S., et al. (2022). *Digital twin creation for slums in Brazil based on UAV data.* The International Archives of the Photogrammetry, Remote Sensing and Spatial Information Sciences, XLVIII-4/W4-2022, pp. 75–81. https://doi.org/10.5194/isprs-archives-XLVIII-4-W4-2022-75-2022
19. Kitchin, R. (2014). The real-time city? Big data and smart urbanism. *GeoJournal, 79*, 1–14.
20. Kitchin, R. (2015). Making sense of smart cities: Addressing present shortcomings. *Cambridge Journal of Regions, Economy and Society, 8*(1), 131–136.
21. Kitchin, R. (2022). Conceptualising smart cities. *Urban Research & Practice, 15*(1), 155–159.
22. Laguerre, M. S., & Laguerre, M. S. (1994). Informal space. In *The informal city* (pp. 27–45). Springer.

23. Lenard, P. T. (2020). Culture. In E. N. Zalta (Ed.), *The Stanford Encyclopedia of Philosophy (Winter 2020 Edition)*.
24. Liu, T., Mostafa, S., Mohamed, S., & Nguyen, T. S. (2021). Emerging themes of public-private partnership application in developing smart city projects: A conceptual framework. *Built Environment Project and Asset Management, 11*(1), 138–156.
25. Moore, M. (2019). Liberal nationalism and the challenge of essentialism. In G. Gustavsson & D. Miller (Eds.), *Liberal nationalism and its critics: Normative and empirical questions* (pp. 188–202). Oxford University Press. https://doi.org/10.1093/oso/9780198842545.003.0011
26. Mylonas, G., et al. (2023). Digital twins for protecting cultural heritage against climate change. *Computer, 56*(9), 100–104. https://doi.org/10.1109/MC.2023.3290687
27. Portmann, E., & Finger, M. (2015). Smart cities-Ein Überblick! *HMD Praxis derWirtschaftsinformatik, 52*, 470–481.
28. Roche, S., Nabian, N., Kloeckl, K., & Ratti, C. (2012). *Are 'smart cities' smart enough*. In Global Geospatial Conference.
29. Sang, F. et al. (2022). Digital twin platform design for Zhejiang rural cultural tourism based on unreal engine. In *2022 International Conference on Culture-Oriented Science and Technology (CoST)* (pp. 274–278). https://doi.org/10.1109/CoST57098.2022.00063
30. Scheibmeir, J., & Malaiya, Y. (2022). A social media-driven digital twin of an invasive species. In *Proceedings of the 10th International Workshop on Simulation for Energy, Sustainable Development & Environment, SESDE, CAL-TEK srl*. https://doi.org/10.46354/i3m.2022.sesde.002
31. Scheibmeir, J. A., & Malaiya, Y. K. (2021). *Social media analytics of the Internet of Things*. https://doi.org/10.21203/rs.3.rs-647683/v1.
32. Sicari, C., Lukaj, V., Celesti, A., Fazio, M., & Villari, M. (2021). GAVIN: A new platform for enriching 3D virtual indoor navigation with social-based geotags. In *Proceedings of the IEEE Symposium on Computers and Communications (ISCC)*. https://doi.org/10.1109/ISCC53001.2021.9631432
33. Song, S. (2005). Majority norms, multiculturalism, and gender equality. *American Political Science Review, 99*(4), 473–489. https://doi.org/10.1017/S0003055405051828

Data-Driven Micromobility Governance—A Stage Model

Felix N. Bäßmann, Daniela G. Waßmann, and Michael H. Breitner

Abstract City authorities are faced with aversions of traditional traffic participants to shared micromobility services albeit these were deemed as a cornerstone of sustainable urban transportation. At the same time, the connectivity of shared vehicles, i.e. bicycles and e-scooters, should allow city authorities to design smart transportation policies. We investigate how cities can and do use micromobility data to reduce aversion and increase the sustainability of personal transportation. Applying design science research, combining knowledge from literature and expert interviews, we derive ten objectives of data-driven micromobility governance. We present and discuss these objectives in a stage model with five maturity levels. Our stage model includes benefits for citizen acceptance, prerequisites for implementation, and provides an actionable agenda for theory and practice.

1 Introduction

City authorities are adopting Information and Communication Technology (ICT) to become smart sustainable cities. One central aim is to increase the quality of life of citizens through smart urban transportation. ICT can collect personal transportation data, citizen sentiment data about services, and assist in managing traffic [33].

Within the aspect of smart urban transportation, shared micromobility was introduced as a sustainable and disruptive service [23]. Promises were among other reduced numbers of private car trips and more convenience on the last mile of public

F. N. Bäßmann (✉) · M. H. Breitner
Information Systems Institute, Leibniz University Hannover, Hannover, Germany
e-mail: baessmann@iwi.uni-hannover.de

M. H. Breitner
e-mail: breitner@iwi.uni-hannover.de

D. G. Waßmann
Leibniz University Hannover, Hannover, Germany
e-mail: wassmann@stud.uni-hannover.de

C. M. Flath et al. (eds.), *Shaping the Digital Future Through Innovation and Practice*,
Lecture Notes in Information Systems and Organisation 85,
https://doi.org/10.1007/978-3-032-08489-7_2

transport. The digital nature of shared micromobility services provides the opportunity to gather data to providers, researchers, and governments, to examine the impact and manage the usage of this new personal transportation service [13] and to interact with users and citizens [16].

However, e-scooter ridership in particular has currently a strong negative effect on the traffic satisfaction of city inhabitants moving by car, bicycle or foot [1]. Gössling [16] stated to mitigate the negative sentiment about shared micromobility, city authorities must carefully intervene and manage the disruptive changes associated with it. They must manage power struggles, social and cultural resistance, and infrastructural as well as technological challenges. To do so, some authorities have implemented policies and expanded their ICTs to cover micromobility [16].

But research has called for more sophisticated interventions to promote this sustainable mode of transport, e.g. joint booking and tariff systems [36]. Public organizations aiming to intervene must adapt to innovation and recognize particular challenges. Practitioners face pressure to deliver innovative services with limited human and funding resources as well as being trained for acquisition processes in which expectations and requirements are defined upfront [20, 28]. It poses the question how city authorities can identify, prioritize, and implement data-driven ICT objectives that mitigate the negative impacts and leverage the strengths of this new type of mobility. In the literature we found little on how city authorities use micromobility data or challenges they face while implementing interventions. Sochor et al. [37] have proposed a five stages model of Mobility-as-a-Service (MaaS) integration. Apart from that we only found in the grey literature Laborda [24] building on this research and suggesting a five-level maturity model of data-led micromobility management derived from MaaS integration levels.

Maturity and stage models are common to assess the quality of an organization its goods and services, to identify solutions for change, and to improve its competitiveness. They "serve to solve the problems of determining a company's status quo of its capabilities and deriving measures for improvement therefrom" [5, p. 214]. Stage models help organizations to effectively manage resources and to achieve complex objectives with acceptable levels of risk. They assist in establishing priorities and provide guidelines [15]. The stages particularly allow for a systematic understanding of the inherent effectiveness and value of different stages of growth, creating awareness on the importance, potentials, requirements, and complexity. Thus, through stage models public administrators can decide on themselves which stage is best for their situation [42].

We hence develop a stage model of data-driven micromobility governance to identify the value for citizens and requirements of the derived objectives. We build upon Lee [25] who proposed a common frame of reference for e-Government stage models. We selected this reference frame, as it evolves around the role and involvement of citizens while including technological and operational requirements. To research the maturity of micromobility data usage in public authorities, to derive an actionable agenda for the continuous improvement of city governments, and to identify opportunities for further research we formulate our Research Question (RQ) as

How can city authorities prioritize micromobility data utilization based on capabilities needed and value provided to adapt to disruptions caused by micromobility?

To address our RQ, we apply a Design Science Research (DSR) approach, following Doyle et al. [11]. Using DSR for the development of maturity models is proposed by Becker et al. [5]. We combine theoretical knowledge about data utilization and sustainability aspects from literature with practical knowledge from different experts in this field. We deduce and classify our findings along the five stages of Lee [25], adapt the reference stage model and present a novel artifact that contributes prescriptive and descriptive knowledge to realize the potential of smart urban transportation and further research opportunities. We then discuss our findings and give recommendations.

2 Research Design and Methods

To address the RQ, we design and evaluate a new artifact following Doyle et al. [11]. Becker et al. [5] suggest to use DSR. Table 1 shows the 6-step research process to formulate the stage model that serves descriptive and prescriptive purposes and to discuss the findings [6].

For Step 1, the problem identification, Becker et al. [5] state three requirements: "the artifact must be relevant to the solution of a heretofore unsolved and important business problem" [29, p. 49], must contribute to current research, and the novel model must be substantiated by comparison with existing models and might be an improvement of a known maturity model. We motivate our research in the Introduction and reflect on current research in Sect. 3 to elaborate on the relevance of our research and existing maturity models.

Table 1 Research design

DSR steps		Results	Sources
Problem	**Step 1:** Identify problem	Research motivation	[5]
Design and build the artifact	**Step 2:** Literature search	42 relevant papers	[40, 41]
	Step 3: Deduce concepts	10 prescriptive concepts	
	Step 4: Expert interviews	12 expert interviews	[14, 27, 31, 35]
	Step 5: Finalizing artifact	Stage model	
Evaluation	**Step 6:** Evaluation of artifact	Evaluated stage model	[34]

In Step 2, the literature search, we applied filters to ensure a feasible number of results [40]. We limited the search to a basket of high quality journals focusing on transportation, i.e. the Journal of Transport Geography, Transport Reviews, Travel Behavior and Society, and Transportation Research Part A, B, C, D, E, and F. We searched the basket with the search string "shared micromobility" in title, abstract, or keywords and date of publication between 2018 and 2024. In consecutive order the title, abstract, and full text were evaluated. Literature was deemed relevant and included, if it provided information on an aspect of data-driven government in the context of micromobility and livability or sustainability. We screened in total 152 papers out of which 42 were considered relevant based on the full text. The search protocol can be found in the online appendix. As suggested by Webster and Watson [41], we developed a concept matrix of the relevant literature in Step 3. Concepts were filtered out if they did not fit to the RQ, e.g., COVID-19 impacts on demand.

After the literature search, we conducted twelve semi-structured interviews in Step 4 to derive practical knowledge. We choose anonymized, semi-structured interviews to engage subjects in a conversation and to get a first-person account of the participant's reality [35]. Following Mayring [27], we gathered and later structured questions along the theoretic concepts deduced from our literature search.

The interview guideline can as well be found in the online appendix. We conducted interviews until saturation was reached [38]. To validate saturation, we selected at least two interview partners from key stakeholders: City Authorities (CAs), Mobility Agencies (MAs), and Sharing Providers (SPs) ensuring that no additional data lead to new insights by adding perspectives from Research (RE), Non-Governmental Organizations (NGOs), and Consulting (CO). Information about the interview partners is displayed in Table 2. Interviews were conducted from August to October 2023, lasted between 20 to 60 min, were recorded, and transcribed afterwards.

In Step 5 the interview data was evaluated by following Mayring [27]. After defining the relevant material, a theory-based, deductive set of initial categories was defined. Utilizing a data sample of four interviews, definitions, anchor examples, and coding rules were adjusted to make them applicable to the data. The coding rules were then applied to the full data set. Any remarks and conflicts of the coding rules and the interview data were noted. These consecutive steps were first individually conducted and then discussed between the first and second author after each step,

Table 2 Interviewed experts

Expert	Affiliation
CA1, CA2, CA3	Representatives of mobility departments in different cities (all cities have more than 500,000 inhabitants)
MA4, MA5, MA6	Employees at different government funded mobility agencies
SP7, SP8	Area managers at different micromobility sharing providers
RE9, RE10	Postdoctoral researchers on urban mobility
NGO11	Representative NGO "VCD Kreisverband Hannover Region"
CO12	Consultant for urban mobility

to achieve validity of the categories. Lastly, the full data set was revised by the first and second author to reflect on the changes. Then, following the content structuring rules of Mayring [27], coded interview references were first paraphrased and then summarized per category to extract information. Anchor examples can be found in the online appendix.

Based on the derived practical knowledge from Step 4 and Step 5, combined with the theoretical knowledge from Step 2 and Step 3, the artifact was created. We applied the design principles for prescriptive and descriptive maturity models proposed by Röglinger et al. [31] to adapt and extend the reference stage model from Lee [25] for the specific purpose of data-driven micromobility governance.

Lastly, evaluating the artifact is a relevant part of DSR [17]. We conducted the ex-post evaluation and justification in Step 6 based on theory as proposed by Schoormann et al. [34] and used Google Scholar, its similarity search, and Research Rabbit to add additional literature to the basket that reflects on the novel findings of our interviews, and that were not covered through the initial literature search.

3 Theoretical Knowledge from Literature

3.1 Stage Models for Public Organizations and Micromobility Services

For shared micromobility and public organizations we found only a few papers that categorized maturity or service levels. Sochor et al. [37] proposed a topology of 5 MaaS integration levels from no integration to integration of societal goals elaborating on responsibility management of MaaS operators on different levels and the incorporation of policy goals. At that time the authors put little emphasis on micromobility and did not include e-scooters which significantly changed the topology of MaaS offers. Later, focusing on e-scooters, Kazemzadeh and Sprei [22] conducted a literature review and proposed a framework to measure the quality level of service and road network infrastructure based on user preferences, reflecting much on cycling literature. In the grey literature Laborda [24] elaborated on the role of mobility data management in the context of the MaaS integration levels proposed by Sochor et al. [37]. Barriers for public and private mobility stakeholders are stated that must be overcome in order to unlock value, i.e. trust in data. On the lowest level integrated information is used for reporting, followed by data-driven policies, succeeded by pricing and subsidies for optimized decisions, and on the highest level societal goals of the cities' mobility plans are supported through multimodal optimization. He stated a need for policymakers to understand this new form of mobility and demanded data-informed mobility policies.

These papers focused on the objectives to improve the quality of mobility services but did not consider the aversion of non-users or emphasized little the perspective of city authorities, i.e. the capabilities needed to implement the stages. To address this gap we select the reference framework of Lee [25]. It contains the stages presenting, assimilating, reforming, morphing, and e-Governance in relation to the two themes operation/technology and citizen/service. Each stage has a focus on data usage in the context of operation/technology, benefits for citizens are covered in the theme citizen/service.

3.2 Data-Driven Micromobility Objectives

In line with the relevant literature on micromobility stage and maturity levels we found the literature on objectives from the citizen/service perspective to be underrepresented. Studies dominantly addressed how micromobility data can be used to identify trip patterns, hotspots, respective parking zones or the sustainability of personal urban transportation. To a lesser extent the results reflect on the potential interaction of citizens with governments and providers through micromobility services. Relevant findings have been made among other by Fitt and Curl [13] who partially focus on spatial conflicts. Gössling [16] screened newspaper reports to identify micromobility concerns reported by these outlets. In recent publications, the role of organizations has been further emphasized. Schumann et al. [36] researched how passively generated big data can improve the safety, social impacts, environmental impacts and system design of micromobility. They suggest among other, increased sensor deployment, data-driven interventions for short-term demand adjustments, and analysis of public transport ridership data to better integrate micromobility in multimodal trip chains. Bigotte and Ferrao [7] studied the future role of e-scooters in urban mobility for cities in Portugal by interviewing experts. We further address this gap in the later sections through the results of our expert interviews.

To comprehensively analyze the literature, we conducted a literature review an aggregated the findings as categories of objectives. We grouped the categories along the individual stages of Lee [25]. On the first stage, Presenting, scattered information is displayed. Visualizations can be positioned towards citizens/services or operation/technology, i.e. city employees, but might only be available and not processed [25]. To reach this stage, micromobility data must be accessible, and capabilities should exist to visualize the data. The literature suggests Visualizing Accidents and Locations [3, 16], to study the positions and quantities of micromobility vehicles and respective accidents.

The second stage, Assimilating, refers to the integration of scattered information bases and applications. During this phase interaction-based services emerge that assimilate informational processes with real-world ones [25]. Through integrated information bases Tailored Operating Areas can be defined based on the built environment and urban characteristics [19, 21]. A Platform for Citizen Interaction helps city employees, according to literature, to better manage conflicts or suggestions, e.g. services for citizens where they can report spatial conflicts caused by micromobility vehicles or users [2].

On the third stage, Reforming, authorities reform processes and services in the real-world, re-engineer and streamline operations and technology, and start to provide digital transactions focusing on increased efficiency [25]. City authorities can target Hotspots for mobility hubs, parking spaces and targeted infrastructure interventions to improve traffic safety [3, 16]. Transactions allow the efficient provision of sharing services in one platform application by Merging and Marketing Services from Different Providers [39].

On the fourth stage, Morphing, the scope of government activities changes as the potential of data usage and micromobility is identified. The focus shifts towards planning and developing new services for the benefit of citizens, focusing on effectiveness not only efficiency. It is expected that citizens can participate more actively in change processes compared to simple interactions and transactions [25]. City authorities then could promote the substitution of less sustainable transport modes [10, 12] or make micromobility services available to disadvantaged communities [9]. Improving Road Networks could then be carried out in a targeted and effective manner to address citizens most willing to switch transportation means [22]. Further, Citizens could request additional services through Sustainable, User-friendly MaaS Provision helping cities to attract or retain users [8, 18].

On the fifth stage, e-Governance, authorities can make use of the full capabilities of advanced ICTs, i.e. technical and operational components being reconfigured almost ad-hoc and citizens and authorities can interact in near real-time [25]. Traffic violations can be monitored and fined precisely in near real-time through Smart Traffic Rules Enforcement and sharing capacities can be dynamically adapted through Dynamic Provision [36].

4 Practical Knowledge from Interviews

Presenting. With regard to data availability and presentation, the reported maturity differed between cities. CA1 is in negotiations with service providers to share the data, while CA2 already has access to dashboards that monitor parked vehicles and hotspots. Consultant CO12 added: "*Some cities oblige providers to share data, others do not. Even though, general permissions give cities great leverage. A general mobility data law is also being drafted at the federal level. Then you have to share your data. That will provide added value for traffic planners and many others in the city.*" CO12 stated negative prejudices as one example: "*Very often, these discussions are only about feelings, so data helps, especially if you can compare yourself with other cities.*"

Providers offer own data products and state data protection as one problem to share relevant data with other stakeholders. SP7: "*We are happy to pass on our knowledge and even have special dashboards where cities can obtain information.*" SP8: "*I would say that the data protection regulation often prevents us from sharing data - it is difficult to share data or new data transfers have to be signed off.*" CA1 argued that data sharing can't be generalized: "*We only want the station data or the location data of the e-scooters for the time being. We don't want to have any personal data, e.g. customer data (…), but if it relates to persons it is indeed problematic regarding data protection.*"

Assimilating. Experts stated that authorities, together with providers, are making targeted adjustments, e.g. tailored operating areas. MA5: "*Are they getting to workplaces where the service area ends 200 meters from the employer? Should the service area be extended? These are things that arise during operations (…) and are then discussed and adjusted together with authorities and providers.*" Further, the importance of interacting with citizens, especially non-users, has been identified by experts, e.g., MA4: "*The 95 percent of the population who don't use it should also be satisfied. The providers need to understand this target group, which is not actually their target group, much better and communicate better.*" CA1: "*From the point of view of citizens, who are not so positive about it, it is extra annoying when they report an e-scooter lying in the pathway and someone only arrives a day later or even later to pick it up.*"

Reforming. On the stage of reforming the dominant topic was the creation of designated parking zones, e.g. CA2: "*The main issue are e-scooters parked in an obstructive way or contrary to traffic regulations.*" RE9: "*The only thing, I think, works well is to define parking zones. (…) I think that contributes to the success because it is an acceptable solution for both sides. For those who are not yet sure if they want to use it or not, it reduces the risk of not finding a vehicle.*" SP7 stated the success of parking zones underpinning it with data: "*We completely turned the city center into a mandatory parking zone in a test. Nobody was allowed to park outside of fixed parking zones. (…) We didn't have fewer customers as a result, but if you walked through the city center, it looked much cleaner.*" It was further suggested by experts to promote appropriate parking with monetary incentives. Interviewees pointed out that increasing citizen interaction and recognizing their needs can further improve the acceptance, e.g. when identifying parking zones. NGO11: "*What is relevant, with regard to fearful spaces and darkness and so on, is that there is social control around the parking zone. (…) A zone in the backyard is always bad, for car sharing, for an e-scooter, or a bicycle.*" Citizens might suggest or rate parking zones. Integrating micromobility service providers can further increase the value and reach of such platforms, as entry barriers to micromobility services are lowered. But implementation challenges and nuanced steps towards MaaS platforms were stated. MA5: "*Cities like Munich or Berlin combine a whole range of providers, e.g. bikes, e-scooter, e-bikes, that are all searchable, bookable and can be paid for using only one app. That is, of course, the ultimate solution, which is where we want to be one day. But that's still a long way off.*"

Morphing. It was pointed out that the road infrastructure is to date in an underdeveloped state which impacts traffic rule enforcement, CO12: "*A set of rules may include restrictions, no-parking zones, no-drive zones and the like. But I can make as many rules as I like, i.e. having to ride on the cycle path, if I don't have a cycle path, then it becomes difficult.*" Interviewees elaborated on the strategic vision of cities and respective mobility plans, e.g. CA2: "*(…) a mobility turnaround, that people use their cars less and shared micromobility more. To get to public transport, for* *example, instead of driving the route in their own car. That's our goal. With fewer conflicts it could increase the overall acceptance among citizens.*" Fully integrated MaaS offers should go hand in hand with public transportation services, i.e. MA5: "*We don't want to cannibalize public transport, but rather ensure that the systems strengthen each other. This is the so-called extended local public transport, and there is a lot of potential in it to encourage more and more people to move around more sustainably.*"

However, the responses of experts indicate that not all the required data is assimilated yet, NGO11: "*You would first have to evaluate what benefit they have. And there would have to be really sound evidence of it. How many journeys were actually saved that might otherwise have been made by car?*" Creating offers that provide a societal net benefit is seen as crucial but data analytics capabilities and respective insights appear not mature enough, to address more potential users, RE9: "*I don't think we currently understand well enough how we can make these services so attractive that they actually reduce car journeys. So how exactly do these services have to look like, where do the vehicles have to be located, what do I have to do with private car ownership or usage to make it possible to switch to other modes of transport?*" In regard to age, CA3: "*To find out how I can address the other age groups and ask them, do you have other needs? That you don't have just one group of users who could also walk.*" NGO11: "*E-mobility on bikes, for example, has an older target group. We can definitely reach them with this. So fewer e-scooters, more bicycles. You're not likely to get older people on e-scooters.*" And income, RE9: "*That it penetrates other income groups. Shared bikes are relatively inexpensive, shared e-scooters are relatively expensive. With the price structure that we currently see on the market, it will hardly appeal to lower income groups. Unless it is included in public transport and you can use it to get to the bus stop.*" And geographically, CA2: "*Cities could issue tenders and can state we don't just want to have the inner-city areas covered, but also the less economically attractive outer areas. However, you have to monitor or track it in some way.*"

e-Governance. Real-time monitoring and enforcement of regulations is seen as an essential part of e-Governance, not only of providers but also in the context of traffic laws. Today, traffic violations are seen as a meaningful problem, e.g. CA2: "*Driving on sidewalks, driving in the opposite direction, cutting other people off (…) simply behaving in a way that endangers traffic.*" Interviewees pointed to solutions that leverage the connectivity of shared devices. CO12: "*If they drive into the pedestrian zone, the e-scooters run out of power and users have to push. That's brilliant, it's great for enforcing laws and road traffic regulations.*" Being able to respond in near real-time to sudden traffic spikes was seen as another promising scenario. SP8: "*There are considerations for live evaluations, e.g., for a soccer match, that you can predict the expected demand. But we haven't got that far yet. Theoretically, it is possible, but today we use historical data and make informed decisions based on that.*"

5 Discussion, Recommendations, and Artifact Evaluation

Based on the theoretical and practical knowledge we derive our stage model, i.e. Fig. 1. The citizen/service perspective shows the increasing value for citizens and growing complexity. Every stage has two objectives, the names were partly modified to incorporate the practical knowledge. After the objective to visualize *Vehicle Locations* and *Accident Locations* on a map to better understand this disruption, two maturity paths emerge for the next three stages. One aims at the acceptance of citizens while using or encountering micromobility in public. From *Tailored Operating Areas* to prevent dead ends and usage in forbidden areas, over targeted measures at *Hotspots* to counter cluttered parking and improve driver safety, to *Improving Road Infrastructure* to effectively steer investments for new road infrastructure. The other path aims at the continuous improvement of the supporting digital services platform, i.e. *Platform for Citizen Interaction,* followed by an initial *Platform for Dispersed Providers,* to *Sustainable, User-friendly MaaS Provision* where curated, incentivized offers allow for integrated multimodal trip chains. On the stage of e-Governance, novel approaches to problems are possible, i.e. automated *Smart Traffic Rules Enforcement* to increase traffic rules compliance and *Dynamic Provider Governance* through which micromobility providers are automatically assessed by defined indicators, based on the results automatically supported or penalized, and allowed fleet sizes adapted based on short-term demand.

The operation/technology perspective highlights the most relevant capabilities to realize the objectives. Each capability is only listed on the lowest stage it first appears. We applied identifying frames to highlight the relationship between capabilities and objectives and lines to connect capabilities that build on each other. To realize an objective on a given stage the capabilities without a frame and with the same frame as the objective must be implemented. To visualize *Vehicle Locations, Geographic Base Data* and *Historic Parking Data* are needed. On the Morphing stage, the objective *Improve Road Infrastructure,* in enabled by *Incentivize Sustainable Trips.* It describes that city authorities use their *Data Analytics Capabilities* to not only identify hotspots for *Data Driven Real World Interventions* but also expand them to a level where they can identify sustainable trips and incentivize these. This capability builds on *Billing and Accounting,* as monetary incentives can be used to incentivize sustainable trips and provided through *Sustainable, User-friendly MaaS Provision.* Similar, the interaction processes with service providers are continuously improved, from labor-intensive *Incident Management,* to digitally *Integrate Provider Offers and Incidents, Static Governing of Providers* with penalizing schemes, and finally *Automated Governing of Providers.*

The generated value of our identified objectives can be of societal or monetary nature, e.g. through improved acceptance or more users. The implementation appears to depend on monetary incentives, governmental prioritization, regulatory frameworks and public relations work of service providers: One city was still in negotiations with providers to receive micromobility data, another one was already using

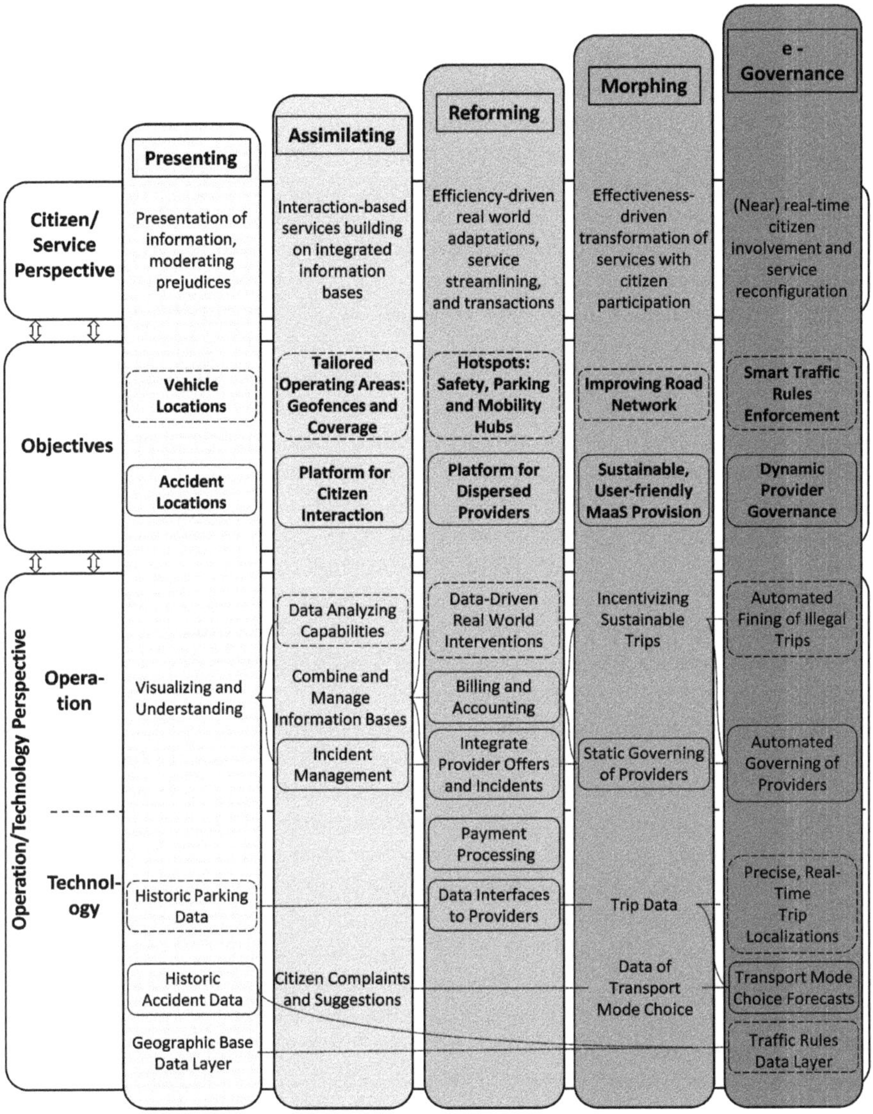

Fig. 1 Stage model of data-driven micromobility governance

dashboards, many micromobility service providers have implemented reporting interfaces for poorly parked vehicles, and software platform providers have rolled out MaaS platforms to some cities. Lee [25] argued that the reference stage model is not normatively rigorous and progressive from a technological standpoint, as ICTs are reproducible and, building on external experience, advanced ICTs can be imported to jump stages. This raises the question how to prioritize and where to jump stages.

We find that implementation actions within cities are often a question of funding, available resources, and data. MA5: "*Very large cities can afford MaaS systems, they monitor everything with dashboards that cost a lot of money per year in order to be able to view and manage shared micromobility digitally.*" CA2: "*We don't necessarily need more data. The issue for us is that we often don't have the capacities to evaluate this data in a way that we can make good use of it.*" Regulations open up leverage for public authorities to outsource the realization of objectives to the private sector. We argue that cities should use their limited resources to be perceived as an equal and serious partner in resulting digital value networks, i.e. by overseeing the removal of poorly parked vehicles in an appropriate time, as highlighted in Sect. 4 under *Assimilating*.

Transforming personal transportation towards sustainability appears to be impeded by a lack of data. To reach higher maturity, insights must be gathered into trips that are environmentally and socially sustainable and trips that could be replaced by such. These could in turn be eligible to government subsidies. Some public transportation providers already offer non-targeted subsidies, e.g., for all short trips on shared bicycles. Cities might start time-limited interventions in underserved areas to test the acceptance and usage of different micromobility forms, to gather potential user and transport mode choice data. We see this as an essential part of data-driven *Sustainable, User-friendly MaaS Provision.* The socially sustainable provision of micromobility services for underserved groups was also examined by Sanguinetti and Alston-Stepnitz [32] and Riggs et al. [30] who researched regulatory policies for e-scooters in 61 cities in the United States of America. The authors recommend policies and pilot programs and emphasize that results will vary strongly based on the city size, climate, and landscape, concluding that individual analysis is needed.

Further, cities must develop transportation strategies for micromobility and objective indicators along which micromobility offers are aligned. This is supported by Sochor et al. [37] who suggest quantified goals, e.g., for user attraction and emission reduction but don't elaborate on the role of service compliance measurements. While dynamic adaptation to demand can increase user numbers, little research has been conducted on the advantages of dynamic or automated provider governance for cities to reduce the need for human oversight [26]. Cities should be able to both dynamically enforce and adapt their micromobility regulatory framework based on objectives and demand. We argue that for *Dynamic Provider Governance* smart public space and curbside management will become increasingly important, to allocate space dynamically to different transportation modes. In this context near real-time processes in city authorities are required, e.g. interfaces to request larger parking zones for events or an automated expansion of parking zones following arrival spikes.

Also, the available technology and public laws can become a determining factor, i.e. for *Smart Traffic Rules Enforcement*. MA6: "*There are specific guidelines as to where e-scooters may be parked, but because the Global Positioning System (GPS) signal is not too precise, vehicles can still be parked incorrectly.*" Bäßmann et al. [4] suggest to use 5G networks to improve the localization accuracy. Also, tenders could require precise, certified GPS hardware in vehicles. To date, fining traffic offenders may not be legally possible through digital tracking and with different types of data varying data protection rules apply. We recommend that stakeholders identify how data regulations can be implemented and that authorities advocate for digital law enforcement.

Lastly, Schumann et al. [36] identify a lack of accident research that was also criticized by MA5: "*That well documented studies are finally launched that put the accident figures in relation to the passenger kilometers traveled, that this information finally becomes facts.*" The authors as well suggested that authorities use big data to identify accident-prone areas and preventive measures like speed throttling.

The mentioned aspects can cause a non-linear maturity path in our stage model. The conflict of multiple and possibly equifinal existing maturity paths is a common criticism [31]. To mitigate this, the authors suggest design science, that we applied. Our resulting stage model is designed to provide a set of objectives and prerequisites that can be executed independently but profit from linear implementation for the two paths, i.e. acceptance improvement and digital platform improvement. Considering the import of external ICTs, Lee [25] argued that from a citizen/service perspective jumping stages in processes and services in the real world is harder and can potentially cause resistance to change. Therefore, implementing objectives and operations from lower stages can pay dividend for organizations by reducing aversion, even though, technologically, jumping stages might appear attractive.

6 Limitations, Conclusions, and Further Research

Our stage model is still limited. Another evaluation round with experts and consecutive improvement can increase the validity of the model. Our practical knowledge originates from experts focusing on large urban agglomerations in Germany and Austria. Thus, results and objectives may vary for other regions and rural areas. For further research, extended interviews for the evaluation and the geographic scope are important.

We contribute to theory our findings on how cities can successively implement data-driven micromobility objectives to continuously improve the quality of life of citizens and reduce aversion. We found that the existing literature has focused much on the operational/technology perspective and less on acceptance from the citizen/service perspective. We add to the latter perspective through our expert interviews. For this we extended and adapted the reference stage model proposed by Lee [25]. For practitioners, we identify as one aspect to further increase the collaboration between cities and service providers, e.g., by designing joint communication and action plans to improve the acceptance and success among the general population. Further, there is a lack of research on detailed accident studies for e-scooters, transport mode choice data and automated service governance from which targeted interventions could be derived. This will help cities to implement sustainable transportation plans. The lack of resources for data analytics in public authorities can be addressed with research projects that provide open source toolboxes on low code or no code basis.

Acknowledgements This research was partially funded by the German Federal Ministry for Digital and Transport under grant number 45FGU121_E. The authors would like to appreciate and thank the interviewees for their participation in this study.

References

1. ADAC. (2023). *ADAC Monitor 2024 „Mobil in der Stadt“* (in German). https://assets.adac.de/image/upload/v1706121441/ADAC-eV/KOR/Text/PDF/ADAC-Monitor-2024-Ergebnisbericht_gsbjf1.pdf. Accessed: 05 March 2024.
2. An, Z., Mullen, C., Zhao, C., & Heinen, E. (2023). Stereotypes and the public acceptability of shared micromobility. *Travel Behaviour and Society, 33*, 1–15.
3. Arias-Molinares, D., Xu, Y., Büttner, B., & Duran-Rodas, D. (2023). Exploring key spatial determinants for mobility hub placement based on micromobility ridership. *Journal of Transport Geography, 110*, 1–14.
4. Bäßmann, F. N., Werth, O., Düffel, T. J., & Breitner, M. H. (2023). *Lost in the city?—A scoping review of 5G enabled location-based urban scenarios.* In Proceedings of the 56th Hawaii International Conference on System Sciences, HICSS, pp. 5072–5083.
5. Becker, J., Knackstedt, R., & Pöppelbuß, J. (2009). Developing maturity models for IT management. *Business & Information Systems Engineering, 1*(3), 213–222.
6. Becker, J., Niehaves, B., Poeppelbuss, J., & Simons, A. (2010). *Maturity models in IS research.* In ECIS 2010 Proceedings.
7. Bigotte, J. F., & Ferrao, F. (2023). The future role of shared e-scooters in urban mobility: Preliminary findings from Portugal. *Sustainability, 15*(23), 16467.
8. Blazanin, G., Mondal, A., Asmussen, K. E., & Bhat, C. R. (2022). E-scooter sharing and bike-sharing systems: An individual-level analysis of factors affecting first-use and use frequency. *Transportation Research Part C: Emerging Markets, 135*, 1–40.
9. Christoforou, Z., de Bortoli, A., Gioldasis, C., & Seidowsky, R. (2021). Who is using e-scooters and how? Evidence from Paris. *Transportation Research Part D: Transport and Environment, 92*, 1–46.
10. de Bortoli, A. (2021). Environmental performance of shared micromobility and personal alternatives using integrated modal LCA. *Transportation Research Part D: Transport and Environment, 93*, 1–18.
11. Doyle, C., Luczak-Roesch, M., & Mittal, A. (2019). *We need the open artefact: design science as a pathway to open science in information systems research.* In International Conference on Design Science Research in Information Systems and Technology, Springer International Publishing, pp. 46–60.
12. Fan, Z., & Harper, C. D. (2022). Congestion and environmental impacts of short car trip replacement with micromobility modes. *Transportation Research Part D: Transport and Environment, 103*, 1–17.
13. Fitt, H., & Curl, A. (2020). The early days of shared micromobility: A social practices approach. *Journal of Transport Geography, 86*, 1–10.
14. Franzke, B., & Zeitner, I. (2023). Qualitative interviews. In *Empirische Sozialforschung für die Polizei- und Verwaltungswissenschaften* (pp. 139–168). Springer Fachmedien Wiesbaden. (in German).
15. Gomes, J., Romão, M., & Calderia, M. (2013). *Linking benefits to maturity models.* In Proceedings of the 15th IAMB Conference.
16. Gössling, S. (2020). Integrating e-scooters in urban transportation: Problems, policies, and the prospect of system change. *Transportation Research Part D: Transport and Environment, 79*, 1–12.

17. Gregor, S., Kruse, L., & Seidel, S. (2020). Research perspectives: The anatomy of a design principle. *Journal of the Association for Information Systems, 21*, 1622–1652.
18. Hong, D., Jang, S., & Lee, C. (2023). Investigation of shared micromobility preference for last-mile travel on shared parking lots in city center. *Travel Behaviour and Society, 30*, 163–177.
19. Huo, J., Yang, H., Li, C., Zheng, R., Yang, L., et al. (2021). Influence of the built environment on e-scooter sharing ridership: A tale of five cities. *Journal of Transport Geography, 93*, 1–9.
20. Jiang, R., Thorogood, A., Joukadar, G., & Harrington, K. (2022). *Enabling digital innovation in the public sector*. In PACIS 2022 Proceedings, pp. 1–16.
21. Karimpour, A., Hosseinzadeh, A., & Kluger, R. (2023). A data-driven approach to estimating dockless electric scooter service areas. *Journal of Transport Geography, 109*, 103579.
22. Kazemzadeh, K., & Sprei, F. (2022). Towards an electric scooter level of service: A review and framework. *Travel Behaviour and Society, 29*, 149–164.
23. Kendziorra, J., Barmann, M. N., Witte, A.-K., & Kusanke, K. (2023). *Gender and mobility—A literature review on women's (non-)use of shared mobility services*. In 'Wirtschaftsinformatik 2023 Proceedings'.
24. Laborda, J. (2022). Mobility data management and its potential to generate value. *Oikonomics, 89*, 1–10.
25. Lee, J. (2010). 10 year retrospect on stage models of e-Government: A qualitative meta-synthesis. *Government Information Quarterly, 27*(3), 220–230.
26. Li, Y. (2019). The role of public authorities in the development of mobility-as-a-service. In *The governance of smart transportation systems* (pp. 229–245). Springer.
27. Mayring, P. (2015). *Qualitative Inhaltsanalyse: Grundlagen und Techniken*. Beltz. (in German).
28. Mergel, I. (2018). Open innovation in the public sector: Drivers and barriers for the adoption of Challenge.gov. *Public Management Review, 20*(5), 726–745.
29. Peffers, K., Tuunanen, T., Rothenberger, M. A., & Chatterjee, S. (2007). A design science research methodology for information systems research. *Journal of Management Information Systems, 24*(3), 45–77.
30. Riggs, W., Kawashima, M., & Batstone, D. (2021). Exploring best practice for municipal e-scooter policy in the United States. *Transportation Research Part A: Policy and Practice, 151*, 18–27.
31. Röglinger, M., Pöppelbuß, J., & Becker, J. (2012). Maturity models in business process management. *Business Process Management Journal, 18*(2), 328–346.
32. Sanguinetti, A., & Alston-Stepnitz, E. (2023). Using emerging mobility data to advocate equitable micromobility infrastructure in underserved communities. *Transportation Research Part D: Transport and Environment, 117*, 1–14.
33. Sarker, I. H. (2022). Smart city data science: Towards Data-driven smart cities with open research issues. *Internet of Things, 19*, 100528.
34. Schoormann, T., Möller, F., Chandra Kruse, L., & Otto, B. (2024). BAUSTEIN —A design tool for configuring and representing design research. *Information Systems Journal, 34*, 1871–1901.
35. Schultze, U., & Avital, M. (2011). Designing interviews to generate rich data for information systems research. *Information and Organization, 21*(1), 1–16.
36. Schumann, H.-H., Haitao, H., & Quddus, M. (2023). Passively generated big data for micromobility: State-of-the-art and future research directions. *Transportation Research Part D: Transport and Environment, 121*, 1–19.
37. Sochor, J., Arby, H., Karlsson, I. M., & Sarasini, S. (2018). A topological approach to mobility as a Service: A proposed tool for understanding requirements and effects, and for aiding the integration of societal goals. *Research in Transportation Business & Management, 27*, 3–14.
38. Strauss, A., & Corbin, J. M. (1990). *Basics of qualitative research: Grounded theory procedures and techniques*. Sage.
39. Vij, A., & Dühr, S. (2022). The commercial viability of Mobility-as-a-Service (MaaS): What's in it for existing transport operators, and why should governments intervene? *Transport Reviews, 42*(5), 695–716.
40. vom Brocke, J., Simons, A., Riemer, K., Niehaves, B., Plattfaut, R., et al. (2015). Standing on the shoulders of giants: Challenges and recommendations of literature search in information systems research. *Communications of the Association for Information Systems, 37*, 205–224.

41. Webster, J., & Watson, R. T. (2002). Analyzing the past to prepare for the future: Writing a literature review. *MIS Quarterly, 26*(2), xiii–xxiii.
42. Wendler, R. (2012). The maturity of maturity model research: A systematic mapping study. *Information and Software Technology, 54*(12), 1317–1339.

Getting to Know Your Customer: Onboarding in an Urban Mobility Ecosystem

Daniel Richter and Jürgen Anke

Abstract In recent years, mobility ecosystems formed in German urban areas, comprising of sharing-based providers and traditional public transport. Access to these ecosystems and service integration is inhibited by multiple onboarding processes during which customer information is exchanged and verified. We conducted a case study investigating the onboarding processes of four mobility providers in an urban mobility ecosystem to show by which means informational demands are satisfied and to enable a discussion on the design space for such processes. We show how different institutions shaping mobility service exchange relationships determine informational demands and the technical procedures used to satisfy these during onboarding processes. This results in diverse technical procedures impacting value co-creation in multiple dimensions, such as identity costs. We introduce the MINTI framework discussing our findings in the light of novel technologies such as digital wallets. Future research is needed to further systematize onboarding design choices and quantify their impacts.

1 Introduction

In recent years, urban mobility has seen a wave of innovation, which includes mobility services based on the principle of sharing [11]. Integrating resources such as rental cars, e-scooters, and bikes, these emergent actors are not only competing with the use of a personal car and traditional public transport systems. They are also co-creating completely novel mobility options for urban dwellers by allowing a demand-based combination of different modes of transport across a journey [38]. Urban mobility, therefore, appears less as a strictly transactional market and more as a service ecosystem of "coopetitive" actors with the common goal of facilitating sustainable, enjoyable, and efficient travel across a city [10, 39]. This vision aligns with urban

---

D. Richter (✉) · J. Anke
HTWD University of Applied Sciences, Digital Service Systems Group, Dresden, Germany
e-mail: daniel.richter@htw-dresden.de

J. Anke
e-mail: juergen.anke@htw-dresden.de

C. M. Flath et al. (eds.), *Shaping the Digital Future Through Innovation and Practice*, Lecture Notes in Information Systems and Organisation 85,
https://doi.org/10.1007/978-3-032-08489-7_3

development efforts aiming to increase the quality of life for citizens and travelers by leveraging digital technologies [7].

While mobility itself is always tied to physical means and work, these new sharing services mainly build on information systems (IS) for most of the coordinating requirements of the service exchange relationship, i.e., locating, reserving, and booking a ride, as well as payment. Typically, before a customer can engage in a sharing-based mobility service exchange, they need to complete an onboarding process. We define customer onboarding as a process during which a service exchange relationship is initiated between a customer and a firm. This includes a decision process checking whether the customer qualifies for that relationship based on their identity, past dealings, and available resources [1]. During these processes, potential customers are asked to share personal information [10]. Depending on the service type, legal obligations, and risk involved, these processes can become lengthy, complex, and thus costly [28]. This impedes facilitating seamless switching between mobility options of different providers in a mobility service ecosystem.

A promising solution to reduce customer onboarding burdens and increase service accessibility is to introduce multi-modal platform solutions following a mobility-as-a-service (MaaS) approach. These encapsulate the value propositions of different mobility providers in a single solution and typically require only a single onboarding process to set up. Such platforms are still in their infancy, however. According to Willing et al., the greatest challenges to MaaS are the integration of diverse actors with differing data requirements and incompatible protocols [38]. Organizationally, Schulz et al. describe how the multiplicity of institutional logics among actors in a mobility ecosystem impedes data sharing and thus technical and processual consolidation [27].

Novel architectural proposals based on digital wallets and verifiable credentials promise a more standardized technical integration of data required during customer onboarding for mobility services [10, 31]. However, there is little to no knowledge about the applicability and economic viability of such solutions considering pre-existing implementations of data exchange and verification mechanisms in mobility ecosystems [14, 29]. Also, recent proposals (see [31] and [10]) do not consider the governance of verifiable credentials, i.e. setting guidelines and constraints for the structure and correct use of the exchanged data to fulfill its informational business purpose [22].

To achieve integrated service offerings in mobility ecosystems, customer onboarding processes of different providers need to be aligned not only technically but also organizationally and institutionally [27, 38]. This requires an understanding of the interplay between the providers' informational demands towards their customers, the technical means to satisfy these demands, and these aspects' impacts on value co-creation. IS research has only sparingly addressed customer onboarding, e.g. in the financial sector [1, 25, 30] or focusing on psychological influences [23, 26]. We aim to contribute to the discussion by pursuing the following research question: *How do mobility providers satisfy their informational demands during customer onboarding processes?*

This paper addresses this issue by analyzing the urban mobility ecosystem MOBI in Dresden, Germany. We built a comprehensive empirical knowledge base on this service ecosystem by analyzing documents and mobile apps. Additionally, we conducted interviews with mobility service providers and city government officials. We then focus on onboarding processes and propose a framework connecting informational demands during a business transaction with technical measures and their impacts.

2 Conceptual Background

2.1 Identity Costs

Transaction cost theory holds that the basic analytic unit of economic exchange is a transaction between economic actors [8, 37]. By analyzing the costs these transactions incur, the theory seeks to explain how to define efficient boundaries for organizations [37]. Based on the human behavioral assumptions of bounded rationality and opportunism [37], uncertainty is seen as a reality to any economic exchange relationship [19, 32].

To deal with this uncertainty at the boundary of the economic actor's sphere of influence, transaction costs are incurred [6]. More recently, these were specifically conceptualized as "identity costs" [4]. Under a transaction cost theoretic lens, identity is an input to exchange, necessarily leading to costs "for the initial identification, and subsequent verification of parties to an exchange, as well as that which is being traded" [4]. These procedures are important for all exchange relationships with an element of temporal continuity or promise, i.e., non-spot contractual and credit relationships because "[p]arties to a contract need some level of assurance it will be settled ex-post" [5].

According to Berg et al., identity costs occur due to commercial and compliance reasons [4]. Commercially, the seller of a good or service needs to identify whether the buyer has both the ability and willingness to pay in exchange [4]. To ascertain these two facets, credit ratings are widely used both in consumer markets [18] and in inter-firm relationships [9]. From a compliance perspective, the most common reason for identity costs is KYC procedures as mandated by international regulations against money laundering and terrorism financing [15]. In Germany, for example, banks must thoroughly check potential customers' legal identity and occupation before engaging in a business relationship with them, as laid out in §§ 10 ff. GwG (Germany). Berg et al. conceptualize the means to exchange such identity information as "identity technologies", including government identification credentials, credit ratings, and reputation [5].

In sum, transaction cost theory explains the need for economic actors to identify each other on commercial or compliance grounds before being able to engage in the desired exchange relationship [4]. This identification is seen as a means to deal with the inherent uncertainty of such relationships based on the assumption of bounded rationality and opportunism of the counterparty [6]. The use of various identity technologies incurs identity costs [5].

2.2 Service Ecosystem Onboarding

Service-dominant logic (SDL) is a meta-theoretical framework emerging from the discipline of marketing, which introduces a shift from the traditional divide between goods and services in economic exchange [33, 35, 36]. Rather, SDL postulates that all exchange, including that of physical goods, is fundamentally the exchange of service, i.e., "using one's resources for the benefit of another entity" [16]. Adopting this view, firms and their customers are both seen as integrators of resources, co-creating value during service exchange [35]. Recently, SDL has moved from a purely dyadic view of exchange to an ecosystems view [2, 34, 35]. Lusch and Vargo define a service ecosystem as "a relatively self-contained, self-adjusting system of resource-integrating actors that are connected by shared institutional logics and mutual value creation through service exchange" [17]. The ecosystems view acknowledges that value co-creation results from service exchange by multiple actors [3].

However, as Akaka et al. note, before an actor can successfully integrate resources, they first need to be accessed via existing relationships and then adapted to the actors' specific needs [2]. What constitutes a valuable and acceptable resource is often governed by the relevant institutions, i.e., "the rules of the game" [20], in a specific context [2, 12]. In service ecosystems, this can be observed in social and symbolic boundaries, "enabling their functioning and defining the rules for membership and access to resources" [21]. Actors inside and outside of a service ecosystem engage in different types of boundary work to competitively and cooperatively establish, configure, and cross boundaries [21]. Actors can use boundary objects to facilitate this type of institutional work, which connect meanings across their differing institutional realities [13, 21, 24].

3 Method

3.1 MOBI: The Case of a Multi-modal Urban Mobility Ecosystem

We carried out our case study on the urban mobility ecosystem MOBI in the city of Dresden, the capital of the German federal state of Saxony. MOBI was established by the city administration in cooperation with the local public transport provider in 2018. The ecosystem's formulated value proposition is "Travel however you want!"

(German: "Fahr doch was du willst!") The establishment of MOBI follows several resolutions of the city council aiming to reduce carbon emissions and improve livability in the city.

The Dresden city administration and the public transport business act as orchestrators of the ecosystem, establishing development goals and membership rules as well as involving and aligning mobility providers' value propositions toward these goals. MOBI's mobility providers include a bike sharing business, a car sharing company, and an on-demand shuttle service. While there are more actors offering mobility value propositions in Dresden, we only focused on the institutionalized MOBI ecosystem, its explicit members, and (potential) mobility customers. A distinct feature of the ecosystem is the physical coupling of the services at more than sixty inter-modal mobility stations, throughout the city territory. While said member businesses also operate outside the ecosystem, they use the common MOBI brand and visual language in the territory of Dresden for vehicles and digital interfaces.

3.2 Data Collection and Analysis

To investigate credential use in the onboarding processes of the MOBI ecosystem and relate that use to the ecosystem's governance, we followed a two-step approach. First, we approached the mobility businesses active in the MOBI ecosystem individually to capture customer onboarding processes, data exchange and used credentials in six workshops. In these workshops, we identified the most relevant onboarding processes, documenting the results in customer journey maps. In the second step, we connected the singular service offerings to inter-actor relationships and the ecosystem's goals and value proposition. For that, we conducted a seventh workshop with members of the city administration and used public information available on the websites of the MOBI ecosystem, the city administration, and the mobility businesses.

Since these workshops, Germany adopted a universal public transport subscription ("Deutschlandticket"), disrupting the traditional transport association boundaries. This resulted in changes to the public transport business onboarding process and ecosystem engagement for customers. Additionally, an on-demand shuttle service joined the commercial ecosystem members. Therefore, we decided to add new data to the knowledge base captured in the previously mentioned seven workshops. Specifically, we conducted observations of customer onboarding processes using the providers' websites and mobile applications. We used screenshots to capture customer interactions and mapped these on a digital whiteboard for further analysis. Additionally, we analyzed documents on terms and conditions and privacy policies related to the onboarding processes.

4 Findings

4.1 Customer Onboarding as Boundary Work

MOBI's ecosystem value proposition of "Travel however you want!" suggests a seamless transition between different mobility options on journeys within Dresden's city boundaries. The establishment of multi-modal mobility points allows the ecosystem's commercial actors to physically provide their means of transport in a way that allows customers to change between them easily. Additionally, the availability of the mobility providers' offerings at separate stations and, in the case of the bike sharing provider, in a free-floating manner, facilitates multi-modal travel by providing a physical coupling of different mobility options.

However, the use of these various offerings for personal mobility is restricted by onboarding processes imposed by the mobility providers on their potential customers. Any engagement with the mobility offerings present in the MOBI ecosystem requires the completion of an onboarding process with one of the commercial actors. These processes generally consist of sharing personal data and contractual agreements regarding the terms of use and data protection. Afterward, customers are generally only able to engage in mobility service exchange with the specific actor imposing the onboarding process. An exception is the case of applying for a public transport subscription with the special MOBI plan, which also enables customers to use bike sharing services. Customers wishing to maximally benefit from MOBI's options for a specific mobility demand, including the ability to switch from one means of transport to another seamlessly, are generally required to undergo three to four separate onboarding processes.

While the terms for membership of mobility providers are given by the city administration and enforced by the public transport provider, the mobility providers decide to engage with potential customers autonomously. Therefore, ecosystem onboarding for mobility customers can be seen as multi-tiered and bound to the quality of service exchange with the mobility businesses. Customer onboarding processes are designed to (1) protect the provider's resources, (2) ensure access to the customer's (mostly financial) resources, and (3) fulfill legal obligations for the specific service exchange relationship under consideration. After onboarding, potential customers are assigned a customer status, which is typically represented in the form of a user account or a customer credential. This status allows customers to engage in service exchange with the mobility provider.

The first two requirements give room for individual risk assessment. For example, all four mobility businesses gather potential customers' legal name during onboarding, three of these gather date of birth, and one the exact place of birth. Methods to validate this data vary from no validation (bike sharing and shuttle service), optional validation with a credit bureau (public transport) to compulsory check with a credit bureau, and matching photos of official documents (car sharing). This is related to the high material and financial risk involved in car sharing, as opposed to, e.g., riding a public bus.

The third requirement, in contrast, forces mobility businesses to employ certain methods and devices to provide information about their customers. For example, the car sharing provider is legally required to ensure only customers with a valid driving license drive their vehicles. Therefore, the check for such a driving license becomes a compulsory part of the onboarding process of any car sharing business in Germany.

In sum, customer onboarding processes and customer membership to the MOBI ecosystem are collectively determined by the mobility businesses' individual risk assessments and legal obligations. They are collective in the sense that membership and access to the full bandwidth of service exchange proposed by mobility businesses require crossing multiple onboarding boundaries set by individual mobility providers.

4.2 *Customer Data Collected During Onboarding*

None of the examined onboarding processes require the same data from potential customers. However, we identified six categories of attributes common to multiple onboarding processes in the MOBI ecosystem. These categories consist of attributes, which serve a common purpose and answer similar questions about a potential customer. An overview of data required by the mobility providers during customer onboarding processes and proof methods are given in Table 1. Across the four onboarding processes and categories, redundancies become visible. Customers wishing to engage in all mobility services in the MOBI ecosystem must submit the same data multiple times, albeit with differing methods. The entries in Table 1 use the following notation with three components $\Omega(\alpha, \beta)$:

1. Optionality of data exchange Ω can assume the characteristics M for mandatory, O for optional, and 1 for mandatorily one of multiple.
2. Data exchange methods α between customer and provider are denoted lower case letters with characteristics f for web form, u for file upload, a for ApplePay clearance, l for account login, and e for external service request.
3. Verification mechanisms β of the transferred data are denoted with lower case letters with 0 for no verification, w for visual verification during web chat, s for SMS code sent to phone number, t for test transaction with payment method, p for PayPal account verification, v for verified data from external system.

Legal identity data is collected by all mobility providers for assurance of contractual duties by the customer. This is connected in part to the second category of contact data. Attributes in this category serve to open channels to the customer not only for billing, marketing, and information about changes to the terms of service but also for dunning and summons in case of violations of the latter. Contact data is also required to deliver physical credentials for service exchange operations, such as transport tickets or fuel cards. Payment data specifies how a payment channel between the mobility provider and the customer is established. The most common payment method supported by all commercial actors but the bike sharing provider is direct debit payment. Other supported methods are credit cards, PayPal, Apple-Pay, and GooglePay. Tied to payment is the credit rating identified in the terms and conditions of the public transport and car sharing providers. While only collected in exceptional cases by the former, the latter requests a credit rating for the potential customers by contacting a credit bureau. Such a rating estimates a person's probability of fulfilling their financial duties during service exchange. The credit rating can also serve as an additional proof method for legal identity, contact, and payment data. The qualifications category comprises attributes only relating to a potential customer's driving license and is only relevant to car sharing. Still, we decided to abstract from a driving license to account for other potentially relevant qualifications a customer might need to prove to partake in a service exchange relationship. Lastly, affiliation data refers to preexisting relationships a customer can use to redeem a discount with the mobility provider. The most important example is various public transport subscriptions a potential customer of the bike and car sharing providers can use to obtain preferential price conditions.

Comparing the collected customer data, the car sharing provider employs the most comprehensive onboarding process. It is also the only one which requires manual labor for data validation. As there is no official digital German driving license, the car sharing provider requires customers to take a photo of the physical credential and upload it during a live web chat with a customer service employee, who then visually validates the entered data and the authenticity of the driving license. This is repeated with an official means of identification, such as a passport or an identity card. Further lacking a digital passport and considering the costly integration of Germany's electronic identity infrastructure, the currently employed procedure for verifying these official credentials is a matter of expediency to the car sharing provider. It is also aligned with the company's insurance policy, signifying the car sharing provider's sensitivity to the risk stemming from both the customer's conduct with rental vehicles and their ability to uphold financial duties. This is also reflected in the request for a credit rating.

In contrast, the bike sharing provider's onboarding process requires the least amount of data from customers to grant access to the rental scheme. While also renting vehicles equipped with modern electronic equipment to customers, the financial risk profile of a bike sharing service exchange is lower than that of car sharing. As a result, only the phone number, the payment method, and an optional affiliation with the public transport provider are verified. In the case of the phone number, an SMS with a login code is sent. Payment methods are tested by deducting 1 Euro from the associated account. The bike sharing provider trusts in anti-money laundering and anti-terrorism legislation requiring legal identification for obtaining a phone number and a bank account to provide the necessary information, if legal actions against a customer are necessary. Without the legal requirement to ensure further qualifications, the bike sharing provider is willingly accepting the risk of onboarding customers with fraudulently obtained phone numbers and payment methods. Lastly, similar to the process of the car sharing provider, the validity of a public transport subscription is determined by checking an identification number with a data set provided by the public transport provider. This step is also not part of the initial

Table 1 Data requested during onboarding by public transport provider, bike sharing provider, car sharing provider, and on-demand shuttle service

Category	Information / Provider	Public transport provider	Bike sharing provider	Car sharing provider	On-demand shuttle service
Legal identity	Legal name	$M(f, 0)$	$M(f, 0)$	$M(f, w)$	$M(f, 0)$
	Birth date	$M(f, 0)$		$M(f, w)$	$M(f, 0)$
	Birth place			$M(f, w)$	
	Identity card no.			$1(f, w)$	
	Passport no.			$1(f, w)$	
	Selfie			$M(u, w)$	$O(u, 0)$
Contact	Postal address	$M(f, 0)$	$M(f, 0)$	$M(f, w)$	$O(f, w)$
	Email address	$M(f, m)$	$M(f, 0)$	$M(f, m)$	$M(f, 0)$
	Phone no.	$O(f, 0)$	$M(f, s)$	$M(f, 0)$	$M(f, 0)$
Payment	International bank account no.	$M(f, 0)$		$M(f, 0)$	$1(f, 0)$
	Credit card details		$1(f, t)$		$1(f, t)$
	PayPal account		$1(f, t)$		$1(l, p)$
	ApplePay account		$1(a, t)$		
	Google account		$1(l, t)$		
Credit rating	Credit rating	$O(e, v)$		$M(e, v)$	
Qualifications	Driving license no.			$M(f, w)$	
	Driving license classes			$M(f, w)$	
	Driving license issuance date			$M(f, w)$	
	Driving license issuer			$M(f, w)$	
Affiliations	Public transport subscription no.		$O(f, v)$	$O(f, v)$	
	Public transport customer no.		$O(f, v)$		

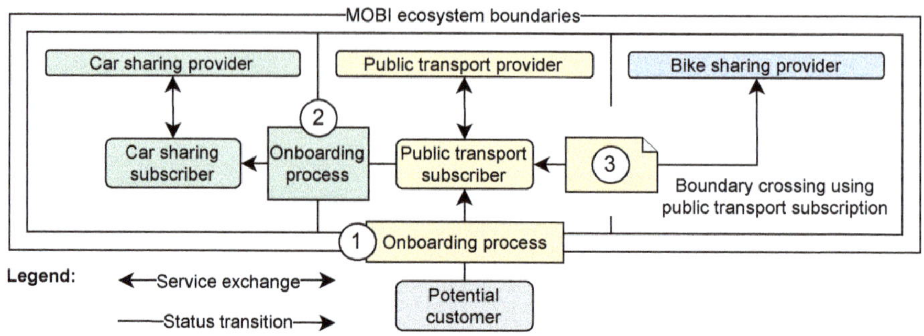

Fig. 1 Exemplary customer status transitions after entering the MOBI ecosystem by onboarding with the public transport provider (1)

onboarding, but can only be completed after access to a personal account has been established. In the MOBI ecosystem, bikes can also be rented without undergoing the onboarding process of the bike sharing provider. Customers already onboarded by the public transport provider with an eligible physical subscription ticket can use the credential's NFC chip to unlock available bikes directly. Payment risk here is outsourced to the public transport provider as an intermediary, which again shows the specific trust-based approach of the bike sharing provider.

4.3 *Crossing Boundaries with Credentials*

Potential customers of MOBI's mobility providers are subject to multiple onboarding processes as a prerequisite for service exchange. By completing such a process, the status of the customer changes. This is reflected in Fig. 1. The on-demand shuttle service is omitted for visual clarity. In this example, a potential customer completes onboarding with the public transport provider to obtain a monthly subscription ticket (Fig. 1, number 1). After this, the potential customer is considered a public transport subscriber. With this newly obtained status, they can now engage in service exchange with the provider, i.e., taking a bus. If they want to rent a car from the car sharing provider, they need to undergo a second onboarding process (Fig. 1, number 2). This process manifests an internal boundary of the MOBI ecosystem, preventing the public transport subscriber from service exchange with the car sharing provider. Despite already being onboarded to the ecosystem and being known and trusted by their business partner, the car sharing provider treats public transport subscribers as if they were outsiders to the ecosystem. Only after they attain the correct customer status can they engage in car sharing.

Onboarding processes are not the only way to cross internal boundaries in the MOBI ecosystem. Public transport subscribers can use the subscription ticket's NFC capabilities to directly engage in bike sharing service exchange (Fig. 1, number 3).

The ticket carries the customer's status and allows them to cross the internal boundary between the public transport and bike sharing provider, i.e. unlocking a bike as well as riding, locking, and returning it. The public transport subscriber, however, does not obtain full bike sharing customership in status. Only after undergoing a regular onboarding process using the provider's website or mobile app can they locate, reserve, and temporarily park bikes.

5 Discussion

Our case study of the MOBI ecosystem shows how service ecosystem boundaries are manifested by various onboarding processes, which determine the eligibility of customers for the desired service exchange relationship with mobility providers. From the provider's perspective customer onboarding fulfills the goals to protect their resources, enable access to customer resources, and to fulfill legal obligations. Customer onboarding processes in the MOBI ecosystem result in status assignments, which are represented by physical credentials or accounts. These are used to engage in mobility service exchange or for customer onboarding with other providers, e.g. to obtain preferential tariffs. Our results show significant overlaps between the data required by different mobility providers. While most data exchange is handled via forms customers have to fill in, there is a diversity of employed technical procedures for the verification of this data. Both required data and the technical procedures are determined by the institutions and institutional arrangements governing the onboarding process and its designated exchange relationship.

The MINTI Framework. To explain how different informational demands arise for actors in service ecosystems, which technical procedures are employed to satisfy these, and which impacts are generated by these configurations, we propose the MINTI framework. The framework is based on an abstraction of our findings and the integration of concepts from the theoretical lenses we used for interpretation, i.e., SDL and transaction cost theory. Its main elements are given in Fig. 2. On the level of a multi-actor business process taking place in a service ecosystem, we localize various institutions and institutional arrangements on micro-, meso- and macro-levels [36] determining the informational demands as well as the technical procedures used to satisfy these, i.e., resource integration [2]. The choice of a specific technical procedure can be restricted by both the relevant institutions, e.g., by laws necessitating them, or by the informational demands themselves, e.g., when only limited data sources are available for a specific identity attribute to be verified [4]. Both informational demand and technical procedures are localized on the level of resource integration, which itself is part of service exchange [34]. They serve to enact the relevant institutional arrangements of a business process in its context by accessing, adapting and integrating informational resources to verify an actor's eligibility for service exchange within these institutional arrangements [2, 12]. In this way, the business processes shaped by the institutional drivers of informational

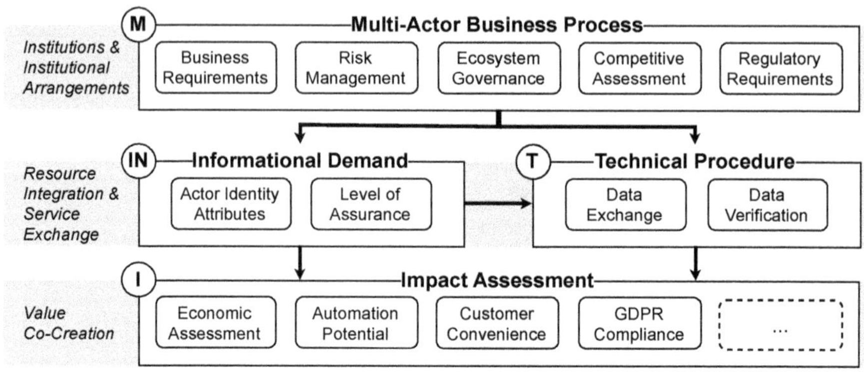

Fig. 2 MINTI framework for informational demand satisfaction in business processes

demand can be viewed as service ecosystem boundaries with specific technical procedures for data exchange and verification as boundary objects for crossing these boundaries [21, 24]. The configuration of informational demand and technical procedures drive the value co-created during the multi-actor business process [2]. The dimensions of the MINTI framework elements are discussed below in detail using the MOBI case as an example.

Multi-Actor Business Process. The most direct influence on informational demands are given by business requirements arising from the operational nature of the service exchange relationship a business process is embedded into. E.g., payment information is collected by all providers in the MOBI ecosystem because financial resources from customers are needed to keep their commercial businesses operational. Since all analyzed service exchange relationships in the MOBI ecosystem have a component of temporal continuity and are in effect credit relationships, providers face the uncertainty of payment from their customers [4]. In this way, risk management determines additional informational demands, e.g., about their customers' credit rating. Similarly, they need to safeguard against opportunistic or fraudulent actors, leading to the necessity to verify payment information [4]. Ecosystem governance also leads to informational demands and determines technical procedures as seen with the public transport subscription ticket, which is issued by the public transport provider and accepted by all mobility providers in the ecosystem. Zooming out of the specific ecosystem to a meso-level, a competitive assessment can determine customary amounts of information demanded and complexity of technical procedures implemented. This is seen with the bike sharing provider, which deliberately allows direct service engagements of public transport subscribers and implements an onboarding process with as little customer information collection as possible. Here, a seamless process for customers is seen as a source of competitive advantage. Lastly, on a macro-level, regulatory requirements might force actors to collect certain actor attributes, possibly with specific methods. This is seen with the car sharing provider's need to verify driving licenses, or in KYC processes.

Informational Demand. The above institutional drivers can determine the demand for both specific identity attributes by an actor and the level of assurance needed to determine the quality of the information. Continuing the example of payment information, the public transport provider opts to only verify payment information in exceptional customer cases with a pre-history of default. On the other hand, the car sharing provider's risk management necessitates a high level of assurance for payment information, involving checks from multiple sources.

Technical Procedure. We extend the concept of "identity technologies" [4] by distinguishing between the necessary information and the mechanisms used for its exchange and verification according to a specific level of assurance. While the public transport provider, e.g., might only carry out plausibility checks against customer bank account numbers, the car sharing provider, while not being able to specifically check the validity of this information, safeguards against opportunistic behavior by employing an additional solvency check and necessitates a deposit. The joint influence of institutional arrangements and informational demand on the choice of a technical procedure can be seen with the example of driving license and identity document checks of the car sharing provider. Competitive assessments and business efficiency goals necessitate a seamless digital onboarding process. However, since the German electronic identity is costly and complex to implement and there is no existing digital driving license, the provider implements a custom process.

Impact Assessment. Value co-creation in the analyzed mobility service exchanges is influenced by the informational demands of actors and technical procedures operated. However, since "[v]alue is always uniquely and phenomenologically determined by the beneficiary" [35], an impact assessment of these two components is necessarily multi-dimensional and dependent on the actor carrying it out. A specific informational demand and accompanying technical procedures can be viewed from an economic standpoint, i.e., which identity costs a specific procedure incurs. This is connected to the potential for automation, which solutions based on digital wallets promise, e.g., [10]. Investments in such technical procedures can be viewed as less asset-specific [37] than, e.g., the car sharing web chat or Germany's electronic ID solution, since the use of standardized digital wallets promise a universal exchange layer for verifiable data [29]. However, whether customers and providers will be able to capitalize on this value proposition, is not definitive, as the willingness to pay for such an infrastructure is low [14].

Limitations. The applicability of our results is subject to several limitations. Firstly, our study is based on a single urban mobility ecosystem. Therefore, our results need to be interpreted in light of MOBI's specific actor configuration and the onboarding processes they implement. As verification methods of customer data vary substantially between mobility providers, further analyses of other mobility ecosystems and customer onboarding therein will likely uncover additional informational demands and technical procedures. Such insights could be used to construct a typology of different configurations. Secondly, we only analyzed the informational demands of mobility providers toward customers during onboarding processes they implement using various technologies. However, customers face a similar decision process when choosing which providers to engage with. Future studies could therefore investigate the demands and means customers use to qualify providers for a service exchange relationship. Finally, our results are based on qualitative data and our subjective interpretation. More objective measurements of the impacts of informational demands and the employed technical procedures on, e.g., onboarding costs and customer convenience could enable better decisions in choosing a specific implementation approach.

Acknowledgements This research was funded as part of the project "Menschenzentrierte digitale Daseinsvorsorge in Stadt und Land" with funds from the European Social Fund Plus (funding code: 100693812) and from tax revenue based on the budget approved by the Saxon state parliament as well as part of the project "ID-Ideal" with funding by the German Federal Ministry of Economic Affairs and Climate Action (funding code: 01MN21001A).

References

1. Aamer, T., & Milani, F. (2023). Improving digital onboarding processes for financial services - a multivocal literature review. *Baltic Journal of Modern Computing, 11*(4) (2023). https://doi.org/10.22364/bjmc.2023.11.4.06
2. Akaka, M. A., Vargo, S. L., & Lusch, R. F. (2012). An exploration of networks in value cocreation: A service-ecosystems view. In S. L. Vargo, & R. F. Lusch (Eds.), *Special issue – Toward a better understanding of the role of value in markets and marketing, Review of marketing research* (Vol. 9, pp. 13–50). Emerald Group Publishing Limited. https://doi.org/10.1108/S1548-6435(2012)0000009006
3. Akaka, M. A., Vargo, S. L., & Lusch, R. F. (2013). The complexity of context: A service ecosystems approach for international marketing. *Journal of International Marketing, 21*(4), 1–20. https://doi.org/10.1509/jim.13.0032
4. Berg, A., Berg, C., Davidson, S., & Potts, J. (2018). Identity as input to exchange. *SSRN Electronic Journal*. https://dx.doi.org/10.2139/ssrn.3171960
5. Berg, A., Berg, C., Davidson, S., & Potts, J. (2018). *The institutional economics of identity.* https://doi.org/10.2139/ssrn.3072823
6. Berg, C., Davidson, S., & Potts, J. (2020). Identity technologies: A transaction cost approach. *SSRN Electronic Journal*. https://dx.doi.org/10.2139/ssrn.3526428
7. Chourabi, H., Nam, T., Walker, S., Gil-Garcia, J. R., Mellouli, S., Nahon, K., Pardo, T. A., & Scholl, H. J. (2012). Understanding smart cities: An integrative framework. In *2012 45th Hawaii International Conference on System Sciences* (pp. 2289–2297). IEEE (2012). https://doi.org/10.1109/HICSS.2012.615
8. Coase, R. H. (1937). The nature of the firm. *Economica, 4*(16), 386–405.https://www.jstor.org/stable/2626876
9. Graham, J. R., & Harvey, C. R. (2001). The theory and practice of corporate finance: Evidence from the field. *Journal of Financial Economics, 60*, 187–243.
10. Hoess, A., Lautenschlager, J., Sedlmeir, J., Fridgen, G., Schlatt, V., & Urbach, N. (2024). Toward seamless mobility-as-a-service. *Business & Information Systems Engineering*. https://doi.org/10.1007/s12599-024-00856-9
11. Jin, S. T., Kong, H., Wu, R., & Sui, D. Z. (2018). Ridesourcing, the sharing economy, and the future of cities. *Cities, 76*, 96–104 (2018). https://doi.org/10.1016/j.cities.2018.01.012
12. Koskela-Huotari, K., Edvardsson, B., Jonas, J. M., Sörhammar, D., & Witell, L. (2016). Innovation in service ecosystems - breaking, making, and maintaining institutionalized rules of resource integration. *Journal of Business Research, 69*(8), 2694–2971.

13. Koskela-Huotari, K., Vink, J., & Edvardsson, B. (2020). The institutional turn in service research: taking stock and moving ahead. *Journal of Services Marketing, 34*(3), 373–387. https://doi.org/10.1108/JSM-02-2019-0101
14. Kubach, M., & Roßnagel, H. (2024). Economically viable identity ecosystems: Value capture and market strategies. In *Open identity summit* (pp. 27–38). Gesellschaft für Informatik e.V. https://dl.gi.de/items/1e80debf-ddd1-4876-ab9b-c4b13be2bc64
15. Levi, M., & Reuter, P. (2006). Money laundering. *Crime and Justice, 34*(1), 289–375. https://doi.org/10.1086/501508
16. Lusch, R. F., & Vargo, S. L. (2006). Service-dominant logic: Reactions, reflections and refinements. *Marketing Theory, 6*(3), 281–288. https://doi.org/10.1177/1470593106066781
17. Lusch, R. F., & Vargo, S. L. (2014). *Service-dominant logic: Premises, perspectives, possibilities*. Cambridge University Press (CUP)
18. Metz, R. (2014). Credit scoring: Will our digital identity replace the real person? In K. Purnhagen & H. Micklitz (Eds.), *Varieties of European economic law and regulation, studies in European economic law and regulation* (pp. 635–650). Springer.
19. Moorman, C., Deshpandé, R., & Zaltman, G. (1993). Factors affecting trust in market research relationships. *Journal of Marketing, 57*(1), 81–101.
20. North, D. C. (1990). *Institutions, institutional change and economic performance*. Political Economy of Institutions and Decisions. Cambridge University Press (1990). https://doi.org/10.1017/CBO9780511808678
21. Razmdoost, K., Alinaghian, L., Chandler, J. D., & Mele, C. (2023). Service ecosystem boundary and boundary work. Journal of Business Research *156*, 113,489 (2023). https://doi.org/10.1016/j.jbusres.2022.113489
22. Richter, D., Praas, C. R., & Anke, J.: Beyond paper and plastic: A meta-model for credential use and governance. In *ECIS 2023 research papers*. https://aisel.aisnet.org/ecis2023_rp/371/
23. Roethke, K., Klumpe, J., Adam, M., & Benlian, A. (2020). Social influence tactics in e-commerce onboarding: The role of social proof and reciprocity in affecting user registrations. *Decision Support Systems, 131*(113), 268. https://doi.org/10.1016/j.dss.2020.113268
24. Sajtos, L., Kleinaltenkamp, M., & Harrison, J. (2018). Boundary objects for institutional work across service ecosystems. *Journal of Service Management, 29*(4), 615–640. https://doi.org/10.1108/JOSM-01-2017-0011
25. Schlatt, V., Sedlmeir, J., Feulner, S., & Urbach, N. (2021). Designing a framework for digital kyc processes built on blockchain-based self-sovereign identity. *Information & Management, 103553*. https://doi.org/10.1016/j.im.2021.103553
26. Schneider, D., Klumpe, J., Adam, M., & Benlian, A. (2020). Nudging users into digital service solutions. *Electronic Markets, 30*(4), 863–881. https://doi.org/10.1007/s12525-019-00373-8
27. Schulz, T., Böhm, M., Gewald, H., Celik, Z., & Krcmar, H. (2020). The negative effects of institutional logic multiplicity on service platforms in intermodal mobility ecosystems. *Business & Information Systems Engineering, 62*(5), 417–433. https://doi.org/10.1007/s12599-020-00654-z
28. Schulz, T., Zimmermann, S., Böhm, M., Gewald, H., & Krcmar, H. (2021). Value co-creation and co-destruction in service ecosystems: The case of the reach now app. *Technological Forecasting and Social Change, 170*(120), 926. https://doi.org/10.1016/j.techfore.2021.120926
29. Sedlmeir, J., Smethurst, R., Rieger, A., & Fridgen, G. (2021). Digital identities and verifiable credentials. *Business & Information Systems Engineering, 63*, 603–613. https://doi.org/10.1007/s12599-021-00722-y
30. Soltani, R., Trang Nguyen, U., & An, A. (2018). A new approach to client onboarding using self-sovereign identity and distributed ledger. In *2018 IEEE International Conference on Internet of Things (iThings) and IEEE Green Computing and Communications (GreenCom) and IEEE Cyber, Physical and Social Computing (CPSCom) and IEEE Smart Data (SmartData)* (pp. 1129–1136). IEEE. https://doi.org/10.1109/Cybermatics_2018.2018.00205
31. Stockburger, L., Kokosioulis, G., Mukkamala, A., Mukkamala, R. R., & Avital, M. (2021). Blockchain-enabled decentralized identity management: The case of self-sovereign identity in public transportation. *Blockchain: Research and Applications, 2*(2),

100,014.https://doi.org/10.1016/j.bcra.2021.100014. https://www.sciencedirect.com/science/article/pii/S2096720921000099
32. Tan, T. M., & Saraniemi, S. (2023). Trust in blockchain-enabled exchanges: Future directions in blockchain marketing. *Journal of the Academy of Marketing Science, 51*(4), 914–939. https://doi.org/10.1007/s11747-022-00889-0
33. Vargo, S. L., & Lusch, R. F. (2004). Evolving to a new dominant logic for marketing. *Journal of Marketing, 68*(1), 1–17. https://doi.org/10.1509/jmkg.68.1.1.24036
34. Vargo, S. L., & Lusch, R. F. (2011). It's all b2b. . .and beyond: Toward a systems perspective of the market. *Industrial Marketing Management, 40*(2), 181–187. https://doi.org/10.1016/j.indmarman.2010.06.026
35. Vargo, S. L., & Lusch, R. F. (2016). Institutions and axioms: an extension and update of service-dominant logic. *Journal of the Academy of Marketing Science, 44*(1), 5–23. https://doi.org/10.1007/s11747-015-0456-3
36. Vargo, S. L., & Lusch, R. F. (2017). Service-dominant logic 2025. *International Journal of Research in Marketing, 34*(1), 46–67. https://doi.org/10.1016/j.ijresmar.2016.11.001
37. Williamson, O. E. (1981). The economics of organization: The transaction cost approach. *American Journal of Sociology, 87*(3), 548–577 (1981). https://www.jstor.org/stable/2778934
38. Willing, C., Brandt, T., & Neumann, D. (2017). Intermodal mobility. *Business & Information Systems Engineering, 59*(3), 173–179. https://doi.org/10.1007/s12599-017-0471-7
39. Zhang, C., & Zhou, H. (2019). The study of coopetition between public bus and bike sharing based on environmental protection. *E3S Web Conference, 136*, 04,015 (2019). DOIurlhttps://doi.org/10.1051/e3sconf/201913604015

Guiding Principles for Government as a Platform

Peter Kuhn, Luca Gastaldi, Dian Balta, and Florian Matthes

Abstract Government as a Platform (GaaP) represents the notion that governments significantly benefit from the adoption of platform concepts from the private sector. While several governments are already implementing this notion, there is an insufficient understanding of what actually constitutes a successful GaaP approach. We apply a design science research strategy and, based on interviews with 26 experts and a survey, iteratively design and evaluate 10 guiding principles for GaaP. The principles show how technological and governance aspects complement each other and which platform concepts constitute GaaP. Our research has implications for scholars towards a detailed conceptualization of GaaP, while practitioners can use the principles as guidelines for implementation.

1 Introduction

Government as a Platform (GaaP) is an approach to the digital transformation of the public sector, which is increasingly followed by governments around the world [1–6]. The underlying idea is that the public sector can profit from the adoption of platform concepts [1], leveraging on principles nurtured in the private sector [4].

P. Kuhn (✉) · D. Balta · F. Matthes
Technical University Munich, Munich, Germany
e-mail: p.kuhn@tum.de

D. Balta
e-mail: balta@fortiss.org

F. Matthes
e-mail: matthes@tum.de

P. Kuhn · D. Balta
Fortiss, Munich, Germany

L. Gastaldi
Politecnico Di Milano, Milan, Italy
e-mail: luca.gastaldi@polimi.it

C. M. Flath et al. (eds.), *Shaping the Digital Future Through Innovation and Practice*, Lecture Notes in Information Systems and Organisation 85,
https://doi.org/10.1007/978-3-032-08489-7_4

While the term GaaP is used to describe a broad range of variations—from political participation via platforms to car sharing organized by local government—we focus on the application of platform concepts to digital public service delivery. Such an application promises both, more efficient and more user-friendly services [1, 4, 7]. In practice, GaaP for digital public service delivery has already been applied by various governments [1–3, 5, 6, 8] successfully, that is, yielding more efficient and user-friendly public services. Furthermore, several governmental digital agencies have publicly advocated the approach, such as the "Government Digital Service" in the UK and "Team Digitale" in Italy [9, 10]. Given its practical relevance, scholars have started investigating and conceptualizing the phenomenon [1, 7, 11], distinguishing different dimensions and constituting elements of GaaP.

However, there is still a lack of understanding of what constitutes a successful implementation of GaaP in practice. Extant research focuses on individual cases [5, 6], emphasising how GaaP implementations differ between countries. Some scholars also started to investigate the similarities of the countries implementing GaaP [1, 11], which suggest that—despite different contexts—there are some underlying principles that successful cases tend to have in common. Identifying these principles would provide "normative and directive statements that guide in decision making" [12], supporting practitioners struggling with GaaP implementation [13], and could contribute to its theoretical conceptualization.

In order to increase the understanding of GaaP, we pose the following research question: *How to successfully guide implementations of GaaP?* To address this question, we apply a design science research strategy [14]. More specifically, we interacted with 26 experts from five countries in three iterations to develop a comprehensive set of ten guiding principles for GaaP. The principles show, on the one hand, how technological and governance aspects complement each other and, on the other, which platform concepts actually constitute GaaP. Moreover, these results confirm previously existing design knowledge but also extend it. Based on our insights, scholars can further conceptualize GaaP while practitioners can use the principles as guidelines. The paper is structured based on [15].

2 Theoretical Background and Objectives for a Solution

GaaP. In his seminal contribution, O'Reilly (2011) introduced the term "Government as a Platform" as the notion of learning from the success of digital platforms in the private sector and transferring the respective concepts to the public one [4]. Since then, various academic publications followed, covering diverse applications of platform concepts in the public sector [1, 2, 6, 11, 16–18]. The examples range from platform-based social funds [19] to platform concepts for digital public service delivery [11, 20]. In this research we focus on the latter, which we will call platform-oriented digital public service delivery. This form of GaaP has been specified as a "government as a platform builder" [21] approach, conceiving central governments as developers of central platforms on which local entities can then build digital public services independently. As described by Thompson and Venters (2021), the "government undertakes architectural work to identify common capabilities, but remains open to a mix of possible delivery models". This role often assumed by a digital agency which therefore plays a central and strategic role in the GaaP approach of many countries. By bundling strategic decisions at such a central entity, GaaP is capable of speeding up digital transformation [4, 7], combining user-friendliness with efficiency [22].

GaaP technology and governance. Literature distinguishes technological and governance aspects of this approach, partially drawing on general information systems literature [1, 11, 23, 24]. From a technological perspective, GaaP is associated with a shared digital infrastructure of software components, such as login and payment [11]. This "platform core" often includes an interoperability layer, such as X-Road in Estonia [1, 3], and serves as an "integration mechanism" [11]. Building on this platform, an ecosystem of digital public services is enabled by platform concepts such as modularity [1] and open standards [4].

Regarding governance, orchestration [2] and co-creation [1] are key elements of GaaP. The latter is based on the openness of the public sector to its stakeholders, enabling platform concepts such as participation [25]. By doing so, the user of public services changes from recipient to being a central part in the ecosystem for public service delivery [26]. The governance of GaaP is therefore connected to the question of how the aforementioned digital agencies can act as a platform owner, orchestrating an ecosystem of public and private actors [2].

Despite these theoretical insights, there is no common definition of GaaP [18]. For the scope of this paper, we build on the works of Bender and Heine (2021) and Thompson and Venters (2021) and use the following working definition: GaaP is the delivery of digital public services using platform concepts for both the technological setup and the governance of its stakeholders.

GaaP in practice. In practice, several countries are implementing platform-oriented digital public service delivery. Explicit references, for instance, can be found in Italy [27], Estonia [3], and the UK [9]. Finland [28], the USA, and Australia [8] also apply platform concepts to their digital public service delivery. While there are successful examples and various aspects already investigated, literature does not specify what actually constitutes a successful GaaP approach [13]. Many publications focus on individual cases (Styrin et al., 2022; Upadhyay et al., 2022), emphasising how GaaP applications differ across countries. At the same time, some publications indicate that successful GaaP approaches tend to follow the same principles [1, 11]. Such principles could guide practitioners, especially in governments struggling with the approach [13]. To our knowledge, however, there is no comprehensive investigation of these principles.

Objectives for a solution. Based on this, our overall objective is to develop a set of guiding principles for GaaP. The design of these principles will seek to meet three objectives: (1) provide normative and directive statements that guide decision makers when designing platform-oriented digital public service delivery, (2) build on successful examples from practice, and (3) provide indications for the further theoretical conceptualization of GaaP.

3 Methodology

To identify the guiding principles of successful GaaP approaches, we followed the Design Science Research (DSR) paradigm [14], which brings detailed understanding about problem and solution domains through building and applying a design artefact [14, 29, 30]. Principles are design artefacts [31] and principle-based design is considered "a specific form of the more general design science research methodology that focuses on extracting principles" [32].

We follow the six-step DSR methodology [15] and go through three iterations (Table 1). The empirical data sampling along the iterations was based on both expert interviews and a survey. In total, 41 interviews were conducted with 26 experts from five countries. Eight experts participated in all three rounds and two experts in two rounds. Eleven experts participated in the survey.

For the selection of experts, we considered people who have or had strategic positions and accountability for platform-oriented digital public service delivery in the respective countries. The experts were contacted via LinkedIn and through the network of the authors. In several cases, interviewees were head of a national digital agency -since those agencies play a central and strategic role in the governance of digital transformation of many governments. We also considered people who have been closely working with them. To avoid potential biases, we collected information from informants who were both in charge at the time of the interview and are not anymore [33]. Furthermore, anonymity has been promised to informants, encouraging candour. Regarding the countries of origin of the experts, we selected countries that have successfully applied GaaP, since principles are typically developed based on successful examples from practice [31]. We chose Estonia for its high ranking in eGovernment scores [34]. We selected Italy and UK since they explicitly pursue GaaP and publicly reflect on it [9, 10]. We added Denmark, for being mentioned by several

Table 1 Overview of the three iterations

	First iteration	Second iteration	Third iteration
Data collection	19 interviews	10 interviews	12 interviews and 11 survey responses
Time of data collection	May to July 2021	January and February 2023	June and July 2023
Resulting artefact	Design decisions	Guiding principles v1	Guiding principles v2

experts as a role model, and Germany, which is progressing but also struggling with GaaP [13]. The interviews were recorded and transcribed for coding.

First iteration. The *problem identification and motivation* was based on research conducted by the authors [13, 35–38], which included a literature review and is retraced in the introduction. The *objectives for a solution* were derived from said publication and literature, as reproduced in the previous section. The *design and development* of the first iteration was based on 19 interviews with British, Estonian and Italian experts. The interviews lasted between 24 and 122 min and were conducted between May and July 2021. The interviews aimed at exploring how GaaP has been applied in the three countries. Exemplary questions were "Which are the main platforms/core services that constitutes the [country's] digital government and ICT infrastructure?" and "Which are the main advantages of GaaP adoption?" The interviews were coded regarding design decisions, distinguishing among decision issue, alternative, and justification [39]. The coding aimed to understand the various aspects and dimensions of GaaP and relative design decisions in the three countries.

Second iteration. The *demonstration and evaluation* of the first iteration was conducted in ten interviews with British, Estonian, and Italian experts. The interviews lasted between 19 and 57 min and were conducted in January and February 2023. The interviews aimed to systematically discuss the identified decisions from the first round. Exemplary questions were "Which governance decisions have been made in your country towards the application of GaaP?" and "Which governance decisions will or should be made in your country towards the application of GaaP?" The second round of interviews was also coded regarding design decisions. The first version of the principles was then *designed and developed* in workshops among the authors. Using dimensions from literature [1, 25], the principles were designed to consider both, governance and technological aspects. Also, principles concerned with the platform core were balanced with principles concerned with the ecosystem. First insights were *communicated* in [36].

Third iteration. The *demonstration and evaluation* of the second iteration was conducted in interviews with twelve experts from the UK, Estonia, Italy, Denmark and Germany. The interviews lasted between 25 and 67 min and were conducted in June and July 2023. The goal of the interviews was to evaluate the principles, preliminary sent to the experts. After a short introduction to the principles, the experts were asked for their opinion on the principles. Exemplary questions were "Do you agree with principle names, statements, rationales and examples? If not, what would you change?" and "Would you recommend them to practitioners from other countries? Why (not)?" The third round was coded regarding the general assessments, examples and potential improvements of the principles. Specifically, all statements about positive and negative features of the principles, missing features and proposals for improvement were extracted. In addition to the semi-structured interviews, the third round included a survey, which eleven out of twelve interviewees responded to. In line with triangulation, the survey was designed to enhance the collected data to compensate for intrinsic biases of the interviews. The survey aimed to collect formalised feedback on the principles and specify their application. Most questions were posed as statements asking for responses on a 5-points Likert scale between "Strongly agree" and "Strongly disagree". Exemplary statements were "The principle is easy to understand" and "The principle has big importance for the success of GaaP in practice." The interviews and the survey results indicated that the principles were mature regarding the objectives for a solution, which is why only small changes to the order and naming were made by the authors. The final artefact is *demonstrated and evaluated* in the later sections of this paper based on an online discussion of the authors with decision makers from Germany. This paper also constitutes the *communication* of the artefact.

4 Results

In the following, we present 10 guiding principles for successful GaaP implementations in practice (cf. Table 2). The principles are targeted at strategists in central roles—such as the head of a country's digital agency.

P1: Political Mandate. The first principle concerns the political mandate for a GaaP approach. In literature, GaaP is associated with transformative changes in the government's structure and governance [1, 2, 7]. The experts explained that, for these changes to happen, political backing is necessary: "*Countries that are successful tend to have very strong mandates.*" (I9, UK). Some experts even argued that this

Table 2 Guiding principles for successful GaaP imlementations

No	Name	Statement
P1	Political mandate	Ensure political backing from the highest office of government
P2	Strong and clear governance	Ensure and enforce a strong and clear governance between and over all relevant stakeholders
P3	Human resources	Invest in hiring and further educating highly qualified personnel
P4	Openness and Co-Creation	Create and cherish a culture of openness and co-creation in and outside the public sector
P5	Carrot and Stick	Incentivise and regulate public entities from all levels of government to participate and contribute
P6	Deployment infrastructure	Provide infrastructure for the performant and easy deployment of all software related to platform-oriented digital public service delivery
P7	Central core functionalities	Provide the core functionalities of digital public services—such as identification/authentication and payment—for all public entities
P8	Interoperability	Enable the seamless exchange of data between all public entities
P9	Decentral business logic	Keep the business logic and business data with the responsible public entities
P10	User-facing frontend	Improve user experience through excellent frontends

mandate needs to be from the very top of government, for instance, from the prime minister. If not, there is the danger of unsolvable conflicts between ministries that hinders the structural changes to be enforced. An example of strong political mandate is the government of prime minister Mart Laar in Estonia from 1999 to 2002, which pushed the digital transformation resulting in the creation of X-Road in 2001. Based on this, we state principle P1: "Ensure political backing from the highest office of government".

P2: Strong and clear governance. The second principle is concerned with the governance of the GaaP approach. In literature, platforms are associated with a central owner that is orchestrating the relevant stakeholders [2]. However, in practice this role cannot only rely on orchestration or quality assurance [11]. The interviewees argue that this platform owner, often a digital agency, needs to be able to make and enforce decisions. "*I would say that this Ministry of Economy and Communication is a digital agency for Estonia. [...] they are definitely leading* " (I10, Estonia). Such strong and clear governance of a digital agency can additionally be strengthened with a strong mandate for its head. In Italy, for instance, the head of the digital agency was also appointed a commissioner of the government: "W*e needed to have a commissioner with the power to substitute the administration in order to give impulse to [...] the implementation of the strategy.*" (I6, Italy). A primus inter pares is crucial for the approach. Based on this, we state principle P2: "Ensure and enforce a strong and clear governance between and over all relevant stakeholders".

P3: Human resources. The third principle is concerned with the people inside the public sector who are working towards the application of GaaP. GaaP is associated with the organization of government and its technology—but with other ideas and rationales than classic public sector bureaucracy [1, 25]. To ensure the effectiveness of this reorganisation, GaaP requires personnel with the ability of "platform thinking" [40, 41]. "*You need a political leader or a leader who has a very good ability to communicate in public and earn trust and negotiate with the politicians. [...] And, then, there has to be a team, an organisation, an agency with very strong technical competencies inside.*" (I5, Italy). In Italy, for instance, this leader was a former Amazon executive, Diego Piacentini, who led the Italian digitalisation efforts from 2016 to 2018. Attracting and keeping qualified personnel is difficult, which is why successful governments use all means available: "*There are many people whose salary is much less because they are working in the public sector [...] whoever is setting up the system, they must create this opportunity for the people to be proud about.*" (I10, Estonia). Taken together, putting major resources and focus on human resources is critical for the success of GaaP approaches. Based on this, we state principle P3: "Invest in hiring and further educating highly qualified personnel".

P4: Openness and Co-Creation. The fourth principle concerns the engagement of the various stakeholders of GaaP. GaaP requires the cooperation of all entities of government but also civil society to achieve user-friendly services. As suggested by literature [4, 25], in the investigated countries this is achieved with a culture of openness and co-creation. A central cornerstone of this culture was the proactive communication of the respective GaaP approaches, for instance, via strategy documents and blog entries [9, 42]. Moreover, a lot of energy was put into convincing people to participate: *"It's effort, effort. Effort of people explaining why you need [them] this thing to do.*" (I6, Italy). Also, in many countries, GaaP approaches are driven by communities: "*This is something that we've seen a lot in the Nordic context, this emergence of these joint collaboration forums, particularly between clusters of different authorities*" (I23, Denmark). Enabling and supporting such collaborations is a central element of GaaP. Based on this, we state principle P4: "Create and cherish a culture of openness and co-creation in and outside the public sector".

P5: Carrot and Stick. The fifth principle concerns public entities' participation in a GaaP approach. GaaP requires a critical mass of involvement of various public entities. To ensure participation, governments need to offer something to those entities [25]. Literature suggests technical support through, for instance, software development kits to incentivise the usage [11]. In practice, financial incentives are even more prevalent, for example the free use of software components or financial transfers: *"You also have to use the financial tools to convince municipalities to participate." (I24, Denmark).* Complementing such "carrots" governments also use "sticks" such as mandatory standards and veto powers: "*Yeah, you need veto power. You need to stop them doing stupid things.*" (I8, UK). However, it is important to find the right balance between incentives and regulation or, in other terms, carrots and sticks: "*I believe that it's not working to do this with rules only, instead I believe in standards*" (I25, Germany). Using a management approach that balances "carrot and stick" policies is an important element of a successful GaaP approach. Based on this, we state principle P5: "Incentivise and regulate public entities from all levels of government to participate and contribute".

P6: Deployment infrastructure. The sixth principle is concerned with the technical foundations for GaaP. GaaP is associated with deeply technical aspects such as IT infrastructure and the design of APIs [43], which enable cross-organizational IT services. As a basis for this technical side of GaaP, the deployment of software needs to be seamless. Deployment can be done via a central cloud infrastructure, such as foreseen by the national cloud strategy of Italy, but not only: "*There is a need for hosting definitely, but is it commercial providers, is it just governmental data centres? And if they want to use cloud technology, fine, but this is not critical by any means.*" (I10, Estonia). An important aspect of deployment infrastructure is the alignment with legal requirements, for instance, regarding data privacy [11]. A working technical basis is a prerequisite for GaaP. Based on this, we state principle P6: "Provide infrastructure for the performant and easy deployment of all software related to platform-oriented digital public service delivery".

P7: Central core functionalities. The seventh principle is concerned with technical functionalities that are necessary for digital public services across public levels and departments. In literature, GaaP is associated with a certain architecture based on modular services [1], in particular shared functionalities, such as a common authentication/identification and payment services [11]. In practice, these common functionalities are sometimes called platforms: "*I think you want actually a number of central platform services and they are experienced as a function in a page.*" (I8, UK). Sharing these functionalities can save resources and increases scalability by simplicity. As a technical implementation, some countries have central components, such as the Italian eID SPID [44], others are built on standards and protocols, such as the Estonian payment functionality: "M*aybe [the GaaP approach] does not provide the core functionality, but the core rules, the core standards at the central level.*" (I3, Italy). The exact set of centrally provided functionalities can vary depending on the context, however, a central IT infrastructure with core functionalities is a commonality of the investigated GaaP countries. Based on this, we state principle P7: "Provide the core functionalities of digital public services—such as authentication and payment—for all public entities".

P8: Interoperability. The eighth principle is concerned with the data exchange between public entities. GaaP is associated with digital public services that exchange data across levels and departments [1]. To ensure that this is possible, data exchange needs to be enabled by the technical architecture of the respective digital infrastructure, for instance, via APIs, middleware, and/or standards and protocols: "*The problem with interoperability is not only the data and the regulation behind the data, but also the integration between the different systems.*" (I24, Denmark). Apart from enabling data exchange, interoperability also simplifies processes on the socio-technical level: "*The decision process, if I want to have, let's say, the tourism ministry agree or the health minister agree on a specific interoperability with the finance ministry. [...] it takes one year to decide that. What, instead, if you have a common digital identity layer on top, it comes out naturally.*" (I6, Italy). This makes interoperability a constituting element of a successful GaaP approach. Based on this, we state principle P8: "Enable the seamless exchange of data between all public entities".

P9: Decentral business logic. The ninth principle is concerned with the business logic and data. Platforms are associated with a balance between centralization and decentralization [23]. To ensure that, common functionalities should be centralized, but at the same time business specific software should remain with the decentral entities: "*The business logic should reside where jurisdiction is.*" (I6, Italy). Keeping the business logic with the responsible entity ensures that the business software is where the know-how is. This allows for agile improvements, better troubleshooting and innovation. Also, "B*usiness logic is power and excessively centralizing power needs to have a safeguard in a democratic state - checks and balances.*" (I6, Italy). Finding the context-specific balance between centralization and decentralisation is critical to GaaP success. Based on this, we state principle P9: "Keep the business logic and business data with the responsible public entities".

P10: User-facing frontend. The tenth principle is concerned with the frontends of digital public services. GaaP is associated with user-friendly services such as integrated and proactive public services [4]. To achieve that, frontends should be designed for excellent user experience: “[It’s] *about providing a user experience that is in line with [...] what the citizen is used to when using digital services on the internet.*“ (I5, Italy). To ensure that countries have introduced unified frontends, such as gov.uk, or set standards, e.g. regarding accessibility and design: “*Providing templates also achieves the goal of harmonizing because you standardize. But you achieve the goal of really good user experience, only if the templates are also top quality, which is not a given.*” (I5, Italy). The success of GaaP is ultimately connected to the success of platform-oriented digital public service delivery with its users. Based on this, we state principle P10: “Improve user experience through excellent frontends”.

5 Demonstration

The use of the principles is demonstrated by their retroactive application to the current GaaP approach of Germany (Table 3). We chose Germany because despite progress in recent years, it is struggling with GaaP [13]. We show how the principles help explain the success and lack of success in Germany’s GaaP implementation. We also show how to principles provide an orientation for strategic decisions and, thus, their ability to serve as guidelines for practitioners. The German GaaP approach has its roots in the Online Access Act of 2017 [45] which regulates that egovernment portals and eIDs of the federal and state governments shall be interoperable. Moreover, a digital agency (FITKO) was founded in 2020 with the task of orchestrating the various stakeholders. FITKO also took ownership of an increasing number of shared components and standards over the years. The following demonstration is based on an online discussion between the authors and decision makers form Germany in November 2023 [46].

The discussion showed that the German GaaP approach is mainly suffering on the governance side. Especially the principles on political mandate (P1) and the strong and clear governance (P2) are not followed. The discussants agreed on the necessity for a clarification of the responsibilities of the various ministries and agencies involved. Also, human resources (P3) are currently not in the focus which is mirrored by the small size of the digital agency FITKO (30 employees). Regarding openness, co-creation (P4) and the integration of public entities via carrot and stick (P5), first steps have been made, for instance, with open sourcing, public documentations and feedback channels. Yet, reservations remain, slowing down progress.

On the technological side, the discussion showed that deployment infrastructure (P6) and central core functionalities (P7), while not perfect, have a decent status in Germany. However, interoperability (P8) is a major open task. This is exemplified by the existence of several components with the same functionality of routing data between IT silos, making the seamless exchange of data complex. The principle of decentral business logic (P9) is followed since Germany retains a strong culture of jurisdiction and federalism. For the same reasons, however, the user-facing frontends (P10) suffer from lack of standards and incentives for user-friendliness.

Table 3 Implementation of the GaaP approach in Germany

No	Principle	Implementation in the German GaaP approach
P1	Political mandate	Not followed because digital government not a priority of chancellor and minister for the interieur
P2	Strong and clear governance	Not followed because unclear responsibilities between several bodies and entities on the federal and state levels
P3	Human resources	Not followed because lack of qualified people in quantity and quality
P4	Openness and Co-Creation	Partially followed because increasing number of core components are publicly documented and feedback channels open
P5	Carrot and Stick	Partially followed because financial schema extended during covid. Yet, participation is only slowly gaining traction
P6	Deployment infrastructure	Partially followed because deployment infrastructure exists but is scattered and not up to date
P7	Central core functionalities	Partially followed because several components exist (eID, payment) but with different owners. Need for consolidation
P8	Interoperability	Partially followed because several solutions exist, but roll-out only slowly gaining traction
P9	Decentral business logic	Followed because the culture of jurisdiction is strong which results in business logic residing where the jurisdiction is
P10	User-facing frontend	Partially followed because, despite efforts toward interoperable portals, there is still a lack of standards and templates

Taken together, further directions for improvement of the German GaaP implementation can be summarized from the discussion: (1) a clarification of ownership, in particular regarding the core elements for interoperability, backed by a strong political mandate, (2) a better orchestration of the various public entities, in particular regarding the adoption of central components and standards, (3) enabling of innovation by opening up to competing frontends, in particular through public documentation of APIs.

6 Evaluation and Discussion

In the following, we evaluate the final form of the principles regarding the three objectives (cf. Chap. 2) and then discuss the implications for theory and practice.

First, the principles provide normative and directive statements for decision makers. The experts approved of the principles and considered them helpful: "*I believe those principles are universal and I believe—independent in which stage [of GaaP] you are—it makes sense to go through these ten principles and say 'Well, where are we?* " (I24, Denmark). Moreover, the survey showed that the catalogue of principles was comprehensive, that the individual principles were easy to understand, and that they were important for the success of GaaP. All experts agreed or strongly agreed that the principles are covering the main aspects of applying GaaP. Finally, the principles overlap with findings from several papers as pinpointed in the results section.

Second, the principles are based on successful examples from practice. The survey confirmed that the principles have been applied in the investigated countries, which speaks to the practical relevance of the principles. Also, existing literature on successful applications of GaaP [1–3] have been systematically integrated into the design process. In addition, we interviewed several heads of digital agencies from internationally recognized role models such as the UK, Estonia, and Denmark. Their experience and examples were incorporated into the principles and are therefore contributing to this objective. Furthermore, our insights can be added to the body of knowledge [14].

Third, the principles provide several indications for the further theoretical conceptualization of GaaP. For example, the term "Government as a platform builder" [21] raises the question what exactly the government is building. According to our results, to apply GaaP for digital public service delivery, governments should build a deployment infrastructure, core functionalities, and an interoperability layer. Similarly, regarding governance, our results suggest that platforms ownership can be broken down into political mandate, clear governance structures and human resources, providing input for theoretical work toward the conceptualization of GaaP.

Based on this evaluation, our results carry implications for theory and practice. We find ten guiding principles of successful GaaP approaches that experts across five different countries consider important and useful. With regard to theory, these findings support the hypothesis that successful GaaP approaches have similarities across countries and therefore relevant aspects of GaaP can be generalized. This also encourages the conceptualization efforts of GaaP, potentially leading to a common definition of GaaP. Moreover, the results confirm aspects that have been discussed in literature before, namely the prevalence of central core functionalities (P7) and interoperability (P8), which have been theorized as constituting (technical) elements of GaaP [11]. Similarly, governance aspects, such as openness and co-creation (P4) have been elaborated by previous literature [25] and are confirmed by our results. Our results suggest additional aspects that play an important role in the implementation of GaaP but are not prevalent in literature yet, for instance, the role of the political mandate (P1) and human resources (P3). The importance of those aspects reconnects to GaaP fundamentally being a form of digital transformation, requiring a holistic approach that is more than yet another platform [1, 4, 7]. Future research can build on these results and investigate the role of these aspects for proper GaaP implementations. With regards to practice, the principles provide guidelines when implementing GaaP, supporting the efforts to profit from the application of platform concepts in the public sector. In particular, decision makers can use the principles to evaluate, develop and speed up their GaaP efforts, for example by governments struggling with GaaP [13].

7 Conclusion

We present 10 principles for the successful implementation of GaaP with several im-plications for theory and practices. However, limitations apply to the results and their implications. First, since the selection of experts was limited to five countries from Europe, the principles might not be generalizable to other contexts, such as emerging economies or countries that differ in their political culture. Future research needs to investigate the applicability of the principles in those contexts. Second, the principles have been developed retrospectively, which means that the experts applied the princi-ples, explicitly or implicitly, before knowing they would be asked to comment on them. Future research could explore introspectively the principles, once applied in practice. Third, the principles are generic and need to be broken down into actionable items to be better applied to the context of the government in question. Future re-search could support this by designing corresponding models and methods. Despite these limitations, we believe the principles to be useful for both practitioners and scholars and hope their publication will support the successful application of GaaP in practice.

References

1. Brown, A., Fishenden, J., Thompson, M., & Venters, W. (2017). Appraising the impact and role of platform models and Government as a Platform (GaaP) in UK Government public service reform: Towards a Platform Assessment Framework (PAF). *Government Information Quarterly, 34*, 167–182. https://doi.org/10.1016/j.giq.2017.03.003
2. Cordella, A., & Paletti, A. (2019). Government as a platform, orchestration, and public value creation: The Italian case. *Government Information Quarterly., 36*, Article 101409. https://doi.org/10.1016/j.giq.2019.101409
3. Margetts, H. & Naumann, A. (2017). *Government as a Platform: What can Estonia Show the World?.*
4. O'Reilly, T. (2011). Government as a platform. *Innovations Technology, Governance, Globalization, 6*, 13–40. https://doi.org/10.1162/INOV_a_00056
5. Styrin, E., Mossberger, K., & Zhulin, A. (2022). Government as a platform: Intergovernmental participation for public services in the Russian Federation. *Government Information Quarterly., 39*, Article 101627. https://doi.org/10.1016/j.giq.2021.101627
6. Upadhyay, P., Kumar, A., Dwivedi, Y. K., & Adlakha, A. (2022). Continual usage intention of platform-based governance services: A study from an emerging economy. *Government Information Quarterly., 39*, Article 101651. https://doi.org/10.1016/j.giq.2021.101651
7. Janssen, M., & Estevez, E. (2013). Lean government and platform-based governance—Doing more with less. *Government Information Quarterly, 30*, S1–S8. https://doi.org/10.1016/j.giq.2012.11.003
8. Gil-Garcia, J. R., Henman, P., & Avila-Maravilla, M.A. (2019). Towards "Government as a Platform"? Preliminary Lessons from Australia, the United Kingdom and the United States. In *Proceedings of Ongoing Research, Practitioners, Posters, Workshops, and Projects of the International Conference EGOV-CeDEM-ePart 2019.*
9. Bracken, M. (2015). *Government as a Platform: The next phase of digital transformation—Government Digital Service.* https://gds.blog.gov.uk/2015/03/29/government-as-a-platform-the-next-phase-of-digital-transformation/. Last accessed 2023/03/29.

10. Digital Transformation Team: Report Digital Transformation Team. (2018).
11. Bender, B. & Heine, M. (2021). Government as a Platform? Constitutive Elements of Public Service Platforms. In A. Kö, E. Francesconi, G. Kotsis, A. M. Tjoa, I. Khalil (Eds.), *Electronic Government and the Information Systems Perspective* (pp. 3–20). Springer. https://doi.org/10.1007/978-3-030-86611-2_1.
12. Janssen, M., Flak, L. S., & Sæbø, Ø. (2013). Government Architecture: Concepts, Use and Impact. In M.A. Wimmer, M. Janssen, H.J. Scholl (Eds.) *Electronic Government: Proceedings of the 12th IFIP WG 8.5 International Conference, EGOV 2013* (pp. 135–147).
13. Kuhn, P., Buchinger, M., Balta, D., & Matthes, F. (2022). Barriers of applying Government as a Platform in Practice: Evidence from Germany. In *Proceedings of the 55th Hawaii International Conference on System Sciences*. https://doi.org/10.24251/HICSS.2022.328.
14. Hevner, A. R. A., March, S. T. S., Park, P. J., & Ram, S. (2004). Design Science in Information Systems Research. *Management Information Systems Quarterly, 28*, 75.
15. Peffers, K., Tuunanen, T., Rothenberger, M. A., & Chatterjee, S. (2007). A Design Science Research Methodology for Information Systems Research. *Journal of Management Information Systems., 24*, 45–77. https://doi.org/10.2753/MIS0742-1222240302
16. Al-Ani, A. (2017). Government as a Platform: Services, Participation and Policies. In M. Friedrichsen, Y. Kamalipour (Eds.), *Digital Transformation in Journalism and News Media: Media Management, Media Convergence and Globalization* (pp. 179–196). Springer. https://doi.org/10.1007/978-3-319-27786-8_14.
17. Jamieson, D., Wilson, R., & Martin, M. (2020). Is the GaaP wider than we think? Applying a sociotechnical lens to Government-as-a-Platform. In *Proceedings of the 13th International Conference on Theory and Practice of Electronic Governance* (pp. 514–517). Association for Computing Machinery. https://doi.org/10.1145/3428502.3428580.
18. Seo, H., & Myeong, S. (2020). The Priority of Factors of Building Government as a Platform with Analytic Hierarchy Process Analysis. *Sustainability., 12*, 5615. https://doi.org/10.3390/su12145615
19. Zaramenskikh, E. & Lyubarskaya, M. (2020). Integration of Digital Services Within the Framework of the Implementation of "Government as a Platform" (GaaP) Model on the Example of a Social Fund. In E. Zaramenskikh, A. Fedorova (Eds.), *Digital Transformation and New Challenges* (pp. 1–10). Springer. https://doi.org/10.1007/978-3-030-43993-4_1.
20. Hautamäki, A. & Oksanen, K. (2018) Digital Platforms for Restructuring the Public Sector. In A. Smedlund, A. Lindblom, L. Mitronen (Eds.), *Collaborative Value Co-creation in the Platform Economy* (pp. 91–108). Springer. https://doi.org/10.1007/978-981-10-8956-5_5.
21. Thompson, M., & Venters, W. (2021). Platform, or technology project? A spectrum of six strategic 'plays' from UK government IT initiatives and their implications for policy. *Government Information Quarterly., 38*, Article 101628. https://doi.org/10.1016/j.giq.2021.101628
22. Fishenden, J., & Thompson, M. (2013). Digital Government, Open Architecture, and Innovation: Why Public Sector IT Will Never Be the Same Again. *Journal of Public Administration Research and Theory, 23*, 977–1004.
23. Baldwin, C. Y., & Woodard, C. J. (2008). The Architecture of Platforms: A Unified View. *SSRN Journal*. https://doi.org/10.2139/ssrn.1265155
24. Hein, A., Schreieck, M., Riasanow, T., Setzke, D. S., Wiesche, M., Böhm, M., & Krcmar, H. (2020). Digital platform ecosystems. *Electron Markets, 30*, 87–98. https://doi.org/10.1007/s12525-019-00377-4
25. Millard, J. (2018). Open governance systems: Doing more with more. *Government Information Quarterly., 35*, S77–S87. https://doi.org/10.1016/j.giq.2015.08.003
26. Rantanen, M. M., Koskinen, J., & Hyrynsalmi, S. (2019). E-Government Ecosystem: A new view to explain complex phenomenon. In *2019 42nd International Convention on Information and Communication Technology, Electronics and Microelectronics (MIPRO)* (pp. 1408–1413). https://doi.org/10.23919/MIPRO.2019.8756909.
27. Piacentini, D. (2023). *Towards the new "operating system" of the country*. https://medium.com/team-per-la-trasformazione-digitale/new-operating-system-country-technological-competence-plans-11b50a750ea7. Last accessed March 29, 2023.

28. Yli-Huumo, J., Päivärinta, T., Rinne, J., & Smolander, K. (2018). Suomi.fi—Towards Government 3.0 with a National Service Platform. In P. Parycek, O. Glassey, M. Janssen, H.J. Scholl, E. Tambouris, E. Kalampokis, S. Virkar (Eds.), *Electronic Government* (pp. 3–14). Springer. https://doi.org/10.1007/978-3-319-98690-6_1.
29. Baskerville, R., Baiyere, A., Gregor, S., Hevner, A., & Rossi, M. (2018). Design science research contributions: Finding a balance between artifact and theory. *Journal of the Association for Information Systems, 19*, 3.
30. Gregor, S., & Hevner, A. R. (2013). Positioning and presenting design science research for maximum impact. *MIS Quarterly, 37*, 337–355.
31. Matheus, R., Janssen, M., & Janowski, T. (2021). Design principles for creating digital transparency in government. *Government Information Quarterly., 38*, Article 101550. https://doi.org/10.1016/j.giq.2020.101550
32. Bharosa, N., & Janssen, M. (2015). Principle-Based Design: A Methodology and Principles for Capitalizing Design Experiences for Information Quality Assurance. *Journal of Homeland Security and Emergency Management, 12*, 469–496. https://doi.org/10.1515/jhsem-2014-0073
33. Leonard-Barton, D. (1990). A Dual Methodology for Case Studies: Synergistic Use of a Longitudinal Single Site with Replicated Multiple Sites. *Organization Science., 1*, 248–266.
34. European Commission: eGovernment Benchmark 2022 - Executive Summary (2022).
35. Kuhn, P., Zavolokina, L., Balta, D., & Matthes, F. (2023). Toward Government as a Platform: An Analysis Method for Public Sector Infrastructure. In *Wirtschaftsinformatik 2023 Proceedings*.
36. Kuhn, P., Maragno, G., Balta, D., Gastaldi, L., & Matthes, F. (2023). Government as a Platform in Practice: Commonalities and Differences Across Three European Countries. In I. Lindgren, C. Csáki, E. Kalampokis, M. Janssen, G. Viale Pereira, S. Virkar, E. Tambouris, A. Zuiderwijk (Eds.), *Electronic Government* (pp. 34–47). Springer. https://doi.org/10.1007/978-3-031-41138-0_3.
37. Kuhn, P., Balta, D., & Matthes, F. (2022). Closing the GaaP: Lessons Learned from a Web-based Analysis Tool for Practitioners. In *Ongoing Research, Practitioners, Posters, Workshops, and Projects of the International Conference EGOV-CeDEM-ePart 2022*. Linköping.
38. Kuhn, P., Dallner, S., Buchinger, M., & Balta, D. (2022). Towards "Government as a Platform": An analysis framework for public sector infrastructure. In *Wirtschaftsinformatik 2022 Proceedings*.
39. Potts, C. & Bruns, G. (1988). Recording the reasons for design decisions. In *ICSE* (pp. 418–427).
40. Leijon, E., Svenheden, J., & Svahn, F. (2017). Platform Thinking in Incumbent Firms: From Concept to Capability. In *HICSS Proceedings*. https://doi.org/10.24251/HICSS.2017.580.
41. Trabucchi, D., & Buganza, T. (2023). *Platform Thinking: Read the past*. Business Expert Press.
42. l'Agenzia per l'Italia Digitale, Dipartimento per la Trasformazione Digitale: Piano Triennale per l'informatica nella Pubblica Amministrazione. (2020).
43. Pope, R. (2019). *Playbook: Government as a Platform*.
44. L'Agenzia per l'Italia Digitale: What is SPID, https://www.spid.gov.it/en/what-is-spid/. Last accessed October 13, 2023.
45. Bundesministerium der Justiz und für Verbraucherschutz: OZG - Gesetz zur Verbesserung des Onlinezugangs zu Verwaltungsleistungen. https://www.gesetze-im-internet.de/ozg/BJNR313800017.html. Last accessed June 10, 2021.
46. NEGZ Spezial: Government as a Platform in Deutschland. (2023).

Supporting the Store-Based Retail with Big Data in German Towns—A Longitudinal Mixed-Method-Study

Cindy Kreuels, Aida Stelter, Bastian Kordyaka, and Björn Niehaves

Abstract Store-based retailers face the challenge of meeting increased customer demands and compete with online marketplaces. Big data (BD) can support store-based retail and engage customers locally. We are therefore conducted a three-year mixed-method-study to identify relevant factors for the German store-based retail in three successive phases. Firstly, we qualitatively identify effectiveness-factors using BD through 13 semi-structured-interviews. Secondly, we quantitatively evaluate the relevance of the identified effectiveness-factors (i.a., over 2.8 million data points) using the 7P-Marketing-Mix, and thirdly analyzed significant factors. Our findings show that many store-based retailers lack knowledge about smart town and BD-use, e.g., by creating a network or running joint retail campaigns to increase the towns attractiveness. We provide an overview and guidance on how BD-analysis can effectively influence the store-based retail transformation in smart towns. Using a mixed-method-study in a German town, we were able to identify which factors influence store-based retail in a smart town and suggest promising interventions.

C. Kreuels · A. Stelter (✉)
University of Siegen, Siegen, Germany
e-mail: Aida.Stelter@uni-siegen.de

C. Kreuels
e-mail: Cindy.Schaefer@uni-siegen.de

B. Kordyaka · B. Niehaves
University of Bremen, Bremen, Germany
e-mail: kordyaka@uni-bremen.de

B. Niehaves
e-mail: niehaves@uni-bremen.de

C. M. Flath et al. (eds.), *Shaping the Digital Future Through Innovation and Practice*, Lecture Notes in Information Systems and Organisation 85,
https://doi.org/10.1007/978-3-032-08489-7_5

1 Introduction

The digital transformation is reshaping various aspects of life, leading to increased urbanization as people seek to balance work and personal needs [1]. This urban shift poses challenges like higher energy and water consumption, increased housing demands, and the need for expanded product and service availability. Additionally, urbanization impacts towns, leading to issues like exodus and limited recreational options [2]. Addressing these challenges requires innovative urban concepts and measures [3]. A holistic approach to support urban transformation towards smart towns, as proposed by Gassmann et al. [4], integrating the power ranges, is valuable. However, applying this approach in towns with the 7P Marketing mix represents a novel strategy.

One power range that became particularly important is 'Smart Economy', and its objective is to maintain the towns economic competitiveness and innovation—this includes the store-based retailers. In Europe, store-based retailers are retailers who sell their products in owner-operated stores (brick-and-mortar stores in US). In recent years, it has become apparent that online retail is preferred over store-based retail—even more since Covid-19 [5, 6]. As a result, store-based retail in towns is coming under increasing pressure and is steadily losing market shares [7]. In addition, demographic change, particularly in towns, is ensuring that fewer walk-in customers are coming to the town and their centers. These structural changes are leading to a variety of negative consequences that hold the potential to substantially reduce the attractiveness of town centers in the long term [8]. These structural problems of store-based retail (especially in towns) can be solved by strengthening and digitizing store-based retail.

To achieve this, key success factors of online retailing can be adapted. In addition to 24/7 availability and customer-friendly delivery concepts, these include the linking of various data sources, that merge the advantages of local retail with digital tools. In summary, previously unused factors should be used in store-based retail. This data can then be analyzed, and the results fed back into store-based retail. A well-functional store-based retail must improve on precisely this point: the toolbox of big data Analytics (BDA) promising to add value to be successful in the future [9, 10]. However, this is not achieved with better data from an individual retailer alone (e.g., cash register data from a store), but through a shared data pool of the towns store-based retailers that is feasible under data protection law and ethically justifiable. 'Smart shops can provide customers with a more enjoyable and satisfactory shopping experience.' [11]. The more detailed the information about towns customer behavior, the more efficiently offers can be set [12]. Aggregating this expanded data from all store-based retailers can reveal potential for strengthening store-based retail.

This paper presents a mixed-method study which is organized into three phases: (1) We qualitatively identify effectiveness factors using BD applications among store-based retailers and consult the 7P Marketing Mix approach from McCarthy [13] and Booms and Bitner [14] as a theoretical framework. (2) We look which factors are feasible. (3) We quantitatively evaluate the relevance of the explored effectiveness factors with questionnaires, collected transaction and sensor data (2.8 million datasets) (e.g., from WLAN) and secondary data (e.g., cash data) from 13 store-based retailers of a German town. In this way, we are able with BDA to identify which factors have an impact on revenue and sales figures for local retail in the town. Against this background, we seek to answer the following research question (RQ): What are big data factors helping data-driven digital transformation of store-based retail in a future smart town?

2 Related Work

Smart town and its Retail Sector. Towns must transform themselves due to a variety of factors, e.g., sustainability, into smart towns. A town is considered 'smart when investments in human and social capital and traditional (transport) and modern (ICT) communication infrastructure fuel sustainable economic growth and a high quality of life, with a wise management of natural resources, through participatory governance' [15]. So, a smart town can be seen as an efficient, sustainable, and livable community [3, 16]. To tackle urban challenges like increased energy consumption and ensuring constant availability of products/services, towns must evolve intelligently. Smart towns leverage existing data to manage resources sustainably and enhance citizens' life quality [4, 17]. Scientifically, smart towns are divided into interconnected power ranges, with 'Smart Economy' playing a vital role in maintaining and enhancing competitiveness and innovation [4, 15]. This involves adopting innovative technologies, improving communication, and bolstering both online and store-based retail [18].

The retail sector has undergone significant changes due to globalization, which has facilitated worldwide retail transactions and altered retail processes [19]. The emergence of information communication technologies (ICT) and smart technologies has led to the rise of new retailing models, transforming traditional retail [11]. Concurrently, increasing digitalization and evolving customer needs necessitate adaptation by retailers, particularly in the realm of online retail [20]. Despite this shift, maintaining store-based retail is crucial for revitalizing town centers and preserving local employment [21]. Moreover, structural changes in towns call for the integration of digital tools and modern payment methods in store-based retail to meet evolving consumer expectations [21]. Adapting to these changes is essential for store-based retailers to remain competitive and meet customer demands.

Amidst numerous challenges, the onset of the Covid-19 pandemic in March 2020 brought additional hurdles for stores worldwide, including Germany [22]. This had varied effects on the retail sector, with decreased sales in certain categories like clothing and toys, while others such as building supplies and medical items saw a surge in demand [23]. Despite these product groups typically being available in store-based stores, many were forced to close, leading to a significant shift to online purchasing due to limited digitization among traditional retailers [20]. This convergence of structural retail changes, digitalization, and the pandemic has created an unprecedented challenge for the industry, often described as a 'triple tsunami' [24]. The outlook for store-based retailers since the pandemic's onset remains bleak, with many facing severe financial constraints and potential insolvency.

Big Data Potential The term big data usually refers only to the size of the data stored, but there are also other factors that play an important role in this context. BDA is seen as the key to many everyday problems in sensible handling of a high data volume. In recent years, the links between big data and smart town have been increasingly investigated [25, 26]. The significant increase in connected devices through the internet of things (IoT) in towns has led to rapid data growth, which has attracted the attention of many researchers. However, until 2016, the combination of IoT and big data was still an unexplored area of research [27]. Towns face a variety of challenges in this regard, as the ongoing digitalization affects almost all areas. Numerous jobs could be eliminated, employees need to be empowered with digital skills to perform new tasks and activities, and clear concepts for data integration and security are needed [28]. In this context, the publication of open public sector datasets is also seen important [29].

Less frequently studied, though growing, is the relationship between BDA and retail. However, even less is the relationship of BDA and store-based retail. Store-based retailers who can link products, time, place, and process data are thus able to implement more targeted strategies and can predict future events based on historical data [30]. Connecting systems through sensors, as well as applications (Apps), provides an opportunity to better understand customer behavior and can provide a competitive advantage for towns [12, 31].

Marketing Mix: 7P Framework The marketing mix is a long-proven marketing method to promote desired behavior and achieve market objectives. This succeeds with the help of different elements. McCarthy [13] developed the 4P model for this purpose. The first four Ps reflect the view of the organization, i.e., the producer. Over time, they have been supplemented by other Ps but an extension of Booms and Bitner [14] became more established because it additionally considered the characteristics of services. The 7P model emerged with the following items [32]:

1. Product: The store-based retail product represents the center of the model. It is needed to satisfy the needs of customers and includes the customer service performance.
2. Price: … as well as its aspects, are included, e.g., the production and social costs. Kotler and Armstrong [33] describe the price as 'the amount of money charged for a product or service, or the sum of all the values that customers give up in order to gain the benefit of having or using a product or service'.
3. Place: … where the products are bought, i.e., the retailer's store and/or website, is called the distribution channel. Lee and Kotler [34] define it as 'where and when the target audience will perform the desired behavior, acquire any related goods, and receive any associated services.

4. Promotion: It is not only about classic advertising, but about any communication ways that reach the customer, regarding e.g., products or orders, to bind customer and convince them.
5. Process: … relates to sales and services and has a strong influence on customer satisfaction as well, e.g., store-based retail must respond to the customers' needs and wishes. This also includes the availability and selection of goods, but also the secure handling of customer data.
6. Physical facilities … encompass external factors beyond the control of store-based retail, alongside social and cultural influences. Also, retailers can influence the success of their offerings; f.i., store furnishings significantly impact customer perceptions of service and quality.
7. Participant: … is about the people who provide the services and has a strong influence on the customers' perception of quality. In our case, the store-based retailer symbolized the center of our study, as it is essential for the consideration. Stakeholders, competitors, or structures are included and summarized here.

In the last ten years (especially through Covid-19) new momentum came into the research and it was shown that the marketing mix is still a strong tool for the study of market processes [35]. This mixed-method study follows the scientific movements and applies the marketing mix in its extended form of Booms and Bitner [14] to the store-based market of retailers to bridge the gap between retail, marketing, and public research.

3 Longitudinal Mixed-Method-Study Setup

This longitudinal mixed-method-study was conducted over three years as part of a research project from January 2018 to February 2021. The study involved 13 store-based retailers which were the store owners (36% female and 64% male). The store-based retailers have not changed over the period of study. The retailers ranged from 38 to 54 years old (average age were 48 years), with stores averaging 74 years in existence, where the youngest is 8 years old and the oldest 229 years. The median is 50.5. Among the retailers were a drugstore, an optician, a bookstore, two pharmacies, three grocery stores, a café, a hotel, a museum, and two furniture stores. To better understand our mixed-method-study, we used a design with three consecutive phases [36, 37]. In phase 1, we exploratory identified effectiveness factors for store-based retailers within qualitative interviews. For more methodical details see Chap. 4—Method Design. We conducted two interviews during the study in order to incorporate the changes caused by Covid-19 into the study and also to do justice to the character of a longitudinal study. Following this, in phase 2 we quantitatively evaluated the 27 identified effectiveness factors by having an expert committee rate the effectiveness of each effectiveness factor on a scale based on the data collected (retailers- and secondary data). For more details see Chap. 5—Method Design & Procedure. It was found that only 12 effectiveness factors have an influence on the revenue and sales figures of the retailors. Finally, significance was evaluated in phase 3. This revealed that there were only four significant factors.

3.1 *Phase 1: Qualitative Exploration of Effectiveness Factors*

3.1.1 Method

Method Design. In our mixed-method study, we first conducted exploratory research [38] to identify effectiveness factors for store-based retailers, focusing on factors impacting revenue or sales. We conducted qualitative interviews with 13 store-based retailers (average length of 60 minutes) initially in-person before the onset of Covid-19 (fourth March 2020), followed by telephone interviews during the pandemic (09/07/2020–10/9/2020). All interviewees were the store owners, and, in both surveys, the interviewees were the same people. To ensure diverse perspectives, we interviewed participants from various sectors (e.g., supermarkets or restaurants) and types of store-based retailers (e.g., experience or stores' existence) [39]. Using a semi-structured interview guide with open-ended questions, we followed established guidelines [38, 40] to ensure comprehensive data collection, including adjustments based on two preliminary interviews and additional questions related to the pandemic in later interviews.

The questionnaire is divided into three or four categories. The first category is about the interviewee itself (age, business, technology status) and the benefits from the project. After that, the status quo of the project and existing issues are briefly clarified and discussed. In the second category, the questions deal with attitudes and behavior towards data sharing as well as worries and fears, i.e. 'What are your concerns about giving your data to the data analysis company as part of the project?'. In the third category we identify which data are available from the store-based retailers and which potentials and expectations they see for the usage of BDA with questions such as: 'What do you hope to gain from participating in the project? How important is the topic of digitization for you? What do you understand specifically by data?' Only in the follow-up study, we asked questions about changes because of Covid-19, e.g., 'What has changed for you because of Covid-19? What alternatives have you found to sell your products? What analytics about data would help you in the current times?'

Data Analysis. The interviews were recorded in German, then transcribed and translated into English for the purpose of analysis using the technique of back-translation. Subsequently, the interviews were analyzed by using MAXQDA 2020 software. Bottom-up coding methods were used to analyze the interviews [41, 42]. The data analysis of the interview results was performed iteratively. To avoid empirical bias, we did not import any preconfigured values. In doing so, the authors independently coded and chose codes that best fit the text excerpt. Then, the codes were merged and grouped (axial coding) that a list of effectiveness factors could be created. We have additionally extended these with the changes due to Covid-19. Differing opinions were discussed with another researcher and clarified by consensus. For example, in the following quote, 'Let's say there is a street festival in my neighborhood […]. When I see there is more happening than normal, I can advertise on the sidewalk.' (RT1), two independent codes ('Outside the store' and 'Running advertising') were found. Finally, 'Outside the store' was used as the axial code. The analysis was terminated at saturation, i.e., when no new effectiveness factors were found. After that we screened the codes for plausibility and fit.

3.1.2 Qualitative Findings

Product. Type of Product. The assortment of products can have a lot of influence on the revenue but also on the attractiveness of the store. For example, a comprehensive analysis can give a store-based retailer in a town information about which products sell well and which do not. Especially in combination with other stores in the town, it gives insights where visitors are more likely to buy the product.

'When it comes to the main product groups, such as skin care cosmetics or fragrances, we are basically on industry's average in terms of the sales shares. Then there are a few products, if I take a shower gel, […] I don't know which one is doing well apart from our bestseller.' (RT9).

Price. Payment methods. In recent years, many new payment methods have been added. Besides cash and EC payment, credit cards, Apple Pay, Google Pay etc. have been added. An analysis of which payment method is more used and preferred can help the store-based retailers to strengthen their innovation character or also show from the pool analysis which payment methods should perhaps be introduced.

'Card payments are increasing as EC devices are used more.' (RT2).

Customer Cards. Customer cards are an important factor for the use of BDA in store-based retail. This allows store-based retailers to keep their data on customers up to date and tailor individualized offers for customers, e.g., by individualized advertising or loyalty point campaigns.

'We have about 50,000 customer addresses stored. But about 20,000 come in regularly […]. And we send them every year promotion, always brand-related promotions, no promotions from ourselves, mostly in combination with the brands. […] Then we record the return at the checkout via the customer number, because the customer gives the card and picks up the gift.' (RT9).

Promotion. Social media marketing. In the twenty-first century, marketing predominantly occurs online, particularly on social media platforms [43, 44]. Therefore, it's crucial for retailers to actively engage online, especially during pandemics, to connect with customers, promote events, offers, and facilitate purchases. However, interviews reveal that older retailers perceive more challenges in this than younger ones. Despite this, there's substantial interest among all retailers in analyzing social media activities, indicating significant potential.

'So, I post on Facebook about our site, and I try not to overdo it. Of course, I'm also watching what our industry is doing and what the others are doing.' (RT3).

Events. Events in the town always attract more visitors and customers to the town than when there is no event. Therefore, especially on these days, customer outreach and promotion are important to create an additional incentive. Based on the data analysis, at event times, the number of visitors to the town has increased significantly and that sales figures have increased significantly with previously advertised promotions.

'When we celebrate festivals, like the Martini market, [...] or the Christmas market [...]. These are all festivals where we make a lot of money, so these are already exorbitant incursions for us [by Corona], you just must put that there.' (RT8).

Place. Online. Addressing customers is enormously important, and especially today, addressing them digitally has become more important than ever. So suitable digital places to address customers are the homepage, social media accounts, or an online store. Reaching customers in this way also increases sales [45].

'We've had a homepage since the beginning, it's indispensable for me. For me, it's a digital shop window, a presentation for the customer.' (RT10).

Participant. Customer frequency during the day. In combination with the analysis of WLAN data and the store-based retailers' cash register data, it is possible to check whether the store-based retailers' gut feeling regarding customer frequency over the course of the day and the week is correct. The store-based retailers hope to gain a lot of insights here, especially in combination with the other store-based retailers as a pool.

'We open at half past eight, then it rises so slowly, peak is usually around 10 o'clock or half past 11 to 12 o'clock. Then it levels off again and then there's another peak, so usually 3:30 to 4:30 or 5:00 p.m. But that's just my feeling.' (RT1).

Process. Covid-19 laws. The pandemic has presented store-based retailers with an unprecedented crisis. Retailers have been forced to close their stores involuntarily, starting in early March 2020 and continuing indefinitely. There was a lot of uncertainty and store-based retailers thought they could reopen in a few weeks. In the phase in the summer of 2020, the stores could partially reopen and sell their products with hygiene concepts until shortly before Christmas 2020. After that, most store-based retailers were closed again until spring 2021.

'This has been even earlier in the county [name of county] than in the rest of the country. Our county administrator said on March 9 that nothing was going to work—we should all close. And then the federal government followed suit on March 16. [...] But we thought that it would take 3-4 weeks.' (RT11).

Impact of Covid-19. The pandemic situation is having a huge impact on store-based retailers. They can no longer sell their products as usual and sometimes must worry about their existence. Digital alternatives have also become established in [name of town], but this does not replace the normal everyday sales routine.

'That has also shown the crisis. There are also many studies in our sector about the fact that these small stores have come through it quite well. The big stores have difficulties because they are often in the top stores in the town centers, where people don't like to go now, and they are just as anonymous, and many customers want to support their local store.' (RT5).

Customer Groups. Knowledge about (potential) customers is an advantage for store-based retailers and offers the deciding factor compared to online retail. Therefore, the analysis of the customers groups, e.g., families, children, seniors, tourist, who are in the town throughout the day, weekdays, months, or year can help store-based retailers to design customer-specific offers and simplify the process enormously.

'It helps me… if I know that […] families are here during the vacations, tourists, or cultural tourists. So, the structure of the strangers. That would interest me.' (RT4).

Physical facilities. Weather. Weather is an uncontrollable influencing factor. Weather forecasts help to control this, but there is still variance. For example, sales figures are also significantly related to the weather.

'[Influence is always exerted] by the weather. If it rains in the summer, that's not so bad for the retail trade, because then people aren't in the garden or at the lake but are simply also out and about in the town, including vacationers.' (RT2).

Seasons. Seasons, including fixed holidays, are external environmental factors that affect retailers' planning. They must accommodate events like Easter and Christmas, alongside other holidays, and periods in between.

'If someone could guarantee us today that we'll have snow by Christmas…that would be fantastic. Then you could really work with it, but … we can't influence that.' (RT11).

3.2 Phase 2: Quantitative Significance

To quantitatively evaluate the identified effectiveness factors, we proceed as follows. First, we describe the design of our quantitative study, and second which effectiveness factors are influencing.

Method Design. In Phase 1, we were able to identify a total of 27 effectiveness factors that are important to retailers in our case of application. We then used a committee of qualified data analysis experts [46] to evaluate the effectiveness factors (Phase 2). The expert committee consists of data analysts, economists, mathematicians, and scientist, in total 12 persons. For this purpose, the data analysts collected data from the store-based retailors from January 2018 to February 2021. The store-based retailers' data included revenue, sales figures, merchandise categories (depending on availability), social media presence, special events, and payment methods. In total, over 2.8 million data points were collected, where a data point is the number of times one or more sales were reported. After data collection, the data was unified, standardized (all data were normalized on a per hour basis), and cleaned for errors. This was done using heuristics in MATLAB. In addition to the store-based retailers' data, the data of the towns public WLAN, which consist of about 40 nodes, was used, as well as other public available data sources regarding weather, events, business hours, etc. (secondary data).

Method Procedure. Some of the identified effectiveness factors could not be verified, meaning that a feasibility check is not possible. This has several reasons e.g., because for some of them the data basis was not available, or the analysis did not take place yet. In the area Place, for example, the effectiveness factors 'Outside the store' and 'Inside the store' could not be proven because the store-based retailers do not keep any lists of when they carried out which advertising measures in or in front of the store. Another example, the effectiveness factors 'Parking situation', 'Effects of road work', or 'Accessibility of public transport' from Process could not be verified because there is no public data regarding the construction site situation or the parking situation. The identified effectiveness factors were rated on a Likert-scale of 1 to 5, with 1 indicating low effectiveness and 5 indicating high effectiveness. All data that could be collected on the effectiveness factor were considered together and evaluated in comparison to the others on the Likert-scale. In a joint evaluation, it was found that a significant statement on the influence on revenue and sales figures is possible for 12 of the 27 effectiveness factors. These are type of products, payment methods, loyalty cards, social media marketing, events, online (location), customer frequency, Covid-19 laws, Covid-19 impact, customer groups, weather, and seasons. How the impact is represented is described in the next chapter, with Fig. 1 showing the 12 effectiveness factors with their impact on sales figures in gray and dashed, and the impact on revenue in dotted blue. The evaluation per area is shown below.

Influencing Factors. In the Product area, the sales figures per product group have a much strong impact. For store-based retailers, this means that the more they know about their product groups and analyze them, the higher is the sales figures. In Price, there is a clear difference between the payment methods before and after the start of the pandemic, which is why in Fig. 1 the effectiveness on revenue is only medium. This is due to the significant increase in cashless payment methods since the start of the pandemic, as well as digital payment methods due to the closed stores. The customer cards made less of a difference here. The area of Promotion is confirmed by

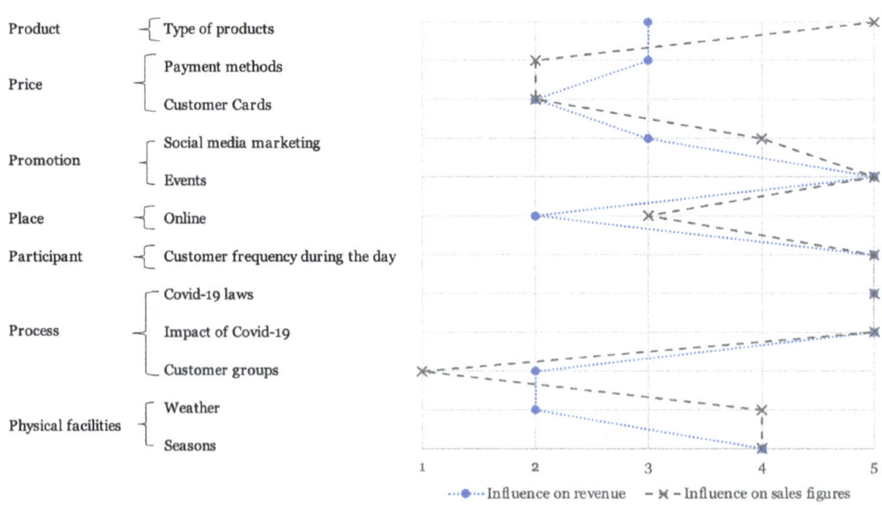

Fig. 1 Quantitative Evaluation of the identified Effectiveness Factors

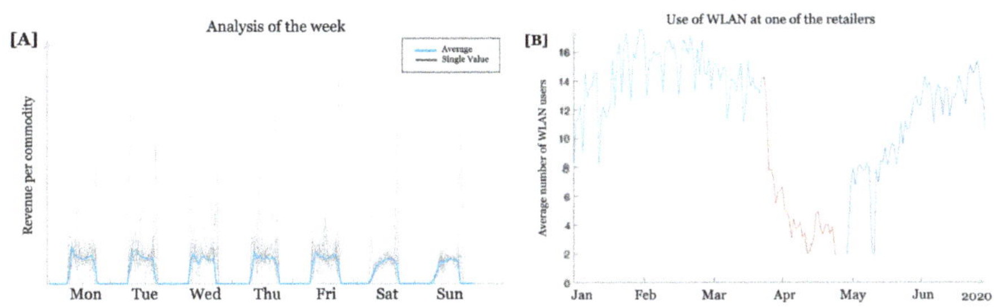

Fig. 2 Analysis of the Revenue per Week [A] and the WLAN Usage [B]

the literature: the more social media marketing by store-based retailers the higher are sales figures and revenue, sales figures are a bit more [45]. However, the most effective events are those that are cancelled due to the pandemic, resulting in significant losses for store-based retailers. Customer outreach (Place) is not as pronounced among the store-based retailers studied. This may be due to the location or the population structure. In the Participants area, sales figures correlate exactly with the number of visitors to the town and thus have a high effectiveness on revenue and sales figures. For this purpose, Fig. 2 [A] shows the course of hourly revenue per product (gray), as well as the average value of these (blue). In the area of Process, the Covid-19 laws and guidelines have a high effectiveness on revenue and sales figures, but in a negative direction. This is confirmed by the influence of both that correlates strongly with the use of the WLAN, which is shown in Fig. 2 [B]. The number of customers on the public WLAN fell steadily from the beginning of March 2020 until the end of May 2021, when it slowly started to rise again. In contrast, the customer groups have little influence on the revenue and almost no significant influence on the sales figures. The external factors (Physical facilities) differ for each effectiveness factor. For example, some store-based retailers suspected in the interviews, that weather has an influence on sales figures, but not on revenue. The analysis shows that only at temperatures above 26 °C does the revenue drop significantly for all store-based retailers. Lastly, seasons have high effectiveness on revenue and sales figures, with Christmas business having the greatest influence.

3.3 Phase 3: Evaluation

Method. Together with the findings from Phase 1 and 2, we were able to evaluate the quantitative significance. Of the 12 feasible influencing factors from Phase 2, 4 of 12 crystallized as significant factors in Phase 3. A very strong influence on both revenue and sales figures were recorded by Events, Customer frequency during the day, Covid-19 laws, and Impact of Covid-19.

Significant Factors. Events have a very strong impact on revenue and sales figures. All store-based retailers surveyed indicated that they experience a strong flow during special opening times, e.g., open Sunday or during events (Christmas markets, or festivals) and therefore notice a difference in sales figures and revenue compared to 'normal days'. The data clearly reflected this, as both revenue and sales figures were higher, as were the number of visitors to the town. This suggests that store-based retailers should open their stores especially during events. Customer frequency during the day had a very strong impact on both revenue and sales figures. All the store-based retailers surveyed indicated that they consistently experience a strong rush at certain times (for two hours in the morning and afternoon) and therefore see a difference in revenue compared to peak hours. From this, we can conclude that especially during peak hours, store-based retailers can sell their products more intensive to the customers and should therefore adjust their individual strategies. Lastly, the days Covid-19 laws and regulations were passed and Covid-19 in general showed a very strong impact on store-based retailers' revenue and sales figures. All store-based retailers interviewed spoke intensely about the impact of closures and Covid-19 consequences. From the time the German government imposed the lockdown, revenue and sales figures dropped dramatically. Compared to previous years, an enormous drop could be observed. Through individual measures individual retailers were able to increase the course numbers and revenue slightly, but never to a pre-Covid-19 level. After the relaxations became known in Germany, visitors to the city rose again, see Fig. 2 [B]. This suggests that store-based retailers need to be prepared for extreme situations and that a digital alternative to sell products is highly advisable.

4 Discussion

In this mixed-method study, we enhance understanding of effective factors for BDA in retail, focusing on store-based retailers. Particularly crucial amid increasing online retail, especially during pandemics, is support for store-based retail. Despite possessing substantial data, many retailers fail to fully utilize it due to constraints like time. By exploring our research model within the context of retail, we aim to derive practical implications. Bridging the 7P-model by Booms and Bitner [14] to retail research, we adapt it to a big data context, revealing various focus areas for effectiveness factors. Our findings indicate a correlation between increased social media usage and revenue, as well as visitor numbers and sales figures. We identify best practices for revenue strategies and highlight pandemic-driven changes. This study contributes to retail and IS research by applying the 7P-Model to a setting with a smart town big data project and integrating pandemic influences into the model. Our results show a high degree of practical relevance for the store-based retail in towns as well as for a smart town itself. Therefore, the results are demonstrated with two examples (very weak influence and a different influence on revenue and sales figures) as the examples with very strong influence have already been presented in detail in chapter Significant Factors. A very low influence on both revenue and sales figures were recorded by Customer cards and -groups. Customer cards are of great relevance for store-based retailers to have an overview and to inform regularly about advertising of their brand partners and to provide small extra gifts only for card-holders [47]. The evaluation demonstrate that this type of customer attachment is popular but has very little impact on revenue and sales figures. However, it indicates customers that their trust and support is valued through their purchase.

A differentiation of the influences on revenue and sales figures was particularly evident in the case of weather, payment methods, online (place), social media marketing, and type of products. For example, the results showed that weather has only a small impact on revenue but a stronger impact on sales figures. Depending on the product range, some store-based retailers reported that a summer rainfall has a positive impact on their sales figures, as customers are not in the garden but rather go shopping in the town. It can be concluded that weather forecasts can help to influence sales figures and should be monitored by store-based retailers. Another example we can derive from the evaluation is that a variety of different payment methods can be offered to reach a range of customers and provide them with different options, but the evaluation show that payment methods have very small influence on sales figures and rather mediocre influence on revenue. It can be deduced that besides the more traditional methods like cash and EC payments, new payment methods like Apple Pay or Google Pay are more attractive and speak for variety but have no significant influence.

Additionally, our findings indicate that leveraging data sources such as social media metrics, weather forecasts, and customer transaction records provides valuable insights into consumer behavior. Specifically, our insights suggest a positive relationship between social media usage and sales figures, highlighting social media's role in understanding customer preferences and engagement. Weather data also showed a differential impact on revenue and sales, with certain conditions driving higher shopping activity. Adapting the 7P-Model to a big data context, we identified strategies like enhanced social media engagement, weather-responsive inventory management, and diverse payment options. These strategies, supported by smart city initiatives, demonstrate the significant impact of big data on rural retail, providing a framework for retailers to prospectively harness data analytics for improved sales and competitiveness.

Furthermore, the results provide valuable insights for a small and town that is transforming into a smart town. Our results show that many store-based retailers in towns lack knowledge about the use of digital technologies as well as big data. A smart town can support this by providing store-based retailers with the knowledge they need, be it through lectures by experts, through a platform, or other possibilities. '[H]igh-frequency, near-real-time data could become the primary input for managers to keep up with sudden pandemic-related developments, and potentially with post-pandemic shopping behavior changes as well' [48]. It is important that every store-based retailer has access to this knowledge and that it is made available without barriers. It is also relevant to note, that despite the comprehensive approach of our mixed-method study, several limitations need to be noted. First, the qualitative phase, which involved 13 semi-structured interviews, may not fully capture the diverse perspectives and experiences across different rural regions, potentially limiting the generalizability of our findings. Accordingly, we invite future research to test the external validity of the derived empirical knowledge of our study. Second, while the quantitative phase analyzed over 2.8 million data points using the 7P-Marketing-Mix, the data was constrained to specific metrics and may not encompass all relevant big data factors affecting rural retail. However, the idea of our study was to test if validated metrics from urban areas can be applied to rural areas as well, which, fortunately, was the case. Nonetheless, our approach should only be considered a preliminary step regarding the implementation of corresponding tools. Moreover, the rapid evolution of big data technologies and smart city initiatives could render some of our recommendations as outdated, making continuous updates and adaptations necessary.

5 Conclusion

As many towns transform to a smart town and one of the many influencing factors of it is Smart Economy, which includes a (successful) towns' retail sector. Our research provides an overview and guide for how the use of BDA can effectively influence the transformation of a store-based retail in a future smart town. By using a mixed-method-study in a German town, we were able to reveal which factors influence the store-based retail in a smart town and we were able to allude to promising interventions.

Our research shows that the store-based retail is enormously influenced by process factors and physical facilities such as legal regulations and the spread and measures of a pandemic. In this regard, retailers need to constantly monitor their process and physical facilities and regularly adjust their own strategy, such as opening hours or the creation of certain offers—this has already started in the participating stores. Especially since external influences such as weather conditions, trends, etc. are not necessarily predictable and can be planned over some longer period.

Our objective was to provide more comprehensive explanations for the use of BDA in retail, as well as to identify the factors that influence the data-driven digital transformation of retail in a future smart town. Considering our findings, future researchers should be able to derive additional factors to strengthen retail in the future. In a next step, the results will be transferred to other store-based retailers and further retailers will be recruited for the project to ensure a larger sample size.

References

1. United Nations: World population prospects 2022: Summary of results. (2022).
2. Parker, K., Horowitz, J., Brown, A., Fry, R., Cohn, D., & Igielnik, R. (2018). *What unites and divides urban.* Suburban and Rural Communities. Pew Research Center.

3. Debbarma, J., & Choi, Y. (2022). A taxonomy of green governance: A qualitative and quantitative analysis towards sustainable development. *Sustainable Cities and Society., 79*, 103693. https://doi.org/10.1016/j.scs.2022.103693
4. Gassmann, O., Böhm, J., & Palmié, M. (2019). *Smart cities: Introducing digital innovation to cities*. Emerald Group Publishing.
5. Statista: eCommerce report 2023. (2023).
6. Hänninen, M., Kwan, S. K., & Mitronen, L. (2021). From the store to omnichannel retail: Looking back over three decades of research. *The International Review of Retail, Distribution and Consumer Research., 31*, 1–35. https://doi.org/10.1080/09593969.2020.1833961
7. Baersch, S., Bollweg, L., Weber, P., Wittermund, T., & Wulfhorst, V. (2021). Local retail under fire: Local shopping platforms revisited pre and during the Corona crisis. In *International conference on Wirtschaftsinformatik*.
8. Momboisse, F., & ten Ham, M. (2018). European e-commerce report 2018. *Brussels*.
9. Meffert, H., Burmann, C., Kirchgeorg, M., Eisenbeiß, M., & Meffert, H. (2019). *Marketing: Grundlagen marktorientierter Unternehmensführung: Konzepte—Instrumente—Praxisbeispiele*. Springer Gabler.
10. Pereira, M. M., & Frazzon, E. M. (2021). A data-driven approach to adaptive synchronization of demand and supply in omni-channel retail supply chains. *International Journal of Information Management., 57*, 102165. https://doi.org/10.1016/j.ijinfomgt.2020.102165
11. Chang, Y.-W., & Chen, J. (2020). What motivates customers to shop in smart shops? The impacts of smart technology and technology readiness. *Journal of Retailing and Consumer Services., 58*, 102325. https://doi.org/10.1016/j.jretconser.2020.102325
12. PhamThi, H., & Ho, T. N. (2024). Understanding customer experience over time and customer citizenship behavior in retail environment: The mediating role of customer brand relationship strength. *Cogent Business & Management., 11*, 2292487. https://doi.org/10.1080/23311975.2023.2292487
13. McCarthy, E.J.: *Basic marketing*. R.D. Irwin (1960).
14. Booms, B. H., & Bitner, M. J. (1981). *Marketing strategies and organizational structures for service firms*. Marketing of Services.
15. Caragliu, A., Bo, C. D., & Nijkamp, P. (2011). Smart cities in Europe. *Journal of Urban Technology., 18*, 65–82. https://doi.org/10.1080/10630732.2011.601117
16. Durán-Sánchez, A., Rama, D., Sereno-Ramírez, A., & Bredis, K. (2017). Sustainability and quality of life in smart cities: Analysis of scientific production. *Presented at the*.
17. Schaefer, C. (2020). Developing a smart city strategy by use of St. *Gallen management model focused in smart mobility and smart environment*. https://doi.org/10.25819/UBSI/1894
18. Kumar, T. M. V., & Dahija, B. (2016). *Smart economy in smart cities | SpringerLink*. Springer.
19. Ortiz-Ospina, E., & Beltekian, D. Trade and globalization. (2014).
20. De Canio, F., Fuentes-Blasco, M., & Martinelli, E. (2023). Exploring channel switching in the aftermath of the Covid-19 pandemic: Are shoppers all driven by the same motivations? *International Journal of Retail & Distribution Management*. https://doi.org/10.1108/IJRDM-10-2022-0414
21. German Retail Association: Trends im Handel 2025. (2016).
22. World Health Organization: World health statistics 2020: monitoring health for the SDGs, sustainable development goals., https://www.who.int/publications/i/item/9789240005105, (2020).
23. Jung, S., Rürup, B., & Schrinner, A. Konsummonitor. (2020).
24. RND: Pleitewelle im Herbst: Innenstädten droht Verödung. Retrieved from April 04, 2023, from https://www.rnd.de/wirtschaft/pleitewelle-im-herbst-innenstadten-droht-verodung-7KF32YFWNX2QS6Q5QVGGXL6JMY.html
25. Malik, K. R., Sam, Y., Hussain, M., & Abuarqoub, A. (2018). A methodology for real-time data sustainability in smart city: Towards inferencing and analytics for big-data. *Sustainable Cities and Society., 39*, 548–556. https://doi.org/10.1016/j.scs.2017.11.031
26. Zeng, D., Tim, Y., Yu, J., & Liu, W. (2020). Actualizing big data analytics for smart cities: A cascading affordance study. *International Journal of Information Management., 54*, 102156. https://doi.org/10.1016/j.ijinfomgt.2020.102156

27. Hashem, I. A. T., Chang, V., Anuar, N. B., Adewole, K., Yaqoob, I., Gani, A., Ahmed, E., & Chiroma, H. (2016). The role of big data in smart city. *International Journal of Information Management., 36*, 748–758. https://doi.org/10.1016/j.ijinfomgt.2016.05.002
28. Kantanen, T., Julkunen, S., Hiltunen, E., & Nickell, D. (2017). Creating employees' motivational paths in the retail trade. *Cogent Business & Management., 4*, 1389332. https://doi.org/10.1080/23311975.2017.1389332
29. van Winden, W., De, L., & Carvalho, L. (2017). *How digitalization changes cities: innovation for the urban economy of tomorrow., 1–24.* https://doi.org/10.13140/RG.2.2.27447.83362
30. Bradlow, E., Gangwar, M., Kopalle, P., & Voleti, S. (2017). The role of big data and predictive analytics in retailing. *Journal of Retailing., 93*, 79–95. https://doi.org/10.1016/j.jretai.2016.12.004
31. Barkham, R., Bokhari, S., & Saiz, A. (2018). Urban big data: City management and real estate markets. In *Artificial intelligence, machine learning, and optimization tools for smart cities: Designing for sustainability*. Springer International Publishing.
32. Rafiq, M., & Ahmed, P. K. (1995). Using the 7Ps as a generic marketing mix: An exploratory survey of UK and European marketing academics. *Marketing Intelligence & Planning., 13*, 4–15. https://doi.org/10.1108/02634509510097793
33. Kotler, P., & Armstrong, G. (2009). *Principles of marketing*. Prentice Hall.
34. Lee, N. R., & Kotler, P. (2015). *Social marketing: Changing behaviors for good*. SAGE Publications.
35. Lim, W. M. (2021). A marketing mix typology for integrated care: The 10 Ps. *Journal of Strategic Marketing., 29*, 453–469. https://doi.org/10.1080/0965254X.2020.1775683
36. Kordyaka, B., Laato, S., Weber, S., Hamari, J., & Niehaves, B. (2024). Exploring the association between engagement with location-based game features and getting inspired about environmental issues and nature. *Presented at the CHI '24: Proceedings of the CHI Conference on Human Factors in Computing Systems*. https://doi.org/10.1145/3613904.364278
37. Kordyaka, B., Pumplun, L., Brunnhofer, M., Kruse, B., & Laato, S. (2023). Gender disparities in esports—An explanatory mixed-methods approach. *Computers in Human Behavior, 149*, 107956. https://doi.org/10.1016/j.chb.2023.107956
38. Sarker, S., Xiao, X., & Beaulieu, T. (2013). Qualitative studies in information systems: A critical review and some guiding principles. *MIS Quarterly., 37*, iii–xviii.
39. Miles, M. B., & Huberman, A. M. (1994). *Qualitative data analysis: An expanded sourcebook*. SAGE.
40. Pumplun, L., Tauchert, C., & Heidt, M. (2019). A new organizational chassis for artificial intelligence-exploring organizational readiness factors. In *European conference on information systems (ECIS)* (pp. 1–15).
41. Corbin, J., & Strauss, A. (2014). *Basics of qualitative research: Techniques and procedures for developing grounded theory*. Sage publications.
42. Glaser, B. G., & Strauss, A. L. (2017). *Discovery of grounded theory: Strategies for qualitative research*. Routledge.
43. Grimmer, L. (2023). The role of local government in marketing small city retailing: Examining the gap between perception and reality. *The International Review of Retail, Distribution and Consumer Research., 33*, 371–395. https://doi.org/10.1080/09593969.2023.2227364
44. Siregar, Y., Kent, A., Perison-Smith, A., & Guan, C. Disrupting the fashion retail journey: Social media and GenZ's fashion consumption | emerald insight. (2023).
45. Sharma, A., & Mehrotra, A. (2007). Choosing an optimal channel mix in multichannel environments. *Industrial Marketing Management., 36*, 21–28. https://doi.org/10.1016/j.indmarman.2006.06.012
46. Wisdom, J., & Creswell, J. W. (2013). Mixed methods: Integrating quantitative and qualitative data collection and analysis while studying patient-centered medical home models. *PCMH Research Methods Series, 13*, 8.
47. Rains, T., & Longley, P. (2021). The provenance of loyalty card data for urban and retail analytics. *Journal of Retailing and Consumer Services., 63*, 102650. https://doi.org/10.1016/j.jretconser.2021.102650
48. Szász, L., Bálint, C., Csíki, O., Nagy, B. Z., Rácz, B. G., Csala, D., & Harris, L. C. (2022). The impact of COVID-19 on the evolution of online retail: The pandemic as a window of opportunity. *Journal of Retailing and Consumer Services., 69*, 103089. https://doi.org/10.1016/j.jretconser.2022.103089

Unlocking Value: Towards a Comprehensive Taxonomy for Commercializing Open Data in the Business Context

Eric Börner

Abstract The increasing availability of open data promises transparency and economic growth. Although several studies have highlighted the value of open data for businesses, the private sector has been slow to adopt it, falling short of expectations. This is due to a lack of knowledge about the real benefits of using open data as a business and few use cases for commercial reuse of open data. Against this backdrop, our study aims to shed light on the commercial use of open data by developing a comprehensive taxonomy consisting of 14 dimensions and deriving five commercial open data user archetypes. Our study contributes to the literature by providing a nuanced understanding of the commercial use of open data, as well as a conceptual framework that structures successful open data use cases, which can be used by businesses and practitioners to identify opportunities for potential open data use scenarios in their respective organizations.

1 Introduction

Data is essential in our knowledge-driven world, driving both societal and economic shifts. Its value increases with reuse [1], making sharing and opening datasets crucial to unlocking its full potential. In this context, the concept of open data has become increasingly popular in recent years. An expanding quantity of data is being made available as open data to promote transparency and stimulate both new businesses and economic growth [2]. The open data movement originated with the release of public data as open data by governments with the goal of enhancing governmental transparency, fostering citizen participation and collaboration, and facilitating economic growth [2, 3]. Open data refers to "data that is freely available, and can be used as well as republished by everyone without restrictions from copyright or patents" [4, p. 1]. Institutional policies and pressures have encouraged both public and private

E. Börner (✉)
Chair of Business Information Systems, Esp. Information Systems in Industry and Trade, TU Dresden, Dresden, Germany
e-mail: eric.boerner1@tu-dresden.de

C. M. Flath et al. (eds.), *Shaping the Digital Future Through Innovation and Practice*, Lecture Notes in Information Systems and Organisation 85,
https://doi.org/10.1007/978-3-032-08489-7_6

entities to provide access to their information [1, 5]. Open Data has the potential to improve governance and democratic processes, empower citizens, adress public problems and create economic opportunities [6]. In terms of economic potential, open data has been the subject of high expectations, being seen as a "gold mine" of business opportunities [7]. According to Manyika et al. [8], the economic value of open data ranges from \$3.2 to \$5.4 trillion annually worldwide. Open data has the potential to enhance growth and prosperity across various industries, including transportation, consumer goods, electricity, finance, agriculture, urban development, and the social sector, as evidenced by prior research [3, 8, 9]. Despite the widespread enthusiasm for the vast potential of open data and the increasing availability of open datasets, the private sector has lagged in its adoption of open data, and the use of open data by businesses is below expectations [10, 11]. While research on the expected benefits of open data provides initial insights, little is known about its potential benefits in the private sector [12]. There is a lack of understanding regarding the precise variables, parameters, and pathways through which open data translates into growth and opportunities [13] and the literature lacks a specific perspective on the use of open data in a business context [14]. Furthermore, there is a shortage of open data use cases that can serve as a foundation for purposeful and precise consumption of open data [15].

This study seeks to examine how economic value can be created through open data in a business environment by viewing this issue from the perspective of enterprises. The research objective is to create a taxonomy for the commercial use of open data by businesses. This will synthesize the relevant knowledge on this topic and expand comprehension of commercial open data reuse in the private sector by improving the still insufficient understanding of open data value creation. The developed taxonomy can assist researchers and practitioners in objectively assessing key facets of the potential business applications of open data. The taxonomy provides various perspectives on the commercial reuse of open data and contains major dimensions that determine the possible use scenarios of open data for businesses. The taxonomy was developed following the approach specified by Nickerson et al. [16]. Throughout the process of four iterations, diverse sources such as research literature, whitepapers, and use cases were examined. Based on the developed taxonomy, we derived five archetypes of commercial open data users. This paper is organized as follows. The second section introduces open data and value creation. In the following two sections, we describe our methodology and the results. In the fifth section, we discuss the contributions and limitations.

2 Theoretical Background

2.1 *Open Data*

Open data is a widely used term and can be defined as "data that is freely available, and can be used as well as republished by everyone without restrictions from copyright or patents" [4, p. 1]. Although there are many definitions of open data, there is no universal approach to determine whether data is open or not. According to Verhulst and Caplan [13], some authors view open data as part of a spectrum of openness. In this regard, Lindman et al. [17] define openness as including technical openness of data (e.g., through the use of interfaces and standards), legal openness (including copyright and licensing), and commercial openness (allowing for commercial use of the data). Open data can be provided by both government and private organizations, resulting in the subsets of Open Government Data (OGD) and Open Private Data [18]. Open government data can be defined as "data collected and held by a government and its agencies, shared and made freely available to anyone in order to pursue open government objectives" [19, p. 3]. Not all published data can be considered 'pure' open data, as they do not always meet strict criteria, such as the Sebastopol Open Government Data Principles [13]. Shared corporate data, i.e. data voluntarily published by companies that were previously internal to the company, is considered by many authors to be a form of open data, although it is often subject to a number of restrictions and is therefore not open data according to a strict interpretation [13]. This work considers open data to be content that is freely accessible, in a machine-readable format, freely usable without licensing restrictions, and free of charge.

2.2 *Value Creation with Open Data*

The literature proposes various concepts to comprehend how value can be created from data or its use. One of the most prominent is the data value chain, which explains how raw data is transformed into actionable information. Open Data Watch [20] has proposed a data value chain with a focus on open data, which is described as follows. The data value chain shows the process that data goes through, from identification of data needs to the impact of data use, as shown in Fig. 1. There are four main stages in the data value chain: collection, publication, uptake, and impact, which are further broken down into sub-stages. First, in the *collection* phase, it is determined what data will be collected and how it will be used before the data is collected, for example, through surveys or by retrieving or using sensors. The data is then processed to ensure its correctness and stored in formats that allow further use. In the *publication* phase, the data must be published in a way that the intended users can access it. This includes analyzing the data to extract useful information and visualize it, releasing the data and associated metadata to make it accessible online and offline, and disseminating it to potential users through appropriate channels such as information intermediaries.

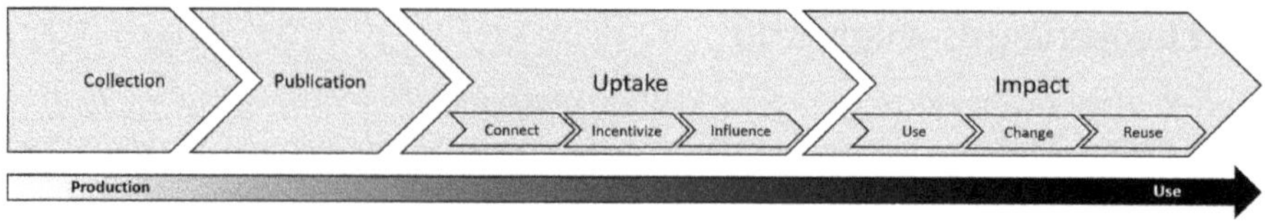

Fig. 1 Data value chain, adapted from Open Data Watch [20]

The *uptake* phase comprises the substages connect, incentivize, and influence. In this phase, connections are established with end users, and the data can be reprocessed to gain new insights. Users are encouraged to utilize the data in their decision-making process and are influenced to value the data. In the final phase (*impact*), the data is used to understand problems or make decisions, change outcomes or improve situations, and finally, the data can be reused by combining it with other data. [20]. The focus of the taxonomy developed within this paper is mainly on the impact phase.

3 Research Method: Taxonomy Development

The objective of this work is to develop a taxonomy that describes different perspectives on the commercial (re)use of open data, due to the absence of suitable frameworks for its commercial use. Taxonomies comprising pertinent dimensions and corresponding attributes can assist researchers in organizing knowledge [21] and can be employed for ex post theory building [22]. For a rigorous classification of commercial open data use scenarios, we chose the approach proposed by Nickerson et al. [16] due to its widespread acceptance as a de facto standard in IS research [21]. Following Nickerson et al. [16], we first specified the meta-characteristics and the ending conditions for the taxonomy development process. As ending conditions, we applied the objective and subjective ending conditions proposed by Nickerson et al. [16]. Next, we developed the Taxonomy with four iterations. During the iterative development process of the taxonomy, new dimensions were added when they were deemed suitable for distinguishing different commercial open data use scenarios. These dimensions were integrated into the taxonomy when they did not overlap with existing dimensions. Dimensions were excluded if they were not suitable for categorizing commercial open data use scenarios because they were too generic or could not cover the entire spectrum of use scenarios. The taxonomy development process is illustrated by Fig. 2. The four employed iterations are described in the following.

First Iteration (Research Literature): In the initial iteration, we employed a conceptual-to-empirical approach, conducting a systematic literature review following the guidelines of Webster and Watson [23]. This approach enabled us to synthesize relevant information on the commercial use of open data in the literature and extract key concepts for the taxonomy. In accordance with the recommendations

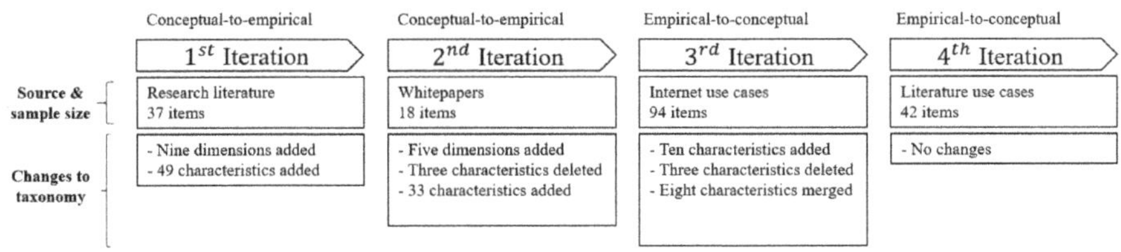

Fig. 2 Summary of the taxonomy development process

set forth by Webster and Watson [23], a four-step process was employed, commencing with an initial search in the 51 key information systems journals on Scopus via litbaskets.io. This was followed by an expanded search on popular databases, including AIS eLibrary, ScienceDirect, and EBSCO. A backward search and a forward search were then conducted. For the database searches, the query "Open Data AND Use OR Re-use OR Reuse" was used. Following the literature extraction, the abstracts and full texts of the identified studies were carefully read to identify patterns of commercial use of open data. The review sample was limited to articles written in English or German and clearly related to the use or consumption of open data by private organizations. Publications that focused on open data disclosure, open data policy, and the use of open data by governments, nonprofits, and citizens were also excluded. After excluding ineligible articles, the final sample contained 37 items. For the literature synthesis, the identified articles were scanned for concepts related to commercial open data reuse. After this scanning, nine concepts relevant to the taxonomy were identified.

Second Iteration (Whitepapers): In the second iteration of the taxonomy development process, grey literature, especially whitepapers from companies and public organizations, were extracted and analyzed. The literature was identified through online and forward–backward searches based on the research literature already identified in the first iteration. The selection and analysis were performed similarly to that of the research literature in the first iteration. The executive summaries and full texts of identified publications were carefully examined and inappropriate papers were removed. From an initial 25 publications identified, seven were removed due to exclusion criteria, resulting in a final sample size of 18 whitepapers. The identified publications were scanned for relevant concepts related to the commercial reuse of open data. Additional six concepts relevant to the taxonomy were identified in this phase.

Third Iteration (Internet Use Cases): For the third iteration, we chose an empirical-to-conceptual approach by examining use cases. Several online sources were identified that contain open data use cases related to the commercial use of open data. For use case identification and extraction, the sources used include European Data Portal, Open Data 500 Project, Open Data Impact Map, Open data means business by ODI.

The open data use cases were limited to scenarios from private, profit-seeking organizations with an active online presence. In addition, there had to be a clear indication of open data use and an accurate description of how open data was being used. The information from the mentioned sources and the respective companies' websites were analyzed and compiled into an Excel sheet. In total, 94 cases from online sources were included in the sample. All cases extracted were grouped according to the existing dimensions of the taxonomy. During this phase of grouping and categorizing cases, there arises a need for new characteristics, while some of the existing ones are proving inadequate.

Fourth Iteration (Literature Use Cases): In the fourth iteration, we shifted the focus to validating our taxonomy using an empirical-to-conceptual approach and applying the taxonomy to a number of use cases extracted from literature sources. As in the previous iteration, the use cases were limited to scenarios from private, profit-oriented companies, with a clear description of the actual usage of open data. Various whitepapers and research papers were used to extract a total of 42 open data use cases. The extracted cases were categorized based on the existing dimensions of the taxonomy. During this phase, there was no need for adaptation or change of the existing dimensions and characteristics of the taxonomy. Therefore, the taxonomy development process concludes with this iteration, as no changes were made and both the subjective and objective ending conditions were met.

Identification of Archetypes: To obtain appropriate archetypes for commercial users of open data, we applied our developed taxonomy to all previously identified open data use cases. We categorized a total of 136 use cases based on the dimensions and related characteristics of our taxonomy. This categorization allowed us to compare the frequencies of each dimension's characteristics with those of every other dimension in the taxonomy to identify common relationships. Through a meticulous comparison of the frequencies of characteristics, we identified several characteristic patterns that resulted in the creation of five distinct archetypes.

4 Results

4.1 Taxonomy for Commercial Open Data Use

This section presents the taxonomy with its 14 dimensions and related characteristics, as depicted in Fig. 3.

Role of Data in Value Proposition: Based on Ferro and Osella [24, 25], the concept of open data in the value proposition is an important categorization for distinguishing between different types of open data use in the enterprise context. It describes the extent to which open data is a component of marketable products or services. In our taxonomy, we distinguish between the characteristics "final good itself", "key ingredient of product/service", "marginal ingredient of product/service" and "no

Dimension									
Role of data in value proposition	Final good itself	Key ingredient of product/service	Marginal ingredient of product/service	No ingredient of product/service					
Process of data use	Data-to-fact	Data-to-data	Data-to-information	Data-to-interface	Data-to-service				
Purpose of data use	Improving internal processes							Product/service development	
	Data management								
	Enrichment	Validation	Cleansing	Intelligence & analytics	Benchmarking	Supply chain management	Risk management	Enhancement of existing products/services	Creation of new products/services
Data source	Government								
	International institutions	National government	Regional government	Municipal government	Corporates	Academic institutions			
Type of data	Geodata	Environmental data	Economic & business data	Traffic & transport data	Agricultural data	Legal data	Demographic data	Science data	
Role of enterprise in value chain		Intermediary							
	Enabler	Aggregator	Developer	Enricher	Service provider				
Role of data in enterprise	Bread and butter for the organization	Bread and butter for a product/service	Addition to existing product/service	Addition for organization					
Type of data elaboration	Aggregation & mash-up	Structuring & classification	Geo-referencing	Validation	Analytics				
Products & services		Services		Digital products					
	Tangible products	Consulting services	Other services	Aggregated information	Open Data repositories	Service platforms	Search- and comparison platforms		
Price mechanism	Premium	Freemium	Free						
Customer segment	Business-to-business (B2B)	Business-to-consumer (B2C)	Business-to-government (B2G)						
Stage of enterprise	Entrepreneurial	Established							
Sector of enterprise	Agriculture	Extractives	Transport	Infrastructure	Consumer products	Finance & insurance	IT & technology	Business services	Health & pharmaceuticals
Business impact	Innovation								
	New products/services	Enhanced products/services	Harmonized data	Improved processes	Improved decision making	Reduced costs			

Fig. 3 Taxonomy for commercial open data use

ingredient of product/service". This categorization can be interpreted as a continuum ranging from maximal to minimal contribution of open data to the enterprise offering. For instance, in the case of the online portal *TrendEconomy*, which provides aggregated open macroeconomic data with visualizations, open data can be considered as "final good itself". If companies use open data solely for internal purposes, such as insurance companies incorporating open data to enhance their risk models, the open data is considered as "no ingredient of product/service".

Process of Data Use: In the realm of open data exploitation processes, various types can be differentiated. Davies [26] initially introduced a distinction between data-to-fact, data-to-data, data-to-information, data-to-interface, and data-to-service. Data-to-fact refers to the extraction of factual information from data for further use, such as in bureaucratic processes [26]. Possible applications of the data-to-fact approach include advocacy and consultancy [27]. Data-to-data involves manipulating data to create new datasets that are more suitable for use by other users [26, 27]. This process is useful for refining and structuring data. Data-to-information covers creating visualizations, infographics, and reports to represent and interpret data [26]. Data-to-interface refers to creating interactive access to data through interfaces, resulting in data platforms and open data portals [26, 27]. Open data portals are repositories for open data, while data platforms are more interactive and allow users to combine open data with other types of data for deeper analysis [27]. When data is used as input for services, it is referred to as data-to-service [28]. This can involve integrating data into existing services or products, or using data to create new services [26].

Purpose of Data Use: The purpose of the data use dimension is to describe the specific purpose for which open data is being utilized. We distinguish between improving internal processes, which includes data management, intelligence and analytics, benchmarking, supply chain management, risk management, and product/service development, which involves enhancing existing products/services and creating new ones. According to Krasikov et al. [15], data management can be distinguished into three usage categories: enrichment, validation, and cleansing.

Data Source: The data source dimension describes the origin of the open data according to the type of data provider. In our taxonomy, we differentiate between open data provided by governments and non-governmental actors such as corporations and academic institutions. In terms of Open Governmental Data, providers can be categorized into international institutions, such as the European Union, and national, regional, and municipal governments.

Type of Data: The type of data dimension distinguishes between different types of open data. The eight most common types of open data with the highest potential for commercial use have been included: geospatial data, environmental data, economic and business data, traffic and transportation data, agricultural data, legal data, demographic data, and scientific data. As indicated by Carrara et al. [29], the most valuable types of information for commercial reuse of open data are geographical, environmental, and economic and business information. Geospatial data encompasses a range of resources, including cadastral and topographic maps, aerial photos, administrative boundaries, and hydrographical maps. Open geospatial data is a commonly utilized resource by insurance companies, as evidenced by the British company *Aviva*'s incorporation of geospatial data into its modeling of floods and other property-related issues, which subsequently informs its pricing models [30]. Economic and business data includes price data, economic trends, trade data, growth projections, industry profiles, market shares, and other pertinent information. This data can be utilized by companies across a diverse array of domains.

Role of Enterprise in Value Chain: This dimension describes where the organization is positioned in the data value chain. Our taxonomy includes five roles: enabler, aggregator, developer, enricher, and service provider. According to Jaakkola et al. [31], aggregators, developers, and enrichers can be grouped as open data intermediaries. Enablers facilitate the supply or use of open data, including storage and hosting, retrieval, categorization, and advisory services [25, 31]. Aggregators collect and combine multiple open data sources and process them to produce insights that are useful to their users [2, 31]. Developers design and build applications around open data [2, 31–33]. Enrichers utilize open data to enable or enhance existing products/services or improve internal processes [2, 31].

Role of Data in the Enterprise: This dimension emphasizes the importance of open data to the organization, as described by Ferro and Osella [24, 25] and Kaasenbrood et al. [28]. If open data is crucial to the organization's operations to the extent that it could not exist without it, it is referred to as the "bread and butter for the organization". Open data can be a crucial component in certain products or services, which is commonly referred to as the "bread and butter for a product or service". Furthermore, open data can be an addition to preexisting products/services or to the organization to strengthen internal capabilities and processes.

Type of Data Elaboration: The type of data elaboration is the process or method used to manipulate or analyze the data. Based on Ferro and Osella [24, 25], the most important techniques in context of commercial open data reuse, such as data aggregation and mash-up, structuring and classification, geo-referencing, validation, and analysis, have been included in our taxonomy.

Products and Services: The product and service dimension encompasses the offerings marketed by the organization. Our taxonomy distinguishes between tangible products, services, and digital products. In terms of services, we differentiate between consulting services and other services. Digital products include aggregated information, open data repositories, service platforms, and search and comparison platforms.

Price Mechanism: The price mechanism describes how monetary profit is generated by offering products and services. Our taxonomy includes the three price mechanisms proposed by Ferro and Osella [25]: premium, freemium, and free.

Customer Segment: The Customer segment refers to the group of individuals or organizations that the company intends to target with its products or services. Our taxonomy includes the business-to-business (B2B), business-to-consumer (B2C), and business-to-government (B2G) segments.

Stage of Enterprise: We added a dimension to our taxonomy, named "stage of enterprise", to assess the enterprise's maturity level. We differentiated between entrepreneurial and established enterprises.

Sector of Enterprise: The sector of the enterprise describes the industry in which the enterprise operates. Our taxonomy includes the nine most important sectors for commercial open data reuse: agriculture, extractives, transport, infrastructure, consumer products, finance and insurance, IT and technology, business services, and health and pharmaceuticals. In our sample of commercial open data use cases, business services, IT and technology, and finance and insurance were the most prevalent sectors of companies using open data.

Business Impact: The dimension of business impact describes the immediate effect of utilizing open data on an organization's business. In our taxonomy, we included innovation (including new or enhanced products/services), harmonized data, improved processes, improved decision-making, and reduced costs. As indicated by Berends et al. [34], the most significant benefit of utilizing open data for businesses is innovation, specifically the introduction of new products and services. This is followed by reduced costs and data harmonization.

4.2 Commercial Open Data User Archetypes

Using our proposed taxonomy, we have identified five common archetypes of commercial open data users. These archetypes are based on open data use cases and represent the most frequent combinations of characteristics from the introduced taxonomy. Although most of them relate to one of the identified roles within the value chain, it is the combination of characteristics that distinguishes the archetypes from the identified roles of the enterprise in the value chain.

Established Enrichers: The established Enricher archetype is a frequently encountered user of open data that enhances its current business model by integrating open datasets to enhance internal processes such as data management. Most established enrichers are large, mature companies in data-intensive industries such as finance and insurance or real estate. Insurance companies, in particular, utilize open data for risk management and improving their predictive models. For example, the lending company *OnDeck* uses open financial data to evaluate the financial health of businesses [13]. Big retailers often use open data to improve store operations, such as identifying optimal store locations and optimizing store assortments using demographic, weather, and consumer data. For example, supermarket *Tesco* used open weather data and sales records to create accurate demand models, reducing overstocking and spoilage [8]. The primary distinction between the established enricher and other archetypes is that the established enrichers exclusively utilize open data to enhance internal issues rather than to improve products or services or create new ones. The offering of this open data archetype includes tangible products or services like insurances, financial services, or distribution electricity. The business impact of open data use is reliant on the intended purpose of its utilization. If open data is utilized for Data Management, it is probable that the outcome will be harmonized data, resulting in a positive business impact. This archetype could potentially achieve harmonized data, improved processes, enhanced decision making, and cost reduction through open data usage.

Search and Comparison Platforms: This archetype utilizes open data to provide a portal or platform for consumers and businesses to find the optimal product, home, contractor, business partner or other based on their needs and preferences. There are various platforms available in different sectors such as finance and insurance and transportation. Some real estate search and comparison platforms, such as *Zillow*, provide property searches for home buyers and sellers or real estate agents, using open demographic data, price indexes, transaction data, etc. [35]. In the transportation sector, some apps and platforms help their customers find the optimal routes and connections using open data on routes and schedules. For these platforms, open data plays an important role, sometimes the platforms rely only on publicly available data. This archetype applies the data to interface and data to information approaches, as data is provided and made available to customers through an interface and may be transformed into valuable and usable information for the customer. The providers of search and comparison platforms can be considered as aggregators or developers, as they aggregate and combine different datasets into their platform and develop the actual platform itself with its inherent search and compare engines and algorithms. The data elaboration methods used by search and comparison platforms are aggregation and mash-up, structuring and classification and analytics. These platforms are mostly provided with a free or freemium price mechanism. The enterprises offering such platforms can be considered for the most parts as small, young entrepreneurial companies.

Aggregation Platforms: This archetype provides aggregated information on specific topics, such as financial reports from companies, patent data, and lawsuit data. Enterprises operating aggregation platforms create value by aggregating datasets from different sources, process them into homogenous, aggregated datasets and provide its customers access to those aggregated datasets via their platform. One example is *OpenCorporates*, which aggregates publicly available corporate data from a variety of sources into corporate and financial data in a standardized format [3]. For this archetype, open data can be considered as a final good itself, processed and marketed on an online platform. Thus, the purpose of utilizing open data is to process it into a new product. The approach of data to interface and data to data is mostly used by aggregation platform providers. Businesses that provide aggregation platforms are considered aggregators in the data value chain. The data elaboration techniques utilized are aggregation and mash-up and structuring and classification to make the datasets easier to understand and discover by the users of the platform. Aggregated information can be considered as the offering of enterprises following this archetype.

Enablers: Enablers provide software and tools for open data analysis, construct open data portals and repositories, and offer assistance with open data publication and distribution. They primarily aid in the construction of repositories and provide guidance to government agencies or companies seeking to open up datasets. The enabler archetype provides products and services, such as open data repositories and consulting services on open data disclosure. These offerings exclude the provision of open data itself. Unlike other archetypes, enablers do not use open data directly for their products. Instead, they work with open data to develop their offerings. Enablers do not elaborate open data for their own use, but provide data elaboration tools to their customers, such as data aggregation or analysis tools. Open data can be considered crucial for this archetype's organization due to its reliance on open data for their business model, even though they do not actually utilize open data in their offerings. An example of the enabler archetype is the U.S. company *3 Round Stones*, which makes a web data publishing platform used by U.S. government agencies to publish and consume data [35].

Business Service Providers: Business service providers utilize open data in their products and services, which they offer to other businesses. They typically aggregate and analyze economic and business data or demographic data to provide useful insights to their customers. The business service provider archetype utilizes the data to service or data to information approach, converting open data into valuable information and insights for their clients. Therefore, open data is used for product/service development purposes, either for the enhancement of the existing offering or for the sake of new business services. The methods used to process this data include aggregation and mash-up, analytics, and in some cases, geo-referencing or structuring and classification. The offering of the business service provider may include service platforms, consulting services, or other services. The relevant sectors in which this archetype operates are predominantly business services, with some overlap in finance, insurance, or IT and technology. *SLR Consulting* is an example of a business service provider that collects open data for research purposes and uses the insights derived from the open data in its advisory and environmental consulting services [36].

5 Discussion and Conclusion

This study aims to identify the characteristics and determinants of open data usage for value creation in a private business setting. Therefore, we identified specific dimensions with respective characteristics across commercial open data use scenarios. For this purpose, we reviewed prior literature and analyzed a broad range of open data use cases from various sources. A taxonomy for creating value with open data in a business context was developed following the guidelines of Nickerson et al. [16], and archetypes for commercial open data users were derived.

The study makes several important contributions to the open data literature. Firstly, the study clarifies and describes the concept of value creation through open data by private for-profit organizations by deriving a taxonomy consisting of 14 key dimensions. We addressed the need for further research in this area, as suggested by Magalhaes and Roseira [27]. Our taxonomy expands on previous research in this area and offers a more comprehensive view of the commercial use of open data. It highlights a wide range of dimensions in which enterprises use open data to create value. Compared to previous studies on the commercial use of open data, our taxonomy offers a more detailed and comprehensive understanding of the elements and relationships that characterize open data value creation in enterprises. Additionally, our taxonomy helps to create a broader understanding of value creation in the business context based on open data, which goes beyond the widespread focus on intermediaries and infomediaries. This includes scenarios with marginal open data utilization. In addition, our taxonomy includes general indicators and determinants that are not specific to open data. Including indicators such as the sector, customer seg-ment, and enterprise stage is crucial for understanding the specific business environment and covering the complex topic of commercial open data utilization in a holistic way. The taxonomy offers a comprehensive and detailed insight into how organizations are incorporating open data into their operations and value chains covering a wide range of industries, business processes, and data sources.

Furthermore, the taxonomy is designed to categorize successful commercial use scenarios of open data, including the roles of open data reusers, sectors, and data types with high commercial potential for open data exploitation. Our taxonomy and the derived archetypes can be regarded as valuable solution space for practitioners and businesses developing open data use cases within their organizations and provide a new perspective on possible business models involving open data. Practitioners and managers can use our taxonomy and archetypes to discover the range of open data use scenarios and identify opportunities for open data exploitation.

The results and implications of our study should be interpreted with several limitations in mind. Firstly, open data use cases can vary in scale and focus, and it is possible for multiple open data use cases to exist in parallel within an organization. Secondly, the development of a taxonomy cannot be entirely objective since it involves interpretation and data classification based on the researcher's comprehension of conceptual frameworks. There may be other possible classifications, as there is no definitive or completely objective approach to this subject matter. Additionally, it is important to note that the development of taxonomies may not always include the full range of concepts or categories within a given field. This is due to limiting factors such as the need for clarity and usability, which can constrain the size of classifications. The application of the taxonomy depends on the specific situation, as not every dimension of the taxonomy is relevant in every case. As Nickerson et al. [16] point out, a taxonomy does not need to be perfect, but it does need to be useful and meet the needs of its users.

Further research is needed due to the complexity of commercial reuse of open data and the still insufficient understanding of the business opportunities that open data offers. Detailed case studies are necessary to better understand the motivations, challenges, and success factors related to the use of commercial open data at the company level. Furthermore, additional research is necessary to quantify the economic impact of using open data on an enterprise-level. This will assist companies in accurately assessing the business potential of open data.

In conclusion, the developed taxonomy and proposed archetypes contribute to the existing open data literature by enhancing the understanding of open data use for commercial purposes and providing a conceptual basis for further research in this area. We hope that our study will stimulate additional work on the promising topic of commercial use of open data in a variety of contexts.

References

1. Hossain, M. A., et al. (2016). State-of-the-art in open data research: Insights from existing literature and a research agenda. *Journal of Organizational Computing and Electronic Commerce., 26*(1–2), 14–40. https://doi.org/10.1080/10919392.2015.1124007
2. Janssen, M., & Zuiderwijk, A. (2014). Infomediary business models for connecting open data providers and users. *Social Science Computer Review., 32*(5), 694–711. https://doi.org/10.1177/0894439314525902
3. Davies, T. et al. (2019). *The state of open data: Histories and horizons*. African Minds and IDRC. https://doi.org/10.47622/9781928331957
4. Braunschweig, K. et al. (2012). The state of open data limits of current open data platforms.
5. Rößler, J. (2022). Sharing is caring: Using open data to improve targeting policies.

6. Ahmadi Zeleti, F., & Kerins, R. (2023). Open data impact taxonomy–Analysis of open data use cases in response to the Ireland's national open data strategy 2017–2022. In *Future of Information and Communication Conference* (pp. 340–357). Springer.
7. The Economist: A new goldmine. (2013). https://www.economist.com/business/2013/05/18/a-new-goldmine
8. Manyika, J. et al. (2013). *Open data: Unlocking innovation and performance with liquid information.* McKinsey Global Institute.
9. Gruen, N. et al. (2014). Open for business: How open data can help achieve the G20 growth target.
10. Krasikov, P. et al. (2020). Is open data ready for use by enterprises? Learnings from corporate registers: In *Proceedings of the 9th International Conference on Data Science, Technology and Applications* (pp. 109–120). SCITEPRESS—Science and Technology Publications. https://doi.org/10.5220/0009875801090120
11. Zuiderwijk, A. et al. (2015). Open data for competitive advantage: Insights from open data use by companies. In *Proceedings of the 16th Annual International Conference on Digital Government Research* (pp. 79–88). ACM, Phoenix Arizona. https://doi.org/10.1145/2757401.2757411
12. Enders, T. et al. (2021). Untangling the open data value paradox: How organizations benefit from revealing data. In F. Ahlemann et al. (Eds.), *Innovation through information systems* (pp. 200–205). Springer International Publishing, Cham. https://doi.org/10.1007/978-3-030-86800-0_15
13. Verhulst, S., & Caplan, R. (2015). Open data: A twenty-first-century asset for small and medium-sized enterprises. *SSRN Journal.* https://doi.org/10.2139/ssrn.3141515
14. Krasikov, P. et al. (2021). Open data in the enterprise context: Assessing open corporate data's readiness for use. In S. Hammoudi, et al. (Eds.), *Data management technologies and applications* (pp. 80–100). Springer International Publishing, Cham. https://doi.org/10.1007/978-3-030-83014-4_4
15. Krasikov, P. et al. (2019). *Open data use cases—Framework for the generation and documentation of open data use cases.*
16. Nickerson, R. C., et al. (2013). A method for taxonomy development and its application in information systems. *European Journal of Information Systems., 22*(3), 336–359. https://doi.org/10.1057/ejis.2012.26
17. Lindman, J. et al. (2013). Open data services: Research agenda. In *2013 46th Hawaii International Conference on System Sciences* (pp. 1239–1246). IEEE. https://doi.org/10.1109/HICSS.2013.430
18. Berends, J., et al. (2017). *Analytical report 9: The economic benefits of open data.* Publications Office of the European Union.
19. Marmier, A., & Mettler, T. (2020). Different shades of perception: How do public managers comprehend the re-use potential of open government data?.
20. The Data Value Chain: Moving from Production to Impact, https://opendatawatch.com/publications/the-data-value-chain-moving-from-production-to-impact, last accessed 2023/11/19.
21. Kundisch, D., et al. (2022). An update for taxonomy designers: Methodological guidance from information systems research. *Business & Information Systems Engineering, 64*(4), 421–439. https://doi.org/10.1007/s12599-021-00723-x
22. Bapna et al. (2004). User heterogeneity and its impact on electronic auction market design: An empirical exploration. *MIS Quarterly, 28*(1), 21. https://doi.org/10.2307/25148623
23. Webster, J., & Watson, R. T. (2002). Analyzing the Past to Prepare for the Future: Writing a Literature Review.
24. Ferro, E., Osella, M. (2012). Business models for PSI re-use: A multidimensional framework. In *Using open data: Policy modeling, citizen empowerment, data Journalism workshop.* European Comission.
25. Ferro, E., Osella, M. (2013). Eight business model archetypes for PSI re-use. Presented at the April.

26. Davies, T. (2010). Open data, democracy and public sector reform. *A look at open government data use from data. gov. uk*, 1–47.
27. Magalhaes, G., & Roseira, C. (2020). Open government data and the private sector: An empirical view on business models and value creation. *Government Information Quarterly, 37*(3), 101248. https://doi.org/10.1016/j.giq.2017.08.004
28. Kaasenbrood, M. et al. (2015). Exploring the factors influencing the adoption of open government data by private organisations. *International Journal of Public Administration in the Digital Age, 2*(2), 75–92. https://doi.org/10.4018/ijpada.2015040105
29. Carrara, W. et al. (2015). *Creating value through open data—Study on the impact of re-use of public data resources.* Publications Office. https://doi.org/10.2759/328101
30. Ordnance Survey, https://www.ordnancesurvey.co.uk/customers/case-studies/aviva-geographic-intelligence-underwriting, last accessed 2023/12/15.
31. Jaakkola, H. et al. (2014). Open data: Opportunities and challenges. In *Proceedings of the 15th International Conference on Computer Systems and Technologies* (pp. 25–39). ACM, Ruse Bulgaria. https://doi.org/10.1145/2659532.2659594
32. Hjalmarsson, A. et al. (2015). Mind the gap: Exploring stakeholders' value with open data assessment. In *2015 48th Hawaii International Conference on System Sciences* (pp. 1314–1323). IEEE. https://doi.org/10.1109/HICSS.2015.160
33. Immonen, A., et al. (2014). Requirements of an open data based business ecosystem. *IEEE Access., 2*, 88–103. https://doi.org/10.1109/ACCESS.2014.2302872
34. Berends, J. et al. (2020). *Reusing open data—A study on companies transforming open data into economic and societal value.* https://doi.org/10.2830/876679
35. Open Data Impact Map, https://opendataimpactmap.org/map#DataView, last accessed 2023/12/14.
36. SLR Consulting | data.europa.eu, https://data.europa.eu/en/publications/use-cases/slr-consulting, last accessed 2023/12/15.

Urban Gamification: Designing Municipal Websites for Enhanced Citizen Trust

Bastian Kordyaka, Sebastian Weber, Luca Bauer, Robin Fritzsche, Gerhard Klassen, Raphael Palombo, Dulce Villegas, Marc Wyszynski, and Bjoern Niehaves

Abstract This short paper addresses the complex relationship dynamics between a municipal website's gamified IS artifact design and the desired goal states of municipal trust. To better understand this relationship, a mixed-methods study is proposed that identifies relevant gamification features in a three-step process in Study 1 and then explores the relationship between gamification and municipal trust using a survey in Study 2. The study results promise added value for (a) user-centered technology design and (b) novel feedback mechanisms to strengthen municipal trust. Additionally, we will contribute to existing gamification literature by identifying relevant gamification features in relation to the design of municipal websites.

B. Kordyaka (✉) · S. Weber · L. Bauer · R. Fritzsche · G. Klassen · R. Palombo · D. Villegas · M. Wyszynski · B. Niehaves
Faculty 3, Digital Public, University of Bremen, Bremen, Germany
e-mail: kordyaka@uni-bremen.de

S. Weber
e-mail: sebweber@uni-bremen.de

L. Bauer
e-mail: bauerl@uni-bremen.de

R. Fritzsche
e-mail: robfri@uni-bremen.de

G. Klassen
e-mail: gerhard.klassen@uni-bremen.de

R. Palombo
e-mail: palombo@uni-bremen.de

D. Villegas
e-mail: villegas@uni-bremen.de

M. Wyszynski
e-mail: m.wyszynski@uni-bremen.de

B. Niehaves
e-mail: niehaves@uni-bremen.de

C. M. Flath et al. (eds.), *Shaping the Digital Future Through Innovation and Practice*, Lecture Notes in Information Systems and Organisation 85,
https://doi.org/10.1007/978-3-032-08489-7_7

1 Introduction

Citizens' trust in the municipalities is vital to ensure a variety of relevant target states in the public sector. Previous research has already shown that citizens' trust enables a municipality to (a) adequately involve citizens in decision-making processes [1, 2], (b) collect relevant information about and from citizens in the form of data to enable a comprehensive understanding of situations [3, 4], and (c) strengthen the sense of community between citizens and the municipality [5, 6]. Accordingly, it can be seen as one of a municipality's central requirements to gain the trust of its citizens. This requirement has various implications. From the Information Systems (IS) perspective, the adequate design of the digital contact situations between citizens and the municipality appears to be of central importance. In line with this idea, the design of the municipal website plays a central role in potentially influencing trust in the interest of the offering municipality, as it is one of the few contact situations that most citizens have to visit sooner or later [7–9]. Surprisingly, existing websites of most municipalities only sporadically use validated tools for designing websites to promote desired target states, such as motivation and engagement. This gap becomes apparent when we consider that insights from validated design concepts, such as serious gaming (e.g., games that are designed with a primary purpose beyond pure entertainment) or gamification (i.e. the application of game design elements and principles in non-game contexts), have not yet been integrated holistically into the municipal context of website design [10–14]. This presents a significant opportunity for research and practical application to enhance citizen interaction and trust through more thoughtfully designed digital interfaces increasing the user experience.

In this short paper, we propose an empirical-based answer to the research gap on which gamification features (e.g., points, badges, personalization) are relevant in designing a municipal website to increase trust in the municipality. To address this research gap, we propose a mixed-methods study consisting of two parts building on theoretical approaches of the sociological theory of trust [15], and the gamification approach [12, 16–18]. In the first part (Study 1), we propose identifying relevant gamification features in the context of municipalities using a three-step selection process based on existing IS literature and player opinions. Subsequently, in the second part, we specify a survey (Study 2) to establish the relationships between the identified list of relevant gamification features and municipal trust. To summarize, our study is guided by the research question:

Research Question: *What is the relationship between gamification and municipal trust regarding website design?*

Implementing our short study promises several added values for existing IS research concerning digital government. First, the results will support (a) user-centered technology design and (b) novel feedback mechanisms to enhance the municipal trust of citizens. Second, we will contribute to existing gamification literature by elucidating the relevant gamification features in the context of municipalities.

The rest of this short study is organized as follows to provide a comprehensible structure. First, we present the literary background and hypotheses (Sect. 2), introducing municipal trust (Sect. 2.1), and gamification (Sect. 2.2). We then present the methodology of the paper (Sect. 3), which introduces the empirical mixed-methods approach (Sect. 3.1), the planned data collection (Sect. 3.2), and the measurements we will use (Sect. 3.3). We conclude with an outlook (Sect. 4).

2 Related Work

2.1 Municipal Trust

The construct of trust has a long multidisciplinary history and is defined as an individual's willingness to depend on another party because of the characteristics of the other party [19]. These perceived characteristics of the other party or so-called trusting beliefs can vary based on the type of the opposite party (e.g., technology or people) [20, 21]. In IS research these two perspectives are evident. Trust in technology is shaped by beliefs about the functionality, reliability, and helpfulness. From a trust in technology perspective, research showed how trust can shape IT-related beliefs and behaviors like perceived usefulness and enjoyment [21], purchase behavior [22–26], or user satisfaction and well-being [27–30]. On the other hand, trust in other people is formed based on beliefs about their competence, benevolence, and integrity [20]. From a trust in people perspective, research highlighted that technology can foster trust in the other party by alternating trusting beliefs through, e.g., perceived website quality [31] or information and system quality [32]. In the specific context of this study, we are interested in municipal trust (e.g., citizens' trust in their own municipality), which also reflects the people's perspective, however, with a focus on a governmental institution. For this purpose, we refer to an established sociological theory of trust [15], consisting of the three trusting beliefs (a) competence (e.g., the extent to which citizens perceive their digital government as capable, effective, skillful or professional in decision-making), (b) benevolence (e.g., the extent to which citizens believe that their digital government genuinely cares about citizens' interests), and (c) honesty (e.g., the extent to which citizens believe that their digital government genuinely cares about citizens' interests) because it captures both citizens' perceptions of government effectiveness, intentions, and integrity, which are critical factors for trust in local government [33].

2.2 Playful Contact Design—Gamification

The playful design of technology, also known as the concepts of serious gaming and gamification has a history in the context of IS research that goes back more than a decade [12, 33–36]. Previous research has already occasionally explored the influence of the gamification concept in the public sector in relation to topics such as (a) parking management [37, 38], (b) public health initiatives [39, 40], and (c) waste management [41, 42]. For our study, we argue that municipal IT artifacts (such as websites) can be viewed as contact situations between citizens and their municipalities. Accordingly, an appealing design is crucial for the activation of motivation and the resulting engagement of citizens. Surprisingly, the websites of most municipalities today only sporadically use available design tools to promote desired target states (such as the participation and the engagement of citizens). This is where gamification comes into play, whereby we argue that the gamified design of a municipal website has an influence on municipal trust. Specifically, we proposed three hypotheses based on empirical insights already gained in other contexts. First, we argue that gamified design can have a positive impact on the trust dimension of competence because it signals a forward-looking and innovative approach, suggesting that the community is competent in its communication and behavior [43, 44]. Secondly, we postulate a positive effect on the trust dimension of benevolence and justify this with the municipality's commitment to creating pleasant and engaging experiences for citizens [45] Thirdly, we assume a reinforcing effect on the trust dimension of honesty, as information is presented transparently through playful elements, thus promoting the perception of openness and integrity [46]. The following are our three hypotheses:

Hypothesis 1: *Gamification is positively connected with municipal competence.*

Hypothesis 2: *Gamification is positively connected with municipal benevolence.*

Hypothesis 3: *Gamification is positively connected with municipal honesty.*

3 Methodology

3.1 Mixed-Methods Research Design

To better understand the relationship between gamification,, and municipal trust, we will use a sequential quantitative design with two consecutive studies [47–51]. Figure 1 illustrates our procedure. Before the start of Study 1, we will conduct a pre-test to identify potential issues with the wording of items and other difficulties in understanding.

Study 1

To identify relevant gamification features in the context of our study (i.e., the design of a municipal website), we will proceed in three subsequent and data-driven steps. First, we will identify a rich list of gamification features by searching previous work. Second, we will conduct a focus group to determine what gamification features are potentially available while designing a municipal website. Third, we will survey

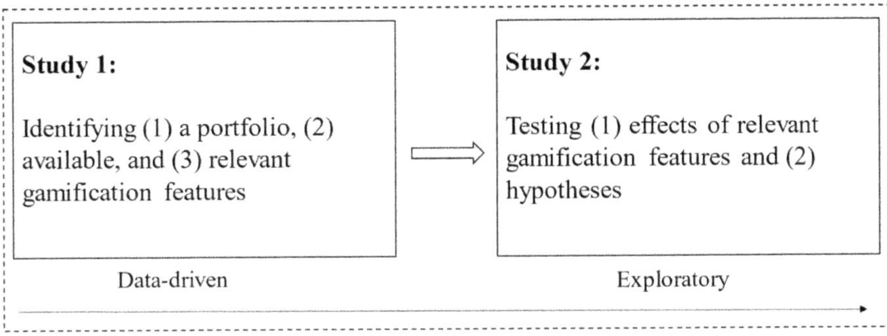

Fig. 1 Mixed-method procedure

potential users of a municipal website and ask them about the potential importance of each gamification feature to derive a shorter list of relevant features.

Study 2

Second, we will use a cross-sectional survey to exploratory test (a) the disjunctive influences of the identified list of relevant gamification features from Study 1 concerning municipal trust.

3.2 *Data Sampling*

Study 1

To identify a suitable study with a large number of gamification features (step 1), we will conduct a literature search (search string "gamification features" AND "list" OR "item" OR "measurement"). To recruit participants for our focus group (step 2), we will contact researchers from our department in other research groups (between 5 and 8 participants). In addition, for step 3 (survey), we will activate a three-digit number of potential users of a municipal website by approaching them through our own networks and research projects.

Study 2

To derive a representative sample of respondents, we will use existing gatekeeper contacts of the group of authors (such as people working in municipalities or citizens) and social media platforms (such as LinkedIn). As prerequisites, we will require participants to be of full age and have experience as municipality citizens. To make sure this prerequisite is fulfilled and ensure data quality, we will ask several knowledge (e.g., "Who is the current mayor of your municipality?") and attention check questions (e.g., "Please multiply two by three and pick the resulting number.") in the course of our survey and exclude participants who will fail one of them.

Table 1 Measurement items

Variable	Id	Example	Source
Gamification	GF	Relevant gamification features will be selected in study 1 out of an initial list of 46 features	[52]
Trust			[33]
Competence	TC_1	My municipality is capable	
	TC_2	My municipality is effective	
	TC_3	My municipality is skillful	
	TC_4	My municipality is professional and successful	
Benevolence	TB_1	If citizens need help, my municipality will do its best to help them	
	TB_2	If anyone is damaged by dealing with risk factors, it quickly becomes my municipalities case	
	TB_3	My municipality acts in the interest of citizens	
	TB_4	My municipality is genuinely interested in the Well-being of citizens, not only in its own	
Honesty	TH_1	My municipality keeps its commitments	
	TH_2	My municipality is honest	
	TH_3	My municipality is sincere	

4 Measurements

Study 1

With the aim of identifying relevant gamification features, in a first step, we already identified a study with a holistic list of 46 features [52].

Study 2

Following the best practices of psychometric research, we will derive a digital questionnaire using empirically validated scales to ask participants about their self-reported perceptions and behaviors. Table 1 illustrates the items that will be included.

5 Outlook

This short paper will examine how the gamification design of municipal websites can influence municipal trust. To this end, a mixed-methods study is proposed to identify key gamification features (Study 1) and investigate their impact on user perceptions (Study 2). We have already conducted the first step of our three-step process of Study 1 and are currently looking for participants for our focus group (second step).

References

1. Alarabiat, A., Soares, D., & Estevez, E. (2021). Determinants of citizens' intention to engage in government-led electronic participation initiatives through Facebook. *Government Information Quarterly, 38*, 101537.
2. Arshad, S., & Khurram, S. (2020). Can governments presence on social media stimulate citizens online political participation? Investigating the influence of transparency, trust, and responsiveness. *Government Information Quarterly, 37*, 101486.
3. Hein, A., Engert, M., Ryu, S., et al. (2023). Building open government data platform ecosystems: A dynamic development approach that engages users from the start. *Government Information Quarterly, 40*, 101878.
4. Mutimukwe, C., Kolkowska, E., & Grönlund, Å. (2020). Information privacy in e-service: Effect of organizational privacy assurances on individual privacy concerns, perceptions, trust and self-disclosure behavior. *Government Information Quarterly, 37*, 101413.
5. Ohmer, M. L. (2007). Citizen participation in neighborhood organizations and its relationship to volunteers self-and collective efficacy and sense of community. *Social Work Research, 31*, 109–120.
6. Macke, J., Sarate, J. A. R., & de Atayde, M. S. (2019). Smart sustainable cities evaluation and sense of community. *Journal of Cleaner Production, 239*, 118103.
7. Scott, J. K. (2005). Assessing the quality of municipal government web sites. *State and Local Government Review, 37*, 151–165.
8. Youngblood, N. E., & Mackiewicz, J. (2012). A usability analysis of municipal government website home pages in Alabama. *Government Information Quarterly, 29*, 582–588.
9. De Jong, M., & Lentz, L. (2006). Scenario evaluation of municipal web sites: Development and use of an expert-focused evaluation tool. *Government Information Quarterly, 23*, 191–206.
10. Karaosmanoglu, S., Cmentowski, S., Nacke, L. E., & Steinicke, F. (2024). Born to run, programmed to play: Mapping the extended reality exergames landscape. In *Proceedings of the CHI conference on human factors in computing systems* (pp. 1–28). Association for Computing Machinery.
11. Abt, C. C. (1987). *Serious games*. University press of America.
12. Deterding S, Dixon D, Khaled R, & Nacke, L. (2011). From game design elements to gamefulness: defining gamification. In: *Proceedings of the 15th international academic MindTrek conference: Envisioning future media environments*. pp 9–15.
13. Contreras-Espinosa, R. S., & Blanco, M. A. (2022). A literature review of E-government services with gamification elements. *International Journal of Public Administration, 45*, 964–980.
14. Weber S, Kordyaka B, & Niehaves B. (2024). *Leveraging Gamification to Facilitate Information-Sharing in the Service Industry*: An Empirical Study.
15. Sztompka, P. (1999). *Trust: A sociological theory*. Cambridge university press.
16. Weber S, Klassen G, Wyszynski M, & Kordyaka B. (2023). Illuminating the Predictive Power of Gamification to Inspire Technology Users. In *Workshopband*. GI, Rapperswil.
17. Jahn, K., Kordyaka, B., Machulska, A., et al. (2021). Individualized gamification elements: The impact of avatar and feedback design on reuse intention. *Computers in Human Behavior, 119*, 106702.
18. Kordyaka, B., Laato, S., Weber, S., et al. (2024). Exploring the association between engagement with location-based game features and getting inspired about environmental issues and nature. In *Proceedings of the CHI conference on human factors in computing systems* (pp. 1–15). ACM.
19. Rousseau, D. M., Sitkin, S. B., Burt, R. S., & Camerer, C. (1998). Not so different after all: A cross-discipline view of trust. *AMR, 23*, 393–404.
20. McKnight, D. H., Carter, M., Thatcher, J. B., & Clay, P. F. (2011). Trust in a specific technology: An investigation of its components and measures. *ACM Transactions on Management Information Systems, 2*, 1–25.

21. Lankton, N., McKnight, D., & Tripp, J. (2015). Technology, humanness, and trust: Rethinking Trust in Technology. *Journal of the Association for Information Systems, 16*.
22. Fang, Y., Qureshi, I., Sun, H., et al. (2014). Trust, satisfaction, and online repurchase intention: The moderating role of perceived effectiveness of E-commerce institutional mechanisms. *MIS Quarterly, 38*, 407–4A9.
23. Sia, C. L., Lim, K. H., Leung, K., Lee, M. K., Huang, W. W., & Benbasat, I. (2009). Web strategies to promote internet shopping: Is cultural-customization needed? *MIS Quarterly, 33*, 491–512.
24. Riedl, R., Hubert, M., & Kenning, P. (2010). Are there neural gender differences in online trust? An fMRI study on the perceived trustworthiness of eBay offers. *MIS Quarterly, 34*, 397–428.
25. Ba, S., & Pavlou, P. A. (2002). Evidence of the effect of trust building Technology in Electronic Markets: Price premiums and buyer behavior. *MIS Quarterly, 26*, 243–268.
26. Gefen, D., Karahanna, E., & Straub, D. W. (2003). Trust and TAM in online shopping: An integrated model. *MIS Quarterly, 27*, 51–90.
27. Söllner, M., Hoffmann, A., & Leimeister, J. M. (2016). Why different trust relationships matter for information systems users. *European Journal of Information Systems, 25*, 274–287.
28. Hoehle, H., Huff, S., & Goode, S. (2012). The role of continuous trust in information systems continuance. *Journal of Computer Information Systems, 52*, 1–9.
29. Benbasat, I., Gefen, D., & Pavlou, P. A. (2010). Introduction to the special issue on novel perspectives on trust in information systems. *MIS Quarterly, 34*, 367–371.
30. Öksüz A, Walter N, Distel B, Räckers, M., & Becker, J. (2016). *Trust in the information systems discipline. Trust and communication in a digitized world*: Models and concepts of trust research 205–223.
31. Mcknight, D. H., Kacmar, C. J., & Choudhury, V. (2004). Shifting factors and the ineffectiveness of third party assurance seals: A two-stage model of initial Trust in a web Business. *Electronic Markets, 14*, 252–266.
32. McKnight D. H, Lankton N. K, Nicolaou A, & Price J (2017). Distinguishing the effects of B2B information quality, system quality, and service outcome quality on trust and distrust. *The Journal of Strategic Information Systems 26*, 118–141. 33.
33. Baptista, G., & Oliveira, T. (2017). Why so serious? Gamification impact in the acceptance of mobile banking services. *Internet Research, 27*, 118–139.
34. Blohm, I., & Leimeister, J. M. (2013). Gamification: Design of IT-based enhancing services for motivational support and behavioral change. *Business and Information Systems Engineering, 5*(4), 275–278.
35. Kordyaka B, Weber S, Klassen G, & Niehaves, B. (2023). Decoding Gamification: A Randomized Within-Subjects Experiment on Affordances. In ACIS 2023 Proceedings. .
36. Karaosmanoglu, S., Schmolzi, T., & Steinicke, F. (2023). Playing with friends or strangers? The effects of familiarity between players in an asymmetric multiplayer virtual reality game. In *Companion proceedings of the annual symposium on computer-human interaction in play* (pp. 76–82). Association for Computing Machinery.
37. Florea, A., Fleaca, V., & Marcu, S. D. (2020). Innovative solution for parking-sharing of private institutions using various occupancy tracking methods. *Advances in Science, Technology and Engineering Systems Journal, 5*, 799–807.
38. Persaud, T., Amadi, U., Duane, A., et al. (2020). Smart City innovations to improve quality of life in urban settings. In *2020 IEEE global humanitarian technology conference (GHTC)* (pp. 1–8). IEEE.
39. De Lima, T. F. M. (2018). A game-based platform to tackle a public health problem. In *Proceedings of the 2018 annual symposium on computer-human interaction in play companion extended abstracts* (pp. 17–25).
40. Selänne, L., Pasanen, M., Aslan, F., & Pakarinen, A. (2024). Gamified intervention for health promotion of families in child health clinics—A cluster randomised trial. *Simulation & Gaming, 55*, 552–569.
41. Pappas, G., Papamichael, I., Zorpas, A., Siegel, J.E., Rutkowski, J., & Politopoulos, K. (2022). Modelling key performance indicators in a gamified waste management tool. *Modelling, 3*, 27.

42. González-Briones, A., Valdeolmillos, D., Casado-Vara, R., Chamoso, P., García Coria, J. A., Herrera-Viedma, E., & Corchado, J. M. (2019). GarbMAS: Simulation of the application of gamification techniques to increase the amount of recycled waste through a multi-agent system. In F. De La Prieta, S. Omatu, & A. Fernández-Caballero (Eds.), *Distributed computing and artificial intelligence, 15th international conference* (pp. 332–343). Springer International Publishing.
43. Campillo-Ferrer, J. M., Miralles-Martínez, P., & Sánchez-Ibáñez, R. (2020). Gamification in higher education: Impact on student motivation and the Acquisition of Social and Civic key Competencies. *Sustainability, 12*, 4822.
44. Martí-Parreño, J., Galbis-Córdova, A., & Currás-Pérez, R. (2021). Teachers beliefs about gamification and competencies development: A concept mapping approach. *Innovations in Education and Teaching International, 58*, 84–94.
45. Li, X., Shi, D., & Wang, S. (2019). Benevolent Deception in Exergame Design. In X. Fang (Ed.), *HCI in Games* (pp. 35–46). Springer International Publishing.
46. Barends, A. J., de Vries, R. E., & van Vugt, M. (2019). Gamified personality assessment: Virtual behavior cues of honesty-humility. *Zeitschrift für Psychologie, 227*, 207–217.
47. Wong, S., & Cooper, P. (2016). Reliability and validity of the explanatory sequential design of mixed methods adopted to explore the influences on online learning in Hong Kong bilingual cyber higher education. *International Journal of Cyber Society and Education, 9*, 45–64.
48. Venkatesh V, Brown S. A, & Bala H (2013). Bridging the qualitative-quantitative divide: Guidelines for conducting mixed methods research in information systems. *MIS Quarterly (MISQ)* 37:21–54.
49. Califf, C. B., Sarker, S., & Sarker, S. (2020). The bright and dark sides of technostress: A mixed-methods study involving healthcare it. *MIS Quarterly, 44*, 809–856.
50. Kordyaka B, Pumplun L, Brunnhofer M, Kruse B, & Laato S. (2023). Gender disparities in esports–An explanatory mixed-methods approach. Computers in Human Behavior 149:107956.
51. Dobbs, P. D., Hodges, E. J., Dunlap, C. M., & Cheney, M. K. (2020). Addiction vs. dependence: A mixed methods analysis of young adult JUUL users. *Addictive Behaviors, 107*, 106402.
52. Koivisto, J., & Hamari, J. (2019). The rise of motivational information systems: A review of gamification research. *International Journal of Information Management, 45*, 191–210.
53. Davoudpour, Z., & Rezapour, M. (2016). The conceptual model of the relationship between institutional transparency, citizen trust and satisfaction (a case study of Tehran city, Iran). *Internatonal Journal Architect Eng Urban Plan, 26*, 131–139.

Practice Track: Innovative Prototypes & Impact of IS

A Drift Detection Prototype for Quality Control in Manufacturing

Dharmil Rajesh Mehta, Safa Omri, Richard Zowalla, and Jens Neuhuettler

Abstract Drift detection is a critical factor in sustaining the performance of Computer Vision (CV) models in modern manufacturing, where it ensures the continuous achievement of high efficiency, quality, and innovation. CV models efficiency is more likely to reduce over time due to environmental changes, equipment wear and tear, or alterations in product specifications. Moreover, the collection of labeled data, essential for monitoring and adjusting these models, is often hindered by constraints such as time, cost, and the lack of domain experts for annotation. Addressing this gap, our research introduces an innovative unsupervised drift detection technique capable of identifying shifts in data distribution without the need for labeled data. This method proactively notifies operators of any decline in data quality that breaches a predetermined safety threshold, thereby preserving the operational integrity of CV applications. Our experimental results confirm the method's efficiency in detecting environmental shifts, changes in product specifications, and an increase in the production of defective parts, highlighting its significant potential to enhance quality control in manufacturing processes through reliable drift detection.

D. R. Mehta (✉) · S. Omri · R. Zowalla · J. Neuhuettler
Fraunhofer Institute for Industrial Engineering IAO, Research and Innovation Center for Cognitive Service Systems (KODIS), Heilbronn, Germany
e-mail: dharmil-rajesh.mehta@iao.fraunhofer.de

S. Omri
e-mail: safa.omri@iao.fraunhofer.de

R. Zowalla
e-mail: richard.zowalla@iao.fraunhofer.de

J. Neuhuettler
e-mail: jens.neuhuettler@iao.fraunhofer.de

C. M. Flath et al. (eds.), *Shaping the Digital Future Through Innovation and Practice*, Lecture Notes in Information Systems and Organisation 85,
https://doi.org/10.1007/978-3-032-08489-7_8

1 Introduction

In the dynamic world of manufacturing, where production environments and processes are continuously evolving, the precision and adaptability of machine learning models, especially those based on Computer Vision (CV) play a key role [17]. These models, integral to various stages of the production process including defect detection, quality control, object recognition, and automation, hinge on the assumption that data distributions remain static over time. Yet, in reality, these distributions are subject to change, a phenomenon known as drift. Drift challenges the foundational assumptions of many machine learning models by altering the statistical properties of the target variable over time, necessitating robust detection mechanisms to ensure models adapt and maintain performance in ever-changing environments [5, 9, 19].

The integration of Artificial Intelligence (AI), particularly through CV, into manufacturing, signifies a substantial shift towards more efficient, quality-driven, and innovative production methods. However, this shift is not without its challenges. The reliability and effectiveness of CV systems in manufacturing are compromised by fluctuations in environmental conditions, equipment integrity, and product specifications. These variations can subtly, yet significantly, affect the data distribution, leading to a decline in model performance if not promptly identified and addressed. Thus, monitoring CV systems for drift becomes imperative, not only for maintaining operational standards but also for upholding quality control and safety regulations.

Despite the recognized importance of drift detection in maintaining the accuracy of CV models, the field faces several hurdles. Among these is the difficulty of acquiring labeled data in manufacturing settings which is hindered by constraints such as cost, time, and the availability of domain experts. This challenge underscores the need for an unsupervised approach to drift detection, capable of identifying shifts in data distribution without relying on labeled datasets [1, 11].

Recent advancements in drift detection have proposed more nuanced approaches that consider the conditional distributions of data given specific contexts that are allowed to change over time [24]. Building upon these methodologies, our paper introduces a framework for context-aware drift detection, which leverages machinery from the causal inference domain to develop a comprehensive detection system built upon a foundation of two-sample tests for conditional distributional treatment effects [2].

This paper presents an innovative unsupervised drift detection methodology designed to tackle these challenges. Our method warns the user of a decline in the data quality that could jeopardize the performance of CV models, ensuring that manufacturing processes continue to benefit from the efficiency and innovation that AI brings. Through rigorous experimentation, we demonstrate the capability of our approach in detecting environmental changes, shifts in product specifications, and rise in the production of defective items. In doing so, we offer a valuable tool for the manufacturing industry to leverage the full potential of computer vision technology, enhancing quality control and ensuring the reliability of AI-driven processes.

Our contributions are twofold:

1. we demonstrate the practical applicability of the drift detection method in the industry by identifying environmental changes and variations in product specifications.
2. we offer a platform where users can not only test our method with sample data but also upload their data to assess and compare drift occurrences.

Through rigorous experimentation and analysis, we aim to establish a new paradigm in maintaining the accuracy and reliability of CV systems in the dynamic and ever-changing environment of manufacturing. This endeavor not only addresses an immediate need within the industry but also paves the way for future innovations in the fields of machine learning and computer vision.

The remainder of the paper is structured as follows. In Sect. 2 we discuss the related work in the field of drift detection. In Sect. 3 we discuss the methodology for drift detection. In Sect. 4 we present the experiment, result, and prototype. In Sect. 5 we conclude the paper and give an outlook of the future work.

2 Related Work

The latest research in drift detection, particularly in machine learning (ML) and its industrial applications, focuses on advanced methods for identifying and addressing both concept drift and data drift. These drifts are crucial for understanding because they directly impact the performance and reliability of ML models in dynamic environments. [16] presented a model for detecting drifts and identifying outliers in IoT sensor data, with a focus on real-time monitoring and early detection. It is used to identify potential outliers and detect both aggressive and progressive drifts, enabling real-time monitoring and early detection. In the field of industrial process modeling, concept drift detection methods have been developed, focusing on regression modeling and addressing the challenges of detecting concept drift in industrial processes. [20] provides a comprehensive overview of concept drift detection methods for industrial process modeling, addressing the need for more research in this area. In the context of business processes, drift detection is used to identify sudden and gradual changes, with a focus on automated and statistically grounded methods [14, 15]. Yeshchenko et al. [23] introduces the Visual Drift Detection tool, which categorizes, drills down, and quantifies process drifts, providing a valuable aid for business process redesign. These methods have been shown to accurately detect typical change patterns and scale up to work for online drift detection. These studies underscore the diverse approaches to understanding and mitigating drift effects but also highlight a common limitation: the heavy reliance on labeled data and the assumption of relatively stable environmental conditions, which are often not present in manufacturing contexts.

The use of drift detection in computer vision has been explored in various studies. Suprem et al. [21] introduced ODIN, a system that uses adversarial auto-encoders to detect and recover from drift in visual data. Liu and Zhou [13] proposed a framework that combines concept drift detection with an online semi-supervised boosting method for robust visual tracking. Rabanser et al. [18] introduced an approach for drift detection using statistical tests and distance-based methods. Liu et al. [12] proposed a Learned Kernel MMD a kernel-based two-sample test method that improves the performance of drift detection by learning the kernels from deep neural nets. Cobb et al. [2] introduced Context-Aware MMD a drift detection framework for conditional distribution effects. dos Reis et al. [4] introduced an approach for drift detection in streaming. The proposed method significantly reduced the insertion and deletion time of the data points for drift detection. Hegedüs et al. [8] presented an approach for detecting concept drift in large-scale, fully distributed networks, using online learners and an adaptive mechanism. These studies collectively demonstrate the potential of drift detection in improving the accuracy and robustness of computer vision systems. Jin et al. [10] proposed the different environmental factors that can affect the performance of the CV model in manufacturing.

3 Methodology

In this section, we will explain the methods used to detect drift in high-dimensional data such as images. We first reduce the dimension and then perform statistical hypothesis testing to compare the distribution of features. In addition, we discuss common issues and challenges for a CV system in an industrial setting, which may influence deep learning model performance in production. The framework for drift detection in the experiment is as shown in Fig. 1.

3.1 Dimensionality Reduction

Convolutional Neural Networks (CNNs) are one of the most suitable methods for feature extraction for image data. The performance of Efficient Net is much better as compared to other network architectures and even obtained the state-of-the-art performance on ImageNet and the CIFAR-100 datasets [22]. The architecture not only increases the accuracy of prediction on the dataset but also penalizes if the network is very computationally heavy. Hence we use Efficient Net B5 for the experiment as a feature extractor.

3.2 Statistical Hypothesis Testing

To analyze potential drift in the input data, we compare the distribution of the feature vectors within a reference data set with the distribution observed in a test data set,

i.e. data collected at a different location or under different environmental conditions. We perform statistical testing using Maximum Mean Discrepancy (MMD) multivariate kernel tests and Kolmogorov-Smirnov Test (KS) with Bonferroni Correction a univariate test and aggregating it with Bonferroni correction.
Multivariate Kernel Two-Sample Tests: MMD is a kernel-based two-sample statistical test that calculates the distance between feature means [7]. A feature map Φ maps X to kernel Hilbert space τ.

$$k(X, Y) = \langle \phi(X), \phi(y) \rangle_{\tau} \tag{1}$$

Given a probability P on X, the feature means μ_P maps $\Phi(X)$ to the mean of every coordinate of $\Phi(X)$.

$$\mu_p(\Phi(X))) = [E[\Phi(X_1)], ..., E[\Phi(X_m)]]^T \tag{2}$$

The inner product of feature means of X and Y can also be written as a kernel function such that:

$$\langle \mu_p(\Phi(X)), \mu_q(\Phi(X)) \rangle_{\tau} \tag{3}$$
$$= E_{p,q}\left[\langle \Phi(X), \Phi(Y) \rangle_{\tau}\right] \tag{4}$$
$$= E_{p,q}[k(X, Y)] \tag{5}$$

MMD is the distance between feature means of X, Y that is of μ_p, μ_q:

$$MMD^2(p, q) = \|u_p - u_q\| \tag{6}$$

By using the norm of the inner product, the Eq. 3 becomes:

$$MMD^2(p, q) = \langle u_p - u_q, u_p - u_q \rangle \tag{7}$$
$$= \langle u_p - u_p \rangle - 2 \langle u_p, u_q \rangle \tag{8}$$
$$+ \langle u_q, u_q \rangle \tag{9}$$

We calculate an unbiased estimate of the squared MMD using samples from both distributions as follows:

$$MMD^2(X, Y) = \frac{1}{m(m-1)} \sum_i \sum_{j \neq i} \kappa(x_i, x_j) - \tag{10}$$

$$\frac{1}{mm} \sum_i \sum_j \kappa(x_i, y_j) \tag{11}$$

$$+ \frac{1}{m(m-1)} \sum_i \sum_{j \neq i} \kappa(y_i, y_j) \tag{12}$$

P-value is calculated by performing a permutation test on the Gaussian Kernel matrix [7].

$$\kappa(x, y) = e^{-\frac{1}{\sigma}\|x-y\|^2} \tag{13}$$

Multiple Univariate Testing: In MMD, K-Dimensional feature vectors are tested at the same time. Hence, we selected KS Test, where each dimension is tested individually. Z is the maximum absolute difference between two empirical cumulative distribution functions $F_p(z)$ and $F_q(z)$. Multiple p-values make it difficult to decide whether there is a drift in overall data because we don't know which p-value to select. Therefore we correct it using Bonferroni correction. It rejects the null hypothesis when the minimum p-value is less than α/K.

$$Z = sup \left\| F_p(z) - F_q(z) \right\| \tag{14}$$

Threshold selection: For selecting the probability of rejecting the null hypothesis (p-value) we could either use a higher p-value (10%) or lower p-value (1% or 0.1%). If we use a lower p-value, the machines would be running where the data might not be similar to the reference dataset and the operator might not be notified until the value drops close to 0 which can be very expensive. If we use a higher p-value value the operator will be notified if there is any slightest change in the environment. The cost of rejecting a true null hypothesis in our scenario is less than failing to reject a false null hypothesis. Hence we have used a p-value of 10% for the experiments.

3.3 Environmental Influences on Image Data Quality

In industrial CV system, the quality of the captured image is important for accurately monitoring product quality via a deployed deep learning model. In the following subsections, we will discuss common environmental influences that can affect image quality and for which a drift detection system needs to be robust. These effects are depicted in Fig. 2. Addressing these issues is critical in maintaining the reliability and effectiveness of the CV system in monitoring product quality and ensuring smooth operations along production lines.

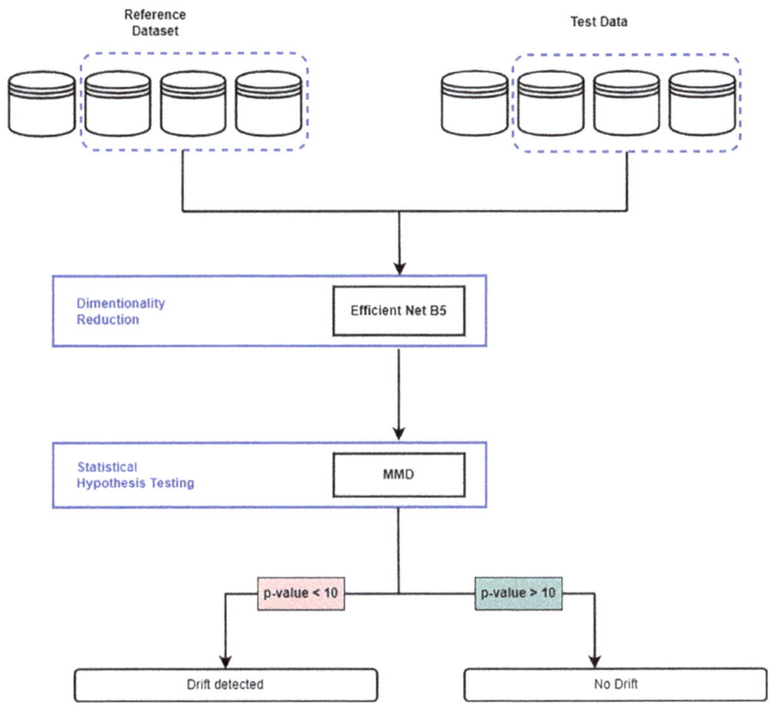

Fig. 1 Drift detection framework

Blurry Images A common problem is the occurrence of `blurred images`, which can be caused by a variety of factors. Poor focusing, where the camera fails to adjust its lens accurately to capture a clear image, is a primary issue [6]. In addition, slower shutter speeds can cause motion blur, especially when monitoring fast-moving production lines or moving objects. Finally, the presence of dirt or damage to the lens can obstruct the light path, causing distortion and blurriness in the captured images. The blurry images are generated using the cv2 Gaussian Blur function using a kernel size of 5×5.
Images in Motion: When products are in motion (e.g. on fast-moving product lines), or when the camera itself is in motion, images can suffer from `motion blur`. This phenomenon occurs when the camera's exposure time is not synchronized with the speed of moving objects, resulting in a smear effect in the captured images that affects the clarity and detail of the captured images. To simulate images in motion we have used a kernel size of 5×5 and the motion direction is 45°.

Changes in Lighting Conditions: Variations of `lightning conditions` pose a significant challenge to the consistency and reliability of image acquisition. Sudden changes in the lightning environment, whether due to natural light variations or artificial sources, can result in images with increased or decreased brightness. These variations can greatly affect the accuracy of image analysis, affecting their ability to

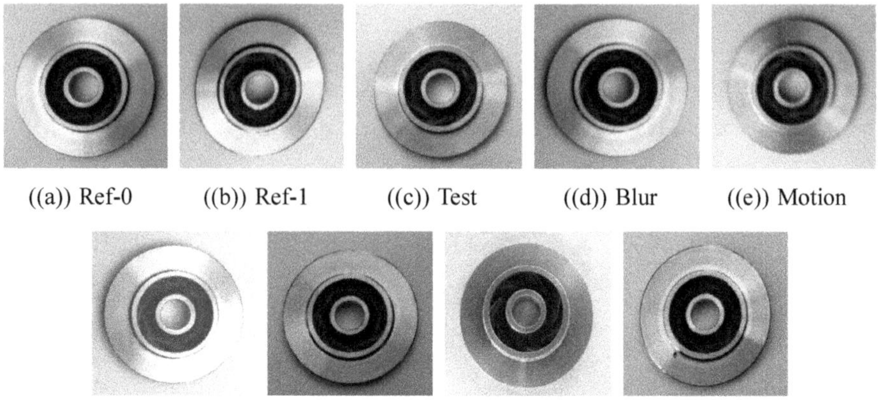

((a)) Ref-0 ((b)) Ref-1 ((c)) Test ((d)) Blur ((e)) Motion

((f)) Bright ((g)) Dark ((h)) Camera ((i)) Defect

Fig. 2 Sample Images. **a** Ref-0: Image from train dataset. **b** Ref-1: Image from train dataset. **c** Test: Image from test dataset. **d** Blur: Gaussian Blur Kernel Size 5×5. **e** Motion: 45° Kernel Size 5×5. **f** Bright: 60% more brightness. **g** Dark: 20% less brightness. **h** Camera: Resolution of 512×512. **i** Defect: Manufacturing Defects

effectively detect defects or anomalies in the captured data. Increased brightness in images can lead to overexposure, washing out important details, and distorting the visual information. Reduced brightness can obscure fine features and reduce contrast between objects. Overexposed images have 60% more brightness than the normal images and underexposed images have 20% less brightness.

Change of Camera: Cameras may be upgraded, replaced, or modified for a variety of reasons, ranging from technological advances to equipment failure. However, such changes can introduce variability in the characteristics and performance of the imaging devices, potentially resulting in images that differ from those contained in the original training dataset. This variability can pose a challenge to CV systems trained on specific images, as the newly captured images may have different resolutions, color profiles, or different focal lengths. The reference dataset has an image size of 300x300 and the images generated by the new camera are of 512×512 size.

Manufacturing of only Defective Parts: The scenario where only defective parts are being produced is not a case of data drift, because the CV model is trained to catch these data and label them as `def`. However, it is economically more favorable to detect this case as drifted data and alert the manufacturers as soon as possible so that they can find the underlying cause.

Images without drift: While deploying drift detection in production most of the time the production process would be working fine under normal circumstances. Hence it is of utmost priority to detect normal running conditions in manufacturing and not send false alarms to operators.

4 Results and Prototype

4.1 Experiments Setup

To observe the performance of drift detection on the industrial use case and verify that it can detect the environmental influences described above we have performed experiments on a submersible pump impeller for quality inspection [3]. The functionality of the impeller is to transfer the energy from the motor to the fluid being pumped. The dataset consists of the top view of the impeller which is made by the casting process. The dataset consists of 8648 images, which are either labeled `ok` or `def` (defect). The class distribution and the datasets used for testing in each experiment are explained in Table 1.

Reference Dataset: For quality control, the best-performing CV models that were trained on these datasets are used in production. The full training dataset may be very large and unavailable during production; to address this issue, we create ten reference datasets by sampling 100 images from train-ok `Ref-1`. In addition, the majority of parts produced during manufacturing will be of label `ok`; however, the proportion of `ok` and `def` in the training dataset is forty-five percent. Therefore, we generate ten reference datasets using train-ok dataset `Ref-1`.

Test Dataset: To ensure that the drift detection works properly and does not give false alarms, we use test datasets for this purpose. The test dataset is ideal since it contains images that are not shown to the model during the training step, but the probability density of the features must be similar to the probability density of the reference dataset. Hence we generate the `Test Samples` dataset by randomly sampling 100 images from test-ok `T-1`. Similarly, we generate images with the environmental influences i.e. `Blurry Images, Images in Motion, Change in Lighting Conditions` by adding noise in the `Test Samples` dataset using the OpenCV library. To test the `Change of Camera` scenario we generated a dataset by sampling 100 images from new-camera-ok `NC-1`. We generate `Parts with defects` dataset by sampling 100 images from test-def `T-2`.

4.2 Statistical Results

In this section, we want to demonstrate that the drift detection method can be deployed in a CV system to ensure that the CV model is deployed in a safe environment. It can trigger an alarm and notify the users when there is any change in the environment or when the machine produces more faulty products. Table 2 shows the drift score using pre-trained Efficient Net B5 as a feature extractor and using MMD and KS Test as a statistical test for drift detection. Test Samples when compared with Reference Datasets should have a p-value of more than 10 as they are from similar distribution. KS Test gave false positive results for the Ref-3 Dataset. KS Test also found it difficult

Table 1 Dataset

Identifier	Dataset	No. of Images	Class	Image size	Experiment
Ref-1	train-ok	2875	ok	300 x 300	Reference Data
Ref-2	train-def	3758	def	300 x 300	Not used
T-1	test-ok	262	ok	300 x 300	Blurry Images, Images in Motion, Changes in Lightning Conditions
T-2	test-def	453	def	300 x 300	Manufacturing of only Defective Parts
NC-1	new-camera-ok	519	ok	512 x 512	Change of Camera
NC-2	new-camera-def	781	def	512 x 512	Not used

to detect environmental changes such as increased intensities, blurred images, and faulty parts. MMD outperformed KS Test in both scenarios by accurately detecting test samples and erroneous samples. Hence, we have developed the prototype using MMD as a hypothesis-testing method.

4.3 *Prototype*

In the progression of our research, we engineered an interactive prototype to facilitate real-world application and evaluation of our unsupervised drift detection methodology. This prototype represents a bridge between theoretical research findings and practical, hands-on experimentation, enabling users to directly engage with the drift detection mechanism within a controlled environment. The design and implementation details, alongside the functionalities of this prototype, are articulated below:

Architectural Framework: The prototype's architecture comprises a React-based frontend interface and a FastAPI-driven backend, implemented in Python. This architectural choice was governed by the need for a responsive user interface that could seamlessly interact with a robust and efficient backend processing unit. React, renowned for its efficient update and rendering capabilities, provides an intuitive interface for users to interact with the prototype. Concurrently, FastAPI offers a high-performance backend solution with asynchronous support, crucial for handling the computationally intensive tasks associated with drift detection in high-dimensional data.

Functional Capabilities: The prototype is designed to perform a dual role: firstly, as a demonstration tool, allowing users to replicate the drift detection experiments highlighted in this study; and secondly, as an analysis platform, enabling users to

Table 2 Drift score on the datasets

Reference	Test sample		Blurry images		Images in motion		Bright images		Dark images		Different camera		Parts with defects	
	MMD	KS	MMD	KS	MMD	KS	MMD	KS	MMD	KS	MMD	KS	MMD	KS
Ref-0	44	44	0	0	1	0	0	6	0	0	3	1	0	**23**
Ref-1	39	27	0	0	2	0	0	2	0	0	1	5	0	**10**
Ref-2	73	33	0	0	2	0	0	4	0	0	0	0	0	3
Ref-3	77	**8**	1	0	3	0	0	**19**	0	0	1	1	0	1
Ref-4	77	100	1	2	2	0	0	9	0	0	0	0	0	2
Ref-5	98	100	2	4	9	0	0	**36**	0	0	0	2	0	2
Ref-6	95	72	1	1	8	0	0	**11**	0	0	0	2	0	2
Ref-7	57	85	0	**80**	1	0	0	8	0	0	0	0	0	0
Ref-8	99	100	2	3	8	0	0	**47**	0	0	0	1	0	0
Ref-9	78	100	1	4	3	0	0	**13**	0	0	0	2	0	1

upload their datasets to evaluate the drift detection capabilities in scenarios specific to their operational environments. This functionality is pivotal for validating the adaptability and effectiveness of the proposed drift detection methodology across various manufacturing settings and conditions. The users have the possibility to run different tests as shown in the experiment and compare the drift scores. If the user has some data available and wants to perform drift detection on them he can even do so by uploading them on the platform. We are planning to publish the code on our platform as open source with a business-friendly OSS license in the near future.

5 Conclusion and Future Work

In this paper, we have addressed the critical need for robust drift detection in the manufacturing sector, paving the way for more resilient and adaptable CV systems. By tackling the challenges of unsupervised drift detection, we contribute to the broader discourse on maintaining the accuracy and reliability of AI applications in dynamic environments, ensuring that the manufacturing industry can continue to reap the benefits of technological advancement without compromise. We have demonstrated the capability of drift detection on a small dataset for a particular use case of quality control in manufacturing.

Our work suggests several open questions that might offer promising paths for future work, we aim to broaden the scope of our investigation to encompass a variety of domains beyond CV, thus expanding the applicability and impact of our findings. A key focus of our future work will involve comprehensive research into the development of an advanced drift detection framework. This framework will not only identify instances of data drift but will also possess the capability to categorize the nature of such drifts accurately. By integrating a 'human-in-the-loop' approach, we envision a system where drift detection is not only automated but is also enhanced by human expertise, enabling precise classification of concept drift types. This dual approach promises to refine the detection process further, ensuring more nuanced and actionable insights for maintaining the integrity of AI-driven systems in the manufacturing industry and beyond.

References

1. Breck, E., Polyzotis, N., Roy, S., Whang, S. E., & Zinkevich, M. A. (2019). Data validation for machine learning. In *USENIX workshop on Tackling computer systems problems with machine learning techniques*.
2. Cobb, O., Van Looveren, A., & Klaise, J. (2022). Sequential multivariate change detection with calibrated and memoryless false detection rates. In *International conference on artificial intelligence and statistics* (pp. 226–239).
3. Dabhi, R., Kantesaria, N., Vaghasia, P., Hirpara, J., & Bhoraniya, R. (2020). Casting product image data for quality inspection. *Kaggle Datasets*. https://www.kaggle.com/datasets/

ravirajsinh45/real-life-industrial-dataset-of-casting-product

4. dos Reis, D. M., Flach, P., Matwin, S., & Batista, G. (2016). Fast unsupervised online drift detection using incremental Kolmogorov-Smirnov test. In *Proceedings of the 22nd ACM SIGKDD international conference on knowledge discovery and data mining, KDD '16*. Association for Computing Machinery. https://doi.org/10.1145/2939672.2939836
5. Engstrom, L., Tsipras, D., Schmidt, L., & Madry, A. (2017). A rotation and a translation suffice: Fooling CNNs with simple transformations. CoRR https://arxiv.org/abs/1712.02779
6. Gedraite, E., & Hadad, M. (2011). Investigation on the effect of a Gaussian Blur in image filtering and segmentation. In *Proceedings* (pp. 393–396).
7. Gretton, A., Borgwardt, M. K., Rasch, J. M., Schölkopf, B., & Smola, A. (2012). A kernel two-sample test. *The Journal of Machine Learning Research, 13*, 723–773.
8. Hegedüs, I., Nyers, L., & Ormándi, R.: Detecting concept drift in fully distributed environments. In *2012 IEEE 10th Jubilee international symposium on intelligent systems and informatics* (pp. 183–188).
9. Hendrycks, D., & Dietterich, T. G. (2019). Benchmarking neural network robustness to common corruptions and perturbations. CoRR https://arxiv.org/abs/1903.12261
10. Jin, M., Mehta Dharmil, R., Xing, W., Schniertshauer, J., Neuhüttler, J., & Zimmermann, F. (2023). Implementation and validation of non-semantic out-of-distribution detection on image data in manufacturing.
11. Klaise, J., Van Looveren, A., Cox, C., Vacanti, G., & Coca, A. (2020). Monitoring and explainability of models in production. arXiv https://arxiv.org/abs/2007.06299
12. Liu, F., Xu, W., Lu, J., Zhang, G., Gretton, A., & Sutherland, D. J. (2021). Learning deep kernels for non-parametric two-sample tests. arXiv https://arxiv.org/abs/2002.09116
13. Liu, Y., & Zhou, Y. (2014). Online detection of concept drift in visual tracking. In *International conference on neural information processing*.
14. Maaradji, A., Dumas, M., La Rosa, M., & Ostovar, A. (2015). Fast and accurate business process drift detection. In *International conference on business process management*.
15. Maaradji, A., Dumas, M., La Rosa, M., & Ostovar, A. (2017). Detecting sudden and gradual drifts in business processes from execution traces. *IEEE Trans. Knowl. Data Eng., 29*, 2140–2154.
16. Munirathinam, S. (2020). Drift detection analytics for IoT sensors. In *IEEE international symposium on multimedia*.
17. Omri, S., Mehta Dharmil, R., & Neuhüttler, J. (2023). Leveraging computer vision for sustainable manufacturing: Potentials, challenges and future perspectives. In *AHFE International Conference, USA*. https://arxiv.org/abs/2007.06299
18. Rabanser, S., Günnemann, S., & Lipton, Z. C. (2019). Failing loudly: An empirical study of methods for detecting dataset shift. https://arxiv.org/abs/1810.11953
19. Recht, B., Roelofs, R., Schmidt, L., & Shankar, V. (2019). Do ImageNet classifiers generalize to ImageNet? CoRR https://arxiv.org/abs/1902.10811
20. Sun, Z., Tang, J., Qiao, J.-f., & Cui, C. (2020). Review of concept drift detection method for industrial process modeling. In *2020 39th Chinese control conference (CCC)* (pp. 5754–5759).
21. Suprem, A., Arulraj, J., Pu, C., & Ferreira, J. E. (2020). *ODIN. Proceedings of the VLDB endowment, 13*, 2453–2465.
22. Tan, M., & Le, Q. V. (2019). EfficientNet: Rethinking model scaling for convolutional neural networks. CoRR https://arxiv.org/abs/1905.11946
23. Yeshchenko, A., Di Ciccio, C., Mendling, J., Polyvyanyy, A.: Comprehensive Process Drift Analysis with the Visual Drift Detection Tool. In: ER Forum/Posters/Demos (2019).
24. Sun, Y., Mi, J., & Jin, C. (2024). Entropy based concept drift detection in information systems. *Knowl.-Based Syst. 290.*

A Method for Performing Ontology-Based Computational Literature Reviews Exemplified for Design Science Research

Sebastian Huettemann, Roland M. Mueller, and Barbara Dinter

Abstract The traditional process of conducting literature reviews requires a significant amount of manual work and is often constrained by the limitations of small sample sizes. Although novel computational approaches to language analysis offer great opportunities, they are rarely applied to literature reviews. We aim to demonstrate the potential of ontology-based computational literature reviews. Therefore, we conducted a Design Science Research (DSR) project to apply and extend a method for this type of review. Since DSR shows a considerable diversity in theoretical foundations and methodological approaches and can serve as an insightful example, we first developed a machine learning classifier to identify DSR articles. Second, we applied and extended a method for ontological annotation and sentence classification. Finally, we conducted a computational literature review of 6235 DSR articles, focusing on the distribution of theories, methods, and topics. We also developed an interactive dashboard prototype with selected results from our study.

1 Introduction

In recent years, there have been significant advances in computational linguistics that could help facilitate automated literature reviews of large collections of documents. For a long time, automatically analyzing language was limited to statistical insights into word distributions. This changed with the seminal paper by [1], which proposed a transformer-based architecture that allowed computers to understand the context

S. Huettemann (✉) · R. M. Mueller
Berlin School of Economics and Law, Berlin, Germany
e-mail: sebastian.huettemann@gmail.com

R. M. Mueller
e-mail: roland.mueller@hwr-berlin.de

B. Dinter
Chemnitz University of Technology, Chemnitz, Germany
e-mail: barbara.dinter@wirtschaft.tu-chemnitz.de

C. M. Flath et al. (eds.), *Shaping the Digital Future Through Innovation and Practice*,
Lecture Notes in Information Systems and Organisation 85,
https://doi.org/10.1007/978-3-032-08489-7_9

and thus the semantics of language, leading to breakthrough developments such as ChatGPT. What if we could go beyond the limits of manual analysis and use novel computational methods to analyze a more extensive body of knowledge?

Research in the field of Information Systems (IS) has explored the use of natural language processing (NLP) technologies to extract knowledge from research articles. This has led to the development of various tools, such as TheoryOn, a search engine for constructs [2], and tools to ensure construct identity [3]. In addition, NLP technologies have been used to extract research methods [4] and to perform question answering on research articles [5]. More recently, Huettemann [6] proposed a method for knowledge extraction through sentence classification and ontological annotation. This method can be used to identify and attribute mentions of research methods, or theories in research articles. However, it may not be suitable for identifying more complex methodologies.

An example of a comprehensive research methodology in IS is DSR. The field of DSR is rapidly expanding, with thousands of articles contributing to its development. In particular, Hevner et al. [7] helped to legitimize the use of DSR as a research methodology in IS. However, before and after this article, many research projects did not explicitly mention DSR as a method, although they shared many of its characteristics. Several articles have analyzed the use of DSR, focusing on different aspects such as overall distribution [8], contributions [9], theories used [10], or their nature and quality [11]. This diversity provides numerous opportunities for further exploration [12–15]. However, literature reviews in major IS outlets are conducted manually with rather small sample sizes, typically ranging from 50 to 300 articles.

In contrast to using manual approaches, we performed a computational literature review of DSR articles in IS. Building on developments in our previous projects [6, 16], we aim to answer the following research question: *How can we apply and extend a method for ontology-based computational literature reviews to comprehensive research methodologies such as DSR?*

In this article, we follow a DSR approach to apply, extend, and demonstrate a method for ontology-based computational literature reviews. We (1) design and develop a machine learning classifier to identify DSR articles, (2) apply and extend a method for ontological annotation and sentence classification, and (3) perform a computational literature review on thousands of DSR articles, providing comprehensive insights into the distribution of theories, methods, and topics. To demonstrate the potential of our approach, we have developed an interactive dashboard prototype that is accessible via a GitHub repository. The link can be found in the references [17].

2 Related Work

The identity and evolution of DSR is of great interest to the IS community. Many articles have analyzed various aspects of this research paradigm. However, a common concern is the limited sample size of articles analyzed, most likely due to the high level of manual work required to conduct literature reviews.

Prat et al. [18] conducted a systematic literature review to analyze DSR evaluation methods in 121 articles from the AIS8 basket from 2004 to 2014. They pointed to future work to analyze a larger sample of research articles. Nagle et al. [9] reviewed 111 DSR articles from the Senior Scholars' basket to understand the presentation, implementation, and contributions of DSR. They noted that future work should include major IS conferences in the analysis. Möller et al. [10] conducted a systematic literature review of DSR articles to identify kernel theories used. They sampled 47 articles from four IS conferences and mentioned that their research covered only a limited snapshot of the last decade. Indulska and Recker [11] analyzed 83 DSR articles from five conferences to determine the proliferation, nature, and quality of DSR articles from 2004–2007, while Deng et al. [8] investigated the identification and distribution of DSR articles in the basket of eight and selected IS conferences. They analyzed 278 articles from 2001–2015.

Typically, literature reviews are conducted in a systematic manner according to established guidelines [19–21]. However, as mentioned in related work, this approach has several drawbacks. The amount of manual work required limits the quantity of material that can be reviewed. Most guidelines were written when automated methods were in their infancy. But in order to analyze a population rather than samples, we need to find ways to automatically generate insights from large volumes of research articles.

Recent examples in the IS discipline include approaches that focus on automatically extracting qualitative insights from research articles. Mueller & Huettemann developed a rule-based approach for extracting constructs and their relationships from the text of articles [22]. A similar approach has been incorporated into the construct search engine TheoryOn [2], focusing primarily on structural equation modeling (SEM) articles. Other studies have used topic modeling to semi-automatically analyze large collections of documents to identify topics, trends, or themes [23, 24]. More recent approaches are based on advanced NLP methods, such as deep learning [4] to classify research methods, or transformer-based methods to classify the context of detected terminology [6]. Table 1 summarizes our findings from related work.

Table 1 Manual literature reviews and automated methods

Type	Author	Limitation
Manual literature reviews	Indulska and Recker [11]	Limited search terms, limited sample size
	Prat et al. [18]	Limited sample size
	Deng et al. [8]	Limited sample size
	Möller et al. [10]	Limited sample size
	Nagle et al. [9]	Limited sample size
Automated methods	Mueller and Huettemann [22]	Focus only on SEM
	Schmiedel et al. [23]	Context of words is not considered
	Li et al. [2]	Focus only on SEM
	Anisienia et al. [4]	Focus only on research methods
	Huettemann [6]	No proof-of-concept for larger samples of data
	Storey et al. [24]	Context of words is not considered

3 Methodology

3.1 Research Design

We follow the DSR methodology of Peffers et al. [25]. The problem is that literature reviews are limited by small sample sizes and current automated approaches cannot replace manual coding. Our objective is therefore to apply and extend a computational approach that can support literature reviews on large collections of documents. The design and development of a DSR classifier and the ontological annotation and sentence classification are illustrated in Sect. 3.1 and 3.2. We demonstrate the capabilities of our method with the results of a computational literature review in this article and in an interactive dashboard prototype. The link to the prototype can be found in the reference section [17]. We evaluated the performance of the DSR classifier against the DSR literature review of Prat et al. [18] and DSR articles from the International Conference on Design Science Research in Information Systems and Technology (DESRIST).

The results in Sect. 4 exemplify the application of an ontology-based computational literature. Therefore, we focused on aspects that are frequently studied: the distribution of DSR articles across major IS publication outlets [8, 9, 11], the use of theories [10, 26, 27], and the use of additional research methods in DSR articles [18, 28–30]. However, the proposed method could be used to create additional types of analyses such as co-occurrence analyses of topics, and theories, or help identify research gaps related to combinations of ontological categories. Figure 1 provides an overview of the key steps of our approach.

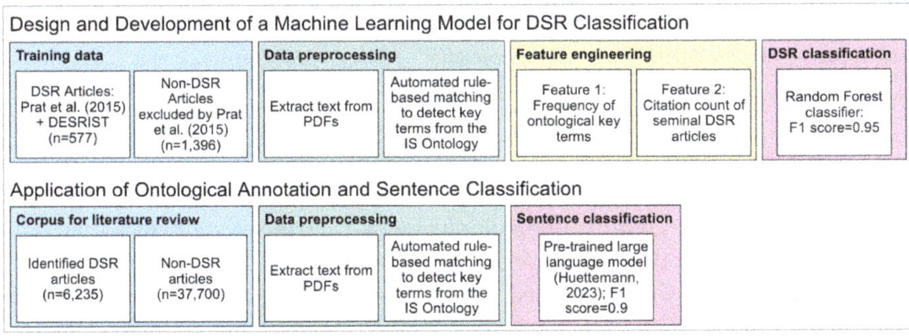

Fig. 1 Methodology overview

In previous work, we developed an approach for automated ontological annotation and sentence classification in IS research articles [6, 16]. Ontological annotation is a method for identifying specific mentions of ontological key terms, such as theories, topics, and research methods in articles. Sentence classification ensures that the extracted key terms can be correctly assigned to a focal article based on their context. However, the definition of DSR articles has changed over time, particularly before and after the legitimizing article by Hevner et al. [7]. In addition, DSR is highly diverse and encompasses many areas—often without an explicit reference to DSR [12]. Therefore, we extended our previous method to include a classifier for DSR articles. We refrained from using tools that implement generative artificial intelligence due to the limitations associated with hallucinations [31–33].

3.2 *Machine Learning Classifier for DSR Papers*

We trained our machine learning classifier based on a corpus of 577 DSR and 1396 non-DSR articles. In 2015, Prat et al. [18] conducted a rigorous literature review to identify DSR articles in IS across the AIS8 basket of journals [34]. They identified 121 DSR articles in the timeframe from 2004 to 2014, and we used these articles as training data. In addition, we collected 456 articles from DESRIST in the period 2009 to 2021, for a total of 577 DSR articles. To create training data with non-DSR articles, we took a random sample of 1396 articles from the AIS8 basket of journals from 2004 to 2014 that were not considered DSR according to Prat et al. [18].

We performed a number of steps to prepare the data and to create features for training the classifier. We extracted the text from all PDF files using Python and Grobid, a machine learning software that extracts information from research articles [35]. To identify IS-specific terminology, we used the IS Ontology [16]. This ontology contains approximately 3000 key terms and 300,000 synonyms covering, for example, research methods, theories, topics, and technologies. We used SpaCy,

Table 2 Training data example

article_id	"design science"	"action research"	...	dsr_citation_count	is_dsr
1	8	2	...	14	Yes
2	0	2	...	1	No

an NLP library [36], to identify all ontological terms and their synonyms in the texts of the research articles through rule-based matching.

As a first feature, we determined the frequency of ontological key terms per article in our corpus. We compared the performance of using the frequency of terms in different categories of the IS Ontology, such as theories, research methods, or topics, and obtained the best results when using the frequency of all terms organized under research methods and data analysis methods (n = 381). As a second feature, we created a count of seminal DSR citations. The intuition was that the more times an article cited a seminal DSR article, the stronger its relationship to DSR. We created a list of seminal DSR papers by analyzing all DESRIST references in our corpus. We selected the top 50 most cited references from DESRIST and manually removed non-DSR papers. We counted how many times an article in our corpus cited one of the DSR papers in this list. Table 2 shows an example of the training data.

We used an 80/20 train-test split and compared the performance of Scikit Learn's random forest classifier [37] with XGBoost [38]. To identify the optimal number of estimators, we performed a grid search with ten-fold cross-validation. After comparing the performance of the models on the test set, we chose the random forest classifier as it performed slightly better than XGBoost. The random forest classifier combines the results of multiple decision trees to make a final classification based on majority voting. The random selection of data and features in each decision tree helps to avoid overfitting. We calculated precision, recall, and weighted average F1-scores where precision = true positives / (true positives + false positives), recall = true positives / (true positives + false negatives), and F1 = 2 * (precision * recall) / (precision + recall). Weighted average F1 scores take into account class imbalance (SciKit Learn, 2023). For comparison, we created a keyword classifier by performing a keyword search in the titles, abstracts, and keywords of the articles in the test set. Whenever any of these elements contained one of the following keywords, we categorized an article as DSR: "DSR", "design science/principle/theory/research/ artifact/ methodology". Table 3 shows that RF outperformed the keyword classifier in terms of recall, retrieving 91% of all DSR articles in the test set compared to 63% for the keyword classifier.

3.3 *Sentence Classification and Ontological Annotation*

To perform the computational literature review, we analyzed a total of 43,925 articles from the basket of eleven [39] and major IS conferences. Using our classifier,

Table 3 DSR classifier performance metrics

Class	Precision (RF | Keyword)	Recall (RF | Keyword)	F1-score (RF | Keyword)	Count of examples
Not DSR	0.96 | 0.86	0.97 | 0.98	0.97 | 0.92	279
DSR	0.93 | 0.94	**0.91 | 0.63**	0.92 | 0.75	116
Weighted average	0.95 | 0.89	0.95 | 0.88	0.95 | 0.87	395

we detected 6235 DSR articles across all outlets. We used a recently introduced sentence classification and ontological annotation method [6] to qualitatively analyze the content of these articles. We used the IS Ontology [16] to detect IS-related key terms such as methods, theories, or technologies. We extracted the text from the PDF files, using Grobid [35], and developed a procedure in Python to perform rule-based matching [36]. As a result, we detected about ten million key terms from the IS Ontology in the texts of the articles in our corpus.

Without considering the context of the detected key terms, the mere occurrence of a term can have different meanings. Consider the term "case study" in different sentences, e.g., "we performed a case study", "Smith et al. 2020 performed a case study", or "a case study is a research method". For this research, we are only interested in key terms that can be attributed to a focal article, such as the first example sentence. Therefore, we performed sentence classification by using a fine-tuned large language model from Huettemann [6] to classify sentences into three classes: describing an article, describing related work, or describing background information. This approach was evaluated on 1000 sentences with an average weighted F1-score of 0.9 [6].

4 Results

4.1 DSR Distribution in Major IS Outlets

Figure 2 shows the proportion of DSR papers in the main IS outlets. In general, we find a higher ratio of DSR articles in conferences (15.5%) than in journals (11.3%). Among the conferences, DESRIST and the International Conference on Business Informatics (WI) have the highest proportion of DSR articles, while the International Conference on Information Systems (ICIS) and Americas Conference on Information Systems (AMCIS) have the lowest. The high proportion of DSR articles in DESRIST is a consequence of our design decision to classify all DESRIST articles as DSR (see Sect. 3.1), while the high proportion of DSR articles in WI could be explained by the high submission rate of the German IS community, which has a strong tradition in DSR. From the basket of eleven journals, Decision Support Systems (DSS) has by far the highest proportion (25.4%) whereas the other journals publish on average only about 10% of DSR articles.

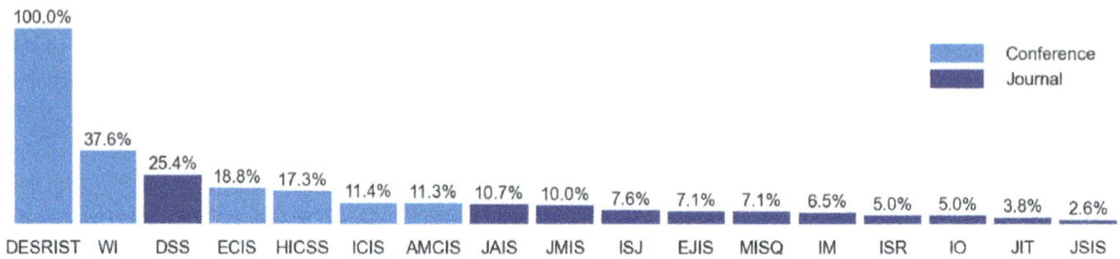

Fig. 2 Ratio of DSR articles by publication outlets

Looking at the average ratio of DSR papers over time, we noticed a slight increase in the number of DSR papers published in conferences. For example, in 1996 the average ratio was about 10%, while in 2022 the average ratio was about 21%. The ratio of DSR articles published in the basket of eleven journals has not exceeded 15% in the last 30 years. The average ratio over this period is about 10%.

Figure 4 shows the top 20 most frequently used DSR-related key terms from the IS Ontology in DSR articles which we found to be consistent with the artifact types described by Prat et al. [18] and Burton-Jones et al. [12]. An interesting observation is that only 51% of the DSR articles used the term design science or one of its synonyms to describe their research approach. This may be due, at least in part, to the fact that our corpus includes articles published before Hevner's seminal article [7]. We also see that most of the key terms refer to conceptualizations rather than implemented prototypes, e.g., *design principle, conceptual modeling, design theory,* or *metamodel.*

4.2 Theories in DSR

To identify DSR articles that use theories, we selected the following theory-related key terms from the IS Ontology as indicators: *Named theories* are existing theories that authors refer to, *design theories* are theories that result from DSR projects, and *theoretical model*, *theory development*, and *kernel theory* refer to theoretical aspects that are frequently mentioned in DSR articles. Of the 6235 DSR articles in our corpus, 1466 DSR articles (23.5%) mention named theories, 508 (8.1%) mention synonyms for the term "design theory" and 2207 (35.4%) mention theoretical aspects. In total, 2833 articles (45.4%) mention at least one of the aforementioned theoretical aspects related to the use of theories.

Figure 5 shows the proportion of DSR articles across the outlets in our corpus. At the high end, we find that 80% or more of DSR articles published in journals such as Journal of the Association for Information Systems (JAIS) and Information and Organization (IO) mention the use of theories. At the lower end, about 40% or less of DSR articles published in journals and conferences such as Hawaii International Conference on System Sciences (HICSS), Information Systems Research (ISR),

AMCIS, or DSS mention the use of theories. Figure 6 shows the average ratio of theory-related DSR articles in journals versus conferences over time.

To better understand the use of existing theories in DSR articles, we identified the top 25 theories by the number of DSR articles. For example, Fig. 7 shows that affordance theory, socio-technical theory, and technology acceptance model form the top three.

We were also interested in the different use of named theories in DSR vs. non-DSR articles. Therefore, we created two visualizations in Fig. 8 showing the largest differences based on 6235 DSR articles (1% = 62.35) and 37,700 non-DSR articles (1% = 377). On the left, we show the top 20 theories with the largest positive difference between DSR and non-DSR articles. For example, we found that articles using the socio-technical theory account for the largest difference where the DSR rate is higher than the non-DSR rate. About 1.3% of all DSR articles use socio-technical theory. In contrast, only about 0.8% of all non-DSR articles use this theory. On the right, we show the top 20 theories with the largest negative difference between DSR and non-DSR articles.

4.3 Non-DSR Methods in DSR Articles

With this analysis, we follow [18, 28–30] to better understand the use and diversity of methodological approaches in DSR. To identify DSR articles using non-DSR methods, we selected articles that contained any method-related key terms that were not related to DSR according to the IS Ontology. Of the 6235 DSR articles in our corpus, 5298 articles (85%) contained additional non-DSR methods. In 937 articles (15%), we found no key terms indicating additional methods.

We analyzed how many additional methods are used in DSR articles, and present the result in Fig. 9, where we show the ratio of DSR articles using additional methods by the count of additional methods. For example, 19% of all DSR articles with additional methods use two of them. In Fig. 10, we show the average number of additional research methods in journal and conference articles over time indicating an upward trend toward the inclusion of more additional research methods.

To determine which additional methods are used in DSR articles, we analyzed the top 25 additional methods in Fig. 11.

To find out what is unique about the use of non-DSR methods in DSR vs non-DSR articles, we created two visualizations. Figure 12 shows the largest differences in the use of methods. The DSR ratio shows the proportion of DSR articles that use a non-DSR method, while the non-DSR ratio shows the proportion of non-DSR articles. For this analysis, we analyzed 5298 DSR articles with non-DSR methods (1% = 52.98) and 31,798 non-DSR articles (1% = 317.98).

On the left, we show the top 20 methods with the largest positive difference between DSR and non-DSR articles. For example, we found that articles using computational algorithms account for the largest difference where the DSR ratio is higher than the non-DSR ratio: about 26% vs. 10%. On the right, we show the top 20 methods with the largest negative difference between DSR and non-DSR articles.

5 Implications and Discussion

Our findings contribute to greater transparency in the publication priorities of major IS outlets (see Figs. 2 and 3). As a result, IS researchers may be able to make more informed decisions about potential submissions to specific outlets. Such overviews could also inform reviewers, editors, or track and program chairs who are managing the diversity of research approaches published in each outlet. This article also contributes to strengthening the position of DSR as a research method in IS. There is an ongoing debate about the identity of the IS discipline [40], but also about the identity and legitimization of DSR in particular [41]. Our findings show that there are a number of theories that are frequently used in DSR but rarely in non-DSR articles, and vice versa. This is also true for the use of (additional) research methods in these studies (see Figs. 8 and 12). Our results show where DSR is enriching the IS discipline and highlight areas that may be underexplored by articles following other, more established research paradigms.

There are also implications for practice, as the presented approach could be applied to different industries. Essentially, three things are needed: (1) a domain ontology that organizes and describes important key terms, (2) a procedure that classifies sentences and isolates statements that relate to the actual documents, (3) a processing pipeline. The processing pipeline takes unstructured documents as input and identifies domain-specific key terms and concepts in sentences describing these documents. The resulting datasets can be further analyzed with dynamic data visualization as proposed in our dashboard prototype. In healthcare, for example, patient records could be analyzed to determine the frequency of symptoms or treatments. Governments could analyze existing policies for similarities to optimize and consolidate duplicative regulations. Larger companies could improve knowledge management and retrieval by ontologically indexing technical reports or project documentations.

However, the approach is not without limitations. By using the IS Ontology to identify key terms in the text of articles, there may be terms that are not included in

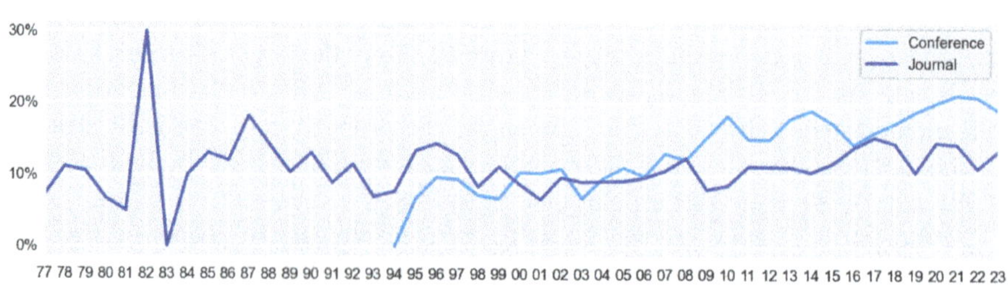

Fig. 3 Average ratio of DSR articles by type of outlet and years

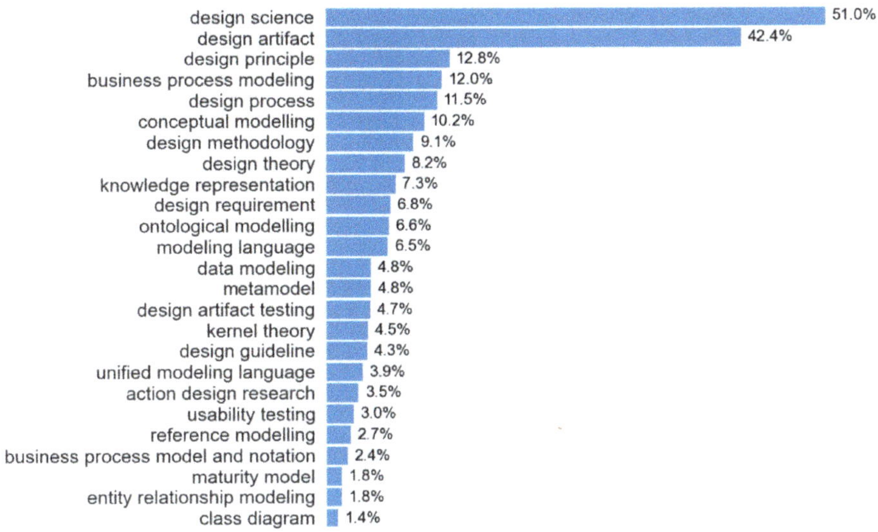

Fig. 4 Ratio of DSR articles that utilize DSR-related key terms (top 20)

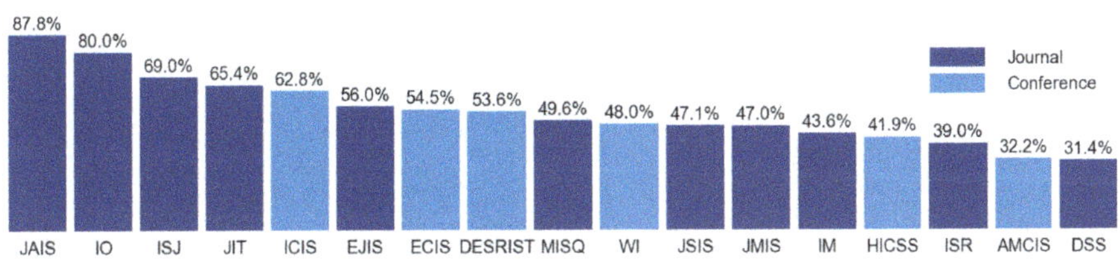

Fig. 5 Ratio of DSR articles that use theories by outlets

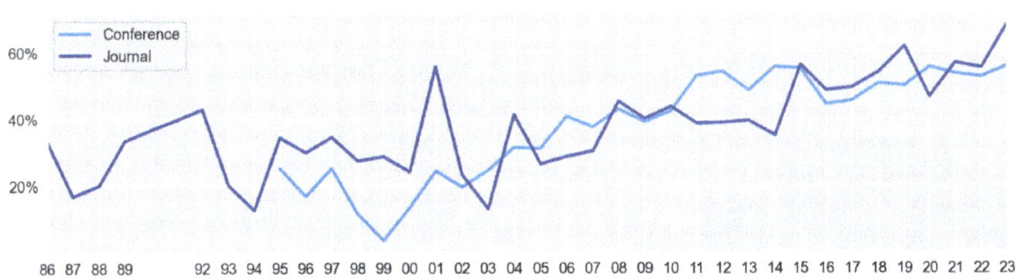

Fig. 6 Average ratio of theory-related DSR articles in conferences versus journals

the ontology, such as emerging theories or methods. Future work could attempt to develop methods to automatically update domain ontologies with new terminology. In addition, we only used sentences that were classified as describing a focal article (see Sect. 3.2). Sentences describing related work or background information may contain additional information that could be attributed to articles. As a result, we

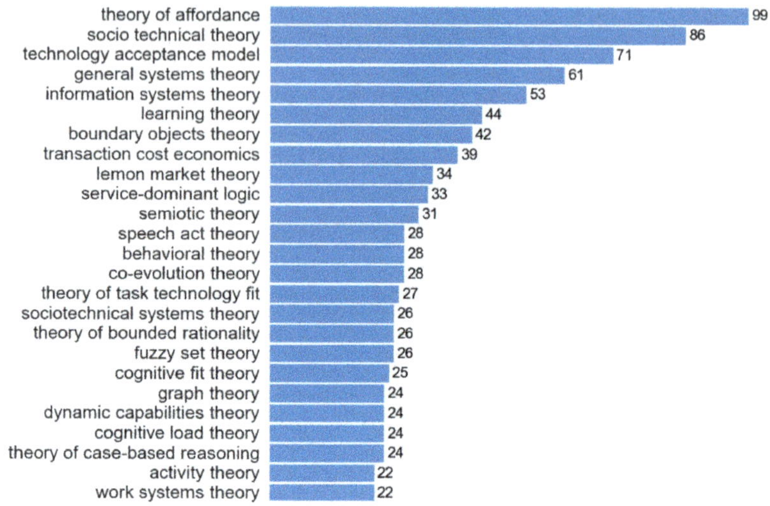

Fig. 7 Top 25 named theories in DSR articles by count of articles

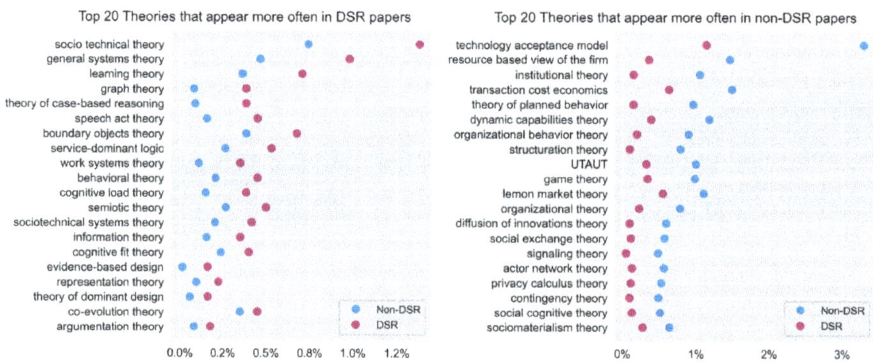

Fig. 8 Largest differences in utilized theories: DSR vs. non-DSR articles

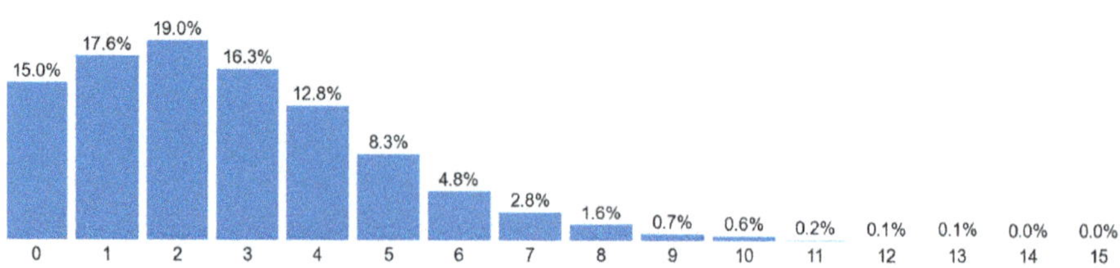

Fig. 9 Ratio of DSR articles by count of additional methods

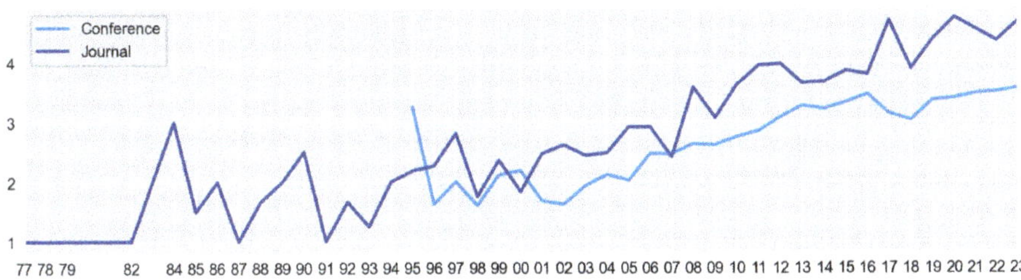

Fig. 10 Average count of additional methods in DSR articles

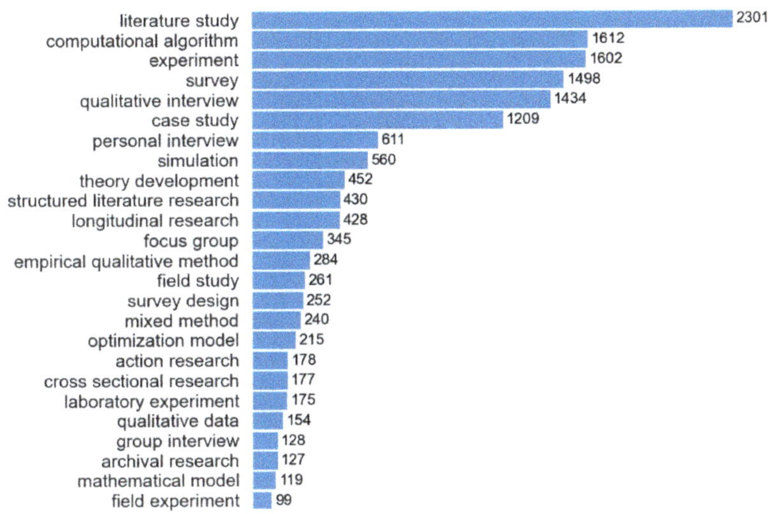

Fig. 11 Top 25 additional methods used in DSR articles by count of DSR articles

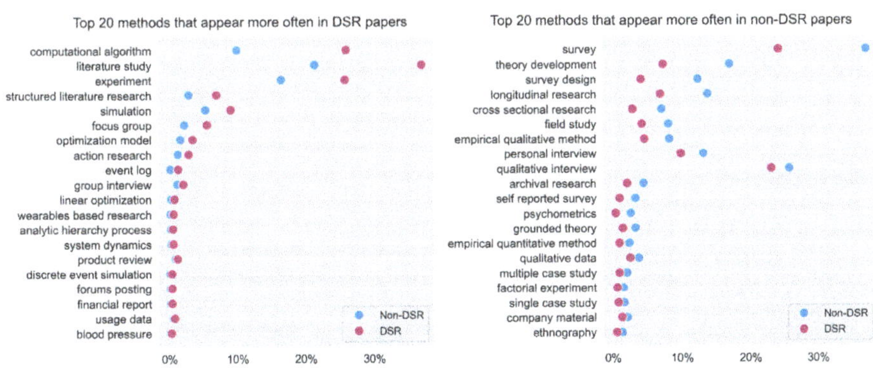

Fig. 12 Biggest differences in methods: DSR vs. non-DSR articles

may have missed key terms in some articles. Furthermore, we took a pragmatic approach in training our classifier with all articles from DESRIST and Prat et al. [18] without checking for misclassifications in their results. In addition, a more nuanced distinction between articles that present advances in DSR methods versus articles that actually apply DSR would be interesting for future work.

6 Conclusion

This research has implications for how we might perform literature reviews. We provided a proof of concept for performing ontology-based computational literature reviews on large collections of research articles. We further demonstrated the flexibility of this approach by integrating a machine learning classifier to identify articles that employ more complex research methodologies. In contrast, manually extracting similar insights from thousands of research articles would be infeasible due to the amount of work required.

Our main contributions are in the following areas: We have presented a method for ontology-based computational literature reviews that combine domain ontologies and sentence classification to derive qualitative insights. In addition, we developed a DSR classifier with high accuracy and gained detailed insights into the distribution of DSR articles, as well as the use of theories and methods that differ from other methodologies in the IS discipline. We also developed and implemented an interactive dashboard prototype that allows users to interactively experience the review results. The prototype can be accessed via a link in the reference section [17].

The results presented in this article inform researchers about the methods and theories used in DSR. They also provide information about the distribution of DSR articles in IS publications. In addition, this research may encourage researchers to use comparable methods for computational literature reviews in order to include a larger number of articles.

References

1. Vaswani, A., Shazeer, N., Parmar, N., Uszkoreit, J., Jones, L., Gomez, A.N., Kaiser, Ł. & Polosukhin, I. (2017). Attention is All you Need. In *Conference on Neural Information Processing Systems (NIPS)*.
2. Li, J., Larsen, K., & Abbasi, A. (2020). TheoryOn: A design framework and system for unlocking Behavioral knowledge through ontology learning. *MIS Quarterly, 44*(4), 1733–1772.
3. Larsen, K. R., & Bong, C. H. (2016). A tool for addressing construct identity in literature reviews and meta-analyses. *MIS Quarterly, 40*(3), 529–551.
4. Anisienia, A., Mueller, R.M., Kupfer, A. & Staake, T. (2021). Research Method Classification with Deep Transfer Learning for Semi-Automatic Meta-Analysis of Information Systems Papers. In *Hawaii International Conference on System Sciences (HICSS)*.

5. Ebert, L.S., Huettemann, S. & Mueller, R.M. (2023). Hey Article, What Are You About? Question Answering for Information Systems Articles through Transformer Models for Long Sequences. In *Hawaii International Conference on System Sciences (HICSS).*
6. Huettemann, S. (2023). Automated Knowledge Extraction from IS Research Articles Combining Sentence Classification and Ontological Annotation. In *International Conference on Business Informatics and Information Systems (WI).*
7. Hevner, A. R., March, S. T., Park, J., & Ram, S. (2004). Design science in information systems research. *MIS Quarterly, 28*(1), 75–105.
8. Deng, Q., Wang, Y. & Ji, S. (2017). Design Science Research in Information Systems: A Systematic Literature Review 2001–2015. In *International Conference on Information Resources Management (CONF-IRM).*
9. Nagle, T., Doyle, C., Alhassan, I. M., & Sammon, D. (2022). The research method we need or deserve? A literature review of the design science research landscape. *Communications of the Association for Information Systems, 50.*
10. Möller, F., Strobel, G., Schoormann, T. & Hansen, M.R.P. (2022). Unveiling the Cloak: Kernel Theory Use in Design Science Research. In *International Conference on Information Systems (ICIS).*
11. Indulska, M., & Recker, J. (2010). Design science in IS research: A literature analysis. In *Information systems foundations: The role of design science.* ANU Press.
12. Burton-Jones, A., Chen, H., Gupta, A., Hevner, A. R., Ketter, W., Jeffrey Parsons, H., Rao, R., Sarkar, S., & Yoo, Y. (2017). Editors comments: Diversity of design science research. *MIS Quarterly, 41*(1), iii–xviii.
13. Cahenzli, M. & Winter, R. (2023). Writing DSR Articles for Maximum Impact, In *European Conference on Information Systems (ECIS).*
14. Peffers, K., Tuunanen, T., & Niehaves, B. (2018). Design science research genres: Introduction to the special issue on exemplars and criteria for applicable design science research. *European Journal of Information Systems, 27*(2), 129–139.
15. Winter, R. (2008). Design science research in Europe. *European Journal of Information Systems, 17*(5), 470–475.
16. Mueller, R.M., Huettemann, S., Larsen, K.R., Yan, S. & Handler, A. (2022). Toward an Information Systems Ontology. In *International Conference on Design Science Research in Information Systems and Technology (DESRIST).*
17. Huettemann, S., Mueller, R.M. & Dinter, B. (2024). *GitHub Repository: Design Science Research Dashboard.* Retrieved March 29, 2024, https://github.com/sebastianhuettemann/dsr_dashboard
18. Prat, N., Comyn-Wattiau, I., & Akoka, J. (2015). A taxonomy of evaluation methods for information systems Artifacts. *Journal of Management Information Systems, 32*(3), 229–267.
19. Kitchenham, B. A., & Charters, S. (2007). *Guidelines for performing systematic literature reviews in software engineering.* Keele University.
20. Okoli, C. (2015). A guide to conducting a standalone systematic literature review. *Communications of the Association for Information Systems, 37.*
21. Webster, J., & Watson, R. T. (2002). Analyzing the past to prepare for the future: Writing a literature review. *MIS Quarterly, 26.*
22. Mueller, R.M. & Huettemann, S. (2018). Extracting Causal Claims from Information Systems Papers with Natural Language Processing for Theory Ontology Learning. In *Hawaii International Conference on System Sciences (HICSS).*
23. Schmiedel, T., Müller, O., & Vom Brocke, J. (2019). Topic Modeling as a strategy of inquiry in organizational research: A tutorial with an application example on organizational culture. *Organizational Research Methods, 22*(4), 941–968.
24. Storey, V. C., Lukyanenko, R., & Castellanos, A. (2023). Conceptual Modeling: Topics, themes, and technology trends. *ACM Computing Surveys, 55*(14s), 1–38.
25. Peffers, K., Tuunanen, T., Rothenberger, M. A., & Chatterjee, S. (2007). A design science research methodology for information systems research. *Journal of Management Information Systems, 24*(3), 45–77.

26. Claver, E., González, R., & Llopis, J. (2000). An analysis of research in information systems (1981–1997). *Information & Management, 37*(4), 181–195.
27. Vessey, I., Ramesh, V., & Glass, R. L. (2002). Research in information systems: An empirical study of diversity in the discipline and its journals. *Journal of Management Information Systems, 19*(2), 129–174.
28. French, A. M., & Shim, J. P. (2011). Multinational diversity in IS research: The effects of education on publication outlets. *Journal of Information Technology, 26*(4), 313–322.
29. Kupfer, A. (2018). Research Methods in the Information Systems Discipline: A Literature Analysis of Conference Papers. In *Americas Conference on Information Systems (AMCIS).*
30. Riedl, R. & Rueckel, D. (2011). Historical Development of Research Methods in the Information Systems Discipline. In *Americas Conference on Information Systems (AMCIS).*
31. Pan, S. L., Nishant, R., Tuunanen, T., & Nah, F. F.-H. (2023). Literature review in the generative AI era - how to make a compelling contribution. *The Journal of Strategic Information Systems, 32*(3), 101788.
32. Schryen, G., Marrone, M. & Yang, J. (2024). Adopting Generative AI for Literature Reviews: An Epistemological Perspective. In *Hawaii International Conference on System Sciences (HICSS).*
33. Susarla, A., Gopal, R., Thatcher, J. B., & Sarker, S. (2023). The Janus effect of generative AI: Charting the path for responsible conduct of scholarly activities in information systems. *Information Systems Research, 34*(2), 399–408.
34. AIS (2021). *Senior Scholars' Basket of Journals.* Retrieved November 15, 2024, https://aisnet.org/page/SeniorScholarBasket
35. GROBID (2024). *GROBID-A machine learning software for extracting information from scholarly documents.* Retrieved May 01, 2024, from https://github.com/kermitt2/grobid
36. Honnibal, M. & Montani, I. (2022). *Spacy usage documentation-rule-based matching.* Retrieved January 12, 2024, from https://spacy.io/usage/rule-based-matching
37. SciKit Learn (2024). *Scikit Learn—Random Forest Classifier*. Retrieved January 5, 2024, from https://www.scikit-learn/stable/modules/generated/sklearn/ensemble/RandomForestClassifier.html
38. Xgboost Developers (2024). XGBoost Documentation—XGBoost 2.0.3 documentation. Retrieved January 05, 2024, from https://xgboost.readthedocs.io/en/stable/index.html
39. AIS (2024). *Senior Scholars' List of Premier Journals.* Retrieved May 01, 2024, https://aisnet.org/page/SeniorScholarListofPremierJournals
40. Schütte, R., Ahlemann, F., Becker, J., Legner, C., Lehrer, C., Wiesche, M., & Richter, G. (2022). Quo Vadis information systems research in times of digitalization? *Business & Information Systems Engineering, 64*(4), 529–540.
41. Frank, U. (2018). *Towards a pluralistic conception of research methods in information systems.*, DuEPublico: Duisburg-Essen Publications Online. University of Duisburg-Essen.

Addressing the Challenge to Measure Information Security Behavior: Toward a Holistic Metric with Scavenger Hunts

Martin Brehmer and Raphaela Stöckl

Abstract Cyberattacks and data breaches lead to high costs for organizations worldwide. Information security education and training awareness programs are one of the most important countermeasures. Here, assessing individuals' level of information security awareness is a crucial task. Regarding this, one of the major challenges is to measure security behavior, a core dimension of security aware- ness. This is because it is often assessed indirectly through questionnaires, which could bias metrics. Therefore, our overarching goal is to develop a more holistic metric that considers and integrates actual human behavior. In this design science research study, we present the status quo of our research, namely a prototypical instance for such a measurement approach, and initial meta-requirements based on two design iterations and pilot tests: a scavenger hunt to measure the consequences of real-world interactions, based on the Human-Aspect-of-Information- Security-Questionnaire as a scientific foundation.

1 Introduction

The annual cost of cyberattacks for German businesses has exceeded EUR 200 billion [1] for three consecutive years since 2021, and data breaches have led to an average cost of USD 4.45 million per incident worldwide [2]. Hereto, information security education, training, and awareness (SETA) programs are one of the major countermeasures [2] mitigating these tremendous business risks (Hiscox [3]). These programs aim to foster secure behavior, typically through classroom or online courses that focus on knowledge transfer as well as hands-on training, such as learning how to store sensitive data. Measuring and interpreting individuals' information security awareness (ISA) level is an essential part of these programs [4] as it

M. Brehmer (✉) · R. Stöckl
Faculty of Business and Economics, University of Augsburg, Augsburg, Germany
e-mail: martin.brehmer@uni-a.de

R. Stöckl
e-mail: raphaela.stoeckl@uni-a.de

C. M. Flath et al. (eds.), *Shaping the Digital Future Through Innovation and Practice*,
Lecture Notes in Information Systems and Organisation 85,
https://doi.org/10.1007/978-3-032-08489-7_10

indicates both the level of awareness and the learning progress within the organization. As a result, evaluated SETA efforts reveal deficiencies in the security chain and indicate areas to improve in subsequent sessions. However, the reliability, accuracy, and transparency of the applied measurement methods, as well as the expressive power of the results, are arguable and consequently pose an enormous challenge for researchers, security educators, and practitioners [5]. A key reason is that security awareness assessments are mostly based on questionnaires in research [6, 7] and practice [8] which means that information security behavior (ISB), a core dimension of ISA [4], is measured indirectly. SETA programs market leaders like KnowB4 aim to tackle this issue by including behavioral security aspects, e.g., providing an additional "personal risk score", predominantly based on responses to phishing simulations or training participation [9]. However, this neglects other critical threats such as brute force attacks on weak passwords, or dumpster diving, where criminals search for sensitive information in discarded files. In essence, questionnaires fail to measure actual ISB [6, 7], and other metrics consider behavior aspects unsatisfactory. This can lead to unwarranted confidence in organizations' resilience against cyber threats due to the inaccurate ISB measurement. For instance, knowing that a found USB stick is potentially malicious does not guarantee that it is not plugged in within the daily work routine. Consequently, organizations are vulnerable to future cyberattacks and data breaches. Beyond practical implications, researchers aiming to improve SETA programs struggle to rigorously evaluate new approaches and generate meaningful theoretical insights. Therefore, research on ISA metrics that considers different aspects of an individual's **actual ISB (aISB)** is essential for rigorous ISA assessment [7].

Our overarching research project aims to address this challenge by developing an instance and design principles for a more holistic ISA metric which includes measuring aISB as a critical dimension of ISA. Thereby, we see the potential to strengthen the effectiveness of SETA programs and their value for both practice and research. In this research-in-progress article, we present our initial steps toward this goal by answering the following research questions:

1. *How can actual security behavior be measured in an authentic environment based on a scientifically grounded information security awareness assessment?*
2. *What are initial meta-requirements and next steps for future research toward a more holistic metric for an information security awareness assessment considering both, questionnaires and actual security behavior?*

To answer these questions, we present an assessment approach implemented as a gamified version of the well-accepted and validated Human-Aspect-of-Information-Security-Questionnaire (HAIS-Q) by Parsons et al. [10]. Specifically, we create tasks for a scavenger hunt based on this questionnaire to assess the participants' level of ISA, including aISB, in an authentic environment. This means, participants follow a storyline and complete security-relevant tasks to earn assessment points. In doing so, this article contributes to design science research (DSR) by providing initial insights from an evaluated instance of a novel approach that addresses the real-world problem of inaccurate ISA metrics. Additionally, we outline meta-requirements for developing

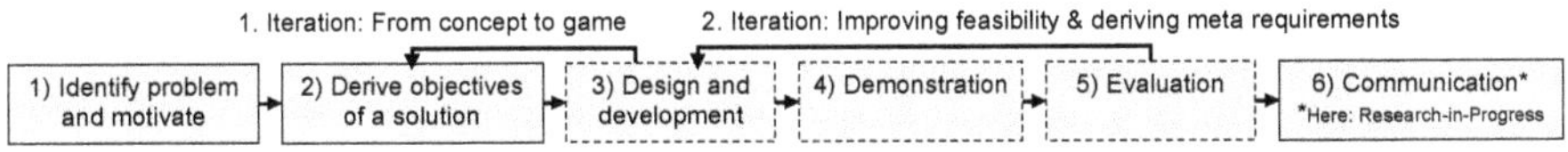

Fig. 1 Metric design process (f. Peffers et al. [11])—dashed lines show ongoing research

a more holistic metric and outline the next steps to revise the artifact and achieve our overarching goal. As we follow the DSR methodology of Peffers et al. [11], this article focuses on two iterations (see Fig. 1). The first iteration addresses the process of (a) how we derive game tasks from a validated questionnaire to cover knowledge, attitudes, and actual behavioral aspects of ISA [10], and (b) how we implement these tasks within a game prototype to measure aISB including a pilot test. The second iteration includes (a) design considerations as well as practical implementation aspects, and (b) meta-requirements derived from a second pilot test.

2 Theoretical Background and Related Work

Measuring ISA is a challenge discussed in several recent literature-review-based studies [5–7]. ISA integrates three core dimensions: security-related "gains in ***knowledge*** and positive changes in ***attitudes*** and ***behaviors***" [5] of individuals in organizations. This definition is rooted in the well-accepted knowledge-attitude-behavior model (KABM) of Kruger and Kearney [4]. Later research addresses criticism for lacking context information and a standardized measurement approach [12] by building on these three core dimensions. For instance, Parsons et al. [10] introduce the HAIS-Q, a modular questionnaire with contextualized items for all three core dimensions, validated in several iterations. However, while it seems feasible to measure knowledge and attitudes through standardized questionnaires, measuring ISB indirectly is heavily criticized as it captures self-reported expected behavior instead of aISB [7]. Thus, more mature and reliable ISA scales that consider aISB are required [7], alongside standardized questionnaires [5].

So far, according to Chaudhary et al. [5], who reference the literature review of Fertig et al. [6], previous studies on metrics mainly address two types of ISA metrics: 'knowledge-based metrics' and 'behavior-based metrics'. Knowledge-based metrics measure, e.g., aspects of the KABM by applying the HAIS-Q. In contrast, behavior-based metrics rely on data logs of security-relevant real-life events, such as the length of an employee's chosen password resulting from a change request [5, 6]. From our perspective, these terms are not entirely distinct, as knowledge-based metrics also appear to indirectly measure ISB according to the KABM, although not aISB. However, they differ in that behavior-based metrics focus on real-world data rather than knowledge-based reporting. [5]

Thus, to develop a more holistic metric, we aim to expand the existing understanding of metrics by building on the concept of knowledge-based metrics, specifically the KABM, while also considering aISB: We apply the HAIS-Q as a theoretical foundation to measure the ***knowledge*** and ***attitude*** dimensions of ISA, and further measure actual ***behavior*** through behavioral data that represent the corresponding HAIS-Q items.

Therefore, we gamify the HAIS-Q [10] by using a digital scavenger hunt (SH) game as a medium. Here, gamification serves as a motivator to (a) engage participants in a SETA context that is often perceived as burdensome [13], and (b) encourage a careful completion of the assessment tasks, potentially enhancing the survey data quality [14]. The SH employs gamification through various game-design functionalities adapted for a non-game context [15]. Technically speaking, SH is a game concept where players solve a set of tasks while interacting with the real world, e.g., searching for specific objects at a designated location. The term 'digital SH' refers to the delivery method using, e.g., a mobile application to present tasks in a motivating manner and to capture the corresponding players' responses. Thus, we utilize the SH mobile application called 'Actionbound' (AB). This platform allows, for example, the inclusion of *storytelling* (to motivate and inform where to go and what to do), *time pressure (*to foster natural behavior and a strong focus on the given task), simple single- or multiple-choice questions that are rated with *points* (to measure the ISA dimensions ***knowledge*** and ***attitude***). Additionally, this allows for tasks where ***behavior*** can be measured through the consequences of their real-life interactions, also rated with *points*. This means we develop tasks based on the HAIS-Q that have to be solved hands-on in the real world. For instance, one task is to find a specific password to access further information for the game. Here, the SH's players first have to walk to a specific location at the university. Second, once there, various general options are presented to solve the task, e.g., extracting a password from a (prepared) USB Stick that is conveniently available at the players' location, or investigating another location for hidden hints on the password. Third, the players evaluate these options, and fourth, they choose an option. Thereby, each option results in a password, but only one of them is the correct password which is awarded with points for the individuals' ranking in the *leaderboard* (to ensure automatic ISA assessments [6]). In summary, our SH includes game-design elements such as *storytelling*, *time pressure*, scorable *points*, and providing a *leaderboard,* which is known to potentially work in a SETA context [16].

This research-in-progress article presents the current state of our research, focusing on meta-requirements for rigorously deriving meaningful SH tasks rather than a final metric. In the following, we offer a preliminary instance of how we strived to measure ISA including aISB. However, a final metric that interprets the measurements requires, e.g., an assessment of the validity and confirmability of the scoring system.

3 Scavenger Hunt Approach to Measure Security Awareness

In order to develop the SH tasks that are implemented in AB, we applied the HAIS-Q [10] as a scaffolding construct. This means that the overall structure of the SH was based on the HAIS-Q's focus areas and all tasks that have been developed related to the content and purpose of the corresponding HAIS-Q items. With that, we basically followed the process (phase 1) for developing an ISA metric of Rohan et al. [7], but with a focus on converting an existing scale (HAIS-Q) toward a more realistic measurement approach that considers not only cybersecurity knowledge and attitudes but also aISB as impact indicators for SETA programs [5].

Consequently, our **first design iteration** focused on a) developing SH tasks based on the HAIS-Q and b) evaluating the approach with a pilot study as a proof of concept to detect technical and procedural errors. To derive the SH tasks, we conducted two initial team workshop days. This included reviewing and implementing the tasks. Since the HAIS-Q is modular [10], we considered 4 out of the 7 focus areas (information handling, social media use, email use, password management) to set the duration of the SH at less than 1.5 h, as the longer the duration, the more likely the results are to be biased. A pilot study was conducted ($n = 17$ participants, students, and research assistants) to find technical and procedural errors and to receive qualitative feedback. The participants reported some technical problems that occurred and found it motivating but slightly too long. It is noteworthy, that no participant mentioned the measurement itself to be burdensome. Examples of SH tasks are provided in Table 1.

Table 1 Examples of SH tasks that are derived from HAIS-Q items of Parsons et al. [10]

HAIS-Q reference item	SH tasks based on the HAIS-Q items
Focus Category: Information handling; Sub-category: Inserting removable media 1. If I find a USB stick in a public place, I shouldn´t plug it into my work computer 2. If I find a USB stick in a public place, nothing bad can happen if I plug it into my work computer 3. I wouldn´t plug a USB stick found in a public place into my work computer	Once you have found the papers and USB sticks, you will receive a cryptic email that gives you hints to find the password needed to open the encrypted file You have the choice to use one of the USB sticks in the room or go to the office mentioned in the email to get the password. Return the USB stick. What is the password?
Focus Category: Email use; Sub-category: Clicking on links in emails from known senders 1. I am allowed to click on any links in emails from people I know 2. It´s always safe to click on links in emails from people I know 3. I don´t always click on links in emails just because they come from someone I know	[...] Your mobile phone is making a noise... What was that? - While walking across the campus, you notice that your work colleague, with whom you have already done some projects has sent you an email. Check your student email inbox. [...] Get the password for the [...] Information Hub, where all information about the university is stored. Enter the password here: [...]

In our **second design iteration**, we focused on (a) shortening the game and eliminating technological errors, e.g., an email that participants were supposed to receive during the game did not reach everyone. Further, we strived to (b) assess the feasibility of our SH regarding its practical operability and potential for a more holistic ISA metric. To achieve (a), we dropped the focus category password management which led to a new duration of ca. 35–45 min. For (b), we followed the first steps of phase 2 (scale development) from Chaudhary et al. [5] and considered the criteria of good ISA metrics [17] for developing a valuable metric approach for practitioners and researchers. To develop a lightweight metric, we adjusted the maximum points for the focus areas among 3 different levels (400 points, 961 points, 1175 points). This enabled us to check whether there is a minimum sum of achievable points without bias. In both tests, the participants were informed that they were in a test situation for research purposes. The use of a pseudonym also ensured no further conclusions concerning individual participants could be drawn. We then conducted a second pilot test ($n = 21$) to receive data for a score comparison. In more detail: All participants completed a pre-test covering the three selected focus areas of the HAIS-Q. Thereby, we calculated Cronbach's α to ensure overall reliability for further comparison. Given that the HAIS-Q is validated [10], the meta-analysis on reported alpha values in leading academic journals by Taber [18], and considering our small sample sizes, we state our values to be acceptable: information handling: $\alpha = .605$,social media use: $\alpha = .736$; email use: $\alpha = .698$. Subsequently, the participants played the SH. Then, we checked whether the ISA scale of Kruger and Kearney [4], e.g. applied by Firsty et al. [19], could be applied to interpret the results of the SH scores. This means, we calculated the corresponding score (HAIS-Q vs. SH) of each construct per participant and interpreted it with the help of the HAIS-Q scale. In 28 construct comparisons (out of *3 focus areas* x $n = 21$ in total) both scales lead to the same conclusion. Then, in 33 comparisons, the SH scale was lower than the corresponding HAIS-Q scale. We state that the SH scale is still valid because the data reveal that these participants lost their points mostly in behavior-based tasks of the SH. This can be an indicator that our approach is successfully measuring and differentiating aISB. In only two comparisons, the SH scaled better than the corresponding HAIS-Q scale, but it must be mentioned that both would have scaled equally if the participants had reached only one point more in the HAIS-Q. Thus, we assume our scales to be comparable to a certain degree. However, the results also indicate that there should be at least ca. 1175 points per AB category to improve overall accuracy (2% avg. difference between HAIS-Q and SH vs. 19–23% avg. diff.). Based on these findings, we suggest six initial meta-requirements for the further development of a more holistic metric which can be seen in Fig. 2.

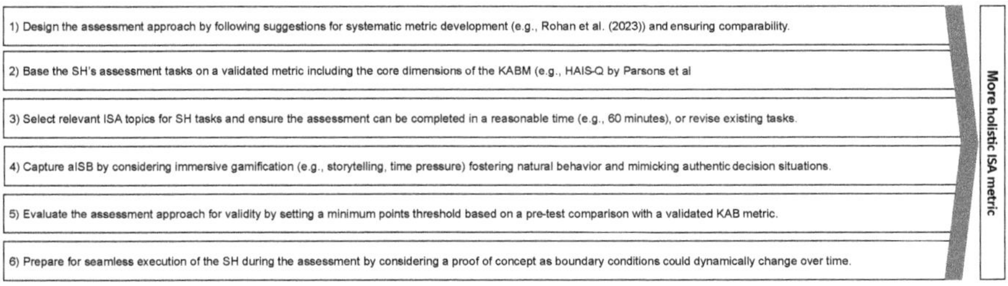

Fig. 2 Meta-requirements toward a more holistic ISA metric that considers aISB

4 Limitations and Future Research

This article provides insight into how to measure ISA, including aISB. Our pilot studies show that the assessment prototype is functional and indicate that the HAIS-Q-based metric might be applicable to our SH scales. Nevertheless, due to the limitations of this study, e.g. the small sample size of our pilot tests, further validation is needed, e.g., by repeating the study with more participants. We also plan to revise the SH prototype toward a more valid reward system. Additionally, expert interviews will be conducted to validate the correctness and practical relevance and to reduce subjectivity that might have influenced the derivation process from the HAIS-Q items to the SH tasks. Moreover, we did not control for existing knowledge. This is consistent with real assessment situations but should be considered as it provides information for further validation of a final metric. We acknowledge that developing such an SH is resource-intensive. However, an SH concept like ours could be reused and customized, e.g., by considering further time savings through the use of generative artificial intelligence to develop content such as a motivating narrative or quizzes [20].

References

1. Wintergerst, R. (2023). *Wirtschaftsschutz 2023*. https://www.bitkom.org/sites/main/files/2023-09/Bitkom-Charts-Wirtschaftsschutz-Cybercrime.pdf. Accessed June 26, 2024.
2. IBM. (2023). *Cost of a Data Breach Report 2023, Ponemon Institute & IBM Security*. https://www.ibm.com/reports/data-breach. Accessed June 26, 2024.
3. Hiscox Ltd. (2023). *Hiscox Cyber Readiness Report 2023*. https://www.hiscoxgroup.com/sites/group/files/documents/2023-10/Hiscox-Cyber-Readiness-Report-2023.pdf. Accessed June 26, 2024.
4. Kruger, H. A., & Kearney, W. D. (2006). A prototype for assessing information security awareness. *Computers & Security, 25*(4), 289–296. https://doi.org/10.1016/j.cose.2006.02.008
5. Chaudhary, S., Gkioulos, V., & Katsikas, S. (2022). Developing metrics to assess the effectiveness of cybersecurity awareness program. *Journal of Cybersecurity, 8*(1), 1. https://doi.org/10.1093/cybsec/tyac006

6. Fertig, T., Schütz, A. E. & Weber, K. (2020). Current Issues Of Metrics For Information Security Awareness. In *Proceedings of the 28th European Conference on Information Systems (ECIS)*. June 15–17, 2020.
7. Rohan, R., Pal, D., Hautamäki, J., Funilkul, S., Chutimaskul, W., & Thapliyal, H. (2023). A systematic literature review of cybersecurity scales assessing information security awareness. *Heliyon, 9*(3), Article e14234. https://doi.org/10.1016/j.heliyon.2023.e14234
8. KnowB4. (2023). *KnowBe4 Technical Documentation for the Security Awareness Proficiency Assessment (SAPA)*. https://www.knowbe4.com/hubfs/KnowBe4-Security-Awareness-Proficiency-Assessment-SAPA-Technical-Document_EN-US.pdf. Accessed June 26, 2024.
9. KnowB4. (2024). *Risk Scores*. https://support.knowbe4.com/hc/en-us/articles/360001358728-Virtual-Risk-Officer-VRO-and-Risk-Score-Guide.
10. Parsons, K., Calic, D., Pattinson, M., Butavicius, M., McCormac, A., & Zwaans, T. (2017). The human aspects of information security questionnaire (HAIS-Q): Two further validation studies. *Computers & Security, 66*, 40–51. https://doi.org/10.1016/j.cose.2017.01.004
11. Peffers, K., Tuunanen, T., Rothenberger, M. A., & Chatterjee, S. (2007). A design science research methodology for information systems research. *Journal of Management Information Systems, 24*(3), 45–77. https://doi.org/10.2753/MIS0742-1222240302
12. McCormac, A., Zwaans, T., Parsons, K., Calic, D., Butavicius, M., & Pattinson, M. (2017). Individual differences and information security awareness. *Computers in Human Behavior, 69*, 151–156. https://doi.org/10.1016/j.chb.2016.11.065
13. Hu, S., Hsu, C., & Zhou, Z. (2022). Security Education, Training, and Awareness Programs: Literature Review. *Journal of Computer Information Systems, 62*(4), 752–764. https://doi.org/10.1080/08874417.2021.1913671
14. Harms, J., Biegler, S., Wimmer, C., Kappel, K. & Grechenig, T. (2015). Gamification of Online Surveys: Design Process, Case Study, and Evaluation. In S. Barbosa, M. Fetter, J.A. González et al. (Eds.), *Proceedings of the 15th IFIP TC 13 International Conference, Bamberg* (pp. 219–236). September 14–18, 2015. Springer.
15. Deterding, S., Dixon, D., Khaled, R., & Nacke, L. (2011). From game design elements to gamefulness. In A. Lugmayr, H. Franssila, C. Safran et al. (Eds.), *Proceedings of the 15th International Academic MindTrek Conference Envisioning Future Media Environments, MindTrek '11: Academic MindTrek 2011, Tampere Finland* (pp. 9–15). September 28–30, 2011. ACM.
16. Brehmer, M. & Reinelt, R. (2023). Gamifying a Learning Management System: Narrative and Team Leaderboard in the Context of Effective Information Security Education. In *Proceedings of the 56th Annual Hawaii International Conference on System Sciences*. January 03–06, 2023.
17. Spitzner, L. (2024). *Security Awareness Metrics*. https://www.sans.org/blog/security-awareness-metrics/. Accessed June 26, 2024.
18. Taber, K. S. (2018). The Use of Cronbach's Alpha When Developing and Reporting Research Instruments in Science Education. *Research in Science Education, 48*(6), 1273–1296. https://doi.org/10.1007/s11165-016-9602-2
19. Firsty Arisya, K., Ruldeviyani, Y., Prakoso, R. & Lailatul Fadhilah, A. (2020). Measurement of Information Security Awareness Level: A Case Study of Mobile Banking (M-Banking) Users. In *2020 Fifth International Conference on Informatics and Computing (ICIC)*. IEEE.
20. Brehmer, M. & Buonassisi, V. (2024). Educators' Friend—Applying Generative AI to Create Effective Digital Learning Objects for Information Security Education: Toward Initial Design Principles. In *Proceedings of the 57th Annual Hawaii International Conference on System Sciences*. January 03–06, 2024.

Cybersecurity Awareness Training for Industrial Software Developers via a Serious Game for Code Review

Research Paper

Andrei-Cristian Iosif, Ulrike Lechner, Maria Pinto-Albuquerque, and Tiago Espinha Gasiba

Abstract Software developers must not only be capable of producing secure code, but must also possess the ability to identify security vulnerabilities when evaluating their peers' work. The necessary awareness of this is crucial in industrial environments that handle critical infrastructure. The present work explores a method to empower software developers on the topic of secure coding, through the practice of code review. We propose a serious game, called the "DuckDebugger", specifically designed for use in industrial settings and to address the needs of software developers, and implement it across 13 events together with over 200 industrial developers. Our research is based on insights gained from deploying this game in an industrial context. The contributions of this work include the design of the serious game and the context in which it is deployed, an analysis of the perceived benefits, and practical recommendations for practitioners seeking to bridge code review and cybersecurity together.

A.-C. Iosif (✉) · T. E. Gasiba
Siemens AG, Munich, Germany
e-mail: andrei-cristian.iosif@siemens.com

T. E. Gasiba
e-mail: tiago.gasiba@siemens.com

A.-C. Iosif · U. Lechner
Universität der Bundeswehr München, Munich, Germany
e-mail: ulrike.lechner@unibw.de

M. Pinto-Albuquerque
Instituto Universitário de Lisboa (ISCTE-IUL), ISTAR, Lisbon, Portugal
e-mail: maria.albuquerque@iscte-iul.pt

C. M. Flath et al. (eds.), *Shaping the Digital Future Through Innovation and Practice*, Lecture Notes in Information Systems and Organisation 85,
https://doi.org/10.1007/978-3-032-08489-7_11

1 Introduction

In the context of accelerated digital transformation, cybersecurity has become more important for businesses, with technology-driven risk management becoming prevalent. Cybersecurity can be ensured through auditing activities. A study from AuditBoard, by Chambers [4], underscores this trend, positioning cybersecurity as a top concern: in their report, over 80% of respondents consider cybersecurity high-risk and give it the top spot for expected audit efforts in 2024. In our study, we focus on code review as an audit activity.

Throughout the software development lifecycle (SDLC), weaknesses can be avoided at multiple stages. By shifting security *left*, in the earlier phases, vulnerabilities in software can be caught at earlier stages of development and this reduces the costs of remediating the flaw. One way to approach this is through automation via DevSecOps.

According to a survey from GitLab [7], resulted from 4000 responses, *"68% of the security professionals surveyed believe it's a programmer's job to write secure code but they also think less than half of developers can spot security holes."*. Advances in automation can lessen the burden of identifiying security weaknesses in code, but some challenges remain. As shown by Gonzalez et al. [8], security testing is complex and requires resources to guide developers. One of the main challenges of application security testing (AppSec) within a DevSecOps environment is collaboration, as per Rajapakse et al. [25].

One way to address non-automatable security activities is by performing code reviews. The challenge to this approach is building awareness on security issues. The associated tradeoff is that time and money is saved later, which offsets the initial resources required to build developer awareness.

We propose a software serious game (SG) that is meant to raise security awareness by empowering practitioners towards performing security-savvy code reviews, and asses their perception of our proposed approach.

The main contributions of this work are:

- **"DuckDebugger" Artifact:** insights into the design lessons across the deployment of the serious game, as distilled from 13 events in the industry, and
- **Artifact Evaluation:** interpretation of the results from our events in the industry. We focus our analysis to cover to following dimensions: the suitability of the proposed serious game as a means of raising practitioner's security awareness, and assessing code review as a means towards empowering developers.

This paper lays out the lessons learned developing and evaluating our proposed SG, for practitioners looking to improve their AppSec posture in an industrial context. Furthermore, we provide a comprehensive reference to the research community wishing to address cybersecurity through code reviews, via SGs for the industry.

This work is organized as follows: Sect. 2 provides related previous work. In Sect. 3 we will introduce the methodology of our research, together with the research questions. Next, Sect. 4 will present the deisgn, context and challenges of the serious game artifact. Section 5 introduces the results of our work together with the resulting discussion. Finally, Sect. 6 concludes our work and, based on our findings, presents further research directions.

2 Background and Related Work

We present the current challenges of the SDLC in terms of ensuring security through code review, introduce concepts used in the evaluations of our SG, and outline the research basis for SGs in the industry.

2.1 Standards

Our work is situated in an industrial context, where standards and compliance are mandatory and guide the work in terms of design requirements.

Ramaj et al. [26] highlight that compliance is currently a blind spot within the DevSecOps paradigm. Regarding standardization within the industry, Moyon et al. [22] have highlighted that integrating security into agile software development presents practical challenges—in heavily regulated industries, scaling agile practices and achieving compliance with security standards leads to enhanced complexity.

Industrial standards serve a dual purpose in our work. They not only enhance the value of compliant software products but also act as a key source for deriving requirements. Such requirements can be converted into actionable guidelines for code reviewers, aiding in the pursuit of secure code reviews in industrial settings.

Relevant to our work, the ISO/IEC 64223-4-1:2018-1 [15] standard on secure product development lifecycle requirements, and ISO/IEC 64223-4-2:2019-12 [16] standard on technical security requirements for IACS components both emphasize secure code review in the development lifecycle. ISO/IEC 20246:2017 [14] offers a framework for work product reviews, and ISO/IEC TR 24772-1:2019 [17] provides language-independent guidance on avoiding programming vulnerabilities. The Common Weakness Enumeration (CWE) Top 25, by MITRE Corporation [21], and OWASP Top 10, by the OWASP Foundation [23], offer secure coding practices.

2.2 Tool Support

Code reviews can benefit from tooling and automation surrounding bugs and vulnerabilities, as such we take inspiration on available tools to be integrated or accounted for in our game.

Although improving AppSec posture within organizations can be handled in multiple ways, e.g. through DevSecOps, there is little research in the area of code review as a means of heightening developers' security awareness. For the remainder of this work, the term *secure code review* shall refer to the concept of performing code review with the explicit purpose of uncovering vulnerabilities in source code.

Sánchez-Gordón & Colomo-Palacios [28] show that automation can lessen the burden of human tasks. On the other hand, Mao et al. [20] highlight how Static Code Analysis (SAST) produce false positives, which still require human filtration. Ami et al. [1] explore the behaviors and assumptions of developers regarding SAST tools and showcase an industrial tendency of tool over-reliance and lack of awareness on *false negatives*. Rindell et al. [27] explore how enriching results from SAST tools is insufficient on their own and propose manual code review as one of the ways to tackle security-related tech debt. SAST tools are unfit to catch business logic or architectural security flaws within source code, making false negatives tedious to resolve. Kupsch & Miller [18] emphasize that, despite the benefits of automation, manual reviews are still required to ensure good coverage to find and address vulnerabilities.

Recent developments in artificial intelligence (AI) through breakthroughs in Large-Language Models (LLMs) and their application show promise in offering more robust decision-supporting tooling, as highlighted by Fu et al. Fu & Tantithamthavorn [6]. Perry et al. [24] investigate the security of code produced when using AI assistants—their findings show that participants with AI Assistants wrote less secure code than those without, all the while being more likely to believe their code was secure.

2.3 Human Factors

As code review can be seen a dialogue between the code author and the reviewer, we look into potential non-technical factors that may influence our design.

Bosu et al. [3] suggest that industry professionals find reviews valuable mainly when they enhance code quality. MacLeod et al. [19] explored what makes a code review useful to code contributors and highlight challenges associated with code review which pertain wholly to human aspects, such as misguided review focus, process ambiguity, and insufficient training.

We draw upon the work of Hänsch & Benenson [9] and Tessem [31] for the concepts of awareness and empowerment respectively.

Hänsch & Benenson [9] outline IT security awareness through three dimensions: understanding vulnerabilities (*perception*), knowledge of protection methods (*protection*), and willingness to engage in secure practices (*behaviour*). Meanwhile, empowerment, as defined by Tessem [31], incorporates both structural and psychological aspects, highlighting the balance between access to resources and personal motivation, aiming to foster an environment that enhances autonomy and effectiveness. Hence, empowerment in an IT context can be loosely defined as the fostering of an environment conducive to enhanced autonomy and effectiveness within the workplace.

Our work aims to bridge technical and human aspects, i.e. security awareness and developer empowerment,9 to enhance cybersecurity awareness and encourage practical application in both user and industrial contexts. We advocate for the use of SGs as an educational tool, supported by the findings of Siami Namin et al. [30] and Hendrix et al. [10], to effectively convey our message and influence behavior.

Our artifact aims to provide practitioners with cybersecurity awareness, empower them and positively shape their future behavior. The game's name, *"DuckDebugger"*, is a reference to the "rubber duck debugging" concept from Hunt & Thomas [12], where explaining a problem to an inanimate object often leads to a solution.

3 Methodology

The present work offers a preliminary set of findings collected from building and evaluating a serious game software artifact focused on empowering software developers on secure code review.

Our research approach is anchored in the Action Design Research (ADR) method by Sein et al. [29], which focuses on creating and assessing IT artifacts within an organizational context to address specific problems. ADR emphasizes iterative collaboration between researchers and practitioners, intertwining problem understanding, action, and evaluation. It operationalizes the principles of Design Science Research by embedding the artifact development process within organizational contexts, thus bridging the gap between theory and practice by iteratively designing and evaluating artifacts in situ.

Starting from a problem formulation, i.e. *"How to empower developers towards performing secure code review?"*, we—a team of practitioners and academics—iteratively gain knowledge and refine our artifact to address the industrial challenge of security-centric code review through our serious game. The present work showcases our design and its evaluation after 3 design iterations and 13 game events. The events took place from May 2023 to February 2024, with a total of more than 200 participants.

Situated in an industrial software setting where cybersecurity is vital, our goal is to enhance code review effectiveness and heighten security awareness. Key to our approach is the design and assessment of a serious game for software developers. With two researchers possessing extensive experience in industrial software development and secure coding, we collaborate with the industry to introduce fresh academic perspectives and rigorously evaluate existing practices. The authors Iosif et al. [13], have shown in a previous work that embedding a serious game within workshops performed in the industry is well-received. This work presents the design after 13 events over 10 months. Table 1 presents an overview of the events that made up our research. The design cycles can be laid out as follows: **(1.)** Initial Design (events 1–3), **v2.)** First refinements (events 4–12) and **(3.)** Usability Refinements (event 13). The participants to the events were all software developers specialized in either

Table 1 Events overview

Event No.	1	2	3	4	5	6	7	8	9	10	11	12	13	Total
Date	05.2023	05.2023	06.2023	11.2023	11.2023	11.2023	12.2023	12.2023	01.2024	01.2024	02.2024	02.2024	02.2024	–
Location	Online	Online	United Kingdom	Germany (Hybrid)	Germany	China	Online	China	Online	Germany	Germany	Online	Germany (Hybrid)	–
No. Participants	14	7	16	9	20	24	30	20	16	15	24	17	12	**224**

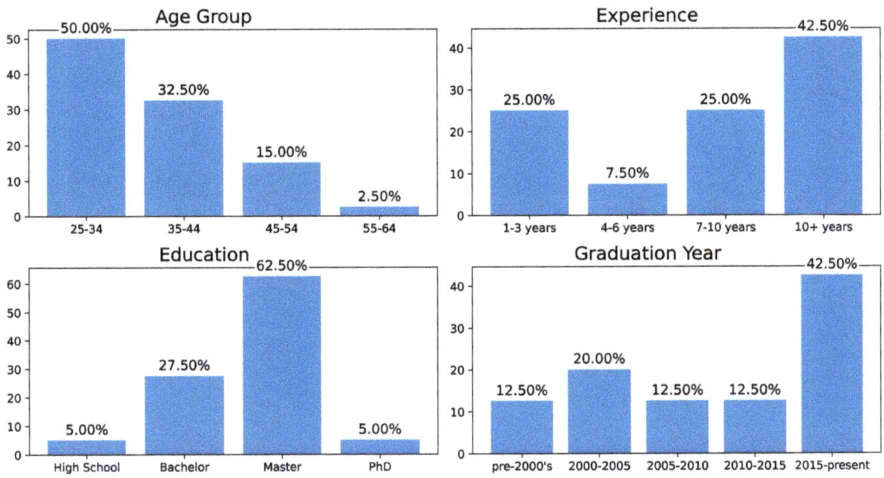

Fig. 1 Surveyee demographics

embedded or web programming. The events took place mostly in Germany, with a few hybrid-setting exceptions (international) and two events in China.

Demographic insights of the participants of the survey are depicted Fig. 1.

The participant sample is organized predominantly in an agile work format (90%), possesses recent higher education (Bachelor's or higher—95%, and 87.5% graduating after 2000) and displays good levels of industry experience.

For the first design cycle (events 1–3), the authors conducted semi-structured interviews to evaluate the game. The participants were asked to provide feedback on the platform in an open discussion, moderated by the authors. The discussion followed two points: keep and change factors. These questions offered insight and guidance towards further improving the game.

The second and (ongoing) third design cycles target to following research question (**RQ**): Is our serious game focused on code review, "*DuckDebugger*", suitable for empowering developers in cybersecurity?

We address the **RQ** by means of a questionnaire, targeting solely the DuckDebugger,4 administered to the participants after the completion of the event. The questionnaire medium was online, and participation in both the semi-structured interviews as well as the questionnaire was voluntary and anonymous. We collected a total of 65 responses.14

Table 2 presents the the questionnaire's contents: there are 14 statements, which respondents are asked to give an agreement level corresponding to a 5-point Likert scale. The questions are grouped into 4 categories, corresponding to the dimensions of empowerment, as adapted from Tessem [31].

Table 2 Questionnaire

ID	Dimension	Statement
I1	Involvement	I learned to initiate changes through code review
I2		I learned to better delegate by participating in the game
I3		The game taught me how to participate in code reviews
T1	Teamwork	The game taught me to evaluate my team's strengths
T2		The game showed how code review can improve knowledge in a project
T3		Code review is useful for information and knowledge sharing
M1	Motivation	I feel reward when performing code review in the game
M2		I gained knowledge by participating in the game
M3		I received new information by participating in the game
M4		I have a sense of power when performing code review
S1	Significance	Participating in this code review game will help me in my daily work
S2		Code reviews bring out my self-determination
S3		By participating in code review, I am aware of my competence
S4		Code reviews bring a sense of meaning to my work

4 Design of the DuckDebugger

This section presents the structure of the events conducted with the software developers. In the following sub-sections, we provide insight into the workshop's design, in terms of both technical architecture and agenda, and offer an overview of the implemented exercises (to be referred to as challenges) in our serious game.

4.1 Context

Each event was structured as a 1–3 day11 workshop, as follows: Participants first receive training on various security concepts, tailored to each event group's background. The delivery method is a combination of presentation slides, live hacking demos, and hands-on exercises. Each workshop concludes with a competitive, full-day session of exercises, similar to a Capture-The-Flag (CTF) event. Participants are asked to form teams and are presented with various types of challenges that they

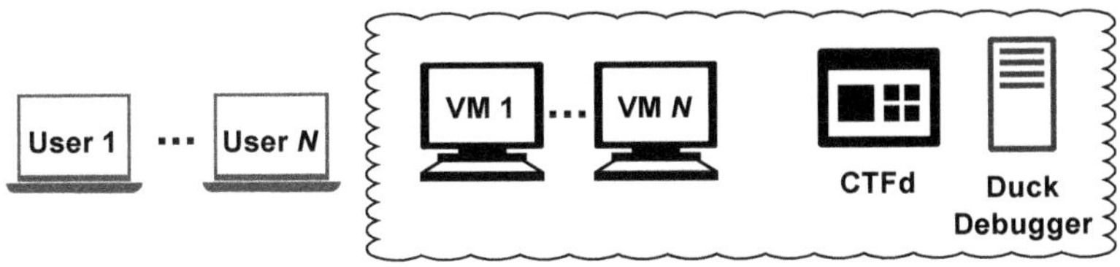

Fig. 2 Event architecture

can solve. The trainers solve an example from each class of challenges, to familiarize them with the infrastructure. The possible challenge types are: code review (the DuckDebugger), web-related, offensive challenges (binary exploitation), and defensive challenges (fixing source code which then gets evaluated against unit tests that check if the vulnerability still exists). The DuckDebugger is a standalone web application, while the rest of the challenges are pre-installed in the Virtual Machines provisioned to the participants. This modularity aims to nullify the players' setup overhead, however, external tools are not prohibited or sanctioned.13 Each correctly solved challenge reveals a code meant to be redeemed for points, as is specific to events following a CTF format. The choice of challenges to be solved is left entirely to the participants. Nonetheless, the questionnaire becomes available only after a player solves at least one DuckDebugger challenge.12 Finally, the winners of the event (i.e. participants in the team with the most points) is congratulated and the event concludes with a feedback session.

4.2 *Architecture*

The technical architecture can be observed in Fig. 2. Participants are only required to have a laptop, the rest of the event's infrastructure is cloud-based. Each participant gets provisioned their own personal virtual machine, with various offensive tooling and locally-running vulnerable applications. Apart from this, the cloud infrastructure hosts a dashboard (open-source project CTFd [5]), where participants can view available challenges and redeem points for the challenges they solve.

4.3 *Review Challenges*

Table 3 presents an overview of the challenges available to players. We show insight into their sizing, by conveying the size of the code snippets and the number of contained vulnerabilities. Based on participant feedback, close to 90% of users find the length of the snippets adequate.

The game's interface is shown in Fig. 3, and is comprised of three columns: `Comment`, `Code` and `Solution`. The vulnerable snippet is presented in the 2nd

Table 3 DuckDebugger: challenges overview

Language	No. challenges	LoC			No. Vulns		
		min	avg	max	min	avg	max
go	5	32	53.2	65	4	6.2	10
javascript	2	54	66.0	78	10	10.5	11
c	6	16	33.5	55	2	4.5	6
csharp	8	12	47.0	116	1	4.88	9
java	9	21	33.0	50	2	2.67	4
python	1	45			22		

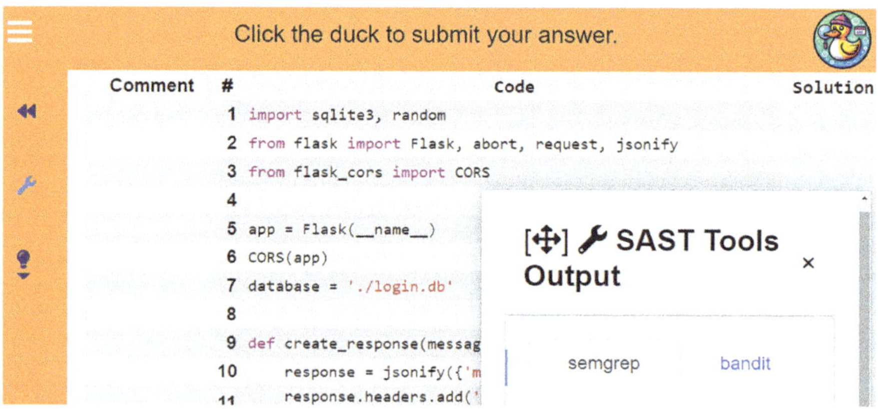

Fig. 3 DuckDebugger interface

column, labeled **`Code`**. Players are expected to insert review comments in the first column (**`Comment`**), for lines in which they recognize vulnerabilities.

Figure 4 presents an example of a vulnerability together with its accompanying solution. In the DuckDebugger platform, challenges are comprised of longer snippets containing multiple such hidden flaws.

Findings from SAST tools can be consulted alongside the code snippet. The objective of including SAST output in the game is twofold: firstly, we emulate a real-world industrial tooling, as a design consideration. Users are expected to gain familiarity and expertise with using SAST findings in their code review; secondly, by observing *false positives/negatives*, developers can understand where human rationalizing is needed and where tools over/under-report findings.

To solve a challenge, a user must find at least 50% of the vulnerabilities in the snippet. As a direct means of feedback, the full intended solution is displayed in the 3rd column for the user to reflect upon after they solve the challenge. The authors chose this threshold based on findings from the first design iteration. It was observed

```
1  int getValueFromarr(int *arr
       , int length, int idx) {
2
3      int value;
4      if (idx < length) {
5          value = arr[idx];
6      } else {
7          printf("Value: %d\n"
       , arr[idx]);
8          value = -1;
9      }
10     return value;
11 }
```

(a) Snippet Containing Vulnerability CWE125

L4: Correct logic should also include the "if 0>=idx" check (CWE125)

L7: Out of bounds read (CWE125) for the 'else' case

(b) Solution for the snippet

Fig. 4 DuckDebugger—Example challenge snippet

that developers undergoing cybersecurity training identify, on average, half of the vulnerabilities that an expert would detect Iosif et al. [13].

When done, the user submits their review. Previous comments are stored between solution attempts. All user interactions are stored for later analysis—a player using the platform generates a "timeline" of events, recorded as a time-series.

Quizzes. Apart from review-type challenges, the *DuckDebugger*'s design also features a quiz-type interface, where players can test their knowledge on various topics (e.g. OWASP topics applied for C#). Answering a multiple-choice question correctly reveals tooltips of why each option was (in)correct before allowing the user to continue to the next question in the quiz. These quiz-type challenges serve as an additional means to enhance developer awareness and create a more varied repertoire of ways for participants to test their knowledge.

5 Results

5.1 First Design Cycle—Events 1 to 3

The first design cycle focused on the following problem formulation: *"How to equip developers to perform security-centric code reviews?"*. To this end, we developed a simplified version of the serious game. We embedded this version of the game within a technical security awareness training. We conducted semi-structured interviews to gauge the participants' reactions to our prototype. Furthermore, participants were requested to offer their input on what aspects of the game should be retained and/or altered. The prototype was positively received, and we recorded the following findings: **(1.)** There should be more variety in the programming languages and style, **(2.)** Challenges should provide more comprehensive solutions **(3.)** Add SAST tool

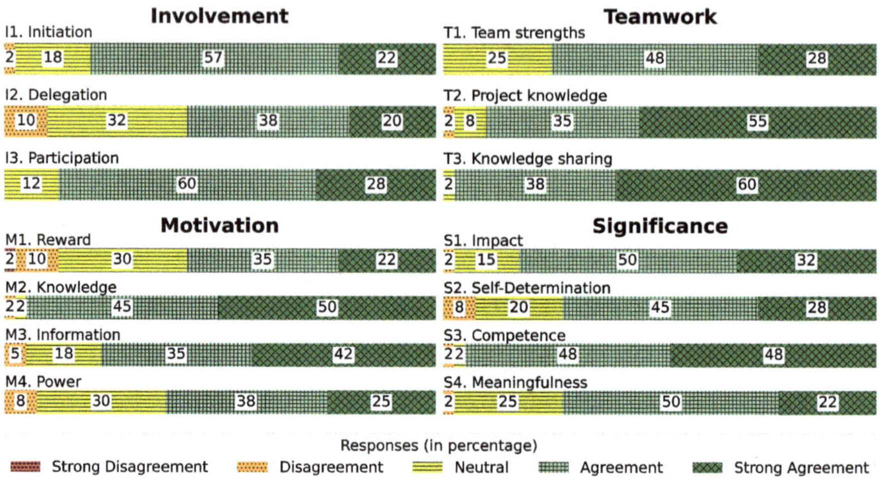

Fig. 5 Empowerment factors

support. Impressions and findings from the first design cycle are further detailed in Iosif et al. [13].

5.2 *Second Design Cycle—Events 4 to 12*

Figure 5 represents the participants' feedback to the questions from Table 2. These results, grouped across the dimensions of developer empowerment, indicate a mixed but generally positive reception of the serious game.

In terms of involvement, there is moderate agreement on the game's role in initiating and participating in code reviews, though skepticism exists about its effectiveness in delegating tasks, with half of responses being neutral (32%) and disagreeing (18%).

When considering teamwork, the game is perceived to facilitate information and skills exchange within teams significantly, with a strong agreement among respondents. However, opinions are more divided regarding the game's ability to enhance knowledge of the project's code base and to highlight individual team strengths, with a substantial number of respondents remaining neutral.

The game's ability to increase developer motivation is viewed variably, with a reasonable level of agreement on its capacity to increase knowledge and provide reward, suggesting some motivational impact. Yet, there is a noticeable level of neutrality, especially concerning code review's ability to empower participants via power dynamics.

The game is seen as significantly contributing to the sense of competence and meaningfulness, with high agreement levels, indicating that participants find value in the game for personal growth and finding significance in their tasks. The impact

and self-determination aspects also receive positive responses, although there's a notable portion of neutrality, suggesting not all participants feel the game strongly supports autonomy or has a transformative impact.
Furthermore, through semi-structured interviews, we identified highly requested areas for improvement in usability: participants suggested visual tweaks for a better user experience, such as highlighting the parts of the intended solution which their solution overlooked.

5.3 *Third Design Cycle (in Progress)—Event 13*

Based on collected feedback across the events of the second design cycle, we have started implementing the most requested usability refinements. Data from a singular event is too sparse to be statistically relevant. Nonetheless, the preliminary feedback from the the 13th event's participants shows higher levels of satisfaction for the users interacting with the serious game. As opposed to the 2nd design cycle, we did not observe any particular recurring improvement request, but rather only small individual desires.

5.4 *Discussion*

In this paper, we have introduced and assessed a developer empowerment training program for industrial software developers. The design of the game was iteratively refined across three design cycles. The 1st iteration consisted of a prototype geared towards requirements elicitation. The 2nd and 3rd design cycles integrated the feedback from the participants to provide a more *satisficing* user experience. Based on the participants' direct feedback, our experience has shown that the review challenges are well received. Furthermore, based on the collected questionnaire data, players of the *DuckDebugger* game claim that the challenges help the developers feel more empowered.

The game shows to illicit overall positive agreement towards the involvement, teamwork, motivation, and significance of the developers. 95% of participants claim to have gained security knowledge and awareness by participating in the game.

We have observed a constant demand for the game and secure code review throughout the 10-month period in which we prototyped and constantly refined the *DuckDebugger*. These events have been welcomed by the participating practitioners and have been endorsed by organizational leadership. Nonetheless, assessing the long-term impact of participation in the games is not feasible, due to several external factors such as: the evolving cybersecurity landscape, both in terms of attack vectors and defense technologies, changing programming standards and paradigms, as well as human factors such as job rotation. Such factors qualify the design of our game to be characterized as a "*wicked problem*", as per Baskerville & Wood-Harper [2] and Hevner et al. [11].

Concentrating on lessons learned designing the game, practitioners looking to adapt our research to their specific deployment context should consider the following: snippets should be adequately sized, and be presented together with findings from SAST tools. Furthermore, the contents of the snippets should be realistic (minimal dummy code) and tailored to the specifics of the participants' professional focus, e.g. web, embedded, and microservices. Lastly, solutions should be comprehensive and offer proactive guidance.

5.5 *Threats to Validity*

Threats to the validity of findings in design research are inevitable. One such threat is the inclusion of mixed workshops, which can introduce bias. While evaluating the impact of empowerment on IT-security, it is difficult to determine if such training has affected code quality due to numerous factors. In an industrial setting, there are external variables that cannot be controlled, which may limit the validity of evaluations. Furthermore, misinterpretation of questionnaire questions may occur due to participants' cultural and language backgrounds. Our data collection process is devoid of demographic segmentation. Therefore, categorizing or analyzing responses on the domains or specific industrial backgrounds of the participants is not possible. Nonetheless, the fact that game participants consist a large sample of industrial software engineers and that answering the questionnaire was voluntary supports the validity of the findings.

Our results show our game as a viable method to empower industrial developers, on the topic of secure code review, as evidenced by the high internal demand for the workshop events and the positive game feedback from the majority of the participants.

6 Conclusions. Further Work

In this work, we present the *DuckDebugger*—a serious game geared towards empowering industrial developers in secure code review, offering insight into its design and implementation. The game has been developed following Action Design Research principles, being iteratively refined throughout 3 design cycles. The research spanned 10 months, during which 13 events were conducted with over 200 industrial software developers.

Our contributions can be classified into two main categories: the design of the *DuckDebugger* and the evaluation thereof. As part of designing the game, we offer an overview of existing resources surrounding secure code review, explore the game's deployment context and technical implementation, as well as provide insight into the lessons learned while refining the game. For the DuckDebugger's evaluation, we provide an analysis of the practitioners' impressions of the game, as collected from semi-structured interviews and questionnaires. Participants enjoy the game and report high agreement towards elicited feelings of empowerment achieved through performing secure code review.

Our design approach is held up by these positive results, together with endorsement from organizational leadership and the constant demand the authors experienced for cybersecurity empowerment events—these outcomes validate the code review serious game as a suitable approach for empowering software developers in cybersecurity topics.

In future work, the authors would like to broaden the collection of available challenges and conduct further empirical studies to assess the needs and pain points of different groups of software developers, extending the prototype towards recognizing contextual and domain knowledge, to more broadly integrate this hands-on workshop module in more diverse settings. Furthermore, we plan to integrate AI reviews as additional tool outputs in the platform.

Acknowledgements This research task was partially supported by Fundação para a Ciência e a Tecnologia, I.P. (FCT) [ISTAR Projects: UIDB/04466/2020 and UIDP/04466/2020]. Ulrike Lechner acknowledges funding for project CONTAIN by the Bundesministerium für Bildung und Forschung (FKZ 13N16581). Andrei-Cristian Iosif and Tiago Gasiba acknowledge the funding provided by the Bundesministerium für Bildung und Forschung (BMBF) for the project CONTAIN (FKZ 13N16585).

References

1. Ami, A. S., Moran, K., Poshyvanyk, D. & Nadkarni, A. (2023). False negative – that one is going to kill you: Understanding industry perspectives of static analysis based security testing, preprint arXiv:2307.16325
2. Baskerville, R. L., & Wood-Harper, A. T. (1996). A critical perspective on action research as a method for information systems research. *Journal of Information Technology, 11*(3), 235–246.
3. Bosu, A., Greiler, M., & Bird, C. (2015). Characteristics of useful code reviews: An empirical study at microsoft. *2015 IEEE/ACM 12th working conference on mining software repositories* (pp. 146–156). IEEE.
4. Chambers, R. (2024). 2024 focus on the future report: Widening risk exposure gap demands internal audit transformation, https://www.auditboard.com/resources/ebook/2024-focus-on-the-future-report-widening-risk-exposure-gap-demands-internal-audit-transformation/. Online, Retrieved 02 March, 2024.
5. CTFd. (2024). CTFd, https://github.com/CTFd/CTFd. Online, Retrieved 28 Feb, 2024.
6. Fu, M. & Tantithamthavorn, C. (2022) , Linevul: A transformer-based line-level vulnerability prediction. In *Proceedings of the 19th international conference on mining software repositories* (pp. 608–620). ACM.
7. GitLab. (2019). No love lost between security specialists and developers, https://about.gitlab.com/developer-survey/. Online, Retrieved 24 Feb, 2024.
8. Gonzalez, D., Perez, P. P., & Mirakhorli, M. (2021). Barriers to shift-left security: The unique pain points of writing automated tests involving security controls. In *Proceedings of the 15th ACM/IEEE international symposium on empirical software engineering and measurement (ESEM)', ESEM '21*. ACM. https://doi.org/10.1145/3475716.3475786

9. Hänsch, N., & Benenson, Z. (2014). Specifying IT security awareness. In *Proceedings - international workshop on database and expert systems applications* (pp. 326–330). IEEE, DEXA'.
10. Hendrix, M., Al-Sherbaz, A. & Bloom, V. (2016) , 'Game based cyber security training: Are serious games suitable for cyber security training?. *International Journal of Serious Games***3**(1).
11. Hevner, A., March, S., Park, J., & Ram, S. (2004). Design science in information systems research. *MISQ, 28*, 75–105.
12. Hunt, A. & Thomas, D. (2019). *The pragmatic programmer* (20th anniversary edition edn.). Addison-Wesley Professional.
13. Iosif, A.-C., Espinha Gasiba, T., Lechner, U. & Albuquerque, M.-P. (2023). Raising awareness in the industry on secure code review practices. In *CYBER 2023: The eighth international conference on cyber-technologies and cyber-systems', IARIA* (pp. 62–68).
14. ISO, IEC 20246:2017. (2017). *Software and systems engineering - Work product reviews*. International Organization for Standardization, Geneva, CH: Standard.
15. ISO, IEC 64223-4-1:2018–1. (2018). *ISO/IEC 62443-4-1:2018 security for industrial automation and control systems - Part 4–1: Secure product development lifecycle requirements*. International Organization for Standardization, Geneva, CH: Standard.
16. ISO, IEC 64223–4-2:2019–12. (2019). *Security for industrial automation and control systems - Part 4–2: Technical security requirements for IACS components*. International Electrical Commission, Geneva, CH: Standard. , 978-2-8322-6597-0
17. ISO, IEC TR 24772–1:2019. (2019). *Programming languages - Guidance to avoiding vulnerabilities in programming languages - Part 1: Language-independent guidance*. International Organization for Standardization, Geneva, CH: Standard.
18. Kupsch, J. A. & Miller, B. P. (2009). Manual versus automated vulnerability assessment: A case study. In *First international workshop on managing insider security threats (MIST)* (pp. 83–97). ACM. pages.cs.wisc.edu/~kupsch/va/ManVsAutoVulnAssessment.pdf
19. MacLeod, L., Greiler, M., Storey, M.-A., Bird, C., & Czerwonka, J. (2017). Code reviewing in the trenches: Challenges and best practices. *IEEE Software, 35*(4), 34–42.
20. Mao, R., Zhang, H., Dai, Q., Huang, H., Rong, G., Shen, H., Chen, L., & Lu, K. (2020). Preliminary findings about DevSecOps from grey literature. In *2020 IEEE 20th international conference on software quality reliability and security* (pp. 450–457). IEEE.
21. MITRE Corporation. (2023). CWE Top 25 most dangerous software weaknesses, http://bit.ly/mitre25. Online, Retrieved 24 July, 2023.
22. Moyon, F., Mendez, D., Beckers, K., & Klepper, S. (2020). How to integrate security compliance requirements with agile software engineering at scale? In M. Morisio, M. Torchiano, & A. Jedlitschka (Eds.), *Product-focused software process improvement* (pp. 69–87). Springer International Publishing.
23. OWASP Foundation. (2021). OWASP Top 10 - 2021, https://owasp.org/Top10. Online, Retrieved 24 July, 2023.
24. Perry, N., Srivastava, M., Kumar, D. & Boneh, D. (2023) , Do users write more insecure code with ai assistants?. In *Proceedings of the 2023 ACM SIGSAC conference on computer and communications security', CCS '23*. ACM. https://doi.org/10.1145/3576915.3623157
25. Rajapakse, R. N., Zahedi, M. & Babar, M. A. (2022). Collaborative application security testing for DevSecOps: an empirical analysis of challenges, best practices and tool support. https://arxiv.org/abs/2211.06953
26. Ramaj, X., Sánchez-Gordón, M., Gkioulos, V., Chockalingam, S., & Colomo-Palacios, R. (2022). Holding on to compliance while adopting DevSecOps: An SLR. *Electronics, 11*(22), 1–19.
27. Rindell, K., Bernsmed, K. & Jaatun, M. G. (2019). Managing security in software: Or: How I learned to stop worrying and manage the security technical debt. In *Proceedings of the 14th international conference on availability, reliability and security* (pp. 1–8). ACM.
28. Sánchez-Gordón, M. & Colomo-Palacios, R. (2020). Security as culture: A systematic literature review of DevSecOps. In *Proceedings of the IEEE/ACM 42nd international conference on software engineering workshops, ICSEW'20* (pp. 266–269). ACM.

29. Sein, M. K., Henfridsson, O., Purao, S., Rossi, M., & Lindgren, R. (2011). Action design research. *MIS Quarterly, 35*, 37–56.
30. Siami Namin, A., Aguirre-Muñoz, Z. & Jones, K. (2016). Teaching cyber security through competition an experience report about a participatory training workshop. In *7th annual international conference on computer science education: Innovation & technology (CSEIT 2016)', CSEIT, global science & technology forum (GSTF).*
31. Tessem, B. (2014). Individual empowerment of agile and non-agile software developers in small teams. *Information and Software Technology, 56*(8), 873–889.

Digital Twins for Haptic Design Thinking: An Innovative Prototype

Alexander Voelz, Christian Muck, and Wilfird Utz

Abstract In an era where digital transformation shapes most facets of business and society, haptic Design Thinking workshops emerge as a valuable driver to foster co-creation and human-centric design among interacting stakeholders. Still, a need persists to capture workshop results in a digital and machine-processable manner. Scene2Model exemplifies these capabilities by enabling an automated transformation of physical scenes into conceptual modeling-based representations. To support this process, novel features are introduced within this work that leverage generative Artificial Intelligence (AI), such as Large Language Model-based object description and attribute generation, along with comprehensive scene summaries. Moreover, the application of the Scene2Model tool in collective intelligence environments is supported by automated postings of results, thus exemplifying the potential to enhance collaborative evaluation and feedback. This approach emphasizes the potential of combining haptic Design Thinking with advanced AI technologies, marking a significant advancement in the refinement of Digital Twins for Haptic Design Thinking.

1 Introduction

Alongside the ongoing digitalization, which redefines today's business landscape as well as the social interactions related to it, the Digital Twin concept has gained popularity across various fields. Traditionally, the concept has been applied in physical settings related to manufacturing and production. Nowadays, the Digital Twin

A. Voelz (✉)
Faculty of Computer Science, University of Vienna, Vienna, Austria
e-mail: alexander.voelz@univie.ac.at

C. Muck · W. Utz
OMiLAB NPO, Berlin, Germany
e-mail: christian.muck@omilab.org

W. Utz
e-mail: wilfrid.utz@omilab.org

C. M. Flath et al. (eds.), *Shaping the Digital Future Through Innovation and Practice*, Lecture Notes in Information Systems and Organisation 85,
https://doi.org/10.1007/978-3-032-08489-7_12

paradigm shifts towards more immersive interpretations that also consider non-tangible aspects as potential application fields, thus requiring the exploration of novel and user-friendly methodologies. In this context, *Digital Twins for Haptic Design Thinking* have been proposed as an intuitive approach to extend the traditional view of Digital Twins.

The aim of this contribution is to showcase an innovative prototype that supports this novel notion, namely Scene2Model.[1] This tool was first introduced in the scientific literature in 2018, enabling the automated "*transformation of tangible Design Thinking artifacts into diagrammatic models with the simultaneous semantic enrichment of the objects*" [12, p. 1]. Scene2Model thus addresses the challenge of capturing the physical results of Design Thinking workshops in a digital form to ease the documentation and sharing with relevant stakeholders beyond the initial participants [8]. Since then, Scene2Model has been applied in research, teaching, and industry projects, which has provided valuable inputs for iterative improvements. The most recent features resulting from these improvements are discussed in this contribution.

For this purpose, the theoretical background regarding Design Thinking, related concepts, and the foundations of the Scene2Model tool are introduced in Sect. 2. Subsequently, the prototypical application of Scene2Model is showcased in Sect. 3, covering new functionalities and current applications within selected research projects. Finally, key takeaways of this contribution are summarized in Sect. 4.

2 Theoretical Background

The foundational concepts of Design Thinking are introduced in the theoretical background, emphasizing the importance of co-creation and collective intelligence. Following this, the Scene2Model tool is presented as a facilitator for digital Design Thinking.

2.1 Design Thinking, Co-Creation, and Collective Intelligence

The trend of adopting Design Thinking across multiple domains has resulted in diverse methodologies, as shown in [8]. Central to each of these approaches is a focus on human-centric design [3] that is particularly valuable in multidisciplinary settings often associated with digital transformation, as it brings together stakeholders from distinct backgrounds to yield collaboration and co-creation of involved entities. Moreover, there is a trend towards interactive workshops utilizing tangible objects based on pen and paper, independent of the employed methodology [15].

[1] https://www.omilab.org/activities/scene2model/.

These materials aid in building a shared understanding among participants, enabling them to convey their insights through physical means. Fundamental aspects supporting this process are collaboration and co-creation, concepts that have been present in human society for millenniums [2]. Nowadays, often associated with involving consumers in the design of products or services, the understanding has shifted towards the general inclusion of all stakeholders relevant to a given design process [1, 5]. These concepts are relevant within the context of Design Thinking workshops as they leverage the integration of varied viewpoints originating from the interacting stakeholders. Addressing this dynamic, the term *Collective Intelligence* has been established to describe the enhanced capabilities that can emerge when diverse groups of individuals synergize their unique knowledge, skills, and perspectives [10]. This phenomenon is exemplified in Design Thinking workshops, where participants from varied domains collaborate actively. Hence, Design Thinking methodologies and corresponding workshops fulfill the foundational principles of collective intelligence by leveraging diverse ideas across disciplines based on collaboration and co-creation to develop creative as well as innovative solutions.

2.2 Digital Design Thinking Using Scene2Model

It has been emphasized in the previous section that Design Thinking methodologies rely on physical workshops and tangible materials to foster collaboration, co-creation, and collective intelligence. The Scene2Model tool addresses the challenge of capturing the results from such workshops by providing an automated mechanism to transform them into digital, conceptual models, currently specific for the storyboard methodology [16] using SAP Scenes.[2] In this context, Scene2Model provides an environment in which a camera stream is harnessed to detect paper figures of a specific scene via an attached QR-Code and then translate these into corresponding modeling objects. Afterward, the transformed objects can be semantically enriched within the environment through further information, additional attributes, or adjusted representations [13]. Detailed explanations of the Scene2Model tool, its implementation based on the ADOxx metamodeling platform [7], and recent applications within an educational setting of the OMiLAB innovation environment have been presented in related works (e.g., [11, 14, 17, 18, 20]). Therefore, these aspects are not discussed hereafter as it would exceed the scope of this contribution focused on newly developed features.

[2] https://apphaus.sap.com/resource/scenes.

3 From Digital Design Thinking Towards Digital Twins for Haptic Design Thinking: The Evolution of the Scene2Model Tool

The Scene2Model tool has been applied in various domains and projects after it was first introduced in the scientific literature. Since then, it has been iteratively evolving towards a novel notion labeled *Digital Twins for Haptic Design Thinking* in recent works [8, 17, 20]. This notion extends the common understanding of the Digital Twin concept, which is traditionally applied in the context of the manufacturing domain. To also account for non-tangible elements being virtually represented by a Digital Twin, wider definitions have been proposed, for example, Digital Twins of a system [9]. Building on this notion of the Digital Twin concept, three foundational components can be identified: (i) Models representing the system under study (ii) that are built upon data traces from the system (iii) while offering services aimed at deriving meaningful implications for the system.

Considering these components, early Scene2Model versions already met the first two. The following section presents how recently developed functionalities contribute to the third component (i.e., deriving meaningful implications). The development of these functionalities is fundamentally driven by the Agile Modeling Method Engineering (AMME) lifecycle [6], which defines a structured process for the realization of modeling methods. Moreover, AMME emphasizes the importance of iteratively refining modeling methods, like Scene2Model, to address changing requirements and integrate new technologies. In line with such iterative refinements, Large Language Models (LLMs) are harnessed to extend the functionalities of Scene2Model for a more context-aware modeling environment, as showcased subsequently.

3.1 Prototypical Functionalities of Digital Twins for Haptic Design Thinking

Subsequently, it is assumed that Design Thinking workshop results (cf. Sect. 2.1) are transformed into digital models using the Scene2Model tool (cf. Sect. 2.2). Based on these assumptions, three prototypical functionalities are showcased below, which aim to derive meaningful implications for a system under study from the inherent model value.

LLM-Based Object Description and Attribute Generation. The first functionality makes use of novel advancements regarding generative Artificial Intelligence (AI) and, more specifically, LLMs with the goal of leveraging their expectations for semantics-driven systems engineering [4]. After the translation of haptic paper figures into digital modeling objects, semantic enrichment can be performed by prompting for further suggestions describing attributes of the individual objects within the scene. Still, this process requires relevant domain knowledge and potentially further

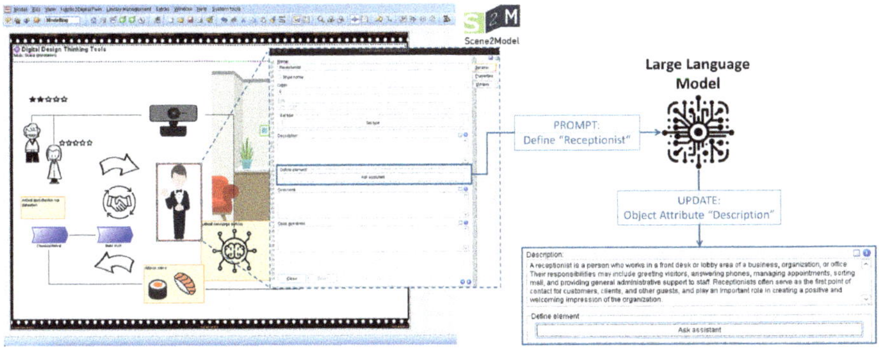

Fig. 1 LLM-based generation of an attribute description for the modeling object "Receptionist"

coordination among workshop participants to reach an agreement regarding generated descriptions. Considering these elaborations, a prototypical feature was added to Scene2Model during the last iteration of the AMME lifecycle [6] to generate object descriptions and attributes for recognized objects automatically.

The following Fig. 1 exemplifies how this functionality is utilized for a scene of hospitality services in Japan,[3] namely for the actor "Receptionist". A corresponding prompt is sent to an LLM via HTTP request to receive a relevant description, which is then saved under the attribute "Description" of the respective object.

LLM-Based Scene Summary. The final result of the storyboard methodology is a collection of scenes that sequentially represent a coherent storyboard. With the goal of providing textual descriptions of each scene for documentation purposes or for visually impaired people, an LLM-based scene summary is provided as a new feature within the most recent Scene2Model version. The summary is created through an engineered prompt that takes every transformed modeling element as input to create a summarizing description for selected scenes. Such summaries serve as additional documentation and can be used for scene validation purposes or advanced sharing functionalities to synergize a collective intelligence that goes beyond the initial workshop participants.

For the scene depicted in Fig. 1, the triggering of this functionality results in the LLM-based generation of the summary displayed in Fig. 2 by sending a corresponding prompt via HTTP request that considers each object represented in the scene.

Scene Evaluation in Collective Intelligence Environments. The third functionality aims to break the limitations of distributed teams by facilitating the transfer of ideas within dedicated platforms. Both created models and the LLM-generated descriptions of scenes can be automatically posted within relevant working platforms, such as Microsoft Teams (cf. Fig. 3). In this way, not only the opinions of workshop participants but also all relevant stakeholders that are included in a specific

[3] This scene will serve as an example throughout the chapter on the prototypical functionalities.

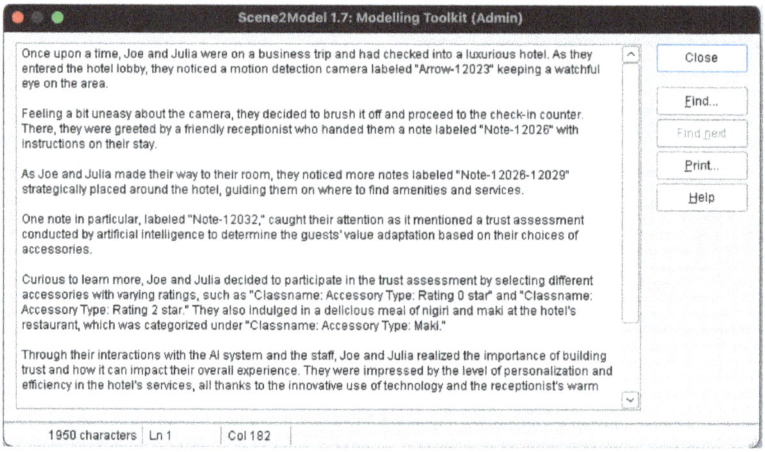

Fig. 2 LLM-based generation of a scene summary for the scene depicted in Fig. 1

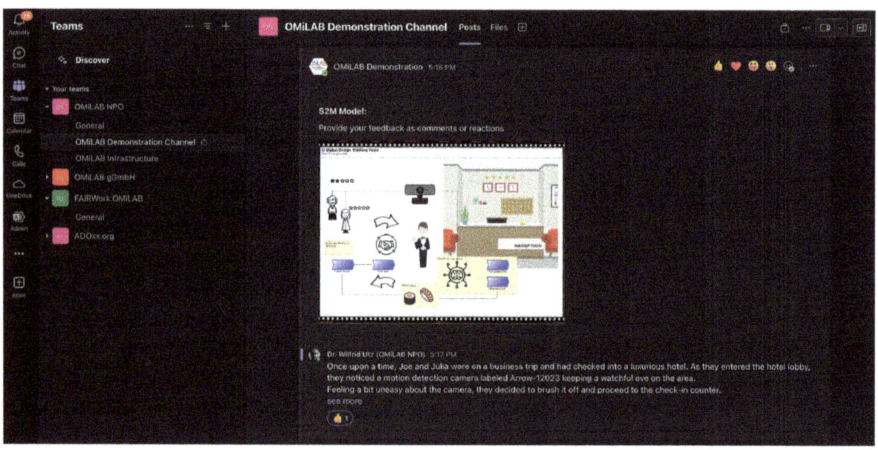

Fig. 3 Automated posting of a scene and its summary (cf. Figs. 1, 2) within Microsoft Teams

design process can be considered. Further, the stakeholders' input can be processed (e.g., using sentiment analysis [22]) to provide an overview of opinions to workshop participants.

3.2 *Current Application Contexts of Scene2Model*

In the following, two selected research projects in which Scene2Model is utilized are presented to provide an overview of the current application contexts.

FAIRWork. is a research project aiming to improve flexibility and worker participation in complex decision-making processes by developing an AI-supported and configurable decision-support system (DSS). Further details about this project can be found on the project webpage[4] and in [21]. Through the Scene2Model tool, decision problems and the related human requirements for complex decision processes can be effectively captured within the FAIRWork project, enabling a comprehensive understanding of the underlying system and scenarios. The captured knowledge is then further utilized in the formalization of decisions that serve as input for a flexible and model-based configuration of the system, thereby allowing non-experts to understand the decisions better and ease the adaptation to changing requirements.

CoDEMO 5.0. is a research project that aims to support decision-makers of organizations from different sectors in transitioning toward sustainable and human-centric strategies in a co-creative manner. Further details on the project and the role of *Digital Twins for Haptic Design Thinking* can be found on the corresponding project webpage[5] and in [19]. By employing the Scene2Model tool, CoDEMO can effectively capture the externalized knowledge from diverse stakeholders, thereby fostering a multi-dimensional understanding of complex systems. This approach supports the project's objectives of advancing sustainable, resilient, and human-centric principles in Organizations 5.0 and also exemplifies the innovative approaches to enhance collaborative decision-making and value co-creation within the European innovation ecosystem.

4 Conclusion

This contribution showcases how prototypical functionalities of the Scene2Model tool can be utilized to open up new opportunities for collaborative and co-creative environments, exemplified through the application within selected research projects. Through our exploration, we highlighted Scene2Model's role in transforming the tangible outputs of haptic Design Thinking workshops into digital representations, enhancing collaborative creativity and decision-making processes. In projects like FAIRWork and CoDEMO 5.0, Scene2Model facilitates a seamless transition from physical objects, serving as data traces, to digital representations of the respective system under study. Subsequently, these objects can be further enriched with added semantics and interoperability, offering a more comprehensive and dynamic approach. Moreover, newly developed features of Scene2Model enable the generation of object descriptions, attributes, and scene summaries, as well as the sharing in dedicated environments to foster evaluation through principles of collective intelligence. The goal of the functionalities is to derive meaningful implications for the original system, thus fulfilling the requirements to be considered *Digital Twins for Haptic Design Thinking*. The insights from corresponding applications illustrate the

[4] https://fairwork-project.eu/.

[5] https://codemo-project.eu/.

growing possibilities that lie at the intersection of traditional Design Thinking and advanced technologies, forming the basis for future developments and applications that can leverage these integrative approaches for innovative solutions.

Acknowledgements This work is supported by both the FAIRWork project (www.fairwork-project.eu), funded by the European Commission's Horizon Europe Programme under contract reference number 101069499, and the CoDEMO 5.0 project (www.codemo-project.eu), funded within the Erasmus+ Programme (ERASMUS-EDU-2022-PI-ALL-INNO) under project reference number 101104819. This paper expresses the opinions of the authors and not necessarily those of the European Commission. The European Commission is not liable for any use that may be made of the information contained in this paper.

References

1. Bhalla, G. (2011). Beyond the business world. In *Collaboration and co-creation: New platforms for marketing and innovation* (pp. 145–163). Springer. https://doi.org/10.1007/978-1-4419-7082-4_8
2. Bhalla, G. (2011). Collaboration and co-creation. In *Collaboration and co-creation: New platforms for marketing and innovation* (pp. 1–16). Springer. https://doi.org/10.1007/978-1-4419-7082-4_1
3. Brown, T. (2008). Design thinking. *Harvard Business Review*, 84–92.
4. Buchmann, R., Eder, J., Fill, H.-G., Frank, U., Karagiannis, D., Laurenzi, E., Mylopoulos, J., Plexousakis, D., & Santos, M. Y. (2024). Large language models: Expectations for semantics-driven systems engineering. *Data & Knowledge Engineering,152*, Article 102324. https://doi.org/10.1016/j.datak.2024.102324
5. Ind, N., & Coates, N. (2013). The meanings of co-creation. *European Business Review, 25*(1), 86–95. https://doi.org/10.1108/09555341311287754
6. Karagiannis, D. (2015). Agile modeling method engineering. In N. Karanikolas, D. Akoumianakis, M. Nikolaidou, D. Vergados & M. Xeno (Eds.), *Proceedings of the 19th Panhellenic conference on informatics* (pp. 5–10). ACM. https://doi.org/10.1145/2801948.2802040
7. Karagiannis, D. (2024). AdoScript: A DSL for developing conceptual modeling methods. In *Essays in Honour of Ulrich Frank informing possible future worlds* (pp. 287–308). Logos.
8. Karagiannis, D. (2024). How digital twins for design thinking support innovative business models. The *Kyoto Economic Review, 198*(Special Issue), 123–146. https://doi.org/10.57475/keizaironso.198.S9
9. Kirchhof, J. C., Michael, J., Rumpe, B., Varga, S., & Wortmann, A. (2020). Model-driven digital twin construction: Synthesizing the integration of cyber-physical systems with their information systems. In *Proceedings of the 23rd ACM/IEEE international conference on model driven engineering languages and systems* (pp. 90–101). ACM. https://doi.org/10.1145/3365438.3410941
10. Leimeister, J. M. (2010). Collective intelligence. *Business & Information Systems Engineering, 2*(4), 245–248. https://doi.org/10.1007/s12599-010-0114-8
11. Miron, E.-T., Muck, C., & Karagiannis, D. (2019). Transforming haptic storyboards into diagrammatic models: The Scene2Model tool. In *Proceedings of the 52nd Hawaii international conference on system sciences* (pp. 541–550). ScholarSpace, Honolulu. https://doi.org/10.24251/HICSS.2019.067
12. Miron, E.-T., Muck, C., Karagiannis, D., & Götzinger, D. (2018). Transforming storyboards into diagrammatic models. In P. Chapman, G. Stapleton, A. Moktefi, S. Perez-Kriz & F. Bellucci (Eds.), *Diagrammatic representation and inference*. LNCS (Vol. 11039, pp. 770–773). Springer. https://doi.org/10.1007/978-3-319-91376-6_78

13. Muck, C. (2024). *A dynamic adaptation framework for haptic modelling methods: Creating digital twins from design thinking*. University of Vienna. https://doi.org/10.25365/thesis.76296
14. Muck, C., & Palkovits-Rauter, S. (2022). Conceptualizing design thinking artefacts: The Scene2Model storyboard approach. In *Domain-specific conceptual modeling: Concepts, methods and ADOxx tools* (pp. 567–587). Springer. https://doi.org/10.1007/978-3-030-93547-4_25
15. Schelle, K. J., Gubenko, E., Kreymer, R., Naranjo, C. G., Tetteroo, D., & Soute, I. A. C. (2015). Increasing engagement in workshops: Designing a toolkit using lean design thinking. In *Proceedings of the multimedia, interaction, design and innovation* (pp. 1–8). ACM. https://doi.org/10.1145/2814464.2814481
16. van der Lelie, C. (2006). The value of storyboards in the product design process. *Personal and Ubiquitous Computing, 10*(2–3), 159–162. https://doi.org/10.1007/s00779-005-0026-7
17. Voelz, A., Muck, C., Amlashi, D. M., & Karagiannis, D. (2023). Bridging haptic design thinking and cyber-physical environments through digital twins using conceptual modeling. In *Joint Proceedings of the BIR 2023 workshops and doctoral consortium co-located with the 22nd international conference on perspectives in business informatics research* (pp. 195–208).
18. Voelz, A., Muck, C., Amlashi, D. M., & Karagiannis, D. (2023). Citizen-centric design of consumable services for smart cities. *Digital Government: Research and Practice,4*(3), 17 (2023). https://doi.org/10.1145/3597420
19. Voelz, A., Vaidian, I., & Muck, C. (2024). Digital twins for haptic design thinking: Application within CoDEMO 5.0. In *Joint proceedings of RCIS 2024 workshops and research projects track co-located with the 18th international conference on research challenges in information science (RCIS 2024).*
20. Völz, A., Vaidian, I. (2024). Digital transformation through conceptual modeling: The NEMO summer school use case. In *Modellierung 2024* (pp. 139–156). Gesellschaft für Informatik e.V. https://doi.org/10.18420/modellierung2024_014
21. Woitsch, R., Muck, C., Utz, W., & Zeiner, H. (2023). Towards a democratic AI-based decision support system to improve decision making in complex ecosystems. In *Joint proceedings of the BIR 2023 workshops and doctoral consortium co-located with the 22nd international conference on perspectives in business informatics research* (pp. 209–223).
22. Yue, L., Chen, W., Li, X., Zuo, W., & Yin, M. (2019). A survey of sentiment analysis in social media. *Knowledge and Information Systems, 60*(2), 617–663. https://doi.org/10.1007/s10115-018-1236-4

Enabling Smart Service Innovation in SMEs: The bi.smart Launchpad

Daniel Heinz, Carina Benz, Hitomi Bremmer, Yevgeni Paliyenko, and Christian Schiller

Abstract In the era of digital transformation, organizations are leveraging digital technologies to innovate through smart services – utilizing sensor-generated data. Despite the rich methodological knowledge available, a significant adoption gap persists in smart service innovation, particularly among small and medium-sized enterprises (SMEs) due to constraints in knowledge dissemination and resources. Addressing this challenge, we collaborated with five SMEs to develop a web application prototype, the "bi.smart Launchpad", aimed at facilitating smart service innovation projects. This paper delineates the design requirements and features instantiated in the prototype, elaborates on its architecture and implementation, and presents the results of a quantitative evaluation. Our findings demonstrate the prototype's potential to bridge the adoption gap, offering SMEs a practical and effective tool to overcome the challenges of smart service innovation.

D. Heinz (✉) · C. Benz
Karlsruhe Institute of Technology, Karlsruhe, Germany
e-mail: daniel.heinz@kit.edu

C. Benz
e-mail: carina.benz@kit.edu

H. Bremmer
EDI GmbH, Karlsruhe, Germany
e-mail: bremmer@edi.gmbh

Y. Paliyenko
University of Stuttgart, Stuttgart, Germany
e-mail: yevgeni.paliyenko@iktd.uni-stuttgart.de

C. Schiller
Fraunhofer IAO, Stuttgart, Germany
e-mail: christian.schiller@iao.fraunhofer.de

C. M. Flath et al. (eds.), *Shaping the Digital Future Through Innovation and Practice*,
Lecture Notes in Information Systems and Organisation 85,
https://doi.org/10.1007/978-3-032-08489-7_13

1 Introduction

Digital technologies such as cloud computing, big data, analytics, and mobile devices are creating transformative opportunities for firms to redefine market offerings and develop new business models [8]. This includes digital services that seamlessly integrate with existing physical products [41, 42], such as John Deere's digital service suite that allows farmers and dealers to manage fleet data online and monitor machines remotely [40]. These smart services rely on conventional products being transformed into smart products augmented by digital technologies, serving as boundary objects in smart service systems [4, 5, 33].

The transition from product-focused markets to integrated smart service systems is not only a technological evolution but also an economic necessity [1, 34]. Firms must shift from linear value chains to interconnected value networks to remain competitive and offer enhanced value propositions [15]. This shift enables new revenue streams and improved customer engagement through data-driven insights and automation [5, 33]. For example, integrating predictive maintenance services can significantly reduce machine downtime and operating costs, providing economic advantages over conventional product models [28].

Despite these benefits, the path to successful smart service innovation (SSI) is fraught with challenges [7, 29]. Many organizations, particularly small and medium-sized enterprises (SMEs) engaged in their core business ('brown-field innovation'), face limited digital skills, perceived risks, and complexity across business functions, as opposed to nascent entrepreneurial activities like startup incubators ('green-field innovation') [2, 16, 43]. Specifically, the lack of established processes, roles, and methods for developing integrated smart product-service systems poses significant barriers for SMEs entering this domain [35].

Various research streams are contributing methodological knowledge to SSI, addressing aspects such as representations of SSI outcomes [23, 32] and generic roles and processes for SSI projects [3, 21, 26]. Despite these advances, a "last mile" gap persists in the widespread adoption and tailored applicability of SSI methods and tools [10, 13, 25]. Efforts like the DIN SPEC 33453 of the [9] aim to bridge this gap by integrating existing methodological knowledge into applicable toolboxes. However, the applied static formats fall short of the potential that digital technologies hold.

A previous review [14] suggests more effective ways of making methodological knowledge accessible to practitioners – which could be provided by academia (as suggested here), consultants (e.g., servicedesigntools.org), or public institutions (e.g., orghandbuch.de). Yet, scholarly efforts beyond traditional publications often face a short lifespan due to insufficient funding for maintenance and updates. To ensure practical impact, SSI researchers must address both "lost before translation" issues by aligning research with practitioner interests and "lost in translation" challenges by effectively translating academic research into SSI practice [36]. Systematically addressing these issues requires that academia integrate and evolve practitioner-oriented artifacts, such as the DIN SPEC 33453, into dynamic research platforms, serving as practitioner-oriented repositories of formalized knowledge to support, for example, SSI efforts [6, 12, 27]. Such integrative resources would promote research in "Pasteur's quadrant," balancing fundamental understanding with practical considerations [39].

Existing approaches often fail to document the implicit design knowledge embedded in such artifacts. To address this gap, we conducted an interdisciplinary multi-year design science research project [18] in collaboration with five SMEs, which aimed to design information systems (here: a web application) to support SSI in SMEs by eliciting design requirements (DRs) and design features (DFs). Our project systematically structured and integrated methodological knowledge for SSI, specifically targeting the usability needs of established SMEs, which often lack the resources for dedicated innovation facilitators and the capacity for extensive exploration.

This paper presents the final artifact built to evaluate our design, the bi.smart Launchpad (available at www.bismart.info). Over the course of the project, this web application proved to be a viable tool for SSI projects in SMEs, providing a streamlined, hands-on process with prescribed activities and applicable resources tailored to SSI. The application builds on existing meta-models for method engineering and SSI-related methodologies (e.g., the DIN SPEC 33453), and it integrates interdisciplinary methodological knowledge from information systems, service design and product engineering. For example, it combines recent SSI methods (e.g., [22]) with broadly applicable frameworks such as the Business Model Canvas [30]. Given the scope of this paper, we focus here primarily on the DRs, DFs, architecture, and implementation of the bi.smart Launchpad rather than providing a comprehensive overview of its content. We also report the results of a quantitative evaluation, reflect on the current state of the prototype, and outline further ways to extend it.

2 Design Requirements for the bi.smart Launchpad

We systematically analyzed a rich set of empirical data to understand the challenges faced by established SMEs today, based on a survey of 71 companies, as well as 24 interviews and five workshops with SMEs that focused on their needs and environment for applying methodological resources in SSI projects [31, 35]. Preliminary insights into these challenges were complemented by a contextual literature review to identify and formulate six distinct empirically and theoretically grounded DRs for information systems to support SSI in SMEs, each aimed at addressing key challenges faced by SMEs today. Table 1 provides an overview of the DRs that guided the design and implementation of the artifact.

Methodological knowledge support (DR1) emerged as a primary requirement, driven by the observation that SMEs often struggle with a lack of accessible, structured and comprehensive methodological knowledge, affecting the effectiveness and efficiency of innovation projects. To address this, the artifact should serve as a central resource that provides SMEs with tailored methodological support to enhance their innovation capabilities as a solid foundation for navigating the complexities of SSI.

Table 1 Overview of design requirements for the bi.smart Launchpad

Design Requirement	The bi.smart Launchpad …
DR1: Methodological Knowledge Support	… should enable SMEs to efficiently navigate smart service innovation projects by providing a comprehensive suite of tailored methodological knowledge
DR2: Independence and Accessibility	… should allow SMEs to independently leverage the web application without external support or specialized training, enhancing accessibility and usability
DR3: Scientifically Rigorous Content	… should incorporate methodological knowledge that adheres to stringent scientific standards, ensuring reliability and effectiveness for smart service innovation in SMEs
DR4: Open Source Availability	… should be provided as an open-source artifact, facilitating the democratization of methodological resources
DR5: User-Friendly Interface	… should offer an intuitive, step-by-step interface to simplify the application of methodological knowledge for users of all expertise levels
DR6: Situational Guidance and Flexibility	… should provide situational guidance and adaptability in the application of methodological knowledge, allowing flexibility and customization to fit individual project needs and contexts

Independence and accessibility (DR2) was identified due to SMEs' limited resources and high dependency on external consultancy to navigate innovation processes. The artifact should be designed to enable SMEs to independently access and use a comprehensive set of innovation resources to enact the right methods that suit their specific needs and context without further external dependencies. This autonomy is essential to enable SMEs to quickly adapt to and capitalize on emerging opportunities in the digital economy, thus fostering a more self-reliant innovation culture. The notion of accessibility here specifically refers to the ease of use and the ability to access and utilize the resources without specialized training or external assistance.

Scientifically rigorous content (DR3) addresses the need for reliable, effective methods based on scientific research. SMEs have highlighted the importance of confidence in the methods they use, underscoring the need for the artifact to curate and present content that adheres to rigorous scientific standards. This requirement ensures that SMEs have access to state-of-the-art, scientifically validated methodological knowledge, thereby fostering confidence in their innovation efforts.

Open source availability (DR4) reflects the importance of knowledge sharing and collaboration in the digital age. Making the content of the web application available without royalties or similar fees invites widespread use and adaptation to individual contexts, fostering a community-driven approach to refining and expanding its utility. While this overlaps with DR2 in promoting accessibility, DR4 specifically emphasizes the availability of the artifact to a wide range of stakeholders who may be involved in SSI projects beyond SMEs themselves, and also to other researchers who seek to build on the current state of the artifact, thus democratizing access to SSI resources.

User-friendly interface (DR5) stems from the recognition that the complexity of innovation tools can inhibit their adoption. An intuitive, step-by-step interface ensures that the artifact is accessible to users with varying levels of expertise. This DR is fundamental to making the methodological resources provided accessible and manageable to a broader segment of stakeholders in SMEs. While DR2 emphasizes the accessibility of its content, DR5 focuses on designing the tool for usability and user experience.

Situational guidance and flexibility (DR6) recognizes the diversity of SSI projects and the need for adaptable methodologies. The bi.smart Launchpad aims to provide tailored guidance, allowing SMEs to adapt methodological knowledge to the specific needs of their projects. This flexibility ensures that the web application can support a wide range of innovation activities, making it a versatile tool for SMEs navigating the digital transformation landscape.

3 Demonstration of the bi.smart Launchpad Prototype

3.1 Architecture of the bi.smart Launchpad

To address the DRs, we iteratively developed, evaluated, and refined design principles for information systems to support SSI in SMEs. We interpreted and transformed these theory-based design principles into actual artifact features, which we formalized by describing DFs. These DFs are implemented in the bi.smart Launchpad as a knowledge portal that provides decision makers and developers in SMEs with focused knowledge and tools to extend their innovation and development processes to innovate smart services and design their product with intelligent components for data collection. Figure 1 provides an overview of the overall architecture of the bi.smart Launchpad.

The bi.smart Launchpad primarily focuses on SMEs that already operate in an existing core business ('brown-field innovation'), as opposed to innovation tools that target early entrepreneurial activities such as startup incubators ('green-field innovation'). Therefore, we expect the users, who are typically managing directors or product and service development teams, to already have extensive knowledge of their existing products, services, and processes, as well as what data is already available in what types and formats, which they apply as their individual input when using the bi.smart Launchpad. Through the provided methodological resources in the web application, those users can derive output for their SSI projects in the form

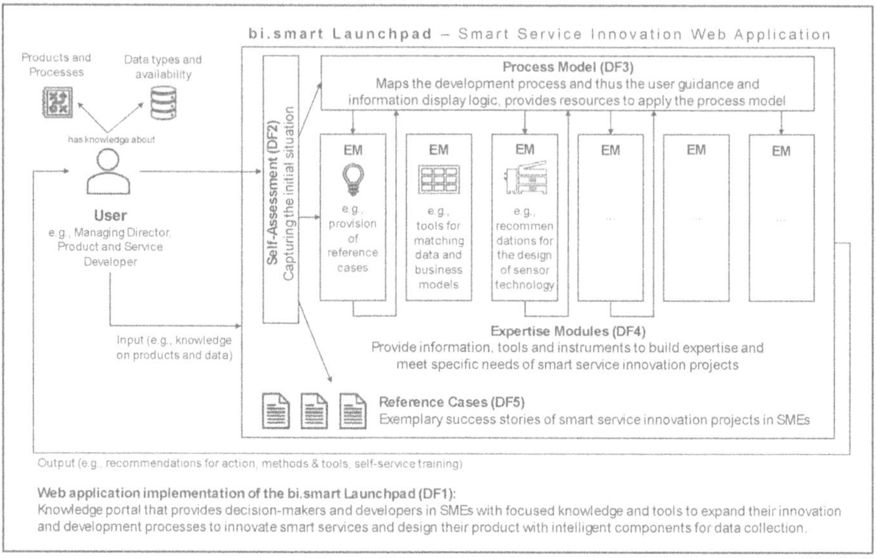

Fig. 1 bi.smart Launchpad architecture

of recommendations for action, applicable methods & tools, as well as self-service training.

The bi.smart Launchpad web application consists of multiple structural components that were individually and collectively designed to meet the above-described DRs to address key challenges that SMEs face in SSI projects. Table 2 provides an overview of these components, which serve as DFs of our protoype to address the DRs. In the next subsection, we present the set of DFs derived through our research and illustrate their implementation in the bi.smart Launchpad prototype in more detail.

Table 2 Overview of the design features of the bi.smart launchpad

Design Feature	DR1	DR2	DR3	DR4	DR5	DR6
DF1: Web application		X	X	X	X	
DF2: Self-assessment	X	X			X	X
DF3: Process model	X	X	X		X	X
DF4: Expertise modules	X	X	X			
DF5: Reference cases	X				X	X

3.2 Design and Implementation of the bi.smart Launchpad Prototype

The design and implementation of the bi.smart Launchpad was primarily guided by five formalized DFs to address the DRs introduced earlier. In the following, we present in detail the components of our prototype along these DFs by describing them their implementation in the bi.smart Launchpad, which can be accessed via www.bismart.info.

DF1: Web application. Central to the design of the bi.smart Launchpad is its development as a publicly available web application that meets the requirements for independence and accessibility (DR2) and the demand for a user-friendly interface (DR5). Using Webflow, we leveraged a comprehensive library of design elements to ensure a responsive, aesthetically pleasing user experience and cross-device accessibility, which is critical for the diverse technology environments of SMEs. The application relies on a content management system to facilitate easy updates and scalability, supporting SMEs' need for a self-sufficient resource (DR2). Accessibility is prioritized by eliminating barriers such as payment or mandatory registration, in line with our goal to democratize access to innovation tools and methods (DR4). These two DRs are further addressed by deliberately providing the content in German, the first language of the primary addressees of this project, while future translations are planned. To build trust and strengthen its credibility, the application includes testimonials from industry and academic partners, as well as information on public funding (DR3). In addition, a repository of academic publications underpins the application, providing users with a foundation of rigorous scientific knowledge (DR3).

DF2: Self-assessment. The self-assessment component serves as the primary entry point for SMEs using the bi.smart Launchpad, ensuring that each SME's unique project context is thoroughly understood and appropriately supported. Through a questionnaire-based interface, SMEs can provide insight into the context of their SSI project and their organizational specifics. This ensures user-friendliness (DR5) and paves the way for customized support in future versions of the bi.smart Launchpad.

By analyzing responses and comparing them with clusters of existing cases that have been studied in more detail in previous research, the tool matches SMEs with the most relevant entry scenario to provide immediate feedback on common challenges identified (Fig. 2). In its current stage of implementation, the scenarios are distinguished along three dimensions: business focus (products/services/solutions), maturity of development processes, and degree of standardization of the business. This matching is consistent with DR6 to provide situational guidance by connecting SMEs to relatable success stories (see DF5) and suggesting methodological resources tailored to the project's respective requirements. Such tailored suggestions fulfill DR1 by facilitating efficient navigation through SSI projects. In addition, the self-assessment tool enables SMEs to start their innovation journey with minimal external

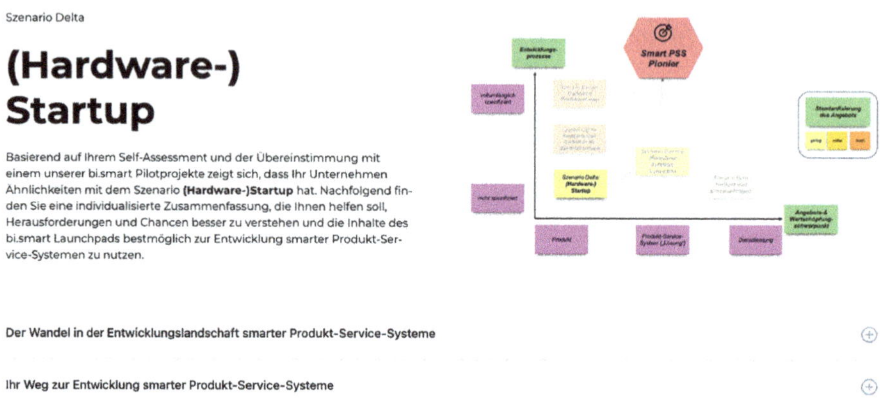

Fig. 2 Excerpt of a scenario description as a self-assessment response

dependencies (DR2). Overall, this DF ensures that SMEs have a personalized, actionable plan based on their self-assessment results, promoting a guided exploration of the bi.smart Launchpad.

DF3: Process model. The process model is a key DF of the prototype, designed to guide SMEs through integrated product and service development for SSI. This model provides a clear sequence of process steps, tasks, and methods, ensuring that SMEs can efficiently navigate the innovation process, directly addressing DR1 (methodological knowledge support). It is equipped with appropriate methods and tools, drawing on both emerging insights from the academic field of SSI and established frameworks such as the Business Model Canvas [30], thus meeting the standards of DR3 (scientifically rigorous content). An assembly of excerpts from the bi.smart Launchpad in Fig. 3 visualizes the layered presentation of the process model – from a general overview of the process, to the overview pages of the implemented process phases, to a detailed outline of a task within the SSI process, which then link to exemplary step-by-step method description for completing one of the tasks (only a visualization of a method template is included in the figure). In total, the bi.smart Launchpad currently includes three process phases further divided into ten process steps and 39 tasks, which are supported by 58 methods with respective templates and descriptions.

Designed for independence and accessibility (DR2), the process model enables SMEs to manage their innovation projects independently without external support (DR2). Its implementation through the user-friendly interface of the bi.smart Launchpad ensures intuitive, step-by-step navigation, making complex methodological knowledge accessible and applicable (DR5). Furthermore, the adaptability of the process model to the specific needs and contexts of SME projects offers situational guidance and flexibility (DF6), providing tailored guidance and tools at key stages of the innovation process.

DF4: Expertise modules. The expertise modules within the bi.smart Launchpad serve as targeted support for SMEs navigating complex aspects of SSI, currently

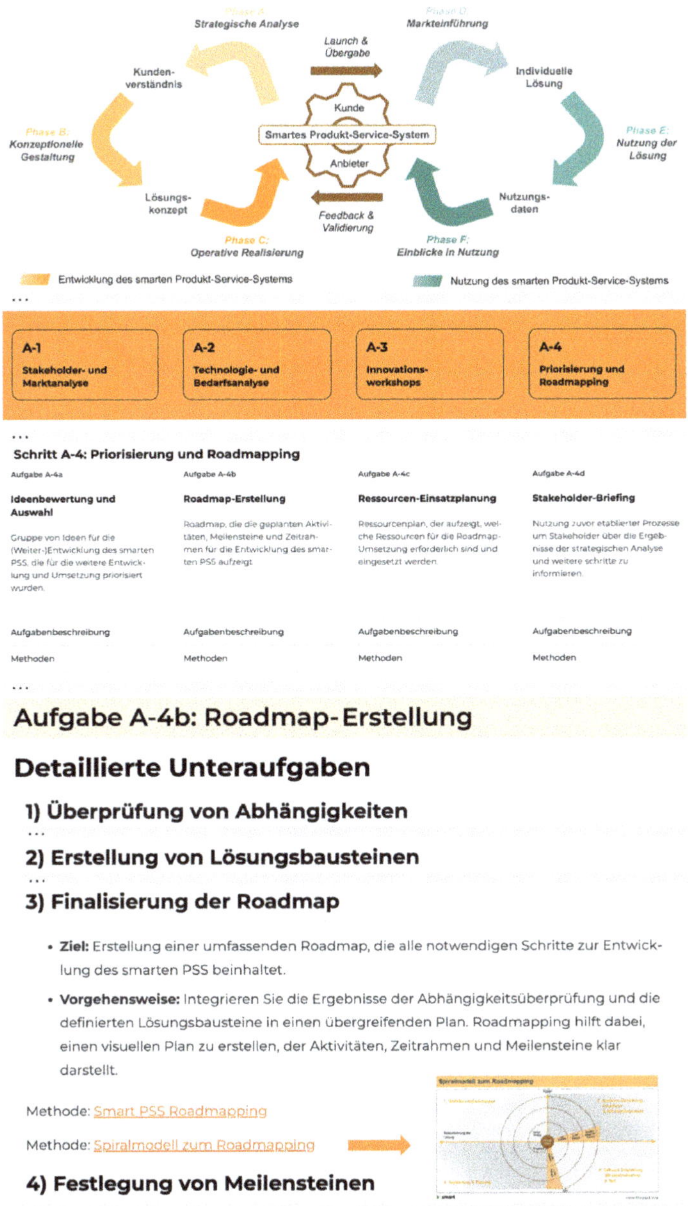

Fig. 3 Overview of the different layers of resources in the process model

covering data and information management, customer (data) integration, business modeling, IIoT platforms and ecosystems, work system design, and sensor integration. These modules distill complex scientific knowledge into practical, accessible guidance by providing SMEs with a collection of tailored methodological knowledge for specific, often challenging aspects of SSI (DR1). For example, the expertise module on IIoT platforms provides an overview of different types and value constellations of data sharing platforms [20], explains the concept of virtual sensors [24], as well as managerial approaches to foster value co-creation in IoT ecosystems [38] among others. These modules allow SMEs to independently explore and implement new technologies and subject areas without external support (DR2) by making the latest scientific knowledge available to SMEs and translating it into practical examples. This ensures that SMEs have access to high quality, scientifically validated information, facilitating informed decision-making and innovation (DR3).

DF5: Reference cases. The reference cases in the bi.smart Launchpad provide SMEs with inspiring success stories from companies that have successfully developed smart products and services through SSI projects. These case descriptions set the context of the company and the initial challenges faced within the SSI project and then detail the project's progress, key solutions employed, and lessons learned, providing SMEs with actionable insights and practical knowledge (Fig. 4). In addition, these reference cases are summarized in videos for an intuitive understanding of the project.

These cases contribute directly to DR1 (methodological knowledge support) by demonstrating practical applications of methodological knowledge in different contexts. The format aligns with DR5 (user-friendly interface) through engaging storytelling and visual summaries that make complex insights accessible. They also support DR6 (situational guidance and flexibility) by providing adaptable insights

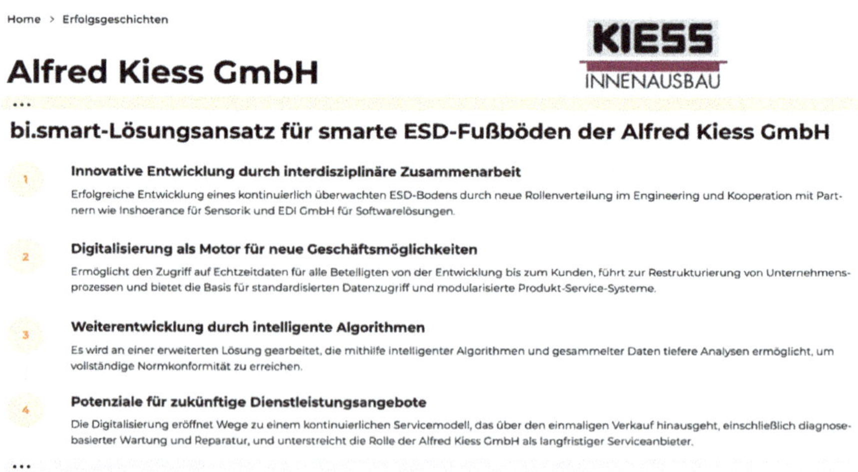

Fig. 4 Exemplary excerpt of a reference case in the bi.smart launchpad

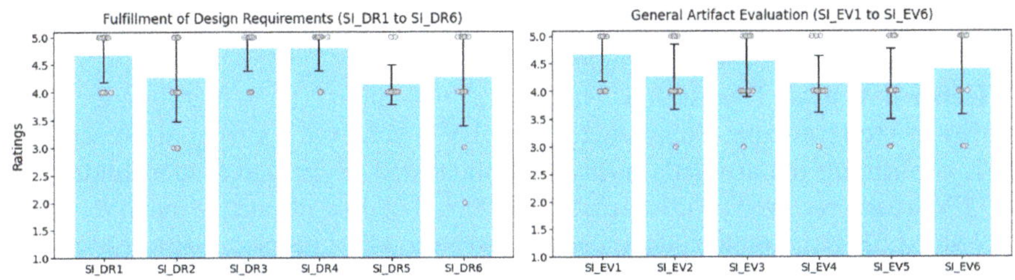

Fig. 5 Evaluation results indicating mean and standard deviation (n = 15)

that SMEs can apply to their unique project needs, demonstrating how different strategies can be tailored to meet specific challenges.

4 Evaluation

Our evaluation used a structured survey to assess the bi.smart Launchpad. The survey instrument was designed to measure satisfaction with the six DRs and six evaluation criteria for the overall artifact derived from Sonnenberg and vom Brocke (2012), with responses collected on a Likert scale from 1 (poorly met) to 5 (excellently met). A total of 15 responses were collected from both researchers and practitioners with expertise in the context of smart service innovation, either from their own company context or from past and current involvement in joint research-industry SSI projects. While three participants had provided feedback at earlier stages of the project, our sampling deliberately focused on leveraging our broader network to gather unbiased feedback. The participants were introduced to our goal of supporting SSI projects in SMEs that already have a core business and asked to familiarize themselves with the structure and content of the bi.smart Launchpad in detail. They then used the survey instrument to provide quantitative feedback. In addition to the quantitative ratings, participants were able to provide comments on each rating to guide further improvement of the artifact.

Fulfillment of design requirements. Data synthesis revealed robust support for the DRs with an overall mean of 4.49. With a mean of 4.67, the prototype fulfills its core objective of providing methodological knowledge support (SI_DR1). The prototype's commitment to open source availability (SI_DR4) received very strong support with a mean of 4.8. Similarly, the mean score of 4.8 for scientifically rigorous content (SI_DR3) underscores the scientific foundation of the prototype's resources. Situational guidance and flexibility (SI_DR6) received a broader range of responses and a lower mean of 4.27, indicating opportunities for refinement, particularly in increasing the system's adaptability to the diverse needs of SME projects, e.g., by incorporating principles from situational method engineering [11, 17]. Independence and accessibility (SI_DR2) and user-friendly interface (SI_DR5) received lower scores with a mean of 4.27 and 4.13 respectively, still signaling support for our current prototype but indicating areas for improvement.

General Artifact Evaluation. The general evaluation criteria highlight the practicality of the prototype. Completeness (SI_EV1) achieved a strong mean score of 4.67, confirming the artifact's utility. Simplicity (SI_EV2) and Understandability (SI_EV3) each received positive reviews, reflected in their respective mean scores of 4.27 and 4.53. Echoing the sentiment of a user-friendly interface, Ease of Use (SI_EV4) and Elegance (SI_EV5), with slightly lower mean scores of 4.13 each, suggest potential areas for streamlining. Fidelity With Real World (SI_EV6), with a mean score of 4.4, indicates that the prototype effectively reflects the practical needs of the industry, although it suggests that additional tuning could better capture the nuances of SSI projects.

The data collected confirms the effectiveness of the bi.smart Launchpad in supporting SSI in SMEs. With high marks for its methodological support and scientific foundation, the prototype is positioned as a strong resource for its purpose. Despite its pronounced strengths, nuanced feedback – enriched by qualitative comments – points to actionable insights for iterative improvement. This includes a focus on increased adaptability and an optimized user experience, guiding the artifact's ongoing evolution.

It is important to acknowledge that our survey-based evaluation cannot fully validate the prototype's utility in practical settings through tangible economic benefits for SMEs, such as enhanced profitability or faster innovation cycles. The absence of metrics on economic success or smart service quality evolution leaves questions about its effectiveness and impact. While these economic implications are beyond this paper's scope, they are crucial for future research, which should connect the prototype's design with measurable business outcomes through longitudinal studies (Fig. 5).

5 Conclusion and Outlook

The demonstration of the bi.smart Launchpad prototype through the elaboration of its DFs illustrates how the artifact aims to address the key DRs identified for supporting SMEs in SSI. Each DF has been designed to ensure that SMEs are equipped with the tools, knowledge, and inspiration necessary to navigate SSI projects. Together, they enhance the usability, accessibility, and applicability of the bi.smart Launchpad, making it a valuable resource for SMEs seeking to leverage smart technologies for competitive advantage. By integrating practical tools with tailored methodological guidance and real-world success stories, the bi.smart Launchpad combines rigorous scientific knowledge with user-friendly design to foster innovation in the SME sector. Through this prototype demonstration, we not only showcase the capabilities of the bi.smart Launchpad, but also set the stage for future developments and enhancements aimed at empowering SMEs for successful SSI projects.

In considering the future trajectory of the bi.smart Launchpad, a number of extensions are being considered to enhance its capacity to facilitate SSI in the SME sector. These potential development paths build on the initial positive evaluations and foundational structure of the prototype to evolve the bi.smart Launchpad in response to the emerging needs of the SME community and the dynamic landscape of digital innovation. The planned enhancements are characterized by a focus on content expansion, enhanced user engagement, and integration of advanced technology features, while maintaining a critical balance between rich functionality and user accessibility.

First, **content expansion** within each bi.smart Launchpad component is expected to address a broader range of SSI projects. This includes incorporating materials that address specific objectives, such as sustainability initiatives or industry-specific challenges. The challenge here is to enrich the Launchpad offerings without overwhelming users, which will require further improvements in interface design and content navigation to maintain usability. Second, the platform aims to open up to scientific contributions by **introducing upload and review functionalities.** This extension aims to democratize the accumulation and dissemination of methodological knowledge by enabling broader participation in content creation and validation. Such a move towards a community-driven model not only enriches the resource base of the Launchpad, but also fosters a collaborative academic environment.

Third, increased customization through the **implementation of a digital representation layer** of individual SSI projects is considered. This would allow for methodological suggestions to be more precisely tailored to the context of SSI projects [11, 19], based on user inputs such as self-assessment results, use case specifics, and project characteristics. The integration of functionalities such as cookies or user accounts could facilitate this personalization, although this requires careful consideration of data integrity and keeping entry barriers low. Finally, exploring the **integration of an intelligent chatbot** within the user interface could be a significant leap toward using advanced technology to assist with methodology application and documentation. This chatbot could provide situational methodological guidance based on both structured and unstructured information available, combining generative AI capabilities with the platform's research-based frameworks.

These potential avenues for extending the bi.smart Launchpad represent a balanced approach to enhancing its utility for SMEs. Each proposed extension is underpinned by the dual objectives of increasing its comprehensiveness and ensuring its continued accessibility and relevance to the target users. As the development of the bi.smart Launchpad progresses, these enhancements will be critically evaluated, guided by ongoing user feedback and the evolving needs of SSI in the SME sector.

Acknowledgements This work was supported by the German Federal Ministry of Education and Research through the research project "Integrated Design of Smart Product-Service Systems in SMEs (bi.smart)" (grant no. 02J19B041). The authors would like to thank Thomas Freudenmann, Thomas Meiren, Daniel Roth and Gerhard Satzger for their support of this publication, as well as the five participating SMEs for their invaluable project insights and feedback during the development of the bi.smart Launchpad.

References

1. Abramovici, M., Gebus, P., & Savarino, P. (2018). Engineering smarter Produkte und Services - Plattform Industrie 4.0 Studie.
2. Anke, J., Ebel, M., Pöppelbuß, J., & Alt, R. (2020a). How to Tame the Tiger - Exploring the Means, Ends, and Challenges in Smart Service Systems Engineering. In *ECIS 2020 Proceedings*.
3. Anke, J., Pöppelbuß, J., & Alt, R. (2020b). It Takes More Than Two to Tango: Identifying Roles and Patterns in Multi-actor Smart Service Innovation. *Schmalenbach Business Review, 72*, 599–634.
4. Becker, J., Beverungen, D., Knackstedt, R., Matzner, M., Müller, O., & Pöppelbuß, J. (2013). Bridging the Gap Between Manufacturing and Service Through IT-Based Boundary Objects. *IEEE Transactions on Engineering Management, 60*(3), 468–482.
5. Beverungen, D., Müller, O., Matzner, M., Mendling, J., & vom Brocke, J. (2019). Conceptualizing smart service systems. *Electronic Markets, 29*(1), 7–18.
6. Böhmann, T., Leimeister, J. M., & Möslein, K. (2014). Service systems engineering. *Business & Information Systems Engineering, 6*(2), 73–79.
7. Bullinger, H.-J., Meiren, T., & Nägele, R. (2015). Smart Services in Manufacturing Companies. In *23rd International Conference on Production Research* (pp. 7–13).
8. Chowdhury, S., Haftor, D., & Pashkevich, N. (2018). Smart Product-Service Systems (Smart PSS) in Industrial Firms: A Literature Review. *Procedia CIRP, 73*, 26–31.
9. German Standards Institute. (2019). *DIN SPEC 33453:2019–09 Entwicklung digitaler Dienstleistungssysteme (Development of digital service systems)*. Beuth.
10. Giray, G., & Tekinerdogan, B. (2018). Situational Method Engineering for Constructing Internet of Things Development Methods. In *Business Modeling and Software Design (BMSD 2018)* (pp. 221–239).
11. Gottschalk, S., Yigitbas, E., Nowosad, A., & Engels, G. (2021). Situation-Specific Business Model Development Methods for Mobile App Developers. In *Enterprise, Business-Process and Information Systems Modeling (BPMDS EMMSAD 2021)* (pp. 262–276).
12. Grisold, T., Kremser, W., Mendling, J., Recker, J., vom Brocke, J., & Wurm, B. (2023). Keeping pace with the digital age: Envisioning information systems research as a platform. *Journal of Information Technology, 38*(1), 60–66.
13. Hagen, S., Jannaber, S., & Thomas, O. (2018). Closing the gap between research and practice – A study on the usage of service engineering development methods in German enterprises. In *Exploring Service Science*. Lecture notes in business information processing (pp. 59–71).
14. Heinz, D., & Anke, J. (2023). Empowering Practitioners: A Conceptual Framework for Value Co-Creation through Smart Service Innovation Methodologies. In *ECIS 2023 Proceedings*.
15. Heinz, D., Benz, C., Bode, J., Hunke, F., & Satzger, G. (2022a). Exploring the Potential of Smart Service Systems: A Multi-actor View on Affordances and Their Actualization. *SMR-Journal of Service Management Research, 6*(2), 132–146.
16. Heinz, D., Park, H.-R., Benz, C., & Satzger, G. (2022b). Innovating Smart Product-Service Systems in Manufacturing SMEs: Current Practices, Affordances, and Constraints. In *IEEE CBI 2022 Proceedings*.
17. Henderson-Sellers, B., & Ralyté, J. (2010). Situational method engineering: State-of-the-art review. *Journal of Universal Computer Science, 16*(3), 424–478.
18. Hevner, A. R., March, S. T., Park, J., & Ram, S. (2004). Design Science in Information Systems Research. *MIS Quarterly, 28*(1), 75–79.
19. Howell, D., Windahl, C., & Seidel, R. (2010). A project contingency framework based on uncertainty and its consequences. *International Journal of Project Management, 28*(3), 256–264.
20. Jussen, I., Fassnacht, M., Schweihoff, J.C., & Möller, F. (2024). Reaching for the Stars: Exploring Value Constellations in Inter-Organizational Data Sharing. In *ECIS 2024 Proceedings*.

21. Jussen, P., Kuntz, J., Senderek, R., & Moser, B. (2019). Smart service engineering. *Procedia CIRP, 83*, 384–388.
22. Kurtz, J., Zinke-Wehlmann, C., Lugmair, N., Schymanietz, M., & Roth, A. (2023). Characterising smart service systems – Revealing the smart value. *SMR-Journal of Service Management Research, 7*(2), 112–128.
23. Maleki, E., Belkadi, F., & Bernard, A. (2018). A Meta-model for Product-Service System based on Systems Engineering approach. *Procedia CIRP, 73*, 39–44.
24. Martin, D., Kühl, N., & Satzger, G. (2021). Virtual Sensors. *Business & Information Systems Engineering, 63*(3), 315–323.
25. Marx, E., Pauli, T., Fielt, E., & Matzer, M. (2020). From services to smart services: Can service engineering methods get smarter as well? In *Wirtschaftsinformatik 2020 Proceedings.*
26. Moser, B., & Faulhaber, M. (2020). Smart Service Engineering. In *Smart Service Management* (pp. 45–61). Springer International Publishing.
27. Nambisan, S., Lyytinen, K., Majchrzak, A., & Song, M. (2017). Digital Innovation Management: Reinventing Innovation Management Research in a Digital World. *MIS Quarterly, 41*(1), 223–238.
28. Neuhüttler, J., Kett, H., Frings, S., Falkner, J., Ganz, W., & Urmetzer, F. (2020). Artificial Intelligence as Driver for Business Model Innovation in Smart Service Systems. In *11th International Conference on Applied Human Factors and Ergonomics (AHFE 2020).* Available at: https://doi.org/10.1007/978-3-030-51057-2_30.
29. Neuhüttler, J., & Nägele, R. (2023). The role of Data and AI during development of Smart Services. In *14th International Conference on Applied Human Factors and Ergonomics (AHFE 2023).*
30. Osterwalder, A., & Pigneur, Y. (2010). *Business Model Generation: A Handbook for Visionaries, Game Changers, and Challengers.* John Wiley & Sons.
31. Paliyenko, Y., Heinz, D., Schiller, C., Tüzün, G.-J., Roth, D., & Kreimeyer, M. (2023). Requirements for a smart product-service system development framework. *Proceedings of the Design Society, 3*, 3085–3094.
32. Pöppelbuß, J., & Durst, C. (2019). Smart Service Canvas – A tool for analyzing and designing smart product-service systems. *Procedia CIRP, 83*, 324–329.
33. Porter, M. E., & Heppelmann, J. E. (2014). How smart, connected products are transforming competition. *Harvard business review, 92*(11), 64–88.
34. Qi, Y., Mao, Z., Zhang, M., & Guo, H. (2020). Manufacturing practices and servitization: The role of mass customization and product innovation capabilities. *International Journal of Production Economics, 228*, Article 107747.
35. Schiller, C., Friedrich, M., & Buchart, S. (2022). Dissemination of smart product-service systems in the corporate world. In *13th International Conference on Applied Human Factors and Ergonomics (AHFE 2022).*
36. Shapiro, D. L., Kirkman, B. L., & Courtney, H. G. (2007). Perceived causes and solutions of the translation problem in management research. *Academy of Management journal, 50*(2), 249–266.
37. Sonnenberg, C., & vom Brocke, J. (2012). Evaluation Patterns for Design Science Research Artefacts. In *Practical Aspects of Design Science* (pp. 71–83). Springer.
38. Sterk, F., Heinz, D., Peukert, C., Fleuchaus, F., Kölbel, T., & Weinhardt, C. (2022). Fostering Value Co-Creation in Incumbent Firms: The Case of Bosch's IoT Ecosystem Landscape. In *ICIS 2022 Proceedings.*
39. Stokes, D. E. (2011). *Pasteur's Quadrant: Basic Science and Technological Innovation.* Brookings Institution Press.
40. Tosato, G. (2021). Enabling the dealer network to deliver smart services. In *Managing Industrial Services* (pp. 173–183). Springer International Publishing.
41. Ulaga, W., & Reinartz, W. J. (2011). Hybrid Offerings: How Manufacturing Firms Combine Goods and Services Successfully. *Journal of marketing, 75*(6), 5–23.
42. Valencia, A., Mugge, R., Schoormans, J. P. L., & Schifferstein, H. N. J. (2015). The design of smart product-service systems (PSSs): An exploration of design characteristics. *International Journal of Design, 9*(1), 13–28.

43. Wolf, V., Franke, A., Bartelheimer, C., & Beverungen, D. (2020). Establishing Smart Service Systems is a Challenge: A Case Study on Pitfalls and Implications. In *Wirtschaftsinformatik 2020 Proceedings* (pp. 103–119).

Two Sides of the Same Coin: An E-Commerce Ecosystem Agent-Based Simulation

Gero Strobel, Tobias Wulfert, and Leonardo Banh

Abstract E-commerce is one of the most important sectors of the economy, with an expected global turnover of USD 7.4 trillion in 2024. Leading companies in the industry like Amazon and Alibaba leverage platform business models that orchestrate complex ecosystems of buyers and sellers. These ecosystems are characterized by globally intertwined networks of independent participants and multifaceted interactions, making their development hard to predict. We propose an agent-based simulation approach, following the three-step process of Haki et al. (2020), to predict the behavior of e-commerce ecosystems with a particular focus on the impact of premium subscription services. Simulation models offer the opportunity to tangibly visualize the effects of a participant's actions on the ecosystem level. Our simulation includes the key actors (i.e., buyer, seller, marketplace), their characteristics, and behaviors to draw conclusions about the evolution of the ecosystem and the strategic role of premium memberships in shaping these digital landscapes.

1 Introduction

Increasing globalization and tremendous digitalization efforts at the societal, company, and individual level have resulted in complex systems of independent but intertwined actors. Platform business models have enriched many industry sectors because the most valuable companies (e.g., Apple, Amazon, and Alibaba) orchestrate multi-sided markets [1]. These companies form digital business ecosystems with their surrounding participants, which serve (end) customers [2]. These business

G. Strobel · T. Wulfert · L. Banh (✉)
University of Duisburg-Essen, Universitätsstraße 2, Essen, Germany
e-mail: leonardo.banh@uni-due.de

G. Strobel
e-mail: gero.strobel@uni-due.de

T. Wulfert
e-mail: tobias.wulfert@uni-due.de

C. M. Flath et al. (eds.), *Shaping the Digital Future Through Innovation and Practice*,
Lecture Notes in Information Systems and Organisation 85,
https://doi.org/10.1007/978-3-032-08489-7_14

models propel ecosystem complexity with an increased division of labor [3]. Due to increasingly interactive processes and global dependencies, even single actors have the power to influence the overall ecosystem (e.g., supply-chain shortages). Precisely the e-commerce sector builds on these mechanisms of complex systems with independent but intertwined actors and represents the most important economic sector with an expected global revenue of USD 7.4 trillion and 24.5% of total retail sales [4]. As it allows electronically supported retail transactions without spatial and temporal restrictions [5], e-commerce is likely to be conducted globally in systems of systems [6]. The most successful organizations in e-commerce operate platform business models exploiting the economic effects of two-sided markets (e.g., matching and subsidizing selected participants) [7]. These platforms form the center of e-commerce ecosystems, which are surrounded by networks of independent participants such as buyers and sellers [8]. These focal platforms (e.g., Amazon Marketplace, Walmart Marketplace, and Alibaba.com) actively orchestrate ecosystem participants by executing governance rules [9]. They match supply- and demand-side participants to enable retail transactions involving additional actors (e.g., content providers) [10, 11]. As focal platforms in e-commerce mature, they alter their business models by providing additional (retail-related) services for ecosystem participants [10]. These services aim at differentiating the company from other competing platforms and locking in participants [12]. A popular means of locking in demand-side participants (i.e., customers) is premium memberships (e.g., Amazon Prime, Walmart + , and Alibaba 88 VIP) that offer privileged services (e.g., free deliveries, exclusive offers, and prioritized order handling) compared to standard members. Membership fees are an important source of revenue for platform owners, although rumors have been raised by recent announcements of price increases for premium memberships [13–15].

Because e-commerce ecosystems are composed of complex and global networks of intertwined but independent participants and a multitude of interacting processes [16], it is worthwhile investigating their behavior. However, the behaviors and interactions of single participants collectively shape the entire ecosystem, making it challenging to predict the evolution of e-commerce ecosystems in general as a consequence of the behavior of single participants within them [17, 18]. Therefore, computationally intensive theory construction approaches, such as simulations, can provide a suitable vehicle to address the complexity and dissect the evolution of e-commerce ecosystems and their participants [19]. Recent studies in information systems research have shown that agent-based simulations are especially suitable for the analysis of complex adaptive systems (i.e., two-sided markets, ecosystems) by simulating the micro-level behaviors that form the macro pattern (i.e., the system under investigation) [20–22]. Against this backdrop, we address the following research question:

How can the behavior of ecosystems and their participants in e-commerce. be predicted when premium services are introduced?

To address the research question, we conceptualized and developed a multi-agent-based simulation of e-commerce ecosystem [8], including the key actors, their characteristics, and their relationships, to analyze their behavior. This paper focuses on the analysis and simulation of the two-sided markets involving buyers and sellers [23, 24] and the central service mechanisms of today's e-commerce platforms [25].

Specifically, this work establishes the foundation for a computationally intensive theory construction endeavor for e-commerce ecosystems by providing an approach to consider the key players in an e-commerce ecosystem (i.e., buyer, seller, and marketplace), their interaction, and the influencing factor of premium membership. Future research will extend the simulation to an overall ecosystem simulation approach, e.g., by including further approaches of simulating agents via generative agents [26, 27]. The remainder of this paper is structured as follows. First, we elicit the fundamentals on agent-based simulations and platforms in e-commerce ecosystems. Second, we present our research approach following 28 [28]. Third, we present our results of the e-commerce ecosystem simulation and the impact of platform memberships on ecosystem development. Finally, we briefly summarize our results and provide an outlook for further research and extending our simulation.

2 Theoretical Background

2.1 Agent-Based Simulation

In natural and social sciences (e.g., chemistry, biology, and economics), the methodological approach of simulation is considered a de facto standard [29]. The use of simulations, and in particular **agent-based simulations**, continues to increase in information systems research due to their suitability for analyzing complex phenomena [20, 28, 30]. This is especially true for the simulation of complex adaptive systems [29], and deployment scenarios include the role of information technology in organizational learning [31], the evolution of information systems architectures [28], the examination of market mechanisms in ecosystems [22], and the efficiency-based tuning of human and machine learning [32]. Regardless of the individual design, agent-based simulations are founded on three central elements: **agents**, **interactions**, and **environment** [33, 34].

Agents are the core actors of the simulation and represent a broad variety of different objects ranging from individuals to technological concepts to entire organizational structures, depending on the phenomenon under investigation [34]. Similar to real-world entities possessing attributes and behaviors (e.g., human beings), agents also possess attributes that characterize themselves and behavior rules that describe how the attributes change or how agents act based on their perception of their environment [35–37].

Interactions describe bidirectional behaviors of agents within the simulation due to the connections and flows between them [34, 35, 37]. Connections define relational links within the simulation that describe which agent or rather which attribute-based instance of an agent (e.g., buyer) may interact with which agent instance of the same or another (e.g., seller) attribute base [34]. Due to the adaptive and dynamic nature of agent-based simulations, the definition of interactions is one of the key challenges in simulation modeling [33]. Flow, on the other hand, characterizes the exchange of resources between agents, which can reflect a range of material or immaterial objects (e.g., goods, money, and information) similar to the agents' attributes depending on the scenario [34, 37]. The exchange of resources between agents serves not only as a realistic representation of real-world phenomena but as fuel for the simulation, keeping it in a stable state and preventing the transition to an entropic state [34, 38].

Environment represents the surroundings and thus the conditions under which the agents behave and interact [28, 36]. The topography of the environment can be modeled by corresponding structures based on the phenomenon under investigation (e.g., valuable resources in a mining simulation). These structures themselves passively influence the simulation through their explicit conditions for the unfolding of actions and interactions [34]. A common example is the predator–prey ecosystem, in which the hunter's access to the prey is blocked by a natural structure such as a rock or reef.

2.2 *Two-Sided Market Theory in E-Commerce Ecosystems*

A **two-sided market** "refers to a market with two distinct sides that benefit from network effects by interacting on a common platform" [23]. Multi-sided markets describe platforms with more than two independent types of actors [39]. Transaction platforms orchestrate two (or more) previously distinct market sides and enable (retail) transactions between them [23, 40, 41]. Thus, **transaction platforms** can be seen as synonymous to digital marketplaces. Network effects describe the benefits of actors caused by the number of participants on the same (i.e., direct) or other (i.e., indirect) market side [23, 42]. These effects can be either positive or negative [39].

Two-sided markets require clearly separable market sides and a strict assignment of participants to a market side to successfully exploit network effects [2]. However, a single actor can also take on multiple roles in multi-sided markets in subsequent transactions [10]. 43 [43] identified demand- and supply-side participants as well as the platform owner as archetypal **actors** in two-sided markets. In the context of e-commerce, they resemble the customer and seller [8]. The platform owner's major source of revenue is transaction fees charged for matching participants and enabling retail transactions [10]. The transaction fee depends on the price of the product or service exchanged. 40 [40] identified volume of network effects, payment type, and multi-homing possibilities as determinants of the price structure in two-sided markets.

Focal platforms (i.e., digital marketplaces) in e-commerce ecosystems can be characterized as multi-sided markets [10, 24]. They intermediate between independent ecosystem participants from separate market sides (e.g., advertising partner, developer, or seller) that can be assigned with unambiguous roles [11]. The independent participants form an e-commerce ecosystem with a common goal (e.g., provide final customers with products or services) [2]. The platform owner can influence the surrounding ecosystem participants by implementing certain governance mechanisms and providing an interaction structure [9, 44]. **E-commerce ecosystems** are digital business ecosystems in the context of e-commerce with focal transaction platforms orchestrating different participants and enabling retail-related transactions between them [8, 24].

3 Research Methodology

Agent-based simulations can be seen as a "third kind of science" [45], besides induction and deduction, that allows us to analyze complex systems, their participants, and the relations among them in a controlled environment. The utilization of such a computationally intensive approach provides us with the methodological groundwork for theory building [19], and the associated achievement of our research goal of predicting the behavior of ecosystems and their participants to pursue. We approach e-commerce ecosystems from a theoretical perspective grounded in the influence of individual actors, the interaction between them, the complex environment, and the dynamic adaptation to this environment as complex adaptive systems (CAS) [8, 34, 35, 37, 38, 46]. Our research process is adapted from the three-phase approach by 28 [28], which followed 20 [20] and 47 [47] for the development of agent-based simulations (Fig. 1).

Phase 1 – Model Development: The simulation is based on a conceptual model that represents the object of investigation. The starting point of our model development was the synthesis of theoretical foundations from the environment of the object of study (e.g., two-sided market theory) combined with the analysis of real-world

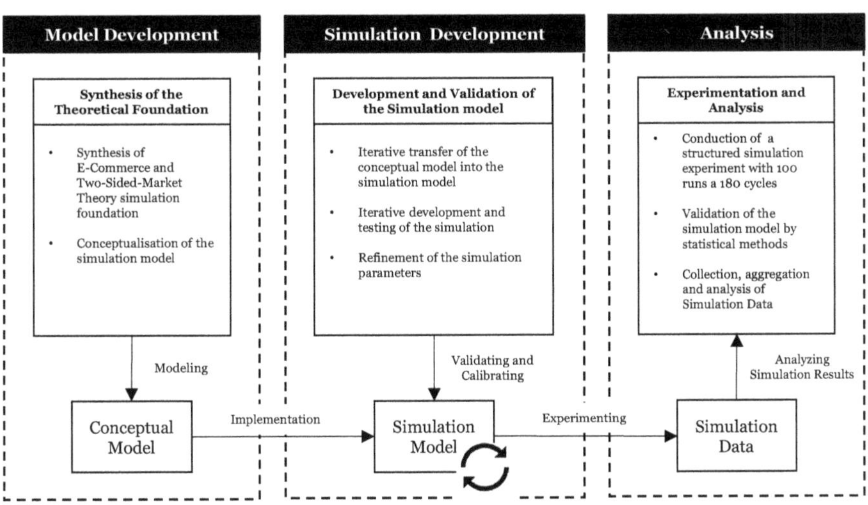

Fig. 1 Research design

scenarios (e.g., Amazon and Walmart) to derive the actors, their behavior, and their relationships. Based on this analysis, we were able to identify key actors (**buyers, sellers**, and **marketplaces**) as agents for the simulation (Table 1).

Marketplaces act as intermediaries between the other agents in the simulation [24]. The central task here is to execute transactions between docked sellers and visiting buyers. If a transaction is successful with the given probability, it is tracked, and the marketplace receives a transaction fee as a share of the transaction price [10]. Primary attributes of the marketplace are the transaction probability in matching buyers and sellers, the number of successful checkouts, and the marketplace's share of transaction fees [48]. Here, the sphere of influence in which the marketplace can interact with the buyer or seller is limited but can grow or shrink depending on the turnover of the marketplace, which is simulated by the success of a marketplace. In addition, a special type of marketplace has been defined that offers a subscription for membership to the platform based on typical premium subscriber models [15].

Buyers search the ecosystem for products or services that match their requirements [10]. When they find a marketplace, they search it for suitable offers and

Table 1 Simulation model conceptualization

Simulation elements		Description	Sources
Agent	Buyer	*Attributes:* Have the need to purchase products and services	[5]
		Behavioral rules: If an interest in buying prevails, searches for marketplaces and offers matching the needs; if matching offer is available, may decide to purchase it; otherwise, continues to search the ecosystem	[11, 43]
	Seller	*Attributes:* Search for opportunities to sell products and services	[5]
		Behavioral rules: Is continuously looking to find sales opportunities; if there is a suitable marketplace with buyers, places offers; otherwise, searches for other marketplaces	[11, 43]
	Marketplace	*Attributes:* Act as an intermediary between supply and demand *Behavioral rules:* Attracts other entities based on their intermediary role; connects supply and demand and creates average price; randomly offers premium membership to buyers	[24] [10]
Interaction	Buyer	*Connection*: Buyer–marketplace *Flow*: Paying energy	[24]
	Seller	*Connection*: Seller–marketplace *Flow*: Receiving energy	[24]
	Marketplace	*Connection*: To all entities in the ecosystem *Flow*: Distributing energy and keeping energy (fees)	[39]
Environment		E-commerce ecosystem with dedicated marketplaces where buyers and sellers can move freely, disappear but also add new ones	[2]

take them accordingly. At selected marketplaces, buyers can sign up for a premium membership, which will provide them with better conditions and increase their preference for this marketplace. In return, a monthly fee must be paid to the marketplace [15].

Sellers offer their products or services on the marketplace [10]. These arise costs, which are estimated per month. If a marketplace becomes occupied by too many other sellers in relation to the number of desired customers, sellers may seek other sales channels [43].

Phase 2 – Simulation Development: The developed conceptual model was iteratively transformed into a simulation. During development of the simulation, we decided to implement the model in the form of a cellular automaton as a grid. The cellular automata represent one of the five basic topologies for agent-based simulation and enable a structured 2D simulation based on the interaction of the cells with their environment. By integrating a multi-cell grid (i.e., the multiple occupancy of a cell), we were able to represent the immaterial infinity of e-commerce marketplaces. To establish a baseline for the parameterization and in particular to obtain the range of the parameters of the simulation, we looked at existing simulation models from the same subject area as a starting point. We also conducted degeneracy tests following 20 [20]. In line with transparency and knowledge accumulation, the full list of parameters is online available (https://bit.ly/TS0tSCabS). Subsequent work will include comprehensive sensitivity analyses that examine the effect of each selected parameter on the system behavior and ultimately help to gain insights in the emergence of patterns and properties generated in the CAS [49]. Further, in the spirit of open science, we plan to publish our simulation, including all code.

Phase 3 – Analysis: In total, the simulation was run as a structured experiment 100 times in a row with 180 cycles each. In the process, 10 million individual data points were collected and aggregated, and the corresponding average for each attribute was formed for each cycle as the basis for the evaluation of the results. To confirm the soundness of the simulation results, we statistically evaluated our data by conducting a multiple linear regression analysis. The regression analysis allowed us to test whether independent variables have a significant effect on a dependent variable. The goal was to investigate the impact of premium memberships and membership fees on e-commerce ecosystem level. Thus, the regression analysis examined the focal platform effect (i.e., the platform type) on economic success. Furthermore, we introduced a premium membership subscription as a second independent variable and assessed how membership fees affect the overall economic success.

The regression was conducted to evaluate if the platform type and price of a premium membership had a significant effect on the marketplace energy. The results revealed that the simulation model was statistically significant, $F(2, 432{,}044) = 211.847$, $p < .001$, $R^2 = .001$. The marketplace energy had a positive and significant coefficient in relation to the platform type, i.e., premium or non-premium ($\beta = 109.34$, $p < .001$), and also a positive and significant coefficient in relation to the membership price ($\beta = 37.554$, $p < .001$). Therefore, a premium focal platform will lead to a 109.34 times higher energy than a standard platform, and the energy will increase 37.553 units for each unit increase of the membership price. This indicates that our simulation showed the expected results, mimicking the competitive advantage of a premium focal platform with membership fees (i.e., higher energy equals more revenue).

4 Results

The execution of our structured simulation experiment with 100 runs of 180 cycles in a 20 by 20 grid with four randomly positioned marketplaces resulted in the distribution of demand-side (i.e., buyers) and supply-side (i.e., sellers) actors depicted in Fig. 2a. Further evaluations (e.g., checkouts, data points) are additionally available online (https://bit.ly/TS0tSCabS).

In contrast to the average of the three standard platforms (solid blue and green curves), the premium platform attracted more participants (dotted orange and red curves). The number of participants indicated the amount of retail transactions orchestrated by each platform per period. While the premium platform orchestrated 4429 transactions, the other platforms only reached 3610 participants on average. This orchestration was monetarized by the platforms with commission fees. Hence, the premium platform generated 5823 fees in total compared to 4055 by the average of other platforms.

The shape of the curves in Fig. 2 resembles a hockey stick form, described in the literature as the typical shape of participants in platform business models exploiting network effects [7, 50]. A tipping point—when the minimum threshold of participants required for network effects to occur—was reached around 10% of the number of total participants after the 89th iteration. A typical tipping point in platforms with network effects has been conceptualized and reflected in previous research [51–53]. All four platforms in our simulation were able to capture network effects and monetize them. Sharp increases in the number of actor curves occurred every 12 iterations (i.e., every year) and resembled the holiday season (Fig. 2a). Moreover, our algorithm then calculated whether the reach of a platform had to be increased

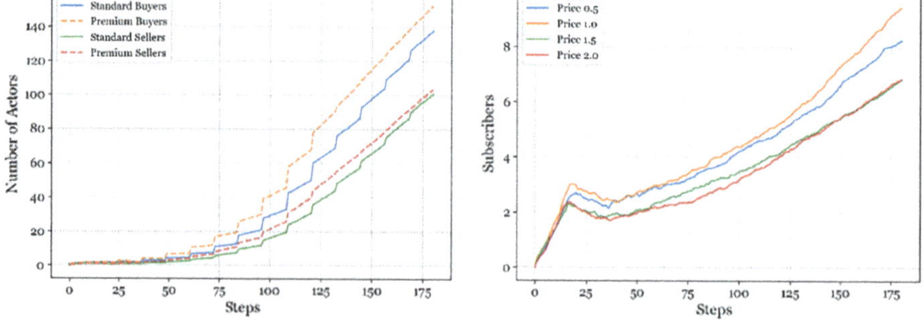

Fig. 2 Number of (a) Actors and (b) Premium subscribers

because of the number of participants. This behavior reflects the effects of word of mouth among participants and was part of the direct network effects [54].

Following the research of 55 [55] on the optimal price for a membership fee (including free shipping) for platforms in e-commerce ecosystems, we applied our agent-based simulation to determine an optimal price for our premium marketplace. We tested premium prices from 0 to 2 in intervals of 0.1 and plotted the number of premium subscribers for the membership fees of 0.5, 1.0, 1.5, and 2.0 (Fig. 2b). The membership fee reduced the total buying power of the demand-side participants, which started at a value of 100 when a new buyer was generated.

The simulation runs revealed that a membership fee of 1.0 resulted in an average of 9.4 premium subscribers after 15 years. Premium membership fees above this threshold seemed too expensive for demand-side participants compared to the benefits of premium memberships and resulted in a decline in the number of premium memberships. Interestingly, the curves for a price of 1.5 and 2.0 converged after 15 years of simulation so that the fees could be increased more dramatically. Amazon's announcements regarding increasing their premium membership fee could be analyzed using these simulation results [14]. Premium subscriptions have proven to be an important and effective loyalty program in e-commerce [56]. On average, premium subscribers spend more money and buy more often compared to non-premium buyers [57]. Additionally, premium subscribers have a higher behavioral loyalty toward the preferred platform, so multi-homing is more unlikely for them [58]. However, premium memberships with free shipping scenarios decreased the number of articles per purchase.

5 Conclusion, Limitations, and Outlook

E-commerce ecosystems are among the most successful business models and the leading companies in this sector, such as Amazon, Walmart, and Alibaba, exert a global influence. Building on the multi-layered interconnectedness of the individual players and the network of globally acting independent actors, these ecosystems can hardly be analyzed with classical methods, let alone their development predicted. However, computationally intensive approaches such as multi-agent simulation provide an approach to address these limitations.

Building on this premise, our paper provides a first approach for simulating e-commerce ecosystems based on their key actors (e.g., buyers, sellers, etc.), their characteristics and dependencies in a two-sided market. We applied our simulation approach to predict the impact of a premium membership platform with demand-side and supply-side participants and determine an optimal membership fee. Simulations are necessary in e-commerce ecosystems because of their complex nature with regard to processes and interactions. Hence, we provide a first tool for guiding actors within these ecosystems. The owners of focal platforms in e-commerce ecosystems can use this simulation to test governance rules (practical contribution). We contribute to existing research on e-commerce ecosystems with a novel approach simulating an excerpt of an e-commerce ecosystem's development at the level of single actors in a two-sided market.

Aside from our contribution to e-commerce research, our work is not without limitations. Currently, the simulation focuses on the key players (e.g., marketplaces, buyers, and sellers), first order within the e-commerce ecosystems. In a next step, we plan to integrate further actors including their behavior and relationships to the already modeled actors into the simulation. On the supply side, manufacturers play an important role by providing the ecosystem with products and services [59]. Supporting actors such as service providers offer value-adding transaction services to other participants [60] and platform providers supply the necessary software for digital platforms [61]. Actors from the surrounding environment such as investors or the government can also have a far reaching impact on all actors by providing necessary monetary foundation for certain participants [62] or enforcing trade and tax laws [63]. Modeling the distinct attributes and actions of each additional participant and their relations among each other allows us to investigate and validate our simulation model, for instance under the aspect of premium memberships or the introduction of external constraints (e.g., trade laws). By expanding our current work with further actors, relations, and actions, we aim at a holistic computationally intensive approach towards simulating the behavior of e-commerce participants and constructing theory regarding our research goal.

Besides the integration of further actors, the integration of additional market and ecosystem mechanisms (e.g., openness etc.) plays a central role in creating a holistic simulation approach. In addition to the simulation of dedicated scenarios at the operational level, this would enable the longitudinal simulation of ecosystems starting from the foundation to the evaluation of different ignition strategies. Detached from the e-commerce context, it would also be conceivable to transfer the simulation to other ecosystem domains such as the topic area of data ecosystems and associated problems such as data sharing. In conclusion, this paper provides another building block for simulation-based analysis and modeling of complex systems in information systems research.

References

1. Gawer, A. (2021). Digital platforms' boundaries: The interplay of firm scope, platform sides, and digital interfaces. *Long Range Planning, 54*, Article 102045. https://doi.org/10.1016/j.lrp.2020.102045
2. Adner, R. (2017). Ecosystem as structure. *Journal of Management, 43*, 39–58. https://doi.org/10.1177/0149206316678451
3. Schüßler, E., Attwood-Charles, W., Kirchner, S., & Schor, J. B. (2021). Between mutuality, autonomy and domination: Rethinking digital platforms as contested relational structures. *Socio-Economic Review, 19*, 1217–1243. https://doi.org/10.1093/ser/mwab038
4. Lebow, S.: Worldwide ecommerce continues double-digit growth following pandemic push to online (2021), Retrieved from: https://www.emarketer.com/content/worldwide-ecommerce-continues-double-digit-growth-following-pandemic-push-online

5. Zwass, V. (1996). Electronic commerce: Structures and issues. *International Journal of Electronic Commerce, 1*, 3–23. https://doi.org/10.1080/10864415.1996.11518273
6. Stallkamp, M., & Schotter, A. P. J. (2021). Platforms without borders? The international strategies of digital platform firms. *Global Strategy Journal, 11*, 58–80. https://doi.org/10.1002/gsj.1336
7. Parker, G., van Alstyne, M., & Choundary, S. (2016). *Platform revolution: How networked markets are transforming the economy and how to make them work for you*. W. W. Norton & Company.
8. Wulfert, T., Woroch, R., Strobel, G., Seufert, S., & Möller, F. (2022). Developing design principles to standardize e-commerce ecosystems: A systematic literature review and multi-case study of boundary resources. *Electronic Markets, 32*, 1–30. https://doi.org/10.1007/s12525-022-00558-8
9. Hein, A., Schreieck, M., Riasanow, T., Setzke, D. S., Wiesche, M., Böhm, M., & Krcmar, H. (2020). Digital platform ecosystems. *Electronic Markets, 30*, 87–98. https://doi.org/10.1007/s12525-019-00377-4
10. Wulfert, T., Seufert, S., Leyens, C. (2021) Developing multi-sided markets in dynamic electronic commerce ecosystems—Towards a taxonomy of digital marketplaces. In: *Proceedings of the 54th Hawaii International Conference on System Sciences (HICSS 2021)*, pp. 6133–6142. Maui, Hawaii
11. Böttcher, T., Rickling, L., Gmelch, K., Weking, J., Krcmar, H.: Towards the Digital Self-Renewal of Retail: The Generic Ecosystem of the Retail Industry. In: Proceedings of the 16th Internationale Tagung Wirtschaftsinformatik (WI2021), pp. 1–9. Essen, Deutschland (2021)
12. Cennamo, C. (2021). Competing in digital markets: A platform-based perspective. *Academy of Management Perspectives, 35*, 265–291. https://doi.org/10.5465/AMP.2016.0048
13. Amazon: Amazon Annual Report 2022 (2023), Retrieved from https://bit.ly/3IoUt1D
14. Herrera, S. (2022). Amazon raises prime membership to $139 a year, citing shipping, labor costs. Retrieved from https://www.wsj.com/articles/amazon-prime-membership-increased-to-139-per-year-due-to-rising-shipping-labor-costs-11643930324
15. Lee, J.-Y., Fang, E., Kim, J. J., Li, X., & Palmatier, R. W. (2018). The effect of online shopping platform strategies on search, display, and membership revenues. *Journal of Retailing, 94*, 247–264. https://doi.org/10.1016/j.jretai.2018.06.002
16. Jacobides, M. G., Cennamo, C., & Gawer, A. (2018). Towards a theory of ecosystems. *Strategic Management Journal, 39*, 2255–2276. https://doi.org/10.1002/smj.2904
17. Hannah, D. P., Tidhar, R., & Eisenhardt, K. M. (2021). Analytic models in strategy, organizations, and management research: A guide for consumers. *Strategic Management Journal, 42*, 329–360. https://doi.org/10.1002/smj.3223
18. Harrison, J. R., Lin, Z., Carroll, G. R., & Carley, K. M. (2007). Simulation modeling in organizational and management research. *AMR, 32*, 1229–1245. https://doi.org/10.5465/amr.2007.26586485
19. Miranda, S., Berente, N., Seidel, S., Safadi, H., Burton-Jones, A. (2022). Editor's comments: Computational intensive theory construction: A primer for authors and reviewer. *MIS Quarterly, 46*, iii–xviii.
20. Davis, J. P., Eisenhardt, K. M., & Bingham, C. B. (2007). Developing Theory Through Simulation Methods. *AMR, 32*, 480–499. https://doi.org/10.5465/amr.2007.24351453
21. Schalowski, J., & Barrot, C. (2019). The long-term diffusion of digital platforms—An agent-based model. ICIS 2019 Proceedings.
22. Schmid, M., Haki, K., Tanriverdi, H., Aier, S., Winter, R. (2021). Platform over market – when is joining a platform beneficial? *ECIS 2021 Research Papers*. Vol. 2021
23. Rochet, J., & Tirole, J. (2003). Platform competition in two-sided markets. *Journal of the European Economic Association, 1*, 990–1029. https://doi.org/10.1162/154247603322493212
24. Hagiu, A., & Wright, J. (2015). Multi-sided platforms. *International Journal of Industrial Organization, 43*, 162–174. https://doi.org/10.1016/j.ijindorg.2015.03.003
25. Turban, E., Whiteside, J., King, D., & Outland, J. (2017). *Introduction to electronic commerce and social commerce*. Springer International Publishing.

26. Park, J.S., O'Brien, J., Cai, C.J., Morris, M.R., Liang, P., Bernstein, M.S. (2023). Generative agents: Interactive simulacra of human behavior. In: Follmer, S., Han, J., Steimle, J., Riche, N.H. (eds.) *Proceedings of the 36th Annual ACM Symposium on User Interface Software and Technology*. (pp. 1–22). ACM. https://doi.org/10.1145/3586183.3606763
27. Wang, L., Ma, C., Feng, X., Zhang, Z., Yang, H., Zhang, J., Chen, Z., Tang, J., Chen, X., Lin, Y. (2024). A survey on large language model based autonomous agents. *Frontiers of Computer Science, 18*. https://doi.org/10.1007/s11704-024-40231-1
28. Haki, K., Beese, J., Aier, S., & Winter, R. (2020). The evolution of information systems architecture: An agent-based simulation model. *MISQ, 44*, 155–184. https://doi.org/10.25300/MISQ/2020/14494
29. Dong, J. Q. (2022). Using simulation in information systems research. *Journal of the Association for Information Systems, 22*, 408–417. https://doi.org/10.17705/1jais.00743
30. Beese, J., Haki, M. K., Aier, S., & Winter, R. (2019). Simulation-based research in information systems. *Business & Information Systems Engineering, 61*, 503–521. https://doi.org/10.1007/s12599-018-0529-1
31. Kane, G. C., & Alavi, M. (2007). Information technology and organizational learning: An investigation of exploration and exploitation processes. *Organization Science, 18*, 796–812. https://doi.org/10.1287/orsc.1070.0286
32. Sturm, T., Gerlacha, J., Pumplun, L., Mesbah, N., Peters, F., Tauchert, C., Nan, N., & Buxmann, P. (2021). Coordinating human and machine learning for effective organization learning. *MISQ, 45*, 1581–1602. https://doi.org/10.25300/MISQ/2021/16543
33. Macal, C., & North, M. (2014). Introductory tutorial: Agent-based modeling and simulation. In: Proceedings of the Winter Simulation Conference 2014. pp. 6–20. IEEE. https://doi.org/10.1109/WSC.2014.7019874
34. Nan, N. (2011). Capturing bottom-up information technology use processes: A complex adaptive systems model. *MIS Quarterly, 35*, 505. https://doi.org/10.2307/23044054
35. Drazin, R., & Sandelands, L. (1992). Autogenesis: A perspective on the process of organizing. *Organization Science, 3*, 230–249. https://doi.org/10.1287/orsc.3.2.230
36. Epstein, J.M., Axtell, R.L. (1996). Growing artificial societies: Social science from the bottom up. The MIT Press
37. Holland, J. H. (2003). *Hidden order perseus books.* Cambridge.
38. Anderson, P. (1999). Perspective: Complexity theory and organization science. *Organization Science, 10*, 216–232. https://doi.org/10.1287/orsc.10.3.216
39. Boudreau, K., & Hagiu, A. (2009). Platform rules: Multi-sided platforms as regulators. In A. Gawer (Ed.), *Platforms, markets and innovation* (pp. 163–191). Edward Elgar Publishing.
40. Armstrong, M. (2006). Competition in two-sided markets. *The RAND Journal of Economics, 37*, 668–691.
41. Hagiu, A., & Wright, J. (2015). Marketplace or reseller? *Management Science, 61*, 184–203. https://doi.org/10.1287/mnsc.2014.2042
42. Shapiro, C., & Varian, H. (1998). *Information rules: A strategic guide to the network economy.* Harvard Business Press.
43. Eisenmann, T., Parker, G., & Alstynevan, M. (2009). Opening platforms: How, when and why? In A. Gawer (Ed.), *Platforms, markets and innovation* (pp. 131–162). Edward Elgar Publishing.
44. Helfat, C. E., & Raubitschek, R. S. (2018). Dynamic and integrative capabilities for profiting from innovation in digital platform-based ecosystems. *Research Policy, 47*, 1391–1399. https://doi.org/10.1016/j.respol.2018.01.019
45. Axelrod, R.M. (1997) *The complexity of cooperation. Agent-based models of competition and collaboration.* Princeton University Press.
46. de Reuver, M., Sørensen, C., & Basole, R. C. (2018). The digital platform: A research agenda. *Journal of Information Technology, 33*, 124–135. https://doi.org/10.1057/s41265-016-0033-3
47. Sargent, R.G. (2010). Verification and validation of simulation models. In: Proceedings of the 2010 Winter Simulation Conference. (pp. 166–183). IEEE. https://doi.org/10.1109/WSC.2010.5679166

48. Reillier, L.C., & Reillier, B. (2017). Platform strategy. How to unlock the power of communities and networks to grow your business. Routledge.
49. Broeke, G. ten, van Voorn, G., Ligtenberg, A.: Which sensitivity analysis method should i use for my agent-based model? *JASSS, 19*(2016). https://doi.org/10.18564/jasss.2857
50. McAfee, A. & Brynjolfsson, E. (2017). *Machine, Platform, Crowd. Harnessing our Digital Future.* W. W. Norton & Company, New York.
51. Evans, D. S., & Schmalensee, R. (2016). *Matchmakers the new economics of multisided platforms.* Harvard Business Review Press.
52. Steur, A. & Bayrle, N. (2020). S-curves in platform-based business—Facing the challenge of the tipping point. *PACIS 2020 Proceedings.* Vol. 2020.
53. Evans, D.S. & Schmalensee, R. (2010). Failure to launch: Critical mass in platform businesses. *Review of Network Economics, 9*(2010). https://doi.org/10.2202/1446-9022.1256
54. Cheung, C. M., & Thadani, D. R. (2012). The impact of electronic word-of-mouth communication: A literature analysis and integrative model. *Decision Support Systems, 54*, 461–470. https://doi.org/10.1016/j.dss.2012.06.008
55. Wen, Z., & Lin, L. (2017). Membership free shipping programs: Effect on competition and optimality of member fees. In: Proceedings of the 50th Hawaii International Conference on System Sciences. Proceedings of the Annual Hawaii International Conference on System Sciences. (pp. 3935–3939). Hawaii International Conference on System Sciences
56. Kumar, V., & Reinartz, W. (2018). Loyalty programs: Design and effectiveness. In: Kumar, V., Reinartz, W. (eds.) *Customer relationship management. Springer Texts in Business and Economics.* (pp. 179–205). Springer Berlin Heidelberg, Berlin, Heidelberg. https://doi.org/10.1007/978-3-662-55381-7_10
57. Ramadan, Z., Farah, M. F., & Bou Saada, R. (2021). Fooled in the relationship: How Amazon Prime members' sense of self-control counter-intuitively reinforces impulsive buying behavior. *Journal of Consumer Behaviour, 20*, 1497–1507. https://doi.org/10.1002/cb.1960
58. Ashley, C., Gillespie, E. A., & Noble, S. M. (2016). The effect of loyalty program fees on program perceptions and engagement. *Journal of Business Research, 69*, 964–973. https://doi.org/10.1016/j.jbusres.2015.09.001
59. Mishra, S., Tripathi, A.R.: Literature review on business prototypes for digital platform. *Journal of Innovation and Entrepreneurship, 9* (2020). https://doi.org/10.1186/s13731-020-00126-4
60. Kaoud, E., Abdel-Aal, M. A. M., Sakaguchi, T., & Uchiyama, N. (2020). Design and optimization of the dual-channel closed loop supply chain with e-commerce. *Sustainability, 12*, 10117. https://doi.org/10.3390/su122310117
61. Aulkemeier, F., Paramartha, M. A., Iacob, M.-E., & Hillegersberg van, J. (2016). A pluggable service platform architecture for e-commerce. *Information Systems and e-Business Management, 14*, 469–489. https://doi.org/10.1007/s10257-015-0291-6
62. Kwak, J., Zhang, Y., & Yu, J. (2019). Legitimacy building and e-commerce platform development in China: The experience of Alibaba. *Technological Forecasting and Social Change, 139*, 115–124. https://doi.org/10.1016/j.techfore.2018.06.038
63. Aulkemeier, F., Iacob, M.-E., & Hillegersbergvan, J. (2017). An architectural perspective on service adoption: A platform design and the case of pluggable cross-border trade compliance in e-commerce. *Journal of Organizational Computing and Electronic Commerce, 27*, 325–341. https://doi.org/10.1080/10919392.2017.1363588

Student Track

Evaluation of Hypothetical Document and Query Embeddings for Information Retrieval Enhancements in the Context of Diverse User Queries

Marten Jostmann and Hendrik Winkelmann

Abstract The task of Information Retrieval (IR) is the foundation of question-answering and information search systems. The complexity of these retrieval systems evolved to enable an effective search of a variety of documents based on users' information needs. However, the quality of the retrieval results highly depends on the question phrasing and structure heavily influenced by the user's age, expertise, background, and aim. This paper aims to close the gap between user-specific query structures and the content of various documents by employing the approaches Hypothetical Document Embeddings (HyDE) and Hypothetical Query Embeddings (HyQE). Both approaches achieve promising results in terms of effectiveness and robustness. An evaluation indicates that HyDE and HyQE outperform traditional retrieval methods such as BM25 and plain embedding methods.

1 Introduction

Large Language Models (LLMs) have demonstrated an extraordinary linguistic understanding and the capability of human-like text generation, reasoning, and question-answering [10, 11, 20]. In addition, LLMs are able to gain and reproduce knowledge through extensive pre-training [19]. However, access to new knowledge is limited and prone to hallucinations, i.e., nonfactual and wrong information [2, 13]. Hence, LLMs should not be utilized directly in organizational settings or critical domains. Recently, Retrieval-Augmented Generation (RAG) has gained attention as a possibility to solve this problem. However, the basis of all RAG systems is an underlying Information Retrieval (IR) the quality of which depends strongly on the question phrasing and structure heavily influenced by the age, expertise, background, and aim of the user [4, 18], thus requiring further tailoring. This research aims to

M. Jostmann (✉) · H. Winkelmann
viadee Unternehmensberatung AG, Münster, Germany
e-mail: marten.jostmann@viadee.de

H. Winkelmann
e-mail: hendrik.winkelmann@viadee.de

C. M. Flath et al. (eds.), *Shaping the Digital Future Through Innovation and Practice*,
Lecture Notes in Information Systems and Organisation 85,
https://doi.org/10.1007/978-3-032-08489-7_15

close the gap between query structures and phrasing and the content of different documents in large collections, hence enabling effective and robust RAG. Hypothetical Document Embeddings (HyDE) and Hypothetical Query Embeddings (HyQE) are investigated in the presence of query variations. Both approaches aim to bridge the lexical gap between the different phrasings of queries and documents by leveraging LLMs.

2 Approach

Hypothetical Document Embeddings (HyDE) and Hypothetical Query Embeddings (HyQE) are alternatives for approaching the concerns of information phrasing and structure. While HyDE is already described in previous work, HyQE is a combination of old ideas and new technology (see [6, 14, 16, 17]).

Hypothetical Document Embeddings Empirically, HyDE has already shown to improve IR results over traditional approaches [9]. HyDE can be used in various domains without requiring a labeled dataset. The core idea is the generation of a hypothetical answer document given a query. The generated document is expected to represent the target documents more effectively than the query itself. Thus, using it for search is expected to increase the effectiveness of IR.

An important aspect not considered in the original publication of HyDE is the handling of query variations and diverse user groups. Still, the creation of hypothetical documents is promising to mitigate these challenges. Compared to methods such as BM25 and dense embeddings, HyDE overcomes the lexical chasm between query and document. This is done by using the language comprehension and reasoning capabilities of LLMs to capture the different linguistic nuances of a query and expand its context.

Furthermore, the vocabulary probability distributions of queries and documents can be aligned by generating hypothetical documents. For instance, question-specific terms such as *what*, *when*, *where*, *why*, and *who* occur less frequently in documents but rather often in questions [3]. Such words would be deemphasized by the context expansion of LLMs, while the content to be searched for is being prioritized.

Hypothetical Query Embeddings A major disadvantage of HyDE is the unawareness of the document corpus. Using the HyDE approach it can never be assumed with absolute certainty whether the generated document is relevant to the given query or not (see [13]). This problem can be avoided by using HyQE since the process is reversed. Instead of generating hypothetical documents that imitate relevant documents, HyQE tries to generate suitable queries for a specific document. Queries are generated during the indexing phase, enabling an efficient IR through the use of dense embeddings. Compared to the HyDE approach, the user query only has to be embedded by an embedding model, leading to a time- and cost-efficient retrieval phase. In Fig. 1 the indexing process of HyQE is depicted.

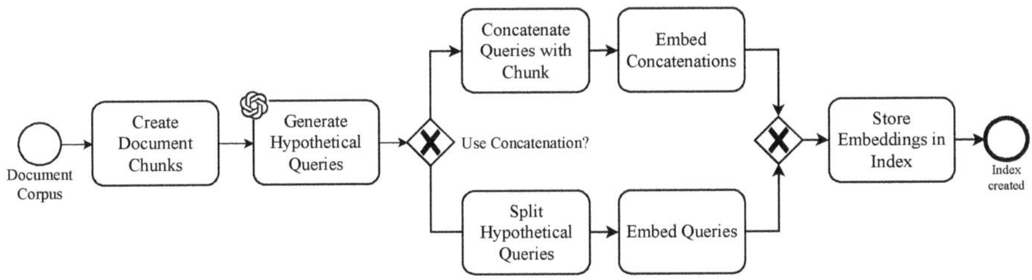

Fig. 1 HyQE indexing process

Initially, the potential target documents have to be split into smaller pieces using an appropriate chunking technique. For each text chunk, an LLM model can generate multiple hypothetical queries. Two options are conceivable. (1) Split generated queries and embed them separately and (2) concatenate all generated queries with the respective chunk. This outcome then is embedded. In the first variant, each query is weighted higher and, therefore, has a greater influence on the IR results in the case of a matching user query. The comparison of hypothetical queries and actual user queries is much more natural and associated with less bias. However, the missing document context can decrease IR performance. This can be mitigated using the second approach where all queries are concatenated with the respective chunk from the target document, thus preserving the document's context.

Moreover, HyQE can also prove advantageous in managing query variations in syntax and semantics: HyQE allows for the generation of specific hypothetical queries in various linguistic variants for the same information need. The underlying information need does not have to be inferred from ambiguous queries but can rather be directly used as the basis for creating questions. In addition, it is possible to create queries from different user perspectives and with consideration of the user's prior knowledge. The effectiveness of the subsequent IR system therefore depends on the number of generated queries, as the broadest coverage of possible variations can only be achieved by scaling up the query amount.

As all time-consuming and expensive steps are processed in the upstream indexing process, the downstream retrieval task can be processed rather quickly. The user is entering a query into the IR system which can be directly embedded without further preprocessing. The next step is to load the respective index from the indexing database. Subsequently, the user embedding is compared to each embedding in the index using a similarity or distance function.

3 Experiments

3.1 Setup

3.1.1 Implementation

Both HyDE and HyQE do not depend on a specific LLM or embedding model. For the experiments the `gpt-3.5-turbo-1106` model from OpenAI (see [7]) with a temperature of 0.3 and a frequency penalty of 0.5 was used to generate hypothetical documents and queries. This generation process was limited to a maximum of 1 500 tokens, allowing the model to freely generate documents and queries but still maintaining a reasonable time and cost effort. The `text-embedding-ada-002` was used as the embedding model (see [15]). The term-based method BM25 and semantic search with plain embeddings serve as the baseline to compare it to the new approaches.

3.1.2 Datasets

Both approaches were evaluated using two real-world test collections out of different domains. The first dataset, abbreviated as DS_1, is an excerpt of the internal Confluence document database of the viadee IT consultancy with over 9400 documents that are different from each other in terms of their subject. The second dataset (DS_2) consists of 30 HTML and PDF files from a public law institute in Germany. Both datasets consist of documents in German and are queried by diverse user groups with different information needs and each represents a different domain.

In order to perform a concise evaluation, not only datasets are required but also test collections containing different queries with their ground truth target documents. A relevance label is defined for each document based on the four-point scale of the TREC 2021 test collection [8]. The first test collection for the Confluence dataset consists of eleven topics with a total of 83 queries. The second test collection contains ten topics with 18 queries.

For the robustness evaluation, both collections were extended with automatically generated query variations based on the variations observed by Penha et al. [18].

3.1.3 Metrics

The effectiveness of the retrieval approaches will be measured using the normalized Discounted Cumulative Gain (nDCG) (see [12]). Furthermore, a measure of the retrieval robustness is required. The robustness evaluation should focus on the degree to which the IR system produces consistent outcomes in the presence of query variations. Hence, by considering only the robustness of the system the retrieval quality is neglected. One possibility to measure the robustness is the Inter-Topic Variance

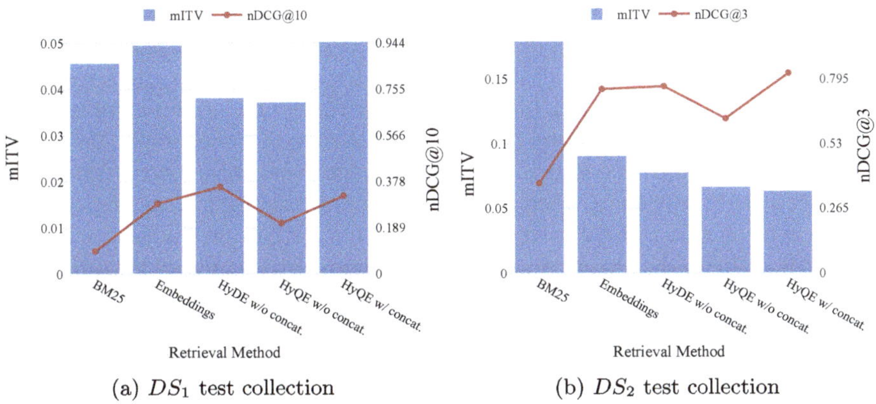

Fig. 2 Effectiveness and robustness of IR approaches

(ITV). For this purpose, the variance of the result of any effectiveness metric Φ_i^n is calculated for each topic $n \in \{1, ..., T\}$ consisting of several queries $i \in \{1, ..., Q\}$. Lastly, the mean Inter-Topic Variance (mITV) is calculated as shown in Eq. 1.

$$mITV = \frac{1}{T}\sum_{n=1}^{T}\sigma_n^2, \quad \text{where } \sigma_n^2 = \frac{1}{Q}\sum_{i=1}^{Q}(\Phi_{n,i} - \bar{\Phi}_n)^2 \tag{1}$$

In the later experiments, the nDCG score is used as the metric Φ, since it is the most informative measurement. A low mITV suggests a more robust system that can handle diverse user queries, as it indicates a reduced variability within the same information need. However, in order to be able to evaluate the overall performance of the IR system, the effectiveness must always be considered.

3.2 Results

In Fig. 2 the effectiveness and robustness of various approaches including the `BM25` and plain `Embeddings` baseline is depicted for two real-world datasets. For DS_1 (see Fig. 2a) both metrics are calculated based on the top 10 retrieval results. Due to the reduced size of DS_2 (see Fig. 2b), only the top 3 retrieval results will be considered.

The results in Fig. 2 indicate that `BM25` is a solid baseline but performs poorly compared to the `Embeddings` baseline. The overall best effectiveness could be achieved by the HyDE approach for the DS_1 test collection. However, for the DS_2 test collection, HyQE with concatenation was able to achieve an `ndcg@3` score of over 80 %.

Concerning the robustness, the results indicate that both baseline approaches are highly sensitive to query variations. By using HyDE, the robustness could be significantly increased compared to the baseline. Simultaneously, the effectiveness of the retrieval results is improved. It is notable that both HyQE variants exhibit significantly stronger deviations across different test collections. For example, the HyQE concatenation approach has both the highest robustness and the highest effectiveness on the second test collection, whereas the same approach has the lowest robustness on the first test collection. HyQE without concatenation exhibits the highest robustness on the DS_2 with the drawback of a lower effectiveness. Irrespective of the robustness deviations, HyQE with concatenation proves to be significantly more effective as the alternative approach in all experiments using Ada embeddings.

3.3 Discussion

The experiments on the effectiveness indicated a strong performance improvement when using HyDE and HyQE with Ada embeddings. The strengths of the HyDE approach originally proposed by Gao et al. could be validated. In addition to the general improvement in the document ranking, HyDE was able to find relevant documents for several queries and topics. Moreover, the HyQE approach demonstrated that the generation of potential user queries can result in a better ranking of relevant documents. The results indicate that the generated queries have to be concatenated with the document to achieve better rankings since the similarity search then can take the document context into account. As the two datasets stem from different domains, generalizability was validated to a certain degree. We expect HyQE to excel in domains where a diverse audience should be able to search for information containing domain-specific language using plain language, as is the case, e.g., in the medical and legal domains. On the other hand, HyDE might benefit from standard document structures in these domains, retrieving required sections.

In addition to the effectiveness, the robustness of the different methods also played a major role in the evaluation. The experiments showed that HyDE was able to deliver constant results even in the presence of various query variations. Contrary to the expectations, HyQE was not able to always improve the robustness of the IR system. While the robustness of HyQE was very low on the DS_1 test collection, it showed the highest robustness on the DS_2 test collection. Overall, the robustness of HyQE strongly depends on the selected dataset, the generated queries as well as the embedding method. Hence, no overarching conclusion can be inferred regarding the effectiveness and robustness of individual retrieval methods. It is promising to further investigate the effect of prompt engineering as a domain-specific hyperparameter tuning-step.

4 Related Work

Traditional retrieval methods based on near-exact match search, such as TF-IDF and BM25, often suffer from the lexical gap [3]. To address this limitation, dense representations in latent semantic spaces have been proposed [21]. In contrast to a sparse representation, dense text embeddings map the text into a fixed-sized, rather low-dimensional vector space. Given a query, similar or relevant texts can be found by comparing the similarity of these embedding vectors.

Based on dense text embeddings, query and document expansion mechanisms aim to refine user queries and documents to enhance the retrieval effectiveness [5]. With the help of query expansion techniques, the query can be extended with additional query terms to minimize the lexical gap between the query and the document. Popular approaches are Doc2Query and Inpars [6, 17]. In contrast to document expansion, query expansion shifts the focus from extending documents to refining queries. The most prominent example is *RM3* which iteratively adapts the user query by considering the retrieved documents as an additional query context [1]. A promising approach leveraging the generative capabilities of LLMs was proposed by GAO et al. [9], namely HyDE. Instead of extending the query with related terms, they suggest generating an intermediate hypothetical document that serves as a better comparison basis.

5 Conclusion

The main goal of this paper was to develop and apply HyDE and HyQE for IR in the context of diverse user queries. In particular, the effectiveness and robustness of these approaches were compared to traditional retrieval methods. The experimental results showed a high effectiveness and robustness of HyDE using both datasets compared to the baseline. However, hypothetical document generation is costly and time-consuming, which is the major drawback of this approach. HyQE mitigates this shortcoming by enabling a faster as well as cheaper retrieval but comes with the drawback of a more expensive indexing phase. The evaluation revealed a high effectiveness for the HyQE concatenation variant. The LLM model was able to generate realistic queries, considering different user perspectives and query types, which led to an increase in the ranking of relevant documents.

References

1. Abdul-Jaleel, N., James Allan, W., Croft, B., Diaz, F., Larkey, L., Li, X., Smucker, M. D., Wade, C., & Umass at trec,. (2004). Novelty and hard. In *Computer science department faculty publication series* (p. 189).

2. and Pascale Fung. Bang, Y., Cahyawijaya, S., Lee, N., Dai, W., Su, D., Wilie, B., Lovenia, H., Ji, Z., Yu, T., Chung, W., Do, Q. V., Xu, Y., & Fung, P. A. (2023). multitask, multilingual, multimodal evaluation of chatgpt on reasoning, hallucination, and interactivity. In J. C. Park, Y. Arase, B. Hu, W. Lu, D. Wijaya, A. Purwarianti & A. A. Krisnadhi (Eds.), *Proceedings of the 13th international joint conference on natural language processing and the 3rd conference of the Asia-Pacific chapter of the association for computational linguistics (Volume 1: Long Papers)* (pp. 675–718). Association for Computational Linguistics.
3. Berger, A., Caruana, R., Cohn, D., Freitag, D., & Mittal, V. (2000). Bridging the lexical chasm: Statistical approaches to answer-finding. In *Proceedings of the 23rd annual international ACM SIGIR conference on research and development in information retrieval* (pp. 192–199).
4. Bilal, D., & Kirby, J. (2002). Differences and similarities in information seeking: children and adults as web users. *Information Processing & Management, 38*(5), 649–670.
5. Billerbeck, B., & Zobel, J. (2005). Document expansion versus query expansion for ad-hoc retrieval. In *ADCS 2005 - proceedings of the tenth Australasian document computing symposium*.
6. Bonifacio, L., Abonizio, H., Fadaee, M., & Nogueira, R. (2022). *Inpars: Data augmentation for information retrieval using large language models*.
7. Brown, T., Mann, B., Ryder, N., Subbiah, M., Kaplan, J. D., Dhariwal, P., Neelakantan, A., Shyam, P., Sastry, G., Askell, A., et al. (2020). Language models are few-shot learners. *Advances in Neural Information Processing Systems, 33*, 1877–1901.
8. Craswell, N., Mitra, B., Yilmaz, E., Campos, D., & Lin, J. (2022). Overview of the trec 2021 deep learning track. In *Text REtrieval Conference (TREC)*. TREC.
9. Gao, L., Ma, X., Lin, J., & Callan, J. (2023). Precise zero-shot dense retrieval without relevance labels. In A. Rogers, J. Boyd-Graber & N. Okazaki (Eds.), *Proceedings of the 61st annual meeting of the association for computational linguistics (Volume 1: Long Papers)* (pp. 1762–1777). Association for Computational Linguistics.
10. Gatt, A., & Krahmer, E. (2018). Survey of the state of the art in natural language generation: Core tasks, applications and evaluation. *Journal of Artificial Intelligence Research, 61*, 65–170.
11. Jiang, Z., Araki, J., Ding, H., & Neubig, G. (2021). How can we know when language models know? on the calibration of language models for question answering. *Transactions of the Association for Computational Linguistics, 9*, 962–977.
12. Järvelin, K., & Kekäläinen, J. (2002). Cumulated gain-based evaluation of ir techniques. *ACM Trans. Inf. Syst., 20*(4), 422–446.
13. Lewis, P., Perez, E., Piktus, A., Petroni, F., Karpukhin, V., Goyal, N., Küttler, H., Lewis, M., Yih, W.-T., Rocktäschel, T., Riedel, S., Kiela, D. (2020). Retrieval-augmented generation for knowledge-intensive nlp tasks. In *Proceedings of the 34th international conference on neural information processing systems, NIPS'20*. Curran Associates Inc.
14. Ma, J., Korotkov, I., Yang, Y., Hall, K., & McDonald, R. (2021). Zero-shot neural passage retrieval via domain-targeted synthetic question generation. In P. Merlo, J. Tiedemann & R. Tsarfaty (Eds.), *Proceedings of the 16th conference of the european chapter of the association for computational linguistics: Main volume, Online, 2021* (pp. 1075–1088). Association for Computational Linguistics.
15. Neelakantan, A., Weng, L., Power, B., & Jang, J. (2022). Introducing text and code embeddings.
16. Nogueira, R., Lin, J., & Epistemic, A. I. (2019). From doc2query to docttttquery. *Online preprint, 6*, 2.
17. Nogueira, R., Yang, W., Lin, J., & Cho, K. (2019). Document expansion by query prediction.
18. Penha, G., Câmara, A., & Hauff, C. (2022). Evaluating the robustness of retrieval pipelines with query variation generators. In M. Hagen, S. Verberne, C. Macdonald, C. Seifert, K. Balog, K. Nørvåg, & V. Setty (Eds.), *Advances in information retrieval*. Lecture notes in computer science (Vol. 13185, pp. 397–412). Springer International Publishing.
19. Petroni, F., Rocktäschel, T., Riedel, S., Lewis, P., Bakhtin, A., Wu, Y, & Miller, A. (2019). Language models as knowledge bases? In K. Inui, J. Jiang, V. Ng & X. Wan (Ed.), *Proceedings of the 2019 conference on empirical methods in natural language processing and the 9th international joint conference on natural language processing (EMNLP-IJCNLP)* (pp. 2463–2473). Association for Computational Linguistics.

20. Wei, J., Wang, X., Schuurmans, D., Bosma, M., Ichter, B., Xia, F., Chi, E., Quoc, L., & Zhou, D. (2022). Chain-of-thought prompting elicits reasoning in large language models.
21. Zhao, W. X., Liu, J., Ren, R., & Wen, J.-R. (2024). Dense text retrieval based on pretrained language models: a survey. *ACM Transactions on Information Systems, 42*(4), 2024.

Exploring Themes in Digital Detox Research: Insights from a Literature Review

Marietta Forster, Fabian J. Stangl, and René Riedl

Abstract In modern society, digital technologies have become essential tools for individuals and organizations, offering unprecedented opportunities for communication and collaboration. However, concerns about the negative effects of digital technology use, such as declined well-being or reduced work productivity, have led to the emergence of digital detoxing as a promising strategy to counteract adverse effects. Digital detoxing refers to the temporary or complete disengagement from digital technologies, including actions such as abstaining from social networking sites and taking breaks during computer work. To guide future research, we conducted a literature review with a focus on empirical research dealing with the voluntary, limited abstinence from use of digital technologies. Thematic analysis of the 61 identified studies revealed eight major themes, including behavioral change, experience, health, motivation, social interaction, strategy, stress perception, and work. Overall, this review provides a comprehensive overview of the digital detox research field.

M. Forster · F. J. Stangl (✉) · R. Riedl
Digital Business Institute, School of Business and Management, University of Applied Sciences Upper Austria, Steyr, Austria
e-mail: fabian.stangl@fh-steyr.at

M. Forster
e-mail: marietta.forster@gmx.at

R. Riedl
e-mail: rene.riedl@jku.at

R. Riedl
Institute of Business Informatics—Information Engineering, Johannes Kepler University Linz, Linz, Austria

C. M. Flath et al. (eds.), *Shaping the Digital Future Through Innovation and Practice*, Lecture Notes in Information Systems and Organisation 85,
https://doi.org/10.1007/978-3-032-08489-7_16

1 Introduction

Digital technologies are essential to modern society, providing unparalleled opportunities for communication, collaboration, and productivity [167] in various domains such as healthcare (e.g., [56]), education (e.g., [27]), or banking (e.g., [10]). However, alongside these benefits, the widespread use of digital technologies has raised concerns about their potential negative impact on well-being (e.g., [148]) and organizational dynamics (e.g., [8]). Issues such as information overload (e.g., [142, 175]), constant interruptions (e.g., [162, 163]), or the blurring of work-life boundaries (e.g., [16, 33]) underscore the need to understand the complex effects of digital technology use (e.g., [144, 166, 176]).

In response to growing concerns about the negative consequences, *digital detoxing* has emerged as a compelling strategy in recent years [112]. Digital detoxing can be defined as temporary or complete disengagement from digital technologies and includes actions such as voluntary, limited abstinence from social networking sites such as Facebook, Instagram, or Snapchat [63, 161, 164]. Research has shown that short-term abstinence from social networking sites like Facebook can significantly increase life satisfaction and reduce stress [165]. Additionally, digital detoxing can involve reducing exposure to digital technologies [63, 161, 164]. For example, reducing daily Facebook use over a 14-day period, with participants limiting their use to 20 min per day, was associated with a decrease in depressive symptoms and an increase in life satisfaction [20]. These findings highlight the importance of maintaining a balanced relationship with digital technologies to promote well-being [63, 111].

Following the call for more research to explore the phenomenon of digital detoxing by Mirbabaie et al. [111], this review aims to analyze the themes of existing empirical studies on digital detoxing. To the best of our knowledge, a review on the themes of empirical digital detox studies has not yet been conducted. Hence, as a companion to Mirbabaie et al. [112] work on conceptualizing of digital detox within the information systems discipline, we address the following research question: **What are the major themes in the existing empirical research on digital detoxing?** More specifically, our analysis focuses on voluntary, limited abstinence from digital technologies, which is supposed to serve as a theoretical foundation for a larger research project on digital detoxing (i.e., a field study examining the effects of voluntary, limited abstinence from digital technologies).

2 Review Methodology

To identify the scope, range, and nature of empirical digital detox studies, we conducted a scoping review to determine the extent of existing literature and the topics addressed therein (for an overview of the different literature review types, please see [133, 151, 152]). To enhance transparency and methodological rigor, we

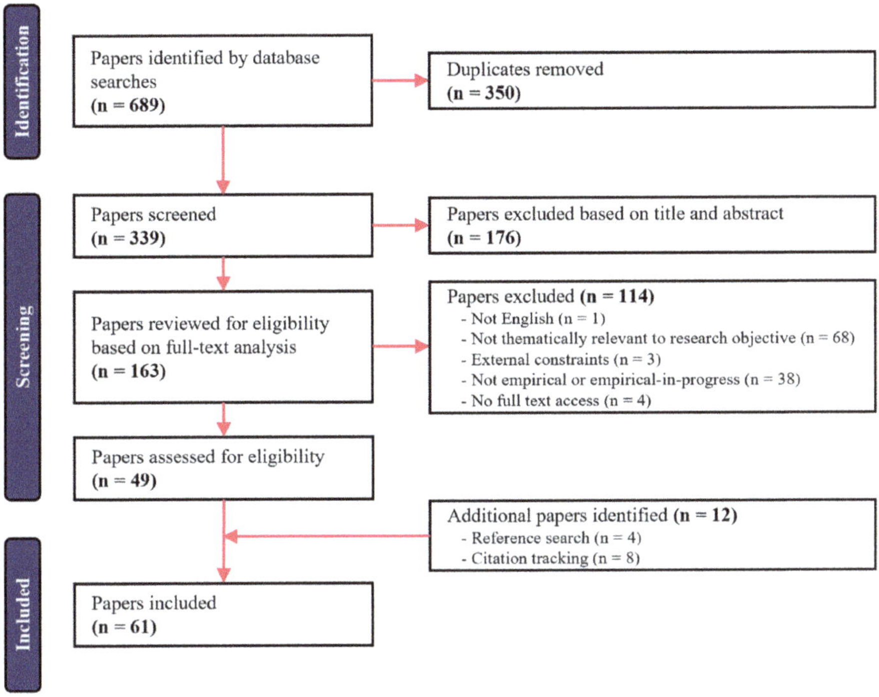

Fig. 1 PRISMA flowchart of literature search and paper selection

followed the Preferred Reporting Items for Systematic Reviews and Meta-Analyses (PRISMA, see Fig. 1) checklist for study identification, selection, and analysis [116, 117]. Also, our review process was aligned with established guidelines for literature searches [198, 200]. Overall, our review methodology consisted of three steps, resulting in a base of 61 empirical digital detox studies relevant to our research objective.

Step 1: Literature Identification—We began our literature search with a recent comprehensive review of empirical digital detox studies [63], which included 65 studies, surpassing previous reviews (e.g., [131, 141]). Keywords were primarily derived from this review, using terms such as "digital abstinence" and "digital disconnection", along with specific terms such as "digital free tourism" and "offline tourism". Due to the conceptual ambiguity of the field [112], we iteratively expanded our search to include terms such as "digital diet", "digital disconnection", and "tech detox", considering variations such as "internet detox" or "online detox." This ensured a comprehensive search syntax, with asterisks indicating generalizations (e.g., detox). The full list of keywords, shown in Table 1, aims to standardize terminology and reduce the proliferation of synonyms [9]. We searched peer-reviewed journals and conference proceedings in eight databases: ACM Digital Library, AIS eLibrary, EBSCO, Emerald, IEEE Xplore, Science Direct, Scopus, and Web of Science.

Table 1 Applied keywords for literature identification

Keyword Type	Keywords
Generic keyword	Digital abstinence, digital detoxification, digital detoxing, digital disconnection, digital reversion, technology non-use, tech detox
Specific keyword	Digital diet, digital disengagement, digital free tourism, digital nudge, offline tourism, unplugged tourism
Synonyms for digital detoxing	Internet detox, online detox

Note We asterisked the term 'digital detox' to generalize the term for the search when it can have multiple meanings (e.g., Internet Detox*, Online Detox*)

Step 2: Literature Screening—Our initial database contained 689 papers. After removing 350 duplicates, 339 unique papers were screened by title and abstract, resulting in the exclusion of 176 papers. The remaining 163 papers underwent full-text analysis based on the following Inclusion Criteria (IC) and Exclusion Criteria (EC):

- **IC1**: Papers must be in English and relevant to voluntary, limited abstinence from digital technologies.
- **IC2**: Papers must be of an empirical or empirical-in-progress nature (for an overview of the different contribution types, please see [145], pp. 18–21).
- **EC1**: Papers were excluded if they did not meet IC1, such as those not written in English (e.g., [91]), irrelevant to the research focus (e.g., social profile and preferences of individuals who abstain from social networking sites; [24]), or dealing with involuntary abstinence [5]. In addition, papers were excluded if they did not meet IC2, including reviews (e.g., [141]), methodological papers (e.g., [155]), or conceptual papers (e.g., [26]).
- **EC2**: Papers without full-text access (e.g., [201]).

Applying these criteria, 49 papers were retained for further analysis, while 114 were excluded due to IC and 4 due to EC2. The excluded papers are listed in Table 2.

Step 3: Literature Inclusion—Following established guidelines for literature searches [198, 200], we conducted a backward search, which identified 4 additional papers (i.e., [20, 29, 51, 65]), and a forward search that identified 8 additional papers (i.e., [36, 67, 88, 94, 146, 153, 168, 185]). This brought the final literature base to 61 empirical digital detox studies published as of April 2024, including 54 journal articles (88.5%), 4 conference papers (6.6%), 2 book chapters (3.3%), and 1 early publication (1.6%).

Table 2 Overview of excluded papers after literature screening

Exclusion Criterion	Number	Reference(s)
EC1: Not english	1	[91]
EC1: Not thematically Relevant to research objective	68	[4, 17, 21, 24, 28, 32, 34, 38–40, 43, 45, 47, 49, 50, 52, 54, 58, 60, 61, 64, 66, 68, 72, 75, 76, 81, 83, 86, 87, 89, 95, 97, 98, 100, 101, 103, 104, 107, 109, 118–121, 127, 128, 132, 134, 135, 137–139, 143, 154, 157, 159, 169, 172–174, 177, 183, 184, 188, 190, 202, 206, 207]
EC1: External constraints	3	[5, 19, 99]
EC1: Not empirical or empirical-in-progress	38	[3, 7, 12, 13, 15, 18, 26, 31, 46, 48, 53, 57, 59, 69, 70, 73, 74, 84, 85, 90, 92, 102, 105, 112, 114, 122, 123, 129, 140, 141, 147, 155, 156, 179, 180, 192–195]
EC2: No Full-Text Access	4	[62, 77, 186, 201]

3 Data Analysis Process of Thematic Analysis

To identify major themes in voluntary, limited abstinence from digital technology use from our literature base, we conducted a thematic analysis based on the methodology outlined by [22, 23]. This approach ensured a systematic analysis process to capture the nuances of the identified empirical digital detox studies. Overall, the data analysis process of the thematic analysis consisted of six phases, which we describe below.

Phase 1: Data Familiarization—In the first phase, we read and reread the 61 empirical digital detox studies to familiarize ourselves with their content. During this phase, we took preliminary notes and highlighted recurring concepts and patterns related to digital detoxing.

Phase 2: Data Coding—Next, we systematically coded the data by identifying features of interest across the dataset. This involved assigning labels to specific segments of text that captured elements related to voluntary, limited abstinence from digital technologies. We used a spreadsheet to manage and organize these codes to ensure a comprehensive coding process.

Phase 3: Generating Initial Themes—We then organized the initial codes into potential themes. This process involved grouping related codes together to form broader categories. We identified eight major themes that represented various aspects of the digital detox research field: behavioral change, experience, health, motivation, social interaction, strategy, stress perception, and work. However, each theme contained multiple codes that shared a common thread.

Phase 4: Review and Developing Themes—The next phase involved reviewing the themes to ensure that they accurately represented the data. We checked the coherence of the themes in relation to the coded excerpts and the entire data set. This iterative process led to the refinement of the themes and sub-themes, resulting in a thematic map that represented the focus of the research.

Phase 5: Refining, Defining and Naming Themes—We further refined each theme to capture its essence and scope. Clear definitions and names were assigned to each theme to provide a structured framework for the analysis. For example, the theme "Behavioral Change" encompasses studies examining how digital detoxing affects individuals' behaviors and habits, including alterations in social media use and offline activities. Table 3 provides definitions and examples of each theme.

Phase 6: Producing the Report—Finally, we compiled a report of our analysis, selecting illustrative examples from the dataset to highlight each theme. These themes are arranged alphabetically, with details of the identified themes presented in the following chapter.

4 Identified Themes from Thematic Analysis

Thematic analysis of the 61 identified studies revealed eight major themes, including behavioral change, experience, health, motivation, social interaction, strategy, stress perception, and work. Each theme is described in detail below, incorporating elements of both a narrative review, which aims to identify existing literature on a topic or issue, and a descriptive review, which analyzes patterns or trends within a body of empirical studies [133].

4.1 Behavioral Change in Empirical Digital Detox Studies

Two empirical digital detox studies were assigned to this theme. These studies examined the effects of digital detoxing on students' information behavior [96] and time distortion [181]. As an example, Lepik and Murumaa-Mengel [96] conducted a five-day digital detox study with students, resulting in 42 of 91 participants submitting diaries documenting their experiences. Content analysis revealed behavioral changes during the digital detoxing, including perceptions of slower time passing, increased productivity, and adoption of offline activities such as reading. Participants also reported experiencing boredom and fear of missing out. After digital detoxing, some changed their use of social media, unfollowing accounts and disabling notifications.

4.2 Experience in Empirical Digital Detox Studies

Fourteen empirical digital detox studies were assigned to this theme. These studies examined digital detox experiences [197] in everyday life [30], tourism [71, 160], students' perceptions of learning experiences during digital detoxing [204], experiences within digital detox communities [170], experiential use of devices central to digital detoxing [55], how the digital detox experience influenced ongoing identity

Table 3 Overview of identified themes

Theme	Definition	Example
Behavioral change	This theme focuses on how digital detoxing affects individuals' behaviors and habits. It includes changes in information processing, time perception, productivity, and engagement in offline activities, with an emphasis on how digital detox interventions lead to changes in social media use or adoption of new offline practices	[96]
Experience	This theme explores individuals' subjective experiences and personal insights during digital detoxing. It includes diverse contexts such as daily life, travel, and community involvement, and highlights how people perceive their digital detox journey, the emotional and psychological impacts they experience, and the challenges they face	[13]
Health	This theme examines the health-related outcomes of digital detoxing. It covers a range of impacts on mental and physical well-being, including reductions in anxiety or depression, as well as improvements in overall cognitive and emotional health due to reduced use of, or temporary disengagement from, digital technologies	[25]
Motivation	This theme addresses the underlying motivations and reasons for engaging in digital detoxing. It includes the personal, social, and health-related drivers that lead individuals to engage in digital detox activities, as well as the challenges and coping strategies associated with these motivations	[106]
Social Interaction	This theme investigates the impact of digital detoxing on social interactions and relationships. It looks at how digital detoxing influences social connections, quality of interactions, and the ability to engage in face-to-face communication	[108]
Strategy	This theme focuses on the strategies and methods used to achieve digital detoxing. It includes various approaches and tools used to limit or reduce the use of digital technology, such as setting time limits, creating technology-free zones, and using specific applications or settings to manage connectivity	[124]
Stress Perception	This theme explores how digital detoxing affects individuals' perceptions of stress. It focuses primarily on stress, but may also examine other health-related outcomes such as mood and overall well-being, including both psychological and physiological effects of reduced use of, or temporary disengagement from, digital technologies	[6]
Work	This theme examines the effects of digital detoxing on work-related aspects, including job performance, cognitive overload, and overall well-being in professional settings, with an emphasis on how digital detox interventions affect work efficiency, satisfaction, and work-life balance	[106]

development [1], return to social networks after digital detoxing [14], risk factors of interactive e-health interventions for digital addiction [2], temporary abstinence from using social networking sites or digital media [80], the experiential effects of abstinence from social networking sites on social connections and well-being [51], and travel experiences during digital detoxing and associated emotional responses [29], and return to daily life [205]. As an example, Baumer et al. [14] provide insights into individuals' return to social networks by analyzing survey data from a convenience sample of 3,539 individuals who voluntarily abstained from Facebook for 99 days, some of whom returned before the designated period. They found that those finding it harder to stay away from Facebook were more likely to resume activity after digital detoxing. Participants' experiences during the digital detoxing were categorized, including perceived dependency and withdrawal. Participants reported missed visual content, inside jokes, or event invitations during their absence from Facebook, among other things.

4.3 Health in Empirical Digital Detox Studies

Twenty-three empirical digital detox studies were assigned to this theme. These studies examined various health-related effects: anxiety, depression, and well-being outcomes after social networking site abstinence [94], changes in cognitive functioning and emotional well-being after reduced social networking site use [189], changes in mood, anxiety, and craving following smartphone abstinence [203], changes in well-being after social networking site abstinence [178], changes in well-being and cognition after reduced smartphone use [130], cognitive dissonance, attitudes toward use, and affect during social media abstinence [185], effects of digital detox programs on electronic screen syndrome in preparatory school students [115], fear of missing out, well-being, and social connectedness before and after abstinence from social networking sites [25], health-related outcomes among university students after abstinence from social networking sites [44], life satisfaction, depressive symptoms, physical activity and smoking behavior [20], loneliness and depression outcomes after social networking site abstinence [78], loneliness, well-being, and quality of day after abstinence or limited use of social networking sites [65], mental health and well-being effects of abstinence from social networking sites [36], mental health effects of social media abstinence [153], mitigating the negative effects of social networking sites using digital detox apps and their effects on problematic smartphone use and well-being [150], self-objectification, self-esteem, and self-compassion after abstinence from social networking sites [146], self-reported affect and motivation among moderate to heavy social networking site users following limited site use [199], smartphone addiction, social media addiction, and health-related outcomes after abstinence from social networking sites [35], smartphone and social media use behaviors following abstinence from social networking sites [168], smartphone withdrawal symptoms, fear of missing out, and mood after smartphone restriction [42], and subjective well-being among passive and active social networking site users [126, 136], particularly distinguishing between passive and active users of social active users of social networking sites [67]. As an example, Brown and Kuss [25] investigated the effects before and after seven days of social media abstinence on fear of missing out, mental health, and social connectedness among 61 participants using a mixed methods within-subjects experimental design with surveys to obtain both quantitative and qualitative data. Results showed that abstinence led to increased well-being and connectedness, and decreased fear of missing out and smartphone use. Participants reported coping, habit, and boredom as reasons for social media use, while notifications were a challenge to abstaining.

4.4 *Motivation in Empirical Digital Detox Studies*

Nine empirical digital detox studies were assigned to this theme. These studies examined motivational strategies for digital detoxing and its effects on well-being [37], motivations and experienced challenges of digital detoxing from social networking sites [125], motivations and tensions during digital detox holidays [41, 171], motivations and practices as an organized activity in a commercial setting (e.g., camp, retreat), where individuals pay for digital detoxing [82], motivations for digital detoxing during holidays [79], motivations for digital detoxing in knowledge work [106], motivations to use digital detox applications to avoid distractions from social networking sites and their relationship to personality traits and technology-related variables [129], and situational motivations to disengage from digital technologies to avoid distractions, improve well-being, and be more present [88]. As an example, Marx et al. [106] conducted interviews with ten knowledge workers to identify six motivations for digital detoxing. These motivations include coping and preventing overload, coping and preventing invasion to achieve work-life separation, improving performance, and seeking a physiological reboot to counteract stress-related physiological effects such as exhaustion, reduced sleep quality, stomach problems, sweating, and tired eyes.

4.5 *Social Interaction in Empirical Digital Detox Studies*

Two empirical digital detox studies were assigned to this theme. These studies examined teenagers' experiences at a phone-free summer camp [108] and varying levels of social networking site use, including abstinence from social networking sites, on well-being, social connection, and social capital [113]. As an example, Megret [108] conducted 31 interviews (individual interviews, focus group interviews) and unstructured conversations at a smartphone-free summer camp. Analysis of the qualitative data revealed that most participants viewed the experience positively, despite significant lifestyle changes. They emphasized increased social interactions and living in the moment, although some felt pressured by constant availability. Challenges included missing personal music and staying informed, especially among older participants approaching voting age. Overall, this study shows how a smartphone-free environment can enhance social interactions, emphasizing the value of face-to-face connections and living in the moment, while acknowledging challenges such as missing personal music and staying informed.

4.6 Strategy in Empirical Digital Detox Studies

Three empirical digital detox studies were assigned to this theme. These studies explored digital detox strategies to abstain from social networking sites and messaging apps and their effects on well-being [124], digital detox strategies to optimize work and maintain well-being with the goal of preventing stress and burnout [158], and the practice of digital detox strategies, the experience of digital well-being, along with the relationship between digital detoxing and digital well-being [191]. As an example, Nguyen [124] conducted interviews with 30 participants and categorized digital detox strategies by device, social media platform or application, and specific features of platforms and apps by using technology to limit connectivity (e.g., through device and app settings). Digital detox strategies included creating technology-free zones, setting time limits, deactivating accounts, limiting screen time, disabling notifications, and using "Do Not Disturb" or "Airplane Mode". Notably, some accounts were also permanently deleted because of the digital detox study.

4.7 Stress Perception in Empirical Digital Detox Studies

Four empirical digital detox studies were assigned to this theme. These studies examined the reduction in stress associated with digital detoxing [6], the effects of abstinence from social networking sites on perceived stress, particularly among heavy users [182], the effects of abstinence from social networking sites on stress, well-being, affect, and perceived loneliness [187], and the effects of abstinence from social networking sites on stress, well-being, and loneliness resulting from social disconnection [196]. As an example, Anrijs et al. [6] conducted a two-week experiment involving 15 participants to investigate the impact of digital detoxing on physiological stress. Participants' smartphone activities were monitored, and physiological stress was measured using wearables based on skin conductance. During the second week, participants engaged in a digital detoxing, using their smartphones only for calls or photos, with the internet connection disabled. Results showed a decrease in physiological stress during the detox period compared to the previous week.

4.8 Work in Empirical Digital Detox Studies

Four empirical digital detox studies were assigned to this theme. These studies examined the effect of digital detoxing on employees' work performance, cognitive overload, and well-being [149], the effect of digital detoxing on employees' individual work performance in various organizations [11], social connectedness in remote work arrangements [110], and its support in preventing and coping with the availability demands of digital technologies for knowledge workers [111]. As an example, Mirbabaie et al. [111] investigated digital detoxing among knowledge workers with a 14-day within-subjects experiment to assess digital technology availability demands, work performance, and satisfaction under normal working conditions versus digital detox conditions. Participants chose one of four digital detox strategies: during breaks, after hours, fixed time windows during work, or notification silence. Results showed a significant decrease in digital technology demands after the detox period, but no detectable effect on work performance or satisfaction.

5 Discussion

5.1 Contributions and Future Research Avenues

The purpose of this review was to systematically examine empirical research on voluntary, limited abstinence from digital technology use to identify and elucidate major themes in digital detox research. Each theme offers valuable insights that not only contextualize current findings, but also pave the way for future research in digital detoxing.

The theme of behavioral change is supported by evidence of changes in behaviors and habits from two empirical digital detox studies (e.g., [96]). Future research could build on this by developing qualitative frameworks and longitudinal studies to document and analyze long-term behavioral changes resulting from digital detoxing. Similarly, the experience theme, enriched by fourteen studies, highlights individuals' subjective experiences and personal insights during digital detoxing while facing the challenges of re-engagement with digital platforms (e.g., [14]). This theme can guide future research in designing comprehensive interview protocols and surveys that capture a wide range of digital detox experiences and related challenges.

The extensive coverage of the health theme with twenty-three studies highlights the potential mental health benefits of digital detoxing, including improved well-being and reduced anxiety (e.g., [25]). Future research could focus on specific interventions and empirical studies to explore the health outcomes associated with digital detoxing, potentially leading to the development of targeted health-focused programs. The motivation theme, drawn from nine studies, reveals diverse motivational factors such as stress reduction and work-life balance (e.g., [106]). This theme provides a basis for exploring how motivations may vary across demographics and contexts, potentially enabling the development of motivational frameworks and behavioral models.

The social interaction theme is based on two studies that show how digital detoxing can enhance social interactions and social engagement (e.g., [108]). However, the limited number of studies suggests that more research is needed to understand, for example, how reduced screen time affects social relationships and social capital. The strategy theme, explored in three studies, examines various digital detox strategies and provides practical insights for managing technology use (e.g., [124]). Future research could focus on designing and evaluating comprehensive digital detox programs, using this theme to test the effectiveness of different strategies across different contexts (e.g., individuals, organizations, demographics).

The stress perception theme, highlighted in four studies, highlights how digital detoxing affects perceived stress, showing a reduction in stress levels during the digital detox period (e.g., [6]). Further research could explore the psychological and physiological mechanisms underlying these effects, which could inform studies on resilience and mental health outcomes. Finally, the work theme, explored in four studies, examines the effects of digital detoxing on work-related aspects (e.g., [111]). This theme suggests the potential benefits of digital detoxing in reducing work-related stress, and future research could focus on developing workplace policies and interventions to promote overall well-being.

Overall, by focusing on these themes, future research can provide evidence-based recommendations for managing digital consumption and promoting healthier digital lifestyles. In addition, they highlight the multifaceted nature of digital detoxing and its potential benefits, advancing the field and contributing to a more nuanced understanding of digital detox practices and outcomes.

5.2 *Limitations*

Our review has several limitations. Language limitation was one factor, as only empirical studies on digital detoxing published in English were included. This limitation may affect the universality of our findings and potentially miss relevant studies published in other languages (e.g., [91]). Furthermore, the focus was on voluntary, limited digital technology abstinence, in line with our aim to serve as a theoretical foundation for a larger research project. Consequently, studies on involuntary technology abstinence (see Table 2) were excluded. The subjectivity of the thematic analysis process is also a limitation. The themes identified represent one interpretation of the literature, and other themes could be developed as some studies may overlap across multiple themes. However, the themes identified provide a parsimonious, yet sufficiently detailed level of analysis that provides a valuable overview of the themes in the digital detox research field (see Table 3). Nevertheless, future research that addresses these limitations may provide additional insights into the field of digital detox research.

6 Conclusion

Digital detoxing is emerging as a promising strategy to address the challenges posed by pervasive digital technologies. As our society becomes increasingly connected, the practice of digital detox is likely to require specific digital skills, such as effective management of screen time and strategies to minimize digital distractions (e.g., [111]). Moreover, digital detoxing requires a proactive and conscious decision-making approach [93], which can enable to reevaluate their use of technology and cultivate a more mindful and balanced digital lifestyle. As such, it will be rewarding to see how the discourse on this relevant research topic will continue to evolve with more contributions from both research and practice.

Acknowledgements This research was funded by the Federal State of Upper Austria through the Austrian Research Promotion Agency (FFG) as part of the project "Interruption" at the University of Applied Sciences Upper Austria.

References

1. Agai, M. S. (2022). Disconnectivity synced with identity cultivation: Adolescent narratives of digital disconnection. *Journal of Computer-Mediated Communication, 27*(6). https://doi.org/10.1093/jcmc/zmac025
2. Alrobai, A., et al. (2019). Exploring the risk factors of interactive e-health interventions for digital addiction. In Information Resources Management Association (Ed.), *Substance Abuse and Addiction* (pp. 375–390). IGI Global. https://doi.org/10.4018/978-1-5225-7666-2.ch020
3. Altmaier, N., et al. (2024). Studying digital disconnection: A mapping review of empirical contributions to disconnection studies. *First Monday, 29*(1). https://doi.org/10.5210/fm.v29i1.13269
4. Anashkina, N., Shmatko, M., & Tkachenko, O. (2020). Digital-detox technology for vocational guidance selection of applicants for media communications area. *Mediaobrazovanie, 60*(4), 570–580.
5. Andersson, L., & Danielsson, M. (2023). Where were you when Facebook went out? Experiences of involuntary disconnection from social media. *Convergence: The International Journal of Research into New Media Technologies*. https://doi.org/10.1177/13548565231223488
6. Anrijs, S. et al. (2018). MobileDNA: Relating physiological stress measurements to smartphone usage to assess the effect of a digital detox. In C. Stephanidis (Ed.), *HCI International 2018 – Posters' Extended Abstracts: 20th International Conference, HCI International 2018, Las Vegas, NV, USA, July 15–20, 2018, Proceedings, Part II*. CCIS, vol. 851, pp. 356–363. Springer. https://doi.org/10.1007/978-3-319-92279-9_48
7. Arenas-Escaso, J. F., Folgado-Fernández, J. A., & Palos-Sanchez, P. R. (2022). Digital disconnection as an opportunity for the tourism business: A bibliometric analysis. *Emerging Science Journal, 6*(5), 1100–1113. https://doi.org/10.28991/ESJ-2022-06-05-013
8. Ayyagari, R., Grover, V., & Purvis, R. (2011). Technostress: Technological antecedents and implications. *MIS Quarterly, 35*(4), 831–858. https://doi.org/10.2307/41409963
9. Barki, H., Rivard, S., & Talbot, J. (1988). An information systems keyword classification scheme. *MIS Quarterly, 12*(2), 299–322. https://doi.org/10.2307/248855
10. Bastari, A., et al. (2020). Digitalization in banking sector: The role of intrinsic motivation. *Heliyon, 6*(12), Article e05801. https://doi.org/10.1016/j.heliyon.2020.e05801

11. Basu, R. (2019). Impact of digital detox on individual performance of the employees. *International Journal of Research and Analytical Reviews, 6*(2), 378–381.
12. Baumer, E. P. S. et al. (2014). Refusing, limiting, departing: Why we should study technology non-use. In *Extended abstracts on human factors in computing systems* (pp. 65–68). https://doi.org/10.1145/2559206.2559224
13. Baumer, E. P. S., Ames, M. G., et al. (2015). Why study technology non-use? *First Monday, 20*(11). https://doi.org/10.5210/fm.v20i11.6310
14. Baumer, E. P. S., Guha, S., et al. (2015). Missing photos, suffering withdrawal, or finding freedom? How experiences of social media non-use influence the likelihood of reversion. *Social Media + Society, 1*(2), 1–14. https://doi.org/10.1177/2056305115614851
15. Bauwens, J., Thorbjornsson, G. B., & Verstrynge, K. (2019). Unplug your life: Digital detox through a Kierkegaardian Lens. *Kierkegaard Studies Yearbook, 24*(1), 415–436. https://doi.org/10.1515/kierke-2019-0017
16. Benlian, A. (2020). A daily field investigation of technology-driven stress spillovers from work to home. *MIS Quarterly, 44*(3), 1259–1300. https://doi.org/10.25300/MISQ/2020/14911
17. Benvenuti, M. et al. (2023). WAITASEC: The development of an application for people'digital wellness. In *Proceedings of the IEEE International Conference on Metrology for eXtended Reality, Artificial Intelligence and Neural Engineering* (pp. 1017–1021). https://doi.org/10.1109/MetroXRAINE58569.2023.10405807
18. Bhattacharya, S., & Raghuvanshi, S. (2019). Digital detoxification: A pressing need for restoring balance in tech-driven life. *IAHRW International Journal of Social Sciences Review, 7*(4), 761–764.
19. Bozan, V., & Treré, E. (2023). When digital inequalities meet digital disconnection: Studying the material conditions of disconnection in rural Turkey. *Convergence: The International Journal of Research into New Media Technologies*, 135485652311745. https://doi.org/10.1177/13548565231174596
20. Brailovskaia, J. et al. (2020). Less Facebook use – More well-being and a healthier lifestyle? An experimental intervention study. *Computers in Human Behavior, 108*, 106332. https://doi.org/10.1016/j.chb.2020.106332
21. Brailovskaia, J., Frahsek, M., & Margraf, J. (2022). Work overload and addictive social media use: A relationship with depression symptoms and life satisfaction. *Journal of Technology in Behavioral Science, 7*(3), 358–367. https://doi.org/10.1007/s41347-022-00258-2
22. Braun, V., & Clarke, V. (2006). Using thematic analysis in psychology. *Qualitative Research in Psychology, 3*(2), 77–101. https://doi.org/10.1191/1478088706qp063oa
23. Braun, V., & Clarke, V. (2023). Thematic analysis. In H. Cooper et al. (Eds.), *APA Handbook of Research Methods in Psychology: Research Designs: Quantitative, Qualitative, Neuropsychological, and Biological* (2nd ed., pp. 65–81). American Psychological Association. https://doi.org/10.1037/0000319-004
24. Brody, N. (2018). Opting out of social media: Online communication attitudes mediate the relationship between personality factors and Facebook non-use. *Southern Communication Journal, 83*(2), 75–88. https://doi.org/10.1080/1041794X.2017.1413415
25. Brown, L., & Kuss, D. J. (2020). Fear of missing out, mental wellbeing, and social connectedness: A seven-day social media abstinence trial. *International Journal of Environmental Research and Public Health, 17*(12), 4566. https://doi.org/10.3390/ijerph17124566
26. Bucher, T. (2020). Nothing to disconnect from? Being singular plural in an age of machine learning. *Media, Culture & Society, 42*(4), 610–617. https://doi.org/10.1177/0163443720914028
27. Bygstad, B., et al. (2022). From dual digitalization to digital learning space: Exploring the digital transformation of higher education. *Computers & Education, 182*, Article 104463. https://doi.org/10.1016/j.compedu.2022.104463
28. Cai, W., & McKenna, B. (2023). Power and resistance: Digital-free tourism in a connected world. *Journal of Travel Research, 62*(2), 290–304. https://doi.org/10.1177/00472875211061208

29. Cai, W., McKenna, B., & Waizenegger, L. (2020). Turning it off: Emotions in digital-free travel. *Journal of Travel Research, 59*(5), 909–927. https://doi.org/10.1177/0047287519868314
30. Caron, A. H., & Mays, K. K. (2021). Breaching perpetual contact: Withdrawing from mobile and social media use in everyday life. *First Monday, 26*(8). https://doi.org/10.5210/fm.v26i8.11652
31. Cecchinato, M. E. et al. (2019). Designing for digital wellbeing: A research & practice agenda. In *Extended Abstracts of the CHI Conference on Human Factors in Computing Systems*. https://doi.org/10.1145/3290607.3298998
32. Cesareo, M., et al. (2021). The ubiquity of social reinforcement: A nudging exploratory study to reduce the overuse of smartphones in social contexts. *Cogent Psychology, 8*(1), 1880304. https://doi.org/10.1080/23311908.2021.1880304
33. Chen, A. J., & Karahanna, E. (2018). Life interrupted: The effects of technology-mediated work interruptions on work and nonwork outcomes. *MIS Quarterly, 42*(4), 1023–1042. https://doi.org/10.25300/MISQ/2018/13631
34. Conroy, D. et al. (2023). "You have to know how to live with it without getting to the addiction part": British young adult experiences of smartphone overreliance and disconnectivity. *Psychology of Popular Media, 12*(4), 471–480. https://doi.org/10.1037/ppm0000425
35. Coyne, P., & Woodruff, S. J. (2023). Taking a break: The effects of partaking in a two-week social media digital detox on problematic smartphone and social media use, and other health-related outcomes among young adults. *Behavioral Sciences, 13*(12), 1004. https://doi.org/10.3390/bs13121004
36. de Hesselle, L. C., & Montag, C. (2024). Effects of a 14-day social media abstinence on mental health and well-being: Results from an experimental study. *BMC Psychology, 12*(1), 141. https://doi.org/10.1186/s40359-024-01611-1
37. Dias, P., Martinho, L., & Jorge, A. (2023). Digital disconnection and Portuguese youth: Motivations, strategies, and well-being outcomes. *Comunicação e Sociedade, 44*, Article e023014. https://doi.org/10.17231/comsoc.44(2023).4466
38. Díaz-Meneses, G., & Estupinán-Ojeda, M. (2022). The outbreak of digital detox motives and their public health implications for holiday destinations. *International Journal of Environmental Research and Public Health, 19*(3), 1548. https://doi.org/10.3390/ijerph19031548
39. Dickinson, J. E., Hibbert, J. F., & Filimonau, V. (2016). Mobile technology and the tourist experience: (Dis)connection at the campsite. *Tourism Management, 57*, 193–201. https://doi.org/10.1016/j.tourman.2016.06.005
40. Dittmar, A., & Görres, A. (2019). A cultural probes study on the (non-)use of digital artefacts. In *Proceedings of Mensch und Computer* (pp. 155–165). https://doi.org/10.1145/3340764.3340785
41. Egger, I., Lei, S. I., & Wassler, P. (2020). Digital free tourism – An exploratory study of tourist motivations. *Tourism Management, 79*, Article 104098. https://doi.org/10.1016/j.tourman.2020.104098
42. Eide, T. A., et al. (2018). Smartphone restriction and its effect on subjective withdrawal related scores. *Frontiers in Psychology, 9*, Article 386218. https://doi.org/10.3389/fpsyg.2018.01444
43. Eitan, T., & Gazit, T. (2024). The "here and now" effect: JoMO, FoMO and the well-being of social media users. *Online Information Review, 48*(5), 1002–1024. https://doi.org/10.1108/OIR-03-2023-0111
44. El-Khoury, J., et al. (2021). Characteristics of social media "detoxification" in university students. *Libyan Journal of Medicine, 16*(1), 1846861. https://doi.org/10.1080/19932820.2020.1846861
45. Enli, G., & Fast, K. (2023). Political solutions or user responsibilization? How politicians understand problems connected to digital overload. *Convergence: The International Journal of Research into New Media Technologies, 29*(3), 675–689. https://doi.org/10.1177/13548565231160618

46. Enli, G., & Syvertsen, T. (2021). Disconnect to reconnect! Self-help to regain an authentic sense of space through digital detoxing. In A. Jansson & P. C. Adams (Eds.), *Disentangling: The geographies of digital disconnection* (pp. 227–252). Oxford University Press.
47. Fan, D. X. F., Buhalis, D., & Lin, B. (2019). A tourist typology of online and face-to-face social contact: Destination immersion and tourism encapsulation/decapsulation. *Annals of Tourism Research, 78*, Article 102757. https://doi.org/10.1016/j.annals.2019.102757
48. Fast, K. (2021). The disconnection turn: Three facets of disconnective work in post-digital capitalism. *Convergence: The International Journal of Research into New Media Technologies, 27*(6), 1615–1630. https://doi.org/10.1177/13548565211033382
49. Fast, K., Lindell, J., & Jansson, A. (2021). Disconnection as distinction: A Bourdieusian study of where people withdraw from digital media. In A. Jansson & P. C. Adams (Eds.), *Disentangling: The Geographies of Digital Disconnection* (pp. 61–90). Oxford University Press.
50. Floros, C., et al. (2021). Imagine being off-the-grid: Millennials' perceptions of digital-free travel. *Journal of Sustainable Tourism, 29*(5), 751–766. https://doi.org/10.1080/09669582.2019.1675676
51. Franks, J., Chenhall, R., & Keogh, L. (2018). The Facebook sabbatical as a cycle: Describing the gendered experience of young adults as they navigate disconnection and reconnection. *Social Media + Society, 4*(3). https://doi.org/10.1177/2056305118801995
52. Fryman, S., & Romine, W. (2021). Measuring smartphone dependency and exploration of consequences and comorbidities. *Computers in Human Behavior Reports, 4*, Article 100108. https://doi.org/10.1016/j.chbr.2021.100108
53. Fuchsberger, V., Murer, M., & Tscheligi, M. (2014). Human-computer non-interaction: The activity of non-use. In *Proceedings of the Companion Publication on Designing Interactive Systems* (pp. 57–60). https://doi.org/10.1145/2598784.2602781
54. Geber, S., Nguyen, M. H., & Büchi, M. (2023). Conflicting norms—How norms of disconnection and availability correlate with digital media use across generations. *Social Science Computer Review*. https://doi.org/10.1177/08944393231215457
55. Ghita, C., & Thorén, C. (2021). Going cold turkey! An autoethnographic exploration of digital disengagement. *Nordicom Review, 42*(s4), 152–167. https://doi.org/10.2478/nor-2021-0047
56. Gjellebæk, C., et al. (2020). Management challenges for future digitalization of healthcare services. *Futures, 124*, Article 102636. https://doi.org/10.1016/j.futures.2020.102636
57. Gong, Y., Schroeder, A., & Plaisance, P. L. (2023). Digital detox tourism: An Ellulian critique. *Annals of Tourism Research, 103*, Article 103646. https://doi.org/10.1016/j.annals.2023.103646
58. Gorokhova, E., & Tsyganova, L. (2021). Techniques of overcoming communication overload. In D. P. Sakas, D. K. Nasiopoulos & Y. Taratuhina (Eds.), *Business Intelligence and Modelling: Unified Approach with Simulation and Strategic Modelling in Entrepreneurship*. SPBE, pp. 387–393. Springer. https://doi.org/10.1007/978-3-030-57065-1_39
59. Gray, B. C. (2023). Digital detox: One strategy for establishing a more ethical relationship to educational technologies on campus. *Collected Essays on Learning and Teaching, 14*(1). https://doi.org/10.22329/celt.v14i1.7162
60. Guha, S., Baumer, E. P. S., & Gay, G. K. (2018). Regrets, I've had a few: When regretful experiences do (and don't) compel users to leave Facebook. In *Proceedings of the ACM Conference on Supporting Groupwork* (pp. 166–177). https://doi.org/10.1145/3148330.3148338
61. Guyard, C., & Kaun, A. (2018). Workfulness: Governing the disobedient brain. *Journal of Cultural Economy, 11*(6), 535–548. https://doi.org/10.1080/17530350.2018.1481877
62. Haba-Rubio, J., et al. (2018). Themenschwerpunkt: Nachtruhe unter Druck - Übermüdung ist unsere neue Realität. *Psychoscope, 39*(3), 10–23.
63. Hager, N., Stangl, F. J., & Riedl, R. (2023). Digital detox research: An analysis of applied methods and implications for future studies. In *Proceedings of the 18th International Conference on Wirtschaftsinformatik*.

64. Haliburton, L. et al. (2022). Think inside the box: Investigating the consequences of everyday physical opt-out strategies for mindful smartphone use. In *Proceedings of the International Conference on Mobile and Ubiquitous Multimedia* (pp. 37–46). https://doi.org/10.1145/3568444.3568452
65. Hall, J. A., et al. (2021). Experimentally manipulating social media abstinence: Results of a four-week diary study. *Media Psychology, 24*(2), 259–275. https://doi.org/10.1080/15213269.2019.1688171
66. Handa, M., & Ahuja, P. (2020). Disconnect to detox: A study of smartphone addiction among young adults in India. *Young Consumers, 21*(3), 273–287. https://doi.org/10.1108/YC-12-2019-1077
67. Hanley, S. M., Watt, S. E., & Coventry, W. (2019). Taking a break: The effect of taking a vacation from Facebook and Instagram on subjective well-being. *PLoS ONE, 14*(6), Article e0217743. https://doi.org/10.1371/journal.pone.0217743
68. Harley, D. (2019). The link between digital disconnection and death anxiety: A preliminary study. *Annual Review of Cybertherapy and Telemedicine, 17*, 115–120.
69. Harmon, J., & Duffy, L. (2023). Turn off to tune in: Digital disconnection, digital consciousness, and meaningful leisure. *Journal of Leisure Research, 54*(5), 539–559. https://doi.org/10.1080/00222216.2023.2220699
70. Hartmann, M. (2022). "Install freedom now!" choosing not to communicate with digital media at work and home. *Javnost - The Public, 29*(1), 17–32. https://doi.org/10.1080/13183222.2021.1889831
71. Hassan, T. H., Salem, A. E., & Saleh, M. I. (2022). Digital-free tourism holiday as a new approach for tourism well-being: Tourists' attributional approach. *International Journal of Environmental Research and Public Health, 19*(10), 5974. https://doi.org/10.3390/ijerph19105974
72. Helsper, E. J., & Reisdorf, B. C. (2013). A quantitative examination of explanations for reasons for internet nonuse. *Cyberpsychology, Behavior, and Social Networking, 16*(2), 94–99. https://doi.org/10.1089/cyber.2012.0257
73. Hesselberth, P. (2018). Discourses on disconnectivity and the right to disconnect. *New Media & Society, 20*(5), 1994–2010. https://doi.org/10.1177/1461444817711449
74. Hesselberth, P. (2021). Retreat culture and therapeutic disconnection. In A. Jansson & P. C. Adams (Eds.), *Disentangling: The Geographies of Digital Disconnection* (pp. 253–272). Oxford University Press. https://doi.org/10.1093/oso/9780197571873.003.0011
75. Hiniker, A. et al. (2016). MyTime: Designing and evaluating an intervention for smartphone non-use. In *Proceedings of the CHI Conference on Human Factors in Computing Systems* (pp. 4746–4757). https://doi.org/10.1145/2858036.2858403
76. Hoang, Q., Cronin, J., & Skandalis, A. (2023). Futureless vicissitudes: Gestural anti-consumption and the reflexively impotent (anti-)consumer. *Marketing Theory, 23*(4), 585–606. https://doi.org/10.1177/14705931231153193
77. Hu, H.-F., & Liu, Y. (2023). Digital-free tourism intention: The effects of message concreteness and intervention. *Tourism Analysis, 28*(3), 505–510. https://doi.org/10.3727/108354223X16758863498791
78. Hunt, M. G., et al. (2018). No more FOMO: Limiting social media decreases loneliness and depression. *Journal of Social and Clinical Psychology, 37*(10), 751–768. https://doi.org/10.1521/jscp.2018.37.10.751
79. Jiang, Y., & Balaji, M. S. (2022). Getting unwired: What drives travellers to take a digital detox holiday? *Tourism Recreation Research, 47*(5–6), 453–469. https://doi.org/10.1080/02508281.2021.1889801
80. Jorge, A. (2019). Social media, interrupted: Users recounting temporary disconnection on Instagram. *Social Media + Society, 5*(4), 1–19. https://doi.org/10.1177/2056305119881691
81. Jorge, A., et al. (2023). Growing out of overconnection: The process of dis/connecting among Norwegian and Portuguese teenagers. *New Media & Society*. https://doi.org/10.1177/14614448231159308

82. Karlsen, F. (2023). The digital detox camp: Practices and motivations for reverse domestication. In M. Hartmann (Ed.), *The Routledge Handbook of Media and Technology Domestication* (pp. 361–373). Routledge.
83. Karlsen, F., & Ytre-Arne, B. (2022). Intrusive media and knowledge work: How knowledge workers negotiate digital media norms in the pursuit of focused work. *Information, Communication & Society, 25*(15), 2174–2189. https://doi.org/10.1080/1369118X.2021.1933561
84. Kaun, A. (2021). Ways of seeing digital disconnection: A negative sociology of digital culture. *Convergence: The International Journal of Research into New Media Technologies, 27*(6), 1571–1583. https://doi.org/10.1177/13548565211045535
85. Kaun, A., & Treré, E. (2020). Repression, resistance and lifestyle: Charting (dis)connection and activism in times of accelerated capitalism. *Social Movement Studies, 19*(5–6), 697–715. https://doi.org/10.1080/14742837.2018.1555752
86. Keller, J., et al. (2021). A mobile intervention for self-efficacious and goal-directed smartphone use in the general population: Randomized controlled trial. *JMIR mHealth and uHealth, 9*(11), Article e26397. https://doi.org/10.2196/26397
87. Kent, R. (2020). Self-tracking health over time: From the use of Instagram to perform optimal health to the protective shield of the digital detox. *Social Media + Society, 6*(3), 1–14. https://doi.org/10.1177/2056305120940694
88. Klingelhoefer, J., Gilbert, A., & Meier, A. (2023). Momentary motivations for digital disconnection: An experience sampling study. *PsyArXiv*. https://doi.org/10.31234/osf.io/qhctd
89. Kour, G. (2016). Digital detoxification: A content analysis of user generated videos uploaded on Youtube by Facebook quitters. *Media Watch, 7*(1), 75–83. https://doi.org/10.15655/mw/2016/v7i1/86493
90. Krischkowsky, A., Fuchsberger, V., & Tscheligi, M. (2021). Making un-use: When humans disengage with technology. In *Proceedings of the CHI Conference on Human Factors in Computing Systems* (pp. 1–10). https://doi.org/10.1145/3411764.3445136
91. Külling, C., & Süss, D. (2018). Einstellungen, Erfahrungen und Emotionen hinsichtlich eines Internetverzichts unter Berücksichtigung der Persönlichkeit. *Psychologie in Österreich, 38*(5), 376–383.
92. Kuntsman, A., & Miyake, E. (2019). The paradox and continuum of digital disengagement: Denaturalising digital sociality and technological connectivity. *Media, Culture & Society, 41*(6), 901–913. https://doi.org/10.1177/0163443719853732
93. Kuntsman, A., & Miyake, E. (2022). *Paradoxes of digital disengagement: In search of the opt-out button.* University of Westminster Press. https://doi.org/10.16997/book61
94. Lambert, J., et al. (2022). Taking a one-week break from social media improves well-being, depression, and anxiety: A randomized controlled trial. *Cyberpsychology, Behavior, and Social Networking, 25*(5), 287–293. https://doi.org/10.1089/cyber.2021.0324
95. Lee, J. et al. (2017). D-TOX: Inducing digital detox for nighttime via smart lamp applied gamification. In *Proceedings of the Conference on Interaction Design and Children* (pp. 497–502). https://doi.org/10.1145/3078072.3084315
96. Lepik, K., & Murumaa-Mengel, M. (2019). Students on a social media "detox": Disrupting the everyday practices of social media use. In S. Kurbanoğlu et al. (Eds.), *Information Literacy in Everyday Life: 6th European Conference, ECIL 2018, Oulu, Finland, September 24–27, 2018, Revised Selected Papers*. CCIS, pp. 60–69. Springer. https://doi.org/10.1007/978-3-030-13472-3_6
97. Li, J., Pearce, P. L., & Low, D. (2018). Media representation of digital-free tourism: A critical discourse analysis. *Tourism Management, 69*, 317–329. https://doi.org/10.1016/j.tourman.2018.06.027
98. Li, J., Pearce, P. L., & Oktadiana, H. (2020). Can digital-free tourism build character strengths? *Annals of Tourism Research, 85*, Article 103037. https://doi.org/10.1016/j.annals.2020.103037

99. Liao, M., & Sundar, S. S. (2022). #facebookdown: Time to panic or detox? Understanding users' reactions to social media outage. In *Proceedings of the CHI Conference on Human Factors in Computing Systems* (pp. 1–8). https://doi.org/10.1145/3491101.3519674
100. Liu, H., et al. (2021). COVID-19 information overload and generation Z's social media discontinuance intention during the pandemic lockdown. *Technological Forecasting and Social Change, 166*, Article 120600. https://doi.org/10.1016/j.techfore.2021.120600
101. Löchtefeld, M., Böhmer, M., & Ganev, L. (2013). AppDetox: Helping users with mobile app addiction. In *Proceedings of the 12th International Conference on Mobile and Ubiquitous Multimedia* (pp. 1–2). https://doi.org/10.1145/2541831.2541870
102. Lomborg, S., & Ytre-Arne, B. (2021). Advancing digital disconnection research: Introduction to the special issue. *Convergence: The International Journal of Research into New Media Technologies, 27*(6), 1529–1535. https://doi.org/10.1177/13548565211057518
103. Lu, X., Lu, Z., & Liu, C. (2020). Exploring TikTok use and non-use practices and experiences in China. In G. Meiselwitz (Ed.), *Social Computing and Social Media. Participation, User Experience, Consumer Experience, and Applications of Social Computing: 12th International Conference, SCSM 2020, Held as Part of the 22nd HCI International Conference, HCII 2020, Copenhagen, Denmark*. LNISA, pp. 57–70. Springer. https://doi.org/10.1007/978-3-030-49576-3_5
104. Magee, R. M., Agosto, D. E., & Forte, A. (2017). Four factors that regulate teen technology use in everyday life. In *Proceedings of the ACM Conference on Computer Supported Cooperative Work and Social Computing* (pp. 511–522). https://doi.org/10.1145/2998181.2998310
105. Markham, A. N. (2021). Echolocation as theory of digital sociality. *Convergence: The International Journal of Research into New Media Technologies, 27*(6), 1558–1570. https://doi.org/10.1177/13548565211047158
106. Marx, J., Braun, L.-M., & Mirbabaie, M. (2022). Motivators of knowledge workers to conduct digital detox. In *Proceedings of the 43rd International Conference on Information Systems.*
107. Matthes, J., et al. (2022). Reflective smartphone disengagement: Conceptualization, measurement, and validation. *Computers in Human Behavior, 128*, Article 107078. https://doi.org/10.1016/j.chb.2021.107078
108. Megret, C. (2024). No connectivity, better connections: Teenagers' experiences of a phone-free summer camp in the United States. *Journal of Adventure Education and Outdoor Learning, 24*(1), 65–78. https://doi.org/10.1080/14729679.2023.2211180
109. Melton, J. et al. (2019). Intentional non-use of the Internet in a digital world: A textual analysis of disconnection narratives. In *Proceedings of the IEEE International Professional Communication Conference* (pp. 65–66). https://doi.org/10.1109/ProComm.2019.00016
110. Mirbabaie, M. et al. (2020). Digital detox – Mitigating digital overuse in times of remote work and social isolation. In *Proceedings of the 31st Australasian Conference on Information Systems.*
111. Mirbabaie, M., Braun, L.-M., & Marx, J. (2022). Knowledge work "unplugged" - Digital detox effects on ICT demands, job performance and satisfaction. In *Proceedings of the 17th International Conference on Wirtschaftsinformatik.*
112. Mirbabaie, M., Stieglitz, S., & Marx, J. (2022). Digital detox. *Business & Information Systems Engineering, 64*(2), 239–246. https://doi.org/10.1007/s12599-022-00747-x
113. Mitev, K. et al. (2021). Social media use only helps, and does not harm, daily interactions and well-being. *Technology, Mind, and Behavior, 2*(1). https://doi.org/10.1037/tmb0000033
114. Moe, H., & Madsen, O. J. (2021). Understanding digital disconnection beyond media studies. *Convergence: The International Journal of Research into New Media Technologies, 27*(6), 1584–1598. https://doi.org/10.1177/13548565211048969
115. Mohamed, S. M., Abdallah, L. S., & Ali, F. N. K. (2023). Effect of digital detox program on electronic screen syndrome among preparatory school students. *Nursing Open, 10*(4), 2222–2228. https://doi.org/10.1002/nop2.1472
116. Moher, D., et al. (2009). Preferred reporting items for systematic reviews and meta-analyses: The PRISMA statement. *PLOS Medicine, 6*(7), Article e1000097. https://doi.org/10.1371/journal.pmed.1000097

117. Moher, D., et al. (2010). Preferred reporting items for systematic reviews and meta-analyses: The PRISMA statement. *International Journal of Surgery, 8*(5), 336–341. https://doi.org/10.1016/j.ijsu.2010.02.007
118. Monge Roffarello, A., & De Russis, L. (2019). The race towards digital wellbeing: Issues and opportunities. In *Proceedings of the CHI Conference on Human Factors in Computing Systems* (pp. 1–14). https://doi.org/10.1145/3290605.3300616
119. Muench, C., et al. (2020). Time to log off: An analysis of factors influencing the willingness to participate in a long-term "Digital Detox" with the smartphone. In C. Stephanidis & M. Antona (Eds.), *HCI International 2020 - Posters: 22nd International Conference, HCII 2020, Copenhagen, Denmark, July 19–24, 2020, Proceedings, Part III*. CCIS, pp. 209–216. Springer. https://doi.org/10.1007/978-3-030-50732-9_28
120. Muench, R., & Muench, C. (2020). Me without my smartphone? Never! Predictors of willingness for smartphone separation and Nomophobia. In C. Stephanidis & M. Antona (Eds.), *HCI International 2020 - Posters: 22nd International Conference, HCII 2020, Copenhagen, Denmark, July 19–24, 2020, Proceedings, Part III*. CCIS, pp. 217–223. Springer. https://doi.org/10.1007/978-3-030-50732-9_29
121. Mutsvairo, B., Ragnedda, M., & Mabvundwi, K. (2022). "Our old pastor thinks the mobile phone is a source of evil." Capturing contested and conflicting insights on digital wellbeing and digital detoxing in an age of rapid mobile connectivity. *Media International Australia*, 1–15. https://doi.org/10.1177/1329878X221090992
122. Nassen, L.-M. et al. (2023). Opt-out, abstain, unplug. A systematic review of the voluntary digital disconnection literature. *Telematics and Informatics, 81*, 101980. https://doi.org/10.1016/j.tele.2023.101980
123. Natale, S., & Treré, E. (2020). Vinyl won't save us: Reframing disconnection as engagement. *Media, Culture & Society, 42*(4), 626–633. https://doi.org/10.1177/0163443720914027
124. Nguyen, M. H. (2021). Managing social media use in an "always-on" society: Exploring digital wellbeing strategies that people use to disconnect. *Mass Communication and Society, 24*(6), 795–817. https://doi.org/10.1080/15205436.2021.1979045
125. Nguyen, M. H. (2023). "Maybe I should get rid of it for a while…": Examining motivations and challenges for social media disconnection. *The Communication Review, 26*(2), 125–150. https://doi.org/10.1080/10714421.2023.2195795
126. Nguyen, M. H., & Hargittai, E. (2023). Digital disconnection, digital inequality, and subjective well-being: A mobile experience sampling study. *Journal of Computer-Mediated Communication, 29*(1). https://doi.org/10.1093/jcmc/zmad044
127. Nguyen, M. H., & Hargittai, E. (2023). Digital inequality in disconnection practices: Voluntary nonuse during COVID-19. *Journal of Communication, 73*(5), 494–510. https://doi.org/10.1093/joc/jqad021
128. Nguyen, M. H., Büchi, M., & Geber, S. (2022). Everyday disconnection experiences: Exploring people's understanding of digital well-being and management of digital media use. *New Media & Society*. https://doi.org/10.1177/14614448221105428
129. Nguyen, V. T. (2022). The perceptions of social media users of digital detox apps considering personality traits. *Education and Information Technologies, 27*(7), 9293–9316. https://doi.org/10.1007/s10639-022-11022-7
130. Olson, J. A., et al. (2022). A nudge-based intervention to reduce problematic smartphone use: Randomised controlled trial. *International Journal of Mental Health and Addiction*. https://doi.org/10.1007/s11469-022-00826-w
131. Özdemir, M. A., & Goktas, L. S. (2021). Research trends on digital detox holidays: A bibliometric analysis, 2012–2020. *Tourism & Management Studies, 17*(3), 21–35. https://doi.org/10.18089/tms.2021.170302
132. Papa, V., & Kouros, T. (2024). 'Slantwise disengagement: Explaining Facebook users' acts beyond resistance/internalization of domination binary'. *Convergence: The International Journal of Research into New Media Technologies, 30*(5), 1762–1778. https://doi.org/10.1177/13548565241227396

133. Paré, G., et al. (2015). Synthesizing information systems knowledge: A typology of literature reviews. *Information & Management, 52*(2), 183–199. https://doi.org/10.1016/j.im.2014.08.008
134. Pawłowska-Legwand, A., & Matoga, Ł. (2021). Disconnect from the digital world to reconnect with the real life: An analysis of the potential for development of unplugged tourism on the example of Poland. *Tourism Planning & Development, 18*(6), 649–672. https://doi.org/10.1080/21568316.2020.1842487
135. Phillips, B., & Shipps, B. (2022). Problematic technology use: The impact of personality and continued use. *The Journal of the Southern Association for Information Systems, 9*(1), 38–63. https://doi.org/10.17705/3JSIS.00021
136. Przybylski, A. K., et al. (2021). Does taking a short break from social media have a positive effect on well-being? Evidence from three preregistered field experiments. *Journal of Technology in Behavioral Science, 6*(3), 507–514. https://doi.org/10.1007/s41347-020-00189-w
137. Purohit, A. K. et al. (2023). Starving the newsfeed for social media detox: Effects of strict and self-regulated Facebook newsfeed diets. In *Proceedings of the CHI Conference on Human Factors in Computing Systems* (pp. 1–16). https://doi.org/10.1145/3544548.3581187
138. Purohit, A. K., Barclay, L., & Holzer, A. (2020). Designing for digital detox: Making social media less addictive with digital nudges. In *Proceedings of the CHI Conference on Human Factors in Computing Systems* (pp. 1–9). https://doi.org/10.1145/3334480.3382810
139. Purohit, A. K., Raggi, M., & Holzer, A. (2023). How pricing and ratings affect perceived value of digital detox apps. In *Extended Abstracts of the CHI Conference on Human Factors in Computing Systems* (pp. 1–7). https://doi.org/10.1145/3544549.3585681
140. Putchavayala, C. K., Singh, D., & Sashidharan, R. K. (2022). A perspective of yoga on smartphone addiction: A narrative review. *Journal of Family Medicine and Primary Care, 11*(6), 2284. https://doi.org/10.4103/jfmpc.jfmpc_1765_21
141. Radtke, T., et al. (2022). Digital detox: An effective solution in the smartphone era? A systematic literature review. *Mobile Media & Communication, 10*(2), 190–215. https://doi.org/10.1177/20501579211028647
142. Ragu-Nathan, T. S., et al. (2008). The consequences of technostress for end users in organizations: Conceptual development and empirical validation. *Information Systems Research, 19*(4), 417–433. https://doi.org/10.1287/isre.1070.0165
143. Reinecke, L., et al. (2017). Digital stress over the life span: The effects of communication load and internet multitasking on perceived stress and psychological health impairments in a German probability sample. *Media Psychology, 20*(1), 90–115. https://doi.org/10.1080/15213269.2015.1121832
144. Riedl, R. (2013). On the biology of technostress: Literature review and research agenda. *ACM SIGMIS Database: The DATA BASE for Advances in Information Systems, 44*(1), 18–55. https://doi.org/10.1145/2436239.2436242
145. Riedl, R., et al. (2020). A decade of NeuroIS research: Progress, challenges, and future directions. *ACM SIGMIS Database: The DATA BASE for Advances in Information Systems, 51*(3), 13–54. https://doi.org/10.1145/3410977.3410980
146. Roberts, T.-A., et al. (2022). "Intermission!" A short-term social media fast reduces self-objectification among pre-teen and teen dancers. *Body Image, 43*, 125–133. https://doi.org/10.1016/j.bodyim.2022.08.015
147. Roffarello, A. M., & De Russis, L. (2023). Achieving digital wellbeing through digital self-control tools: A systematic review and meta-analysis. *ACM Transactions on Computer-Human Interaction, 30*(4), 1–66. https://doi.org/10.1145/3571810
148. Salo, M., et al. (2022). Formation and mitigation of technostress in the personal use of IT. *MIS Quarterly, 46*(2), 1073–1108. https://doi.org/10.25300/MISQ/2022/14950
149. Schmitt, J. B., Breuer, J., & Wulf, T. (2021). From cognitive overload to digital detox: Psychological implications of telework during the COVID-19 pandemic. *Computers in Human Behavior, 124*, Article 106899. https://doi.org/10.1016/j.chb.2021.106899

150. Schmuck, D. (2020). Does digital detox work? Exploring the role of digital detox applications for problematic smartphone use and well-being of young adults using multigroup analysis. *Cyberpsychology, Behavior, and Social Networking, 23*(8), 526–532. https://doi.org/10.1089/cyber.2019.0578
151. Schryen, G., et al. (2017). Literature reviews in IS research: What can be learnt from the past and other fields? *Communications of the Association for Information Systems, 41*(30), 759–774. https://doi.org/10.17705/1CAIS.04130
152. Schryen, G., et al. (2020). A knowledge development perspective on literature reviews: Validation of a new typology in the IS field. *Communications of the Association for Information Systems, 46*(7), 134–186. https://doi.org/10.17705/1CAIS.04607
153. Schwarz, D., et al. (2022). The effect of a 1-week abstinence from Instagram on mental health in youth and young adults. *Kindheit und Entwicklung, 31*(4), 200–210. https://doi.org/10.1026/0942-5403/a000392
154. Schwarzenegger, C., & Lohmeier, C. (2021). Creating opportunities for temporary disconnection: How tourism professionals provide alternatives to being permanently online. *Convergence: The International Journal of Research into New Media Technologies, 27*(6), 1631–1647. https://doi.org/10.1177/13548565211033385
155. Senabre Hidalgo, E., & Greshake Tzovaras, B. (2023). "One button in my pocket instead of the smartphone": A methodological assemblage connecting self-research and autoethnography in a digital disengagement study. *Methodological Innovations, 16*(2), 149–162. https://doi.org/10.1177/20597991231161093
156. Serrano-Puche, J. (2017). Developing healthy habits in media consumption: A proposal for dealing with information overload. In R. P. F. Marques & J. C. L. Batista (Eds.), *Information and Communication Overload in the Digital Age* (pp. 202–222). IGI Global. https://doi.org/10.4018/978-1-5225-2061-0.ch009
157. Sheldon, K. M., Abad, N., & Hinsch, C. (2011). A two-process view of Facebook use and relatedness need-satisfaction: Disconnection drives use, and connection rewards it. *Journal of Personality and Social Psychology, 100*(4), 766–775. https://doi.org/10.1037/a0022407
158. Šimunjak, M. (2023). "You Have to Do That for Your Own Sanity": Digital disconnection as journalists' coping and preventive strategy in managing work and well-being. *Digital Journalism*, 1–20. https://doi.org/10.1080/21670811.2022.2153711
159. Spiliotopoulos, T., & Oakley, I. (2020). An exploration of motives and behavior across Facebook and Twitter. *Journal of Systems and Information Technology, 22*(2), 201–222. https://doi.org/10.1108/JSIT-12-2019-0258
160. Stäheli, U., & Stoltenberg, L. (2024). Digital detox tourism: Practices of analogization. *New Media & Society, 26*(2), 1056–1073. https://doi.org/10.1177/14614448211072808
161. Stangl, F. J., & Riedl, R. (2023). Digital Detoxing als Maßnahme gegen digitalen Stress: Auf die Verwendung digitaler Technologien temporär verzichten. *Theologisch-praktische Quartalschrift, 171*(3), 274–283.
162. Stangl, F. J., & Riedl, R. (2023). Interruption science as a research field: Towards a taxonomy of interruptions as a foundation for the field. *Frontiers in Psychology, 14*, Article 1043426. https://doi.org/10.3389/fpsyg.2023.1043426
163. Stangl, F. J., & Riedl, R. (2023). Interruptions in the workplace: An exploratory study among digital business professionals. In F. F.-H. Nah & K. Siau (Eds.), *HCI in Business, Government and Organizations: 10th International Conference, HCIBGO 2023, Held as Part of the 25th HCI International Conference, HCII 2023, Copenhagen, Denmark, July 23–28, 2023, Proceedings, Part II*. LNCS, vol. 14039, pp. 400–422. Springer. https://doi.org/10.1007/978-3-031-36049-7_29
164. Stangl, F. J., & Riedl, R. (2024). Neurophysiological measurements in the research field of digital detoxing: Review and implications for future research. In F. D. Davis et al. (Eds.), *Information Systems and Neuroscience: NeuroIS Retreat 2023, Vienna, Austria*. LNISO, vol. 68, pp. 105–121. Springer. https://doi.org/10.1007/978-3-031-58396-4_10
165. Stangl, F. J., et al. (2023). Negative psychological and physiological effects of social networking site use: The example of Facebook. *Frontiers in Psychology, 14*, Article 1141663. https://doi.org/10.3389/fpsyg.2023.1141663

166. Stangl, F. J., Seiler, V., & Riedl, R. (2025). Revealing the benefits and burdens of workplace digitalization: Preliminary insights from a qualitative study. In Siau, K. L. & Nah, F. F.-H. (Eds.), *HCI in Business, Government and Organizations: 12th International Conference, HCIBGO 2025, Held as Part of the 27th HCI International Conference, HCII 2025, Gothenburg, Sweden, June 22–27, 2025, Proceedings, Part II*. LNCS, vol. 15805, pp. 219–235. Springer. https://doi.org/10.1007/978-3-031-92826-0_14
167. Stephanidis, C., et al. (2019). Seven HCI grand challenges. *International Journal of Human-Computer Interaction, 35*(14), 1229–1269. https://doi.org/10.1080/10447318.2019.1619259
168. Stieger, S., & Lewetz, D. (2018). A week without using social media: Results from an ecological momentary intervention study using smartphones. *Cyberpsychology, Behavior, and Social Networking, 21*(10), 618–624. https://doi.org/10.1089/cyber.2018.0070
169. Sutton, T. (2017). Disconnect to reconnect: The food/technology metaphor in digital detoxing. *First Monday, 22*(6). https://doi.org/10.5210/fm.v22i6.7561
170. Sutton, T. (2020). Digital harm and addiction: An anthropological view. *Anthropology Today, 36*(1), 17–22. https://doi.org/10.1111/1467-8322.12553
171. Syvertsen, T. (2022). Offline tourism: Digital and screen ambivalence in Norwegian mountain huts with no internet access. *Scandinavian Journal of Hospitality and Tourism, 22*(3), 195–209. https://doi.org/10.1080/15022250.2022.2070540
172. Syvertsen, T. (2023). Framing digital disconnection: Problem definitions, values, and actions among digital detox organisers. *Convergence: The International Journal of Research into New Media Technologies, 29*(3), 658–674. https://doi.org/10.1177/13548565221122910
173. Syvertsen, T., & Enli, G. (2020). Digital detox: Media resistance and the promise of authenticity. *Convergence: The International Journal of Research into New Media Technologies, 26*(5–6), 1269–1283. https://doi.org/10.1177/1354856519847325
174. Tai, Z., Yu, X., & He, B. (2021). Locked down through virtual disconnect: Navigating life by staying on/off the health QR code during COVID-19 in China. *Convergence: The International Journal of Research into New Media Technologies, 27*(6), 1648–1662. https://doi.org/10.1177/13548565211047157
175. Tams, S., et al. (2020). Worker stress in the age of mobile technology: The combined effects of perceived interruption overload and worker control. *Journal of Strategic Information Systems, 29*(1), Article 101595. https://doi.org/10.1016/j.jsis.2020.101595
176. Tarafdar, M., et al. (2007). The impact of technostress on role stress and productivity. *Journal of Management Information Systems, 24*(1), 301–328. https://doi.org/10.2753/MIS0742-1222240109
177. Treré, E. (2021). Intensification, discovery and abandonment: Unearthing global ecologies of dis/connection in pandemic times. *Convergence: The International Journal of Research into New Media Technologies, 27*(6), 1663–1677. https://doi.org/10.1177/13548565211036804
178. Tromholt, M. (2016). The Facebook experiment: Quitting Facebook leads to higher levels of well-being. *Cyberpsychology, Behavior, and Social Networking, 19*(11), 661–666. https://doi.org/10.1089/cyber.2016.0259
179. Trujillo Pons, F. (2023). The "Digital Disconnect" on the back of occupational health and safety. *Journal of Leadership, Accountability and Ethics, 20*(4), 188–200. https://doi.org/10.33423/jlae.v2023i20.6521
180. Trujillo Pons, F., & Megino Fernández, D. (2023). Mental health and the right to digital disconnection at work: A panoramic vision from the Spanish experience and the recent approaches of the European Parliament. *Labor Law Journal*, 79–90.
181. Turel, O., & Cavagnaro, D. R. (2019). Effect of abstinence from social media on time perception: Differences between low-and at-risk for social media "addiction" groups. *Psychiatric Quarterly, 90*(1), 217–227. https://doi.org/10.1007/s11126-018-9614-3
182. Turel, O., Cavagnaro, D. R., & Meshi, D. (2018). Short abstinence from online social networking sites reduces perceived stress, especially in excessive users. *Psychiatry Research, 270*, 947–953. https://doi.org/10.1016/j.psychres.2018.11.017
183. Ugur, N. G., & Koc, T. (2015). Time for digital detox: Misuse of mobile technology and phubbing. *Procedia - Social and Behavioral Sciences, 195*, 1022–1031. https://doi.org/10.1016/j.sbspro.2015.06.491

184. Umasankar, M., et al. (2022). Disconnect to reconnect: Employee wellbeing through digital detoxing. *Journal of Positive School Psychology, 6*(2), 4463–4673.
185. Vaghefi, I. (2021). Sustaining abstinence from social media: Results from a seven-day Facebook break: Social media abstinence. In *Proceedings of the 24th International Academic Mindtrek Conference* (pp. 221–229). https://doi.org/10.1145/3464327.3464337
186. Vaghefi, I. et al. (2018). Digital detox? Understanding users' abstinence from social networking sites use. In *Proceedings of the 39th International Conference on Information Systems.*
187. Vally, Z., & D'Souza, C. G. (2019). Abstinence from social media use, subjective well-being, stress, and loneliness. *Perspectives in Psychiatric Care, 55*(4), 752–759. https://doi.org/10.1111/ppc.12431
188. Van Bruyssel, S., De Wolf, R., & Vanden Abeele, M. (2023). Who cares about digital disconnection? Exploring commodified digital disconnection discourse through a relational lens. *Convergence: The International Journal of Research into New Media Technologies.* https://doi.org/10.1177/13548565231206504
189. van Wezel, M. M. C., Abrahamse, E. L., & Vanden Abeele, M. M. P. (2021). Does a 7-day restriction on the use of social media improve cognitive functioning and emotional well-being? Results from a randomized controlled trial. *Addictive Behaviors Reports, 14*, 100365. https://doi.org/10.1016/j.abrep.2021.100365
190. Vanden Abeele, M. M., & Mohr, V. (2021). Media addictions as apparatgeist: What discourse on TV and smartphone addiction reveals about society. *Convergence: The International Journal of Research into New Media Technologies, 27*(6), 1536–1557. https://doi.org/10.1177/13548565211038539
191. Vanden Abeele, M. M., & Nguyen, M. H. (2024). Digital media as ambiguous goods: Examining the digital well-being experiences and disconnection practices of Belgian adults. *European Journal of Communication, 39*(2), 122–144. https://doi.org/10.1177/02673231231201487
192. Vanden Abeele, M. M. P. (2021). Digital wellbeing as a dynamic construct. *Communication Theory, 31*(4), 932–955. https://doi.org/10.1093/ct/qtaa024
193. Vanden Abeele, M. M. P., & Nguyen, M. H. (2022). Digital well-being in an age of mobile connectivity: An introduction to the Special Issue. *Mobile Media & Communication, 10*(2), 174–189. https://doi.org/10.1177/20501579221080899
194. Vanden Abeele, M. M. P., et al. (2024). Why, how, when, and for whom does digital disconnection work? A process-based framework of digital disconnection. *Communication Theory, 34*(1), 3–17. https://doi.org/10.1093/ct/qtad016
195. Vanden Abeele, M. M. P., Halfmann, A., & Lee, E. W. J. (2022). Drug, demon, or donut? Theorizing the relationship between social media use, digital well-being and digital disconnection. *Current Opinion in Psychology, 45*, 101295. https://doi.org/10.1016/j.copsyc.2021.12.007
196. Vanman, E. J., Baker, R., & Tobin, S. J. (2018). The burden of online friends: The effects of giving up Facebook on stress and well-being. *The Journal of Social Psychology, 158*(4), 496–508. https://doi.org/10.1080/00224545.2018.1453467
197. Vialle, S. J., Machin, T., & Abel, S. (2023). Better than scrolling: Digital detox in the search for the ideal self. *Psychology of Popular Media.* https://doi.org/10.1037/ppm0000496
198. vom Brocke, J. et al. (2009). Reconstructing the giant: On the importance of rigour in documenting the literature search process. In S. Newell et al. (Eds.), *Proceedings of the 17th European Conference on Information Systems* (pp. 2206–2217).
199. Wadsley, M., & Ihssen, N. (2023). Restricting social networking site use for one week produces varied effects on mood but does not increase explicit or implicit desires to use SNSs: Findings from an ecological momentary assessment study. *PLoS ONE, 18*(11), Article e0293467. https://doi.org/10.1371/journal.pone.0293467
200. Webster, J., & Watson, R. T. (2002). Analyzing the past to prepare for the future: Writing a literature review. *MIS Quarterly, 26*(2), xiii–xxiii.

201. White, T. R. (2013). Digital social media detox (DSMD): Responding to a culture of interconnectivity. In B. Pătruţ, M. Pătruţ & C. Cmeciu (Eds.), *Social Media and the New Academic Environment* (pp. 414–430). IGI Global. https://doi.org/10.4018/978-1-4666-2851-9.ch020
202. Widdicks, K., et al. (2022). Escaping unsustainable digital interactions: Toward "more meaningful" and "moderate" online experiences. *International Journal of Human-Computer Studies, 165*, Article 102853. https://doi.org/10.1016/j.ijhcs.2022.102853
203. Wilcockson, T. D. W., Osborne, A. M., & Ellis, D. A. (2019). Digital detox: The effect of smartphone abstinence on mood, anxiety, and craving. *Addictive Behaviors, 99*, Article 106013. https://doi.org/10.1016/j.addbeh.2019.06.002
204. Wood, N. T., & Muñoz, C. (2021). Unplugged: Digital detox enhances student learning. *Marketing Education Review, 31*(1), 14–25. https://doi.org/10.1080/10528008.2020.1836973
205. Zhang, M., & Zhang, X. (2022). Between escape and return: Rethinking daily life and travel in selective unplugging. *Tourism Management, 91*, Article 104521. https://doi.org/10.1016/j.tourman.2022.104521
206. Zhu, Z. (2022). Developing intentional relationships with technologies: Exploring players' tension between play and non-play and designing built-in interventions to contribute to digital well-being. In *Extended Abstracts of the CHI Conference on Human Factors in Computing Systems* (pp. 1–4). https://doi.org/10.1145/3491101.3503815
207. Zhu, Z., Mitchell, A., & Zhang, R. (2022). Developing intentional relationships with technologies: An exploratory study of players' experiences with built-in interventions in games. In *Proceedings of the ACM Designing Interactive Systems Conference* (pp. 745–758). https://doi.org/10.1145/3532106.3533460

Fostering Inclusivity—Towards Principles for Inclusive Information Systems Design

Naveen Vimalan, Markus P. Zimmer, and Paul Drews

Abstract Social inclusion of impaired individuals through information systems (IS) design is pivotal yet challenging. Current IS designs and designers often prioritize functionality, neglecting critical societal and structural aspects. Existing inclusive design approaches fall short in fully addressing the multifaceted challenges faced by impaired individuals, resulting in a lack of clear guidance for creating truly inclusive IS. To address this gap, we conducted a systematic literature review, unveiling six inclusive design principles. These principles integrate insights from various disability models and span different inclusive design approaches. They offer guidance in crafting IS that meet the diverse needs and abilities of impaired individuals while addressing societal and structural barriers, ultimately fostering greater inclusivity of IS designs.

1 Introduction

In the landscape of information systems (IS) design, the social inclusion of impaired individuals is both essential and complex [1, 2]. Researchers within the IS discipline have identified that designers face obstacles in creating inclusive IS, often prioritizing technical solutions over ethical and social considerations [3]. For instance, designers often wrongly assume that impaired individuals prioritize functionality over aesthetics [4]. This misconception can lead to situations where websites for visually impaired individuals prioritize text size but neglect visually appealing layouts [5]. Moreover, impaired individuals are often pressured to adapt to the standards designed

N. Vimalan (✉) · M. P. Zimmer · P. Drews
Leuphana University Lüneburg, Lüneburg, Germany
e-mail: naveenvimalan209@outlook.de

M. P. Zimmer
e-mail: markus.zimmer@leuphana.de

P. Drews
e-mail: paul.drews@leuphana.de

C. M. Flath et al. (eds.), *Shaping the Digital Future Through Innovation and Practice*, Lecture Notes in Information Systems and Organisation 85,
https://doi.org/10.1007/978-3-032-08489-7_17

for non-impaired individuals [6, 7]. Ultimately, impaired individuals face challenges, including discriminatory attitudes of designers and barriers entrenched both in design practices and society. To tackle these hurdles, designers need to understand how existing inclusive design approaches reflect specific models of disability.

Disability models—such as functional, social, and critical model—shape designers' perspectives on disability [6]. These models provide insights into the multifaceted nature of disability and barriers to effective IS use [8, 9]. Prominent inclusive design approaches like Inclusive Design and Universal Design integrate these models but often prioritize functional aspects over critical social considerations [10]. Approaches such as User-Sensitive Inclusive Design seek to eliminate societal barriers through user involvement and social inclusion strategies [4, 11]. Despite this, they may not always provide detailed technical guidance on ensuring accessibility in IS design [4]. This creates a notable gap: the absence of comprehensive principles tailored specifically to inclusive IS design that integrate insights from various disability models and existing inclusive design approaches.

With respective principles being absent, the challenge of fostering inclusive designs persists, prompting important questions to designers: How can they determine which design approach best serves each disability model? Alternatively, how can they derive principles that encompass the requirements of all three disability models? To explore these issues, our research question is: *How can principles for inclusive design be developed based on models of disability and inclusive design approaches?*

To answer this question, we delve into various disability models and inclusive design approaches, recognizing their pivotal role in shaping designers' perspectives. Through a systematic literature review (SLR), we unveil principles rooted in the models of disability and inclusive design approaches that help to foster inclusivity of IS designs. Moreover, we provide principles that can be utilized to compare different design approaches or shed light on the design process regarding inclusivity. Ultimately, the results of our work provide designers with a focused set of principles that embody the core concepts of inclusivity and offer guidance in developing equitable and accessible IS for impaired individuals.

2 Theoretical Background

As we delve into inclusive IS design, understanding its theoretical underpinnings is crucial. Thus, we examine various disability models and inclusive design approaches. Analyzing these models alongside inclusive design approaches, we gain insights into how individual needs, societal perceptions, and structural factors intersect to inform inclusive IS design.

2.1 Models of Disability

The *functional model of disability* (FM), also known as the medical model, focuses on individual biological defects and characteristics [12, 13]. It sees disability as resulting from limitations or impairments, such as illness or injury, requiring medical treatment and rehabilitation [14]. The functional model encompasses not only physical but also sensory or cognitive abilities [15]. Sensory abilities pertain to our sense organs such as vision, hearing, or speech abilities, while cognitive abilities refer to mental or emotional capabilities. Although the functional model considers a broad range of abilities, it places the problem on the individual and often leads to a normative view where disability is seen as an inability to function like a "normal" person [14, 16, 17].

The *social model of disability* (SM) represents a shift in understanding, focusing on societal barriers rather than individual deficits. A central idea of the social model is the distinction between "disability" and "impairment". According to Shakespeare and Watson [18], society disables impaired people by isolating them, making disability a societal construct rather than solely an individual condition. This distinction is crucial as it highlights that societal factors, not just individual impairments, contribute to disability [13, 19, 20]. Hence, the social model emphasizes the right of impaired people to fully participate in all aspects of life and calls for designing inclusive social structures and environments.

The *critical model of disability* (CM) focuses on political, cultural, and social mechanisms that marginalize individuals with impairments [21]. It highlights how societal norms contribute to the stigmatization and marginalization of individuals with impairments, shaping their opportunities for full participation [22, 23]. The critical model of disability addresses these barriers, emphasizing how attitudes shape the environment for individuals with impairments and impact their societal participation [10, 24]. Hence, similar to the social model, the critical model recognizes that disability is not solely individual but influenced by societal, cultural, and political norms. It emphasizes understanding and challenging these dimensions of disability.

2.2 Inclusive Design Approaches

The existing inclusive design approaches are deeply intertwined with the three models of disability (i.e., FM, SM and CM), forming the foundation upon which perceptions and responses to diverse impairments are built [9, 15, 25]. Thus, deriving principles based on disability models is essential because existing inclusive design approaches are intricately linked with these models. In exploring the realm of inclusive design, we encounter a diverse array of approaches, each offering unique perspectives on inclusivity (see Table 1).

Among the historically prominent approaches is *Inclusive Design* (ID), which takes a holistic view in emphasizing the creation of products, environments, and services accessible to a diverse group of people [26, 27]. ID emphasizes individual

Table 1 Inclusive design approaches and their groundings in the models of disability

Design approach	Key concepts	Models of disability		
		FM	SM	CM
Inclusive design	Emphasizes the creation of products, environments, and services accessible to a diverse group of people	x	x	
Universal design	Focusses on designing for general accessibility rather than specific needs	x		
Design for all	Focuses on universal usability and social inclusion, but encompasses broader aspects of social differences beyond functional needs	x	x	
User-centered design	Involves cooperative interaction between designers and impaired individuals to understand their needs, behaviors, and preferences		x	
Participatory design	Emphasizes collaborative interaction between designers and impaired individuals to foster their participation and engagement in design activities		x	
Ability based design	Advocates focusing on the strengths and capabilities of impaired individuals, rather than their limitations	x		
User-sensitive inclusive design	Emphasizes that designers need to build real empathy with impaired individuals to deeply understand their needs	x	x	x
Responsive inclusive design	Focuses on software that adapts to varying abilities and requirements of impaired individuals, and fostering engagement throughout the design process	x	x	x

adaptability and strives to eliminate social barriers, aligning with the functional and social model of disability [28]. In contrast, *Universal Design* (UD) shares a similar goal of promoting usability for everyone [29]. However, UD solely draws inspiration from the functional model of disability, focusing on designing for general accessibility rather than specific individual needs [15]. Synonym to UD, *Design for All* (DfA) focuses on universal usability and social inclusion but encompasses broader aspects of social differences (e.g. age, gender, ethnicity,...) beyond functional needs, reflecting dimensions of the functional and social disability model [15, 29].

Beyond these prominent methodologies, a plethora of other approaches contribute to the rich tapestry of inclusive design. For instance, *User-Centered Design* (UCD) and *Participatory Design* (PD) focus on collaborative interaction between designers and impaired individuals to foster their engagement in design activities [9], aligning with the social model of disability by promoting social inclusion. *Ability Based*

Design (ABD) advocates to focus on the strengths and capabilities of impaired individuals, rather than their limitations, aligning with the functional disability model [28]. Contrary, *User-Sensitive Inclusive Design* (USID) emphasizes that designers need to build real empathy with impaired individuals to deeply understand their needs [4]. It also recognizes that human functionality e.g., hearing capabilities can change over time depending on factors like age [4]. By recognizing building empathy and changing abilities over time, USID blends aspects of the functional, social and critical model of disability. Similarly, *Responsive inclusive Design* (RiD) integrates functional, social, and critical disability aspects into the software life cycle, adapting to changes in abilities and requirements of impaired individuals, and fostering their engagement throughout the design process [30].

As we delve deeper into each inclusive design approach, it becomes evident that they possess distinct strengths and limitations, and root in different disability models. While some approaches excel in promoting universal usability and intuitive design, others prioritize participatory processes and stakeholder engagement. By critically evaluating these capabilities and limitations in relation to disability models, we can better understand how to align design approaches with the diverse needs of impaired individuals. Having laid the theoretical foundation, we next outline our research approach.

3 Methodology

3.1 Literature Search and Selection

We conducted a SLR based on Wolfswinkel et al. [31]. We collected literature on inclusive design approaches in the fields of IS, Human–Computer Interaction (HCI), and social sciences. The literature search covers the databases Scopus and AIS eLibrary (AISeL), targeting top IS journals and conferences, and started with defining keywords and criteria for our literature search (see Fig. 1). We included terms like disability, impairment, inclusion, design, and IS, while excluding keywords such as Big Data, Data Analytics, and Blockchain, which do not directly relate with our research on inclusive IS design. Our focus was on articles, conference papers, and reviews that specifically addressed inclusion or disability in IS design, or provided information on the models of disability as well as inclusive design approaches. We excluded documents not mentioning inclusion or disability in IS design or not written in English.

In the first phase, we used Scopus to search for literature within the field of IS, restricted to articles from the "Basket of 11" [32]. We filtered for articles, conference papers, and reviews, published between 2000 and 2023. The literature search was carried out using the following search string: (("inclus*" OR "disab*" OR "impair*") AND ("design" OR "develop*")). This produced a total of 48 articles. Additionally, we undertook the same literature search process in the AISeL targeting leading IS

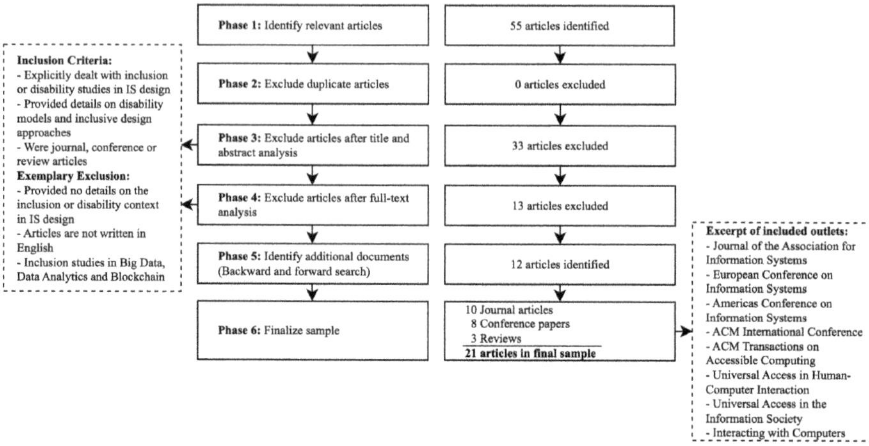

Fig. 1 Selection and filtering process

conferences. For this, we used the same combination of keywords as in Scopus. We also limited the timeframe to the years 2000 to 2023. This produced no relevant literature on inclusive IS design focusing on impaired individuals in the IS conferences ICIS, PACIS, HICSS, or WI. However, in ECIS, we found one article on accessibility in the context of user interface design for visually impaired individuals; and in AMCIS, we identified six articles on IS design for impaired individuals. Overall, we collected 55 articles from the IS discipline (see Fig. 1).

In the second, third and fourth phase, we selected articles for our analysis based on the defined inclusion and exclusion criteria (see Fig. 1). We exported the identified articles from Scopus and AISeL to a spreadsheet. Using filter functions, we excluded possible duplicates, but we found none. Next, we reviewed the articles' titles and abstracts. This led to exclusion of 33 articles that neither focused on IS design nor on individuals with impairments. Subsequently, we conducted a full-text analysis of the remaining 22 articles, revealing that 13 were not relevant as they did not address inclusive IS design. Thus, the selection process produced nine articles from the IS discipline.

In the fourth phase, we also performed forward and backward searches in Scopus and AISeL across various disciplines, including IS, HCI, and social sciences. This resulted in 30 additional articles. After we excluded irrelevant articles, which provided no details on inclusive IS design, we added 12 additional articles to our sample. In total, we selected 21 articles, conference papers, and reviews, primarily from the fields of IS and HCI (see Fig. 1).

3.2 Literature Analysis

The literature analysis followed grounded theory in three sequential steps: open, axial, and selective coding, adhering to the methodology outlined by Wolfswinkel et al. [31]. We used MAXQDA, a text analysis tool, for coding. In a preparatory step, we highlighted important text passages—to which we refer as "codes"—from a randomly selected article from the literature sample. Then, we gradually coded the remaining articles. All articles underwent this preparatory highlighting step at least once. Afterwards, we continued with open coding.

During open coding, we formed "1st Order Concepts" based on the created codes from the preparatory step. We aimed at developing 1st order concepts that reflected inclusive design approaches and/or the models of disability (see Fig. 2). We started creating a 1st order concept related to the adaptability of IS based on ID [3], RiD [30] and ABD [28], along with a concept addressing accessibility and usability in IS design [5, 7, 11, 33, 34]. Subsequently, we formed a 1st order concept associated with the overlook of social diversity of impaired individuals in IS design [7, 8, 25, 35], and a concept with promoting participation and empowerment of impaired individuals through collaborative design efforts [9, 36]. These concepts involve applying design approaches like ID [37], DfA [3], UCD [9, 38], PD [4, 25, 36] and USID [4, 38]. Additionally, we developed a 1st order concept related to social barriers, including stereotypes and biases towards impaired individuals, which can be addressed by design approaches like ID, UCD, PD and USID [10, 15, 25]. Lastly, we formed a 1st order concept associated with structural barriers within existing design practices, including cost-related challenges and issues with current inclusive design guidelines [3, 10, 35]. The structural barriers can be addressed through design approaches like USID [4] and RiD [30]. As we progressed with open coding, we observed that certain 1st order concepts, such as adaptability and usability, were closely aligned with the functional model of disability, emphasizing individual needs. Similarly, concepts focusing on empowerment of impaired individuals and societal barriers resonated with the social and critical model of disability, highlighting the role of societal structures and attitudes in shaping disability experiences.

In axial coding, we summarized our 1st order concepts into so-called "2nd Order Themes" (see Fig. 2). For this, we compared the characteristics of our 1st order concepts. This made it possible to classify them into themes, producing a meaningful subdivision of our 1st order concepts. A total of six themes emerged, encapsulating principles derived from insights into disability models and inclusive design approaches, aimed at fostering inclusivity of IS designs (see Fig. 2).

Lastly, during selective coding, we formed core categories, or "Aggregate Dimensions" based on the 2nd order themes' characteristics. These aggregate dimensions further categorize the principles for inclusive IS design and help us in answering our research question. These dimensions are functional, social, and critical inclusion principles reflecting the disability models and the complex interplay between individual needs, societal structures, and critical factors in design processes (see Fig. 2).

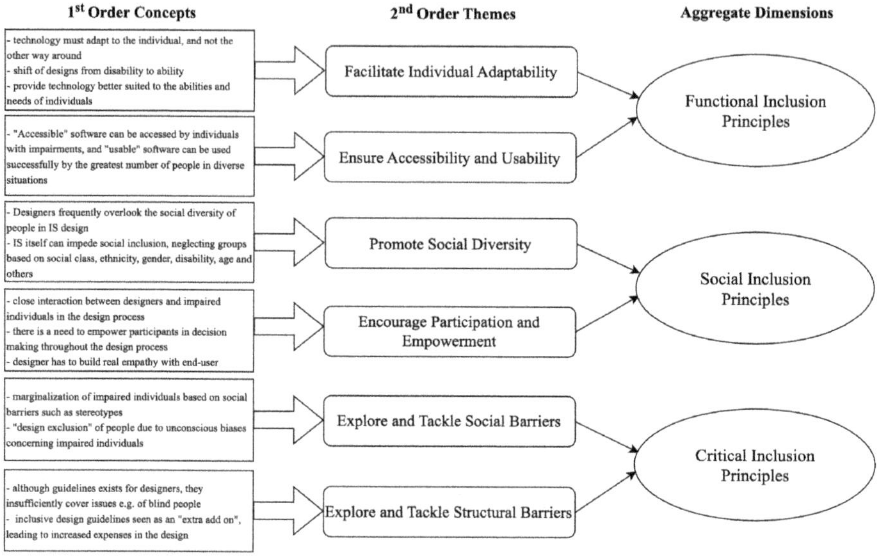

Fig. 2 Compiled data structure from coding the literature sample on inclusive IS design

After thoroughly reviewing all articles in the literature sample and conducting the necessary coding steps, we reached "theoretical saturation". This occurred when no new concepts, properties, or connections emerged, indicating a comprehensive understanding of the data.

4 Findings

Having conducted a literature analysis using grounded theory, we identified a set of principles aimed at guiding designers in inclusive IS design. Categorized into functional, social, and critical dimensions, these principles address the complex interplay between individuals' needs, societal challenges as well as structural barriers in design processes. Now, we present these principles in detail, shedding light on their significance and implications for inclusive IS design through practical examples.

4.1 Functional Inclusive Principles

In the realm of inclusive design, traditional boundaries dictated by the functional model of disability are being challenged [8, 9]. Rather than solely focusing on impairments, there is a growing recognition that IS design should prioritize the diverse abilities of individuals [28]. The ABD approach, demonstrated by the SUPPLE project, focuses on individual abilities [28]. SUPPLE uses decision-theoretic optimization to generate user interfaces tailored to a person's abilities, preferences, and tasks, significantly improving speed, accuracy, and user satisfaction for individuals with motor impairments compared to default interfaces [28]. Furthermore, both ID and RiD highlight the need for technology to adapt to the individual's needs and abilities, not the other way around [30]. For instance, the EDICO application was developed using RiD and allows the inclusion of people with visual impairments into classrooms by incorporating adaptations based on the use of refreshable braille displays [30]. Therefore, the following principle for inclusive IS design emerges:

> ***Facilitate Individual Adaptability***: Design should enable individual adjustments to meet the changing needs and abilities of impaired individuals.

Accessibility and usability are paramount in ensuring that IS cater to the needs of diverse individuals. Unfortunately, many existing IS suffer from a lack of accessibility and usability, posing significant challenges for impaired individuals [6, 34]. For instance, individuals with visual impairments may struggle to access websites that are not optimized for screen readers [33]. Similarly, poor usability can hinder user interaction and satisfaction, making it difficult for impaired individuals to effectively engage with the environment [2]. Integrating UD related guidelines, such as the Web Content Accessibility Guidelines (WCAG), ensures that IS accommodate various abilities and preferences seamlessly [38]. Wentz et al. [7] developed a touch-based web app following WCAG, specifically designed for inclusive learning environments. By following WCAG and integrating user feedback from blind individuals through usability tests, the app ensures seamless accessibility and usability [7]. This approach not only accommodates diverse needs but also enhances user engagement and learning outcomes [2]. Thus, we can define the following principle for inclusive IS design:

> ***Ensure Accessibility and Usability***: Design should ensure accessibility and usability through WCAG guidelines and usability tests with impaired individuals.

4.2 Social Inclusion Principles

The social model of disability highlights social barriers within society, faced by impaired individuals, such as the overlook of social diversity [8, 25]. In the IS field, there is limited research integrating social diversity into IS design, leading to sparsity of guidelines for designers to navigate inclusive designs [35]. Consequently, designers often overlook demographics such as gender, ethnicity, age, and social class in IS design [8, 35]. By adopting existing design approaches, designers can address both individual needs and societal barriers [9]. For instance, ID focuses on eliminating barriers and facilitating participation for diverse individuals [3, 4]. In contrast, DfA take a comprehensive approach, accommodating the needs of everyone in the design of IS, thereby fostering social inclusion in both design and society [4]. Moreover, tools like GenderMag help designers identify and address gender biases in their software [39]. GenderMag has been shown to be effective in evaluating and improving software inclusivity, which can lead to higher user satisfaction and broader user adoption [40]. Additionally, methods like persona creation or user journey mapping help to learn more about the diversity of impaired individuals [9]. Thus, the following principle for inclusive IS design can be defined:

> ***Promote Social Diversity***: Design should promote social diversity, recognizing the diverse demographics of impaired individuals in the design process.

Benton et al. [9] stress that excluding individuals with impairments from the design process gives undue influence to other stakeholders, like designers, leading to less transparent outcomes. Both UCD and PD advocate for active involvement of individuals with impairments throughout the design process, fostering their social inclusion in IS design [4, 36]. They suggest that combining end-users and designers' expertise is key to an optimal IS design [9]. Achieving this requires not only participation, but also empowerment of individuals with impairments. In the study of Sitbon & Farhin [41] participants showed heightened engagement when presented with prototypes, especially during interactive phases. They demonstrated increased visual attention and enthusiastic facial expressions, particularly when experiencing the text-to-speech output. Therefore, continual encouragement of contributions is vital to maintain engagement [42]. Additionally, USID recommends cultivating genuine empathy to deeply understand people's needs and experiences, integrating them into design from the outset [4]. Therefore, we can define the following principle for inclusive IS design:

> ***Encourage Participation and Empowerment***: Design should encourage the participation and empowerment of impaired individuals, to ensure their meaningful involvement throughout the design process.

4.3 Critical Inclusion Principles

The critical model of disability addresses inequalities embedded within design and society, such as stereotypes. Negative stereotypes persist among impaired individuals due to various factors like demographics, socio-economic status, and culture [10, 43]. For instance, a job-matching platform may lack specific accommodations for impaired individuals, making them feel excluded or skeptical about using it, ultimately fearing bias towards non-impaired individuals [10]. Design approaches such as ID tackle design exclusion, aiming to eliminate barriers to access created by unconscious biases and assumptions about individuals' abilities [28]. Additionally, UCD, PD, and USID emphasize co-creation between designers and impaired individuals, integrating their voices, needs, and experiences directly into the design process [4, 36, 41], thereby challenging biases and stereotypes. Thus, we define the following principle for inclusive IS design:

> ***Explore and Tackle Social Barriers***: Design should explore and tackle social barriers that contribute to the marginalization of impaired individuals.

Beyond social barriers, there are challenges within design practices that hinder inclusive IS design. For instance, current inclusive design guidelines for blind people are still incomplete or difficult to implement in practical design contexts, hindering designers' ability to create accessible and usable IS [2]. Therefore, USID suggests that designers should not solely rely on guidelines, but they need to develop real empathy with the impaired individuals to deeply understand their needs [4]. Additionally, challenges related to costs impede the design of specialized IS. Designers often integrate inclusive design guidelines as an afterthought, leading to increased expenses toward the end of the design phase [3, 4]. To overcome this hurdle, RiD focusses on incorporating requirements of impaired individuals throughout the software lifecycle, resulting in reduced unnecessary expenses [30]. Thus, we can formulate the following principle for inclusive IS design:

> ***Explore and Tackle Structural Barriers***: Design should explore and tackle structural barriers entrenched within design resources and practices.

Overall, these fundamental principles are crucial for designers to consider individuals' needs as well as societal and structural barriers in the creation of inclusive IS designs. The principles for inclusive IS design reflect key considerations derived from various inclusive design approaches and dimensions of the disability models, each offering unique perspectives on how to approach inclusive IS design. Table 1 provides an overview of the six principles and maps which of these principles the analyzed approaches for inclusive IS design reflect. Hence, our findings provide two key insights: the six principles for fostering inclusive IS design and how existing inclusive IS design approaches reflect these principles. The latter shows that none of the analyzed inclusive design approaches reflects all principles or—put differently—the approaches feature different groundings in the models of disability (see Table 2).

5 Discussion

This paper tackles the critical gap in existing inclusive design approaches that fail to comprehensively consider various models of disability, focusing primarily on functional design aspects but neglecting broader societal and structural barriers faced by individuals with impairments. Moreover, designers often lack the necessary knowledge and resources to foster inclusivity, ultimately hindering the creation of inclusive IS [35]. This emphasizes the need for design principles tailored to inclusive IS design that recognize and combine insights from disability models and existing inclusive design approaches, providing guidance for creating inclusive designs.

To bridge this gap, we conducted a systematic literature review to conceptualize six principles for fostering inclusive IS designs. These principles root in the different models of disability (i.e., functional, social and critical). The *functional inclusion principles* of "Facilitate Individual Adaptability" and "Ensure Accessibility and Usability" root in the functional model of disability that regards the individual

Table 2 Principles for inclusive IS design and their reflection in design approaches

				Inclusive design approaches							
		Principles for inclusive IS design	Definition	ID	UD	DfA	UCD	PD	ABD	USID	RiD
Dimensions of the disability models	Functional Inclusion Principles	*Facilitate individual adaptability*	Design should enable individual adjustments to meet the changing needs and abilities of impaired individuals	x					x		x
		Ensure accessibility and usability	Design should ensure accessibility and usability through WCAG guidelines and usability tests with impaired individuals		x						
	Social Inclusion Principles	*Promote social diversity*	Design should promote social diversity, recognizing the diverse demographics of impaired individuals in the design process	x		x					
		Encourage participation and empowerment	Design should empower impaired individuals, fostering their meaningful involvement throughout the design process				x	x		x	

(continued)

Table 2 (continued)

				Inclusive design approaches							
		Principles for inclusive IS design	Definition	ID	UD	DfA	UCD	PD	ABD	USID	RiD
	Critical Inclusion Principles	*Explore and tackle social barriers*	Design should explore and tackle social barriers that contribute to the marginalization of impaired individuals	**x**			x	x		x	
		Explore and tackle structural barriers	Design should explore and tackle structural barriers entrenched within design resources and practices							x	x

as the focal point for inclusive design. These principles emphasize the importance of designing intuitive IS to accommodate the diverse needs of impaired individuals by utilizing design approaches like ID, UD, ABD, and RiD. In contrast, the *social inclusion principles* of "Promote Social Diversity" and "Encourage Participation and Empowerment" reflect the social model of disability by acknowledging that societal barriers can disable and exclude impaired individuals from participating in design activities. Design approaches such as ID, DfA, UCD, PD, and USID are instrumental in operationalizing these principles, as they provide guidance on interacting and collaborating with impaired individuals. Lastly, the *critical inclusion principles* of "Explore and Tackle Social Barriers" and "Explore and Tackle Structural Barriers" address and challenge systemic inequalities embedded within design practices and society, as posited by the critical model of disability. These principles accentuate that designers can utilize design approaches such as ID, UCD, PD, USID and RiD to dismantle social barriers like stereotypes or structural barriers like cost-related obstacles within design practices.

As we delve into these principles, it becomes clear that each set of principles highlights different aspects of the models of disability and that the various inclusive design approaches for inclusive IS design emphasize different models; and thus, sets of principles (see Table 2). The functional inclusion principles focus on IS design that prioritizes overall accessibility, whereas the social inclusion principles extend IS design to encompass societal inclusion by recognizing that impaired individuals can face exclusion from society due to factors like overlooking social diversity. Contrary, the critical inclusion principles challenge inequalities such as stereotypes faced by impaired individuals and barriers in the design process itself. Hence, we answer our research question, "How can principles for inclusive design be developed based on models of disability and inclusive design approaches?", by providing principles for inclusive IS design based on existing inclusive design approaches and the models of disability. The provided principles bridge the identified research gap of a lack of comprehensive principles tailored to inclusive IS design that cut across different inclusive design approaches and reflect insights from the three models of disability. With these principles, we paved a way for designers to navigate inclusive design, addressing diverse individuals' needs alongside societal and structural barriers, ultimately fostering greater inclusivity of IS designs. For example, these principles can inform IS design processes that use one of the existing inclusive design approaches or future developments and modifications of inclusive design approaches to better reflect the three models of disability.

While these principles can provide valuable guidance, we acknowledge limitations. One limitation arises from the methodology of the SLR, which was based on a selection of 21 articles predominantly from core IS journals and conferences. This approach may have overlooked literature from design-related fields, essential for developing inclusive design principles. Additionally, the derivation of these principles may be restricted by their focus on the functional, social, and critical disability model, potentially overlooking other critical viewpoints such as political or ethical considerations.

The adoption of these principles can have significant implications for the design of digital products and services. By incorporating the principles, organizations can enhance user satisfaction, expand their market reach, and foster social inclusion, thereby contributing to their digital responsibility [44, 45]. Moreover, implementing the principles and prioritizing inclusivity in IS design can lead to innovation, as designers are challenged to think beyond traditional design paradigms.

In conclusion, the principles for inclusive IS design outlined in this paper offer valuable insights into creating IS that prioritize the diverse needs and abilities of individuals with impairments, while also tackling societal and structural barriers that impede inclusive design practices. Although limitations exist, the adoption of these principles can lead to tangible benefits for both impaired individuals and organizations. Moving forward, the next steps would involve conducting interviews or focus groups with relevant stakeholders to test these principles in real-life scenarios. This process will help refine and expand the principles to address emerging trends in inclusive design.

References

1. Díaz Andrade, A., & Techatassanasoontorn, A. A. (2021). Digital enforcement: Rethinking the pursuit of a digitally-enabled society. *Information Systems Journal, 31*, 184–197. https://doi.org/10.1111/isj.12306
2. Babu, R., & Singh, R. (2009). Evaluation of web accessibility and usability from blind user' s perspective: The context of online assessment. In *AMCIS Proceedings 2009* (pp. 1–10).
3. Abascal, J., & Nicolle, C. (2005). Moving towards inclusive design guidelines for socially and ethically aware HCI. *Interacting with Computers, 17*, 484–505. https://doi.org/10.1016/j.intcom.2005.03.002
4. Newell, A. F., Gregor, P., Morgan, M., Pullin, G., & Macaulay, C. (2011). User-sensitive inclusive design. *Univers Access Inf Soc., 10*, 235–243. https://doi.org/10.1007/s10209-010-0203-y
5. Adipat, B., & Zhang, D. (2005) Interface design for mobile applications. In *AMCIS Proceedings 2005* (pp. 2281–2290).
6. Saqr, R., & Bhattacherjee, A. (2012). Web accessibility: Factors enabling the visually impaired to using websites. In *AMCIS Proceedings 2012* (pp. 1–10).
7. Wentz, B., Null, J., Dickson, E., Skinner, W., Swogger, J., & Thompson, A. (2015). Developing and implementing an accessible, touch-based web app for inclusive learning. In *AMCIS Proceedings 2015* (pp. 1–9).
8. Keller, S., Owens, J., Parker, C., Keller, S., Owens, J., & Craig, P. (2000). Improving online access for people with disabilities. In *ECIS Proceedings 2000*.
9. Benton, L., & Johnson, H. (2015). Widening participation in technology design: A review of the involvement of children with special educational needs and disabilities. https://doi.org/10.1016/j.ijcci.2015.07.001
10. Pethig, F., & Kroenung, J. (2019). Specialized information systems for the digitally disadvantaged. *Journal of the Association for Information Systems, 20*(5). https://doi.org/10.17705/1jais.00573
11. Neerincx, M. A., Cremers, A. H. M., Kessens, J. M., van Leeuwen, D. A., & Truong, K. P. (2009). Attuning speech-enabled interfaces to user and context for inclusive design: Technology, methodology and practice. *Universal Access in the Information Society, 8*, 109–122. https://doi.org/10.1007/S10209-008-0136-X/FIGURES/5

12. Adam, A., & Kreps, D. (2009). Disability and discourses of web accessibility. *Information, Communication & Society, 12*, 1041–1058. https://doi.org/10.1080/13691180802552940
13. Haegele, J. A., & Hodge, S. (2016). Disability discourse: Overview and critiques of the medical and social models. *Quest, 68*, 193–206. https://doi.org/10.1080/00336297.2016.1143849
14. Mitra, S. (2006). The capability approach and disability. *Journal of Disability Policy Studies, 16*, 236–247.
15. Toboso, M. (2011). Rethinking disability in Amartya Sen's approach: ICT and equality of opportunity. https://doi.org/10.1007/s10676-010-9254-2
16. Talcott, P. (1975). The sick role and the role of the physician reconsidered. *Health and Society, 53*, 257–278.
17. Pfeiffer, D. (2001). The conceptualization of disability. *Research in Social Science and Disability, 2*, 29–52. https://doi.org/10.1016/S1479-3547(01)80019-1
18. Shakespeare, T., & Watson, N. (2001). The social model of disability: An outdated ideology? *Research in Social Science and Disability, 2*, 9–28. https://doi.org/10.1016/S1479-3547(01)800 18-X
19. Barney, K. W. (2012). Disability simulations: Using the social model of disability to update an experiential educational practice. *SCHOLE: A Journal of Leisure Studies and Recreation Education, 27*, 1–11. https://doi.org/10.1080/1937156X.2012.11949361
20. Roush, S. E., & Sharby, N. (2011). Disability reconsidered: The paradox of physical therapy. *Physical Therapy, 91*, 1715–1727. https://doi.org/10.2522/PTJ.20100389
21. Vehmas, S., & Watson, N. (2014). Moral wrongs, disadvantages, and disability: A critique of critical disability studies. https://doi.org/10.1080/09687599.2013.831751
22. Goodley, D. (2011). Disability studies: An interdisciplinary introduction. *Disability & Society, 26*, 503–505. https://doi.org/10.1080/09687599.2011.567809
23. Campbell, F. K. (2009) Contours of ableism: The production of disability and abledness, 1–231. https://doi.org/10.1057/9780230245181/COVER.
24. Steele, C. M. (1997). A threat in the air. How stereotypes shape intellectual identity and performance. *American Psychologist, 52*, 613–629. https://doi.org/10.1037//0003-066X.52.6.613
25. Wass, S., Thygesen, E., & Purao, S. (2023). Principles to facilitate social inclusion for design-oriented research. *Journal of the Association for Information Systems, 24*, 1204–1247. https://doi.org/10.17705/1jais.00814
26. Clarkson, J., Coleman, R., Keates, S., & Lebbon, C. (2003). *Inclusive design: Design for the whole population*. Springer.
27. Waller, S., Bradley, M., Hosking, I., & Clarkson, P. J. (2015). Making the case for inclusive design. *Applied Ergonomics, 46*, 297–303. https://doi.org/10.1016/j.apergo.2013.03.012
28. Wobbrock, J. O., Kane, S. K., Gajos, K. Z., Harada, S., & Froehlich, J. (2011). Ability-based design: Concept, principles and examples. *ACM Transactions on Accessible Computing, 3*, 1–27. https://doi.org/10.1145/1952383.1952384
29. Stephanidis, C. (2001). User interfaces for all: New perspectives into human-computer interaction. In C. Stephanidis (Ed.), *User interfaces for all - concepts, methods, and tools* (pp. 3–17). Lawrence Erlbaum Associates.
30. Martínez, C. M., Piorno, J. R., Escribano Otero, J. J., & Guijarro Mata-García, M. (2023). Responsive inclusive design (RiD): A new model for inclusive software development. *Universal Access in the Information Society, 22*, 893–902. https://doi.org/10.1007/S10209-022-00893-9/FIGURES/4
31. Wolfswinkel, J. F., Furtmueller, E., & Wilderom, C. P. M. (2013). Using grounded theory as a method for rigorously reviewing literature. *European Journal of Information Systems, 22*, 45–55. https://doi.org/10.1057/EJIS.2011.51
32. AIS: Senior Scholar's List of Premier Journals.
33. Leal Ferreira, S. B., de Silveira, D. S., Chauvel, M. A., & do Amaral Leal Ferreira, M. G.: e-Accessibility: Making the web accessible to the visually impaired persons. In *AMCIS Proceedings 2008* (pp. 1–8).

34. Djamasbi, S., Tullis, T., Girouard, M., Hebner, M., & Krol, J. (2006). Web accessibility for visually impaired users: Extending the technology acceptance model (TAM). In *AMCIS Proceedings 2006*.
35. Olbrich, S., Trauth, E. M., Niederman, F., & Gregor, S. (2015). Inclusive design in IS: Why diversity matters. *Communications of the Association for Information Systems, 37*, 767–782. https://doi.org/10.17705/1CAIS.03737
36. Brereton, M., Sitbon, L., Abdullah, M. H. L., Vanderberg, M., & Koplick, S. (2015). Design after design to bridge between people living with cognitive or sensory impairments, their friends and proxies. *CoDesign, 11*, 4–20. https://doi.org/10.1080/15710882.2015.1009471
37. Hosking, I., Waller, S., & Clarkson, P. J. (2010). It is normal to be different: Applying inclusive design in industry. *Interacting with Computers, 22*, 496–501. https://doi.org/10.1016/J.INTCOM.2010.08.004
38. Newell, A. F., & Gregor, P. (2002). Design for older and disabled people - where do we go from here? *Universal Access in the Information Society, 2*, 3–7. https://doi.org/10.1007/s10209-002-0031-9
39. Stumpf, S., Peters, A., Bardzell, S., Burnett, M., Busse, D., Cauchard, J., & Churchill, E. (2020). Gender-inclusive HCI research and design: A conceptual review. *Foundations and Trends in Human-Computer Interaction, 13*, 1–69. https://doi.org/10.1561/1100000056
40. Szlavi, A., & Guedes, L. S.(2023). *Gender inclusive design in technology: Case studies and guidelines*. Lecture Notes in Computer Science (including subseries Lecture Notes in Artificial Intelligence and Lecture Notes in Bioinformatics). 14030 LNCS (pp. 343–354). https://doi.org/10.1007/978-3-031-35699-5_25/FIGURES/1
41. Sitbon, L., & Farhin, S. (2017). Co-designing interactive applications with adults with intellectual disability: A case study. *ACM International Conference Proceeding Series, 5*, 487–491. https://doi.org/10.1145/3152771.3156163
42. Mazzone, E., Read, J. C., & Beale, R. (2008). Design with and for disaffected teenagers. *ACM International Conference Proceeding Series, 358*, 290–297. https://doi.org/10.1145/1463160.1463192
43. Farina, A. (1981). Are women nicer people than men? Sex and the stigma of mental disorders. *Clinical Psychology Review, 1*, 223–243. https://doi.org/10.1016/0272-7358(81)90005-2
44. Zimmer, M. P., Järveläinen, J., Stahl, B. C., & Mueller, B. (2023). Responsibility of/in digital transformation. *Journal of Responsible Technology, 16*, Article 100068. https://doi.org/10.1016/J.JRT.2023.100068
45. Trier, M., Kundisch, D., Beverungen, D., Müller, O., Schryen, G., Mirbabaie, M., & Trang, S. (2023). Digital responsibility: A multilevel framework for responsible digitalization. *Business and Information Systems Engineering, 65*, 463–474. https://doi.org/10.1007/S12599-023-00822-X/FIGURES/1

Hate Speech and Sentiment of YouTube Video Comments From Public and Private Sources Covering the Israel-Palestine Conflict

Simon Hofmann, Christoph Sommermann, Mathias Kraus, Patrick Zschech, and Julian Rosenberger

Abstract This study explores the prevalence of hate speech (HS) and sentiment in YouTube video comments concerning the Israel-Palestine conflict by analyzing content from both public and private news sources. The research involved annotating 4983 comments for HS and sentiments (neutral, pro-Israel, and pro-Palestine). Subsequently, machine learning (ML) models were developed, demonstrating robust predictive capabilities with area under the receiver operating characteristic (AUROC) scores ranging from 0.83 to 0.90. These models were applied to the extracted comment sections of YouTube videos from public and private sources, uncovering a higher incidence of HS in public sources (40.4%) compared to private sources (31.6%). Sentiment analysis revealed a predominantly neutral stance in both source types, with more pronounced sentiments towards Israel and Palestine observed in public sources. This investigation highlights the dynamic nature of online discourse surrounding the Israel-Palestine conflict and underscores the potential of moderating content in a politically charged environment.

S. Hofmann · C. Sommermann
Friedrich-Alexander Universität Erlangen-Nürnberg, Nürnberg, Germany
e-mail: simon1995.hofmann@fau.de

C. Sommermann
e-mail: christoph.sommermann@fau.de

M. Kraus · J. Rosenberger (✉)
Universität Regensburg, Regensburg, Germany
e-mail: julian.rosenberger@ur.de

M. Kraus
e-mail: mathias.kraus@ur.de

P. Zschech
TU Dresden, Dresden, Germany
e-mail: patrick.zschech@tu-dresden.de

C. M. Flath et al. (eds.), *Shaping the Digital Future Through Innovation and Practice*,
Lecture Notes in Information Systems and Organisation 85,
https://doi.org/10.1007/978-3-032-08489-7_18

1 Introduction

In the digital era, the prevalence of hate speech (HS) on online platforms has notably escalated, particularly within the discourse surrounding contentious socio-political issues. A vivid example is the Israel-Palestine conflict, where the region's complex and longstanding geopolitical tensions frequently manifest in heated online interactions that can escalate into HS [6, 10]. The impact of such speech extends beyond mere words, affecting not only the psychological health of individuals but also the overall harmony within their social communities [11, 17]. In 2021, approximately 40% of U.S. residents reported encountering online hate speech, with young adults showing heightened vulnerability to its psychological consequences [25, 31]. Against this backdrop, our study focuses on HS detection and sentiment analysis within the context of the Israel-Palestine conflict. HS detection refers to the identification and classification of language that denigrates individuals or groups based on inherent characteristics such as race, religion, or gender [10, 16]. Sentiment analysis assesses the emotional tone behind a text to understand the attitudes, opinions, and emotions being expressed [22, 39]. By integrating these analytical dimensions, our research aims to provide deeper insights into the nature of social media discourse, particularly in politically sensitive contexts.

Research underscores that platforms like YouTube not only reflect but can amplify ethno-racial and religious hatred, potentially transforming online spaces into arenas for aggressive and polarized exchanges [28, 35]. This growing prevalence of HS, intensified by the interconnected nature of online platforms, underscores an urgent need for sophisticated machine learning (ML) methods to support more effective content moderation, implement legal regulation, and enhance digital safety [6, 34].

This paper addresses the dual challenges of detecting HS and analyzing sentiment in the aftermath of significant events like the Hamas attack on Israel on the 7th of October in 2023 [2]. By analyzing comments from YouTube videos related to this conflict, we aim to develop ML models that not only detect HS but also gauge public sentiment, thereby contributing to the mitigation of online toxicity and promoting digital responsibility [38]. Our study makes several contributions. First, we provide a carefully annotated dataset of 4983 YouTube comments labeled for HS and sentiment.[1] Second, we develop ML models with promising predictive capabilities with AUROC scores between 0.83 to 0.90 for tasks of hate speech detection and sentiment analysis. Finally, through this work, we gain novel insights into how different platforms may influence user interactions and the broader dynamics of online discourse [38].

This paper is structured as follows: Sect. 2 reviews relevant literature to establish a theoretical foundation for our methods. Section 3 details the methodologies employed in data collection, cleaning, labeling, and analysis. Section 4 presents our findings, followed by a discussion in Sect. 5 on the broader impacts of these results on online discourse moderation. Finally, Sect. 5.1 outlines the limitations of our

[1] Our dataset is publicly available here: doi.org/10.17605/OSF.IO/Q45CT.

study and suggests directions for future research. This structured approach ensures a comprehensive exploration of the dynamics of HS and sentiment within the context of the Israel-Palestine conflict, offering clear insights and actionable findings.

2 Related Work

The increasing prevalence of HS on online platforms, particularly during discussions on sensitive topics like the Israel-Palestine conflict, has highlighted the need for effective moderation tools [37]. ML techniques have been widely adopted to tackle this challenge, with a focus on developing accurate and efficient HS detection models [6].

Traditional ML approaches, such as Logistic Regression (LR) and Support Vector Machines (SVM), have been extensively used for HS detection and sentiment analysis tasks. LR, a probabilistic model that uses a logistic function to model the relationship between input features and binary outcomes, has shown promising results in text classification tasks [4]. SVM, on the other hand, aims to find the optimal hyperplane that maximizes the margin between different classes in a high-dimensional space [8]. Both LR and SVM have been successfully applied to HS detection and sentiment analysis in various contexts [10, 32].

While more advanced techniques like deep learning and Transformer architectures have gained popularity in recent years [33], traditional ML methods still hold value due to their simplicity, interpretability, and effectiveness, especially when dealing with smaller datasets. For instance, Davidson et al. [9] employed LR and SVM for detecting toxic language in social media comments, achieving promising results. Similarly, Burnap and Williams [5] used LR and SVM to classify hateful and antagonistic content on Twitter, demonstrating the effectiveness of these methods in capturing the nuances of online HS.

Despite these advancements, significant challenges remain in HS detection and sentiment analysis, particularly in managing the complex socio-political discourse surrounding the Israel-Palestine conflict. The nuanced language and evolving nature of online interactions further complicate the automated detection of HS. Moreover, research highlights distinct behaviors among authors of HS, who tend to exhibit higher activity levels, use specific and non-trivial language, and maintain dense connections within their networks [19, 29]. This trend is especially pronounced in the Global South, where social media plays a critical role in spreading fear and animosity towards minorities, often using historical events and political symbols to stir up emotions [7, 13].

Future research should focus on refining ML techniques, improving their adaptability to different contexts, and reducing biases that may affect the fairness of HS detection systems [37]. In this study, we aim to contribute to the existing body of work by developing LR and SVM models for HS detection and sentiment analysis in the context of the Israel-Palestine conflict. By focusing on these traditional ML

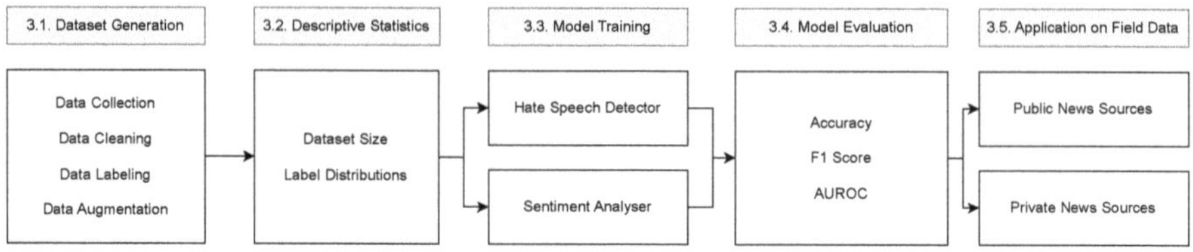

Fig. 1 Framework of our work

approaches and leveraging a carefully annotated dataset of YouTube comments, we seek to provide insights into the dynamics of online discourse and the effectiveness of these methods in capturing the nuances of HS and sentiment in this context.

3 Methods

In the following, we describe the steps taken in order to build a dataset, train models, and then apply these models on field data. Figure 1 illustrates these steps.

3.1 Dataset Generation

We created a unique dataset for this research by collecting comments from YouTube videos related to the Israel-Palestine conflict using web scraping techniques [20]. We gathered comments from videos of German public and private news services to ensure diverse perspectives. The data collection process was conducted in two rounds, spanning seven weeks from October 2 to November 20, 2023. In the first round, we collected a total of 19 047 comments from 13 videos. To capture the evolving nature of the conflict and its impact on public discourse, we carried out a second scraping process to obtain comments from an additional six videos that covered events occurring on a weekly basis after October 18, 2023.

Given the noisy nature of user-generated content on YouTube, we extensively cleaned the collected dataset to ensure data quality and consistency. We removed empty lines, duplicates, non-German comments, numbers, special characters, and emojis. We standardized the text by converting it to lowercase, normalizing umlauts and special letters, and applying tokenization. We utilized the Natural Language Toolkit (NLTK) to filter out stop words while retaining negations for sentiment analysis [3]. We employed lemmatization using the WordNet Lemmatizer from NLTK to reduce words to their base form, accounting for the complexities of the German language [26].

To train supervised machine learning models for hate speech detection and sentiment analysis, we manually labeled the cleaned dataset. Three annotators conducted

Table 1 Summary of data augmentation techniques

Data augmentation technique	Source	Comments added
Back Translation	HateCheck via DeepL	2000
GPT-4	Generated Content	1095

a detailed and iterative labeling process, following recommendations by Artstein and Poesio [1] to ensure consistency and reliability. We used a binary system to label comments for the presence of hate speech, with an expanded definition including derogatory, sexist, vulgar, or profane language. For sentiment labeling, we employed a ternary classification (pro-Palestine, pro-Israel, and neutral) based on keywords, phrases, and overall tone. Regular meetings among annotators ensured consistent application of labeling criteria.

To mitigate class imbalance and increase dataset diversity, we employed data augmentation techniques. We adapted the "HateCheck" English dataset [30] into German through back-translation, enhancing linguistic variety. We also utilized language models, particularly GPT-4, to generate additional comments for sentiment analysis. The augmented dataset included 2000 comments for hate speech detection and 1095 comments for sentiment analysis, increasing robustness for model training [40]. Table 1 summarizes the data augmentation techniques and their contributions.

3.2 Descriptive Statistics

Following the preprocessing, two distinct datasets emerged. The initial dataset, comprised of the original scraped comments, included 19 074 entries. From this dataset and the augmented comments, a total of 4983 comments were manually classified for HS and sentiment by the annotators. The subsequent, more concise dataset evolved from the nearly five thousand annotated comments, encapsulating 944 distinctly labeled entries. The distribution between public (55.08%, n=520) and private (44.92%, n=424) sources was noted, with the sampled videos spanning seven weeks from October 2 to November 20, 2023. A majority of the comments (62.12%, n=577) originated from the initial three weeks up to October 18, 2023, while the remainder (38.88%, n=367) came from the concluding four weeks. Comment length varied widely within the dataset, enriching it for sentiment analysis and subsequent model training.

In labeling, efforts were concentrated on achieving label balance. The label distribution shows a higher prevalence of HS (64.55% Yes vs. 35.45% No), which may slightly bias the model towards detecting HS, potentially increasing false positives. Sentiment distribution is predominantly neutral (46.39%), with more pro-Palestine (33.15%) than pro-Israel (20.45%) comments, which may affect the model's sentiment detection accuracy. The relatively balanced public/private source distribution

Table 2 Distribution of hate speech and sentiment labels in the annotated dataset

Hate Speech			Sentiment		
Label	Count	Percentage (%)	Label	Count	Percentage (%)
Yes	609	64.55	Neutral	438	46.39
No	335	35.45	Pro-Israel	193	20.45
			Pro-Palestine	313	33.15

and temporal spread of comments help ensure diverse perspectives, though the higher initial activity may influence overall representativeness. The distribution of labels for both HS and sentiment is detailed in Table 2.

3.3 Model Training

Machine learning has been widely used for hate speech detection and sentiment analysis in recent years, with various techniques employed to represent text data and train classification models [10, 36]. Our decision to combine hate speech detection with sentiment analysis is grounded in several key considerations from existing literature. Schmidt and Wiegand [32] highlight that sentiment analysis can provide valuable context for hate speech detection, as extreme negative sentiment often correlates with hate speech. This complementary relationship allows for a more nuanced understanding of the text. Moreover, Davidson et al. [9] argue that sentiment analysis helps in distinguishing between hate speech and merely offensive language, which often share negative sentiment but differ in intent and severity. By integrating these two tasks, we aim to provide a more comprehensive analysis of the YouTube comments related to the Israel-Palestine conflict, leveraging the strengths of both approaches to gain deeper insights into the nature and tone of the discourse.

We experimented with two methods for text representation: Bag of Words (BoW) and Term Frequency-Inverse Document Frequency (TF-IDF) [33]. BoW represents text as a vector of word frequencies, disregarding grammar and word order but keeping multiplicity. This method is simple and effective for converting text into a numerical format for machine learning models [41]. TF-IDF, on the other hand, weights the frequency of terms inversely with their occurrence across documents, highlighting unique words within the corpus [27]. We opted for BoW due to its simplicity and effective performance during our initial experimentation phase.

For the hate speech detection task, we trained separate LR and SVM models. The LR model used the 'lbfgs' solver, which is an optimizer in the family of quasi-Newton methods. The regularization strength was set to 0.1 to mitigate potential overfitting issues, and the L2 norm was employed for regularization. This configuration provided a good balance between bias and variance, ensuring the model's robustness and reliability. The SVM model for hate speech detection used a linear kernel function, as it is well-suited for this classification problem [8]. The hyperparameter tuning for the SVM involved testing a range of values for the regularization parameter from 0.01 to 1.0 to determine the best performing configuration.

Similar to the hate speech detection task, we trained separate LR and SVM models for sentiment analysis. The LR model for sentiment analysis also used the 'lbfgs' solver and L2 regularization, with the regularization strength set to 0.1. The SVM model for sentiment analysis employed a linear kernel function, and the hyperparameter tuning process was conducted in the same manner as for the hate speech detection SVM model.

By training separate models for hate speech detection and sentiment analysis, we developed a Hate Speech Detector and a Sentiment Analyser. This approach allows for a more targeted and specialized analysis of the YouTube comments, enabling us to gain insights into the prevalence of hate speech and the sentiment expressed towards the Israel-Palestine conflict.

3.4 Model Evaluation

To evaluate our ML models, we followed common practice. The prepared datasets (see Sects. 3.1–3.2) were divided into training (80%) and testing (20%) sets to facilitate the evaluation of the models' performance on unseen data. 10-fold cross-validation was implemented on the training data to provide a comprehensive view of the models' predictive capabilities and to identify any biases or vulnerabilities in their performance [14].

For measuring the model performance, we used various threshold dependent and threshold independent metrics. First, we used the prediction accuracy to obtain first insights into the performance of the ML models. Second, we used F1-score to address the issue of our unbalanced dataset. Finally, we used the are under the receiver operating characteristic (AUROC) as a threshold independent metric.

3.5 Application on Field Data

To assess the practical applicability of our developed hate speech detection and sentiment analysis models, we applied our trained models on two large datasets comprising YouTube comments. The first dataset, consisting of 19 074 comments, partially served as training material for the models, while the second dataset, containing 12 000 entirely new comments, was used to apply the model to unfamiliar data in order to gain insights into the political discourse and the dynamics behind it. For each comment, our trained models are used to detect hate speech and evaluate the sentiment expressed.

Figure 2 shows a word cloud to visualize the most common words that appear in the field data, where the size of the words represents their occurrence, offering

Fig. 2 Word cloud of field data

a visual representation of key terms from our data. In this analysis, certain words such as 'raus' and 'waffen' stand out due to their size, each appearing in 1.5 percent of the comments. The most dominant term, 'raus,' a German word meaning 'out' or 'outside', suggests themes of expulsion, removal, or a call to action to leave, which are central in the text. This is confirmed by other prominently featured words like 'volk', 'waffen', 'eigenen', and 'haben', indicating discussions around national identity, defense, and possession. Additionally, words such as 'israeli', 'allah', and 'volk' point to the Israeli-Palestine conflict. Smaller, yet still significant terms like 'verstehen', 'thema', and 'berichterstattung' imply a focus on understanding reports or discussions. It is important to remember that word clouds, while providing a snapshot of frequency, do not offer context or the relationships between terms. They guide us toward the main subjects and the possible tone or stance but do not replace thorough textual analysis.

4 Results

4.1 Hate Speech Detection

The evaluation results of our HS detection model using LR present a comprehensive picture of its performance. It yielded a training accuracy of 77.46% and a testing accuracy of around 73.94%. While lower than the testing accuracy, this figure is still indicative of good model reliability. The classification report illustrates precision, recall, and F1-scores of about 0.74 for both classes. Specifically, for class 0 (No HS), the precision, recall, and F1-score were 0.74, 0.71, and 0.72, respectively, while for class 1 (HS), these metrics were 0.74, 0.76, and 0.75, respectively. The macro and weighted average F1-scores were both approximately 0.74, indicating a balanced performance across classes. A key metric in classification tasks, AUROC, stood at

0.83 for both classes. These results underscore the effectiveness of the LR model in the context of our HS detection task. The careful tuning of model parameters, such as the regularization strength, has contributed to this solid performance, helping to mitigate overfitting while maintaining the model's ability to generalize well to new, unseen data.

The SVM model achieved an AUROC score of 0.82 for both classes, slightly performing worse than the LR. The confusion matrix shows that the model correctly classified 225 instances as negative and 263 instances as positive, while misclassifying 91 negative instances as positive and 81 positive instances as negative. The results for both models are close together. Based on the slightly better values of the AUROC and in the confusion matrix it was decided to continue with the LR model and apply it to the field data for hate speech detection.

4.2 Sentiment Analysis

The LR model for the sentiment analysis achieved an accuracy of 76.92% on the training set, while on the testing set, it maintained a relatively strong performance with an accuracy of 72.06%. Furthermore, the model's discrimination ability across classes was highlighted by the AUROC scores. For class 0 (Neutral), the AUROC was 0.90, indicating robust predictive power. Class 1 (Israel) exhibited an AUROC of 0.85, suggesting reliable discrimination, while class 2 (Palestine) showed a respectable AUROC of 0.84. These findings underscore the model's capability to differentiate between classes relatively well.

4.3 Field Analysis

4.3.1 Hate Speech Detection.

The comparison between the incidence of HS in private and public domains reveals that in private sources, a smaller proportion of content is classified as hate (31.6%), while a larger portion (68.4%) is categorized as no hate. In public sources, the proportion of content identified as hate is slightly higher at 40.4%, with 60.2% being no hate. These numbers suggest that HS is more frequently detected in public sources than in private ones according to this analysis. However, it is important to consider the context of the data, the methodology used for detection, and the definitions applied to what constitutes HS.

Figure 3 shows four lines tracking the percentage of content identified as hate versus no hate over time. The hate lines fluctuate over time, indicating variability in the comments of public and private sources during the specified periods. There appears to be a general difference of no hate content being higher than hate content across all the dates shown. The dates on the x-axis range from October 2 to November

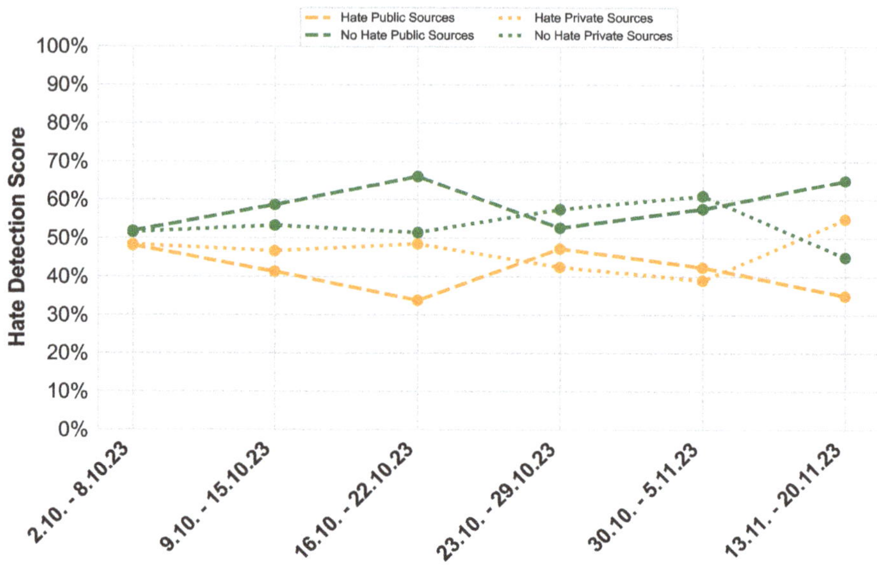

Fig. 3 Hate progression over time

20, 2023. The highest peak for the hate line, representing public sources, occurs in the week of '02.10.–08.10.23', which may be related to the onset of escalated military actions and hostilities, potentially contributing to a surge in online hate speech as communities reacted to the sudden escalation and heavy casualties [18]. Accordingly, the lowest point for the hate line from public sources is seen in the week of '16.10.–22.10.23', which could align with periods of relative calm or effective diplomatic interventions that temporarily moderated discussions [21]. The no hate lines also fluctuate, but in an inverse relationship to the hate line. The reasons for these fluctuations could be influenced by many factors such as current events or changes in public discourse. These fluctuations highlight the dynamic nature of online content moderation and the challenges involved in monitoring HS over time.

Figure 3 further shows fluctuations in the detection of HS in private sources over time. The green lines representing no HS in private and public sources shows a wave-like pattern with peaks and troughs. The highest peak for HS occurs in the week of '13.11.–20.11.23', where the detection rate in private sources rises to just under 55%. This peak likely reflects the public reaction to ongoing military operations and particularly impactful events, such as airstrikes on hospitals and densely populated areas reported during this week, which could drive spikes in hateful and polarized online content [12, 23]. The hate detection rate for private sources reaches its lowest point in the fifth week, '30.10.–05.11.23', at around the 40% mark. This dip may be associated with brief periods of ceasefire or calls for peace that could lead to a temporary reduction in online hostility [15]. The green line, representing no HS, and the orange line, representing HS, both of which representing public and private sources, intersect before the week of '13.11.–20.11.23'. At this point, the rates of hate and no hate detection are equal, indicating a balance between detected HS and non-HS content. As with public sources, the reasons behind these fluctuations in private sources are not provided by the graph alone. These data points underscore the complexity of tracking and understanding HS patterns within different domains of communication.

4.3.2 Sentiment Analysis.

A majority of the content from private sources is categorized as neutral, comprising 68.4%. In private sources, sentiment towards Israel accounts for 18.6%, while sentiment towards Palestine is at 13%. Conversely, a slightly lower percentage of content from public sources is neutral, at 63.6%. Public sources exhibit a higher sentiment towards Israel at 21.2%, and sentiment towards Palestine is also more pronounced at 15.2%. Neutral sentiment still dominates in both private and public sources, suggesting that most content does not express a strong bias towards either Israel or Palestine. Notably, sentiments towards Israel and Palestine are more elevated in public sources than in private ones. The lesser prevalence of neutral sentiment in public sources could suggest that public platforms or media may feature more opinionated or specific content related to Israel and Palestine.

Figure 4 illustrates the distribution of sentiment across private and public sources on the topic of Israel and Palestine, categorized into three key sentiments: Neutral (N), representing comments that neither support nor oppose either side; pro-Israeli (I), representing comments that support or favor Israel; and pro-Palestinian (P), representing comments that support or favor Palestine. The graph shows six lines representing these sentiment categories across sources: Neutral sentiment is shown in gray; pro-Israeli sentiment is shown in blue; pro-Palestinian sentiment is shown in orange. The difference between public and private news sources is represented by the dotted line for private sources and the dashed line for public sources. This visualization helps to understand how each sentiment fluctuates over time and varies between public and private contexts.

Neutral sentiment generally peaks at around 80% by the end of October across both private and public sources, though it shows slight fluctuations before and afterwards. Sentiment towards Israel in public sources starts just above 20% in early October, experiences a dip towards the end of the month, and then rises again, occasionally surpassing initial levels. Conversely, sentiment towards Palestine in public sources begins below 20%, increases in early October, then dips below its initial level in the third week to around 10%, before climbing towards the end of the month. The orange dotted line, representing pro-Palestinian sentiment in private sources, shows a fluctuating pattern, starting at 13.61% in early October, peaking at 17.82% in mid-October, before a significant drop to 5.68% at the end of the month, and finally diminishing to a mere 1.19% by mid-November. This suggests a marked decrease in private pro-Palestinian sentiment as the month progresses. In contrast, the orange dashed line, which charts pro-Israeli sentiment in public sources, begins at 15.81%, peaks notably

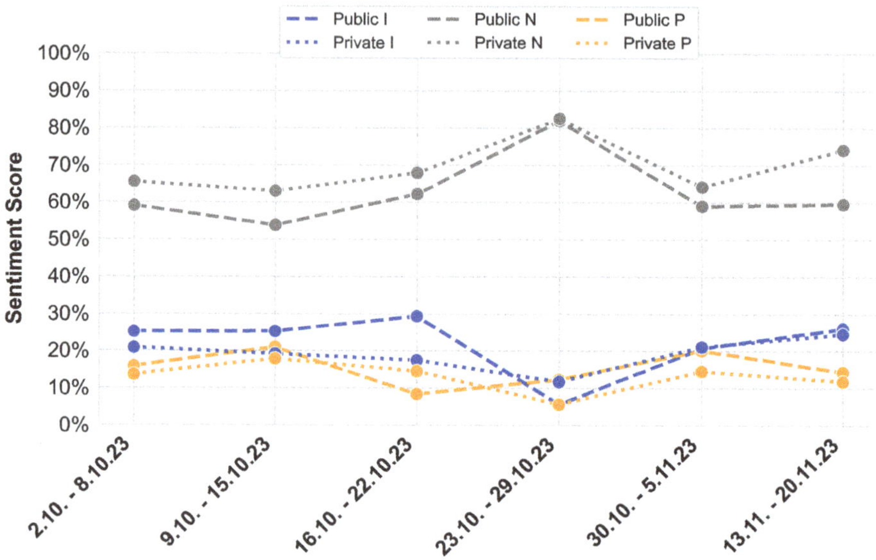

Fig. 4 Sentiment progression over time

to 20.96% in mid-October, then dips to 8.42% before recovering back to 20.20% at the start of November, and stabilizes at 14.38% by mid-November, indicating a more resilient public sentiment towards Palestine throughout the period. Despite these fluctuations, neutral sentiment remains consistently the highest, indicating that the majority of content does not express a strong bias towards either Israel or Palestine. This graph demonstrates similar patterns of sentiment movement in both private and public sources, with fluctuations particularly pronounced in private sources, where neutral sentiment notably spikes around October 23rd, and sentiments towards Israel and Palestine demonstrate similar trends of increase and decrease, concluding the month with noticeable shifts.

5 Discussion

The analysis of online discourse from YouTube comments over a seven-week period concerning the Israel-Palestine conflict, which encompassed 19 074 comments with 4983 specifically annotated for HS and sentiment, provides an insightful look into the complex dynamics of public sentiment on digital platforms. This period, marked by intensified geopolitical tensions, saw an interplay of opinions that the application of sentiment analysis and HS detection has helped to decode, echoing findings from previous research that highlights how negative sentiments typically dominate direct content interactions [24]. Furthermore, Figure 2, featuring terms like 'palestina', 'israeli', 'free', and 'god', highlights the conflict's historical, territorial, and nationalistic core, as well as its deep religious dimensions. The term 'free' especially highlights the ongoing struggles for independence, sovereignty, and liberation, which are central to the geopolitical discourse on the Israel-Palestine conflict. Studies like Oh et al. [24] highlight that while negative sentiment often pervades direct interactions, positive sentiment tends to spread more broadly across social platforms. This understanding of sentiment distribution is critical because it informs the strategies that can be employed to effectively moderate and engage with content.

The predominance of neutral sentiments in both private and public sources, as revealed in this study, suggests a general reluctance among users to openly declare their stance on such a controversial issue. However, the analysis also reveals that pro-Palestine sentiments, even within comments classified as HS, are notably vocal, sometimes crossing into HS territory. This observation is crucial for content moderators as it highlights the importance of nuanced and balanced labeling practices to avoid mistakenly conflating strong sentiments with HS. It is imperative that short comments like "free Palestine" are carefully scrutinized to prevent oversimplification, while longer comments, which offer more context, require advanced analytical tools to accurately discern underlying sentiments. In addition, the data suggests significant fluctuations in sentiment that may be influenced by specific external events, be they political, military, or social. These fluctuations indicate a potential impact of real-world events on online expression and highlight the possibility for sentiment analysis to serve as a barometer for public opinion and discourse dynamics. Such insights could be crucial not only for developing more effective communication strategies but also for potentially enhancing our understanding of how global events may shape online communities.

This comprehensive analysis highlights the critical need for robust HS detection mechanisms, particularly in discussions on contentious topics like the Israel-Palestine conflict. By refining these tools and approaches, we can cultivate constructive online environments and maintain digital platforms for balanced, informed discussions, not fostering hostility. Implementing moderation strategies, such as warning labels and sentiment analysis alerts, can balance debate while flagging harmful content for review.

5.1 Limitations and Further Research

This study has several limitations. Firstly, scraping comments from 13 videos, mainly from public and private channels, introduces uniqueness that may affect reproducibility when using different selection criteria. Additionally, disabled comments on some videos limited data access, potentially impacting model outcomes. Also, training the models on a limited dataset could affect their robustness and applicability. Furthermore, during data cleaning, emojis were removed due to their frequent sarcastic use, which complicates sentiment and hate speech interpretation. This may limit analysis by excluding non-textual expressions that provide additional context. This study focused on descriptive analysis to provide a clear overview of the data, while a thorough exploration of underlying reasons requires a separate study. Moreover, analyzing user demographics was not feasible with the available data, as the YouTube Data API does not provide this information. The research setting, including the time, location, and researchers' preferences, adds to the peculiarities and uniqueness of this study, thus potentially limiting the generalizability of the findings. Future research could adopt a longitudinal approach to studying the Israel-Palestine conflict, analyzing sentiment over an extended period to capture evolving public opinion more accurately. Increasing the proportion of precisely labeled comments and further refining the models could provide deeper insights into which sources or topics are most associated with HS, aiding the development of specialized HS detection models. Such efforts could help make online interactions more pleasant by effectively mitigating HS and abusive language on various platforms. Additionally, the researchers' German background influenced the choice of German videos for analysis, ensuring highest linguistic proficiency. This study focuses solely on analyzing online discourse and does not address potential biases from a dominant German perspective on the conflict, which is a limitation. Lastly, this study does not analyze the content or sentiment of the videos themselves, excluding potential insights into how media framing influences the comments.

References

1. Artstein, R., & Poesio, M. (2008). Inter-coder agreement for computational linguistics. *Computational Linguistics,34*(4), 555–596.
2. Barnea, A. (2024). Israeli intelligence was caught off guard: The hamas attack on 7 october 2023—a preliminary analysis. *International Journal of Intelligence and CounterIntelligence*, 1–27
3. Bird, S. (2006). Nltk: The natural language toolkit. In *Proceedings of the COLING/ACL 2006 interactive presentation sessions* (pp. 69–72).
4. Blümel, J., & Zaki, M. (2022). Comparative analysis of classical and deep learningbased natural language processing for prioritizing customer complaints. In *Proceedings of the 55th Hawaii international conference on system sciences (HICSS)*
5. Burnap, P., & Williams, M. L. (2015). Cyber hate speech on twitter: An application of machine classification and statistical modeling for policy and decision making. *Policy Internet, 7*(2), 223–242.
6. Caron, M., Bäumer, F., & Müller, O. (2022). Towards automated moderation: Enabling toxic language detection with transfer learning and attention-based models. In *Proceedings of the 55th Hawaii international conference on system sciences*
7. Chandra, M., Reddy, M., Sehgal, S., Gupta, S., Buduru, A. B., & Kumaraguru, P. (2021). A virus has no religion: Analyzing islamophobia on twitter during the covid-19 outbreak. In *Proceedings of the 32nd ACM conference hypertext social media* (pp. 67–77).
8. Cortes, C., & Vapnik, V. (1995). Support-vector networks. *Mach Learn, 20*, 273–297.
9. Davidson, T., Warmsley, D., Macy, M., & Weber, I. (2017). Automated hate speech detection and the problem of offensive language. In *Proceedings of the international AAAI conference web social media* (vol. 11, pp. 512–515).
10. Fortuna, P., & Nunes, S. (2018). A survey on automatic detection of hate speech in text. *ACM Computing Surveys, 51*(4), 1–30.

11. Frenda, S., Patti, V., & Rosso, P. (2023). Killing me softly: Creative and cognitive aspects of implicitness in abusive language online. *Natural Language Engineering, 29*(6), 1516–1537.
12. Hancock, S. (2023). Israel-gaza violence: The conflict explained. https://www.bbc.com/news/world-middle-east-67424064, Retrieved May 02 2024
13. Jafri, F. A., Siddiqui, M. A., Thapa, S., Rauniyar, K., Naseem, U., & Razzak, I. (2023). Uncovering political hate speech during indian election campaign: A new low-resource dataset and baselines. arXiv preprint arXiv:2306.14764
14. Kohavi, R., et al. (1995). A study of cross-validation and bootstrap for accuracy estimation and model selection. *Proceedings of the International Joint Conference on Artificial Intelligence (IJCAI), 14*, 1137–1145.
15. Lau, C., Raine, A., Qiblawi, T., Tanno, S., Smith-Spark, L., Vogt, A., & Powell, T. B. (2023) Israel-hamas war in gaza: Live updates. https://edition.cnn.com/middleeast/live-news/israel-hamas-war-gaza-news-11-04-23/index.html, Retrieved May 14 2024
16. Loebbecke, C., Luong, A. C., & Obeng-Antwi, A. (2021). AI for tackling hate speech. In *Proceedings of the 29th European conference on information systems (ECIS), Marrakesh, Morocco.*
17. Maarouf, A., Pröllochs, N., & Feuerriegel, S. (2024). The virality of hate speech on social media. In *Proceedings of the ACM on Human-Computer Interaction (CSCW1)* (Vol. 8, pp. 186:1–186:22).
18. Martinez, A. R. (2023). Timeline: A look back at the gaza-israel conflict. https://www.nytimes.com/2023/10/08/world/middleeast/timeline-gaza-israel-attacks-hamas.html, Retrieved May 10 2024.
19. Mathew, B., Illendula, A., Saha, P., Sarkar, S., Goyal, P., & Mukherjee, A. (2020). Hate begets hate: A temporal study of hate speech. *Proceedings of the ACM on Human Computer Interaction, 4*(CSCW2), 1–24.
20. Mitchell, R. (2018). *Web scraping with Python: Collecting more data from the modern web.* O'Reilly Media.
21. Mogul, R., Raine, A., Picheta, R., Tanno, S., Powell, T. B., & Almasy, S. (2023). Israel-hamas war in gaza: Live updates. https://edition.cnn.com/middleeast/live-news/israel-hamas-war-gaza-news-10-22-23/index.html, Retrieved April 20 2024
22. Mukkamala, R., Kauffman, R. J., & Henriksen, H. Z. (2023). Champions for social good: How can we discover social sentiment and attitude-driven patterns in prosocial communication? *Journal of the Association for Information Systems, 24*(6), 1562–1593.
23. New York Times. (2023). W.h.o. says gaza hospitals are near collapse. https://www.nytimes.com/live/2023/11/20/world/israel-hamas-gaza-war-news#who-gaza-hospitals, Retrieved May 15 2024
24. Oh, H., Goh, K. Y., & Phan, T. Q. (2023). Are you what you tweet? The impact of sentiment on digital news consumption and social media sharing. *Information Systems Research, 34*(1), 111–136.
25. Pew Research Center. (2021). The state of online harrassment. https://www.pewresearch.org/internet/2021/01/13/the-state-of-online-harassment/, Retrieved May 20 2024
26. Plisson, J., Lavrac, N., Mladenic, D., et al. (2004). A rule based approach to word lemmatization. *Proceedings of the Informatics Society (IS), 3*, 83–86.
27. Ramos, J., et al. (2003). Using tf-idf to determine word relevance in document queries. In *Proceedings of the 1st instructional conference on machine learning* (Vol. 242, pp 29–48).
28. Ray, A., & George, J. (2021) Online hate and its routes to aggression: A research agenda. In: *Proceedings of the 54th Hawaii international conference on system sciences (HICSS).*
29. Ribeiro, M., Calais, P., Santos, Y., Almeida, V., & Meira, Jr W. (2018). Characterizing and detecting hateful users on twitter. In *Proceedings of the internatinal AAAI conference web social media* (Vol. 12).
30. Röttger, P., Vidgen, B., Nguyen, D., Waseem, Z., Margetts, H., & Pierrehumbert, J. B. (2020). Hatecheck: Functional tests for hate speech detection models. arXiv preprint arXiv:2012.15606
31. Saha, K., Chandrasekharan, E., & De Choudhury, M. (2019). Prevalence and psychological effects of hateful speech in online college communities. In *Proceedings of the 10th ACM conference web science* (pp. 255–264).

32. Schmidt, A., & Wiegand, M. (2017). A survey on hate speech detection using natural language processing. In *Proceedings of the 5th international workshop natural language processing and social media* (pp. 1–10).
33. Siebers, P., Janiesch, C., & Zschech, P. (2022). A survey of text representation methods and their genealogy. *IEEE Access, 10*, 96492–96513.
34. Slivko, O., & Andres, R. (2021). Regulation of hate speech and Hatefulness on German Twitter. In *Proceeding of the 42nd international conference on information systems (ICIS), Austin, Texas*.
35. Susarla, A., Oh, J. H., & Tan, Y. (2012). Social networks and the diffusion of user-generated content: Evidence from youtube. *Information Systems Research, 23*(1), 23–41.
36. Thoms, B., Eryilmaz, E., Mercado, G., Ramirez, B., & Rodriguez, J. (2017). Towards a sentiment analyzing discussion-board. In *Proceeding of the 50th Hawaii international conference on systems and science (HICSS)*.
37. Vosoughi, S., Roy, D., & Aral, S. (2018). The spread of true and false news online. *Science, 359*(6380), 1146–1151.
38. Wlömert, N., Papies, D., Clement, M., & Spann, M. (2024). Frontiers: The interplay of user-generated content, content industry revenues, and platform regulation: Quasi-experimental evidence from youtube. *Marketing Science, 43*(1), 1–12.
39. Xie, J., Liu, X., Zeng, D. D., & Fang, X. (2022). Understanding medication nonadherence from social media: A sentiment-enriched deep learning approach. *MIS Q, 46*(1), 341–372.
40. Yang, K., Lau, R. Y., & Abbasi, A. (2023). Getting personal: A deep learning artifact for text-based measurement of personality. *Information Systems Research, 34*(1), 194–222.
41. Zhang, Y., Jin, R., & Zhou, Z. H. (2010). Understanding bag-of-words model: A statistical framework. *International Journal of Machine Learning and Cybernetics, 1*, 43–52.

Investigation of Success Factors for Co-Creation Platforms for SMEs

Hanna Fritzke, Ann-Kristin Cordes, and Mitja Kulczynski

Abstract Flexibility and innovation are crucial for companies to remain competitive in the digital age. However, companies' innovation efforts are often focused on internal processes and proprietary platforms, which can lead to the development of redundant knowledge and ideas in any organisation. The integration of co-creation offers a way out by facilitating access to external resources such as external knowledge and ideas, which in turn can increase the effectiveness of the innovation process. Therefore, in this article we identify success factors for the use of co-creation platforms in small and medium-sized enterprises (SMEs), which play a significant role in remaining competitive in today's business world. Through a hermeneutic literature review, opportunities, challenges and success factors are identified. The results serve as a guide for SMEs to implement and optimise co-creation platforms in order to improve their innovation processes and strengthen their competitiveness.

1 Introduction

In today's dynamic business environment, flexibility and innovation are crucial for organisations to remain competitive [3, 30, 36]. Often, organisations' innovation efforts are focused on internal processes and proprietary platforms, which can lead to the development of redundant knowledge and ideas within each company [15]. One solution is to create access to external resources such as external knowledge and external ideas. This approach of involving external sources in the innovation process is known as co-creation and helps to increase the effectiveness of the innovation process [3]. Co-creation is an interactive process in which different actors work

H. Fritzke (✉) · A.-K. Cordes · M. Kulczynski
Department of Computer Science, Kiel University, 24098 Kiel, Germany
e-mail: stu227511@mail.uni-kiel.de

A.-K. Cordes
e-mail: akc@informatik.uni-kiel.de

M. Kulczynski
e-mail: mku@informatik.uni-kiel.de

C. M. Flath et al. (eds.), *Shaping the Digital Future Through Innovation and Practice*, Lecture Notes in Information Systems and Organisation 85,
https://doi.org/10.1007/978-3-032-08489-7_19

together and create value together [22, 29]. The integration of digital technologies facilitates the implementation of this process [2, 27]. Co-creation platforms, which not only support the exchange of resources and knowledge between companies and customers, but also enable the involvement of other stakeholders such as employees, universities and suppliers, are central to promoting this collaboration [4, 14]. Overall, co-creation has the potential to promote innovation, deepen understanding of market changes and customer needs and open up access to new markets [7, 16]. This participatory approach enables companies not only to improve their ability to innovate, but also to respond more flexibly to market changes and to position themselves successfully in a changing business environment.

In this article we focus on the study of co-creation for SMEs. The importance of co-creation for SMEs is emphasized due to their limited innovation resources and the fact that they often operate in dynamic markets [14]. Due to limited time and financial resources and smaller research and development departments, SMEs are increasingly reliant on external input and collaboration with other companies [4]. Co-creation in the SME sector is therefore an exciting topic that is the focus of this article. The use of a co-creation platform can be of great benefit to SMEs, as it facilitates access to external resources, promotes innovation and increases customer satisfaction. [9, 18, 30, 37, 49, 52, 61]. The central research question of this article is therefore which success factors are decisive for the implementation and operation of co-creation platforms in small and medium-sized enterprises (SMEs).

The identification of success factors for co-creation platforms for SMEs is essential in order to gain targeted insights into the decisive elements that make these platforms successful. Unfortunately, the aforementioned references and those listed in the theoretical foundation section do not yet examine the effects and developments of co-creation platforms in SMEs. This research gap is partially closed with the help of the development of success factors.

The focus on success factors enables the targeted development of strategies to use resources efficiently, minimize risks and maximize the chances of successful implementation. The result of this article contributes to recognizing the potential of co-creation platforms for SMEs and making optimal use of it in order to strengthen the innovative power of these companies and thus increase their competitiveness. This article thus provides a scientific contribution to the design of future digital strategies and how these can be prepared and developed.

2 Method

A hermeneutic literature search is conducted in the scientific databases Web of Science, Science Direct, AIS database, Scopus and Google Scholar [5]. The search is not limited to specific journals. The search begins with the search terms *Co-Creation* and *Co-Creation Platform*. Scientific papers are then selected from the resulting results according to title, abstract and content, provided that they are considered relevant to the research objective of this article. Special attention is initially paid to review articles and summaries in order to capture the basic concepts of the topic [6].

Once a basic understanding has been established, a targeted literature search is carried out using the previously identified key concepts as search terms, such as *Co-Creation Engagement Platform* or *Co-Creation Actors*. In addition, search terms specifically aimed at SMEs such as *Co-Creation SME* and *Open Innovation SME* are included in the search. The resulting search results are subjected to an in-depth analysis in which the titles and abstracts of the identified publications are examined in order to select thematically relevant ones. Some publications are excluded, for example, because they are out of date or focus too strongly on specific topics. After this selection phase, 152 publications remain. A detailed analysis of the selected scientific publications is then carried out in order to eliminate unsuitable or non-relevant content. This reduces the number of publications to 44. This process is supplemented by the use of backward and forward searches to identify both the cited literature and the literature that refers to the selected articles [60]. In this way, an additional 16 relevant publications were identified. This methodical approach ensures that this research work in the field of co-creation is based on a solid information base. At the end of the selection process, 60 scientific papers remain, which are intensively analyzed and provide a comprehensive basis for the identification of success factors for co-creation platforms for SMEs.

3 Theoretical Background

There is no uniform definition of co-creation in the literature to date [14, 29, 40]. In order to obtain an overview of the various co-creation perspectives and the components of co-creation, a concept matrix according to Webster & Watson [60] is created (see Table 1) in order to develop a clear definition and delimitation of the various concepts.

3.1 Co-Creation Definition

Co-creation aims to share human experiences with each other and thereby create added value [1, 50]. The exchange of these experiences enables all parties involved to develop a deeper understanding of the situation of the other parties and to jointly create new and improved experiences [48]. This form of interactive collaboration aims to create value for all parties involved by sharing resources, experience and knowledge [3, 7, 35, 48]. In many companies, the promotion of innovation is a central goal of co-creation [55]. A common platform can be used to enable stakeholders to share and integrate their resources and develop new resources and ideas in learning processes [19, 35].

Table 1 Concept matrix for co-creation. ✔ marks an occurrence in the publication

Authors	Co-creation from different perspectives				Components							
	General Def.	Marketing	Service	Innovation	Value					Actor	Platform	
					General Def.	in-exchange	in-use	in-context	experiential		Engagement P.	Digital P.
(Abbate et al. 2019)				✔	✔					✔	✔	✔
(Abendroth et al. 2021)	✔											✔
(Arina & Rustiadi 2018)	✔				✔		✔					
(Chandna & Salimath 2022)				✔							✔	✔
(Cova et al. 2011)			✔			✔	✔					
(de Reuver et al. 2018)												✔
(Eckhardt et al. 2021)	✔									✔		
(Eikebrokk et al. 2018)	✔											
(Eikebrokk et al. 2021)	✔											
(Fehrer et al. 2020)				✔							✔	
(Frow et al. 2015)	✔						✔			✔	✔	
(Galvagno & Dalli 2014)		✔	✔	✔								
(Garmann-Johnsen et al. 2021)	✔											
(Grover & Kohli 2012)				✔	✔							✔
(Grönroos 2008)			✔			✔	✔					
(Grönroos & Voima 2013)			✔		✔	✔	✔			✔		
(Hein et al. 2020)												✔
(Hossain & Islam 2015)												✔
(Hossain & Lassen 2017)				✔								✔
(Ind & Coates 2013)			✔	✔	✔		✔					
(Jiang et al. 2023)				✔								✔
(Kleber & Volkova 2017)		✔	✔	✔		✔	✔	✔	✔	✔	✔	
(Leclercq et al. 2016)		✔	✔	✔		✔	✔	✔	✔	✔	✔	
(Lee et al. 2012)				✔	✔							
(Leino & Puumala 2021)	✔									✔	✔	
(Leipämaa-Leskinen et al. 2022)										✔	✔	
(Li & Tuunanen 2022)			✔	✔			✔			✔	✔	✔
(Lusch & Nambisan 2015)			✔			✔	✔			✔		
(Nambisan & Baron 2007)				✔		✔						
(Nambisan & Nambisan 2008)				✔	✔							
(Payne et al. 2008)			✔				✔		✔			
(Prahalad & Ramaswamy 2004*b*)			✔	✔		✔			✔			
(Prahalad & Ramaswamy 2004*a*)			✔	✔					✔			
(Ramaswamy 2011)	✔						✔		✔		✔	
(Ramaswamy & Gouillart 2010*a*)	✔				✔							
(Ramaswamy & Gouillart 2010*b*)	✔									✔	✔	
(Ramaswamy & Ozcan 2014)	✔				✔					✔	✔	
(Russell & Smorodinskaya 2018)	✔									✔		
(Russo-Spena & Mele 2012)		✔	✔	✔			✔	✔		✔		
(Schreieck & Wiesche 2017)				✔								✔
(Staub et al. 2021)												✔
(Vargo 2008)			✔				✔	✔		✔		

Co-creation is often seen in the design context as a method for promoting participatory practices [12, 54]. Co-creation serves as a design method for collaborative processes with different stakeholders to generate ideas and ensure that all relevant stakeholders are actively involved in the early development phases of a future solution [12]. However, current definitions understand co-creation not only as a method, but as a continuous process that involves various stakeholders in the phases of an innovation process [12, 35]. This process-oriented view emphasizes the long-term, interactive and dynamic relationship between the actors [53]. Definitions of co-creation vary in terms of their scope, ranging from the joint development of products and services to the transformation of corporate structures [1]. Some publications emphasize the collaboration of companies with customers, while others include a broader range of actors such as universities and governments [10, 12, 38, 45].

As this article focuses on co-creation platforms and innovation support for SMEs, it is important that the definition of co-creation focuses on the joint development of innovations. At the same time, it is crucial that the definition focuses on the platform as the central component of co-creation. We therefore define co-creation as follows:

> *Co-creation is an interactive process in which different actors share resources and collaborate on a common platform to develop innovative products and services and create value for all stakeholders.*

3.2 Co-Creation from Different Perspectives

The analysis by Galvagno & Dalli [17] identifies three central theoretical perspectives: Service science, innovation and technology management, and marketing and consumer research. In service science, the focus is on the consideration of companies as service providers for customers [17]. In contrast to the product-centric way of thinking, which focuses on material goods, the exchange of services is emphasized, in which skills and competencies are used to create benefits for others [41]. Co-creation is understood here as joint value creation in which different actors work together to create value [21]. Co-creation is therefore considered an essential element of services [17]. This perspective aims to better understand co-creation mechanisms [35]. Among other things, the roles, activities and organizational structures in the co-creation process are examined [17].

The technology and innovation management perspective views co-creation as an interactive process that brings different actors together to jointly create value and develop innovations [13] and focuses on how technologies can be used to optimize the interaction between the actors [13, 17]. The focus is on the framework conditions that enable actors to create value together [32, 35]. In particular, the virtual interaction between customers and companies is considered [17].

Marketing and consumer research emphasizes the active role of customers in the co-creation process [17, 53]. The motives for participating in a co-creation process and the possible outcomes are being intensively investigated [35]. One focus is on the question of how companies can systematically use the skills and experience of individuals and communities [53]. In particular, it examines how the direct involvement of customers in the value creation process leads to a more intensive exchange of experience [17].

This article focuses on the perspective of innovation and technology management, as it is relevant to the main objective of identifying success factors for co-creation platforms in the SME context.

4 Components of Co-Creation

The basic components are the value created, the actors involved and the engagement platform. These terms are often used very differently. Therefore, their role in the co-creation process is explained below.

4.1 The Value

In the traditional view, suppliers have control over value creation and customers primarily value product characteristics such as price, quality and individuality. Today, the focus is on the perceived benefits of products and services and the experience of using them [41]. Customers are increasingly looking for enriching experiences such as security, comfort or social affiliation, and the relationship that customers have with the offer is not just about individual product features [36, 44].

There are four conceptualizations of value in the co-creation literature: 1. *value-in-exchange:* Value-in-exchange refers to the user's perception of the value achieved through the exchange of different resources such as monetary, mental or physical resources [35]. Co-creation research examines value-in-exchange to understand the motivation for active participation, i.e. why stakeholders contribute their resources to the process of co-creation [32, 42]. 2. *value-in-use:* An extension of value-in-exchange is value-in-use [58]. This describes how the use of products or services increases individual well-being [22, 35]. The emphasis is on the user as an active value creator and the value is created through the act of use over time [22, 35, 58]. The focus is therefore on the customer's experience and skills in order to create value from the products and services [22]. 3. *Value-in-context:* Value-in-context emphasizes the joint creation of value in a social and spatial context [35, 58]. Value creation is viewed in a broader context and customers can also generate value from indirect sources such as imagination or recommendations from others [32, 35, 58]. For example, value can be created in a social context [32] 4. *Experiential value:* Experiential value comprises different types of value such as value-in-use, value-in-context, value-in-exchange and the hedonic dimension, which can be differentiated on the basis of intrinsic/extrinsic, self/other-oriented and active/reactive dimensions [35].

Co-creation emphasizes the active role of users as value creators. Successful innovations should offer unique, enriching experiences that go beyond traditional functional aspects [36]. The place of value and new knowledge thus lies in the interactions between individuals [1].

4.2 The Actors

The stakeholders in the co-creation process are individuals, members of organizations or communities who participate in the co-creation process by sharing resources and expertise [35]. The active participation of both internal and external stakeholders is crucial to the co-creation process. Internal stakeholders, such as management, have a deep understanding of internal processes and resources and support change processes through their credibility [20]. External stakeholders such as customers, public institutions and suppliers bring new perspectives and resources [20]. Identifying suitable stakeholders and strengthening their motivation is essential in the co-creation process [1].

Since all actors create equal value in the co-creation process, there is often no distinction between the roles and actions of customers and suppliers, for example [22]. Every actor has the potential to be an innovator [41]. In the process of resource exchange, actors can take on both the role of providers by sharing resources and the role of receivers by integrating external resources and thereby creating value [35, 44]. Actors switch between these roles throughout the value creation process.

The traditional distribution of roles between companies and customers has thus changed. In the past, producers were regarded as dominant, value-creating actors and customers as passive recipients [41, 46]. Today, customers are active, informed and an integral part of the value creation process, as they actively create value through interaction, feedback and co-creation of their experiences [46].

It is of great importance to not only focus on customers, but also to include other stakeholders such as public institutions, suppliers, business partners and competitors in the co-creation process [32, 35, 59]. This extension to a larger group of stakeholders contributes to the diversity of value creation activities and to increasing efficiency [16].

4.3 The Platform

The literature on co-creation emphasizes the importance of engagement platforms and digital platforms. Engagement platforms are crucial for the implementation of co-creation, as co-creation takes place on these platforms with a large number of actors in a participatory process [1, 39]. The platforms enable continuous interaction between companies, customers and other stakeholders [47]. They provide the infrastructure for value creation and serve as a source of innovation [19, 41]. Engagement platforms support the concentration of resources and thus actively contribute to promoting the co-creation process [1, 41]. Not only companies, but also online communities and institutions, for example, have the opportunity to set up such platforms or use existing mediation platforms [1, 26].

Digital platforms, on the other hand, are technical artifacts that facilitate collaboration and knowledge exchange between different actors by efficiently coordinating resources [2, 26, 56]. These platforms not only facilitate the search for resources, but are also characterized by the ability to independently search for opportunities to integrate resources and identify synergies [1, 41]. For example, a digital platform can recognize that certain users have special skills that fit well with the needs of others and actively recommend their collaboration to create added value [41].

An engagement platform can be a digital platform, such as a website, but also an offline platform, such as a workshop [48]. There are engagement platforms that are not digital, just as there are digital platforms that are not engagement platforms. Offline engagement platforms remain important for co-creation, but digital platforms are becoming more relevant and dominant because they make communication and information exchange between users more efficient [35]. The focus of this paper is therefore particularly on digital engagement platforms.

5 Success Factors of Co-Creation Platforms for SMEs

SMEs are an important part of the economy, as they make up a large part of the business landscape, especially in Germany [28]. Limited time and financial resources pose a challenge for SMEs and often mean that their research and development departments are smaller and have less multidisciplinary expertise compared to larger companies [4]. SMEs are therefore often dependent on external input and collaboration with other companies [13]. However, they often lack the resources to initiate co-creation processes on their own [14], and they are usually unable to manage the entire innovation process on their own [37]. This is why networks are crucial for creating the conditions for successful co-creation in SMEs [14].

Co-creation platforms open up multiple opportunities for SMEs by enabling effective collaboration with external partners such as users, universities and suppliers [4, 35]. These platforms promote the rapid adaptability of SMEs by efficiently identifying market changes and customer needs through the active involvement of customers and other stakeholders [7, 30]. This enables a rapid response and adaptation to new trends and customer requirements and thus contributes to further strengthening competitive advantages. Co-creation platforms also help to promote innovation, as they enable an efficient exchange of information and the integration of resources between different actors, which promotes the identification of previously overlooked potential and the development of innovative approaches [2, 18]. They also make it possible to adapt products and services to individual customer needs and actively involve customers in the various phases of the innovation process. This leads to higher customer satisfaction and loyalty, as they experience that their ideas and opinions are taken seriously [49, 53, 61]. Networks and co-creation platforms also enable SMEs to tackle challenges together and minimize risks by sharing the burden [4, 28, 37, 51, 57].

However, there are also challenges that can stand in the way of the successful implementation of co-creation platforms for SMEs. Among other things, there is a risk of falling into misguided partnerships and losing important core resources, especially if there is no shared vision [13, 30]. Another challenge is a lack of trust, which can negatively impact the success of the collaboration by not honoring agreements and withholding information [13, 31]. Rivalry, which on the one hand can be a source of innovative solutions, can on the other hand hinder cooperation by reinforcing deficits in communication and information exchange [14, 30]. Scarce resources are also an obstacle for SMEs, as their limited financial resources put them at a disadvantage compared to larger companies, which can lead to increased dependence on external funding [13, 27]. Lack of incentives is an obstacle as it can affect the motivation of actors to actively participate in co-creation processes and thus jeopardize the effectiveness of collaboration on co-creation platforms [13].

The following discusses the success factors that can help overcome these barriers, capitalize on the opportunities and promote the effective implementation of co-creation platforms for SMEs. Success factors play a central role in any industry and enable companies to leverage their competitive strengths [8]. In the context of this article, success factors are defined as crucial elements that contribute significantly to the successful implementation and operation of a co-creation platform for SMEs. They focus in particular on the requirements and framework conditions for the implementation and use of such platforms. The success factors are identified by deriving them from the identified challenges and opportunities for SME co-creation platforms.

1. *Clear goals and shared vision*: When developing a co-creation platform, a shared vision and objectives are crucial to commit all participating SMEs and other stakeholders to a common direction [27]. The shared vision serves as a guide and promotes collaborative solution finding by providing orientation and facilitating the prioritization of important platform features [28]. This strengthens management, creates trust and increases the willingness to share resources [18].
2. *Dialogue*: Continuous dialog is essential to promote collaboration. It makes it possible to reduce information asymmetries, exchange ideas, build trust and find joint solutions [30, 40]. The dialog should be transparent and conducted via various communication channels such as forums, blogs, wikis or social media to ensure comprehensive knowledge integration and open discussion [7, 30, 41].
3. *Transparency*: Transparency plays a central role in effective dialog and refers to the open exchange of information and equal access to this information for all participants [7, 45]. This includes role, process and outcome transparency, which ensures that all participants have a clear understanding of their role, the innovation process and the outcomes [43]. Transparency promotes trust, facilitates innovation and increases customer satisfaction as customers can see how their contributions are used and have realistic expectations [7, 43, 45]. In addition, transparency minimizes risks by helping to avoid misunderstandings and conflicts [41].
4. *Network governance:* The effective handling of rivalry and the regulation of competition in co-creation platforms require well thought-out network governance [14]. This includes ecological-institutional norms that define rules of conduct, minimize potential risks and curb opportunistic behavior [30]. With

clear rules and a fair governance structure, SMEs can derive greater innovation benefits from the platform [41]. This governance structure should define clear rules for resource sharing, data protection, information security and value creation approaches such as incentive systems to encourage active participation [24, 27, 41]. It must be decided whether ownership should be centralized, in consortia or decentralized [23]. The decision-making powers of the platform must also be defined [2] with a balanced approach between stability and flexibility [11].

5. *Shared adaptive knowledge base:* A shared adaptive knowledge base is crucial for SMEs to overcome resource challenges [27]. This knowledge base should not be static, but should be constantly expanded through the integration of digital and non-digital information. Clear agreements on common terminology and technical standards ensure that this knowledge base is used effectively so that SMEs can develop innovative ideas more quickly. A shared adaptive knowledge base enables SMEs to adapt flexibly to market changes and develop innovative ideas faster by accessing the collective knowledge of a network of stakeholders, thereby increasing their innovative capacity.
6. *Incentives*: In order to promote the motivation of the actors, the co-creation platforms should offer a variety of incentives [51]. These incentives can include extrinsic elements such as financial rewards as well as intrinsic motivation, for example the social value of participation. Intrinsic motivation in particular, which is based on a recognizable personal benefit, promotes the problem-solving creativity of users [34]. The involvement of users in the co-creation process is most successful when the users are intrinsically motivated and recognize a clear personal benefit [34].
7. *Positive user experience*: A positive user experience on co-creation platforms is crucial for satisfaction and active participation [33]. This experience not only influences interaction on the platform, but also the perception of the company and its products or services [43]. The user experience is made up of pragmatic, social, user-friendly and hedonic components [33, 43]. Through a clear navigation structure, multimedia elements for conveying information, customer recognition programs, social networking functions and the integration of playful elements, companies can promote a positive user experience and thus increase the ability to innovate.
8. *Further development and flexible technological infrastructure:* Co-creation networks are dynamic structures that need to maintain their adaptability to changes in a changing competitive landscape and to technological developments [14]. To support this adaptation process, it is important to obtain regular feedback from the network players. This provides a direct insight into the experiences, concerns and needs of network members. By systematically analyzing this feedback, weaknesses can be identified and strengths highlighted. The continuous collection and evaluation of feedback enables targeted optimization and further development of the co-creation platform. A flexible technological infrastructure must be created so that the platform can adapt dynamically to the needs of users [49]. Flexibility is achieved through a modular structure with clear interfaces to ensure easy adaptation and integration [27].

6 Conclusion

Co-creation has the potential to fundamentally change the way SMEs collaborate and innovate. In addition to opportunities such as recognizing untapped potential and the ability to adapt quickly, challenges such as the lack of a shared vision and limited resources must be overcome. Success factors such as clear goals, transparency and a positive user experience are therefore crucial to overcoming the challenges and taking advantage of the opportunities offered by co-creation platforms. The identified success factors provide guidance for the implementation of such platforms, whereby the individual context must always be taken into account and adjustments may be necessary. This article thus provides a scientific contribution to the design of future digital strategies and how these can be prepared and developed.

The literature review was hermeneutic and restricted to a limited number of databases and selected academic sources, which may result in a limited perspective. It is important to emphasize that this article does not claim to cover all aspects completely and that some facets may have been less illuminated due to the limited selection of sources. Another aspect is that the hermeneutic approach is based on theoretical assumptions and concepts without a comprehensive practical validation through e.g. expert interviews. The article is limited to general findings on co-creation platforms for SMEs without considering specific details on actors, responsibilities, financing and ownership structure. This could affect the applicability of the derived recommendations to individual contexts and further investigation of these aspects would be necessary. The transferability of the results to large companies is limited due to the specific consideration of SMEs and could be investigated in more detail in future research.

Despite these limitations, the findings provide an insight into the importance of co-creation in SMEs and serve as a basis for future, in-depth research. Future research could carry out a differentiated analysis of the actors on co-creation platforms for SMEs, shedding light on the interactions and individual contributions to the co-creation process. An in-depth investigation of the influence of co-creation platforms on different sectors within SMEs and the integration of artificial intelligence into co-creation processes would also be of interest.

References

1. Abbate, T., Codini, A. P., & Aquilani, B. (2019). Knowledge co-creation in open innovation digital platforms: Processes, tools and services. *Journal of Business and Industrial Marketing, 34*(7), 1434–1447.
2. Abendroth, J., Riefle, L., & Benz, C. (2021). Opening the black box of digital b2b co-creation platforms: A taxonomy. In *Wirtschaftsinformatik 2021 Proceedings*.
3. Arina, N., & Rustiadi, S. (2018). Cooperation, collaboration, and co-creation: A review of existing literature and applications. *International Journal of Family Business Practices, 1*.
4. Aschehoug, S. H., & Ringen, G. (2013). Open innovation and idea generation in SMEs. *Proceedings of the International Conference on Engineering Design, ICED, 1*, 169–178.

5. Boell, S. K., & Cecez-Kecmanovic, D. (2014). A hermeneutic approach for conducting literature reviews and literature searches. *Communications of the Association for Information Systems, 34*, 257–286.
6. Brocke, J. V., Simons, A., Niehaves, B., Riemer, K., Plattfaut, R., & Cleven, A. (2009). Reconstructing the giant: On the importance of rigour in documenting the literature search process. In *17th European Conference on Information Systems (ECIS)*.
7. Chandna, V., & Salimath, M. S. (2022). Co-creation of value in platform-dependent entrepreneurial ventures. *Electronic Commerce Research*.
8. Chen, M.-K., Wu, S.-W., Huang, Y.-P., & Chang, F.-J. (2022). The key success factors for the operation of SME cluster business ecosystem. *Sustainability, 14*(14), 8236.
9. Costa, A., Crupi, A., Marco, C. E. D., & Minin, A. D. (2023). SMEs and open innovation: Challenges and costs of engagement. *Technological Forecasting and Social Change, 194*, Article 122731.
10. Cova, B., Dalli, D., & Zwick, D. (2011). Critical perspectives on consumers' role as 'producers': Broadening the debate on value co-creation in marketing processes. *Marketing Theory, 11*(3), 231–241.
11. de Reuver, M., Sørensen, C., & Basole, R. C. (2018). The digital platform: A research agenda. *Journal of Information Technology, 33*(2), 124–135.
12. Eckhardt, J., Kaletka, C., Krüger, D., Maldonado-Mariscal, K., & Schulz, A. C. (2021). Ecosystems of co-creation. *Frontiers in Sociology, 6*.
13. Eikebrokk, T., Lind, E., & Olsen, D. (2018). Co-creation of it-value in a cluster of small enterprises. *Procedia Computer Science, 138*, 492–499.
14. Eikebrokk, T. R., Garmann-Johnsen, N. F., & Olsen, D. H. (2021). Co-creation in networks of SMEs: A conceptual model of the cocreation process. *Procedia Computer Science, 181*, 360–366.
15. Fehrer, J. A., Brodie, R. J., Kaartemo, V., & Reiter, M. (2020). 12 the role of engagement platforms in innovation ecosystems. *Innovating in the Open Lab* (pp. 129–140). De Gruyter.
16. Frow, P., Nenonen, S., Payne, A., & Storbacka, K. (2015). Managing co-creation design: A strategic approach to innovation. *British Journal of Management, 26*(3), 463–483.
17. Galvagno, M., & Dalli, D. (2014). Theory of value co-creation: A systematic literature review. *Managing Service Quality, 24*(6), 643–683.
18. Garmann-Johnsen, N. F., Olsen, D. H., & Eikebrokk, T. R. (2021). The co-creation canvas. *Procedia Computer Science, 181*, 189–197.
19. Grover, V., & Kohli, R. (2012). Cocreating it value: New capabilities and metrics for multifirm environments. *MIS Quarterly, 36*(1), 225–232.
20. Grunwald, G. (2022). Sustainability co-creation in digitalized global value chains. *Strategic Change, 31*(1), 19–29.
21. Grönroos, C. (2008). Service logic revisited: Who creates value? and who co-creates? *European Business Review, 20*(4), 298–314.
22. Grönroos, C., & Voima, P. (2013). Critical service logic: Making sense of value creation and co-creation. *Journal of the Academy of Marketing Science, 41*(2), 133–150.
23. Hein, A., Schreieck, M., Riasanow, T., Setzke, D. S., Wiesche, M., Böhm, M., & Krcmar, H. (2020). Digital platform ecosystems. *Electronic Markets, 30*(1), 87–98.
24. Hein, A., Weking, J., Schreieck, M., Wiesche, M., Böhm, M., & Krcmar, H. (2019). Value co-creation practices in business-to-business platform ecosystems. *Electronic Markets, 29*(3), 503–518.
25. Hossain, M., & Islam, K. M. Z. (2015). Ideation through online open innovation platform: Dell ideastorm. *Journal of the Knowledge Economy, 6*(3), 611–624.
26. Hossain, M., & Lassen, A. (2017). How do digital platforms for ideas, technologies, and knowledge transfer act as enablers for digital transformation? *Technology Innovation Management Review, 7*(9), 55–60.
27. Hönigsberg, S. (2020). A platform for value co-creation in SME networks. In *Designing for Digital Transformation. Co-Creating Services with Citizens and Industry: 15th International Conference on Design Science Research in Information Systems and Technology* (pp. 285–296). Springer-Verlag.

28. Hönigsberg, S., Dinter, B., & Wache, H. (2020). The impact of digital technology on network value co-creation. In *Proceedings of the Annual Hawaii International Conference on System Sciences* (pp. 5233–5242). IEEE Computer Society.
29. Ind, N., & Coates, N. (2013). The meanings of co-creation. *European Business Review, 25*(1), 86–95.
30. Jiang, H., Yang, J., & Gai, J. (2023). How digital platform capability affects the innovation performance of SMEs–evidence from china. *Technology in Society, 72*, Article 102187.
31. Järvi, H., Kähkönen, A. K., & Torvinen, H. (2018). When value co-creation fails: Reasons that lead to value co-destruction. *Scandinavian Journal of Management, 34*(1), 63–77.
32. Kleber, D.M.-S., & Volkova, T. (2017). Value co-creation drivers and components in dynamic markets. *Marketing and Branding Research, 4*(3), 249–263.
33. Kohler, F., Matzler, S., & Füller. (2011). Co-creation in virtual worlds: The design of the user experience. *MIS Quarterly, 35*(3), 773–788.
34. Kristensson, P., Matthing, J., & Johansson, N. (2008). Key strategies for the successful involvement of customers in the co-creation of new technology-based services. *International Journal of Service Industry Management, 19*(4), 474–491.
35. Leclercq, T., Hammedi, W., & Poncin, I. (2016). Ten years of value cocreation: An integrative review. *Recherche et Applications en Marketing (English Edition), 31*(3), 26–60.
36. Lee, S. M., Olson, D. L., & Trimi, S. (2012). Co-innovation: Convergenomics, collaboration, and co-creation for organizational values. *Management Decision, 50*(5), 817–831.
37. Lee, S., Park, G., Yoon, B., & Park, J. (2010). Open innovation in SMEs-an intermediated network model. *Research Policy, 39*(2), 290–300.
38. Leino, H., & Puumala, E. (2021). What can co-creation do for the citizens? applying co-creation for the promotion of participation in cities. *Environment and Planning C: Politics and Space, 39*(4), 781–799.
39. Leipämaa-Leskinen, H., Närvänen, E., & Makkonen, H. (2022). The rise of collaborative engagement platforms. *European Journal of Marketing, 56*(13), 26–49.
40. Li, M., & Tuunanen, T. (2022). Information technology–supported value co-creation and co-destruction via social interaction and resource integration in service systems. *The Journal of Strategic Information Systems, 31*(2), Article 101719.
41. Lusch, R. F., & Nambisan, S. (2015). Service innovation: A service-dominant logic perspective. *MIS Quarterly: Management Information Systems, 39*(1), 155–175.
42. Nambisan, S., & Baron, R. A. (2007). Interactions in virtual customer environments: Implications for product support and customer relationship management. *Journal of Interactive Marketing, 21*(2), 42–62.
43. Nambisan, S., & Nambisan, P. (2008). How to profit from a better 'virtual customer environment. *MIT Sloan Management Review, 49*(3), 53–61.
44. Payne, A. F., Storbacka, K., & Frow, P. (2008). Managing the co-creation of value. *Journal of the Academy of Marketing Science, 36*(1), 83–96.
45. Prahalad, C. K., & Ramaswamy, V. (2004a). Co-creation experiences: The next practice in value creation. *Journal of Interactive Marketing, 18*(3), 5–14.
46. Prahalad, C., & Ramaswamy, V. (2004b). Co-creating unique value with customers. *Strategy and Leadership, 32*(3), 4–9.
47. Ramaswamy, V. (2011). It's about human experiences...and beyond, to co-creation. *Industrial Marketing Management, 40*(2), 195–196.
48. Ramaswamy, V., & Gouillart, F. (2010a). Building the co-creative enterprise. *Harvard Business Review, 88*(10), 1–9.
49. Ramaswamy, V., & Gouillart, F. (2010b). *The power of co-creation: Build it with them to boost growth, productivity, and profits*. Free Press.
50. Ramaswamy, V., & Ozcan, K. (2014). *The co-creation paradigm*. Stanford University Press.
51. Roser, T., DeFillippi, R., & Samson, A. (2013). Managing your co-creation mix: Co-creation ventures in distinctive contexts. *European Business Review, 25*(1), 20–41.
52. Russell, M. G., & Smorodinskaya, N. V. (2018). Leveraging complexity for ecosystemic innovation. *Technological Forecasting and Social Change, 136*, 114–131.

53. Russo-Spena, T., & Mele, C. (2012). "five co-s" in innovating: A practice-based view. *Journal of Service Management, 23*(4), 527–553.
54. Sanders, E.B.-N., & Stappers, P. J. (2008). Co-creation and the new landscapes of design. *CoDesign, 4*, 5–18.
55. Schreieck, M., & Wiesche, M. (2017). How established companies leverage it platforms for value co-creation-insights from banking. In *Twenty-Fifth European Conference on Information Systems (ECIS)*.
56. Staub, N., Haki, K., Aier, S., & Winter, R. (2021). Taxonomy of digital platforms: A business model perspective. In *Proceedings of the Annual Hawaii International Conference on System Sciences* (pp. 6163–6172). IEEE Computer Society.
57. Ulvenblad, P., & Barth, H. (2021). Liability of smallness in SMEs—using co-creation as a method for the 'fuzzy front end' of HRM practices in the forest industry. *Scandinavian Journal of Management, 37*(3), Article 101159.
58. Vargo, S. L. (2008). Customer integration and value creation. *Journal of Service Research, 11*(2), 211–215.
59. Vargo, S. L., & Lusch, R. F. (2011). It's all b2b...and beyond: Toward a systems perspective of the market. *Industrial Marketing Management, 40*(2), 181–187.
60. Webster, J., & Watson, R. T. (2002). Analyzing the past to prepare for the future: Writing a literature review. *MIS Quarterly, 26*(2).
61. Zhang, T., Lu, C., Torres, E., & Cobanoglu, C. (2020). Value co-creation and technological progression: A critical review. *European Business Review, 32*(4), 687–707.

Knowledge Management Through Knowledge Repositories: Deriving Design Principles From Practice

Christian Gussew and Philipp zur Heiden

Abstract Knowledge management is an important discipline as it organizes the knowledge resources necessary for innovation and sustainable competitive advantage. Thus, it becomes increasingly important in times of high fluctuation and retirements. With the rise of (generative) artificial intelligence (AI) and related technological advances, information systems supporting knowledge management processes are expected to improve. Still, research has not yet provided prescriptive knowledge on such AI-supported knowledge management systems. Therefore, we apply the design archaeology methodology and analyze the functionalities of successful knowledge repositories as a special class of knowledge management systems. We derive nine design principles and evaluate them using interviews with practitioners, showing a high relevance of the topic and the design knowledge. This study contributes to knowledge management and information systems literature by uncovering (already starting) change due to technological (AI) advances, deriving prescriptive knowledge on knowledge management systems, and providing rigor to the design archaeology methodology.

1 Introduction

In the modern business environment, knowledge is widely regarded as one of the key resources for sustainable competitive advantage and innovation [9, 11, 13, 16, 46]. Knowledge can be referred to as a mix of experiences, values, and information that influences how new experiences and information are processed [18]. With products and services becoming more complex, organizations compete for the scarce resource that is knowledge [51]. On top of that, organizations are confronted with the potential loss of their knowledge as developed countries face a demographic change in the

C. Gussew · P. zur Heiden (✉)
Department of Management Information Systems, Paderborn University, Paderborn, Germany
e-mail: philipp.zur.heiden@uni-paderborn.de

C. Gussew
e-mail: cgussew@mail.uni-paderborn.de

C. M. Flath et al. (eds.), *Shaping the Digital Future Through Innovation and Practice*, Lecture Notes in Information Systems and Organisation 85,
https://doi.org/10.1007/978-3-032-08489-7_20

form of aging workforce, which is expected to get worse in the coming years [17]. In the 27 member states of the European Union, more than 60 million of the 447 million citizens in 2020 were in the age of 55–64 years, with an expected retirement in the next few years [44]. Additionally, research suggests that employees increasingly focus on self-directed career paths—protean career orientation [65, 67]—linked to lower loyalty and higher employee turnover [32, 77]. With employees retiring or switching organizations, these organizations loose implicit knowledge, i.e., knowledge that is not explicated or codified. This potential loss of knowledge happens while technological and business trends like data-driven decision making and Artificial Intelligence (AI) usage are dependent on data [56] or alternatively put codified knowledge [72].

The discipline that deals with ensuring, developing, and using knowledge in an organization is called Knowledge Management (KM) [13]. In this paper, knowledge management is regarded as "the capability to manage knowledge such as gathering internal or external knowledge of organizations, converting them to new idea or strategy, and applying them and protecting them" [76, p. 31]. Some regard KM as critical for organizational survival as it drives innovativeness and organizational performance [19, 32, 51, 76]. KM is also associated with reducing redundancy, minimizing errors, and reducing training and onboarding times [24, 75, 77]—leading to less time invested, less money spent, and an overall more profitable organization [24, 75, 77].

Studies show that in order for KM to be effective it needs information systems support in the form of Knowledge Management Systems (KMS) [77]. These tools facilitate knowledge management processes and help to ensure the implementation of knowledge-sharing strategies [19, 77]. Various types of software can be put under the umbrella term KMS [77]. The most used type of KMS in practice are Knowledge Repositories (KRs) [6], typically coming in the form of wikis or article bases [43, 77] used for the codification of knowledge in easily accessible databases [14]. KRs can be defined as a digital place to store all information of an organization marked as relevant and is used for the codification of knowledge in easily accessible databases [14, 43]. Our research is focused on KRs as the most prominent class of KMS.

Recently, there have been massive technological advances, especially in the area of AI [10]. Conversational AI is able to fully generate comprehensive texts and inspire and improve the writing of individuals [74], while AI is also able to generate images based on text [10]. In combination with expert knowledge, AI is able to augment existing knowledge and derive reasoned decisions [34]. While the possible implications of AI in business decision-making are discussed [15], other areas like maintenance planning already use AI to derive actions based on predictions [23]. However, the hype of AI in the software industry leads to rushed implementations, inflated expectations, and false marketing of traditional software functionalities as AI capabilities [45]. As KM is closely linked to the enabling technology of the time [20], it is expected that KMS will once again undergo a change, similar to the evolution in the context of Web 2.0 in the early 2000s [3, 58, 66, 77]. To be able to enhance KMS and especially KRs with new technologies, however, there is a need for prescriptive knowledge on how to design them. Existing literature is missing an overview of key functionalities and design options, especially with regard to AI. Such a review is important to identify truly new AI functionalities, assess their potential impact on how to perform KM, and provide an outlook on the further development of KRs and their potential business benefit.

This study addresses the identified research gap by deriving and evaluating prescriptive knowledge on the basis of market-leading KRs. Therefore, the research goal is to provide a comprehensive overview of current KRs and their design. Using the design science-oriented design archaeology methodology [12], we derived prescriptive knowledge from successful KMS instantiations. The manifestation of such prescriptive knowledge can be, e.g., done by formulating design principles (DPs) [30]. More specifically, we followed the suggested approach by Gnewuch and Maedche [27] in order to analyze KRs for their functionalities, which in turn were used to derive nine prescriptive DPs. These were later evaluated for relevance in two interviews with practitioners.

The remainder of the paper is structured as follows. Section 2 provides the background on KM processes and KMS. Section 3 outlines the design archaeology methodology used in this research. Section 4 presents the findings in form of derived DPs as well as the evaluation results. In Sect. 5 we conclude our work by discussing the results and limitations of our research.

2 Theoretical Background

In the literature, the term knowledge is often understood, used, and explained as one part of the data-information-knowledge-wisdom (DIKW) hierarchy [60]. While the DIKW hierarchy typically supports the hypothesis that wisdom ultimately emerges from data [72], the relationship can also be put in a way that data is created from wisdom/knowledge [72]. Thus, we refer to the term knowledge in a more broad sense that partly captures other areas of the DIKW hierarchy: "Knowledge is a fluid mix of framed experience, values, contextual information, and expert insight that provides a framework for evaluating and incorporating new experiences and information. It originates and is applied in the minds of knowers. In organizations, it often becomes embedded not only in documents or repositories but also in organizational routines, processes, practices, and norms" [18, p. 5].

In the same way that knowledge can be put in context in the DIKW hierarchy, the term itself is also commonly categorized into different subdimensions [5, 52]. The most established categorization is the one of *tacit* and *explicit* knowledge [41, 52]. Explicit knowledge is also referred to as codified knowledge and describes knowledge that can be expressed in words and numbers to be shared in a formal way [64]. Tacit knowledge is seen as unconscious, personal, and context-specific knowledge that is embedded in actions and beliefs [64, 69]. In order to be shared, tacit knowledge needs to be externalized, i.e., transformed into explicit knowledge [51]. Typically, a distinction can be made between the four knowledge processes of (1) knowledge creation, (2) knowledge storage, (3) knowledge sharing and transfer, and (4) knowledge application [2]. Knowledge creation is the process of forming new ideas in order to obtain new knowledge or adapt existing knowledge on the basis of both external and internal sources [16, 73]. Knowledge storage refers to the process of identifying knowledge that is relevant to the organization and codifying it in a suitable way [40]. Knowledge sharing and transfer is seen as the process of exchanging knowledge between individuals, groups, and organizations by searching and accessing knowledge that is needed (pull) or by distributing knowledge to recipients (push) [38, 70]. Knowledge application is the process of using knowledge for decision-making, problem solving and turning knowledge into innovations [50]. This process realizes the advantages and benefits of KM [50, 51].

In general, two main KM strategies are known—the personalization strategy and the codification strategy [7]. The former focuses on the tacit aspects of KM to facilitate the dialogue between individuals, build networks between people, and in general link knowledge tightly to the person holding it [33]. The codification strategy, in contrast, has a strong focus on the explicit aspects of knowledge that are independent of the person who developed it [1, 31].

The type of KM strategy that is selected by a firm also has major implications on the type of information systems that are used to support that process. Organizations with a personalization strategy use KMS to create a knowledge network, while organizations with a codification strategy use KMS in the form of KRs [43]. Software of the knowledge network type is used to connect people for interactions in forms of electronic forums or communities of practice [2]. In contrast, software of the KR type enables the codification of corporate knowledge and best practices [43]. Some examples of KMS that can be seen as knowledge network applications are chat rooms, forums, net conferencing tools, expert catalogues, and overall groupware tools [3, 77]. In distinction, web 2.0 tools like wikis, blogs, and webpages for the creation of articles and guides can be seen as KRs [43, 77]. Further KMS include knowledge maps, full-text indexing tools, and document management tools [77]. Some even consider service desk solutions as KMS, as they are mainly focused on solving the needs of internal and/or external customers through knowledge transfer [71].

The most prominently used KMS in practice are KRs [6]. These can be defined as a digital place to store all information of an organization marked as relevant, is used for the codification of knowledge in easily accessible databases, and supports all four knowledge processes [14, 43]. Many KRs follow the overall structure and principles of wikis, which are generally characterized by an easy creation of web pages (articles, handbooks, etc.) without the need to have skills in mark-up languages [54]. One central aspect of wikis is shared authorship, which describes that pages can be created and updated by all (eligible) individuals in an organization, that knowledge is typically not owned by just one person or instance, and that interaction and collaboration is desired [36]. In addition, wikis implement extensive versioning which allows for rollbacks to former versions of a page and helps in identifying contributions to certain pages [55]. Links to and between pages as well as search functions are typically found in wikis, enabling the interconnectedness of knowledge [54]. Other functions include the support of media file attachments, annotations, permission settings, reporting functionality, and notification mechanisms [39, 62].

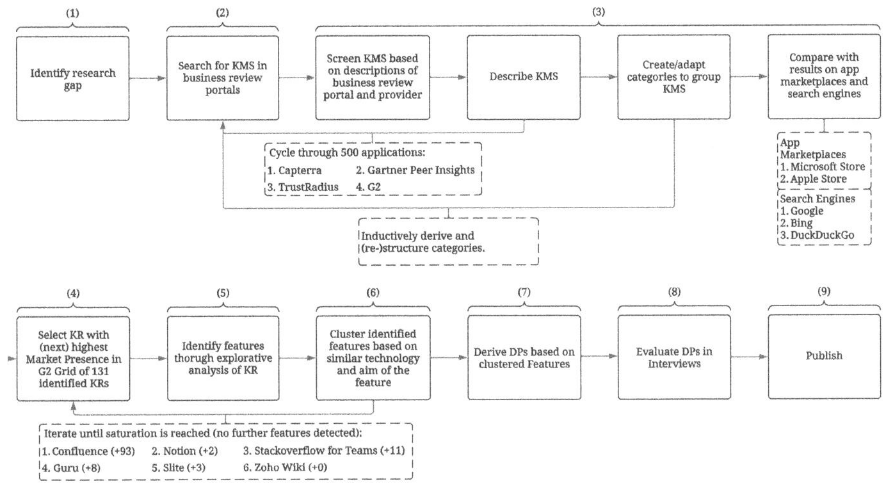

Fig. 1 Process diagram of the applied design archaeology method.

3 Research Design

To address the research gap of a lack of prescriptive knowledge on KRs, we applied the design archaeology approach [12], which enabled us to derive DPs from existing and acknowledged artifacts in use. Design archaeology is a research methodology following the design science research paradigm [12]. As such, it is used to create prescriptive knowledge in the form of artifacts that guide both the problem solving in practice and further academic research [29, 37, 53]. The underlying assumption of design archaeology is that digital artifacts (i.e., software) are created, adapted, and optimized in the economy and society to solve practical problems and may evolve faster than corresponding academic research [12, 27]. Traditional design science seeks to create DPs on the basis of theories/models, and methods/instantiations on the basis of DPs. However, design archaeology uses the opposite approach to derive and understand the abstract knowledge that constitutes working artifacts [12].

As a concrete procedure for evaluating software artifacts from practice, Gnewuch and Maedche [27] suggest a process that is similar to a structured literature review which was applied in an extended nine step form (see Fig. 1): (1) problem identification and formulation, (2) systematic search for instantiations, (3) first screening and categorization of the found instantiations, (4) selection of instantiations for more detailed analysis, (5) analysis of structure and functionalities, (6) clustering of findings, (7) derivation of design principles, (8) evaluation of the derived design principles and (9) publication of results.

(1) The research started with the identification of the problem that current literature on KMS, specifically KRs, does not depict the recent technological changes. (2) With the target set, a systematic search for KMS was conducted in the business

review portals Capterra, Gartner Peer Insights, TrustRadius, and G2, using the terms "knowledge management" and "knowledge management systems".

(3) For each result of the search, an initial screening based on the information available on the business software review portal as well as the website of the provider was done to classify the type of software by one of the researchers. This process of step 2 and 3 was done iteratively per application. The categories were derived in an inductive form during the search by describing the main use case and structure per software and grouping similar applications. Based on the groups formed, categories were defined and frequently revised as the grouping changed. After 500 entries of KMS, the search was stopped using business review portals. A comparative search was then conducted in the Microsoft Store as well as the Apple App Store revealing that these marketplaces mainly included types of software that were unrelated to the research. Lastly, another comparative search was done using the search engines Google, Bing, and DuckDuckGo, which to the vast majority revealed applications that were already included in the list of 500 KMS, with no new type of software discovered. Therefore, we assumed that our search results are representative of the market landscape of KMS.

Of the 500 results, 131 applications are KRs (26%), 82 applications are service desk and customer support applications (16%), 75 applications are software for the storage, management and retrieval of files (15%), 42 applications are used for collaboration (8%), 37 application are learning management systems (7%), and the remaining 133 applications (27%) are others which for example includes intranet, customer relationship management software, and asset management tools.

(4) As not all 131 KRs can be analyzed in detailed form, a selection on the applications needed to be made. Out of these applications, the most popular ones should be investigated, as they offer the best picture on what is acknowledged and used in practice. Due to the heterogeneity of the market, research institutions like Gartner Inc. do not publish reports on the usage or popularity [21]. As the next best available information, the KRs were selected based on the *Market Presence* of the G2 Grid, which is calculated by user reviews on the business software review portal and includes metrics like employee numbers and social followers [25].

(5) The selected applications were analyzed in an explorative approach. For each KR, a workspace was created in order to try out the core application and collect a list of features this application offers. Most of the collected features were directly tested in the applications while other features could not be tested as they needed certain infrastructure (e.g. active directory for single-sign-on configuration) or were only available in premium versions, without the option for a free trial. In addition, documentations and guides by the provider and third parties were used in order to get a full understanding of the software and minimize the risk of missing out on specific functionalities.

(6) The analysis was stopped after six KMS as the number of new discovered features was decreasing with each new application and the feature analysis was saturated during the sixth analyzed KMS. The 117 features, which were collected in a spreadsheet, were clustered by the type of feature and afterwards by the aim of the feature group and which KM processes they support. Features which were only

available in one or two KRs and which were not considered to be a possible unique selling point of the application were excluded. (7) The resulting overview served as the basis for deriving DPs, which were structured in the form suggested by Gregor et al. [30]. Using the taxonomy by Möller et al. [49], our approach can be described as primarily reflective, as we evaluated existing artifacts ex-post without a definition of meta-requirements a priori. In a first iteration, aim, context, and mechanism were defined for the features grouped in the analysis, while a second iteration was done in a more supportive approach to collect meta-requirements which provide rigor to the DPs in form of a rationale. (8) Afterwards, the DPs were evaluated by conducting two expert interviews with practitioners with regards to relevance. (9) The research is concluded by the publication in form of this paper.

4 Results

4.1 Design Principles of Knowledge Repositories

Based on the analysis of six KRs, a total of nine DPs were derived. Six of these DPs are considered as being specific to KRs, while the other three can be applied in the same way to other information systems. The focal point is set to these six DPs. For each KR specific DP, we provide an Aim (A) in form of the knowledge processes it supports, the Mechanism (M) used for achieving that, and a Rationale (R) [30]. Across all nine DPs, the context is always an organization that wants to facilitate successful KM while the users of the application are always members of the organization (i.e., employees). The DPs are presented in the order of the knowledge processes they support.

DP1: Versatile Knowledge Storing. The ability to input and codify knowledge is a minimum requirement for KRs. (A) Beyond just offering any form of codification, the DP of versatile knowledge storing describes that KRs need to enable employees to create and store their knowledge in a suitable form. (M) KRs can do this by offering a variety of content forms like articles, blogs, and Question & Answer (Q&A) formats. But also drawings, and in general the incorporation of visuals, should be supported. In addition to that, rich text formatting options, links between pages and paragraphs, and support for various media file types (audio, video, images, presentations, etc.) are implemented in modern KRs. (R) This variety of formats is considered to be important as the format the knowledge is presented in has an effect on how other employees process and perceive this knowledge [63]. While some formats are more suited to one type of knowledge, other formats may be more suited to different knowledge types [76].

DP2: Knowledge Creation & Storage. (A) To foster knowledge storage as well as aid employees in creating and storing knowledge in both effective and time efficient ways, current KRs offer a range of mechanisms. (M) Some of these mechanisms include more classic functionalities like page templates, copy features, or the possibility to import content. In addition, some KRs check for duplicates when creating new content to avoid redundancy. Next to it, most of the KRs offer newly available assistances by AI, e.g., helping in writing pages by suggesting titles, fixing grammar and spelling, functionalities to translate full pages, and changing the tone to more formal or emotional language. Also, creating new paragraphs and pages based on prompts in a conversational chatbot is possible. So far, these functionalities are limited to text processing and text formatting but advances to the generation of pictures and the general incorporation of visuals are possible as generative text-to-image models like DALL-E are already available [4]. (R) The relevance of these mechanisms is justified in the reduction of time effort for knowledge storage. The codification of knowledge is considered to be an high expense of time and effort [43] that has a significant negative relationship to the amount of KMS usage [28]. With lower time invest, users are more likely to store their knowledge [74]. Beyond time savings, the new AI support has the potential to positively influence the quality of content by offering more precise vocabulary choices and enhance grammar and spelling [74] as well as the potential to help overcome possible writer's block and inspire to write in different perspectives [74].

DP3: Version Control. (A) To assure good quality of stored knowledge when sharing, (M) KRs should support autosave, have functionalities for setting the visibility of content and scheduling when changes are made visible, have a process for the verification of content, and log all changes made, so that older versions can be restored at any point of time. (R) The basis for the rationale is the fact that finding current, relevant, and accurate knowledge is the main goal of knowledge seekers [68]. Also, trust into the KR is seen as an important factor for the acceptance of a KMS [35]. By using mechanisms like versioning, it is possible to ensure the quality of documents that have been edited by multiple users [47], simultaneously building trust.

DP4: Usage Analytics. (A) To identify needs for knowledge creation and storage and optimize knowledge sharing, (M) KRs should provide reports and analytics for content views, usage and engagement, the option to create custom dashboards and key performance indicators, and allow to report on what knowledge users are searching for. In some KRs, AI evaluates search prompts by users to display what knowledge users need and how likely they have found what they searched for. Further developments in this area could go into a more detailed analysis of user behavior on single pages to derive suggestions for possible improvements. Going even further, knowledge that employees searched for in vain could trigger notifications to people who have been identified as possibly having this knowledge, to ask for the creation of an entry in the KR. (R) The justification for this DP can be partly given due to knowledge being more likely to be stored when an individual gets credit for their codification effort and sees that the knowledge is used appropriately [43]. In addition, it has been identified that removement of irrelevant or incorrect knowledge from the KRs is important [26]. Using reporting and analytics measures, the knowledge that needs action can be determined.

DP5: Collaborative Knowledge Exchange. (A) To encourage exchange between employees in knowledge creation, storage and sharing, (M) KRs should support same time editing with multiple users, commenting, tagging of users, leaving reactions, the option to follow other users, and the functionality to chat with others. AI brings about change here, too, by suggesting users who might be able to answer specific questions in a Q&A. In the near future, these recommendations may also be extended to the creation of knowledge pages, with suggestions on which colleagues might contribute to certain topics or paragraphs. (R) The rationale comes from the fact that knowledge is more likely to be stored when an individual gets credit for their codification effort and sees that his knowledge is used appropriately [43]. Furthermore, commenting, reworking, and extending existing knowledge is a key driver for successful KM, as it gets people to engage with knowledge and improves its quality [68]. On the other hand, getting tagged in too many pages may lead to over-work and create technostress for some users [57].

DP6: Knowledge Discoverability. (A) To encourage employees in sharing the existing knowledge as well as applying stored knowledge, (M) KMS should implement mechanisms for the organization and search of knowledge. These include features like bookmarking pages, organizing pages into folders and workspaces, (automatic) labeling of pages, notifications and announcements in the application or via e-mail, exporting content in a variety of formats, and search and filter functions. One of the KRs offers context-based recommendations of knowledge, if a pre-defined keyword is identified by the web browser of the user. Extending on these mechanisms, current KRs offer conversational AI chatbots for finding pages or even directly provide answers to questions, by combining knowledge that is spread across multiple pages. Pages which contain interesting knowledge can be summarized by the AI with regards to certain aspects to avoid reading long documentations. Individual recommendations for knowledge, which might be relevant, are provided in the application. In the near future, the recommendation systems may be extended to also recommend context-based knowledge in the web browser search, without the need to define rules when something should be shown. (R) This DP is justified by the importance of finding and applying knowledge [50]. Seeking for and finding the correct knowledge takes time and effort and is therefore to be seen as an opportunity cost of the knowledge seeker [28]. As not finding the needed knowledge can lead to the abortion of the search [42], KRs that reduce the search effort are more likely to be used [42]. In addition, the ease of finding knowledge is also positively related to the willingness of others to store further knowledge [68].

Apart from the six DPs specific for KRs, three additional ones were derived which all have the aim of supporting the full set of KM processes. **DP7: System Administration** refers to a set of mechanisms that allows for the general management and customization of the KMS, e.g., in the form of login settings, appearance settings, as well as user and permission settings. Such control over the system is needed to ensure availability, efficiency, and security for all users [8]. **DP8: Multi Device Support** refers to the access of the KMS using different devices and without the need for installation, as the application is accessible using a browser. This is important due to the increasing amount of different devices used in the work context with the expectation that applications support an access independent from the device [61]. **DP9: Adaptability** refers to the option of extending the core application by standard integrations, APIs, and Add-Ons. Justification comes from general need in IS to loosely couple applications to connect business processes and build a sustainable system architecture [59].

4.2 Evaluation

The evaluation of the prescriptive knowledge was done in the form of two expert interviews. *Interview A* was conducted with a Knowledge Manager in a German IT company with 251–500 employees. *Company A* is using a KR since a number of years and was in a transitioning phase between two KRs at the time of the interview. Their codified knowledge can take various forms like step-by-step guides, how to's, alerting plans, and complex documentations, e.g., of system architectures. *Interview B* was conducted with a learning & development expert in a German energy grid provider with 501–1000 employees. *Company B* is mainly using learning management software for training, in addition to a KR that contains how to's for office applications. In both companies, KRs are used to facilitate internal KM. While company B stores and distributes knowledge centrally from the human resources department, company A has a more decentral KM approach, with everyone being able to document their process knowledge. Both interviews lasted around 1.5 hours each and were structured as follows: First, each DP was presented, discussed, and assessed with regards to relevance. After that, the interviewees were asked if they are missing any DPs. Lastly, all DPs were ranked among each other and put in an order, from least to most relevant (high number indicating higher relevance).

With two exceptions, seven of the nine DPs were evaluated as being important (see Table 1). DP6 (*Knowledge Discoverability*) as well as DP2 (*Knowledge Creation & Storage*) were mentioned as the most crucial DPs, as the risk of users not finding the content they are searching for and the time effort for codification are critical components. In contrast, DP8 (*Multi Device Support*) was seen ambiguously. In company A, almost all employees are always using a computer. In company B the quality of content was regarded as being very important, even if this results in people not being able to do the training on mobile devices. Also, DP9 (*Adaptability*) was seen ambiguously by company A as it can foster or hinder the KR usage, dependent on how the integrations are built. In addition, integrations were regarded as not too important for KMS in company B. Extending on the nine DPs presented, in interview A, a call was made for an additional DP that helps in capturing knowledge. A problem that was described is that important knowledge is not always codified in KRs. Therefore, the KMS should help in finding this content and ask people to store such knowledge. This could, for example, happen by scanning available files and notes in other databases to check for gaps or by supporting knowledge capture processes in the case of employee termination.

AI features were recognized as an important trend in KM, with more and deeper changes to be expected in the near future The experts also underlined that future

Table 1 Evaluated design principles

Design principle	Ranks (A/B)	Arguments
DP1: Versatile Knowledge Storing	6/2	(A) Standard mechanisms that are important but do not drive successful KM (B) Knowledge should be offered in different formats because of diverse learning preferences
DP2: Knowledge Creation & Storage	1/3	(A) Deviating descriptions for the same process could lead to dissatisfied customers (need for duplicate check) (B) Storing knowledge is very time consuming (A+B) AI functions are regarded as possibly very interesting/beneficial but are not yet used (A) Risk of loss of company uniqueness, in case of extensive AI usage in business critical process descriptions (B) Storing new or abstract topics need more assistance than storing everyday knowledge
DP3: Version Control	3/4	(A+B) Ensuring knowledge quality is important for KM (A) Mechanisms greatly assist in ensuring quality but processes like four-eyes principles are still necessary (B) Knowledge on strictly regulated processes need more control than knowledge with regards to e.g. soft skills
DP4: Usage Analytics	5/6	(A+B) Reporting is regarded as very important as it helps in monitoring the usage and be able to act when needed (A) Analytics are more important for knowledge managers than employees/users
DP5: Collaborative Knowledge Exchange	7/8	(A) Collaboration mechanisms can be helpful but are used seldom (B) Clear responsibilities on knowledge storing may be more helpful than open collaboration by everyone
DP6: Knowledge Discoverability	2/1	(A) "The sentence 'I could not find anything' is the worst thing a user can say" (B) Organizing knowledge is especially important for new hires who need to familiarize themselves with a new topic (A+B) AI search options are not in use at the moment but they are seen as a potential big step of improvement (B) Obtaining knowledge when needed in contrast to learning in advance would be beneficial
DP7: System Administration	4/5	(A) Important to ensure stability & accessibility of KMS (A) Permission management is especially important (B) Allows for targeted distribution of content
DP8: Multi Device Support	10/9	(A) Unimportant - most employees are mainly using PC's (B) Can be important for field workers, but content quality is more important than availability on every device
DP9: Adaptability	9/7	(A) Ambiguous: May foster KMS usage or may result in knowledge storing in different applications (B) Less important for KMS than for other software
Knowledge Capture	8/–	(A) Loss of not stored knowledge is a big business issue (A) Not needed for organizations with perfect KM

learning might be more demand-based, which could also be supported by AI recommending suitable knowledge in real-time.

5 Discussion and Conclusion

This study followed a design archaeology methodology to derive DPs from KRs in practice. By this, a current overview of the structure and possibilities of KRs was created. Through the application of design archaeology [12, 27], this research provides rigor to the methodology as it is a very recently publicized methodology, that was not used extensively in other research so far. The study shows that the most recent advances, especially in AI, do also have an influence on KRs. The impact of technological innovations does not result in changes that can be encapsulated in one DP. Quite contrary, the changes are to be found across almost all aspects of KRs. The most striking advances are found in DP1 (*Knowledge Creation & Storage*) as well as DP6 (*Knowledge Discoverability*), as new AI features offer completely new ways of generating, optimizing, processing, and finding knowledge. Also, due to the AI developments, these two DPs were evaluated as being especially important. The relevance gain is also to be highlighted by the fact that former studies have not identified the assistance in knowledge storage as a separate DP [39, 62]. Despite all the novel mechanisms, this research also shows that the overall structure of KRs has not changed completely as some of the DPs, e.g., DP3 (*Version Control*), DP4 (*Usage Analytics*), DP5 (*Collaborative Knowledge Exchange*), DP7 (*System Administration*), and DP8 (*Multi Device Support*) were also identified by prior research, albeit under a different name [39, 62]. In addition to the findings mentioned above, this research contributes to the literature by providing an overview of the overall market situation on KMS. Based on the 500 applications screened, we could show that KRs are still the most common type of KMS, followed by service desk applications and software for storage, management, and retrieval of files. With this being said, the overall market is very heterogenous and a high variety of different types of KMS exist.

The heterogenity also acts as a limitation of this study as we only looked at one class of systems, namely KRs, and the structure and functionalities they provide. On top of that, it is imaginable that the technological advances through generative AI are so disruptive, that we will face a new type of KMS that goes beyond just changes in how a KR or a collaboration software is used. In future research, other types of KMS should be investigated to understand how these system have changed due to most recent technological advances. Also, an investigation on possible new types of KMS seems promising. At the time of the research, most of the AI functions were just very recently introduced into the software and were oftentimes still in a beta version. We are only at the beginning of the (next) AI revolution and cannot yet fully evaluate the impact these technological advances will have. Therefore, further studies may be needed in a few years to see which other (AI) mechanisms have established in KRs in comparison to the results of this study. Besides that, literature suggests that there is a difference between how small and medium enterprises do KM, compared to big corporations [22, 48]. A distinction on how the mechanisms effect organizations in relation to the size was not made and may be incorporated into future research.

While the evaluation in two expert interviews already shows tendencies regarding the relevance of specific DPs, the results of this study may be analyzed in more detail. The evaluation of acceptance of the features by measuring the real usage by users could be one interesting possibility. Another interesting research avenue would be based on the question whether the existence of AI mechanisms is a reliable predictor for the acceptance and usage of a KR. Additionally, the hallucinating behavior of (generative) AI is a topic that has to be researched further. Hallucinations might become a problem, especially for KM and KR, as users often rely on the information that can be found in these systems. Concluding the research, it needs to be said that both the literature and the practitioners from the interviews argue that KMS are very important for the facilitation of KM, but the success of KM is still, to a high degree, dependent on how KM is introduced, used, and facilitated in the company [77].

References

1. Ajith Kumar, J., & Ganesh, L. (2011). Balancing knowledge strategy: Codification and personalization during product development. *Journal of Knowledge Management, 15*(1), 118–135.
2. Alavi, M., & Leidner, D. E. (2001). Review: Knowledge management and knowledge management systems: Conceptual foundations and research issues. *MIS Quarterly, 25*(1), 107–136.
3. Beylier, C., Pourroy, F., Villeneuve, F., & Mille, A. (2009). A collaboration-centred approach to manage engineering knowledge: A case study of an engineering SME. *Journal of Engineering Design, 20*(6), 523–542.
4. Bird, C., Ungless, E. & Kasirzadeh, A. (2023). Typology of risks of generative text-to-image models. In *Proceedings of the 2023 AAAI/ACM conference on AI, ethics, and society, AIES '23* (pp. 396–410). ACM.
5. Blackler, F. (1995). Knowledge, knowledge work and organizations: An overview and interpretation. *Organization Studies, 16*(6), 1021–1046.
6. Bock, G.-W., Kankanhalli, A., & Sharma, S. (2006). Are norms enough? the role of collaborative norms in promoting organizational knowledge seeking. *European Journal of Information Systems, 15*(4), 357–367.
7. Bolisani, E., Padova, A., & Scarso, E. (2020). The continuous recombination of codification and personalisation KM strategies: A retrospective study. *Electronic Journal of Knowledge Management, 18*(2), 185–195.
8. Burgess, M. (2003). On the theory of system administration. *Science of Computer Programming, 49*(1–3), 1–46.
9. Cambra-Fierro, J., Florin, J., Perez, L., & Whitelock, J. (2011). Inter-firm market orientation as antecedent of knowledge transfer, innovation and value creation in networks. *Management Decision, 49*(3), 444–467.
10. Cao, Y., Li, S., Liu, Y., Yan, Z., Dai, Y., Yu, P. S., & Sun, L. (2023). *A comprehensive survey of AI-generated content (AIGC): A history of generative AI from GAN to ChatGPT.*
11. Carneiro, A. (2000). How does knowledge management influence innovation and competitiveness? *Journal of Knowledge Management, 4*(2), 87–98.

12. Chandra Kruse, L., Seidel, S., & vom Brocke, J. (2019). Design archaeology: Generating design knowledge from real-world artifact design. In B. Tulu, S. Djamasbi, & G. Leroy (Eds.), *Extending the boundaries of design science theory and practice* (pp. 32–45). Springer International Publishing.
13. Chang, C.L.-H., & Lin, T.-C. (2015). The role of organizational culture in the knowledge management process. *Journal of Knowledge Management, 19*(3), 433–455.
14. Chhim, P. P., Somers, T. M., & Chinnam, R. B. (2017). Knowledge reuse through electronic knowledge repositories: A multi theoretical study. *Journal of Knowledge Management, 21*(4), 741–764.
15. Chuma, E. L., & De Oliveira, G. G. (2023). Generative AI for business decision-making: A case of ChatGPT. *Management Science and Business Decisions, 3*(1), 5–11.
16. Costa, V., & Monteiro, S. (2016). Key knowledge management processes for innovation: A systematic literature review. *VINE Journal of Information and Knowledge Management Systems, 46*(3), 386–410.
17. Crandall, P. G., Houser, R. H. & O'Bryan, C. A. (2022). Becoming the employer of choice: Anticipating and preparing for a graying workforce in industry. *SN Social Sciences,* **2**(173).
18. Davenport, T., & Prusak, L. (1998). *Working knowledge: How organizations manage what they know*. Harvard Business School Press.
19. Di Vaio, A., Palladino, R., Pezzi, A., & Kalisz, D. E. (2021). The role of digital innovation in knowledge management systems: A systematic literature review. *Journal of Business Research, 123*, 220–231.
20. Dotsika, F., & Patrick, K. (2013). Collaborative KM for SMEs: A framework evaluation study. *Information Technology & People, 26*(4), 368–382.
21. Drakos, N. (2021). Quick answer: Why isn't there a magic quadrant for knowledge management?. https://www.gartner.com/en/documents/4003610. Retrieved 2023-12-29.
22. Edvardsson, I. R. (2009). Is knowledge management losing ground? developments among icelandic SMEs. *Knowledge Management Research & Practice, 7*(1), 91–99.
23. Efthymiou, K., Papakostas, N., Mourtzis, D., & Chryssolouris, G. (2012). On a predictive maintenance platform for production systems. *Procedia CIRP, 3*, 221–226.
24. Epetimehin, F. M., & Ekundayo, O. (2011). Organisational knowledge management: Survival strategy for nigeria insurance industry. *Interdisciplinary Review of Economics and Management, 3*(2), 53–64.
25. G2 Grid Explained (n.d.). https://sell.g2.com/resources/guides/g2-grid-explained. Retrieved 2024-01-03.
26. García, J., Amescua, A., Sánchez, M.-I., & Bermón, L. (2011). Design guidelines for software processes knowledge repository development. *Information and Software Technology, 53*(8), 834–850.
27. Gnewuch, U., & Maedche, A. (2022). Toward a method for reviewing software artifacts from practice. In A. Drechsler, A. Gerber, & A. Hevner (Eds.), *The transdisciplinary reach of design science research* (pp. 337–350). Springer International Publishing.
28. Goodman, P. S., & Darr, E. D. (1998). Computer-aided systems and communities: Mechanisms for organizational learning in distributed environments. *MIS Quarterly, 22*(4), 417–440.
29. Gregor, S., & Hevner, A. R. (2013). Positioning and presenting design science research for maximum impact. *MIS Quarterly, 37*(2), 337–355.
30. Gregor, S., Kruse, L., & Seidel, S. (2020). Research perspectives: The anatomy of a design principle. *Journal of the Association for Information Systems, 21*, 1622–1652.
31. Greiner, M. E., Böhmann, T., & Krcmar, H. (2007). A strategy for knowledge management. *Journal of Knowledge Management, 11*(6), 3–15.
32. Gresty, M. (2013). What role do information systems play in the knowledge management activities of SMEs? *Business Information Review, 30*(3), 144–151.
33. Hansen, M. T., Nohria, N. & Tierney, T. (1999). What's your strategy for managing knowledge?. *Harvard Business Review*, 55–69.
34. Harfouche, A., Quinio, B., Saba, M., & Saba, P. B. (2023). The recursive theory of knowledge augmentation: Integrating human intuition and knowledge in artificial intelligence to augment organizational knowledge. *Information Systems Frontiers, 25*(1), 55–70.

35. He, W., Fang, Y., & Wei, K. (2008). The role of trust in promoting organizational knowledge seeking using knowledge management systems: An empirical investigation. *Journal of the American Society for Information Science and Technology, 60*(3), 526–537.
36. Hester, A. J. (2010). Increasing collaborative knowledge management in your organization: Characteristics of wiki technology and wiki users. In *Proceedings of the 2010 special interest group on management information system's 48th annual conference on computer personnel research on computer personnel research', SIGMIS-CPR '10*. Association for Computing Machinery (pp. 158–164).
37. Hevner, A. R. (2007). A three cycle view of design science research. *Scandinavian Journal of Information Systems 19*(2).
38. Holdt Christensen, P. (2003), Knowledge sharing: Time sensitiveness and push-pull strategies in a non-hype organisation, Working Paper 12/2003, Department of Management, Politics and Philosophy, CBS, Denmark.
39. Hung, W.-H. & Wang, W.-H. (2020). Design principles of wiki system for knowledge transfer and sharing in organizational education and training. *Sustainability 12*(17).
40. Hussain, A., Reyad, S., & Gupta, V. (2021). The knowledge creation, capture, sharing and transfer - to what extent they are interrelated in higher education institutions? *International Journal of Innovation, Creativity and Change, 15*(9), 814–834.
41. Joia, L. A., & Lemos, B. (2010). Relevant factors for tacit knowledge transfer within organisations. *Journal of Knowledge Management, 14*(3), 410–427.
42. Kankanhalli, A., Tan, B. C., & Wei, K. (2005). Understanding seeking from electronic knowledge repositories: An empirical study. *Journal of the American Society for Information Science and Technology, 56*(11), 1156–1166.
43. Kankanhalli, A., Tan, B. C. Y., & Wei, K.-K. (2005). Contributing knowledge to electronic knowledge repositories: An empirical investigation. *MIS Quarterly, 29*(1), 113–143.
44. Kiss, M., Negreiro, M., Niestadt, M., Nijenhuis, C., Van Lierop, C. & Van der Linde, A. (2022). *Demographic outlook for the European Union 2022*, Publications Office of the European Union.
45. LaGrandeur, K. (2023). The consequences of ai hype. *AI and Ethics*.
46. Lee, M. R., & Lan, Y.-C. (2011). Toward a unified knowledge management model for SMEs. *Expert Systems with Applications, 38*(1), 729–735.
47. Lukosch, S., & Leisen, A. (2009). Comparing and merging versioned wiki pages. In J. Cordeiro, S. Hammoudi, & J. Filipe (Eds.), *Web information systems and technologies* (pp. 159–173). Springer.
48. Massaro, M., Handley, K., Bagnoli, C., & Dumay, J. (2016). Knowledge management in small and medium enterprises: A structured literature review. *Journal of Knowledge Management, 20*(2), 258–291.
49. Möller, F., Guggenberger, T. M., & Otto, B. (2020). Towards a method for design principle development in information systems. In S. Hofmann, O. Müller, & M. Rossi (Eds.), *'Designing for digital transformation* (pp. 208–220). Co-Creating Services with Citizens and Industry. Springer International Publishing.
50. Ngah, R., & Wong, K. Y. (2020). Linking knowledge management to competitive strategies of knowledge-based SMEs. *The Bottom Line, 33*(1), 42–59.
51. Omotayo, F. O. (2015). Knowledge management as an important tool in organisational management: A review of literature. *Library Philosophy and Practice, 1*(1238), 1–23.
52. Pathirage, C. P., Amaratunga, D. G., & Haigh, R. P. (2007). Tacit knowledge and organisational performance: Construction industry perspective. *Journal of Knowledge Management, 11*(1), 115–126.
53. Peffers, K., Tuunanen, T., Rothenberger, M. A., & Chatterjee, S. (2007). A design science research methodology for information systems research. *Journal of Management Information Systems, 24*(3), 45–77.
54. Pei Lyn Grace, T. (2009). Wikis as a knowledge management tool. *Journal of Knowledge Management, 13*(4), 64–74.
55. Prasarnphanich, P. & Wagner, C. (2009). The role of wiki technology and altruism in collaborative knowledge creation. *Journal of Computer Information Systems*, **49**(4).

56. Provost, F., & Fawcett, T. (2013). Data science and its relationship to big data and data-driven decision making. *Big Data, 1*(1), 51–59.
57. Ragu-Nathan, T. S., Tarafdar, M., Ragu-Nathan, B. S., & Tu, Q. (2008). The consequences of technostress for end users in organizations: Conceptual development and empirical validation. *Information Systems Research, 19*(4), 417–433.
58. Razmerita, L., & Kirchner, K. (2011). How wikis can be used to manage knowledge in SMEs: A case study. *Business Information Review, 28*(3), 175–178.
59. Ren, M. & Lyytinen, K. J. (2008), 'Building enterprise architecture agility and sustenance with soa', *Communications of the Association for Information Systems***22**.
60. Rowley, J. (2007). The wisdom hierarchy: representations of the dikw hierarchy. *Journal of Information Science, 33*(2), 163–180.
61. Santosa, S. & Wigdor, D. (2013). A field study of multi-device workflows in distributed workspaces. In *Proceedings of the 2013 ACM international joint conference on pervasive and ubiquitous computing', UbiComp '13*. Association for Computing Machinery (pp. 63–72).
62. Schaffert, S. (2006). Ikewiki: A semantic wiki for collaborative knowledge management. In *15th IEEE international workshops on enabling technologies: Infrastructure for collaborative enterprises (WETICE'06)* (pp. 388–396).
63. Schnotz, W. (2002). Towards an integrated view of learning from text and visual displays. *Educational Psychology Review, 14*(1), 101–120.
64. Seidler-de Alwis, R., & Hartmann, E. (2008). The use of tacit knowledge within innovative companies: Knowledge management in innovative enterprises. *Journal of Knowledge Management, 12*(1), 133–147.
65. Sullivan, S. E., & Baruch, Y. (2009). Advances in career theory and research: A critical review and agenda for future exploration. *Journal of Management, 35*(6), 1542–1571.
66. Sultan, N. (2013). Knowledge management in the age of cloud computing and web 2.0: Experiencing the power of disruptive innovations. *International Journal of Information Management, 33*(1), 160–165.
67. Supeli, A., & Creed, P. A. (2015). The longitudinal relationship between protean career orientation and job satisfaction, organizational commitment, and intention-to-quit. *Journal of Career Development, 43*(1), 66–80.
68. Sutanto, J., & Jiang, Q. (2013). Knowledge seekers' and contributors' reactions to recommendation mechanisms in knowledge management systems. *Information & Management, 50*(5), 258–263.
69. Takeuchi, H. & Nonaka, I. (2000). *Classic Work: Theory of organizational knowledge creation* (pp. 139–182). The MIT Press.
70. Tangaraja, G., Mohd Rasdi, R., Abu Samah, B., & Ismail, M. (2016). Knowledge sharing is knowledge transfer: A misconception in the literature. *Journal of Knowledge Management, 20*(4), 653–670.
71. Tehrani, A. R. F., & Mohamed, F. Z. M. (2011). A CBR-based approach to ITIL-based service desk. *Journal of Emerging Trends in Computing and Information Sciences, 2*(10), 476–484.
72. Tuomi, I. (1999). Data is more than knowledge: Implications of the reversed knowledge hierarchy for knowledge management and organizational memory. In *Proceedings of the 32nd annual hawaii international conference on systems sciences (HICSS-32)*.
73. Turner, J. R., Zimmerman, T., & Allen, J. M. (2012). Teams as a sub-process for knowledge management. *Journal of Knowledge Management, 16*(6), 963–977.
74. Washington, J. (2023). The impact of generative artificial intelligence on writer's self-efficacy: A critical literature review. *SSRN Electronic Journal* .
75. Wu, I.-L., & Chen, J.-L. (2014). Knowledge management driven firm performance: The roles of business process capabilities and organizational learning. *Journal of Knowledge Management, 18*(6), 1141–1164.
76. Xue, C. T. S. (2017). A literature review on knowledge management in organizations. *Research in Business and Management, 4*(1), 30–41.
77. Zouari, C., Ben, M., Dakhli, D., & Ben, S. (2018). A multi-faceted analysis of knowledge management systems. *Procedia Computer Science, 138*, 646–654.

Perception and Management of Work Interruptions among Digital Business Professionals: An Updated Study

Volker Seiler, Fabian J. Stangl, and René Riedl

Abstract The modern workplace has been profoundly transformed by the widespread integration of digital technologies, fundamentally changing the way individuals conduct business and interact within their work environments. However, this digital transformation has also created a major problem relevant to both research and practice: the ubiquitous prevalence of work interruptions (e.g., receiving unexpected emails or instant messages while focused on a task). Against this background, we conducted a qualitative study to allow digital business professionals to describe their general perception and management of interruptions. As a result, we validate and refine a category system developed in a previous study on specific interruption types, quantify their outcomes on psychological well-being and work performance, and examine how they are handled, thus filling gaps in the existing literature on interruption perception and management. Overall, this category system can serve as a valuable foundation for future interruption science research.

1 Introduction

Interruption science, an interdisciplinary research field, rigorously examines the ubiquitous occurrence of interruptions [54]. The study of interruptions, defined as "*an unexpected suspension of the behavioral performance of, and/or attentional*

V. Seiler
School of Management, Carinthia University of Applied Sciences, Villach, Austria
e-mail: volkerseiler1@gmail.com

F. J. Stangl (✉) · R. Riedl
Digital Business Institute, School of Business and Management, University of Applied Sciences Upper Austria, Steyr, Austria
e-mail: fabian.stangl@fh-steyr.at

R. Riedl
Institute of Business Informatics – Information Engineering, Johannes Kepler University Linz, Linz, Austria
e-mail: rene.riedl@jku.at

C. M. Flath et al. (eds.), *Shaping the Digital Future Through Innovation and Practice*, Lecture Notes in Information Systems and Organisation 85,
https://doi.org/10.1007/978-3-032-08489-7_21

focus from, an ongoing work task" ([44], p. 817), is critical to better understanding their effects on cognitive functioning (e.g., [22]), emotional responses (e.g., [41]), and task completion (e.g., [38]) in various settings. For example, in the context of the modern workplace, the pervasive digital transformation and the ubiquitous presence of digital technologies have fundamentally changed business practices and work environments [21]. Along with their widespread adoption, digital technologies have thereby also introduced a new barrier that challenges focus and productivity: *work interruptions* (e.g., [1–3, 9, 14, 16, 38, 63]).

An illustrative example of interruptions encountered in professional life are those resulting from computer-mediated communication [50]. These interruptions are transmitted through information and communication technologies (ICTs), which are digital technologies used to communicate and process, store, and disseminate information [4], such as MS Teams or Slack. While such interruptions may serve to enhance communication and streamline decision-making processes in the workplace [16, 24, 33], they also dramatically contribute to interruptions during work-related activities [63], which can lead to increased stress levels and detrimental effects on overall performance and productivity (for reviews and a meta-analysis, please see [15, 39, 48]). Interestingly, even frequent interruptions containing information relevant to the primary task may not necessarily disrupt users' flow or impair their task performance [38]. However, to mitigate constant distraction or loss of focus on essential tasks, it is critical to explore the use and function of digital technologies to counteract any potential "dark side" [64].

Against this background, our study aims to examine the perception and management of work interruptions by professionals in digital business environments. Indeed, unlike their counterparts in other professional domains, digital business professionals operate in information-rich digital ecosystems and are constantly immersed in digital tools and technologies. Having the necessary digital competencies to navigate these modern workplaces can be vital to mitigating the negative impact of interruptions on cognitive functioning, emotional responses, or task completion [40]. For example, experimental studies by Galluch et al. [16] revealed that interruptions mediated by ICTs can induce stress, although control over timing can help alleviate stress levels. Additionally, digital business professionals, such as digital business managers, rely heavily on ICTs, such as collaboration tools for task planning and execution (e.g., [16]), email (e.g., [2]), and videoconferencing systems (e.g., [49]). As a result, work interruptions, particularly in collaborative work settings, may be unavoidable. However, a recent study by Tiilikainen et al. [66] investigated this characteristic of the modern workplace and found that groups engaged in such collaborative tasks are resilient and can effectively withstand frequent interruptions by leveraging the capabilities of ICT (e.g., adjusting the volume and vibration intensity of their ICT).

Given this unique context surrounding digital business professionals, they are particularly suitable for our study. Hence, we seek to answer the following main research question (RQ): **How do digital business professionals perceive and manage work interruptions?** More specifically, the focus of the present study is to validate a category system developed in a previous exploratory study with digital business professionals [55], which is also part of a larger research project on interruption science (for details, see [56]).

2 Research Background

This present study extends a previous exploratory study in which we investigated the perception and management of work interruptions among digital business professionals [55]. Our present research serves as confirmatory research aimed at validating a category system developed for the purpose of future research activities in interruption science. In the following, we will frame the research problem [46] by outlining three gaps in the existing literature that are in line with our archetypal research objective [47] on the perception and management of work interruptions among digital business professionals. This approach abstracts our main RQ into three specific sub-RQs (S-RQs), which are essential for developing a deeper understanding and a stronger impact relevant to both scientific research and practice.

The literature on interruptions reveals a rich array of attributes that define their multifaceted nature, stemming from pioneering experimental investigations such as those conducted by Kurt T. Lewin and his experimental research program in the 1920s (e.g., [29, 42, 68]). Over time, researchers have delineated different perspectives on the classification of interruptions, distinguishing attributes such as technology mediation, criticality, timing (during or outside of working hours), and the nature of initiation (endogenous or exogenous) [54]. For example, the typology proposed by Jett and George [23] categorize interruptions into breaks, discrepancies, distractions, and intrusions within organizational contexts. These categories reflect differences in origin and impact, ranging from endogenous breaks that provide personal time to exogenous intrusions that disrupt primary tasks. By investigating the specific interruption types prevalent among digital business professionals, our study aims to deepen the understanding of the dynamics of interruptions in this context and their implications, thereby addressing the following S-RQ1: **What specific types of work interruptions can be classified among digital business professionals?**

Numerous studies have explored the multiple effects of interruptions and shed light on their complex implications. These studies have revealed consequences ranging from performance deficits, such as forgetting or delaying tasks and decreased accuracy, to profound psychological effects. For example, seminal research by Maria A. Rickers-Ovsiankina [42] revealed a tendency to resume interrupted actions, even when incomplete, with far-reaching personal and organizational consequences, including work-family conflict (e.g., [67]) and increased resistance to new information systems (e.g., [28]). In addition, the widespread use of work-related technology during non-work hours has been observed to disrupt recovery processes and exacerbate psychological distress (e.g., [11, 45, 51]). However, amidst these negative effects, interruptions have also been associated with positive effects, such as alleviating boredom [71] and promoting positive affect [52]. Hence, our study also seeks to deepen the understanding of how interruptions affect the psychological well-being and work performance of digital business professionals by addressing the following S-RQ2: **How do work interruptions affect psychological well-being and work performance of digital business professionals?**

The study of interruptions in research has expanded to include various aspects, particularly the core challenge of managing interruptions and identifying individual strategies for dealing with them. Several studies have outlined different methods that individuals use to effectively manage interruptions. For example, Kirmeyer's [26] observational study of police radio dispatchers identified three coordination methods: sequential processing, preemption, and simultaneity. In sequential processing, individuals prioritize completing the primary task before addressing the interruption, whereas preemption involves immediately addressing the interruption while temporarily suspending the primary task. Simultaneity involves rapidly switching between the interrupting activity and the primary task to manage both simultaneously. Similarly, McFarlane's [31, 32] research on human-computer interaction design identified four coordination methods: immediate, negotiated, mediated, and scheduled, each offering different approaches to managing interruptions. For example, in scheduled coordination, the individual chooses an appropriate time to deal with the interruption, ensuring minimal disruption to ongoing tasks. Importantly, given the complex nature of interruptions [54], insights from interruption management research, including coping strategies and factors that influence decisions about managing interruptions (e.g., [61]), could contribute to the development of more effective coping mechanisms and a better understanding of the factors that influence individuals' decisions about managing interruptions to mitigate adverse effects on workflow (e.g., [69]), cognitive processes (e.g., [70]), stress levels (e.g., [48]), and job satisfaction (e.g., [5]). Given this complexity in managing interruptions, our study also aims to investigate how digital business professionals manage interruptions in their workplace, addressing the following S-RQ3: **How do digital business professionals deal with work interruptions?**

3 Research Methodology

Consistent with our previous exploratory study of how digital business professionals perceive and manage work interruptions [55], we chose a qualitative research design using interviews as the data collection method and qualitative content analysis for analysis. This decision reflects the views of many scholars who emphasize the flexibility of qualitative methods in identifying and exploring emerging patterns in data, which aligns with the main objective of our qualitative study [13, 17, 34]. Notably, none of the participants in the previous study participated in the current study.

The interview itself consisted of five sets of questions. For the present paper, we focus on three sets of questions that collected demographic information about the interview participants and their perceptions and management of work interruptions. To meet the requirements of the sample frame, we provided participants with screening questions based on the ICT examples from Ayyagari et al. [4]. These questions were designed to assess the frequency and types of ICTs used by participants, rather than relying solely on self-reported skill levels. This approach helped to mitigate potential self-report bias and ensure a more accurate representation of participants' digital competencies. Participants who demonstrated sufficient engagement with ICT at work were included in the study, targeting digital business professionals with the necessary digital competencies to navigate modern workplaces [40], which can also be considered an exemplary sample frame for information systems studies [4]. We then analyzed the data related to the second set of questions dealing with the perception of work interruptions and the third set of questions dealing with the management of work interruptions.

3.1 Interview Participants

Prior to the interviews of the main study, a pilot interview was conducted with another person to validate our interview guide. This person is an expert in the field of digital business. Some minor adjustments were then made based on his suggestions. Notably, the interview protocol also followed Spradley's [53] interview approach, which consisted of descriptive (e.g., What kind of interruptions do you mainly experience during your working hours? Please give some examples?), structural (e.g., Can you give me an example of whether an interruption during your work can be important or unimportant and why?), and contrastive (e.g., Do interruptions distract you from your primary task? Or does the original primary task remain present?) questions. Table 1 provides a sample of the questions from our final interview protocol on the perception and management of work interruptions.

In this qualitative study, we recruited 50 digital business professionals. Interview participants were recruited through the personal network of one of the authors of this paper. Respondents were gender balanced and age ranged from 23 to 44 years (mean [$\pm$SD] age: 30.2 $\pm$ 4.84 years; median 29 years). Most participants had an undergraduate degree (16), followed by a graduate degree (14) or a general qualification for university entrance (11). Additionally, a few participants had completed an apprenticeship (5) or obtained a Master's degree (4). The participants were recruited from Austrian companies in different business sectors (e.g., retail, management consulting), and work in a variety of roles relevant to digital business (e.g., consultant for digitalization projects, specialist for digital products and processes). Their work experience ranged from 1.5 to 22 years (mean [$\pm$SD]: 8.75 $\pm$ 4.77 years; median 7.5). Overall, following Myers and Newman [37], we focused on ensuring that the interviewees represented a diverse voice to investigate the perception and management of work interruptions among digital business professionals.

To assess the overall ICT use at work, we used the variable "Total ICT Use at Work". This variable consists of a 5-point Likert scale (1 being "Never", 5 being "Always"), with the examples adopted from Ayyagari et al. [4], which includes all ratings of the different ICTs per participant in daily work. The resulting data

Table 1 Interview Questions on Perception and Management of Work Interruptions

Sample of Interview Questions on Perception of Work Interruptions
• Are you regularly interrupted by digital technologies at work? • What kind of interruptions do you mainly experience during your working hours? Please give some examples. • What do these interruptions mean to you in your professional life? For example, do these interruptions help you do your work because they are relevant? Or are these interruptions rather unimportant for you in a professional context? Again, give some examples. • How do you feel when you are interrupted at work? For example, can interruptions affect your work performance, or do you feel disturbed by them? Please give examples. • Are there certain interruptions that you ignore while others are considered? If so, what criteria do you use to make this decision? • Is an interruption always annoying or only when it occurs during an important task, for example? • Can you give me an example of whether an interruption during your work can be important or unimportant and why? • Can you give an example of a task that can be interrupted and why? • Do you think that interruptions can be relevant to your task? If so, can you give an example? • Do you feel better when you are occasionally interrupted, especially when you are doing a challenging task? Can you give an example?
Sample of Interview Questions on Management of Work Interruptions
• How do you react when you are interrupted? For example, do you try to manage both the task and the interruption at the same time, or do you manage the interruption first and then resume the original task? Please provide examples. • Are there interruptions that you must manage immediately? If so, what factors influence this decision? Please provide examples. • Do interruptions distract you from your primary task? Or does the original primary task always remain present? • Do you sometimes fail to resume your current task or resume it late due to interruptions? If so, how often does this happen? • What do you do when interruptions prevent you from completing your work on time? Do you complete these tasks the next day during working hours or the same day outside of regular working hours? Are there any specific factors that you consider when making your decision? Please provide examples. • Do you have any other tips or tricks for effectively managing interruptions? • Does your company create a supportive environment to reduce interruptions?

indicate that our sample of digital business professionals possess the necessary digital competencies to use ICT effectively in modern work environments [40]. With an overall rating of 4.51 ($\pm$ 0.45; median 4.64) for ICT use at work, the data suggest that our sample of digital business professionals are highly proficient in using ICT at work.

3.2 Interview Procedure

Before the interviews were conducted, each participant was contacted individually by one of the authors of this paper. The primary purpose of this initial communication was to encourage participants to reflect on the perception and management of work interruptions. In addition, participants were assured of complete anonymity throughout the data collection and analysis process and were given the opportunity to clarify the purpose and objectives of the study.

Over a period of approximately 1.5 months, all 50 respondents were contacted by the end of 2023 and invited to express their interest in participating in the study. Upon consent, each respondent received an email containing a comprehensive study briefing along with attached questionnaires for personal and demographic information, as well as a privacy statement to be reviewed, signed, and returned prior to the interview. This initial questionnaire aimed, among other things, to assess participants' suitability for the interview, particularly regarding their daily use of ICT.

Subsequently, semi-structured interviews with open-ended questions (see Table 1) were conducted with each participant, either in person (30) or via videoconference (20). The part of the interviews with questions relating to the perception and management of work interruptions lasted approximately 30 minutes. All interviews were recorded and transcribed in verbatim to serve as the foundation for subsequent coding.

3.3 Interview Data Coding and Analysis

Qualitative content analysis was the chosen approach to examine the collected interview data. The analysis followed a systematic and structured methodology based on Mayring's [30] qualitative content analysis. This approach is characterized by the initial development of a category system and a sequence of steps for coding and analysis, ensuring a thorough examination of the data [12].

First, we immersed ourselves in the interview data, reading and re-reading the transcripts to develop a deep understanding of the content. This step is consistent with Mayring's [30] emphasis on fully understanding the material before categorizing it.

Second, we used our previously developed category system [55] as the foundation for analyzing the perception and management of work interruptions among digital business professionals. This former category system was also developed according to Mayring's [30] theory-oriented and rule-bound procedure to systematically analyze the data from the collected interviews. Moreover, it was structured along the identified context-specific constructs (i.e., categories) with corresponding definitions for interruption types and interruption management methods from the interruption literature and exemplary studies from the interruption research and formed into the category system using examples from the material.

However, during the analysis and the initial coding of the interview data, it became apparent that the developed category system needed to be adjusted due to limitations of the previous study: a small sample size of seven digital business professionals and written responses that may not have fully captured interruption characteristics. These adjustments to the category system were then structured along the already identified context-specific constructs, with corresponding definitions from interruption research, and integrated into the category system using examples from the data. To ensure the applicability of our coding process, we then engaged an independent expert to review our categorization scheme. The feedback helped to refine our coding approach, resulting in minor adjustments to improve the accuracy and consistency of the analysis. Table 2 shows the adapted category system derived from this qualitative study.

Third, two authors of this paper independently coded the interviews using the adapted category system, extracting all textual elements to ensure that 100% of the interview material was considered. This approach ensured that varying perspectives were considered during the coding process, which increased the robustness of our analysis. Upon completion of the independent coding process, discrepancies between the two authors' codes were identified and discussed to reach consensus. This collaboration helped to resolve any inconsistencies and ensure the reliability of the coding process.

Forth and finally, we compared and validated the coding results by assessing intercoder agreement using Cohen's [10] established procedures. The intercoder agreement was 87%, exceeding the accepted threshold of >61% [27]. To ensure full consensus on the coding of the interview data, we resolved any discrepancies through discussion and clarification of divergent codes.

4 Research Results

In this section, we present the main findings of our content analysis. We also include interviewee statements that provide insight into the perception and management of work interruptions among digital business professionals. Note that the interviews were conducted in German and the exemplary statements were translated in verbatim. Overall, the present study largely confirms the trends observed in our previous exploratory study on the perception and management of work interruptions among digital business professionals [55], although the necessary adjustments to the category system due to the limitations of the earlier study may explain the differences between the earlier and the present study to some extent.

Table 2 Overview of Category System on Interruption Constructs

Category: Interruption Types		
Code	**Definition**	**Reference**
Break	Endogenous event that results in time off from work to accommodate personal needs and the rhythm of the day (e.g., take time to have lunch).	Jett and George [23]
Distraction	Exogenous event that triggers psychological reactions due to external stimuli or secondary activities that interrupt focused attention on primary task activities (e.g., individual is exposed to noise while performing a task).	Jett and George [23]
Instruction	Exogenous event that temporarily interrupts the execution of the primary task activities due to an event that is relevant to the task fulfilment of another person (e.g. explanation of a work step).	Tiedge [65]
Intervention	Exogenous event that reveals a discrepancy between task performance expectations and actual performance of primary task activities (e.g., individual receives feedback relevant to task performance).	Addas and Pinsonneault [1]
Intrusion	Exogenous event that temporarily interrupts the execution of primary task activities due to an event that is irrelevant to task performance (e.g., unscheduled phone call).	Jett and George [23] & Addas and Pinsonneault [1]
Category: Interruption Consequences		
Code	**Definition**	**Exemplary Study**
Negative performance outcomes	The subject's work performance is negatively affected by the interruption (e.g., interruptions lead to decreased task accuracy).	Morgan et al. [35]
Negative psychological outcomes	The subject's psychological Well-being is negatively affected by the interruption (e.g., interruptions lead to work exhaustion).	Chen and Karahanna [8]
Neutral outcomes	The subject's work performance or psychological Well-being is not affected by the interruption (e.g., interruptions tend to have no effect on performance at the start of a task).	Murray and Khan [36]
Positive performance outcomes	The subject's work performance is positively affected by the interruption (e.g., interruptions lead to a work strategy change).	Zijlstra et al. [71]
Positive psychological outcomes	The subject's psychological Well-being is positively affected by the interruption (e.g., interruptions lead to the triggering of positive emotions).	Sonnentag et al. [52]

(continued)

Table 2 (continued)

Category: Interruption Management		
Code	**Definition**	**Reference**
Preemption	The interrupting activity is processed immediately, while the primary activity remains temporarily unfinished.	Kirmeyer [26]
Scheduled	The interrupting activity is processed later, whereby the individual chooses a suitable time to process it.	McFarlane's [31, 32]
Sequential processing	The primary activity is processed first, before the interrupting activity is started.	Kirmeyer [26]
Simultaneity	The interrupting activity and the primary activity are processed with rapid task switching to accomplish both activities.	Kirmeyer [26]

4.1 S-RQ1: What Specific Types of Work Interruptions Can Be Classified among Digital Business Professionals?

Our qualitative content analysis revealed a total of 5 interruption types, which we ranked based on their frequency distribution. Interview participants provided statements related to the following interruption types: intrusion, distraction, break, intervention, and instruction. Table 3 provides a breakdown of these interruption types, supported by our participants' statements.

4.2 S-RQ2: How Do Work Interruptions Affect Psychological Well-being and Work Performance of Digital Business Professionals?

Our qualitative content analysis revealed a total of 5 interruption consequences, which we ranked based on their frequency distribution. Interview participants provided statements related to the following interruption consequences: neutral outcomes, negative psychological outcomes, positive psychological outcomes, negative performance outcomes, and positive performance outcomes. Table 3 provides a breakdown of these interruption consequences, supported by our participants' statements.

Table 3 Result of Content Analysis and Exemplary Statements

Interruption Types	**Frequency Distribution**	**Exemplary Statement**
Break	23.2%	"Time is also often overlooked. Taking just five minutes to catch your breath or think about something else during a break can help motivate you to keep working."
Distraction	24.8%	"Interruptions can be distracting, and you may find yourself switching from one task to another."
Instruction	3.6%	"Then I have to stop what I am doing and show my colleague the folder path or show him something in the graphics program that he needs. Either directly at his computer or I leave my workstation and move away from my current task."
Intervention	11.7%	"When I receive a phone call from my supervisor instructing me to send certain documents to the auditor within the next thirty minutes, I am forced to interrupt my current task and attend to this urgent matter. This intervention disrupts the flow of my work and requires immediate attention to comply with the instructions."
Intrusion	36.7%	"When I'm working and someone engages in small talk nearby, it's intrusive because it's something that should be done elsewhere. This distracts me, making it difficult to concentrate. I find it challenging to ignore interruptions like this."
Interruption Consequences	**Frequency Distribution**	**Exemplary Statement**
Negative performance outcomes	20.2%	"For more complex tasks, interruptions often take me out of my thoughts and require considerable effort to refocus on the original task. It actually interferes with work performance."
Negative psychological outcomes	20.6%	"Most of the interruptions I encounter are often insignificant in nature, and they tend to distract me rather than help me accomplish my tasks."
Neutral outcomes	24.1%	"The interruptions are usually brief, and I don't personally mind them. For me, they're just a part of working life."
Positive performance outcomes	14.9%	"If it's input that I can use or that I'm ultimately interested in, then the interruption is meaningful and has a positive impact on the outcome of the work."
Positive psychological outcomes	20.2%	"Most of the interruptions I experience are relevant, informative, and sometimes even amusing, such as when colleagues share something funny in the chat."
Interruption Management	**Frequency Distribution**	**Exemplary Statement**
Preemption	37.7%	"A website outage is an example where many people are affected, and for me, the urgency is clear that it needs immediate attention."

(continued)

Table 3 (continued)

Scheduled	28.6%	"I continue with the more important task and set a reminder for the interruption or problem that occurred in between."
Sequential processing	13.2%	"If I notice that it's not necessarily an important interruption, or it's not directly related to my task, I don't deal with it right away, but after I've finished my current task."
Simultaneity	20.5%	"I quickly check to see if it's a Microsoft teams message, who it's from, and what the message is about. It only takes a few seconds."

4.3 S-RQ3: How Do Digital Business Professionals Deal with Work Interruptions?

Our qualitative content analysis revealed a total of 4 interruption management methods, which we ranked based on their frequency distribution. Interview participants provided statements related to the following methods for managing interruptions: preemption, scheduling, simultaneity, and sequential processing. Table 3 provides a breakdown of these interruption management methods, supported by our participants' statements.

5 Research Discussion

5.1 Contributions and Implications

We contribute to interruption science research by providing practical insight into how digital business professionals perceive and manage work interruptions. Based on interview data and qualitative content analysis, this study effectively categorizes specific interruption types, quantifies their outcomes on psychological well-being and work performance, and examines how they are handled (see Table 3). Overall, the category system we developed (see Table 2) provides a theory-oriented and rule-bound perspective [30] on the perception and management of work interruptions, enriching interruptions science research.

The main scientific contribution of this qualitative study lies in the validation and refinement of a category system previously developed in an exploratory study [55]. By focusing on filling gaps in the existing literature on the perception and management of interruptions, our research contributes to both scientific research and practical applications. Through careful analysis of interview data and qualitative content, we were able to confirm and extend the trends identified in our previous exploratory study regarding the perception and management of work interruptions among digital business professionals. Despite the similarities between the findings of the previous and present studies, it is important to acknowledge the necessary adjustments to the category system that were prompted by the limitations inherent in the earlier research. These adjustments, while essential to refining the category system, provide insight into the dynamic nature of interruption management strategies and highlight areas for further exploration in the field of interruption science. Thus, our qualitative study not only validates the existing framework, but also lays the groundwork for future research efforts aimed at enhancing our understanding of how individuals perceive and manage interruptions in different professional contexts.

By examining work interruptions and their real-world applications, researchers can provide valuable insights into how individuals perceive and manage interruptions in different work settings, ultimately informing the development of strategies to improve productivity (e.g., [16]), performance (e.g., [62]), and overall well-being (e.g., [25]). For example, understanding how interruptions are perceived and managed is critical to optimizing productivity and minimizing disruptions in contexts ranging from emergency response (e.g., [18]) to the office environments (e.g., [61]). Thus, continued research in interruption science, guided by a validated category system from a comprehensive qualitative study that provides an overview of interruption types, their psychological and performance outcomes, and management methods (see Table 2), promises to advance our understanding in these areas. This research can also enhance resilience to interruptions and support individual work efforts, particularly in optimizing employee effectiveness and efficiency [6, 63].

In this context, several research approaches could be used to further explore patterns, preferences, and challenges in the perception and management of interruptions, which could also potentially advance the category system we have developed (see Table 2). For example, shadowing is a method in which an observer unobtrusively records how an individual performs tasks in a field setting. Empirical research using shadowing has found, for example, that information workers who frequently switch between different collaborative contexts constantly monitor the actions of their colleagues to gain an overview of progress, which helps them to adjust their own actions [19]. Such interruption management behavior results in the need to constantly redirect attention to the ongoing work task, which can have detrimental effects on performance [35]. To mitigate the negative effects, the design of ICT technology could increase individuals' awareness of their current workload and subsequently improve performance outcomes [19]. Another conceivable qualitative research approach is the analysis of activity logs, which can serve as a basis for identifying specific time management behaviors [43] and also allow for classifying the antecedents of specific types of interruptions. For example, Pammer and Bratic [43] analyzed data from activity logs to identify antecedents of interruptions related to software and self-induced fragmentation of work time. Such individual analyses can, for example, help identify ineffective time management habits (e.g., distractions that regularly interrupt focused attention on primary task activities, [43]), which is important for managing interruptions, as research has shown that one loses between 5% [20] and approximately 28% [7] of work time due to interruptions. Irrespective of the research approach chosen, such approaches may be suitable for interruption science research to advance the discourse on the perception and management of interruptions.

5.2 Limitations and Future Research Avenues

Our qualitative study is not without its limitations. First, our research methodology may be susceptible to biases such as recall bias and impression management. To mitigate these biases, however, we asked participants to reflect on their experiences with work interruptions in advance. Second, while we identified specific interruption types, quantified their outcomes on psychological well-being and work performance, and examined how they are handled among digital business professionals, there are additional interruption attributes that warrant investigation, as outlined in more detail in a review of the conceptual and descriptive structure of interruptions [54]. For example, recent reviews suggest examining physiological responses to interruptions, such as increased heart rate and cortisol levels, which may affect arousal and cognitive performance [57–60]. Addressing these limitations offers significant potential for advancing interruption science research and motivating future studies.

Acknowledgments This research was funded by the Federal State of Upper Austria through the Austrian Research Promotion Agency (FFG) as part of the project "Interruption" at the University of Applied Sciences Upper Austria. Also, we would like to thank the digital business professionals who participated in this study.

References

1. Addas, S., & Pinsonneault, A. (2015). The many faces of information technology interruptions: A taxonomy and preliminary investigation of their performance effects. *Information Systems Journal, 25*(3), 231–273. https://doi.org/10.1111/isj.12064
2. Addas, S., & Pinsonneault, A. (2018a). E-mail interruptions and individual performance: Is there a silver lining? *MIS Quarterly, 42*(2), 381–405. https://doi.org/10.25300/MISQ/2018/13157
3. Addas, S., & Pinsonneault, A. (2018b). Theorizing the multilevel effects of interruptions and the role of communication technology. *Journal of the Association for Information Systems, 19*(11), 1097–1129. https://doi.org/10.17705/1jais.00521
4. Ayyagari, R., Grover, V., & Purvis, R. (2011). Technostress: Technological antecedents and implications. *MIS Quarterly, 35*(4), 831–858. https://doi.org/10.2307/41409963
5. Baethge, A., & Rigotti, T. (2013). Interruptions to workflow: Their relationship with irritation and satisfaction with performance, and the mediating roles of time pressure and mental demands. *Work & Stress, 27*(1), 43–63. https://doi.org/10.1080/02678373.2013.761783
6. Baham, C., et al. (2023). Generational differences in handling technology interruptions: A qualitative study. *European Journal of Information Systems, 32*(5), 858–878. https://doi.org/10.1080/0960085X.2022.2070557
7. Chen, A. J., & Karahanna, E. (2014). Boundaryless technology: Understanding the effects of technology-mediated interruptions across the boundaries between work and personal life. *AIS*

Transactions on Human-Computer Interaction, 6(2), 16–36. https://doi.org/10.17705/1thci.00059
8. Chen, A. J., & Karahanna, E. (2018). Life interrupted: The effects of technology-mediated work interruptions on work and nonwork outcomes. *MIS Quarterly, 42*(4), 1023–1042. https://doi.org/10.25300/MISQ/2018/13631
9. Cheng, X., Bao, Y., & Zarifis, A. (2020). Investigating the impact of IT-mediated information interruption on emotional exhaustion in the workplace. *Information Processing and Management, 57*(6), 102281. https://doi.org/10.1016/j.ipm.2020.102281
10. Cohen, J. (1960). A coefficient of agreement for nominal scales. *Educational and Psychological Measurement, 20*(1), 37–46. https://doi.org/10.1177/001316446002000104
11. Derks, D., et al. (2016). Work-related smartphone use, work–family conflict and family role performance: The role of segmentation preference. *Human Relations, 69*(5), 1045–1068. https://doi.org/10.1177/0018726715601890
12. Dey, I. (1993). *Qualitative data analysis: A user friendly guide for social scientists*. Routledge.
13. Eisenhardt, K. M. (1989). Building theories from case study research. *Academy of Management Review, 14*(4), 532–550. https://doi.org/10.5465/amr.1989.4308385
14. Feldman, E., & Greenway, D. (2021). It's a matter of time: The role of temporal perceptions in emotional experiences of work interruptions. *Group and Organization Management, 46*(1), 70–104. https://doi.org/10.1177/1059601120959288
15. Fischer, T., & Riedl, R. (2017). Technostress research: A nurturing ground for measurement pluralism? *Communications of the Association for Information Systems, 40*(17), 375–401. https://doi.org/10.17705/1CAIS.04017
16. Galluch, P. S., Grover, V., & Thatcher, J. B. (2015). Interrupting the workplace: Examining stressors in an information technology context. *Journal of the Association for Information Systems, 16*(1), 1–47. https://doi.org/10.17705/1jais.00387
17. Glaser, B. G., & Strauss, A. L. (2017). *Discovery of grounded theory: Strategies for qualitative research*. Routledge. https://doi.org/10.4324/9780203793206
18. Gontar, P., et al. (2017). Hate to interrupt you, but... analyzing turn-arounds from a cockpit perspective. *Cognition, Technology & Work, 19*(4), 837–853. https://doi.org/10.1007/s10111-017-0440-4
19. González, V. M., & Mark, G. J. (2005). Managing currents of work: Multi-tasking among multiple collaborations. In Gellersen, H. et al. (eds), *ECSCW 2005: Proceedings of the Ninth European Conference on Computer-Supported Cooperative Work, 18–22 September 2005, Paris, France* (pp. 143–162). Springer. https://doi.org/10.1007/1-4020-4023-7_8
20. Gupta, A., & Sharda, R. (2008). SIMONE: A simulator for interruptions and message overload in network environments. *International Journal of Simulation and Process Modelling, 4*(3/4), 237. https://doi.org/10.1504/IJSPM.2008.023685
21. Hess, T., et al. (2016). Options for formulating a digital transformation strategy. *MIS Quarterly Executive, 15*(2), 103–119.
22. Hirsch, P., et al. (2024). Examining the cognitive processes underlying resumption costs in task-interruption contexts: Decay or inhibition of suspended task goals? *Memory & Cognition, 52*(2), 271–284. https://doi.org/10.3758/s13421-023-01458-8
23. Jett, Q. R., & George, J. M. (2003). Work interrupted: A closer look at the role of interruptions in organizational life. *Academy of Management Review, 28*(3), 494–507. https://doi.org/10.5465/amr.2003.10196791
24. Jia, L., et al. (2019). The importance of policy to effective IM use and improved performance. *Information Technology & People, 33*(1), 180–197. https://doi.org/10.1108/ITP-09-2018-0409
25. Keller, A. C., et al. (2020). Please wait until I am done! Longitudinal effects of work interruptions on employee well-being. *Work & Stress, 34*(2), 148–167. https://doi.org/10.1080/02678373.2019.1579266
26. Kirmeyer, S. L. (1988). Coping with competing demands: Interruption and the type A pattern. *Journal of Applied Psychology, 73*(4), 621–629. https://doi.org/10.1037/0021-9010.73.4.621
27. Landis, J. R., & Koch, G. G. (1977). The measurement of observer agreement for categorical data. *Biometrics, 33*(1), 159–174. https://doi.org/10.2307/2529310

28. Laumer, S., et al. (2016). Work routines as an object of resistance during information systems implementations: Theoretical foundation and empirical evidence. *European Journal of Information Systems, 25*(4), 317–343. https://doi.org/10.1057/ejis.2016.1
29. Lewin, K. T. (1926). *Vorsatz Wille und Bedürfnis: Mit Vorbemerkungen über die psychischen Kräfte und Energien und die Struktur der Seele.* Springer. https://doi.org/10.1007/978-3-642-50826-4
30. Mayring, P. (2014). Qualitative content analysis: Theoretical foundation, basic procedures and software solution.
31. McFarlane, D. C. (1997). *Interruption of people in human-computer interaction: A general unifying definition of human interruption and taxonomy.* Naval Research Laboratory (NRL Formal Report NRL/FR/5510-97-9870).
32. McFarlane, D. C. (1998). *Interruption of people in human-computer interaction.* Doctoral Dissertation. George Washington University.
33. McMurtry, K. (2014). Managing email overload in the workplace. *Performance Improvement, 53*(7), 31–37. https://doi.org/10.1002/pfi.21424
34. Mintzberg, H. (1979). An emerging strategy of "direct" research. *Administrative Science Quarterly, 24*(4), 582–589. https://doi.org/10.2307/2392364
35. Morgan, P. L., et al. (2009). Improving memory after interruption: Exploiting soft constraints and manipulating information access cost. *Journal of Experimental Psychology: Applied, 15*(4), 291–306. https://doi.org/10.1037/a0018008
36. Murray, S. L., & Khan, Z. (2014). Impact of interruptions on white collar workers. *Engineering Management Journal, 26*(4), 23–28. https://doi.org/10.1080/10429247.2014.11432025
37. Myers, M. D., & Newman, M. (2007). The qualitative interview in IS research: Examining the craft. *Information and Organization, 17*(1), 2–26. https://doi.org/10.1016/j.infoandorg.2006.11.001
38. Nadj, M., et al. (2023). What disrupts flow in office work? The impact of frequency and relevance of IT-mediated interruptions. *MIS Quarterly, 47*(4), 1615–1646. https://doi.org/10.25300/MISQ/2023/17200
39. Nastjuk, I., et al. (2023). Integrating and synthesising technostress research: A meta-analysis on technostress creators, outcomes, and IS usage contexts. *European Journal of Information Systems*, 1–22. https://doi.org/10.1080/0960085X.2022.2154712
40. Oberländer, M., Beinicke, A., & Bipp, T. (2020). Digital competencies: A review of the literature and applications in the workplace. *Computers & Education, 146*, 103752. https://doi.org/10.1016/j.compedu.2019.103752
41. Ortiz de Guinea, A., Titah, R., & Léger, P.-M. (2014). Explicit and implicit antecedents of users' behavioral beliefs in information systems: A neuropsychological investigation. *Journal of Management Information Systems, 30*(4), 179–210. https://doi.org/10.2753/MIS0742-1222300407
42. Ovsiankina, M. A. (1928). Die Wiederaufnahme unterbrochener Handlungen. *Psychologische Forschung, 11*(1), 302–379. https://doi.org/10.1007/BF00410261
43. Pammer, V., & Bratic, M. (2013). Surprise, surprise: Activity log based time analytics for time management. *Extended Abstracts on Human Factors in Computing Systems*, 211–216. https://doi.org/10.1145/2468356.2468395
44. Puranik, H., Koopman, J., & Vough, H. C. (2020). Pardon the interruption: An integrative review and future research agenda for research on work interruptions. *Journal of Management, 46*(6), 806–842. https://doi.org/10.1177/0149206319887428
45. Ragsdale, J. M., & Hoover, C. S. (2016). Cell phones during nonwork time: A source of job demands and resources. *Computers in Human Behavior, 57*, 54–60. https://doi.org/10.1016/j.chb.2015.12.017
46. Rai, A. (2017a). Editor's comments: Avoiding type III errors: Formulating IS research problems that matter. *MIS Quarterly, 42*(2), iii–vi.
47. Rai, A. (2017b). Editor's comments: Seeing the forest for the trees, MIS Quarterly, 41(4), pp. iii–viii.

48. Riedl, R. (2013). On the biology of technostress: Literature review and research agenda. *ACM SIGMIS Database: The DATA BASE for Advances in Information Systems, 44*(1), 18–55. https://doi.org/10.1145/2436239.2436242
49. Riedl, R., et al. (2023). Videoconference fatigue from a neurophysiological perspective: Experimental evidence based on electroencephalography (EEG) and electrocardiography (ECG). *Scientific Reports, 13*(1), 18371. https://doi.org/10.1038/s41598-023-45374-y
50. Russell, E., Jackson, T., & Banks, A. (2021). Classifying computer-mediated communication (CMC) interruptions at work using control as a key delineator. *Behaviour & Information Technology, 40*(2), 191–205. https://doi.org/10.1080/0144929X.2019.1683606
51. Schlachter, S., et al. (2018). Voluntary work-related technology use during non-work time: A narrative synthesis of empirical research and research agenda. *International Journal of Management Reviews, 20*(4), 825–846. https://doi.org/10.1111/ijmr.12165
52. Sonnentag, S., et al. (2018). Feeling interrupted—Being responsive: How online messages relate to affect at work. *Journal of Organizational Behavior, 39*(3), 369–383. https://doi.org/10.1002/job.2239
53. Spradley, J. P. (2016). *The ethnographic interview*. Waveland Press.
54. Stangl, F. J., & Riedl, R. (2023a). Interruption science as a research field: Towards a taxonomy of interruptions as a foundation for the field. *Frontiers in Psychology, 14*, 1043426. https://doi.org/10.3389/fpsyg.2023.1043426
55. Stangl, F. J., & Riedl, R. (2023b). Interruptions in the workplace: An exploratory study among digital business professionals. In Nah, F. F.-H., & Siau, K. (eds), *HCI in Business, Government and Organizations: 10th International Conference, HCIBGO 2023, Held as Part of the 25th HCI International Conference, HCII 2023, Copenhagen, Denmark, July 23–28, 2023, Proceedings, Part II*. LNCS, vol. 14039, pp. 400–422. Springer. https://doi.org/10.1007/978-3-031-36049-7_29
56. Stangl, F. J., & Riedl, R. (2023c). Perception and management of work interruptions: A qualitative study, in *Extended Abstracts of the 6th International Digital Business Research Day*.
57. Stangl, F. J., & Riedl, R. (2024). Neurophysiological measurements in the research field of interruption science: Insights into applied methods for different interruption types based on an umbrella review. In F. D. Davis et al. (eds), *Information Systems and Neuroscience: NeuroIS Retreat 2023, Vienna, Austria*. LNISO, vol. 68, pp. 123–152. Springer. https://doi.org/10.1007/978-3-031-58396-4_11
58. Stangl, F. J., & Riedl, R. (2025a). Autonomic nervous system activity measurements in the research field of interruption science: Insights into applied methods. In Davis, F. D. et al. (eds), *Information Systems and Neuroscience: NeuroIS Retreat 2024, Vienna, Austria*. LNISO, vol. 66, pp. 47–69. Springer. https://doi.org/10.1007/978-3-031-71385-9_6
59. Stangl, F. J., & Riedl, R. (2025b). Brain imaging methods in the research field of interruption science: An analysis of applied methods. In Davis, F. D. et al. (eds), *Information Systems and Neuroscience: NeuroIS Retreat 2024, Vienna, Austria*. LNISO, vol. 66, pp. 71–93. Springer. https://doi.org/10.1007/978-3-031-71385-9_7.
60. Stangl, F. J., & Riedl, R. (2025c). Hormone measurements in the research field of interruption science: Review of applied methods. In Davis, F. D. et al. (eds), *Information Systems and Neuroscience: NeuroIS Retreat 2024, Vienna, Austria*. LNISO, vol. 66, pp. 95–114. Springer. https://doi.org/10.1007/978-3-031-71385-9_8.
61. Stangl, F. J., Seiler, V., & Riedl, R. (2025). How do digital business professionals manage work interruptions? A pilot study on coping strategies. In Siau, K. L., & Nah, F. F.-H. (eds), *HCI in Business, Government and Organizations: 12th International Conference, HCIBGO 2025, Held as Part of the 27th HCI International Conference, HCII 2025, Gothenburg, Sweden, June 22–27, 2025, Proceedings, Part II*. LNCS, vol. 15805, pp. 198–218. Springer. https://doi.org/10.1007/978-3-031-92826-0_13.
62. Tams, S., Thatcher, J. B., & Grover, V. (2018). Concentration, competence, confidence, and capture: An experimental study of age, interruption-based technostress, and task performance. *Journal of the Association for Information Systems, 19*(9), 857–908. https://doi.org/10.17705/1jais.00511

63. Tams, S., et al. (2020). Worker stress in the age of mobile technology: The combined effects of perceived interruption overload and worker control. *Journal of Strategic Information Systems, 29*(1), 101595. https://doi.org/10.1016/j.jsis.2020.101595
64. Tarafdar, M., Gupta, A., & Turel, O. (2013). The dark side of information technology use. *Information Systems Journal, 23*(3), 269–275. https://doi.org/10.1111/isj.12015
65. Tiedge, J. T. (1975). Clarifying the concept of distraction. *Public Opinion Quarterly, 39*(2), 178–188. https://doi.org/10.1086/268214
66. Tiilikainen, S., et al. (2024). Toward a process-based, interpretive understanding of how collaborative groups deal with ICT interruptions. *MIS Quarterly, 48*(1), 167–218. https://doi.org/10.25300/MISQ/2023/16434
67. Wan, M., et al. (2019). The knife cuts on both sides: Examining the relationship between cross-domain communication and work–family interface. *Journal of Occupational and Organizational Psychology, 92*(4), 978–1019. https://doi.org/10.1111/joop.12284
68. Zeigarnik, B. W. (1927). Das Behalten erledigter und unerledigter Handlungen. *Psychologische Forschung, 9*(1), 1–85. https://doi.org/10.1007/BF02409755
69. Zellmer-Bruhn, M. E. (2003). Interruptive events and team knowledge acquisition. *Management Science, 49*(4), 514–528. https://doi.org/10.1287/mnsc.49.4.514.14423
70. Zickerick, B., et al. (2020). Differential effects of interruptions and distractions on working memory processes in an ERP study. *Frontiers in Human Neuroscience, 14*, 84. https://doi.org/10.3389/fnhum.2020.00084
71. Zijlstra, F. R. H., et al. (1999). Temporal factors in mental work: Effects of interrupted activities. *Journal of Occupational and Organizational Psychology, 72*(2), 163–185. https://doi.org/10.1348/096317999166581

The Role of Data Management in Scaling AI Startups: A Practical Framework

Tilman Friedrich, Lukas Sanwald, and Isabelle Keutner

Abstract This study examines data management and scaling in AI startups. It uncovers the distinctive scaling dynamics of AI startups, where data emerges as a central resource. Through qualitative research and interviews with 13 AI startups, operational complexities and strategic approaches in data management are unveiled. The research employs a practical Framework of Data Conceptualisation for AI startups, which we developed based on our findings, enriching both scientific understanding and entrepreneurial theory in the AI domain.

1 Introduction

In the digitisation era, artificial intelligence (AI) enables new products, business models and processes, marking a transformative period in information systems management [4]. With this new potential, the number of AI startups has risen to 508 in Germany alone and is rising every year [10]. These startups are positioned at the intersection of adapting AI and effective data management. With the need for training data to build, optimise, and extend their AI products, data is playing an essential role in the success and growth of this firms [20]. The quality of the output of the AI is depending of the availability, quality and accessibility of its training data [15]. Therefore, the understanding of critical data management practices becomes essential [22].

Existing research highlights the role of AI across industries and the challenges of scaling [21, 26], yet there remains a notable gap in understanding how early-stage AI startups manage their training data specifically. This paper seeks to bridge this gap by exploring the specific training data management practices essential for the growth and innovation of early-stage AI startups. We aim to answer the research question: *What factors and data management practices are to be considered for AI startups to scale?* Using a newly developed framework to answer this question, this study integrates

T. Friedrich (✉) · L. Sanwald · I. Keutner
Freie Universität Berlin, Berlin, Germany
e-mail: tilmaf99@zedat.fu-berlin.de

C. M. Flath et al. (eds.), *Shaping the Digital Future Through Innovation and Practice*, Lecture Notes in Information Systems and Organisation 85,
https://doi.org/10.1007/978-3-032-08489-7_22

insights from [9], who identify inadequate planning, scope creep, and insufficient skills as relevant challenges, and [22], who emphasize the need to manage technological issues and data-related factors for AI project success. By employing qualitative research methods and conducting 13 semi-structured interviews with AI startup executives, this study draws upon the methodological framework of [11] to investigate the different aspects of training data procurement, quality management and usage. Our investigation reveals that the successful scaling of AI startups is closely linked to an interplay between the necessary technological infrastructure, procurement and processing of training data, while also addressing regulatory requirements as highlighted by [5] and developing an comprehensive data strategy. The paper contributes to the academic discourse on AI startups, expanding the understanding of training data management's role in scaling and innovating within these companies. It offers practical guidelines for AI startups to effectively design and adapt their data strategies, securing competitive advantages and developing successful AI products.

2 Background

2.1 Theoretical Background

The theoretical background for this paper is based on [24], which links value creation in dynamic environmental contexts to the management of firm resources using the resource-based view. This perspective highlights the strategic importance of intangible assets, such as data, in driving sustainable competitive advantage. By effectively managing and leveraging data resources, startups can enhance their innovation capabilities, better understand customer needs, and respond swiftly to market changes. For AI startups, data is even more critical due to their reliance on large volumes of high-quality data to train AI models, setting them apart from other types of startups and organizations, highlighting the unique challenges they face in data management. This highlights data as a crucial component of their resource portfolio, contributing significantly to its long-term success and growth trajectory. Startups are seen as resource bundles that build capabilities, offering value to customers and competitive advantage. In this context, we conceptualise startups as composed of resource bundles that can be utilised to build and leverage capabilities to provide value to customers, gain a competitive advantage, and generate wealth for the owners. Following this perspective, we understand data which is needed to develop the AI as a resource of AI startups. The data can be used to build capabilities of the AI, which can be leveraged to offer value to customers.

2.2 Relevance of Training Data in AI Startups

AI startups are digital startups, where AI is a central aspect of its business model [23]. In the domain of AI startups, data is a critical asset, often described as the fuel for artificial intelligence technologies [20]. Highlighting the distinct approach AI startups must take towards data management compared to conventional digital startups not centered around AI, especially training data, is fundamental to their innovation, growth, and their value proposition, requiring strategic acquisition, processing, and use [14]. The success and expansion of these companies significantly depend on data, as it is crucial for developing and fine-tuning their AI products [20]. Data's role in AI encompasses availability, quality, accessibility, and flow, essential for AI solutions. Jöhnk et al. [15] emphasize these aspects, noting the direct impact of data quality and availability on AI outcomes and the necessity of data accessibility and smooth data flow for AI development. The quality of the output of the AI is directly linked to the quantity and the quality of the training data. Therefore, AI startups have to invest more resources in the data processing processes than conventional digital startups [29]. Data management and regulatory compliance also add layers of complexity. Eitle and Buxmann [8] highlight the importance of regulatory adherence, especially in sensitive data contexts, suggesting that compliance influences data management strategies. Bessen et al. [6] point out the need for proprietary training data, crucial for AI model training, product customisation, and aligning with data privacy and intellectual property considerations.

2.3 Scaling AI Startups

Scaling is the way in which size-related concepts behave relative to each other during the growth process, such as the relationship between the number of employees and the operational profit of startups. Scaling, therefore, refers to how individual components of a system react when its size changes [27]. The ability to scale accordingly is a crucial point for AI startups, especially concerning fundraising, productivity, and the distribution of new product and technology innovations [23]. In comparison to other types of startups, AI startups seem to be able to expand known types of scaling, such as by being capable of transferring machine learning models to other business applications [1].

3 Methodology

Our research is dedicated to unravelling the complex processes of how AI startups manage their training data, spanning from initial acquisition through to the formulation of comprehensive data strategies. Utilising a qualitative research framework, we delved into the operational complexities that support scalable and replicable value creation within these startups. Our methodological approach follows a modified Grounded Theory Methodology (GTM), [7, 11]. The approach is particularly suited to exploring and understanding the nuances of information systems in the dynamic landscape of AI startups. In preparing for our empirical exploration, we diverged from the traditional GTM data collection pathways. Instead, we employed a theory-informed approach as recommended by [12]. It was essential to navigate the different dimensions of AI and its business implications effectively. Our separate literature review included sources on AI, data, and the challenges of scaling in AI startups. We identified 20 relevant papers from five databases that address the topic and highlight key factors and data management practices for AI startups.

By structuring the data according to [11], we were able to gain a theoretical overview of the in-depth data in the field of AI startups. Building on this, we reasoned that given the critical role of interviews in gaining further in-depth insights, especially in the context of GTM studies [7], we selected semi-structured expert interviews according to [18]. The method allowed us to capture the complex experiences and perspectives of entrepreneurs who are deeply involved in the data management processes of AI startups. Langley and Meziani [18] differentiates between different genres, whereby our research had to be oriented towards the "investigative". The main purpose of this is to identify specific events. Specific techniques such as event tracking, indirect questioning and a modification of the courtroom questioning method were used to gain these insights [18].

The structure of the interview guide was systematically divided into three subdivisions. The initial part collected general data, probing into the integration of AI into the startups' value propositions. The second section poses open-ended questions on data-related scaling issues, aiming for a detailed discussion. In the final part, we addressed with specific categories of data management in the context of AI startups, which we were able to define through our literature research.

3.1 Data Collection

Our data collection process includes a range of perspectives on how AI startups navigate the complexities of scaling, leveraging resources for value creation and capture. To achieve a comprehensive understanding, we targeted a varied sample of respondents, including (Co-)founders, managing directors, operation officers and data scientists. We also ensured our sample encompassed a balanced mix of different early stage startups which are operating in various industries. While some are at the very beginning, some already scaled up to a certain level, employing more people and making substantial revenue. We only included startups where AI is central to their value proposition, a distinction not always straightforward given the common marketing of AI capabilities.

To collect our interviewees, we reached out to 262 individuals from 146 startups via various communication channels, resulting in 11 interviews. Additional inquiries

Table 1 Overview data properties

ID	Function interviewee	Industry	Founding year	Market	Interview duration	Headquarters
ID1	Founder	IT consulting	2017	B2B	45:11 min	Berlin, Germany
ID2	Data scientist	Construction	2021	B2B	16:58 min	Brandenburg, Germany
ID3	Founder	Construction	2024	B2C	15:44 min	Berlin, Germany
ID4	Founder	Real estate management	2023	B2B	35:09 min	Berlin, Germany
ID5	Co-founder	Healthtech	2022	B2C	45:13 min	Berlin, Germany
ID6	Co-founder	Biotechnology	2022	B2B	44:41 min	Berlin, Germany
ID7	Co-founder	Healthtech	2023	B2B	30:54 min	Charleston, USA
ID8	Managing director	HR system	2022	B2B	49:22 min	Gothenburg, Sweden
ID9	Founder	E-Learning	2023	B2G	36:02 min	Berlin, Germany
ID10	Founder	E-Learning	2021	All	64:30 min	Berlin, Germany
ID11	Co-founder	Aviation	2016	B2B	35:13 min	Amsterdam, Netherlands
ID12	COO	IT consulting	2020	B2B	36:57 min	Province of Jönköping, Sweden
ID13	Head of marketing	Publishing	2017	B2B	22:04 min	Linköping, Sweden

within personal networks yielded 2 more interviews, totalling 13 participants. As AI had to be central to their value proposition, numerous interviews conducted during this process had to be eliminated. A comprehensive overview of the interviews, including details such as industry, interview duration, and other relevant specifics, can be found in Table 1. With participants' consent, interviews were recorded and stored as audio files, which have been transcribed.

3.2 *Data Analysis*

Table 1 presents a detailed profile of all conducted interviews, categorising the AI startups into relevant sectors. The categorisation illustrates a broad distribution of AI solutions and applications that AI startups are confronted with in various areas. Additionally, the table provides an overview of the startups' sizes, ranging from micro teams of 1 to 32 employees, with a notable mention that three startups exceed the 15-employee mark. Highlighting the differing levels of operational and scaling complexities encountered within our dataset, this variation stands out. The startups' founding years stretch from 2016 to 2024, with a noticeable cluster of six startups begun in the recent years of 2022 and 2023. The temporal clustering indicates that many participating ventures are relatively new, navigating the initial or ongoing challenges of scaling. The roles of our interviewees within their startups predominantly include founders and co-founders, primarily positioned at the C-level. These individuals are offering insights into strategic decision-making, resource allocation, and scaling strategies due to their comprehensive understanding of the company's direction and challenges. Our sample's geographical distribution extends beyond Germany and Europe, including an interview conducted in the United States, thus enriching our research with a broader international perspective. The duration of interviews varied from 15 to 64 min, averaging 36 min per discussion. The range reflects our flexible interviewing strategy, which was adjusted according to the respondent's availability and the depth of insights they were able to provide.

For the data analysis phase, we employed a modified grounded theory approach facilitated by the use of the coding software MAXQDA software to analyse our interview transcripts and perform open coding. The process began with open coding of all interviews, leading to an initial set of codes based on single statements that laid the foundation for our abstraction process into first-order categories, as outlined by [11]. Further coding helped us develop a conceptual framework to explore the influence of digital infrastructure on the scalability of AI startups. Progressing from raw data to strategic themes and aggregated dimensions, this methodical approach allows us to take an unbiased perspective on the critical role of data in the scaling processes of AI startups. The subsequent section delves deeper into these thematic codes and the insights derived from them.

4 Results

In adherence to the methodology adopted by [11], our data analysis process facilitated the construction of an data structure, which is visually represented in Fig. 1. The structure allowed us to structure the qualitative insights extracted from our interviews and investigate the factors and data management practices AI startups require to scale as defined by the research question. Herein, we delineate each identified dimension in relation to the overarching themes and concepts. For AI startups scaling, they need to consider prerequisites for training data handling and external factors for a successful data management. Essential data management practices include data strategy, training data acquisition, and data processing.

4.1 Prerequisites for Training Data Handling

Our analysis exposed two critical themes, which AI startups need to incorporate to successfully acquire and utilise their training data. The first one is a flexible IT architecture and infrastructure, as expert 5 underlines: *"Future requirements must be taken into account when making infrastructure decisions"*. Because of the high demand of AI regarding storage and computing capacities, all interviewed startups used external cloud infrastructure. As there is a high density of innovation in the AI field, a flexible IT architecture is needed to quickly adapt to emerging requirements. The second theme is the availability of AI and data expertise to identify relevant data and ensure high data quality, as expert 5 further describes: *"Testing, training and optimising AI algorithms requires "man power" and qualified personnel"*. As such personnel is highly sought after, early recruitment of AI and data specialists is crucial, as expert 11 further underlines: *"It's quite difficult to find people with a solid AI background"*.

4.2 Data Strategy

In the AI startup ecosystem, scaling depends on creating universal models that can adapt to varied applications, reducing the typically high expenses associated with AI adjustments. The strategy is emphasized by a necessity for iterative refinement through continuous data acquisition, ensuring AI systems evolve in alignment with user needs and experiences. Reflective of this approach, expert 13's perspective on customised solutions—*"We have a customised solution. So we're basing the customer solution on [their] content."*—illustrates a commitment to user-centered development. Similarly, expert 7's emphasis on speed for user experience enhancement—*"(...) the speed of the AI, so at the end of the day, to increase the user experience, it is particularly important that the documentation we generate is as fast as possible and that you get feedback as quickly as possible when you are sitting in front of our software."*—further validates the importance of rapid, user-responsive AI systems. Collectively, these insights inform the 'Data Strategy' dimension of our framework, reinforcing the essentially of a user-focused approach in AI development and the perpetual cycle of feedback and fine-tuning that drives innovation and growth in the field.

4.3 Training Data Acquisition

Training data acquisition is a critical concern for AI startups, which must balance the use of external sources with the generation of proprietary datasets. From our interviews, expert 6 highlighted a common challenge, regarding public data sets *"(...) the measurements very often that were done so far were not optimised for (training) AI algorithm"* a view shared in the other interviews. Emphasizing the need for startups to critically assess and often reconfigure external training datasets for their specific AI applications. Expert 10 underlines the importance of sourcing data diversity: *"(...) you want to have a healthy mix of external data (...) and data that you have captured from your products, from your services"*. The approach not only

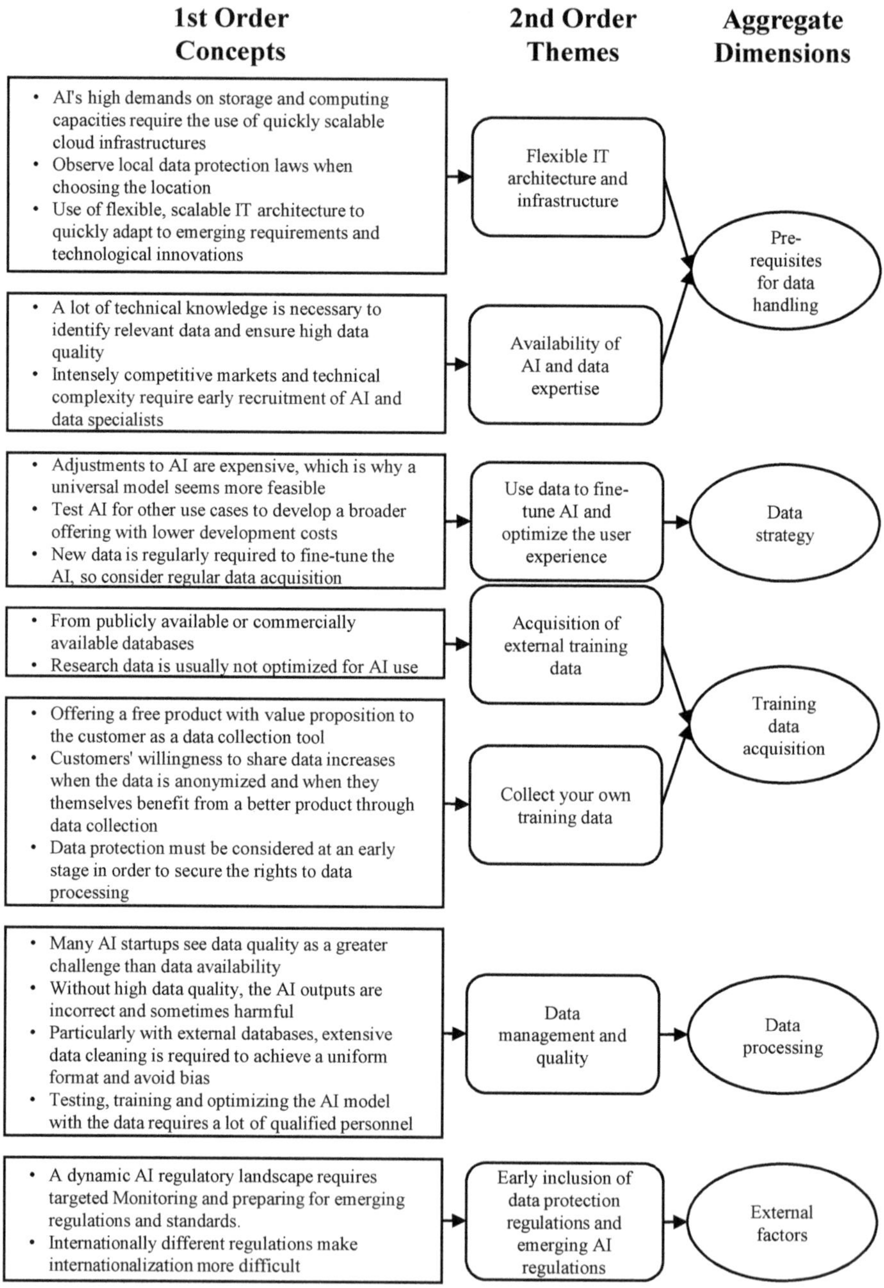

Fig. 1 Data structure

broadens the data spectrum but also infuses the AI with real-world insights from the startup's own operations. It shows the importance of combining publicly available or commercially available databases with the startup's own data collection tools, such as free products that incentives customer participation, as expert 12 states: *"We give out software for free just for testing purposes."* or as its mentioned in ID5, ID8 and ID11. Anonymization and customer benefit from data sharing are key drivers of customer willingness to contribute their data (ID8).

4.4 Data Processing

In AI startups, ensuring high-quality data is crucial for effective data processing. As illuminated by the interviews, ensuring high data quality is essential because inaccurate AI outputs can be detrimental, sometimes leading to adverse outcomes (ID4). Expert 6 stresses the complexity of achieving data quality, which is intricately linked to data availability. Diversification of data sets is also pivotal, as expert 5 points out the need for varied data, *"not only (...) patients but also healthy people or those with similar diseases"* to train the AI for a wider range of use cases. Moreover, the potential for customer dissatisfaction due to AI errors is a pressing concern, with expert 4 emphasising the necessity of quality assurance to mitigate risks associated with AI technology: *"We try to have quality assurance (at exactly these points) to minimise that."*. These insights highlight the strategic importance placed on data management and quality within the data processing dimension. Effective data cleaning techniques and a diversity of data in testing are not just operational requirements but strategic necessities to ensure that AI systems are reliable, equitable, and fit for their intended purpose. Furthermore, the role of qualified personnel, as highlighted by expert 5, adds up to this process. They contribute in closing the gap between the data potential and the valuable AI results that are realized.

4.5 External Factors

AI startups operate within a dynamic regulatory landscape that requires monitoring and proactive preparation for emerging regulations and standards. The adaptability to swiftly respond to such regulatory changes ensures compliance, which is fundamental to scalable operations. Interview insights reinforce this perspective, with expert 10 discussing the necessity of adhering to digital rights management and local data laws, *"So, for example, if we have users in India (...) we shouldn't be transmitting the data of Indian users outside of India"*. Expert 5 highlights the importance of incorporating data protection regulations like GDPR from the onset: *"If you set it up right from the start, then it's not a too big obstacle"*. Furthermore, expert 9 anticipates *"Data protection will be a big issue for us (...)"*. These insights attest to the importance of early inclusion of data protection regulations and awareness of the evolving AI

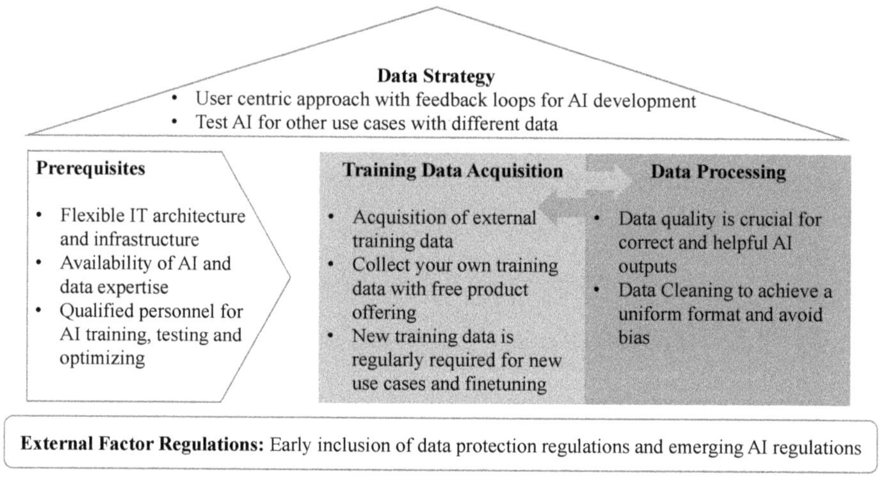

Fig. 2 Framework with data management practices and factors for AI startups to consider when scaling

regulatory environment, as shown in our data structure. The strategic integration of cloud computing also emerges as a crucial element to be agile and able to scale up while maintaining regulatory compliance and high security standards.

5 Discussion

Built upon the insights we gained from preceding analyses, we have developed a strategic framework which answers the defined research question. The framework (Fig. 2) is derived from our research findings and provides a structured representation of factors and data management practices to be considered for AI startups to scale. It is centred on data strategy, encompassing prerequisites, training data acquisition and data processing, as well as the essential compliance with regulatory requirements. Looking from the perspective of the resource management processes from [24], the framework links to the structuring and leveraging components. Defining a data strategy can be seen as the mobilising process of the leveraging component. To handle the data, AI startups need capabilities in the field of AI and data expertise, infrastructure and personnel. This refers to the prerequisites part of the framework. Training data acquisition and data processing are directly linked to the structuring component. The critical resource data needs to be acquired and accumulated by AI startups to train their AI models. Further detailed explanations provide deeper understanding the interconnections among the framework's components.

5.1 Data Prerequisites

As our interviews showed, emerges a foundational IT infrastructure's scalability as essential prerequisites to utilise training data. Aligning with the statements made by [19], the need considers cloud computing technology not just a utility but the basis upon which modern AI startups can pivot, scale, and innovate with agility. The cloud's inherent scalability enables startups to expand or contract their resources to match operational demands dynamically. Moreover, [25] insights on choosing appropriate and scalable data storage systems resonate with the importance of having robust and accessible AI and data expertise. The extensive data needs of AI startups—*speedy access, security, and efficiency*—necessitate data storage solutions that are not just adequate for current needs but also future requirements, an understanding also deepened by the work of [2]. Further compounding these operational necessities is the critical factor of data risk management. References [3, 14] bring to the fore the importance of identifying and mitigating data risks, be it through securing data or ensuring compliance with regulatory standards. Such proactive measures are critical for creating a trustful environment.

5.2 Data Strategy

The development of a data strategy in AI startups constitutes a systematic integration of foundational IT infrastructure and expertise with the nuanced aspects of training data acquisition and processing. This integrated approach is critical for ensuring the continuous improvement and relevance of AI technologies. According to our research, the effectiveness of a data strategy depends on a continuous feedback mechanism, whereby training data is systematically collected, cleaned, and applied, driving the iterative refinement of AI solutions. The approach, as delineated in our framework, is not just conceptual but operational. It emphasises the need for agility and adaptability in data strategies to accommodate rapid technological shifts and changing regulatory frameworks. Additionally, AI startups face unique hurdles due to their limited resources and lack of established compliance processes. Unlike large firms with existing infrastructure and protocols, AI startups must build these from the ground up. The literature reinforces this perspective, offering empirical evidence and theoretical insights into the strategic utilisation of data. For instance, [16, 28] advocate for the strategic exploitation of big data, which is pivotal in informing data strategy and guiding decision-making processes. Complementing this is [2, 17], who stress the importance of centralized data management. Such an approach not only optimizes operations but also secures data coherence, aligning closely with a startup's overarching objectives. Moreover, the insistence on data quality, highlighted both in our findings and in the literature by [2], is crucial. A significant" data strategy necessitates the utilisation of datasets that are both standardised and devoid of bias, catering to the diverse requirements of AI training and application.

5.3 Training Data Acquisition

The training data acquisition phase for AI startups is characterised by utilising both external and internal data sources. The strategy is reflected in the literature and in the feedback loops our interviewees described. The necessity to combine varied data sources to construct a comprehensive understanding of both the problem space and the customer base is integral for AI-driven insights and innovations. Bessen et al. [6] discuss the imperative of acquiring sufficient proprietary training data, emphasising the need for startups to accumulate their own datasets. The approach ensures data fits with the startup's specific use cases. Complementing this perspective, [13] highlight the significance of leveraging customer behaviour data to sharpen the AI models continuously. As startups collect and process customer interaction data, they can fine tune their offerings to better match customer expectations and needs, ultimately enhancing the user experience. Embedding the customer's preferences into the AI itself, this customer-centric approach to data analysis goes beyond just tailoring products and services.

5.4 Data Processing

In AI startups, data processing is driven by the necessity to preserve data integrity and ensuring quality, a task consistently reflected by the startups we interviewed. The effort to refine data into a usable format is a critical for the product's accuracy and reliability. The literature strengthens our findings, with [2] shedding light on the needs of data in training versus its application in end-use scenarios. They argue that the discrepancy in statistical distribution between these stages necessitates tailored processing methodologies to ensure the AI models developed during the training phase perform optimally when deployed. The importance of foreseeing the eventual application of the data from the onset of the processing phase speaks volumes about this aspect. Adding to the complexity of data processing is the challenge of encryption, as noted by [25]. He points out that with a significant amount of valuable data being encrypted for security reasons, startups must equip themselves with appropriate decryption methodologies to access and utilise this data effectively.

5.5 Data Regulations and Ethics

Data protection regulations, including the General Data Protection Regulation (GDPR), are integral to the ethical deployment of AI technologies. Baier et al. [2] emphasize that managing data centrally in a single location confers several secondary benefits beyond compliance. The approach improves security, enables better integration across systems, and solidifies data ownership, which are critical for developing

Table 2 Actionable recommendations

Scalable IT infrastructure	Invest in cloud computing technologies and scalable data storage systems to ensure agility and growth adaptability
Data expertise acquisition	Prioritize early recruitment of AI and data specialists to enhance data quality and processing capabilities
Training data strategy	Blend internal and external data sources, utilizing customer behavior insights and big data analytics to enrich AI models
Data processing excellence	Implement sophisticated data cleaning and encryption decryption methods, ensuring high data quality for training and application
Regulatory compliance	Embed GDPR and other data protection regulations into the foundation of data strategies, ensuring ethical deployment
Centralized data management	Manage data centrally to enhance security, integration, and ownership, paving the way for a robust internal data platform
Feedback-driven strategy	Foster a continuous feedback loop between data acquisition and processing to perpetually refine AI products and services

an internal data platform. Such a platform can meet cross-departmental needs while meeting privacy and data protection standards. Furthermore, the requirement to integrate data silos, as dictated by various regulatory frameworks, poses a significant challenge for AI startups. Moreover, there is the need to adhere to data localisation laws, which dictate that user data be stored within specific geographical boundaries. These regulatory requirements need to be included into the data strategy. Balancing the need for seamless data integration with the imperative of regulatory compliance, as highlighted by [2], is essential for this strategy. Therefore, it is imperative for startups to embed data protection and ethical considerations into their operational processes from the beginning. Taking a proactive approach is not only defensive but serves as a strategic asset. By prioritising compliance, AI startups lay a foundation for scaling that is ethical, legal, and sustainable.

The framework acts as a practical roadmap, guiding startups toward achieving scalable growth by leveraging their resources to archive an effective data management. To apply the theory to real-world scenarios, we've created a table summarising a selection of insights generated by our research (Table 2). The table breaks down our thorough analysis into specific, actionable steps. It lists key considerations and their related recommendations, offering AI startups a clear plan for strategic action.

6 Conclusions

The research contributes to the scientific understanding of AI startups by providing insights into their data practices. The developed framework offers a practical guide for AI startups and contributes to the understanding of their data management strategies. It reveals the interplay between internal resources, data strategies, and the data acquisition and processing of AI startups.

While the research provides valuable insights, it is not without limitations. The study is based on a limited sample of 13 interviews, potentially affecting the generalisation of the results. There could also be a certain bias in the interview data and the data is based on self-reporting statements by interviewees who were founders or managers of the company, so there is a risk of distortion and idealised representation. The rapidly evolving nature of the AI industry may render some findings time-sensitive. Additionally, the proposed actionable recommendations, while practical, may be context-dependent, varying based on individual circumstances within AI startups. In essence, our research serves as a robust foundation for future investigations into the dynamic landscape of AI startups, acknowledging these limitations as catalysts for further exploration and refinement of the presented frameworks and insights [9]. Future research could adopt a Mixed-Methods approach, expand the sample size, and explore emerging technologies to provide a more comprehensive understanding of AI startups' data management practices. One approach is to analyze the documented data management processes of AI startups and assess them through interviews with responsible personnel to identify key success factors.

References

1. Agrawal, A., Gans, J., & Goldfarb, A. (2019). *Prediction, judgment, and complexity: A theory of decision-making and artificial intelligence*. University of Chicago Press.
2. Baier, L., Jöhren, F., & Seebacher, S. (2019). Challenges in the deployment and operation of machine learning in practice. In *Proceedings of the 27. European Conference on Information Systems (ECIS2019), Stockholm-Uppsala, Sweden, presented by Karlsruhe Service Research Institute (KSRI).*
3. Bauer, M., Dinther, C., & Kiefer, D. (2020). Machine learning in SME: An empirical study on enablers and success factors. In *AMCIS 2020 Proceedings - Advancings in information systems research: August 10-14, 2020, Association for Information Systems (AIS).*
4. Berente, N., Gu, B., Recker, J., & Santhanam, R. (2021). Managing artificial intelligence. *Managing Artificial Intelligence," MIS Quarterly, 45*(3), 1433–1450.
5. Bessen, J., Impink, S., Reichensperger, L., & Seamans, R. (2020). GDPR and the importance of data to AI startups. *Journal of Artificial Intelligence Regulation.*
6. Bessen, J., Impink, S., Reichensperger, L., & Seamans, R. (2022, June). The role of data for AI startup growth. *Research Policy, 51*(5), Article 104513.
7. Corbin, J., & Strauss, A. (1998). *Basics of qualitative research: Techniques and procedures for developing grounded theory*. Sage Publications.
8. Eitle, V., & Buxmann, P. (2020). Cultural differences in machine learning adoption: An international comparison between Germany and the united states. In *Association for Information*

Systems AIS Electronic Library (AISeL), ECIS 2020 Proceedings, presented by Technical University of Darmstadt.
9. Ermakova, T., Blume, J., Fabian, B., & and Fomenko, E. (2021). Beyond the hype: Why do data-driven projects fail? In *Proceedings of the 54th Hawaii International Conference on System Sciences | 2021*.
10. *German AI Startup Landscape*. (2023). https://www.appliedai-institute.de/hub/2023-ai-german-startup-landscape
11. Gioia, D., Corley, K., & Hamilton, A. (2012). Seeking qualitative rigor in inductive research: Notes on the Gioia methodology. *Sage Journals*.
12. Goldkuhl, G., & Cronholm, S. (2019). Grounded theory in information systems research — from themes in is discourse to possible developments. In *ICIS 2019 Proceedings. 4*.
13. Huy, P., Shavkatovich, S., Abdul-Samad, Z., Agrawal, D., Ashifa, K., & Arumugam, M. (2023, November). Resource management projects in entrepreneurship and retain customer based on big data analysis and artificial intelligence. *The Journal of High Technology Management Research, 34*(2), Article 100471.
14. Jia, P., & Stan, C. (2021). Artificial intelligence factory, data risk, and VCs' mediation: The case of ByteDance, an AI-powered startup. *Journal of Risk and Financial Management*.
15. Jöhnk, J., Weißert, M., & Wyrtki, K. (2020). Ready or not, AI comes– an interview study of organizational AI readiness factors. *Business & Information Systems Engineering: The International Journal of WIRTSCHAFTSINFORMATIK, Springer, Gesellschaft für Informatik e.V. (GI), 63*(1), 5–20.
16. Koronios, A., Gao, J., & Selle, S. (2014). Big data project success - a meta analysis. In *Pacific Asia Conference on Information Systems (PACIS) 2014 Proceedings. 376*.
17. Kühne, B., & Böhmann, T. (2019). Data-driven business models — building the bridge between data and value', *Proceedings 27. European Conference on Information Systems (ECIS2019), Stockholm-Uppsala, Sweden, presented by University of Hamburg, Germany*.
18. Langley, A., & Meziani, N. (2020). Making interviews meaningful. *The Journal of Applied Behavioral Science*.
19. Li, J., & Yao, M. (2021). New framework of digital entrepreneurship model based on artificial intelligence and cloud computing. *Mobile Information Systems, 6*, 1–11.
20. Pumplun, L., Tauchert, C., & Heidt, M. (2019). A new organizational chassis for artificial intelligence - exploring organizational readiness factors. In *Proceedings of the 27th European Conference on Information Systems (ECIS), Stockholm & Uppsala, Sweden, June 8–14* .
21. Rahwan, I., Cebrian, M., Obradovich, N., Bongard, J., Bonnefon, J., Breazeal, C., Crandall, J., Christakis, N., Couzin, I., Jackson, M., Jennings, N., Kamar, E., Kloumann, I., Larochelle, H., Lazer, D., McElreath, R., Mislove, A., Parkes, D., Pentland, A., Wellman, M., et al. (2019). Machine behaviour. *Nature, 568*(7753), 477–486.
22. Schlegel, D., Schuler, K., & Westenberger, J. (2023). Failure factors of AI projects: Results from expert interviews. *International Journal of Information Systems and Project Management*.
23. Schulte-Althoff, M., Fürstenau, D., & Lee, G. M. (2021). A scaling perspective on AI startups. In *54th Hawaii International Conference on System Sciences (HICSS-54)*.
24. Sirmon, D., Hitt, M., & Duane Ireland, R. (2007). Managing firm resources in dynamic environments to create value: Looking inside the black box. *Article of Management Review, 32*(1), 273–292.
25. Thomasian. (2022). Storage technologies and their data. In *Storage systems: Organization, performance, coding, reliability, and their data processing*.
26. Weber, M., Beutter, M., Weking, J., Böhm, M., & Krcmar, H. (2022). AI startup business models. *Springer Link, Business & Information Systems Engineering, Business & Information Systems Engineering, 64*, 91–109.
27. West. (2017). *Scale: The universal laws of growth, innovation, sustainability, and the pace of life in organisms, cities, economies, and companies*. Penguin Press.
28. Yu, H., Zhang, R., & Kim, C. (2023). Intelligent analysis system of college students' employment and entrepreneurship situation: Big data and artificial intelligence-driven approach. *Computers and Electrical Engineering, 110*, Article 108823.

29. Zebhauser, J., Rothe, H., & Sundermeier, J. (2023). Scaling AI ventures: How to navigate tensions between automation and augmentation. In *Proceedings of the 56th Hawaii International Conference on System Sciences*.

Understanding Similarities and Differences of Digital Health Platforms: Towards a Taxonomy

Finn Schubert, Jan Maschewski, and Paul Drews

Abstract The increasing importance of Digital Health Platforms (DHPs) necessitates the development of a systematic approach to their categorisation and evaluation in order to optimise the integration of DHPs into the healthcare system. The paper develops a taxonomy for DHPs comprising 19 dimensions along the four meta-characteristics Legal and Economic Aspects, Technology and Standards. By applying the taxonomy to the Apple Health platform, we demonstrate its practicability and potential to identify platform-specific characteristics, which can help with strategic positioning within the healthcare sector. The taxonomy also helps managers and developers to identify DHP's characteristics and act according to needs. Further research opportunities exist in adapting and extending the taxonomy to account for evolving trends and innovations in the field.

1 Introduction

The digital transformation of the healthcare sector presents significant challenges and opportunities. Digital Health Platforms (DHPs) play a central role in this transition by enhancing the integration and efficiency of healthcare delivery [16]. DHPs are complex digital systems that extend beyond simple health apps to create integrated ecosystems by connecting multiple sides (e.g. patients, physicians and developers) through code. The market for digital health solutions, including telemedicine and mobile health (mHealth), is projected to exceed $650 billion by 2025 [51]. The COVID-19 pandemic has further underscored the importance of DHPs, with the telemedicine market expected to grow to $280 billion by 2025 [51].

F. Schubert · J. Maschewski (✉) · P. Drews
Institute of Information Systems, Leuphana University, Lüneburg, Germany
e-mail: jan.maschewski@leuphana.de

P. Drews
e-mail: paul.drews@leuphana.de

C. M. Flath et al. (eds.), *Shaping the Digital Future Through Innovation and Practice*,
Lecture Notes in Information Systems and Organisation 85,
https://doi.org/10.1007/978-3-032-08489-7_23

Current research highlights the need for detailed analysis and categorization of digital health platforms (DHPs) [17, 18]. Meister et al. [34] underscore the importance of a comprehensive taxonomy to fully leverage digitalization in healthcare. The absence of such a taxonomy creates challenges in evaluating DHPs, hindering comparison and generalization of research findings [12, 14, 25, 52]. Therefore, a systematic taxonomy is essential to consolidate existing knowledge about DHPs, guide their design, assure external and internal fit, and assess risks, patterns, and characteristics [48, 54]. A DHP taxonomy is essential for improving clarity, comparison, integration, compliance, market understanding, patient care, and research within the rapidly evolving field of digital health. In light of these considerations, our study aims to address the following research question:

> How does a comprehensive taxonomy of DHPs look like that enhances DHP cate-gorization, evaluation, and integration within the healthcare system?

This question will guide the development of a taxonomy that captures the diverse dimensions of DHPs. We develop the taxonomy following the taxonomy development method by [37]. The derived taxonomy encompasses 19 dimensions along four meta-characteristics. Our taxonomy provides a conceptual framework for better understanding DHPs and facilitating future research and theorizing regarding DHPs by establishing comparability among DHPs thereby enhancing their effective utilization.

2 Research Background

Digital platforms (DPs) represent a complex phenomenon that cannot be fully captured by a single definition due to their diverse functions and manifestations [26, 50]. According to [50], they are best understood as software-based systems built upon a modular technological architecture. This architecture facilitates the coordination of external actors within an ecosystem, who may either drive innovation or compete with each other. As central hubs, DPs connect businesses or individuals to enhance the exchange of complementary services and products. From a service perspective, DPs act as bridges, facilitating interaction between different user groups such as providers and consumers. From a technological perspective, they are seen as tailored technical solutions designed to support and enhance digital interactions and exchange of digital information. Additionally, an ecosystems perspective views DPs as expansive digital ecosystems where numerous actors interact and cooperate to collectively create and share value.

The field of digital health encompasses the use of information and communication technologies within the healthcare sector, aiming to enhance both the treatment of diseases and the promotion of health. This is achieved through the targeted utilisation of digital data, images and other forms of information [57]. The field of digital health is expansive, encompassing various sub-disciplines such as mobile health (mHealth), health informatics, wearable technologies, telemedicine and personalised medicine [2]. Digital health thereby demonstrated the capability to enhance therapeutic results and overall well-being of the population while offering opportunities for more efficient delivery of care [27, 49, 56].

DHPs are digital multi-sided platforms in the healthcare sector that foster coordination, interaction, and exchange among otherwise independent parties [21, 22, 23]. Broadly, DHPs do this via their extensible codebase “that provides core functionality shared by the modules that interoperate with it and the interfaces through which the agents interoperate” [55]. The delivery of healthcare is especially complex as multiple highly specialized actors are involved, which different initiatives around the world found out in their efforts to enhance the sector’s capacity and efficiency, increase service quality or reduce its costs [2, 32]. DHPs need to be differentiated from individual health apps. While health apps often serve as access points to DHPs for end users, DHPs represent an integrative ecosystem that goes far beyond the functionalities of a single app. DHPs connect various actors, applications and services, and are central to digital health.

3 Methodology

Taxonomies are important tools used to “bring order to complex areas” by categorizing dimensions or characteristics and identifying similarities within the topics under study [37]. To develop a comprehensive taxonomy for DHPs, we employed a structured approach integrating a systematic literature review with the taxonomy development framework as proposed by [37].

At the outset we defined three meta-characteristics for selecting and classifying DHPs within the taxonomy. Reflecting our interest in a socio-technological description of DHPs we formed the two characteristics of “Economic Aspects” and “Technology”. We supplemented them with “Legal Aspects” as the healthcare sector is highly regulated. Like [37] observed, it was later in the development process that another meta-characteristic’s (“Standards”) high importance for the healthcare sector and hence for our taxonomy became apparent to us and was added.

As outlined by [37], both subjective and objective criteria were established as ending conditions for the taxonomy development. These included a thorough examination of our sample and ensuring that no new dimensions or characteristics were added in the final iteration (saturation). The ending conditions of the taxonomy were designed to ensure conciseness, robustness, completeness, extendibility, and explanatory power. This was done to guarantee that the taxonomy was subjected to a rigorous review and adjustment process, thus maintaining its applicability and relevance for the systematic evaluation of DHPs [37].

We initiated the review of relevant literature with multiple searches of academic databases using the search strings as outlined in Table 1.

This process initially yielded 331 papers. We first examined the titles and abstracts to filter out what did not meet the inclusion criteria (articles focusing on either DPs, digital health or DHPs). We then reviewed the full texts and discarded those that did

Table 1 Search string for data collection

Search String	Applied Databases
"Digital Platform" OR "Digital Health*" AND ("Taxonomy" OR "legal" OR "compliance" OR "technology" OR "*Management" OR "economic" OR "Business Models" OR "Research Methodology" OR "Health Impact" OR "characteristics" OR "strengths" OR "weaknesses"	PubMed, Journal of Medical Research IEEE, AIS Electronic Library, ScienceDirect, Google Scholar

not meet our follow-up criteria (e.g. articles that lacked detailed information about DHPs, dealt with processes like implementation or development of DHPs or had a very narrow focus [as we thrive to gain a general understanding of DHPs]). To further enrich our literature sample, we conducted a forward and backward search. We also included gray literature, such as practice reports or white papers in our analysis, which supplemented our understanding from a practical perspective. In the end, 61 articles formed the basis of our study.

Throughout the literature search and taxonomy development we adopted both conceptual-to-empirical (C2E) and empirical-to-conceptual (E2C) approaches [37]. This allowed us to utilize deductive and inductive strategies, as described by [37]. Following an E2C analysis of existing DP taxonomies and the limited literature on DHPs, the taxonomy was designed and progressively refined through the C2E approach as outlined in Fig. 1.

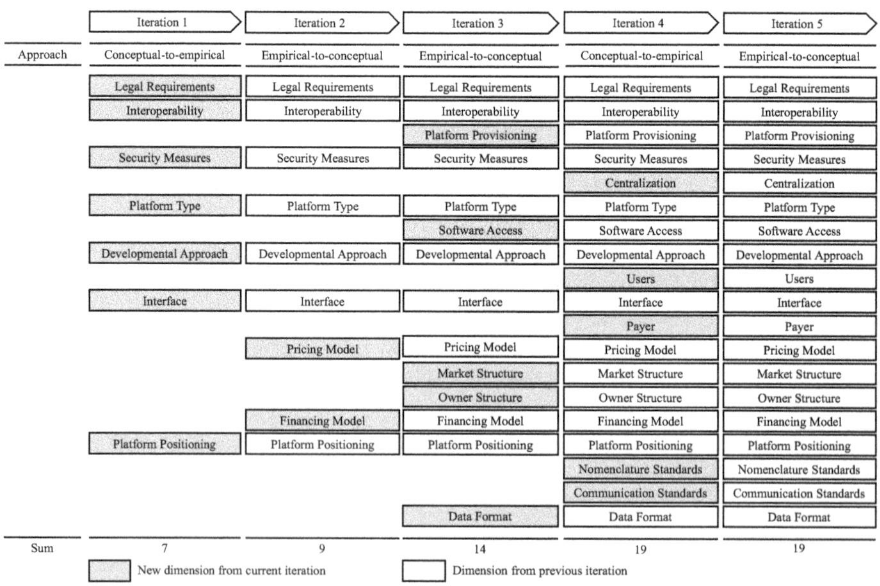

Fig. 1 Development of dimensions for the digital health platform taxonomy (presentation following [41] adjusted for our research).

The subsequent stage involved the demonstration and evaluation of the taxonomy's relevance and efficacy in real-world contexts, with the objective of validating its practicality and usefulness for future applications [37]. We selected Apple Health for this analysis due to its wide adoption, comprehensive integration of various health data sources, its significant impact on the digital health landscape and availability of data.

4 Digital Health Platform Taxonomy

Our DHP taxonomy showcased in Table 2 comprises four meta-characteristics: Legal, Technology, Economic, and Standards. Within these four meta-characteristics, a total of 19 dimensions are included. We classify dimensions as either exclusive (E) or non-exclusive (N), enabling precise analysis by indicating whether individual or multiple attributes can simultaneously apply to a DHP.

4.1 Meta-Characteristic Legal

This meta-characteristic addresses the required security measures DHPs have to comply with for maintaining security, privacy, and operational integrity [13]. It emphasizes the importance of aligning DHP operations with legal standards to ensure compliance with privacy laws that protect sensitive health information. The dimension focuses on two critical areas: legal requirements and interoperability.

The integration of **Legal Requirements** is a legal necessity for the security and privacy of DHPs. Adhering to legal requirements for security practices such as encryption, anonymization, and access control is crucial to ensure the protection of sensitive health data and to comply with especially strict regulatory standards [13, 40, 43]. Depending on the sensitivity of the data, the legislator may impose varying degrees of stringent requirements for data handling. Advanced encryption techniques and strict access permissions protect against data misuse and promote user trust [19, 39, 44].

Interoperability is a key element in the operation of DHPs and is encouraged by regulatory frameworks. The ability of different systems and applications to efficiently exchange data and collaborate is critical to achieving comprehensive healthcare. Open platforms use APIs to facilitate the development of new services and encourage innovation, while closed systems provide a high level of security and continuity through their restrictive measures. The choice of platform architecture must meet both regulatory requirements and the technical and functional needs of DHPs [12, 32, 38].

Table 2 Taxonomy for digital health platforms

Dimensions		Characteristics			E/N
Legal	Legal Requirements	Encryption	Anonymisation	Access control	N
	Interoperability	Open	Closed		E
Technology	Platform Provisioning	Private Cloud	Public Cloud	Hybrid Cloud	N
		On-Premises	On-Device		
	Security Measures	Encryption	Authentification	Physical Access	N
	Centralization	Central	Hybrid	Decentral	E
	Platform Types	Dataplatform	Metaplatform	Marketplace	N
		Horizontally-integrated	Vertically-integrated		
	Software Access	Open-Source-Software	Proprietary Software		E
	Developmental Approach	User-centric	Technology-centric		N
		Institution-centric	Information-centric		
	Users	Professionals	Patients	Insurances	N
		Developers	Researchers		
	Interfaces	Third-Party (API)	Web-based	PC-Client	N
		Mobile	Wearable		
Economic	Payer	Professionals	Patients	Partner / Developer	N
		Insurances	Public		
	Pricing Model	per Use(r)	One-Off	Subscription	N
		Provisions	Advertisement	Data Brokerage	
	Market Structure	First healthcare market	Second healthcare market	Third healthcare market	N
	Owner Structure	Government	Private Company		E
		Non-Governmental Org	Public–Private Partnership		
	Financing Model	Commercial	Public welfare oriented	Hybrid	E
	Platform Positioning	Specialized	Integrative		N
Standards	Nomenclature Standards	SNOMED	LOINC	ICD	N
		CPT	RxNorm		
	Communication Standards	HL7	FHIR	XDS	N
	Data Formats	DICOM	CCD	CDA	N

4.2 Meta-Characteristic Technology

The Technology meta-characteristic employs a critical evaluation of the technological configuration that is essential to DHPs. It emphasizes key components and their functional characteristics, thereby illuminating the technological foundations that shape the efficiency and flexibility of digital solutions.

Platform Provisioning is a crucial aspect of DP structure, as highlighted in different contexts (e.g. [11, 43]. It covers configurations such as private, public, and hybrid clouds, as well as on-premises setups. Private clouds provide enhanced control and security, which is vital for maintaining data privacy [31, 53]. Although public clouds are cost-effective and scalable, they present inherent security risks [29, 31]. Hybrid clouds combine the benefits of both, offering flexi-ble data management ideal for digital health [29, 31]. On-premises configurations ensure maximal data control [20, 46, 58], and on-device models reduce data breach risks by processing data locally on user devices.

The technical **Security Measures** dimension encompasses encryption, authentication, and physical access controls—key mechanisms to protect data integrity and confidentiality. As highlighted by [43], encryption secures data confidentiality by restricting access to unauthorized users. Authentication verifies identities to secure access [30]. Physical access control limits access to essential infrastructure to authorized personnel only [43]. These measures collectively play a vital role in mitigating data breaches and boosting trust in digital infrastructures, which must continually adapt to evolving cyber threats.

The **Centralization** dimension categorizes DHPs into centralized, decentralized, and hybrid control structures, as detailed by [24] and the [57]. Centralized DHPs centralize processes on the platform, utilizing external applications as front-end interfaces [24, 57]. Decentralized DHP structures distribute processes and responsibilities while enhancing data management flexibility [24, 57]. Hybrid models integrate both centralized and decentralized elements, thereby improving both flexibility and functionality [57].

The **Platform Types** dimension distinguishes data platforms, which analyze large datasets to enhance diagnosis and treatment; horizontally integrated platforms, which offer comprehensive care in specific medical domains; vertically integrated platforms, which connect various stages of healthcare for a holistic approach; meta-platforms, which combine horizontal and vertical elements to form extensive healthcare net-works; and marketplace platforms, which facilitate the commerce of healthcare products and services, furthering healthcare digitization [17, 18].

The **Software Access** dimension examines the rights and permissions granted to users and stakeholders to engage with, utilize, or modify DHPs. For instance, open-source software permits direct interaction with the software code, fostering innovation and customization [1]. Conversely, proprietary software restricts access to its source code to the owning company, thereby providing controlled environments and professional support strengthening operational security [42].

Recent advances in IS in healthcare are characterized by a multidimensional **Developmental Approach** that incorporates various academic perspectives. [43] emphasize the integration of technological infrastructure and user information requirements for comprehensive DP designs. Aanstad et al. [2] explore the integration of scalable and interoperable information infrastructures in healthcare, underscoring the need for systems that adapt to varying environmental demands. Maschewski and Lemmer [33] advocate for a patient-centric framework that prioritizes patient enablement, empowerment, and engagement, reinforcing the user-centric dimension.

DHPs serve a diverse range of **Users**, unique to the healthcare sector and each with individual needs, preferences, and roles [2, 33]. By addressing the needs, preferences and roles of each group, DHPs empower individuals and organizations to collaborate, communicate, and leverage technology to enhance health outcomes and promote well-being across the continuum of care [27, 32, 49].

DHPs utilize a variety of **Interfaces** to facilitate interaction, data exchange, and engagement between users, systems, and devices [52, 57]. These interfaces are designed to accommodate a wide range of needs, prefer-ences, and technical requirements, ensuring seamless access to healthcare services and information. Interfaces play a pivotal role in extending the reach, accessibility, and functionality of DHPs, empowering its users [5257].

4.3 Meta-Characteristic Economic

In the Economic meta-characteristic of DHPs, the economic setup is illuminated in order to shed light on the operational and strategic dynamics of DHPs.

The **Payer** dimension illuminates the various motivations that compel stakeholders to pay for DHPs. Due to the distinctive nature of the healthcare sector, a multitude of actors may be inclined or compelled to bear a portion of the cost for developing or running a DHP [2, 22]. Depending on the general configuration of the DHP, patients are frequently subsidized in order to facilitate adoption [2, 54].

The **Pricing Model** dimension reveals how DHPs employ pricing models to meet the needs and preferences of the platform operator and the platform's strategic positioning, ensuring compliance with applicable laws [18, 22, 52]. The pricing models vary in terms of cost structure, payment flexibility, and value proposition [54]. A platform may employ multiple pricing strategies concurrently, contingent on the targeted payer. Also factors such as user demographics, use cases, payer structure, and desired outcomes within the highly regulated healthcare sector are reflected [54, 22, 18].

The dimension **Market Structure** allows for the classification of DHPs into three distinct healthcare markets: traditional medical treatment systems (often paid for by insurances), preventive care markets (often paid for by patients themselves), and shared economy models enhancing community health networks. This classification helps elucidate the roles DHPs play in healthcare delivery and wellfare, with each market presenting unique challenges and opportunities for system innovation and efficiency [18]. DHPs may engage in one or multiple of these markets depending on the individual users condition. For instance, diet tracking DHPs functions might be part of health prevention (second healthcare market) or treatment (first healthcare market).

Owner Structure examines the influence of different ownership forms on DHPs' strategic direction, operational priorities, and regulatory compliance. Ownership can range from government entities ensuring transparency and strict regulation to private companies potentially prioritizing profits. In addition, non-governmental organizations (NGOs) and public–private partnerships (PPPs) offer models that blend public oversight with private sector efficiency, aligning closely with public health objectives [3, 36, 47].

The **Financing Model** dimension examines financial frameworks that enable DHPs to sustain and scale operations. Commercial models prioritize profitability, focusing on innovation and efficiency to remain competitive [35, 40]. Public welfare-oriented models, supported by nonprofit organizations or public funding and using open-source technologies, emphasize accessibility and quality of healthcare, prioritizing societal benefits over financial returns [40]. Hybrid models combine free basic services with premium features, promoting scalability and user engagement by allowing users to test services before committing financially [15, 40].

The **Platform Positioning** dimension determines the architectural design and functionality of DHPs within the healthcare ecosystem. Specialized DHPs are designed to focus on specific services or functions. As a result, they require strong integration with other systems to address interoperability and sustainability challenges [43]. Integrative DHPs support a centralized system with interoperable interfaces and open standards. This enables effective communication and collaboration across various healthcare services, fostering a cohesive healthcare environment [43].

4.4 Meta-Characteristic Standards

In the evolving landscape of digital healthcare, standards play a crucial role in ensuring interoperability, data integrity, and patient safety. These standards are guidelines or frameworks that define unique ways how data in the healthcare sector is structured, communicated, and utilized across various actors [45].

Nomenclature Standards: primarily focus on establishing uniformity in the terminology used within digital health systems. This includes the naming conventions for medical conditions procedures, medications, and other health-related entities. By adhering to standardized nomenclature, DHPs can communicate effectively with stakeholders and accurately interpret and exchange information. Nomenclature standards provide comprehensive sets of codes and terms for various clinical concepts [28, 45, 57].

Communication Standards address the protocols and formats used for exchanging health information between different systems. These standards ensure seamless interoperability and data exchange, regardless of the underlying technology or platforms involved. Communication standards define messaging and interface specifications for health data exchange and facilitate the transfer of clinical and administrative information between healthcare applications, electronic health records (EHRs), and other health IT systems [28, 45, 57].

Data Formats delineate the specific categories and formats of health data that are standardized for collection, storage, and transmission. For instance, DICOM standardizes the formats for medical imaging data or CCD and CDA specify the structure and content of clinical summaries and documents. These standards ensure consistency and accuracy in capturing different types of clinical and administrative information. They standardize the formats enabling interoperability and compatibility among various imaging devices and systems. Additionally, they specify the structure and content of clinical summaries and documents, facilitating the exchange of patient information across different care settings [28, 45, 57].

4.5 Taxonomy Application

To demonstrate the taxonomy's applicability, we evaluated Apple Health as a representative DHP. The results in Table 3 show how the taxonomy systematically categorizes DHPs. This structured analysis aids researchers in comparative studies and best practices. For management, it highlights the platform's uniqueness, guiding strategic decisions and fostering innovation.

Legal. Apple Health's cybersecurity is reinforced by end-to-end encryption and controls like Passcode, Touch ID, and Face ID, ensuring that data is accessible only on trusted devices and parties [6]. Apple is unable to access encrypted data without user consent, and Differential Privacy further anonymizes user data (Hargitai et al., 2018). Interoperability is maintained through a closed platform model, where data sharing with third-party apps requires explicit user consent and reasoning for access requests [6, 12].

Technology. Apple Health emphasizes on-device processing to handle health data locally and protect user privacy [6]. The platform's security measures demonstrate its commitment to encryption, authentication, and physical access controls. HealthKit data is encrypted on-device and end-to-end for users with iOS 12 or later, and access to the Health app requires two-factor authentication and a passcode, ensuring that only authorized users can access the data. Health and fitness data is encrypted and only accessible with a passcode, ensuring user control and security [6]. Apple Health's hybrid nature allows for centralized data collection and processing on Apple devices and integration with external data sources, while maintaining full user control over their data [6, 9]. As a data platform, Apple Health collects and processes health data from Apple devices and authorized third-party applications. As a horizontal integration platform, it consolidates disparate sources of health data. As a meta-platform, it shares data with healthcare providers to create a comprehensive network of health information and services [8]. The software access for Apple Health is proprietary [6]. Apple Health is both user-centric and technology-centric, prioritizing patient empowerment and engagement while leveraging advanced technologies such

Table 3 Taxonomy application apple health

Dimensions		Characteristics			E/N
Legal	Legal Requirements	**Encryption**	**Anonymisation**	**Access control**	N
	Interoperability	Open	**Closed**		E
Technology	Platform Provisioning	Private Cloud	Public Cloud	Hybrid Cloud	N
		On-Premises	**On-Device**		
	Security Measures	**Encryption**	**Authentification**	**Physical Access**	N
	Centralization	Central	**Hybrid**	Decentral	E
	Platform Types	**Dataplatform**	**Metaplatform**	Marketplace	N
		Horizontally-integrated	Vertically-integrated		
	Software Access	Open-Source-Software	**Proprietary Software**		E
	Developmental Approach	**User-centric**	**Technology-centric**		N
		Institution-centric	Information-centric		
	Users	Professionals	**Patients**	Insurances	N
		Developers	Researchers		
	Interfaces	**Third-Party (API)**	Web-based	PC-Client	N
		Mobile	Wearable		
Economic	Payer	Professionals	**Patients**	**Partner / Developer**	N
		Insusrances	Public		
	Pricing Model	per Use(r)	One-Off	Subscription	N
		Provisions	Advertisement	Data Brokerage	
	Market Structure	First healthcare market	**Second healthcare market**	Third healthcare market	N
	Owner Structure	Government	**Private Company**		E
		Non-Governmental Org	Public–Private Partnership		
	Financing Model	**Commercial**	Public welfare oriented	Hybrid	E
	Platform Positioning	**Specialized**	**Integrative**		N
Standards	Nomenclature Standards	SNOMED	**LOINC**	ICD	N
		CPT	**RxNorm**		
	Communication Standards	HL7	**FHIR**	XDS	N
	Data Formats	**DICOM**	**CCD**	CDA	N

as end-to-end encryption and on-device processing. This dual focus enhances the user experience and ensures data security [6, 9]. It offers the Health SDK as an API and a mobile interface in the Health App [6, 9].

Economic. Apple Health is funded by patients who pay for the devices and by developers who pay to publish apps linked to Apple Health [6, 9]. It is part of the second healthcare market, focused on individual wellness and prevention, and illustrates how DHPs are disrupting traditional market structures. The integration of external data sources, such as Adidas Running, underscores this dynamic [6, 9]. Apple Health is a private company [9] and uses a provision-based pricing model. It supports the development of third-party apps through the Apple Developer Program, charges fees to deploy apps in the App Store, and benefits from an extensive ecosystem [5, 7]. Apple Health's business strategy promotes a dynamic and diverse offering of apps while supporting the distribution of Apple devices optimized for the use of these apps [5, 7]. Apple Health represents a specialized platform with significant integrative capabilities, combining advanced health monitoring tools with comprehensive data aggregation capabilities [6].

Standards. Apple Health utilizes standardized nomenclature systems to ensure that data recorded and shared across different devices and health systems is consistent and interpretable. One of the key nomenclature systems used is the LOINC [10]. Additionally, for medication, Apple HealthKit supports coding systems like RxNorm, which provides normalized names for clinical drugs and is commonly used in pharmacy management and drug interaction software [10]. Apple Health primarily uses HealthKit, its proprietary framework, to manage the health data on iOS devices. HealthKit provides a secure container for storing health-related information and offers an API for developers to access and interact with that data. For interoperability with external health systems and EHRs, Apple supports the FHIR standard [4].

5 Discussion, Limitations, and Future Research

Our study aimed to address the lack of a systematic taxonomy for understanding DHPs, which have gained significant attention but lack a comprehensive classification framework. Existing research focuses on specific requirements or architectural elements without a holistic view. This limitation hinders the comparability of DHPs and the ability to draw broader conceptual insights. To address this we developed a taxonomy following [37] method. By validating the taxonomy with the example of Apple Health we prove to that our work helps to enhance DHP categorization and evaluation, which in turn can support integrative efforts with the healthcare system.

Our taxonomy comprises four meta-characteristics and 19 related dimensions, providing a structured approach to categorizing DHPs. Our work contributes to both academic and practical fields by providing a detailed classification scheme that enhances understanding of the multifaceted nature of DHPs. The taxonomy allows researchers to better capture the unique characteristics of DHPs, supporting further theoretical developments and the design of more effective platforms. For practitioners, this taxonomy serves as a valuable tool for analyzing and distinguishing between different DHPs, facilitating platform development and optimization, promoting sustainable health improvements, and enhancing both patient satisfaction and therapeutic outcome.

Despite its contributions, this study has its limitations. First, the static nature of a taxonomy and the rapidly evolving field of digital health mean that we only provide a snapshot of the current state of DHPs. This limitation means that we cannot guarantee the completeness of the dimensions and characteristics identified. Second, we did not explore in detail the potential interrelationships between individual characteristics and dimensions. Third, some dimensions, such as cybersecurity, may have limited utility in distinguishing different types of DHPs, as robust cybersecurity measures are a universal requirement for all platforms. Nevertheless, we included this dimension to highlight its critical importance and the need for detailed future research on cybersecurity implementations to improve differentiation. Although we followed established guidelines and used both E2C and C2E approaches, additional empirical validation is encouraged to verify the robustness of the taxonomy.

Future research should focus on identifying specific archetypes of DHPs to allow for a more nuanced classification. By examining these archetypes, researchers could explore whether certain types of DHPs are more effective than others in certain setting, leading to the derivation of specific design principles for DHPs. In addition, further exploration of the relationships between dimensions and their characteristics may provide deeper insights into the design and performance of DHPs, contributing to the continuous improvement of DHPs. In conclusion, while our taxonomy provides a structured and comprehensive framework for understanding DHPs, ongoing research and empirical validation are essential to adapt and refine our taxonomy in response to the evolving digital health landscape.

References

1. Aalami, O., Hittle, M., Ravi, V., Griffin, A., Schmiedmayer, P., Shenoy, V., Gutierrez, S., & Venook, R. (2023). CardinalKit: Open-source standards-based, interoperable mobile development platform to help translate the promise of digital health. *JAMIA Open, 6*(3). https://doi.org/10.1093/jamiaopen/ooad044
2. Aanestad, M., Grisot, M., Hanseth, O., & Vassilakopoulou, P. (2017). Information infrastructures within European health care. In *Computers in health care*. https://doi.org/10.1007/978-3-319-51020-0
3. Anttiroiko, A.-V., Valkama, P., & Bailey, S. J. (2014). Smart cities in the new service economy: Building platforms for smart services. *AI & SOCIETY, 29*(3), 323–334. https://doi.org/10.1007/s00146-013-0464-0
4. Apple Inc. (2024e). *Empower your patients with their health data*. https://www.apple.com/healthcare/health-records/
5. Apple Inc. (2020). *Apple announces App Store Small Business Program*. https://www.apple.com/newsroom/2020/11/apple-announces-app-store-small-business-program/
6. Apple Inc. (2023). *Health privacy overview—Whitepaper*. https://www.apple.com/ios/health/pdf/Health_Privacy_White_Paper_May_2023.pdf

7. Apple Inc. (2024a). *Choosing a membership*. https://developer.apple.com/support/compare-memberships/
8. Apple Inc. (2024b). *Einführung zu Gesundheitsdaten auf dem iPhone*. https://support.apple.com/de-de/guide/iphone/iphbb8259c61/ios
9. Apple Inc. (2024c). *Gesundheitsdaten auf dem iPhone, iPad oder der Apple Watch* verwal-ten. https://support.apple.com/de-at/108779
10. Apple Inc. (2024d). *The future of healthcare is in your hands*. https://www.apple.com/healthcare/
11. Arnold, L., Jöhnk, J., Vogt, F., & Urbach, N. (2022). IIoT platforms' architectural features—A taxonomy and five prevalent archetypes. *Electronic Markets, 32*(2), 927–944. https://doi.org/10.1007/s12525-021-00520-0
12. Asadullah, A., Faik, I., & Kankanhalli, A. (2018). *Digital platforms: A review and future directions*. https://aisel.aisnet.org/pacis2018/248/
13. Biasin, E., Yaşar, B., & Kamenjašević, E. (2023). New cybersecurity requirements for medical devices in the EU: The forthcoming European Health Data Space, Data Act, and Artificial Intelligence Act. *Law, Technology and Humans, 5*(2), 43–58. https://doi.org/10.5204/lthj.3068
14. Blaschke, M., Haki, K., Aier, S., & Winter, R. (2019). *Taxonomy of digital platforms: A platform architecture perspective*. https://aisel.aisnet.org/cgi/viewcontent.cgi?article=1220&context=wi2019
15. Bruhn, M., & Hadwich, K. (2018). Service Business Development—Entwicklung und Durchsetzung serviceorientierter Geschäftsmodelle. In *Springer Fachmedien Wiesbaden GmbH* (pp. 3–37). Springer Fachmedien Wiesbaden. https://doi.org/10.1007/978-3-658-22424-0_1
16. Bundesministerium für Gesundheit. (2023). *Digitalisierung im Gesundheitswesen*. https://www.bundesgesundheitsministerium.de/themen/digitalisierung/digitalisierung-im-gesundheitswesen.html
17. Choueiri, P., Hosseini, M., Kaltenbach, T., Kleipass, U., Neumann, K., & Rong, O. (2020). *Future of health 2 | The rise of healthcare platforms*.
18. Chrobok, T. (2023). Design von Digital-Health-Geschäftsmodellen – Vorgehensweise, Herausforderungen und Erfolgsfaktoren. In *Springer Fachmedien Wiesbaden* (pp. 221–253). Springer Fachmedien Wiesbaden. https://doi.org/10.1007/978-3-658-35991-1_1
19. De Oliveira, M. T., Amorim, L. H., Marquering, H., Zwinderman, A. H., & Olabarriaga, S. D. (2022). Perceptions of a secure cloud-based solution for data sharing during Acute Stroke care: Qualitative interview study. *JMIR Formative Research, 6*(12). https://doi.org/10.2196/40061
20. Fisher, C. (2018). Cloud versus on-premise computing. *American Journal of Industrial and Business Management, 8*(9), 1991–2006. https://doi.org/10.4236/ajibm.2018.89133
21. Frishammar, J., Essén, A., Bergström, F., & Ekman, T. (2023). Digital health platforms for the elderly? Key adoption and usage barriers and ways to address them. *Technological Forecasting and Social Change, 189*. https://doi.org/10.1016/j.techfore.2023.122319
22. Fürstenau, D., Auschra, C., Klein, S., & Gersch, M. (2019). A process perspective on platform design and management: Evidence from a digital platform in health care. *Electronic Markets, 29*(4), 581–596. https://doi.org/10.1007/s12525-018-0323-4
23. Gawer, A., & Cusumano, M. A. (2013). Industry platforms and ecosystem innovation. *The Journal of Product Innovation Management, 31*(3), 417–433. https://doi.org/10.1111/jpim.12105
24. Gelhaar, J., Groß, T., & Otto, B. (2021). *A taxonomy for data ecosystems*. 53rd Hawaii International Conference on System Sciences (HICCS). https://hdl.handle.net/10125/71359
25. Gregor. (2006). The nature of theory in information systems. *MIS Quarterly, 30*(3), 611–642. https://doi.org/10.2307/25148742
26. Hein, A., Schreieck, M., Riasanow, T., Setzke, D. S., Wiesche, M., Böhm, M., & Krcmar, H. (2019). *Digital platform ecosystems. EM, 30*(1), 87–98. https://doi.org/10.1007/s12525-019-00377-4
27. Hibbard, J. H., & Greene, J. (2013). What the evidence shows about patient activation: Better health outcomes and care experiences; fewer data on costs. *Health Affairs, 32*(2), 207–214. https://doi.org/10.1377/hlthaff.2012.1061

28. ISO. (2024). *Standards by ISO/TC 215 health informatics*. https://www.iso.org/committee/54960/x/catalogue/p/1/u/0/w/0/d/0
29. Knapcikova, L., Peraković, D., Perisa, M., & Balog, M. (2022). Sustainable Management of manufacturing systems in industry 4.0. *EAI/Springer Innovations in Communication and Computing*. https://doi.org/10.1007/978-3-030-90462-3
30. Kwon, J., & Johnson, M. E. (2018). Meaningful healthcare security: Does meaningful-use attestation improve information security performance? *MIS Quarterly: Management Information Systems, 42*(4), 1043–1067. https://misq.org/meaningful-healthcare-security-does-meaningful-use attestation-improve-information-security-performance.htm
31. Mahmoudi, C. (2017). Cloud and mobile cloud architecture, security and safety. In *Hand-book of system safety and security: Cyber risk and risk management, cyber security, threat analysis, functional safety, software systems, and cyber physical systems* (pp. 199–223). Elsevier Inc. https://doi.org/10.1016/B978-0-12-803773-7.00010-3
32. Malm-Nicolaisen, K., Pedersen, R., & Fagerlund, A. J. (2019). Open or closed: A project proposal for investigating two different EHR platform approaches. In *Studies in Health Technology and Informatics, 265*, 207–212. IOS Press. https://doi.org/10.3233/SHTI190165
33. Maschewski, J., & Lemmer, K. (n.d.). *Patient centricity in IS healthcare—A framework proposing enablement, empowerment, and engagement of patients as individual IS users*. AIS Electronic Library (AISeL). https://aisel.aisnet.org/wi2023/79
34. Meister, S., Becker, S., Leppert, F., & Drop, L. (2017). Digital Health, Mobile Health und Co. – Wertschöpfung durch Digitalisierung und Datenverarbeitung. In *Springer Gabler* (pp. 185–212). Springer Fachmedien Wiesbaden. https://doi.org/10.1007/978-3-658-12258-4_13
35. Mettler, T., & Eurich, M. (2012). A "design-pattern"-based approach for analyzing e-health business models. *Health Policy and Technology, 1*(2), 77–85. https://doi.org/10.1016/j.hlpt.2012.04.005
36. Mineraud, J., Mazhelis, O., Su, X., & Tarkoma, S. (2016). *A gap analysis of Internet-of-Things platforms*. Computer Communications.
37. Nickerson, R. C., Varshney, U., & Muntermann, J. (2013). A method for taxonomy development and its application in information systems. *European Journal of Information Systems, 22*(3), 336–359. https://doi.org/10.1057/ejis.2012.26
38. Nikayin, F., & de Reuver, M. (2012). *Governance of smart living service platforms: state-of-the-art and the need for collective action.*
39. Oh, S. R., Seo, Y. D., Lee, E., & Kim, Y. G. (2021). A comprehensive survey on security and privacy for electronic health data. *International Journal of Environmental Research and Public Health, 18*(18). MDPI. https://doi.org/10.3390/ijerph18189668
40. Rasche, C., & Raab, E. (2023). Digitale Gesundheitsplattformen. Strategien – Geschäftsmodelle – Entwicklungslinien. In *Springer Fachmedien Wiesbaden* (pp. 73–97). Springer Fachmedien Wiesbaden. https://doi.org/10.1007/978-3-658-35991-1_5
41. Remane, G., Nickerson, R. C., Hanelt, A., Tesch, J. F., & Kolbe, L. M. (2016, 14.12). *A taxonomy of carsharing business models*. ICIS Proceedings 2016. International Conference on Information Systems, Dublin, Ireland. https://aisel.aisnet.org/icis2016/Crowdsourcing/Presentations/18
42. Reynolds, C. J., & Wyatt, J. C. (2011). Open source, open standards, and health care information systems. *Journal of Medical Internet Research, 13*(1). JMIR Publications Inc. https://doi.org/10.2196/jmir.1521
43. Richter, K., Zimmer, M. P., & Lemmer, K. (2023). *Decoding the landscape of smart city platforms: A taxonomy approach*. https://aisel.aisnet.org/wi2023/90
44. Rodrigues, J. J. P. C., de La Torre, I., Fernández, G., & López-Coronado, M. (2013). Analysis of the security and privacy requirements of cloud-based electronic health records systems. *Journal of Medical Internet Research, 15*(8). https://doi.org/10.2196/jmir.2494
45. Roehrs, A., da Costa, C. A., da Rosa Righi, R., & De Oliveira, K. S. F. (2017). Personal health records: A systematic literature review. In *Journal of Medical Internet Research, 19*(1). JMIR Publications Inc. https://doi.org/10.2196/jmir.5876

46. Saa, P., Moscoso-Zea, O., & Luján-Mora, S. (2017). *Data security issues in cloud-based software-as-a-service ERP Andrés Cueva Costales DGPCTI Public Company Yachay Quito, Ecuador*.
47. Santana, E. F. Z., Chaves, A. P., Gerosa, M. A., Kon, F., & Milojicic, D. (2018). Software platforms for smart cities: concepts, requirements, challenges, and a unified reference architecture. *ACM Computing Surveys, 50*(6), 1–37. https://doi.org/10.1145/3124391
48. Schermuly, L., Schreieck, M., Wiesche, M., & Krcmar, H. (2019). *Developing an industrial IoT platform—Trade-off between horizontal and vertical approaches.*
49. Shortell, S. M., Poon, B. Y., Ramsay, P. P., Rodriguez, H. P., Ivey, S. L., Huber, T., Rich, J., & Summerfelt, T. (2017). A multilevel analysis of patient engagement and patient-reported outcomes in primary care practices of accountable care organizations. *Journal of General Internal Medicine, 32*(6), 640–647. https://doi.org/10.1007/s11606-016-3980-z
50. Sidorenko, E. L. (2022). Definition of "digital platforms." In *The platform economy: Designing a supranational legal framework* (pp. 77–92). Springer Singapore. https://doi.org/10.1007/978-981-19-3242-7_6
51. Statista. (2024). *Digital health—Statistics & facts*. https://www.statista.com/topics/2409/digital-health/#topicOverview/
52. Staub, N., Haki, K., Aier, S., & Winter, R. (2021). *Taxonomy of digital platforms: A business model perspective*. Proceedings of the 54th Hawaii International Conference on System Sciences.
53. Stephanie, L., & Sharma, R. S. (2020). Digital health eco-systems: An epochal review of practice-oriented research. *International Journal of Information Management, 53*,. https://doi.org/10.1016/j.ijinfomgt.2019.10.017
54. Tiwana, A. (2014). Platform governance. In *Elsevier eBooks* (pp. 117–151). https://doi.org/10.1016/b978-0-12-408066-9.00006-0
55. Tiwana, A., Konsynski, B.R., & Bush, A.A. (2010). *Platform evolution: Coevolution of platform architecture, governance, and environmental dynamics*.
56. U.S. Food & Drug Administration. (2020). *What is digital health?* https://www.fda.gov/medical-devices/digital-health-center-excellence/what-digital-health
57. WHO & ITO. (2020). *Digital health platform handbook: Building a digital information infrastructure (infostructure) for health*. World Health Organization. https://iris.who.int/handle/10665/337449. Lizenz: CC BY-NC-SA 3.0 IGO
58. Winkler, T. J., & Brown, C. v. (2013). Horizontal allocation of decision rights for on-premise applications and software-as-a-service. *Journal of Management Information Systems, 30*(3), 13–48. https://doi.org/10.2753/MIS0742-1222300302

AI Act Workshop

Assuring EU AI Act Compliance and Adversarial Robustness of LLMs

Tomas Bueno Momcilovic, Beat Buesser, Giulio Zizzo, Mark Purcell, and Dian Balta

Abstract Large language models are prone to misuse and vulnerable to security threats, raising significant safety and security concerns. The European Union's Artificial Intelligence Act seeks to enforce AI robustness in certain contexts, but faces implementation challenges due to the lack of standards, complexity of LLMs and emerging security vulnerabilities. Our research introduces a framework using ontologies, assurance cases, and factsheets to support engineers and stakeholders in understanding and documenting AI system compliance and security regarding adversarial robustness. This approach aims to ensure that LLMs adhere to regulatory standards and are equipped to counter potential threats.

24.1 Introduction

Large language models (LLMs) have shown great results in generating content from the data they were trained or fine-tuned on, when prompted in natural language [1]. However, recent work shows that training, fine-tuning, prompting and generating can be vulnerable to malicious or accidental misuse [2], as the models themselves are brittle to adversarial attacks [3]. By exploiting unknown properties of LLMs, attacks

T. Bueno Momcilovic (✉) · D. Balta
fortiss GmbH Research Institute, Munich, Germany
e-mail: momcilovic@fortiss.org

D. Balta
e-mail: balta@fortiss.org

B. Buesser
IBM Research Europe, Zurich, Switzerland
e-mail: beat.buesser@ibm.com

G. Zizzo · M. Purcell
IBM Research Europe, Dublin, Ireland
e-mail: giulio.zizzo2@ibm.com

M. Purcell
e-mail: markpurcell@ie.ibm.com

C. M. Flath et al. (eds.), *Shaping the Digital Future Through Innovation and Practice*, Lecture Notes in Information Systems and Organisation 85,
https://doi.org/10.1007/978-3-032-08489-7_24

can negatively impact the privacy and fundamental rights of EU citizens by leaking information or generating toxic content [4]. In combination with advanced capabilities (e.g., robotic control; [5]), applications (e.g., autonomous decision-making; [6]) or contexts (e.g., medical diagnosis; [7]), compromised LLMs can also have safety implications.

The recently adopted EU Artificial Intelligence Act (further: EUAIA; [8]) aims to mitigate the negative impact of "high-risk" AI systems by imposing demands on providers and deployers in designated contexts. Two foreseeable issues will make implementation of the Act considerably challenging if such systems have LLM components. First, the standards that operationalize the legal language into technical requirements are yet to be established, and rapid pace of development could render some parts obsolete. Second, the architecture of an LLM is substantially more dynamic, opaque and extensible than that of many predecessor models. Their performance, generality and trainable "harmlessness" are relatively novel breakthroughs that are not yet well-understood and brittle to even small changes. Thus, ensuring security with stable, proactive and mature practices is difficult.

In this work-in-progress, we investigate the problem and potential resolution for fulfilling the LLM- and robustness-relevant duties in EUAIA. We argue that to have justifiable confidence that LLMs are compliant and trustworthy, engineers need to continuously integrate, monitor, patch and communicate about the implemented defenses against adversarial attacks. We introduce a framework for knowledge representation and reasoning about the provenance, necessity and sufficiency of demands and defenses. Using ontologies, assurance cases and factsheets, the framework is intended to assist engineers and legal stakeholders in establishing a complete and dynamic picture of the safety, security and compliance of the LLM.

24.2 Background

The EUAIA [8] is a law covering particular aspects of AI usage in the EU, which was proposed in April 2021 and adopted in March 2024.[1] It is expected to enter into force in 2026, whereby technical standards and guidelines that interpret the Act will be available at the earliest in mid-2025 [12], or no later than 2028 (Art. 6 Para. 5; Art. 15 Para. 2; EUAIA).

The core of EUAIA are duties placed upon the providers[2] of any AI system that will be used in high-risk domains (Art. 6–49; Annex I Section B; Annex III) or within regulated products (Annex I Section A). Other duties include: responsibilities of other stakeholders; prohibitions of using AI systems in particular domains (Art. 5); transparency-relevant duties for providers of user-oriented and generative AI systems

[1] The original text [9] has been drafted before the breakthrough of conversational LLMs in 2022 (e.g., ChatGPT; [10]), and subsequently revised to include stipulations for LLM-like models [8]. We refer to the revised version that is made available by the [11].

[2] i.e., those who develop or commission it, and put it on the market or into service; Art. 3, EUAIA.

(Art. 50); and provisions for structuring the regulatory administration (Art. 57–100). Although most duties are model-agnostic, providers of general-purpose AI models[3] have specific obligations regardless of the domain (Art. 51–56).

While LLMs are not inherently classified as high-risk, EUAIA duties may apply in at least three scenarios. First, stakeholders in the regulated contexts may find the general capabilities and user-friendliness of LLM-based chatbots to be worth the compliance effort. Second, as first of its kind globally, the EUAIA may become the standard framework for how to structure voluntary risk management. Third, regular reviews by the legislators (Chapter IX & Art. 112) and any detected incidents (Art. 73) may result in the risk classification, domain coverage or model-specific duties being amended.

The law requires that providers establish quality properties such as unbiasedness, privacy, cybersecurity and safety to the user at an appropriate level. Compliance, however, means translating those properties into technical measures, interpreting their appropriateness in a given context, and managing risk to ensure their stability over time. This stability in performance, safety and security across contexts and time is known as **robustness**, which has long been a difficult problem in AI. For example, even after extensive training, LLMs can be brittle to adversarial attacks that elicit harmful responses with randomized, automated or manual prompting [3]. Despite attempts of many providers to reduce that risk by setting guardrails, simple attacks still tend to succeed [13].

Ensuring robustness and compliance with EUAIA over time implies testing, surveilling, reasoning about and reacting to newly discovered attacks. Thus, providers need to monitor and evaluate the impact of developments potentially affecting the safety and security of their LLM-based systems. Given the novelty of the field, valuable data about attacks and defenses is found in gray literature such as preprints [13] and technical reports [14], or online repositories [15] for replicating experiments. Assurance, or establishing justifiable evidence-based confidence that a property has been achieved [16], thus depends on effective knowledge management, which in turn depends on proper formalization of that knowledge.

24.3 Methodology

Our research methodology centers on knowledge representation from three parallel streams. First, we perform a simple legal analysis [17, 18] of the EUAIA to identify relevant duties[4] and stakeholders. Second, we elicit information about adversarial attacks and defenses in unstructured expert interviews and literature review (cf. [19]). Third, we use the Goal Structuring Notation (GSN; [20]) to express the confidence

---

[3] i.e., those that can easily perform and integrate in a wide-range of applications, regardless of the intended purpose, e.g., LLMs; Art. 3, EUAIA.

[4] i.e., legal obligations that a particular stakeholder should satisfy [18].

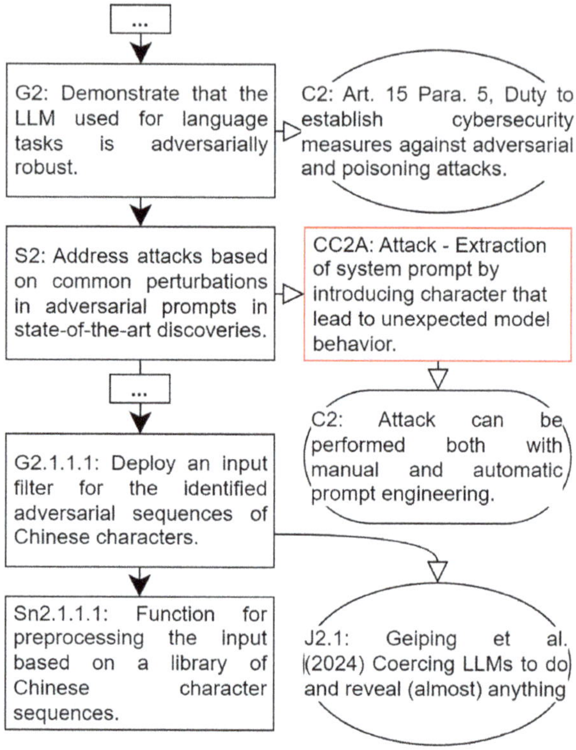

Fig. 24.1 Excerpt from a GSN-based assurance argument, operationalizing the duty in Art. 15 Para. 5. Legend: goals (G), strategies (S), justifications (J), contexts (C), solutions (Sn) and counterclaims (CC)

about EUAIA compliance and adversarial robustness in an exemplary assurance argument, comprising claims and evidence about appropriate defenses. We then combine and formalize this information in an ontology[5] using the Web Ontology Language [21], and display it as a human-readable narrative FactSheet report [22].

24.4 Proposed Framework

We identify 23 duties in EUAIA (cf. Table 24.1) that directly refer to safety, cybersecurity or robustness, or proximate terms such as incident, risk or misuse. Providers of high-risk AI systems need to satisfy fifteen of those duties, and providers of general-purpose AI models four; other duties relate to deployers, market surveillance authorities and national competent authorities. While not representative of all

[5] i.e., specification of concepts, categories and relations in a particular domain. In this stage, we focus on expressing concepts in a graph of semantic triples, i.e., subject-predicate-object statements.

Table 24.1 Overview of robustness-relevant EUAIA duties. Text is paraphrased, and qualifiers emphasized by authors for readability; see original text alongside Art. 3 for corresponding definitions.

#	§	S.*	Relevant duties
1	9.2	A	Identify, evaluate and mitigate *reasonably foreseeable* risks of the system
2	9.5	A	Ensure *appropriate* and *adequate* risk management measures
3	10.2	A	Establish confidentiality and security of private data collected for assurance of other duties (e.g., bias mitigation)
4	13.3, An. IV	A	Include information about robustness and cybersecurity (e.g., metrics) and their limitations in instructions for use
5	14.2	A	Design system for *effective* human oversight regarding safety monitoring and prevention/minimization of *reasonably foreseeable* misuse
6	14.4	A	Design *appropriate* functionalities for human overseers to: understand the system; monitor for "anomalies, dysfunctions and unexpected performance"; understand, override, and reverse the output; and intervene or interrupt the system's operation in a *safe* state
7	15.1	A	Establish an *appropriate* level of robustness and cybersecurity
8	15.4	A	Establish robustness and resilience of system regarding "errors, faults or inconsistencies."
9	15.5	A	Establish cybersecurity measures against adversarial and poisoning attacks
10	17.1	A	Establish security-of-supply measures
11	31.2	B	Satisfy *suitable* cybersecurity requirements
12	50.2	C	Ensure that AI-generated content is *robustly* and *reliably* watermarked
13	53.1, An.XI	C	Report on measures used to detect *unsuitable* data sources and biases; evaluation of *systemic* risk; measures for adversarial testing, model alignment and fine-tuning; system architecture and dependencies
14	55.1	C	Establish cybersecurity and adversarially test with respect to systemic risks
15	57.6	D	Support safety risk identification, testing, and mitigation in regulatory sandboxes
16	58.4	D, A	Prespecify safeguards and conditions for real-world testing
17	70.3	D	Establish safety and cybersecurity expertise
18	70.4	D	Ensure an *adequate* level of cybersecurity
19	73.1,7-8,11	A, E, F, D	Notify supervising stakeholder of a *serious* incident
20	73.2-6	A, E	Establish and report on the definite, *reasonably likely* or suspected causal link between the system and a serious incident
21	74.12	A	Securely provide documentation and data on system
22	78.2	D	Establish cybersecurity measures for data obtained from providers
23	92.5,7	C	Supply information on testing, safeguards and risk mitigation measures at the request of the AI Office

*Stakeholders—A: High-risk AI System Provider; B: Notified Body; C: General-Purpose AI Provider; D: National Competent Authority; E: Deployer; F: Market Surveillance Authority relevant demands or conditions,[6] the list is a starting overview of the intersection between compliance and robustness.

Much of the legal text includes context-specific adjectives or qualifiers such as "reasonably foreseeable", "suitable", "appropriate" or "effective." Lacking the technical requirements that operationalize what is suitable, providers would need to devise strategies to comply, and justify their suitability in the given context. This is a common case for building an assurance argument, as visualized in Fig. 24.1.

One possible strategy includes mitigating attacks based on character combinations, as described by [13]. Experiments show that specific characters in prompts can trigger profanity or leak hidden instructions in responses. They demonstrated the effectiveness of such attacks across various pre-trained open-source LLMs (e.g., LLaMa-2-7B-chat) using different scripts (e.g., Latin or Chinese).

Engineers can deploy several defenses here. Initially, a simple static input filter may be used to screen out prompts with characters that more frequently lead to such responses. Over time, this filter can be refined by testing how particular characters and combinations thereof affect the particular model; filter parameters can be adjusted to better and dynamically distinguish between benign and adversarial prompts. Ultimately, a more robust but costly solution would be to retrain the LLM to be less vulnerable to any character.

We developed an ontology (Fig. 24.2) to formalize and link the concepts that are used for evaluating, implementing and tracing the effectiveness of defenses. First, it contains information about a prompt, its contents and characters in a way that allows providers to retrieve and calculate of values needed for both static and dynamic filters. Second, it traces the sources of successful adversarial prompts (Fig. 16 of [13]) and allows comparison with example data previously used to adversarially train the model. Third, it traces the provenance of the EUAIA duty (i.e., Art. 15 Para. 5), and links it with the assurance argument, so that this information can be systematically documented in a factsheet. This allows engineers and other stakeholders to track their status of compliance, perform causal analyses, and maintain LLM defenses, making their systems' robustnes auditable with respect to the EUAIA.

24.5 Conclusion

The EU Artificial Intelligence Act aims to mitigate risks of AI systems by imposing obligations on the robustness of various properties. However, for systems with LLM components, the implementation of these duties will be significantly challenging due to the inherent complexity and opacity of LLMs, alongside the continuous emergence of new security threats. Our proposed framework seeks to make the process of ensuring compliance and robustness effective, by allowing engineers (i.e., providers and deployers) to more easily represent and reason about LLM defenses through

[6] e.g., transferability of Cybersecurity Act certificates (Art. 42 Para. 2) or conditional exemption of providers of free and open-source models (Art. 2 Para. 12; Art. 53 Para. 2).

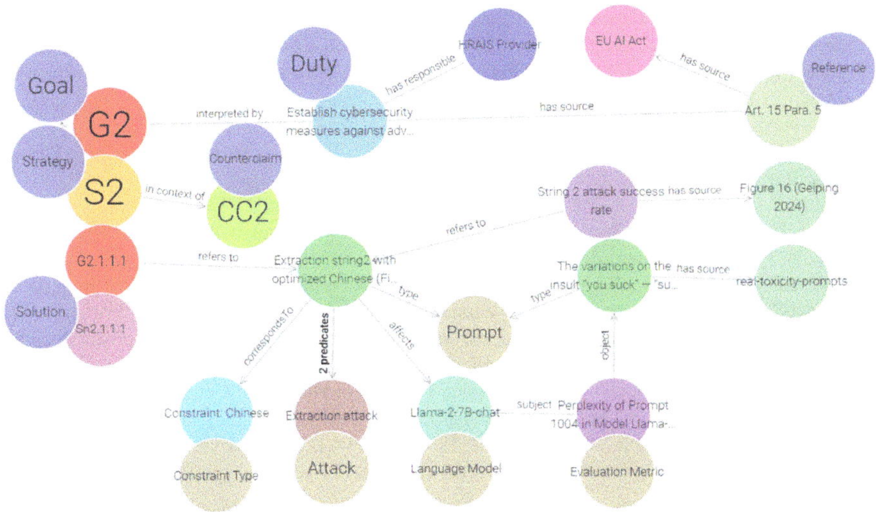

Fig. 24.2 Excerpt from the ontology. Left-most circles make the argument (Fig. 24.1), while all remaining circles represent attacks, defenses, duties and sources. Coloring is arbitrary

ontologies and assurance cases. The framework allows legal stakeholders and users to audit these systems with a complete, accurate and up-to-date snapshot.

Nonetheless, we recognize that this approach currently relies on manual work in creating arguments. This limits its usefulness for documenting and evaluating changes to law, system or attack vectors. Our future research centers on integrating the framework with techniques and tools that would allow arguments, concepts and relations to be expressed automatically, and evaluating it experimentally.

Acknowledgements This work was partially supported by financial and other means by the following research projects: DUCA (EU grant agreement 101086308), FLA (supported by the Bavarian Ministry of Economic Affairs, Regional Development and Energy), the DiProLeA (German Federal Ministry of Education and Research, grant 02J19B120 ff), as well as our industrial partners in the FinComp project. We thank the reviewers for their valuable comments.

References

1. Kojima, T., Gu, S. S., Reid, M., Matsuo, Y., & Iwasawa, Y. (2022). Large language models are zero-shot reasoners. *Advances in Neural Information Processing Systems, 35*, 22199–22213.
2. Yao, Y., Duan, J., Xu, K., Cai, Y., Sun, Z., & Zhang, Y. (2024). A survey on large language model (llm) security and privacy: The good, the bad, and the ugly. *High-Confidence Computing, 4*(2), Article 100211.
3. Zou, A., Wang, Z., Kolter, J. Z., & Fredrikson, M. (2023). Universal and transferable adversarial attacks on aligned language models. CoRR abs/2307.15043

4. European Parliament, Council of the European Union: Regulation (EU) 2016/679 of the European Parliament and of the Council of 27 April 2016 on the protection of natural persons with regard to the processing of personal data and on the free movement of such data, and repealing Directive 95/46/EC (General Data Protection Regulation). (2016). Retrieved May 15, 2024, from https://data.europa.eu/eli/reg/2016/679/oj
5. Vemprala, S., Bonatti, R., Bucker, A., & Kapoor, A. (2023). Chatgpt for robotics: Design principles and model abilities
6. Wang, L., Ma, C., Feng, X., Zhang, Z., Yang, H., Zhang, J., Chen, Z., Tang, J., Chen, X., Lin, Y., Zhao, W. X., Wei, Z., & Wen, J. (2024). A survey on large language model based autonomous agents. *Frontiers of Computer Science, 18*(6), Article 186345.
7. Thirunavukarasu, A. J., Ting, D. S. J., Elangovan, K., Gutierrez, L., Tan, T. F., & Ting, D. S. W. (2023). Large language models in medicine. *Nature Medicine, 29*(8), 1930–1940.
8. European Parliament, Council of the European Union: Corrigendum to the position of the European Parliament adopted at first reading on 13 March 2024 with a view to the adoption of Regulation (EU) 2024/......) of the European Parliament and of the Council laying down harmonised rules on artificial intelligence and amending Regulations (EC) No 300/2008, (EU) No 167/2013, (EU) No 168/2013, (EU) 2018/858, (EU) 2018/1139 and (EU) 2019/2144 and Directives 2014/90/EU, (EU) 2016/797 and (EU) 2020/1828 (Artificial Intelligence Act). (2024). Accessed 2024-05-15
9. European Parliament, Council of the European Union: Proposal for a Regulation of the European Parliament and of the Council laying down harmonised rules on artificial intelligence (Artificial Intelligence Act) and amending certain union legislative acts. (2021). Accessed 2024-05-15
10. OpenAI. (2022). Introducing ChatGPT. Retrieved February 25, 2024, fromhttps://openai.com/index/chatgpt
11. Future of Life Institute: The AI Act explorer. (2024). Retrieved May 17, 2024, from https://artificialintelligenceact.eu/ai-act-explorer/
12. CEN-CENELEC: CEN/CLC/JTC 21-Artificial Intelligence-Work Programme. (2024). Retrieved May 17, 2024, from https://standards.cencenelec.eu/dyn/www/f?p=205:22:0::::FSP_ORG_ID,FSP_LANG_ID:2916257,25&cs=1827B89DA69577BF3631EE2B6070F207D
13. Geiping, J., Stein, A., Shu, M., Saifullah, K., Wen, Y., & Goldstein, T. (2024). Coercing llms to do and reveal (almost) anything. arXiv preprint arXiv:2402.14020
14. Russinovich, M., Salem, A., & Eldan, R. (2024). Great, now write an article about that: The crescendo multi-turn llm jailbreak attack
15. Anthropic: HuggingFace Dataset Card for HH-RLHF. (2024). Retrieved May 17, 2024, from https://huggingface.co/datasets/Anthropic/hh-rlhf
16. National Institute of Standards and Technology (NIST). (2018). Risk management framework for information systems and organizations. NIST special publication 800-37. https://nvlpubs.nist.gov/nistpubs/SpecialPublications/NIST.SP.800-37r2.pdf
17. van Engers, T., & van Doesburg, R. (2015). First steps towards a formal analysis of law. In D. Malzahn & G. Granja (Eds.), *eKNOW 2015: The Seventh International Conference on Information, Process, and Knowledge Management: February 22–27, 2015, Lisbon, Portugal* (pp. 36–42). Wilmington, DE: IARIA.
18. Hohfeld, W. N., Campbell, D., & Thomas, P. A. (2001). Some fundamental legal conceptions as applied in judicial reasoning. *Yale Law Journal*. http://lawcat.berkeley.edu/record/1178561, first published 2001 by Ashgate Publishing.
19. Bueno Momcilovic, T., Buesser, B., Zizzo, G., Purcell, M., & Balta, D. (September 2024). Towards assurance of LLM adversarial robustness using ontology-driven argumentation. In *xAI'24: 2nd World Conference on eXplainable Artificial Intelligence*, July 17–19, 2024, Valletta, Malta (pp. 1–8). Springer (2024), upcoming publication.
20. Assurance Case Working Group (ACWG). (2021). Goal Structuring Notation Community Standard, Version 3. Retrieved February 25, 2024, from https://scsc.uk/scsc-141c

21. World Wide Web Consortium (W3C). (2012). OWL 2 web ontology language, (second edition). https://www.w3.org/TR/owl2-rdf-based-semantics/
22. Arnold, M., Bellamy, R. K., Hind, M., Houde, S., Mehta, S., Mojsilović, A., Nair, R., Ramamurthy, K. N., Olteanu, A., Piorkowski, D., et al. (2019). FactSheets: Increasing trust in AI services through supplier's declarations of conformity. *IBM Journal of Research and Development, 63*(4/5), 6–1.

The Impact of the AI-Act on the Implementation of Conversational Agents in Healthcare Processes

Björn-Lennart Eger, Daniel Rose, and Barbara Dinter

Abstract In view of the growing significance of artificial intelligence (AI) in healthcare, compliance with the European Union's AI-Act (AI-Act) is crucial for ensuring patient safety, data security and legal conformity. This research-in-progress paper examines the impact of the AI-Act on the design of healthcare processes that are supported conversational agents. It highlights the challenges arising from the new regulatory requirements of the AI-Act and discusses preliminary approaches for integrating these provisions into healthcare processes. The focus is on analyzing the regulatory effects on the automation of healthcare processes. Our first findings provide a basis for further research and the eventual implementation of the AI-Act's requirements. The paper underlines the need for clear risk classifications and precise definitions of AI systems, as well as their potential effects on efficiency and patient safety in healthcare.

1 Introduction

In today's fast-paced environment, companies must act dynamically and continuously adapt to technological developments and regulatory requirements. The healthcare sector faces similar challenges, especially in light of the increasing importance

B.-L. Eger (✉) · D. Rose · B. Dinter
Chair of Business Information Systems—Business Process and Information Management, Chemnitz University of Technology, Chemnitz, Germany
e-mail: bjoern-lennart.eger@wirtschaft.tu-chemnitz.de

D. Rose
e-mail: daniel.rose@wirtschaft.tu-chemnitz.de

B. Dinter
e-mail: barbara.dinter@wirtschaft.tu-chemnitz.de

C. M. Flath et al. (eds.), *Shaping the Digital Future Through Innovation and Practice*, Lecture Notes in Information Systems and Organisation 85,
https://doi.org/10.1007/978-3-032-08489-7_25

of artificial intelligence (AI). Compliance with the European Union's AI-Act (AI-Act)[1] becomes crucial to ensure data security, patient safety and legal conformity. In particular, healthcare processes are affected by these dynamics and must be designed flexibly to meet the new requirements. Vasilecas et al. [1] identify regulatory adjustments, market developments, changes in patient behavior, process improvements, and policy modifications as driving forces. In recent years, regulatory adaptations have been especially necessary in healthcare with regard to data protection. The AI-Act introduces additional challenges through new regulations. AI applications in healthcare—for instance, diagnostic and treatment support systems—represent a central focus of these new regulations, even though the precise interpretation of the AI-Act's specific requirements remains unclear.

Thus, this research-in-progress paper is primarily intended as an outlook on how this work can be advanced in future phases. In the subsequent steps of this ongoing project, we plan to apply a methodological approach following the Design Science Research (DSR) paradigm described by Peffers et al. [2]. DSR comprises six activities that can be executed sequentially and iteratively: problem identification and motivation, definition of objectives for a solution, design and development, demonstration, evaluation, and communication.

As an initial step for our further research, we apply a problem-oriented approach. In doing so, the problem situation is analyzed in greater detail and assessed for its relevance. To approach the thematic areas—healthcare processes, the AI-Act, and process management—an iterative literature review is conducted. This review provides a solid basis for defining the problem, which is induced by the new requirements of the AI-Act, as well as for formulating the objectives for designing healthcare processes. A primary focus is on existing concepts that incorporate changes in regulations and laws into process designs. These concepts are compared with the requirements of the AI-Act in order to derive recommendations for the implementation of AI-driven agents in processes while considering the AI-Act. The development of such recommendations is intended to be the central focus of the design phase. The demonstration phase will be carried out using an example of a healthcare process, specifically within the framework of an upcoming research project aimed at integrating conversational agents into healthcare processes. In a subsequent evaluation, experts from the healthcare sector will assess the effectiveness and applicability of the recommendations.

This paper aims, as a first step, to illustrate the impact of the AI-Act on the design of dynamic healthcare processes and to investigate how the principles of the AI-Act influence the application of AI in the healthcare sector. We place particular emphasis on conversational agents in healthcare processes. These initial findings lay the groundwork for further research and for the later implementation of the AI-Act's

---

[1] European Union (2024) Regulation (EU) 2024/1689 of the European Parliament and of the Council laying down harmonised rules on artificial intelligence and amending Regulations (EC) No 300/2008, (EU) No 167/2013, (EU) No 168/2013, (EU) 2018/858, (EU) 2018/1139 and (EU) 2019/2144 and Directives 2014/90/EU, (EU) 2016/797 and (EU) 2020/1828 (Artificial Intelligence Act). https://eur-lex.europa.eu/eli/reg/2024/1689/oj.

requirements. The article seeks to contribute to answering the following two research questions:

1. How does the AI-Act influence the design and implementation of AI-based symptom assessment systems in healthcare?
2. What challenges and conflicts arise from the AI-Act's requirements in the use of conversational agents?

2 Healthcare Processes

The European Union's AI-Act imposes new regulatory requirements on the healthcare sector that call for comprehensive adjustments to existing healthcare processes. In particular, both medical and non-medical processes must be reviewed and adapted. Medical processes, also known as care pathways, are directly tied to the treatment course of a patient [3]. Non-medical processes support medical treatment processes and coordinate collaboration among various professionals and organizational units. The healthcare sector is already heavily regulated, especially regarding data protection and the security of health data in accordance with the General Data Protection Regulation (GDPR) (Art. 4—Paragraph 15 GDPR—Definitions of "health data", 2015). In addition to the GDPR, the Medical Device Regulation (MDR) [4] influences the design of software that supports the monitoring or treatment of diseases or injuries (Art. 2, Para. 1 of Regulation (EU) 2017/745).

The AI-Act creates further challenges through new regulations. Processes in healthcare are particularly complex compared to other industries and are characterized by an ever-changing environment. This multidisciplinarity in healthcare, which brings together various fields and expertise, as well as the high density of regulations, requires flexible and adaptable processes. A model-based representation of these processes can help visualize and integrate the diverse requirements. Swoboda [5] emphasizes that the modeling language BPMN (Business Process Model and Notation) is particularly suitable for describing processes in healthcare. To incorporate the requirements of the AI-Act into process design, an extended graphical modeling language would be necessary. Such a language should comprehensively represent the diverse regulations and activities, enabling their integration into healthcare processes. A clear and structured representation could support the implementation of the new regulations and ensure compliance with legal requirements.

3 Risk Classification of Conversational Agents in Healthcare

Conversational agents that are based on AI use machine learning and deep learning algorithms to recognize users' intentions and generate appropriate, context-sensitive responses [6]. In healthcare, they offer significant advantages in symptom assessment and preliminary diagnosis, as they understand natural language and can process complex queries—for example, in capturing symptoms and providing initial diagnostic hints [7].

Because conversational agents are considered as AI systems under the AI-Act, it is especially important to determine their risk level accurately. The AI-Act differentiates between systems with minimal, limited, and high risk, which significantly affects regulatory requirements and safety measures. A precise assignment to the appropriate risk level is crucial for ensuring regulatory compliance. Against this background, in the following section, we examine the risk classification of conversational agents in the healthcare sector in detail.

The AI-Act introduces a risk grading for AI systems that is divided into four categories:

- **Prohibited Systems:** Systems posing an unacceptable risk (e.g., social scoring systems) are assigned to the first category and are banned (Art. 5 AI-Act).
- **High-Risk Systems:** These systems have significant impact on health, safety, or fundamental rights, such as AI used in critical infrastructure or in healthcare, and belong to the second category (Art. 6; Annex III AI-Act).
- **Limited-Risk Systems:** These systems are primarily subject to transparency requirements, such as general chatbots (Art. 52 AI-Act).
- **Minimal-Risk Systems:** Systems that do not pose significant risks, such as spam filters, are placed into the fourth category and are subject to hardly any regulatory requirements.

Accurately classifying conversational agents in healthcare within these categories is essential. While they might generally be viewed as limited-risk systems, they may, in certain situations, be considered high-risk—especially if they perform diagnostic functions or generate user profiles that could lead to incorrect treatments and significant health risks (Art. 6; Annex III AI-Act). This classification highlights the need for precise definitions and clear differentiation criteria for high-risk systems.

However, uncertainties remain about exactly which technologies fall under "artificial intelligence" in the AI-Act, which critics argue does not provide enough clarity. Prof. Dr. Patrick Glauner highlighted this issue during his statement at the public hearing of the Committee on Digital Affairs in the German Bundestag on 15 May 2024 [8]. The subsequent discussion underscored the need to develop clear and practicable definitions that are robust both legally and in practical application.

In this context, the Committee on Digital Affairs in the Parliament of the Federal Republic of Germany is working on implementing the European AI-Act into national law. According to inquiries within the committee, the goal is to establish a regulatory framework that not only ensures the safety of citizens but also fosters the potential of technological development [9].

4 Exemplary Problem Statement in Healthcare Processes Triggered by the AI-Act

As outlined earlier, this paper presents preliminary work for an upcoming research project. In collaboration with an industry partner, we will examine the use of conversational agents in healthcare processes with a focus on the modeling and implementation of such processes. Consequently, we are confronted with the regulations of the AI-Act. These regulations, for example, come into play when conversational agents analyze entered personal data regarding the emotions and intentions of patients and react accordingly. Such analysis is necessary when healthcare processes are modeled to recognize and deduce patient intentions and to capture symptoms. According to Recital 18 of the AI-Act, an AI system is defined as an emotion recognition system if it detects or deduces emotions or intentions of natural persons based on biometric data [10]. Furthermore, Recital 44 of the AI-Act highlights serious concerns regarding the detection and deduction of emotions (European Commission, 2024). Additionally, Art. 6 Para. 1 of the AI-Act classifies systems that intend to integrate AI under the harmonization requirements specified in Annex 1 as high-risk systems [10]. Affected systems also include medical products, which, according to Regulation (EU) 2017/745 of the European Parliament, may also include software products [4].

The introduction of the AI-Act will, therefore—similar to the GDPR—necessitate profound changes in processes and in process modeling. The AI-Act will force similar structural changes by setting specific requirements for the assessment and management of AI risks. One consequence of these various regulations is the central challenge of how providers and operators of such conversational agents can integrate the new regulatory requirements of the AI-Act—for example, the definitions and stipulations regarding emotion recognition and high-risk classification—into their healthcare processes. To date, detailed guidelines for practical implementation have not been published. Art. 6 Para. 5 of the AI-Act stipulates that these guidelines should be available no later than 18 months after the regulation comes into force. They are expected to provide a comprehensive list of practical examples for both high-risk and non-high-risk use cases of AI systems [10].

Our aim in this paper is to discuss approaches for considering the AI-Act's requirements in the development of healthcare processes. Early consideration of their impact enables a sound basis for integrating new technologies such as conversational AI. A comprehensive knowledge base that gathers all relevant details of the AI-Act and its effects on processes can be supportive in this context. When these requirements are embedded in the processes, clarity is enhanced and, as a consequence, decision-making is improved through a consistent and complete data foundation. A solid knowledge base thereby increases process efficiency, promotes regulatory compliance, and minimizes the risk of errors by ensuring that relevant information is always available.

Applied to an exemplary healthcare process, this could mean that the objectives regarding increased automation can only be partially achieved, as outlined below. For instance, the process of symptom assessment could be made more efficient through the use of conversational AI. In such a scenario, the digital agent would manage the communication for capturing patient data and issues. However, conflicts with the AI-Act's requirements may arise during the analysis and classification of symptoms by the conversational AI for further treatment. According to AI-Act Article 9, systems for emotion recognition and classification must always be supervised. Unsupervised operation by AI is not permissible, as it may pose risks to the affected patients.

A similar issue exists regarding the transparency requirement in the AI-Act. According to Article 13 of the AI-Act, when using AI, the algorithms employed and their decision-making processes must be transparent. Transferred to the symptom assessment process, this means that the digital agent must inform the patient that the symptom data is captured and analyzed by an AI system. Moreover, an explanation must be provided regarding how the AI reaches its conclusions. These explanations should be given in comprehensible language and elucidate the logic behind the AI's decisions. However, given that current AI models cannot entirely preclude the occurrence of hallucination effects, the decisions made must be reviewed and approved by human personnel.

This implies that despite automation through conversational AI, human interaction remains necessary, thereby reducing the degree of automation. The required human oversight ensures that ethical and regulatory requirements are met, yet it simultaneously counteracts complete automation. An early examination of the requirements and potential impact of the AI-Act can aid in planning the implementation of conversational AI in processes and help set realistic expectations.

5 Conclusion

The considerations initiated in this paper regarding the integration of the AI-Act's requirements into the design of dynamic healthcare processes show that the current delineation of terms such as emotion recognition and AI systems remains impractical. In particular, risk grading must be more clearly defined to enable a concrete application in healthcare. Emotion recognition is likely to emerge as a future point of contention due to the lack of clear regulation for practical application.

The stringent considerations of the AI-Act might lead to a delays in the development and implementation of conversational agents in healthcare, as additional resources and time must be allocated to comply with the regulations. This could pose a particular challenge for smaller companies and start-ups. On the other hand, the AI-Act could also contribute to strengthening patients' trust in these technologies by ensuring that their data is used securely and ethically. Ultimately, the success of conversational agents in healthcare will depend on how well they can balance regulatory compliance with the provision of valuable and efficient services for patients.

There is a clear need for further discussions and more precise interpretations of the AI-Act to ensure a practicable and legally secure implementation in healthcare. Future research should focus on the development of clear regulatory guidelines and practical applications to promote the safety and efficiency of AI systems in healthcare.

References

1. Vasilecas, O., Kalibatiene, D., & Lavbič, D. (2016). Rule- and context-based dynamic business process modelling and simulation. *Journal of Systems and Software, 122*, 1–15. https://doi.org/10.1016/j.jss.2016.08.048
2. Peffers, K., Tuunanen, T., Rothenberger, M., & Chatterjee, S. (2007). A design science research methodology for information systems research. *Journal of Management Information Systems, 24*, 45–77.
3. Lenz, R., & Reichert, M. (2007). IT support for healthcare processes—Premises, challenges, perspectives. *Data & Knowledge Engineering, 61*, 39–58. https://doi.org/10.1016/j.datak.2006.04.007
4. European Commission. Medical device regulation (2017), https://eur-lex.europa.eu/legal-content/DE/TXT/PDF/?uri=CELEX:32017R0745
5. Swoboda, W. (2014). IT-unterstützte Modellierung klinischer Prozesse. In R. B. Bouncken, M. A. Pfannstiel, & A. J. Reuschl (Eds.), *Dienstleistungsmanagement im Krankenhaus II. Prozesse, Produktivität, Diversität* (pp. 81–102). Springer Gabler, Fachmedien [Germany], Wiesbaden [Germany]. https://doi.org/10.1007/978-3-658-05134-1_4
6. Tudor Car, L., Dhinagaran, D. A., Kyaw, B. M., Kowatsch, T., Joty, S., Theng, Y. L., & Atun, R. (2020). Conversational agents in health care: Scoping review and conceptual analysis. *Journal of Medical Internet Research, 22*, e17158. https://doi.org/10.2196/17158
7. Prasad, M. L., Srinivasulu, C., Meenakshi, M., & Rohitha, P. (2023). *Chatbots in Healthcare. IJRASET, 11*, 1087–1091. https://doi.org/10.22214/ijraset.2023.55295
8. Glauner, P. Schriftliche Stellungnahme von Prof. Dr. Patrick Glauner. Anhörung am 15.05.2024 zu Nationale Spielräume bei der Umsetzung des europäischen Gesetzes über Künstliche Intelligenz (2024), https://www.bundestag.de/resource/blob/1002474/773fbf5b7ff6943097c45b097e8d8b3c/Glauner.pdf
9. Deutscher Bundestag. Nationale Aufsicht bei Künstlicher Intelligenz komplex (2024), https://www.bundestag.de/dokumente/textarchiv/2024/kw20-pa-digitales-ki-1001728
10. European Commission. AI Act (2024), https://digital-strategy.ec.europa.eu/en/policies/regulatory-framework-ai

GPSR Compliance
The European Union's (EU) General Product Safety Regulation (GPSR) is a set of rules that requires consumer products to be safe and our obligations to ensure this.

If you have any concerns about our products, you can contact us on

ProductSafety@springernature.com

In case Publisher is established outside the EU, the EU authorized representative is:

Springer Nature Customer Service Center GmbH
Europaplatz 3
69115 Heidelberg, Germany

www.ingramcontent.com/pod-product-compliance
Ingram Content Group UK Ltd.
Pitfield, Milton Keynes, MK11 3LW, UK
UKHW022108180926
475695UK00001B/41
9783032084880